Formulation, Implementation, and Control of Competitive Strategy

Eighth Edition

John A. Pearce II
College of Commerce and Finance
Villanova University

Richard B. Robinson, Jr.
Moore School of Business
University of South Carolina

Boston   Burr Ridge, IL   Dubuque, IA   Madison, WI   New York   San Francisco   St. Louis
Bangkok   Bogotá   Caracas   Kuala Lumpur   Lisbon   London   Madrid   Mexico City
Milan   Montreal   New Delhi   Santiago   Seoul   Singapore   Sydney   Taipei   Toronto

McGraw-Hill Higher Education

A Division of The **McGraw-Hill** *Companies*

FORMULATION, IMPLEMENTATION, AND CONTROL OF COMPETITIVE STRATEGY

Published by McGraw-Hill/Irwin, a business unit of The McGraw-Hill Companies, Inc., 1221 Avenue of the Americas, New York, NY, 10020. Copyright © 2003, 2000, 1997, 1994, 1991, 1988, 1985, 1982 by The McGraw-Hill Companies, Inc. All rights reserved. No part of this publication may be reproduced or distributed in any form or by any means, or stored in a database or retrieval system, without the prior written consent of The McGraw-Hill Companies, Inc., including, but not limited to, in any network or other electronic storage or transmission, or broadcast for distance learning.
Some ancillaries, including electronic and print components, may not be available to customers outside the United States.
This book is printed on acid-free paper.

1 2 3 4 5 6 7 8 9 0 DOW/DOW 0 9 8 7 6 5 4 3 2

ISBN 0-07-248852-2

Publisher: *John E. Biernat*
Senior sponsoring editor: *Andy Winston*
Editorial coordinator: *Sara E. Ramos*
Marketing manager: *Lisa Nicks*
Producer, Media technology: *Jennifer Becka*
Senior project manager: *Kimberly D. Hooker*
Production supervisor: *Rose Hepburn*
Senior designer: *Jennifer McQueen*
Supplement producer: *Matthew Perry*
Senior digital content specialist: *Brian Nacik*
Cover design: *Kiera Cunningham*
Typeface: *10/12 Times New Roman*
Compositor: *Shepherd Incorporated*
Printer: *R. R. Donnelley*

Library of Congress Cataloging-in-Publication Data

Pearce, John A.
   Formulation, implementation, and control of competitive strategy / John A. Pearce II,
Richard B. Robinson, Jr.—8th ed.
      p. cm.
   Includes bibliographical references and index.
   ISBN 0-07-248852-2 (alk. paper)
   1. Strategic planning. 2. Strategic planning—Case studies. I. Robinson, Richard B.
(Richard Braden), 1947-II. Title.
   HD30.28 .P3385 2003
   652.4'01—dc21

                                                            2002067159

www.mhhe.com

To
Mary Frances and Jack Pearce
Mattie and Frank Fletcher

Preface

This eighth edition of *Formulation, Implementation, and Control of Competitive Strategy* is both the culmination of over 20 years of work by many people and a major revision designed to accommodate the needs of strategy students in the 21st century. These are exciting times and they are reflected in the many new developments in this book and the accompanying McGraw-Hill supplements. This preface describes what we have done to make the eighth edition uniquely effective in preparing students for strategic decisions in tomorrow's fast-paced global business arena. It also allows us the opportunity to recognize many outstanding contributors.

The eighth edition of *Formulation, Implementation, and Control of Competitive Strategy* is divided into 11 chapters that provide a thorough, state-of-the-art treatment of the critical business skills needed to plan and manage strategic activities. Each chapter has been filled with new, current real-world examples to illustrate concepts in companies that students recognize and regularly read about in the news around the world. Strategic ramifications of topics like executive compensation, e-commerce, the Internet, entrepreneurship, ethics, continuous improvement, virtual organization, cultural diversity, outsourcing, strategic alliances, and global competition can be found across several chapters. While the text continues a solid academic connection, students will find the text material to be practical, skills oriented, and relevant to their jobs.

We are excited and honored to be selected by *BusinessWeek* as its exclusive partner among strategic management textbooks. Their editors were very comfortable with the framework we use to explain strategic management and our emphasis on practical, relevant coverage. We were thrilled to have unlimited access to the world's best business publication to create examples, illustration modules, and various cases. The result is an extensively enhanced text and cases benefiting from hundreds of contemporary examples and illustrations provided by *BusinessWeek* writers worldwide. You will see *BusinessWeek*'s impact on our discussion case feature, our Strategy in Action modules, our cases, and our website. Of course, we are also pleased with several hundred examples blended into the text material, which came from recent issues of *BusinessWeek* or www.businessweek.com.

AN OVERVIEW OF OUR TEXT MATERIAL

The eighth edition continues to use a model of the strategic management process as the basis for the organization of the text material. Previous adopters have identified that model as a key distinctive competence for our text because it offers a logical flow, distinct elements, and an easy-to-understand guide to strategic management. The model has been modestly refined to reflect strategic analysis at different organizational levels as well as the importance of internal analysis in the strategic management process. Adopters see quickly and feel comfortable that the model and subsequent structure continue to provide a student-friendly approach to the study of strategic management.

We reduced the number of chapters to 11 to accommodate excellent reviewer suggestions about a simplified organization and focused coverage of strategic management topics. We reduced the overall text length while ensuring state of the art topical coverage. Focused wording, elimination of seldom used reference lists and other features have helped ensure a more concise, readable coverage of strategic management.

The first chapter provides an overview of the strategic management process and explains what students will find as they use this book. The remaining 10 chapters cover each part of the strategic management process and techniques that aid strategic analysis, decision making, implementation, and control.

The literature and research in the strategic management area have developed at a rapid pace in recent years in both the academic and business press. This eighth edition includes several upgrades designed to incorporate major developments from both these sources. While we include cutting-edge concepts, we emphasize straightforward, logical, and simple presentation so that students can grasp these new ideas without additional reading. The following are a few of the revisions that deserve particular note:

Corporate Social Responsibility

This eighth edition gives added emphasis to the issue of corporate social responsibility. Many collegiate business schools have decided that stand-alone courses in business ethics and social responsibility are no longer necessary. Such decisions make it important that all other business courses accept a greater role in discussing the relevant topics. Our revision helps professors fulfill this obligation by presenting a balanced discussion and useful guidelines to students and managers on key topics in corporate social responsibility.

Agency Theory

Of the recent approaches to corporate governance and strategic management, probably none has had a greater impact on managerial thinking than agency theory. While the breadth and measurement of its usefulness continue to be hotly debated, students of strategic management need to understand the role of agency in our free enterprise, capitalistic system. This edition presents agency theory in a coherent and practical manner. We believe that it arms students with a cutting-edge approach to increasing their understanding of the priorities of executive decision making and strategic control.

Resource-Based View of the Firm

One of the most significant conceptual frameworks to systematize and "measure" a firm's strategic capabilities is the resource-based view (RBV) of the firm. The RBV has received major academic and business press attention during the last decade, helping to shape its value as a conceptual tool by adding rigor during the internal analysis and strategic analysis phases of the strategic management process. This edition provides a revised treatment of this concept in Chapter 5. We present the RBV in a logical and practical manner as a central underpinning of sound strategic analysis. Students will find several useful examples and a straightforward treatment of different types of "assets" and organizational capabilities culminating in the ability to determine when these resources create competitive advantage. They will see different ways to answer the question "what makes a resource valuable?" and be able to determine when that resource creates a competitive advantage in a systematic, disciplined, creative manner.

Value Chain Analysis

Outsourcing is becoming a standard business practice in virtually every facet of business operations. This trend enhances the usefulness of the value chain approach in strategic analysis. We have simplified our treatment of this useful conceptual framework and added several contemporary examples to enable students to quickly incorporate the value chain perspective into their strategic thinking process. Chapter 5 includes new Strategies in Action about the use of a value chain perspective at Volkswagen and about its contribution to the impressive strides that UPS is making in overtaking FedEx in the domestic and international package transportation industry.

Executive Compensation

While our text has led the field in providing a practice-oriented approach to strategic management, we have redoubled our efforts to treat topics with an emphasis on application. Our new section on executive compensation in Chapter 9 is a clear example in this edition. You will find an extended discussion of executive bonus options that provides a comparison of the relative merits of the five most popular approaches in use today.

Balanced Scoreboard

A recent evolution in the motivation that underpins strategic management is reflected in the adoption of the Balanced Scoreboard approach to corporate performance evaluation. While the maximization of shareholder wealth retains the top spot in executive priorities, the guideline is now widely accepted that strategic initiatives must produce favorable outcomes over a range of stakeholder objectives. We try to help our readers gain an appreciation for this perspective in our eighth edition.

Bankruptcy

Many times revisions in this book are driven by changes in business trends. Nowhere is that more evident than in our discussion of company bankruptcy. In the 1980s bankruptcy was treated as a last option that precluded any future for the firm. In the first decade of the 2000s the view has dramatically changed. Bankruptcy has been elevated to the status of a strategic option, and executives need to be well versed in its potentials and limitations, as you will see in Chapter 6.

Strategic Analysis and Choice

We have divided the discussion of strategic analysis and choice into two chapters. Chapter 7 examines the single business setting. Chapter 8 looks at the multibusiness company and the diversification decision. We have added an interesting new section delineating the advantages of diversification and the case against it. *BusinessWeek* has helped us add numerous outstanding examples to these two chapters from business writers around the world. DaimlerChrysler, Nokia, Caterpillar, and Amazon.com are just a few of the names students will quickly recognize in coverage that illustrates and helps them more easily understand how strategic analysis is conducted and choices made.

Strategy Implementation

New Chapter 9 focuses on reward systems, short-term objectives, and empowerment mechanisms as part of strategy implementation. It eliminates approximately 10 pages of previous discussion of functional tactics that have served as a convenient but sometimes unnecessary review of functional courses leading up to the capstone strategy class. Doing so allows students to move quickly into strategy implementation considerations from an executive perspective.

Structuring an Effective Organization

Chapter 10 provides a new perspective on the issue of organizational structure as a central mechanism for strategy implementation, particularly in larger companies. It explores three fundamental driving forces on contemporary organizational structure—globalization, the Internet, and speed. From this beginning, it covers research by academics and prominent business analysts to identify guidelines relevant to matching structure to strategy in the 21st century. Carly Fiorina's pioneering new structure at Hewlett-Packard provides a starting point, six contemporary guidelines to structuring an effective organization are explored in depth, providing students with useful conceptual tools to take into their postgraduation companies and contribute to specific structural challenges. A concise appendix is provided to Chapter 10 detailing the pros and cons of different basic organizational structures. It is included there rather than in the chapter to increase the readability and contemporary focus of the chapter material.

Organizational Leadership

New Chapter 10 has added coverage of outsourcing, virtual organizations, and the recruitment/development process as key contemporary considerations in building effective management teams. How to get and keep top-management talent is an issue of critical importance examined in this new edition.

Strategic Control and Continuous Improvement

New Chapter 11 offers a major revision in our treatment of these topics. First, a reduced and concise treatment of four broad strategic controls used in the formulation and implementation phases of strategic management are discussed and illustrated. Second, the link between quality/continuous improvement initiatives and the strategic management process receive new, in-depth treatment in this chapter. ISO9003 and Six Sigma are examined as contemporary approaches to the continuous improvement of a company's value chain and a mechanism to guide strategic control. The experiences of several well known companies in adopting these tools help illustrate their value in a comprehensive strategic management commitment. Finally, the increasingly popular use of the Balanced Scoreboard approach is also explored in this new chapter because of its value in supporting strategic control and continuous improvement.

OUR STRATEGIC ALLIANCE WITH *BUSINESSWEEK*

Thanks to the leadership at McGraw-Hill and *BusinessWeek,* we have completed a strategic alliance of our own that benefits every professor and student that uses this book. Our book is *BusinessWeek*'s exclusive partner among strategic management textbooks in the collegiate market. We have long felt *BusinessWeek* to be the unquestionable leader among business periodicals for its coverage of strategic issues in businesses, industries, and economies worldwide. Personal surveys of collegiate faculty teaching strategic management confirmed our intuition: While there are many outstanding business magazines and new publications, none match the consistent quality found in *BusinessWeek* for the coverage of corporate strategies, case stories, and topics of interest to students and professors of strategic management.

Through this partnership, we get unconditional access to *BusinessWeek* material for this book and the insights of their writers and editorial staff in the use of their cutting-edge stories and topical coverage. *BusinessWeek* gets to become more involved in the educational market as a supplements provider and they get increased exposure to strategic management teachers and students entering the business world. They plan to make their publication available on very favorable terms with the expectation that those initial users will roll over into long-term subscribers. From our point of view, this is a unique four-way win-win; teachers, students, authors, and *Business Week* all stand to gain in many ways. We are most proud of their selection criteria: they judged this strategy book as providing the most logical, proven framework to explain strategic management while prioritizing practical, frequent illustrations. The most direct way you can see the impact of the *Business Week* alliance is in three book features: discussion cases, Strategy in Action modules, and 25 short cases.

The Discussion Case Feature

We pioneered the cohesion case innovation several years ago and continue to be pleased by notes and comments from adopters that consider it very useful. For this eighth edition, we created a *Business Week* Discussion Case at the end of each chapter that illustrates key topics from that chapter. In this way, we examine a variety of companies across the 11 chapters. We think that you will find the variety of exciting companies covered, in combination with the depth of the *Business Week* research that underlies these stories, to make this feature a true pedagogical innovation once again. Amazon.com, Toyota-Japan, DaimlerChrysler, Caterpillar, and General Electric are just a few of the exciting situations examined in depth by *Business Week*'s senior staff and shared in detail with students in a very readable fashion.

Strategy in Action Modules

Another pedagogical feature we pioneered, Strategy in Action modules, has become standard in most strategy books. While such affirmation is pleasing, we have long seen the need to obtain quality illustrations to be a difficult permissions and editorial task. No more. Our strategic alliance with *Business Week* lets us once again pioneer an innovation. We have worked with *Business Week* field correspondents worldwide to fill over 60 new *Business Week* Strategy in Action modules with short, hard-hitting current illustrations of key chapter topics. We are the only strategy book to have *Business Week*–derived illustration modules, and we are energized by the excitement, interest, and practical illustration value our students tell us they provide.

OUR WEBSITE

A substantial website has been designed to aid your use of this book. It includes areas accessible only to instructors and areas specifically designed to assist students. The instructor section includes downloadable supplements, which keep your work area less cluttered and let you quickly obtain information. *Business Week* provides access to the article archives through the instructor website. The site offers an elaborate array of linkages to company websites and other sources that you might find useful in your course preparation. The student resources section of the website provides interactive discussion groups where students and groups using the book may interact with other students around the world doing the same thing. Students are provided company and related business periodical (and other) website linkages to aid and expedite their case research and preparation efforts. Practice quizzes and tests are provided to help students prepare for tests on the text material and attempt to lower their anxiety in that regard. Access to *Business Week* articles that update the cases and key illustration modules in the book are provided. We expect students will find the website useful and interesting. Please visit us at www.mhhe.com/pearce8e.

SUPPLEMENTS

Components of our teaching package include a revised, comprehensive instructor's manual, test bank, PowerPoint presentation, and a computerized test bank. These are all available to qualified adopters of the text.

Professors can also choose between two simulation games as a possible package with this text: The International Business Management Decision Simulation (McDonald/ Neelankavil), or the Business Strategy Game (Thompson/Stappenbeck).

- The International Business Management Decision Simulation is also a Windows-based simulation that provides an international business analysis and plan simulation that allows students to create multinational business plans and compete with other student groups. Fifteen countries representing three regions of the world along with four product categories are included in the simulation. Students assess business plans by using the financial reports contained in the simulation.

- The Business Strategy Game provides an exercise to help students understand how the functional pieces of a business fit together. Students will work with the numbers, explore options, and try to unite production, marketing, finance, and human resource decisions into a coherent strategy.

ACKNOWLEDGMENTS

We have benefited from the help of many people in the evolution of this project over eight editions. Students, adopters, colleagues, reviewers, and business contacts have provided hundreds of insightful comments, suggestions, and contributions that have progressively enhanced this book and its supplements. We are indebted to the researchers and practicing managers who have accelerated the development of the literature on strategic management.

We are particularly indebted to the talented case researchers who have produced the cases used in this book, as well as to case researchers dedicated to the revitalization of case research as an important academic endeavor. First-class case research is a major avenue through which top strategic management scholars should be recognized.

The development of this book through eight editions has benefited from the generous commitments of time, energy, and ideas from the following colleagues. The valuable ideas, recommendations, and support from these outstanding scholars, teachers, and practitioners have added quality to this book (we apologize if affiliations have changed):

Mary Ackenhusen
INSEAD

A. J. Almaney
DePaul University

James Almeida
Fairleigh Dickinson University

B. Alpert
San Francisco State University

Alan Amason
University of Georgia

Sherry Anderson
Sonoma State University

Sonny Aries
University of Toledo

Katherine A. Auer
The Pennsylvania State University

Amy Vernberg Beekman
George Mason University

Patricia Bilafer
Bentley College

Robert Earl Bolick
Metropolitan State University

Bill Boulton
Auburn University

Charles Boyd
Southwest Missouri State University

Jeff Bracker
University of Louisville

Dorothy Brawley
Kennesaw State College

James W. Bronson
Washington State University

Eric Brown
George Mason University

Robert F. Bruner
INSEAD

William Burr
University of Oregon

Gene E. Burton
California State University–Fresno

Edgar T. Busch
Western Kentucky University

Charles M. Byles
Virginia Commonwealth University

Gerard A. Cahill

Jim Callahan
University of LaVerne

James W. Camerius
Northern Michigan University

Richard Castaldi
San Diego State University

Gary J. Castogiovanni
Louisiana State University

Jafor Chowdbury
University of Scranton

James J. Chrisman
University of Calgary

Neil Churchill
INSEAD

J. Carl Clamp
University of South Carolina

Joyce Claterbos
University of Kansas

Issac Cohen
San Jose State University

Earl D. Cooper
Florida Institute of Technology

Louis Coraggio
Troy State University

Jeff Covin
Indiana University

John P. Cragin
Oklahoma Baptist University

Larry Cummings
Northwestern University

Peter Davis
Memphis State University

William Davis
Auburn University

Julio DeCastro
University of Colorado

Philippe Demigne
INSEAD

Robert Dennehy
Pace University

D. Keith Denton
Southwest Missouri State University

F. Derakhshan
California State University–San Bernardino

Brook Dobni
University of Saskatchewan

Mark Dollinger
Indiana University

Jean–Christopher Donck
INSEAD

John Dory
Pace University

Max E. Douglas
Indiana State University

Pat DeMouy
University South Carolina

Yves Doz
INSEAD

Julie Driscoll
Bentley College

Derrick Dsouza
University of North Texas

Thomas J. Dudley
Pepperdine University

John Dunkelberg
Wake Forest University

Soumitra Dutta
INSEAD

Harold Dyck
California State University

Norbert Esser
Central Wesleyan College

Alan Eisner
Pace University

Forest D. Etheredge
Aurora University

Liam Fahey
Babson College

Mary Fandel
Bentley College

Mark Fiegener
Oregon State University

Calvin D. Fowler
Embry-Riddle Aeronautical University

Debbie Francis
Auburn University–Montgomery

Elizabeth Freeman
Southern Methodist University

Mahmound A. Gaballa
Mansfield University

Donna M. Gallo
Boston College

Diane Garsombke
University of Maine

Betsy Gatewood
Indiana University

Michael Geringer
Southern Methodist University

Bertrand George
INSEAD

Manton C. Gibbs
Indiana University of Pennsylvania

Armand Gilinsky
Sonoma State University

Nicholas A. Glaskowsky, Jr.
University of Miami

Tom Goho
Wake Forest University

Jon Goodman
University of Southern California

Pradeep Gopalakrishna
Hofstra University

R. H. Gordon
Hofstra University

Barbara Gottfried
Bentley College

Peter Goulet
University of Northern Iowa

Walter E. Greene
University of Texas–Pan American

Sue Greenfeld
California State University–San Bernardino

David W. Grigsby
Clemson University

Daniel E. Hallock
St. Edward's University

Don Hambrick
Columbia University

Barry Hand
Indiana State University

Jean M. Hanebury
Texas A&M University

Karen Hare
Bentley College

Earl Harper
Grand Valley State University

Paula Harveston
Berry College

Samuel Hazen
Tarleton State University

W. Harvey Hegarty
Indiana University

Edward A. Hegner
California State University–Sacramento

Marilyn M. Helms
University of Tennessee–Chattanooga

Lanny Herron
University of Baltimore

D. Higginbothan
University of Missouri

Roger Higgs
Western Carolina University

William H. Hinkle
Johns Hopkins University

Charles T. Hofer
University of Georgia

Alan N. Hoffman
Bentley College

Richard Hoffman
College of William and Mary

Eileen Hogan
George Mason University

Phyllis G. Holland
Valdosta State University

Gary L. Holman
St. Martin's College

Don Hopkins
Temple University

Cecil Horst
Keller Graduate School of Management

Mel Horwitch
Theseus

Henry F. House
Auburn University–Montgomery

William C. House
University of Arkansas–Fayetteville

Frank Hoy
University of Texas–El Paso

Warren Huckabay

Eugene H. Hunt
Virginia Commonwealth University

Tammy G. Hunt
University of North Carolina–Wilmington

John W. Huonker
University of Arizona

Stephen R. Jenner
California State University

Shailendra Jha
Wilfrid Laurier University–Ontario

C. Boyd Johnson
California State University–Fresno

Troy Jones
University of Central Florida

Jon Kalinowski
Mankato State University

Al Kayloe
Lake Erie College

Michael J. Keefe
Southwest Texas State University

Kay Keels
Louisiana State University

James A. Kidney
Southern Connecticut State University

John D. King
Embry-Riddle Aeronautical University

Raymond M. Kinnunen
Northeastern University

John B. Knauff
University of St. Thomas

Rose Knotts
University of North Texas

Dan Kopp
Southwest Missouri State University

Michael Koshuta
Valparaiso University

Jeffrey A. Krug
The University of Illinois

Jerome Kuperman
Minnesota State University

Myroslaw Kyj
Widener University of Pennsylvania

Dick LaBarre
Ferris State University

Joseph Lampel
New York University

Ryan Lancaster
The University of Phoenix

Sharon Ungar Lane
Bentley College

Roland Larose
Bentley College

Anne T. Lawrence
San Jose State University

Joseph Lampel
McGill University

Stephen Leavenworth
Pace University

Joseph Leonard
Miami University–Ohio

Robert Letovsky
Saint Michael's College

Michael Levy
INSEAD

Benjamin Litt
Lehigh University

Frank S. Lockwood
University of Wisconsin

John Logan
University of South Carolina

Sandra Logan
Newberry College

Jean M. Lundin
Lake Superior State University

Rodney H. Mabry
Clemson University

Donald C. Malm
University of Missouri–St. Louis

Charles C. Manz
Arizona State University

John Maurer
Wayne State University

Denise Mazur
Aquinas College

Edward McClelland
Roanoke College

Rich McCline
San Franciso State University

Bob McDonald
Central Wesleyan College

Patricia P. McDougall
Indiana University

S. Mehta
San Jose State University

Ralph Melaragno
Pepperdine University

Richard Merner
University of Delaware

Linda Merrill
Bentley College

Timothy Mescon
Kennesaw State College

Philip C. Micka
Park College

Bill J. Middlebrook
Southwest Texas State University

Robert Mockler
St. John's University

James F. Molly, Jr.
Northeastern University

Cynthia Montgomery
Harvard University

W. Kent Moore
Valdosta State University

Jaideep Motwani
Grand Valley State University

Karen Mullen
Bentley College

Gary W. Muller
Hofstra University

Terry Muson
Northern Montana College

Daniel Muzyka
INSEAD

Stephanie Newell
Bowling Green State University

Michael E. Nix
Trinity College of Vermont

Kenneth Olm
University of Texas–Austin

Benjamin M. Oviatt
Georgia State University

Joseph Paolillo
University of Mississippi

Gerald Parker
St. Louis University

Paul J. Patinka
University of Colorado

James W. Pearce
Western Carolina University

Michael W. Pitts
Virginia Commonwealth University

Douglas Polley
St. Cloud State University

Carlos de Pommes
Theseus

Valerie J. Porciello
Bentley College

Mark S. Poulous
St. Edward's University

John B. Pratt
Saint Joseph's College

Oliver Ray Price
West Coast University

John Primus
Golden Gate University

Srivinivasa Rangan
Babson College

Norris Rath
Shepard College

Paula Rechner
University of Illinois

Richard Reed
Washington State University

J. Bruce Regan
University of St. Thomas

H. Lee Remmers
INSEAD

F. A. Ricci
Georgetown University

Keith Robbins
Winthrop University

Gary Roberts
Kennesaw State College

Lloyd E. Roberts
Mississippi College

John K. Ross III
Southwest Texas State University

George C. Rubenson
Salisbury State University

Alison Rude
Bentley College

Les Rue
Georgia State University

Carol Rugg
Bentley College

J. A. Ruslyk
Memphis State University

Ronald J. Salazar
Idaho State University

Bill Sandberg
University of South Carolina

Harry Sapienza
University of Minnesota

Uri Savoray
INSEAD

Jack Scarborough
Barry University

Paul J. Schlachter
Florida International University

David Schweiger
University of South Carolina

John Seeger
Bentley College

Martin Shapiro
Iona College

Arthur Sharplin
McNeese State University

Frank M. Shipper
Salisbury State University

Rodney C. Shrader
Georgia State University

Lois Shufeldt
Southwest Missouri State University

Bonnie Silvieria
Bentley College

F. Bruce Simmons III
The University of Akron

Mark Simon
Georgia State University

Michael Skipton
Memorial University

Fred Smith
Western Illinois University

Scott Snell
Michigan State University

Coral R. Snodgrass
Canisius College

Rudolph P. Snowadzky
University of Maine

Neil Snyder
University of Virginia

Melvin J. Stanford
Mankato State University

Romuald A. Stone
James Madison University

Warren S. Stone
Virginia Commonwealth University

Ram Subramanian
Grand Valley State University

Paul M. Swiercz
Georgia State University

Robert L. Swinth
Montana State University

Norihito Tanaka
Kanagawa University

Chris Taubman
INSEAD

Marilyn Taylor
University of Missouri at Kansas City

Russell Teasley
University of South Carolina

James Teboul
INSEAD

George H. Tompson
University of New Zealand

Jody Tompson
University of New Zealand

Melanie Trevino
University of Texas–El Paso

Howard Tu
Memphis State University

Craig Tunwall
Ithaca College

Elaine M. Tweedy
University of Scranton

Arieh A. Ullmann
SUNY–Binghamton

P. Veglahn
James Madison University

George Vozikis
The Citadel

William Waddell
California State University–Los Angeles

Bill Warren
College of William and Mary

Kirby Warren
Columbia University

Steven J. Warren
Rutgers University

Michael White
University of Tulsa

Randy White
Auburn University

Sam E. White
Portland State University

Frank Winfrey
Kent State University

Joan Winn
University of Denver

Joseph Wolfe
University of Tulsa

Robley Wood
Virginia Commonwealth University

Edward D. Writh, Jr.
Florida Institute of Technology

John Young
University of New Mexico

S. David Young
INSEAD

Jan Zahrly
Old Dominion University

Alan Zeiber
Portland State University

We are affiliated with two separate universities, both of which provide environments that deserve thanks. As the Endowed Chair of the College of Commerce and Finance at Villanova University, Jack is able to combine his scholarly and teaching activities with his coauthorship of this text. He is grateful to Villanova University and his colleagues for the support and encouragement they provide.

Richard appreciates the support provided within the Moore School of Business by Mr. Dean Kress. Mr. Kress provides multifaceted assistance on projects, classes, and research that leverages the scope of what can be accomplished each year. Moore School colleagues in the management department along with Dean Joel Smith and Program Director Hoyt Wheeler provide encouragement while staff members Cheryl Fowler, Susie Gorsage, and Carol Lucas provide logistical support for which Richard is grateful.

Leadership from McGraw-Hill/Irwin deserves our utmost thanks and appreciation. Gerald Saykes got us started and continues his support. Andy Winston's editorial leadership has enhanced our quality and success. Editorial and production assistance from Sara Ramos and Kim Hooker helped this to become a much better book. The McGraw-Hill/Irwin field organization deserves particular recognition and thanks for the success of this project.

We also want to thank the *BusinessWeek* editors who listened to the strategic alliance proposal, selected our book, and are proving to be excellent strategic partners.

We hope that you will find our book and ancillaries all that you expect. We welcome your ideas and recommendations about our material. Please contact us at the following addresses:

Dr. John A. Pearce II
College of Commerce and Finance
Villanova University
Villanova, PA 19085-1678
610-519-4332
john.pearce@villanova.edu

Dr. Richard Robinson
Moore School of Business
University of South Carolina
Columbia, SC 29205
803-777-5961
Robinson@sc.edu.

We wish you the utmost success in teaching and studying strategic management.

Jack Pearce and Richard Robinson

About the Authors

John A. Pearce II, PhD, is the holder of the College of Commerce and Finance Endowed Chair in Strategic Management and Entrepreneurship at Villanova University. Previously, Dr. Pearce was holder of the Eakin Endowed Chair in Strategic Management at George Mason University and was a State of Virginia Eminent Scholar. In 1994, he received the Fulbright U.S. Professional Award for service in Malaysia. Professor Pearce has taught at Penn State, West Virginia University, the University of Malta, where as a Fulbright Senior Professor in International Management he served as the Head of Business Faculties, and at the University of South Carolina, where he was Director of PhD Programs in Strategic Management. He received a PhD degree in Business Administration from the Pennsylvania State University.

Professor Pearce is coauthor of 36 books that have been used to help educate more than one million students and managers. He has also authored more than 250 articles and professional papers. These have been published in journals that include the *Academy of Management Journal, California Management Review, Journal of Applied Psychology, Journal of Business Venturing, Sloan Management Review,* and *Strategic Management Journal.* Several of these publications have resulted from Professor Pearce's work as a principal on research projects funded for more than $2 million. He is a recognized expert in the field of strategic management, with special accomplishments in the areas of strategy formulation, implementation, control, management during recessions, mission statement development, competitive assessment, industry analysis, joint ventures, and tools for strategy evaluation and design.

Dr. Pearce is a frequent leader of executive development programs and an active consultant to business and industry, whose client list includes domestic and multinational firms engaged in manufacturing, service, and nonprofit industries.

Richard B. Robinson, Jr., PhD, is a Business Partnership Foundation Fellow in Strategic Management and Entrepreneurship in the Moore School of Business, University of South Carolina. He also serves as Director of the Faber Entrepreneurship Center at USC and Associate Director of the Center for Manufacturing and Technology in USC's College of Engineering and Information Technology. Dr. Robinson received his PhD in Business Administration from the University of Georgia. He graduated from Georgia Tech in Industrial Management.

Professor Robinson has coauthored over 30 books addressing strategic management and entrepreneurship issues that students and managers use worldwide. He has authored over 250 articles, professional papers, and case studies that have been published in major journals including the *Academy of Management Journal, Academy of Management Review, Strategic Management Journal, Academy of Entrepreneurship Journal,* and the *Journal of Business Venturing.*

Dr. Robinson has previously held executive positions with companies in the pulp and paper, hazardous waste, building products, lodging and restaurant industries. He currently serves as a director or advisor to entrepreneurial companies that are global leaders in niche markets in the log home, building products, animation and computer chip thermal management industries. Dr. Robinson also supervises over 50 student teams each year that undertake field consulting projects and internships with entrepreneurial companies worldwide.

Brief Contents

Contents

Chapter 11
Strategic Control and Continuous Improvement   318

Overview of Strategic Management

The first chapter of this book introduces strategic management, the set of decisions and actions that result in the design and activation of strategies to achieve the objectives of an organization. The chapter provides an overview of the nature, benefits, and terminology of and the need for strategic management. Subsequent chapters provide greater detail.

The first major section of Chapter 1, "The Nature and Value of Strategic Management," emphasizes the practical value and benefits of strategic management for a firm. It also distinguishes between a firm's strategic decisions and its other planning tasks.

The section stresses the key point that strategic management activities are undertaken at three levels: corporate, business, and functional. The distinctive characteristics of strategic decision making at each of these levels affect the impact of activities at these levels on company operations. Other topics dealt with in this section are the value of formality in strategic management and the alignment of strategy makers in strategy formulation and implementation. The section concludes with a review of the planning research on business, which demonstrates that the use of strategic management processes yields financial and behavioral benefits that justify their costs.

The second major section of Chapter 1 presents a model of the strategic management process. The model, which will serve as an outline for the remainder of the text, describes approaches currently used by strategic planners. Its individual components are carefully defined and explained, as is the process for integrating them into the strategic management process. The section ends with a discussion of the model's practical limitations and the advisability of tailoring the recommendations made to actual business situations.

Chapter One

Strategic Management

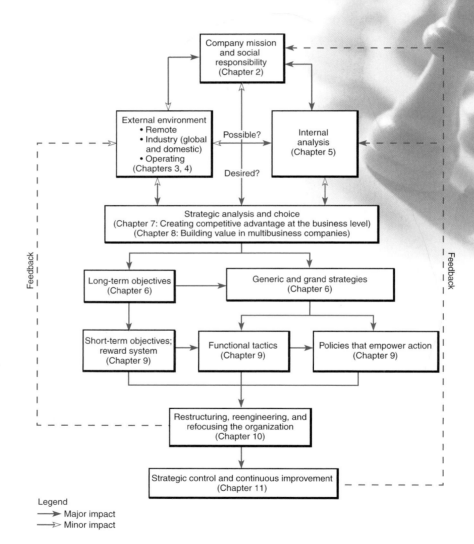

THE NATURE AND VALUE OF STRATEGIC MANAGEMENT

Managing activities internal to the firm is only part of the modern executive's responsibilities. The modern executive also must respond to the challenges posed by the firm's immediate and remote external environments. The immediate external environment includes competitors, suppliers, increasingly scarce resources, government agencies and their ever more numerous regulations, and customers whose preferences often shift inexplicably. The remote external environment comprises economic and social conditions, political priorities, and technological developments, all of which must be anticipated, monitored, assessed, and incorporated into the executive's decision making. However, the executive often is compelled to subordinate the demands of the firm's internal activities and external environment to the multiple and often inconsistent requirements of its stakeholders: owners, top managers, employees, communities, customers, and country. To deal effectively with everything that affects the growth and profitability of a firm, executives employ management processes that they feel will position it optimally in its competitive environment by maximizing the anticipation of environmental changes and of unexpected internal and competitive demands.

Broad-scope, large-scale management processes became dramatically more sophisticated after World War II. These processes responded to increases in the size and number of competing firms; to the expanded role of government as a buyer, seller, regulator, and competitor in the free enterprise system; and to greater business involvement in international trade. Perhaps the most significant improvement in management processes came in the 1970s, when "long-range planning," "new venture management," "planning, programming, budgeting," and "business policy" were blended. At the same time, increased emphasis was placed on environmental forecasting and external considerations in formulating and implementing plans. This all-encompassing approach is known as strategic management.

Strategic management is defined as the set of decisions and actions that result in the formulation and implementation of plans designed to achieve a company's objectives. It comprises nine critical tasks:

1. Formulate the company's mission, including broad statements about its purpose, philosophy, and goals.

2. Conduct an analysis that reflects the company's internal conditions and capabilities.

3. Assess the company's external environment, including both the competitive and the general contextual factors.

4. Analyze the company's options by matching its resources with the external environment.

5. Identify the most desirable options by evaluating each option in light of the company's mission.

6. Select a set of long-term objectives and grand strategies that will achieve the most desirable options.

7. Develop annual objectives and short-term strategies that are compatible with the selected set of long-term objectives and grand strategies.

8. Implement the strategic choices by means of budgeted resource allocations in which the matching of tasks, people, structures, technologies, and reward systems is emphasized.

9. Evaluate the success of the strategic process as an input for future decision making.

As these nine tasks indicate, strategic management involves the planning, directing, organizing, and controlling of a company's strategy-related decisions and actions. By *strategy,* managers mean their large-scale, future-oriented plans for interacting with the competitive environment to achieve company objectives. A strategy is a company's game plan. Although that plan does not precisely detail all future deployments (of people, finances, and material), it does provide a framework for managerial decisions. A strategy reflects a company's awareness of how, when, and where it should compete; against whom it should compete; and for what purposes it should compete.

Dimensions of Strategic Decisions

What decisions facing a business are strategic and therefore deserve strategic management attention? Typically, strategic issues have the following dimensions.

Strategic Issues Require Top-Management Decisions   Since strategic decisions overarch several areas of a firm's operations, they require top-management involvement. Usually only top management has the perspective needed to understand the broad implications of such decisions and the power to authorize the necessary resource allocations. As top manager of Volvo GM Heavy Truck Corporation, Karl-Erling Trogen, president, wanted to push the company closer to the customer by overarching operations with service and customer relations empowering the work force closest to the customer with greater knowledge and authority. This strategy called for a major commitment to the parts and service end of the business where customer relations was first priority. Trogen's philosophy was to so empower the work force that more operating questions were handled on the line where workers worked directly with customers. He believed that the corporate headquarters should be more focused on strategic issues, such as engineering, production, quality, and marketing.

Strategic Issues Require Large Amounts of the Firm's Resources   Strategic decisions involve substantial allocations of people, physical assets, or moneys that either must be redirected from internal sources or secured from outside the firm. They also commit the firm to actions over an extended period. For these reasons, they require substantial resources. Whirlpool Corporation's "Quality Express" product delivery program exemplified a strategy that required a strong financial and personnel commitment from the company. The plan was to deliver products to customers when, where, and how they wanted them. This proprietary service uses contract logistics strategy to deliver Whirlpool, Kitchen Aid, Roper, and Estate brand appliances to 90 percent of the company's dealer and builder customers within 24 hours and to the other 10 percent within 48 hours. In highly competitive service-oriented businesses, achieving and maintaining customer satisfaction frequently involve a commitment from every facet of the organization.

Strategic Issues Often Affect the Firm's Long-Term Prosperity   Strategic decisions ostensibly commit the firm for a long time, typically five years; however, the impact of such decisions often lasts much longer. Once a firm has committed itself to a particular strategy, its image and competitive advantages usually are tied to that strategy. Firms become known in certain markets, for certain products, with certain technologies. They would jeopardize their previous gains if they shifted from these markets, products, or technologies by adopting a radically different strategy. Thus, strategic decisions have enduring effects on firms—for better or worse.

Global Strategy in Action
Revising Toyota's Image

Exhibit 1–1

BusinessWeek The hearty appetite for fancy German metal has Toyota Motor Co. (TM) spooked. "Higher-priced sedans are a traditional base of strength for Toyota," says Yasuhiko Fukatsu, managing director for domestic luxury sales. "But BMW and Mercedes-Benz are doing a better job attracting younger buyers." Toyota also is increasingly worried about a resurgent Nissan Motor Co. (NSANY), which is staging a comeback in the sedan niche.

Toyota's answer: Run its rivals off the road. To do so, it is unleashing on Japan a dozen-plus new or improved vehicles. Besides updating such midrange standbys as the Camry, Toyota is bulking up on eye-candy luxury models, most of which sell for $30,000 to $60,000. Among them: fully loaded versions of the muscular and decidedly BMW-ish Verossa, the remodeled Lexus ES 300 (known in Japan as the Windom), and a Mercedes-like sedan called the Brevis. Toyota is even debating marketing cars at home under the Lexus badge, which now exists only overseas.

Aging customers are a problem for Toyota everywhere, but nowhere more than in Japan. Most of the folks buying such luxury Toyota sedans as the best-selling Crown are graying executives who started out with entry-level Toyotas in the 1950s and 1960s. By contrast, upwardly mobile Japanese wouldn't be caught dead in a Crown, a $30,000 sedan often used as a taxi. Consider Shunsuke Kurita, a 46–year-old interior designer who drives a black 1999 BMW 318i. "It's a status symbol more than anything else, but I figure a BMW has better resale value than domestic cars," he says. "Toyota sedans have a fuddy-duddy image."

Still, why all the fuss? After all, foreign imports account for less than 10% of the Japanese auto market. Well, what worries Toyota is that up-and-coming Japanese drivers will develop the kind of loyalty to their German imports that their parents had to Toyota. Were that to happen, Toyota could lose out on future sales to drivers now in their late thirties and early forties.

Source: Extracted from C. Dawson, "Toyota: Taking on BMW," *BusinessWeek,* July 30, 2001.

Exhibit 1–1, Global Strategy in Action, is a *BusinessWeek* excerpt that provides an excellent example of a firm's strategy tied to its image and competitive advantage. For years, Toyota had a successful strategy of marketing its sedans in Japan. With this strategy came an image, a car for an older customer, and a competitive advantage, a traditional base for Toyota. The strategy was effective, but as its customer base grew older its strategy remained unchanged. A younger customer market saw the image as unattractive and began to seek out other manufacturers. Toyota's strategic task in foreign markets is to formulate and implement a strategy that will reignite interest in its image.

Strategic Issues Are Future Oriented Strategic decisions are based on what managers forecast, rather than on what they know. In such decisions, emphasis is placed on the development of projections that will enable the firm to select the most promising strategic options. In the turbulent and competitive free enterprise environment, a firm will succeed only if it takes a proactive (anticipatory) stance toward change.

Strategic Issues Usually Have Multifunctional or Multibusiness Consequences Strategic decisions have complex implications for most areas of the firm. Decisions about such matters as customer mix, competitive emphasis, or organizational structure necessarily involve a number of the firm's strategic business units (SBUs), divisions, or program units. All of these areas will be affected by allocations or reallocations of responsibilities and resources that result from these decisions.

Strategic Issues Require Considering the Firm's External Environment All business firms exist in an open system. They affect and are affected by external conditions that are largely beyond their control. Therefore, to successfully position a firm in competitive situations, its strategic managers must look beyond its operations. They must consider what relevant others (e.g., competitors, customers, suppliers, creditors, government, and labor) are likely to do.

Three Levels of Strategy

The decision-making hierarchy of a firm typically contains three levels. At the top of this hierarchy is the corporate level, composed principally of a board of directors and the chief executive and administrative officers. They are responsible for the firm's financial performance and for the achievement of nonfinancial goals, such as enhancing the firm's image and fulfilling its social responsibilities. To a large extent, attitudes at the corporate level reflect the concerns of stockholders and society at large. In a multibusiness firm, corporate-level executives determine the businesses in which the firm should be involved. They also set objectives and formulate strategies that span the activities and functional areas of these businesses. Corporate-level strategic managers attempt to exploit their firm's distinctive competencies by adopting a portfolio approach to the management of its businesses and by developing long-term plans, typically for a five-year period. A key corporate strategy of Airborne Express's operations involved direct sale to high-volume corporate accounts and developing an expansive network in the international arena. Instead of setting up operations overseas, Airborne's long-term strategy was to form direct associations with national companies within foreign countries to expand and diversify their operations.

Another example of the portfolio approach involved a plan by state-owned Saudi Arabian Oil to spend $1.4 billion to build and operate an oil refinery in Korea with its partner, Ssangyong. To implement their program, the Saudis embarked on a new "cut-out-the-middleman" strategy to reduce the role of international oil companies in the processing and selling of Saudi crude oil.

In the middle of the decision-making hierarchy is the business level, composed principally of business and corporate managers. These managers must translate the statements of direction and intent generated at the corporate level into concrete objectives and strategies for individual business divisions, or SBUs. In essence, business-level strategic managers determine how the firm will compete in the selected product-market arena. They strive to identify and secure the most promising market segment within that arena. This segment is the piece of the total market that the firm can claim and defend because of its competitive advantages.

At the bottom of the decision-making hierarchy is the functional level, composed principally of managers of product, geographic, and functional areas. They develop annual objectives and short-term strategies in such areas as production, operations, research and development, finance and accounting, marketing, and human relations. However, their principal responsibility is to implement or execute the firm's strategic plans. Whereas corporate- and business-level managers center their attention on "doing the right things," managers at the functional level center their attention on "doing things right." Thus, they address such issues as the efficiency and effectiveness of production and marketing systems, the quality of customer service, and the success of particular products and services in increasing the firm's market shares.

Exhibit 1–2 depicts the three levels of strategic management as structured in practice. In alternative 1, the firm is engaged in only one business and the corporate- and business-level responsibilities are concentrated in a single group of directors, officers, and managers. This is the organizational format of most small businesses.

Alternative 2, the classical corporate structure, comprises three fully operative levels: the corporate level, the business level, and the functional level. The approach taken throughout this text assumes the use of alternative 2. Moreover, whenever appropriate,

EXHIBIT 1–2
Alternative Strategic Management Structures

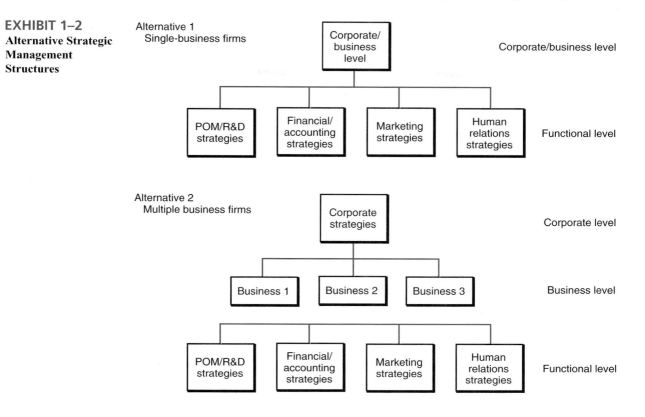

Alternative 1
Single-business firms

Corporate/business level — Corporate/business level

POM/R&D strategies | Financial/accounting strategies | Marketing strategies | Human relations strategies — Functional level

Alternative 2
Multiple business firms

Corporate strategies — Corporate level

Business 1 | Business 2 | Business 3 — Business level

POM/R&D strategies | Financial/accounting strategies | Marketing strategies | Human relations strategies — Functional level

topics are covered from the perspective of each level of strategic management. In this way, the text presents a comprehensive discussion of the strategic management process.

Characteristics of Strategic Management Decisions

The characteristics of strategic management decisions vary with the level of strategic activity considered. As shown in Exhibit 1–3, decisions at the corporate level tend to be more value oriented, more conceptual, and less concrete than decisions at the business or functional level. For example, at Alcoa, the world's largest aluminum maker, chairman Paul O'Neill made Alcoa one of the nation's most centralized organizations by imposing a dramatic management reorganization that wiped out two layers of management. He found that this effort not only reduced costs but also enabled him to be closer to the frontline operations managers. Corporate-level decisions are often characterized by greater risk, cost, and profit potential; greater need for flexibility; and longer time horizons. Such decisions include the choice of businesses, dividend policies, sources of long-term financing, and priorities for growth.

Functional-level decisions implement the overall strategy formulated at the corporate and business levels. They involve action-oriented operational issues and are relatively short range and low risk. Functional-level decisions incur only modest costs, because they are dependent on available resources. They usually are adaptable to ongoing activities and, therefore, can be implemented with minimal cooperation. For example, the corporate headquarters of Sears, Roebuck & Company spent $60 million to automate 6,900 clerical jobs by installing 28,000 computerized cash registers at its 868 stores in the United States. Though this move eliminated many functional-level jobs, top management believed that reducing annual operating expenses by at least $50 million was crucial to competitive survival.

EXHIBIT 1–3   Hierarchy of Objectives and Strategies

Ends (What is to be achieved?)	Means (How is it to be achieved?)	Strategic Decision Makers			
		Board of Directors	Corporate Managers	Business Managers	Functional Managers
Mission, including goals and philosophy		✓✓	✓✓	✓	
Long-term objectives	Grand strategy	✓	✓✓	✓✓	
Annual objectives	Short-term strategies and policies		✓	✓✓	✓✓

Note: ✓✓ indicates a principal responsibility; ✓ indicates a secondary responsibility.

Because functional-level decisions are relatively concrete and quantifiable, they receive critical attention and analysis even though their comparative profit potential is low. Common functional-level decisions include decisions on generic versus brandname labeling, basic versus applied research and development (R&D), high versus low inventory levels, general-purpose versus specific-purpose production equipment, and close versus loose supervision.

Business-level decisions help bridge decisions at the corporate and functional levels. Such decisions are less costly, risky, and potentially profitable than corporate-level decisions, but they are more costly, risky, and potentially profitable than functional-level decisions. Common business-level decisions include decisions on plant location, marketing segmentation and geographic coverage, and distribution channels.

Formality in Strategic Management

The formality of strategic management systems varies widely among companies. *Formality* refers to the degree to which participants, responsibilities, authority, and discretion in decision making are specified. It is an important consideration in the study of strategic management, because greater formality is usually positively correlated with the cost, comprehensiveness, accuracy, and success of planning.

A number of forces determine how much formality is needed in strategic management. The size of the organization, its predominant management styles, the complexity of its environment, its production process, its problems, and the purpose of its planning system all play a part in determining the appropriate degree of formality.

In particular, formality is associated with the size of the firm and with its stage of development. Methods of evaluating strategic success also are linked to formality. Some firms, especially smaller ones, follow an *entrepreneurial* mode. They are basically under the control of a single individual, and they produce a limited number of products or services. In such firms, strategic evaluation is informal, intuitive, and limited. Very large firms, on the other hand, make strategic evaluation part of a comprehensive, formal planning system, an approach that Henry Mintzberg called the *planning mode*. Mintzberg also identified a third mode (the *adaptive mode*), which he associated with medium-sized firms in relatively stable environments.[1] For firms that follow the adaptive mode, the identification and evaluation of alternative strategies are closely related to existing strategy. It is not unusual to find different modes within the same organization. For example, Exxon might follow an entrepreneurial mode in developing and evaluating the strategy of its solar subsidiary but follow a planning mode in the rest of the company.

[1] H. Mintzberg, "Strategy Making in Three Modes," *California Management Review* 16, no. 2 (1973), pp. 44–53.

The Strategy Makers

The ideal strategic management team includes decision makers from all three company levels (the corporate, business, and functional)—for example, the chief executive officer (CEO), the product managers, and the heads of functional areas. In addition, the team obtains input from company planning staffs, when they exist, and from lower-level managers and supervisors. The latter provide data for strategic decision making and then implement strategies.

Because strategic decisions have a tremendous impact on a company and require large commitments of company resources, top managers must give final approval for strategic action. Exhibit 1–3 aligns levels of strategic decision makers with the kinds of objectives and strategies for which they are typically responsible.

Planning departments, often headed by a corporate vice president for planning, are common in large corporations. Medium-sized firms often employ at least one full-time staff member to spearhead strategic data-collection efforts. Even in small firms or less progressive larger firms, strategic planning often is spearheaded by an officer or by a group of officers designated as a planning committee.

Precisely what are managers' responsibilities in the strategic planning process at the corporate and business levels? Top management shoulders broad responsibility for all the major elements of strategic planning and management. It develops the major portions of the strategic plan and reviews, and it evaluates and counsels on all other portions. General managers at the business level typically have principal responsibilities for developing environmental analysis and forecasting, establishing business objectives, and developing business plans prepared by staff groups.

A firm's president or CEO characteristically plays a dominant role in the strategic planning process. In many ways, this situation is desirable. The CEO's principal duty often is defined as giving long-term direction to the firm, and the CEO is ultimately responsible for the firm's success and, therefore, for the success of its strategy. In addition, CEOs are typically strong-willed, company-oriented individuals with high self-esteem. They often resist delegating authority to formulate or approve strategic decisions.

However, when the dominance of the CEO approaches autocracy, the effectiveness of the firm's strategic planning and management processes is likely to be diminished. For this reason, establishing a strategic management system implies that the CEO will allow managers at all levels to participate in the strategic posture of the company.

In implementing a company's strategy, the CEO must have an appreciation for the power and responsibility of the board, while retaining the power to lead the company with the guidance of informed directors. The interaction between the CEO and board is key to any corporation's strategy. Empowerment of the board has been a recent trend across major management teams. Exhibit 1–4, Strategy in Action, presents descriptions of the changes that companies have made in an attempt to monitor the relationships between the role of the board and the role of CEO.

Benefits of Strategic Management

Using the strategic management approach, managers at all levels of the firm interact in planning and implementing. As a result, the behavioral consequences of strategic management are similar to those of participative decision making. Therefore, an accurate assessment of the impact of strategy formulation on organizational performance requires not only financial evaluation criteria but also nonfinancial evaluation criteria—measures of behavior-based effects. In fact, promoting positive behavioral consequences also enables the firm to achieve its financial goals. However, regardless

Company	Innovation
Dayton Hudson Corporation	Requires the inside directors to conduct an annual evaluation of the CEO.
Medtronic	Solicits opinions on board procedures by requiring all directors to complete a questionnaire, then the full board reviews the results at an annual meeting and tries to make improvements.
Stanhome	Developed a formal document that specifies the board's purpose, size, proportion of outside directors, annual calendar, and expectations of directors and management.
Mallinckrodt	Separated the roles of chair and CEO.
Lukens	Formed a committee of outside directors to study a major acquisition proposal, hold discussions with management, and recommend action to the full board.
Campbell Soup Company	Designated a lead director with the title of vice chairman.
Monsanto	Increased the proportion of the board's time that would be focused on strategic direction and considered specific capital proposals within that framework.
General Motors	Developed an explicit set of guidelines that outline how the board will function and be structured.

Source: Reprinted by permission of *Harvard Business Review*. An exhibit from "Empowering the Board," by Jay W. Lorsch, January–February 1995. Copyright © 1995 by the President and Fellows of Harvard University, all rights reserved.

of the profitability of strategic plans, several behavioral effects of strategic management improve the firm's welfare:

1. Strategy formulation activities enhance the firm's ability to prevent problems. Managers who encourage subordinates' attention to planning are aided in their monitoring and forecasting responsibilities by subordinates who are aware of the needs of strategic planning.

2. Group-based strategic decisions are likely to be drawn from the best available alternatives. The strategic management process results in better decisions because group interaction generates a greater variety of strategies and because forecasts based on the specialized perspectives of group members improve the screening of options.

3. The involvement of employees in strategy formulation improves their understanding of the productivity-reward relationship in every strategic plan and, thus, heightens their motivation.

4. Gaps and overlaps in activities among individuals and groups are reduced as participation in strategy formulation clarifies differences in roles.

5. Resistance to change is reduced. Though the participants in strategy formulation may be no more pleased with their own decisions than they would be with authoritarian decisions, their greater awareness of the parameters that limit the available options makes them more likely to accept those decisions.

Risks of Strategic Management

Managers must be trained to guard against three types of unintended negative consequences of involvement in strategy formulation.

First, the time that managers spend on the strategic management process may have a negative impact on operational responsibilities. Managers must be trained to minimize that impact by scheduling their duties to allow the necessary time for strategic activities.

Second, if the formulators of strategy are not intimately involved in its implementation, they may shirk their individual responsibility for the decisions reached. Thus, strategic managers must be trained to limit their promises to performance that the decision makers and their subordinates can deliver.

Third, strategic managers must be trained to anticipate and respond to the disappointment of participating subordinates over unattained expectations. Subordinates may expect their involvement in even minor phases of total strategy formulation to result in both acceptance of their proposals and an increase in their rewards, or they may expect a solicitation of their input on selected issues to extend to other areas of decision making.

Sensitizing managers to these possible negative consequences and preparing them with effective means of minimizing such consequences will greatly enhance the potential of strategic planning.

Executives' Views of Strategic Management

How do managers and corporate executives view the contribution of strategic management to the success of their firms? To answer this question, a survey was conducted that included over 200 executives from the Fortune 500, Fortune 500 Service, and INC 500 companies.[2] Their responses indicate that corporate America sees strategic management as instrumental to high performance, evolutionary and perhaps revolutionary in its ever-growing sophistication, action oriented, and cost effective. Clearly, the responding executives view strategic management as critical to their individual and organizational success.

THE STRATEGIC MANAGEMENT PROCESS

Businesses vary in the processes they use to formulate and direct their strategic management activities. Sophisticated planners, such as General Electric, Procter & Gamble, and IBM, have developed more detailed processes than less-formal planners of similar size. Small businesses that rely on the strategy formulation skills and limited time of an entrepreneur typically exhibit more basic planning concerns than those of larger firms in their industries. Understandably, firms with multiple products, markets, or technologies tend to use more complex strategic management systems. However, despite differences in detail and the degree of formalization, the basic components of the models used to analyze strategic management operations are very similar.

Because of the similarity among the general models of the strategic management process, it is possible to develop an eclectic model representative of the foremost thought in the strategic management area. This model is shown in Exhibit 1–5. It serves three major functions. First, it depicts the sequence and the relationships of the major components of the strategic management process. Second, it is the outline for this book. This chapter provides a general overview of the strategic management process, and the major components of the model will be the principal theme of subsequent chapters. Notice that the chapters of the text that discuss each of the strategic management process components are shown in each block. Finally, the model offers one approach for analyzing the case studies in this text and thus helps the analyst develop strategy formulation skills.

[2] V. Ramanujam, J. C. Camillus, and N. Venkatraman, "Trends in Strategic Planning," in *Strategic Planning and Management Handbook,* ed. W. R. King and D. I. Cleland (New York: Van Nostrand Reinhold, 1987), pp. 611–28.

EXHIBIT 1–5   **Strategic Management Model**

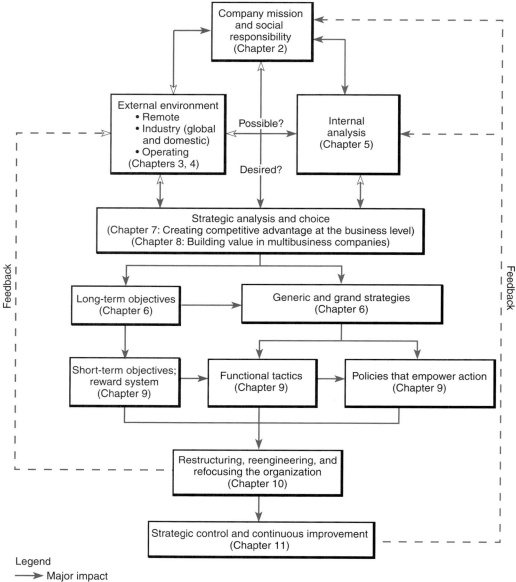

Legend
⟶ Major impact
⟶⇢ Minor impact

Components of the Strategic Management Model

This section will define and briefly describe the key components of the strategic management model. Each of these components will receive much greater attention in a later chapter. The intention here is simply to introduce them.

Company Mission

The mission of a company is the unique purpose that sets it apart from other companies of its type and identifies the scope of its operations. In short, the mission describes the company's product, market, and technological areas of emphasis in a way that reflects the values and priorities of the strategic decision makers. For example, Lee Hun-Hee, the new chairman of the Samsung Group, revamped the company mission by stamping his own brand of management on Samsung. Immediately, Samsung separated Chonju Paper Manufacturing and Shinsegae Department Store from other operations. This corporate act of downscaling reflected a revised management philosophy that favored specialization, thereby changing the direction and scope of the organization.

Social responsibility is a critical consideration for a company's strategic decision makers since the mission statement must express how the company intends to contribute to the societies that sustain it. A firm needs to set social responsibility aspirations for itself, just as it does in other areas of corporate performance.

Internal Analysis

The company analyzes the quantity and quality of the company's financial, human, and physical resources. It also assesses the strengths and weaknesses of the company's management and organizational structure. Finally, it contrasts the company's past successes and traditional concerns with the company's current capabilities in an attempt to identify the company's future capabilities.

External Environment

A firm's external environment consists of all the conditions and forces that affect its strategic options and define its competitive situation. The strategic management model shows the external environment as three interactive segments: the remote, industry, and operating environments.

Strategic Analysis and Choice

Simultaneous assessment of the external environment and the company profile enables a firm to identify a range of possibly attractive interactive opportunities. These opportunities are *possible* avenues for investment. However, they must be screened through the criterion of the company mission to generate a set of possible and *desired* opportunities. This screening process results in the selection of options from which a *strategic choice* is made. The process is meant to provide the combination of long-term objectives and generic and grand strategies that optimally position the firm in its external environment to achieve the company mission.

Strategic analysis and choice in single or dominant product/service businesses center around identifying strategies that are most effective at building sustainable competitive advantage based on key value chain activities and capabilities—core competencies of the firm. Multibusiness companies find their managers focused on the question of which combination of businesses maximizes shareholder value as the guiding theme during their strategic analysis and choice.

Long-Term Objectives

The results that an organization seeks over a multiyear period are its *long-term objectives*. Such objectives typically involve some or all of the following areas: profitability, return on investment, competitive position, technological leadership, productivity, employee relations, public responsibility, and employee development.

Generic and Grand Strategies

Many businesses explicitly and all implicitly adopt one or more *generic strategies* characterizing their competitive orientation in the marketplace. Low cost, differentiation, or focus strategies define the three fundamental options. Enlightened managers seek to create ways their firm possesses both low cost and differentiation competitive advantages as part of their overall generic strategy. They usually combine these capabilities with a comprehensive, general plan of major actions through which their firm intends to achieve its long-term objectives in a dynamic environment. Called the *grand strategy,* this statement of means indicates how the objectives are to be achieved. Although every grand strategy is, in fact, a unique package of long-term strategies, 14 basic approaches can be identified: concentration, market development, product development, innovation, horizontal integration, vertical integration, joint venture, strategic alliances, consortia, concentric diversification, conglomerate diversification, turnaround, divestiture, and liquidation.

Each of these grand strategies will be covered in detail in Chapter 6.

Action Plans and Short-Term Objectives

Action plans translate generic and grand strategies into "action" by incorporating four elements. First, they identify specific functional *tactics and actions* to be undertaken in the next week, month, or quarter as part of the business's effort to build competitive advantage. The second element is a clear time frame for completion. Third, action plans create accountability by identifying who is responsible for each "action" in the plan. Fourth, each "action" in an action plan has one or more specific, immediate objectives that are identified as outcomes that action should generate.

Functional Tactics

Within the general framework created by the business's generic and grand strategies, each business function needs to identify and undertake activities unique to the function that help build a sustainable competitive advantage. Managers in each business function develop tactics that delineate the functional activities undertaken in their part of the business and usually include them as a core part of their action plan. *Functional tactics* are detailed statements of the "means" or activities that will be used to achieve short-term objectives and establish competitive advantage.

Policies That Empower Action

Speed is a critical necessity for success in today's competitive, global marketplace. One way to enhance speed and responsiveness is to force/allow decisions to be made whenever possible at the lowest level in organizations. *Policies* are broad, precedent-setting decisions that guide or substitute for repetitive or time-sensitive managerial decision making. Creating policies that guide and "preauthorize" the thinking, decisions, and actions of operating managers and their subordinates in implementing the business's strategy is essential for establishing and controlling the ongoing operating process of the firm in a manner consistent with the firm's strategic objectives. Policies often increase managerial effectiveness by standardizing routine decisions and empowering or expanding the discretion of managers and subordinates in implementing business strategies.

The following are examples of the nature and diversity of company policies:

A requirement that managers have purchase requests for items costing more than $5,000 cosigned by the controller.

The minimum equity position required for all new McDonald's franchises.

The standard formula used to calculate return on investment for the 43 strategic business units of General Electric.

A decision that Sears service and repair employees have the right to waive repair charges to appliance customers they feel have been poorly served by their Sears appliance.

Restructuring, Reengineering, and Refocusing the Organization

Until this point in the strategic management process, managers have maintained a decidedly market-oriented focus as they formulate strategies and begin implementation through action plans and functional tactics. Now the process takes an internal focus—getting the work of the business done efficiently and effectively so as to make the strategy successful. What is the best way to organize ourselves to accomplish the mission? Where should leadership come from? What values should guide our daily activities—what should the organization and its people be like? How can we shape rewards to encourage appropriate action? The intense competition in the global marketplace has made this tradition "internally focused" set of questions—how the activities within their business are conducted—recast themselves with unprecedented attentiveness to the marketplace. *Downsizing, restructuring,* and *reengineering* are terms that reflect the critical stage in strategy implementation wherein managers attempt to recast their organization. The company's structure, leadership, culture, and reward systems may all be changed to ensure cost competitiveness and quality demanded by unique requirements of its strategies.

Strategic Control and Continuous Improvement

Strategic control is concerned with tracking a strategy as it is being implemented, detecting problems or changes in its underlying premises, and making necessary adjustments. In contrast to postaction control, strategic control seeks to guide action on behalf of the generic and grand strategies as they are taking place and when the end results are still several years away. The rapid, accelerating change of the global marketplace of the last 10 years has made continuous improvement another aspect of strategic control in many organizations. *Continuous improvement* provides a way for managers to provide a form of strategic control that allows their organization to respond more proactively and timely to rapid developments in hundreds of areas that influence a business's success.

An early entrant, Yahoo emerged as an Internet giant. Yet, despite the success of its product, the management team never developed a strategy to ensure sustainable growth. Ignoring both threats from the AOL–Time Warner merger and opportunities in a merger with eBay, Yahoo misjudged its strategic environment. Even after Yahoo's revenues had significantly decreased, it did not shift its strategy to be less reliant on online advertising. As you will read in Exhibit 1–6, E-commerce Strategy in Action, Yahoo's e-commerce strategy was significantly undermined by its management's failure to see fundamental shifts in its industry.

Strategic Management as a Process

A *process* is the flow of information through interrelated stages of analysis toward the achievement of an aim. Thus, the strategic management model in Exhibit 1–5 depicts a process. In the strategic management process, the flow of information involves historical, current, and forecast data on the operations and environment of the business. Managers evaluate these data in light of the values and priorities of influential individuals and groups—often called *stakeholders*—that are vitally interested in the actions of the business. The interrelated stages of the process are the 11 components discussed in the previous section. Finally, the aim of the process is the formulation and implementation of strategies that work, achieving the company's long-term mission and near-term objectives.

Viewing strategic management as a process has several important implications. First, a change in any component will affect several or all of the other components. Most of the arrows in the model point two ways, suggesting that the flow of information usually is reciprocal. For example, forces in the external environment may influence the nature of a company's mission, and the company may in turn affect the external environment and

E-commerce Strategy in Action
Inside Yahoo!

Exhibit 1–6

BusinessWeek The first sign that the game had changed for Yahoo! Inc. (YHOO) came just days after its stock hit an all-time high—of $237.50. An investment banker had a juicy tip that chief rival America Online Inc. (AOL) was about to buy old-media giant Time Warner Inc. The move would rearrange the planets in the media universe—and rock Yahoo's world.

The next morning, CEO Timothy A. Koogle, President Jeffrey Mallett, and co-founder Jerry Yang held a council of war at the company's Santa Clara (Calif.) headquarters. Should Yahoo stick to its guns and remain an independent assembler of news and entertainment supplied by others? Or should it take advantage of its $110 billion market cap to make an old-media purchase of its own? They would not follow AOL's lead. All of Yahoo's chips would remain on the Net.

It was Yahoo's first big mistake. Over the next 13 months, Yahoo's management troika would commit a series of blunders that would downgrade the No. 1 Internet portal from powerhouse to Milquetoast. Corner-office intrigue, consensus management in gridlock, a souring economy, and plain old bad judgment would conspire to send Yahoo's revenues plummeting.

Yahoo's problems couldn't be fixed by a little cost-snipping and an upsurge in the economy. Its reliance on advertising revenues turned into a liability as dot-com advertisers die off like mayflies and corporate advertisers pony up 50% less for online ads than they did a year ago. Meanwhile, AOL Time Warner boasts a $221 billion market cap and controls a vast empire of online properties, magazines, movie studios, and book publishers. Its advertising and commerce revenues rose 10% last quarter.

Yahoo got a second chance to alter its fate. Again, it blew it. Seeking to beef up its e-commerce revenues, Yahoo began negotiating to buy Web auction leader eBay Inc. in late March 2000. But as acquisition talks heated up, so did Yahoo's internal politics. Koogle wanted the deal. But Mallett was concerned about having eBay CEO Margaret C. Whitman in Yahoo's executive lineup. Koogle and Mallett also differed on the strategic importance of the deal. "Tim could see the wisdom of challenging the Yahoo culture through a deal with eBay. Others were more threatened." With Koogle outnumbered, the potential deal unraveled. "This was Yahoo's most fundamental problem. It was always management by persuasion, not management by dictation," says former manager Rich Rygg. And Yahoo paid for it. Yahoo's fortunes flagged. If the merger had gone through, Yahoo would not have to rely on advertising for 90% of its revenues.

Yahoo's take-the-money-and-run style, along with its dearth of media veterans, prevented it from spotting fundamental changes in the Net advertising market. Together, Koogle and Mallett will be remembered as the management duo that built Yahoo into one of the mightiest Internet companies. But the bad mix of Koogle's disengagement and Mallett's headstrong ways kept them from anticipating vital adjustments, and this left the company vulnerable when Yahoo's world began to spin out of control.

Source: Excerpted form Ben Elgin, "Inside Yahoo!," *BusinessWeek*, May 21, 2001.

heighten competition in its realm of operation. A specific example is a power company that is persuaded, in part by governmental incentives, to include a commitment to the development of energy alternatives in its mission statement. The company then might promise to extend its R&D efforts in the area of coal liquefaction. The external environment has affected the company's mission, and the revised mission signals a competitive condition in the environment.

A second implication of viewing strategic management as a process is that strategy formulation and implementation are sequential. The process begins with development or reevaluation of the company mission. This step is associated with, but essentially followed by, development of a company profile and assessment of the external environment. Then follow, in order, strategic choice, definition of long-term objectives, design of the grand strategy, definition of short-term objectives, design of operating strategies, institutionalization of the strategy, and review and evaluation.

The apparent rigidity of the process, however, must be qualified.

First, a firm's strategic posture may have to be reevaluated in response to changes in any of the principal factors that determine or affect its performance. Entry by a major new competitor, the death of a prominent board member, replacement of the chief executive officer, and a downturn in market responsiveness are among the thousands of changes that can prompt reassessment of a firm's strategic plan. However, no matter where the need for a reassessment originates, the strategic management process begins with the mission statement.

Second, not every component of the strategic management process deserves equal attention each time planning activity takes place. Firms in an extremely stable environment may find that an in-depth assessment is not required every five years. Companies often are satisfied with their original mission statements even after a decade of operation and spend only a minimal amount of time addressing this subject. In addition, while formal strategic planning may be undertaken only every five years, objectives and strategies usually are updated each year, and rigorous reassessment of the initial stages of strategic planning rarely is undertaken at these times.

A third implication of viewing strategic management as a process is the necessity of feedback from institutionalization, review, and evaluation to the early stages of the process. *Feedback* can be defined as the collection of postimplementation results to enhance future decision making. Therefore, as indicated in Exhibit 1–5, strategic managers should assess the impact of implemented strategies on external environments. Thus, future planning can reflect any changes precipitated by strategic actions. Strategic managers also should analyze the impact of strategies on the possible need for modifications in the company mission.

A fourth implication of viewing strategic management as a process is the need to regard it as a dynamic system. The term *dynamic* characterizes the constantly changing conditions that affect interrelated and interdependent strategic activities. Managers should recognize that the components of the strategic process are constantly evolving but that formal planning artificially freezes those components, much as an action photograph freezes the movement of a swimmer. Since change is continuous, the dynamic strategic planning process must be monitored constantly for significant shifts in any of its components as a precaution against implementing an obsolete strategy.

Changes in the Process

The strategic management process undergoes continual assessment and subtle updating. Although the elements of the basic strategic management model rarely change, the relative emphasis that each element receives will vary with the decision makers who use the model and with the environments of their companies.

A recent study describes general trends in strategic management, summarizing the responses of over 200 corporate executives. This update shows there has been an increasing companywide emphasis on and appreciation for the value of strategic management activities. It also provides evidence that practicing managers have given increasing attention to the need for frequent and widespread involvement in the formulation and implementation phases of the strategic management process. Finally, it indicates that, as managers and their firms gain knowledge, experience, skill, and understanding in how to design and manage their planning activities, they become better able to avoid the potential negative consequences of instituting a vigorous strategic management process.

Summary

Strategic management is the set of decisions and actions that result in the formulation and implementation of plans designed to achieve a company's objectives. Because it involves long-term, future-oriented, complex decision making and requires considerable resources, top-management participation is essential.

Strategic management is a three-tier process involving corporate-, business-, and functional-level planners, and support personnel. At each progressively lower level, strategic activities were shown to be more specific, narrow, short term, and action oriented, with lower risks but fewer opportunities for dramatic impact.

The strategic management model presented in this chapter will serve as the structure for understanding and integrating all the major phases of strategy formulation and implementation. The chapter provided a summary account of these phases, each of which is given extensive individual attention in subsequent chapters.

The chapter stressed that the strategic management process centers on the belief that a firm's mission can be best achieved through a systematic and comprehensive assessment of both its internal capabilities and its external environment. Subsequent evaluation of the firm's opportunities leads, in turn, to the choice of long-term objectives and grand strategies and, ultimately, to annual objectives and operating strategies, which must be implemented, monitored, and controlled.

Questions for Discussion

1. Find a recent copy of *BusinessWeek* and read the "Corporate Strategies" section. Was the main decision discussed strategic? At what level in the organization was the key decision made?

2. In what ways do you think the subject matter in this strategic management–business policy course will differ from that of previous courses you have taken?

3. After graduation, you are not likely to move directly to a top-level management position. In fact, few members of your class will ever reach the top-management level. Why, then, is it important for all business majors to study the field of strategic management?

4. Do you expect outstanding performance in this course to require a great deal of memorization? Why or why not?

5. You undoubtedly have read about individuals who seemingly have given singled-handed direction to their corporations. Is a participative strategic management approach likely to stifle or suppress the contributions of such individuals?

6. Think about the courses you have taken in functional areas, such as marketing, finance, production, personnel, and accounting. What is the importance of each of these areas to the strategic planning process?

7. Discuss with practicing business managers the strategic management models used in their firms. What are the similarities and differences between these models and the one in the text?

8. In what ways do you believe the strategic planning approach of not-for-profit organizations would differ from that of profit-oriented organizations?

9. How do you explain the success of firms that do not use a formal strategic planning process?

10. Think about your postgraduation job search as a strategic decision. How would the strategic management model be helpful to you in identifying and securing the most promising position?

Chapter 1 Discussion Case

BusinessWeek

Kraft's Global Strategy: Can Kraft Be a Big Cheese Abroad?

1   When Aussies stroll down the aisles of their local supermarket, what catches their eyes are snacks from Unilever (UL) and Nestlé (NSRGY). Kraft Macaroni & Cheese and Oscar Mayer hot dogs, on the other hand, are hard to find and far from first choice. "They would be classified as a slow-moving line," says Terry Walters, the owner of an IGA store in Cairns, Queensland, about the classic American macaroni-and-cheese dinner. As for hot dogs: "We have the meat pie."

2   Kraft may be ubiquitous in U.S. grocery stores, but overseas it's a far different picture. Kraft isn't one of Walters' top five food suppliers, ranking below even H.J. Heinz Co. (HNZ), despite its ownership of Australia's famed Vegemite spread. Only 27% of its total revenues come from overseas, vs. 44% for Heinz, more than 50% for McDonald's Corp. (MCD), and more than 80% for Coca-Cola Co. (KO)

3   That will have to change. As Kraft embarks on a giant initial public offering, expected in mid-June, its challenge is to once again become a growth company. Widely admired for the astute management of its brand lineup, Kraft's nevertheless stuck in a slow-growth industry in the United States. Smart marketing and methodical cost cutting helped it boost earnings 14.1% last year, but Kraft's sales actually dipped slightly, to $26.53 billion. In fact, Kraft's annual sales have dropped 16.2% since 1994. The company took a big step toward building revenues in December with its $19.2 billion purchase of Nabisco Group Holdings Corp. (NGH-U), whose cookie and cracker brands are growing faster than Kraft's top brands.

4   That deal should boost Kraft's sales to an expected $35.05 billion this year. But analysts say that if Kraft is to spark long-term growth, it must do a better job of tapping foreign consumers. Kraft acknowledged as much when it announced that once the IPO is completed, Betsy D. Holden, CEO of Kraft Foods North America, would share the chief executive office with Roger K. Deromedi, a 13-year Kraft veteran who has been president and CEO of Kraft Foods International Inc. for the past two years. The company declined to comment or make top executives available to *BusinessWeek,* citing the quiet period before the IPO, as did parent Philip Morris Cos. (MO).

5   AMERICAN ICONS. The largest food company in North America by far, Kraft has dominated U.S. grocery-store shelves for decades. Its powerhouse brands are American icons: Philadelphia Cream Cheese, Oreo cookies, Tang, Jell-O, Kool-Aid, Life Savers, Planters peanuts, Lunchables prepackaged meals for kids. Its portfolio comprises a remarkable 61 brands with more than $100 million in sales last year. Supermarket consultants say it would be nearly impossible to run a U.S. grocery store without its products.

6   But these aren't the best of times, even for strong supermarket brands. Shopper loyalty has waned as the grocery chains' in-house brands compete for shelf space, and big brands such as Kraft's tend to be mature. Take salad dressing. Even though Kraft is the market leader, "there's Kraft, there's Wish-Bone, there's Hellmann's," says John P. Mahar, operations director at the Green Hills Farms supermarket in Syracuse, N.Y. "If we have Wish-Bone on sale, shoppers pick up Wish-Bone. They don't care. The majority of Kraft's brands are just another commodity."

7   TOBACCO TAINT. Boosting sales will become even more urgent once Kraft has outside shareholders to answer to. Cigarette maker Philip Morris, which has owned Kraft since 1988, is putting 16.1% of the company on the market in an offering that could raise as much as $8.4 billion. That would be the second-largest IPO on record, behind only AT&T Wireless Group's $10.5 billion stock market debut last year. Philip Morris will remain firmly in control, but its goal is to realize more of Kraft's value by distancing the business from the tobacco taint that has held Philip Morris' stock price down.

8   The first concern for investors might be whether Kraft's co-CEO structure can work. Deromedi, 47, and Holden, 45, who started at Kraft as an assistant product manager in 1982, will both report to Geoffrey Bible, chairman of Philip Morris. Analysts wonder how long the arrangement will last, citing a long list of prominent companies, from

DaimlerChrysler to Citigroup, where co-CEO set-ups fizzled. "The co-CEO structure calls into question if this is truly an independent company," says Goldman, Sachs & Co. analyst Romitha S. Mally. "At the end of the day, it will be the chairman and the board, which is controlled by Philip Morris, who will be the ultimate decision makers for Kraft."

9   In this case, though, the co-CEOs have well-defined management areas. Another plus: Their personalities seem to complement each other. James J. Drury, vice-chairman of Spencer Stuart, an executive-search firm in Chicago, describes Deromedi, who holds a math degree, as "more focused on problem solving and more likely to make tough decisions in complex situations." Holden, he says, is creative, charismatic, and more people-oriented: "She's more the one to take into consideration how a business situation may impact people."

10   A top task for the new CEOs will be figuring out how to expand outside North America. Overseas, Kraft faces a lineup of tough global competitors—Unilever, Nestlé, Groupe Danone—that were quicker to break into fast-growing markets in Asia, Latin America, and Eastern Europe. Unilever and Nestlé, for example, each get 32% of their sales in developing countries. Western Europe, Kraft's strongest international market, is almost as saturated as the United States. Even in Great Britain, Kraft is only the eighth-largest food company. "A truly global organization would have a quarter to one-third of their business in North America, not three-quarters," says Adrian Richardson, global consumer and retail-sector head at BT Funds Management, a large money manager in Sydney.

11   FORTRESS. One problem is that Kraft's strength, convenience products, doesn't go over well in emerging markets, where scarce shopping dollars are concentrated on necessities. Unilever, for example, sells staples in India such as rice with added protein and salt with iodine. Kraft, on the other hand, has only a tiny presence there. But Kraft plans to jump-start sales in emerging markets by introducing additional snack, beverage, cheese, and other brands in countries where it already has a presence. It also plans to enter countries where it has no operations and to make acquisitions, especially in snacks and beverages, according to its filings with the Securities & Exchange Commission.

Richardson believes Kraft could make up to three significant acquisitions in the next few years to beef up its offshore operations: "If they just build, build, build [new plants], they won't meaningfully move the dial," he says. For Kraft, "the U.S. domestic base is an absolute fortress that provides a very good cash cow" with which to go shopping. "They're not too late."

12   Close to home, Kraft is getting a much-needed shot of adrenaline from the Nabisco purchase. Last year, Kraft's sales dipped 1%, vs. gains of 7.3% at General Mills Inc. (GIS) and 6.3% at Hershey Foods Corp. (HSY) Many older Kraft products are in aging categories with flat or declining volumes, such as cereal and traditional store-bought coffee. But with Nabisco, Kraft picked up faster-growing product lines such as Chips Ahoy! cookies and Ritz crackers that will fuel earnings growth. Overnight, Kraft moved from a 6% to a 20% market share in crackers and cookies, a category that's expanding at more than twice the rate of the food-industry average. Goldman's Mally expects Kraft sales to rise 3.5% in each of the next three years, just ahead of the industry average. And with the cost savings it expects to squeeze from Nabisco, Kraft estimates that its earnings will grow at an above-average 18% to 22% annually over the same period.

13   That additional growth will be needed to cover the cost of the Nabisco deal. The newly public Kraft will carry an $18.5 billion debt load, even after using the offering proceeds to pay off a portion of the $11 billion it borrowed through Philip Morris to buy Nabisco. Next year, $7 billion of this debt comes due, and Kraft won't be able to meet that payment, according to its prospectus. But it says it plans to use its good credit rating to refinance.

14   Kraft has long been a leader in product development—in 1989 it launched the novel Lunchables line that's now a $750 million-a-year product. Innovations like that put Kraft on top of the U.S. food industry. Now investors will be counting on Deromedi and Holden to sprinkle some of that magic overseas.

Source: Julie Forster and Becky Gaylord, "Can Kraft Be a Big Cheese Abroad? It needs more global clout to offset a mature U.S. market," *BusinessWeek,* June 4, 2001.

Part **Two**

Strategy Formulation

Strategy formulation guides executives in defining the business their firm is in, the ends it seeks, and the means it will use to accomplish those ends. The approach of strategy formulation is an improvement over that of traditional long-range planning. As discussed in the next eight chapters—about developing a firm's competitive plan of action—strategy formulation combines a future-oriented perspective with concern for the firm's internal and external environments.

The strategy formulation process begins with definition of the company mission, as discussed in Chapter 2. In that chapter, the purpose of business is defined to reflect the values of a wide variety of interested parties. Social responsibility is discussed as a critical consideration for a company's strategic decision makers since the mission statement must express how the company intends to contribute to the societies that sustain it.

Chapter 3 deals with the principal factors in a firm's external environment that strategic managers must assess so they can anticipate and take advantage of future business conditions. It emphasizes the importance to a firm's planning activities of factors in the firm's remote, industry, and operating environments. A key theme of the chapter is the problem of deciding whether to accept environmental constraints or to maneuver around them.

Chapter 4 describes the key differences in strategic planning and implementation among domestic, multinational, and global firms. It gives special attention to the new vision that a firm must communicate in a revised company mission when it multinationalizes.

Chapter 5 shows how firms evaluate their company's strengths and weaknesses to produce an internal analysis. Strategic managers use such profiles to target competitive advantages they can emphasize and competitive disadvantages they should correct or minimize.

Chapter 6 examines the types of long-range objectives strategic managers set and specifies the qualities these objectives must have to provide a basis for direction and evaluation. The chapter also examines the generic and grand strategies that firms use to achieve long-range objectives.

Comprehensive approaches to the evaluation of strategic opportunities and to the final strategic decision are the focus of Chapter 7. The chapter shows how a firm's strategic options can be compared in a way that allows selection of the best available option. It also discusses how a company can create competitive advantages for each of its businesses.

Chapter 8 extends the attention on strategic analysis and choice by showing how managers can build value in multibusiness companies.

Chapter **Two**

Defining the Company's Mission and Social Responsibility

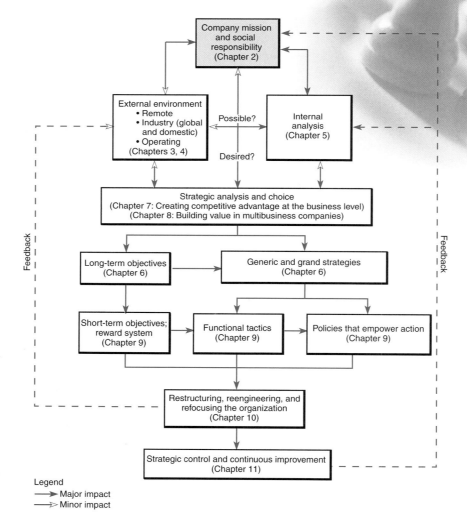

Company mission and social responsibility (Chapter 2)

External environment
• Remote
• Industry (global and domestic)
• Operating
(Chapters 3, 4)

Possible?

Desired?

Internal analysis (Chapter 5)

Strategic analysis and choice
(Chapter 7: Creating competitive advantage at the business level)
(Chapter 8: Building value in multibusiness companies)

Long-term objectives (Chapter 6)

Generic and grand strategies (Chapter 6)

Short-term objectives; reward system (Chapter 9)

Functional tactics (Chapter 9)

Policies that empower action (Chapter 9)

Restructuring, reengineering, and refocusing the organization (Chapter 10)

Strategic control and continuous improvement (Chapter 11)

Feedback

Feedback

Legend
⟶ Major impact
⟶▷ Minor impact

WHAT IS A COMPANY MISSION?

Whether a firm is developing a new business or reformulating direction for an ongoing business, it must determine the basic goals and philosophies that will shape its strategic posture. This fundamental purpose that sets a firm apart from other firms of its type and identifies the scope of its operations in product and market terms is defined as the company mission. As discussed in Chapter 1, the company mission is a broadly framed but enduring statement of a firm's intent. It embodies the business philosophy of the firm's strategic decision makers, implies the image the firm seeks to project, reflects the firm's self-concept, and indicates the firm's principal product or service areas and the primary customer needs the firm will attempt to satisfy. In short, it describes the firm's product, market, and technological areas of emphasis, and it does so in a way that reflects the values and priorities of the firm's strategic decision makers. An excellent example is the company mission statement of Nicor, Inc., shown in Exhibit 2–1, Strategy in Action.

The Need for an Explicit Mission

No external body requires that the company mission be defined, and the process of defining it is time-consuming and tedious. Moreover, it contains broadly outlined or implied objectives and strategies rather than specific directives. Characteristically, it is a statement, not of measurable targets but of attitude, outlook, and orientation.

The mission statement is a message designed to be inclusive of the expectations of all stakeholders for the company's performance over the long run. The executives and board who prepare the mission statement attempt to provide a unifying purpose for the company that will provide a basis for strategic objective setting and decision making. In general terms, the mission statement addresses the following questions:

Why is this firm in business?

What are our economic goals?

What is our operating philosophy in terms of quality, company image, and self-concept?

What are our core competencies and competitive advantages?

What customers do and can we serve?

How do we view our responsibilities to stockholders, employees, communities, environment, social issues, and competitors?

FORMULATING A MISSION

The process of defining the company mission for a specific business can perhaps be best understood by thinking about the business at its inception. The typical business begins with the beliefs, desires, and aspirations of a single entrepreneur. Such an owner-manager's sense of mission usually is based on the following fundamental beliefs:

1. The product or service of the business can provide benefits at least equal to its price.

2. The product or service can satisfy a customer need of specific market segments that is currently not being met adequately.

PREAMBLE

We, the management of Nicor, Inc., here set forth our belief as to the purpose for which the company is established and the principles under which it should operate. We pledge our effort to the accomplishment of these purposes within these principles.

BASIC PURPOSE

The basic purpose of Nicor, Inc., is to perpetuate an investor-owned company engaging in various phases of the energy business, striving for balance among those phases so as to render needed satisfactory products and services and earn optimum, long-range profits.

WHAT WE DO

The principal business of the company, through its utility subsidiary, is the provision of energy through a pipe system to meet the needs of ultimate consumers. To accomplish its basic purpose, and to ensure its strength, the company will engage in other energy-related activities, directly or through subsidiaries or in participation with other persons, corporations, firms, or entities.

All activities of the company shall be consistent with its responsibilities to investors, customers, employees, and the public and its concern for the optimum development and utilization of natural resources and for environmental needs.

WHERE WE DO IT

The company's operations shall be primarily in the United States, but no self-imposed or regulatory geographical limitations are placed upon the acquisition, development, processing, transportation, or storage of energy resources, or upon other energy-related ventures in which the company may engage. The company will engage in such activities in any location where, after careful review, it has determined that such activity is in the best interest of its stockholders.

Utility service will be offered in the territory of the company's utility subsidiary to the best of its ability, in accordance with the requirements of regulatory agencies and pursuant to the subsidiary's purposes and principles.

---

3. The technology that is to be used in production will provide a cost- and quality-competitive product or service.

4. With hard work and the support of others, the business can not only survive but also grow and be profitable.

5. The management philosophy of the business will result in a favorable public image and will provide financial and psychological rewards for those who are willing to invest their labor and money in helping the business to succeed.

6. The entrepreneur's self-concept of the business can be communicated to and adopted by employees and stockholders.

As the business grows or is forced by competitive pressures to alter its product—market—technology, redefining the company mission may be necessary. If so, the revised mission statement will contain the same components as the original. It will state the basic type of product or service to be offered, the primary markets or customer groups to be served, and the technology to be used in production or delivery; the firm's fundamental concern for survival through growth and profitability; the firm's managerial philosophy; the public image the firm seeks; and the self-concept those affiliated with the firm should have of it. This chapter will discuss in detail these components. The examples shown in Exhibit 2–2 provide insights into how some major corporations handle them.

Basic Product or Service; Primary Market; Principal Technology

Three indispensable components of the mission statement are specification of the basic product or service, specification of the primary market, and specification of the principal technology for production or delivery. These components are discussed under one

Strategy in Action
Identifying Mission Statement Components: A Compilation of Excerpts
from Actual Corporate Mission Statements

Exhibit 2–2

1. Customer-market	We believe our first responsibility is to the doctors, nurses, and patients, to mothers and all others who use our products and services. (Johnson & Johnson)
	To anticipate and meet market needs of farmers, ranchers, and rural communities within North America. (CENEX)
2. Product-service	AMAX's principal products are molybdenum, coal, iron ore, copper, lead, zinc, petroleum and natural gas, potash, phosphates, nickel, tungsten, silver, gold, and magnesium. (AMAX)
3. Geographic domain	We are dedicated to total success of Corning Glass Works as a worldwide competitor. (Corning Glass)
4. Technology	Control Data is in the business of applying microelectronics and computer technology in two general areas: computer-related hardware and computing-enhancing services, which include computation, information, education, and finance. (Control Data)
	The common technology in these areas relates to discrete particle coatings. (NASHUA)
5. Concern for survival	In this respect, the company will conduct its operation prudently, and will provide the profits and growth which will assure Hoover's ultimate success. (Hoover Universal)
6. Philosophy	We are committed to improve health care throughout the world. (Baxter Travenol)
	We believe human development to be the worthiest of the goals of civilization and independence to be the superior condition for nurturing growth in the capabilities of people. (Sun Company)
7. Self-concept	Hoover Universal is a diversified, multi-industry corporation with strong manufacturing capabilities, entrepreneurial policies, and individual business unit autonomy. (Hoover Universal)
8. Concern for public image	We are responsible to the communities in which we live and work and to the world community as well (Johnson & Johnson)
	Also, we must be responsive to the broader concerns of the public, including especially the general desire for improvement in the quality of life, equal opportunity for all, and the constructive use of natural resources. (Sun Company)

heading because only in combination do they describe the company's business activity. A good example of the three components is to be found in the business plan of ITT Barton, a division of ITT. Under the heading of business mission and area served, the following information is presented:

> The unit's mission is to serve industry and government with quality instruments used for the primary measurement, analysis, and local control of fluid flow, level, pressure, temperature, and fluid properties. This instrumentation includes flow meters, electronic readouts, indicators, recorders, switches, liquid level systems, analytical instruments such as titrators, integrators, controllers, transmitters, and various instruments for the measurement of fluid properties (density, viscosity, gravity) used for processing variable sensing, data collecting, control, and transmission. The unit's mission includes fundamental loop-closing control and display devices, when economically justified, but excludes broadline central control room instrumentation, systems design, and turnkey responsibility.
>
> Markets served include instrumentation for oil and gas production, gas transportation, chemical and petrochemical processing, cryogenics, power generation, aerospace, government, and marine, as well as other instrument and equipment manufacturers.

In only 129 words, this segment of the mission statement clearly indicates to all readers—from company employees to casual observers—the basic products, primary markets, and principal technologies of ITT Barton.

Often the most referenced public statement of a company's selected products and markets appears in "silver bullet" form in the mission statement; for example, "Dayton-Hudson Corporation is a diversified retailing company whose business is to serve the American consumer through the retailing of fashion-oriented quality merchandise." Such an abstract of company direction is particularly helpful to outsiders who value condensed overviews.

Company Goals: Survival, Growth, Profitability

Three economic goals guide the strategic direction of almost every business organization. Whether or not the mission statement explicitly states these goals, it reflects the firm's intention to secure *survival* through *growth* and *profitability*.

A firm that is unable to survive will be incapable of satisfying the aims of any of its stakeholders. Unfortunately, the goal of survival, like the goals of growth and profitability, often is taken for granted to such an extent that it is neglected as a principal criterion in strategic decision making. When this happens, the firm may focus on short-term aims at the expense of the long run. Concerns for expediency, a quick fix, or a bargain may displace the assessment of long-term impact. Too often, the result is near-term economic failure owing to a lack of resource synergy and sound business practice. For example, Consolidated Foods, maker of Shasta soft drinks and L'eggs hosiery, sought growth through the acquisition of bargain businesses. However, the erratic sales patterns of its diverse holdings forced it to divest itself of more than four dozen companies. This process cost Consolidated Foods millions of dollars and hampered its growth.

Profitability is the mainstay goal of a business organization. No matter how profit is measured or defined, profit over the long term is the clearest indication of a firm's ability to satisfy the principal claims and desires of employees and stockholders. The key phrase here is "over the long term." Obviously, basing decisions on a short-term concern for profitability would lead to a strategic myopia. Overlooking the enduring concerns of customers, suppliers, creditors, ecologists, and regulatory agents may produce profit in the short term, but, over time, the financial consequences are likely to be detrimental.

The following excerpt from the Hewlett-Packard statement of mission ably expresses the importance of an orientation toward long-term profit:

> To achieve sufficient profit to finance our company growth and to provide the resources we need to achieve our other corporate objectives.
>
> In our economic system, the profit we generate from our operation is the ultimate source of the funds we need to prosper and grow. It is the one absolutely essential measure of our corporate performance over the long term. Only if we continue to meet our profit objective can we achieve our other corporate objectives.

A firm's growth is tied inextricably to its survival and profitability. In this context, the meaning of growth must be broadly defined. Although the product impact market studies (PIMS) have shown that growth in market share is correlated with profitability, other important forms of growth do exist. Growth in the number of markets served, in the variety of products offered, and in the technologies that are used to provide goods or services frequently lead to improvements in a firm's competitive ability. Growth means change, and proactive change is essential in a dynamic business environment.

Hewlett-Packard's mission statement provides an excellent example of corporate regard for growth:

Objective: To let our growth be limited only by our profits and our ability to develop and produce technical products that satisfy real customer needs.

We do not believe that large size is important for its own sake; however, for at least two basic reasons, continuous growth is essential for us to achieve our other objectives.

In the first place, we serve a rapidly growing and expanding segment of our technological society. To remain static would be to lose ground. We cannot maintain a position of strength and leadership in our field without growth.

In the second place, growth is important in order to attract and hold high-caliber people. These individuals will align their future only with a company that offers them considerable opportunity for personal progress. Opportunities are greater and more challenging in a growing company.

The issue of growth raises a concern about the definition of the company mission. How can a firm's product, market, and technology be specified sufficiently to provide direction without precluding the exercise of unanticipated strategic options? How can a firm so define its mission that it can consider opportunistic diversification while maintaining the parameters that guide its growth decision? Perhaps such questions are best addressed when a firm's mission statement outlines the conditions under which the firm might depart from ongoing operations. General Electric Company's extensive global mission provided the foundation for its GE Appliances (GEA) in Louisville, Kentucky. GEA did not see consumer preferences in the world market becoming Americanized. Instead, its expansion goals allowed for flexibility in examining the unique characteristics of individual foreign markets and tailoring strategies to fit them.

The growth philosophy of Dayton-Hudson also embodies this approach:

The stability and quality of the corporation's financial performance will be developed through the profitable execution of our existing businesses, as well as through the acquisition or development of new businesses. Our growth priorities, in order, are as follows:

1. Development of the profitable market preeminence of existing companies in existing markets through new store development or new strategies within existing stores.
2. Expansion of our companies to feasible new markets.
3. Acquisition of other retailing companies that are strategically and financially compatible with Dayton-Hudson.
4. Internal development of new retailing strategies.

Capital allocations to fund the expansion of existing Dayton-Hudson operating companies will be based on each company's return on investment (ROI), in relationship to its ROI objective and its consistency in earnings growth and on the ability of its management to perform up to the forecasts contained in its capital requests. Expansion via acquisition or new venture will occur when the opportunity promises an acceptable rate of long-term growth and profitability, an acceptable degree of risk, and compatibility with Dayton-Hudson's long-term strategy.

Company Philosophy

The statement of a company's philosophy, often called the *company creed,* usually accompanies or appears within the mission statement. It reflects or specifies the basic beliefs, values, aspirations, and philosophical priorities to which strategic decision makers are committed in managing the company. Fortunately, the philosophies vary little from one firm to another. Owners and managers implicitly accept a general, unwritten, yet pervasive code of behavior that governs business actions and permits them to be largely self-regulated. Unfortunately, statements of company philosophy are often so similar and so platitudinous that they read more like public relations handouts than the commitment to values they are meant to be.

We, the Saturn Team, in concert with the UAW and General Motors, believe that meeting the needs of customers, Saturn members, suppliers, dealers, and neighbors is fundamental to fulfilling our mission.

To meet our customer's needs . . .

- our products and services must be world leaders in value and satisfaction.

To meet our members' needs, we . . .

- will create a sense of belonging in an environment of mutual trust, respect, and dignity;

- believe that all people want to be involved in decisions that affect them, care about their jobs and each other, take pride in themselves and in their contributions, and want to share in the success of their efforts;

- will develop the tools, training, and education for each member, recognizing individual skills and knowledge;

- believe that creative, motivated, responsible team members who understand that change is critical to success are Saturn's most important asset.

To meet our suppliers' and dealers' needs, we . . .

- will strive to create real partnerships with them;

- will be open and fair in our dealings, reflecting trust, respect, and their importance to Saturn;

- want dealers and suppliers to feel ownerships in Saturn's mission and philosophy as their own.

To meet the needs of our neighbors, the communities in which we live and operate, we . . .

- will be good citizens, protect the environment, and conserve natural resources;

- will seek to cooperate with government at all levels and strive to be sensitive, open, and candid in all our public statements.

Saturn's statement of philosophy, presented in Exhibit 2–3, Strategy in Action, indicates the company's clearly defined initiatives for satisfying the needs of its customers, employees, suppliers, and dealers.

Despite the similarity of these statements, the intentions of the strategic managers in developing them do not warrant cynicism. Company executives attempt to provide a distinctive and accurate picture of the firm's managerial outlook. One such statement of company philosophy is that of Dayton-Hudson Corporation. As Exhibit 2–4, Strategy in Action, shows, Dayton-Hudson's board of directors and executives have established especially clear directions for company decision making and action.

Perhaps most noteworthy in the Dayton-Hudson statement is its delineation of responsibility at both the corporate and business levels. In many ways, the statement could serve as a prototype for the three-tier approach to strategic management. This approach implies that the mission statement must address strategic concerns at the corporate, business, and functional levels of the organization. Dayton-Hudson's management philosophy does this by balancing operating autonomy and flexibility on the one hand with corporate input and direction on the other.

As seen in Exhibit 2–5, Global Strategy in Action, the philosophy of Nissan Motor Manufacturing is expressed by the company's People Principles and Key Corporate Principles. These principles form the basis of the way the company operates on a daily basis. They address the principal concepts used in meeting the company's established goals. Nissan focuses on the distinction between the role of the individual and the corporation. In this way, employees can link their productivity and success to the productivity and success of the company. Given these principles, the company is able to concentrate on the issues most important to its survival, growth, and profitability.

Strategy in Action Exhibit 2–6 provides an example of how General Motors uses a statement of company philosophy to clarify its environmental principles.

The corporation will:

Set standards for return on investment (ROI) and earnings growth.

Approve strategic plans.

Allocate capital.

Approve goals.

Monitor, measure, and audit results.

Reward performance.

Allocate management resources.

The operating companies will be accorded the freedom and responsibility:

To manage their own business.

To develop strategic plans and goals that will optimize their growth.

To develop an organization that can ensure consistency of results and optimum growth.

To operate their businesses consistent with the corporation's statement of philosophy.

The corporate staff will provide only those services that are:

Essential to the protection of the corporation.

Needed for the growth of the corporation.

Wanted by operating companies and that provide a significant advantage in quality or cost.

The corporation will insist on:

Uniform accounting practices by type of business.

Prompt disclosure of operating results.

A systematic approach to training and developing people.

Adherence to appropriately high standards of business conduct and civic responsibility in accordance with the corporation's statement of philosophy.

Public Image

Both present and potential customers attribute certain qualities to particular businesses. Gerber and Johnson & Johnson make safe products; Cross Pen makes high-quality writing instruments; Étienne Aigner makes stylish but affordable leather products; Corvettes are power machines; and Izod Lacoste stands for the preppy look. Thus, mission statements should reflect the public's expectations, since this makes achievement of the firm's goals more likely. Gerber's mission statement should not open the possibility for diversification into pesticides, and Cross Pen's should not open the possibility for diversification into $0.59 brand-name disposables.

On the other hand, a negative public image often prompts firms to reemphasize the beneficial aspects of their mission. For example, in response to what it saw as a disturbing trend in public opinion, Dow Chemical undertook an aggressive promotional campaign to fortify its credibility, particularly among "employees and those who live and work in [their] plant communities." Dow described its approach in its annual report:

> All around the world today, Dow people are speaking up. People who care deeply about their company, what it stands for, and how it is viewed by others. People who are immensely proud of their company's performance, yet realistic enough to realize it is the public's perception of that performance that counts in the long run.

Firms seldom address the question of their public image in an intermittent fashion. Although public agitation often stimulates greater attention to this question, firms are concerned about their public image even in the absence of such agitation. The following excerpt from the mission statement of Intel Corporation is an example of this attitude:

Global Strategy in Action
Principles of Nissan Motor Manufacturing (UK) Ltd.

Exhibit 2–5

	People Principles **(All Other Objectives Can Only Be Achieved by People)**
Selection	Hire the highest caliber people; look for technical capabilities and emphasize attitude.
Responsibility	Maximize the responsibility; staff by devolving decision making.
Teamwork	Recognize and encourage individual contributions, with everyone working toward the same objectives.
Flexibility	Expand the role of the individual: multiskilled, no job description, generic job titles.
Kaizen	Continuously seek 100.1 percent improvements; give "ownership of change."
Communications	"Every day, face to face."
Training	Establish individual "continuous development programs."
Supervisors	Regard as "the professionals at managing the production process"; give them much responsibility normally assumed by individual departments; make them the genuine leaders of their teams.
Single status	Treat everyone as a "first class" citizen; eliminate all illogical differences.
Trade unionism	Establish single union agreement with AEU emphasizing the common objective for a successful enterprise.
	Key Corporate Principles
Quality	Building profitably the highest quality car sold in Europe.
Customers	Achieve target of no. 1 customer satisfaction in Europe.
Volume	Always achieve required volume.
New products	Deliver on time, at required quality, within cost.
Suppliers	Establish long-term relationship with single-source suppliers; aim for zero defects and just-in-time delivery; apply Nissan principles to suppliers.
Production	Use "most appropriate" technology; develop predictable "best method" of doing job; build in quality.
Engineering	Design "quality" and "ease of working" into the product and facilities; establish "simultaneous engineering" to reduce development time.

We are sensitive to our *image with our customers and the business community.* Commitments to customers are considered sacred, and we are upset with ourselves when we do not meet our commitments. We strive to demonstrate to the business world on a continuing basis that we are credible in describing the state of the corporation, and that we are well organized and in complete control of all things that determine the numbers.

Exhibit 2–7, Strategy in Action, presents a marketing translation of the essence of the mission statements of six high-end shoe companies. The impressive feature of the exhibit is that it shows dramatically how closely competing firms can incorporate subtle, yet meaningful, differences into their mission statements.

Company Self-Concept

A major determinant of a firm's success is the extent to which the firm can relate functionally to its external environment. To achieve its proper place in a competitive situation, the firm realistically must evaluate its competitive strengths and weaknesses. This

As a responsible corporate citizen, General Motors is dedicated to protecting human health, natural resources, and the global environment. This dedication reaches further than compliance with the law to encompass the integration of sound environmental practices into our business decisions.

The following environmental principles provide guidance to General Motors personnel worldwide in the conduct of their daily business practices:

1. We are committed to actions to restore and preserve the environment.

2. We are committed to reducing waste and pollutants, conserving resources, and recycling materials at every stage of the product life cycle.

3. We will continue to participate actively in educating the public regarding environmental conservation.

4. We will continue to pursue vigorously the development and implementation of technologies for minimizing pollutant emissions.

5. We will continue to work with all governmental entities for the development of technically sound and financially responsible environmental laws and regulations.

6. We will continually assess the impact of our plants and products on the environment and the communities in which we live and operate with a goal of continuous improvement.

---

idea—that the firm must know itself—is the essence of the company self-concept. The idea is not commonly integrated into theories of strategic management; its importance for individuals has been recognized since ancient times.

Both individuals and firms have a crucial need to know themselves. The ability of either to survive in a dynamic and highly competitive environment would be severely limited if they did not understand their impact on others or of others on them.

In some senses, then, firms take on personalities of their own. Much behavior in firms is organizationally based; that is, a firm acts on its members in other ways than their individual interactions. Thus, firms are entities whose personality transcends the personalities of their members. As such, they can set decision-making parameters based on aims different and distinct from the aims of their members. These organizational considerations have pervasive effects.

Ordinarily, descriptions of the company self-concept per se do not appear in mission statements. Yet such statements often provide strong impressions of the company self-concept. For example, ARCO's environment, health, and safety (EHS) managers were adamant about emphasizing the company's position on safety and environmental performance as a part of the mission statement. The challenges facing the ARCO EHS managers included dealing with concerned environmental groups and a public that has become environmentally aware. They hoped to motivate employees toward safer behavior while reducing emissions and waste. They saw this as a reflection of the company's positive self-image.

The following excerpts from the Intel Corporation mission statement describe the corporate persona that its top management seeks to foster:

> Management is self-critical. The leaders must be capable of recognizing and accepting their mistakes and learning from them.
>
> Open (constructive) confrontation is encouraged at all levels of the corporation and is viewed as a method of problem solving and conflict resolution.
>
> Decision by consensus is the rule. Decisions once made are supported. Position in the organization is not the basis for quality of ideas.
>
> A highly communicative, open management is part of the style.
>
> Management must be ethical. Managing by telling the truth and treating all employees equitably has established credibility that is ethical.

Allen-Edmonds

Allen-Edmonds provides high-quality shoes for the affluent consumer who appreciates a well-made, finely crafted, stylish dress shoe.

Bally

Bally shoes set you apart. They are the perfect shoe to complement your lifestyle. Bally shoes project an image of European style and elegance that ensures one is not just dressed, but well-dressed.

Bostonian

Bostonian shoes are for those successful individuals who are well-traveled, on the "go" and want a stylish dress shoe that can keep up with their variety of needs and activities. With Bostonian, you know you will always be well dressed whatever the situation.

Cole-Hahn

Cole-Hahn offers a line of contemporary shoes for the man who wants to go his own way. They are shoes for the urban, upscale, stylish man who wants to project an image of being one step ahead.

Florsheim

Florsheim shoes are the affordable classic men's dress shoes for those who want to experience the comfort and style of a solid dress shoe.

Johnston & Murphy

Johnston & Murphy is the quintessential business shoe for those affluent individuals who know and demand the best.

Source: "Thinking on Your Feet, the Johnston & Murphy Guerrilla Marketing Competition" (Johnston & Murphy, a GENESCO Company).

We strive to provide an opportunity for rapid development.

Intel is a results-oriented company. The focus is on substance versus form, quality versus quantity.

We believe in the principle that hard work, high productivity is something to be proud of.

The concept of assumed responsibility is accepted. (If a task needs to be done, assume you have the responsibility to get it done.)

Commitments are long term. If career problems occur at some point, reassignment is a better alternative than termination.

We desire to have all employees involved and participative in their relationship with Intel.

Newest Trends in Mission Components

Recently, three issues have become so prominent in the strategic planning for organizations that they are increasingly becoming integral parts in the development and revisions of mission statements: sensitivity to consumer wants, concern for quality, and statements of company vision.

Customers

"The customer is our top priority" is a slogan that would be claimed by the majority of businesses in the United States and abroad. For companies including Caterpillar Tractor, General Electric, and Johnson & Johnson this means analyzing consumer needs before as well as after a sale. The bonus plan at Xerox allows for a 40 percent annual bonus, based on high customer reviews of the service that they receive, and a 20 percent penalty if the feedback is especially bad. For these firms and many others, the overriding concern for the company has become consumer satisfaction.

In addition many U.S. firms maintain extensive product safety programs to help assure consumer satisfaction. RCA, Sears, and 3M boast of such programs. Other firms including Calgon Corporation, Amoco, Mobil Oil, Whirlpool, and Zenith provide toll-free telephone lines to answer customer concerns and complaints.

EXHIBIT 2–8
**Key Elements
of Customer
Service–Driven
Organizations**

1. A mission statement or sense of mission makes customer service a priority.
2. Customer service goals are clearly defined.
3. Customer service standards are clearly defined.
4. Customer satisfaction with existing products and services is continuously measured.
5. Ongoing efforts are made to understand customers to determine where the organization should be headed.
6. Corrective action procedures are in place to remove barriers to servicing customers in a timely and effective fashion.
7. Customer service goals have an impact on organizational action.

Source: An excerpt from "Peters, 1987," p. 78. Reprinted from *Business Horizons,* July–August 1995. Copyright 1995 by the Foundation for the School of Business at Indiana University. Used with permission.

The focus on customer satisfaction is demonstrated by retailer J.C. Penney in this excerpt from its statement of philosophy: "The Penney Idea is (1) To serve the public as nearly as we can to its complete satisfaction; (2) To expect for the service we render a fair remuneration, and not all the profit the traffic will bear; (3) To do all in our power to pack the customer's dollar full of value, quality, and satisfaction."

A focus on customer satisfaction causes managers to realize the importance of providing quality customer service. Strong customer service initiatives have led some firms to gain competitive advantages in the marketplace. Hence, many corporations have made the customer service initiative a key component of their corporate mission. Some key elements of customer service–driven organizations are listed in Exhibit 2–8.

Quality

"Quality is job one!" is a rallying point not only for Ford Motor Corporation but for many resurging U.S. businesses as well. Two U.S. management experts fostered a worldwide emphasis on quality in manufacturing. W. Edwards Deming and J. M. Juran's messages were first embraced by Japanese managers, whose quality consciousness led to global dominance in several industries including automobile, TV, audio equipment, and electronic components manufacturing. Deming summarizes his approach in 14 now well-known points:

1. Create constancy of purpose.
2. Adopt the new philosophy.
3. Cease dependence on mass inspection to achieve quality.
4. End the practice of awarding business on price tag alone. Instead, minimize total cost, often accomplished by working with a single supplier.
5. Improve constantly the system of production and service.
6. Institute training on the job.
7. Institute leadership.
8. Drive out fear.
9. Break down barriers between departments.
10. Eliminate slogans, exhortations, and numerical targets.
11. Eliminate work standards (quotas) and management by objective.

CADILLAC

The Mission of the Cadillac Motor Company is to engineer, produce, and market the world's finest automobiles known for uncompromised levels of distinctiveness, comfort, convenience, and refined performance. Through its people, who are its strength, Cadillac will continuously improve the quality of its products and services to meet or exceed customer expectations and succeed as a profitable business.

MOTOROLA

Dedication to quality is a way of life at our company, so much so that it goes far beyond rhetorical slogans. Our ongoing program of continued improvement out for change, refinement, and even revolution in our pursuit of quality excellence.

It is the objective of Motorola, Inc., to produce and provide products and services of the highest quality. In its activities, Motorola will pursue goals aimed at the achievement of quality excellence. These results will be derived from the dedicated efforts of each employee in conjunction with supportive participation from management at all levels of the corporation.

ZYTEC

Zytec is a company that competes on value; is market driven; provides superior quality and service: builds strong relationship with its customers; and provides technical excellence in its products.

12. Remove barriers that rob workers, engineers, and managers of their right to pride of workmanship.

13. Institute a vigorous program of education and self-improvement.

14. Put everyone in the company to work to accomplish the transformation.

Firms in the United States responded aggressively. The new philosophy is that quality should be the norm. For example, Motorola's production goal is 60 or fewer defects per every billion components that it manufactures.

Exhibit 2–9, Strategy in Action, presents the integration of the quality initiative into the mission statements of three corporations. The emphasis on quality has received added emphasis in many corporate philosophies since the Congress created the Malcolm Baldrige Quality Award in 1987. Each year up to two Baldrige Awards can be given in three categories of a company's operations: manufacturing, services, and small businesses.

Vision Statement

Whereas the mission statement expresses an answer to the question "What business are we in?" a company *vision statement* is sometimes developed to express the aspirations of the executive leadership. A vision statement presents the firm's strategic intent that focuses the energies and resources of the company on achieving a desirable future. However, in actual practice, the mission and vision statement are frequently combined into a single statement. When they are separated, the vision statement is often a single sentence, designed to be memorable. For example:

Federal Express: "Our vision is to change the way we all connect with each other in the New Network Economy."

Lexmark: "Customers for Life."

Microsoft: "A computer on every desk, and in every home, running on Microsoft software."

OVERSEEING THE STRATEGY MAKERS

Who is responsible for determining the firm's mission? Who is responsible for acquiring and allocating resources so the firm can thoughtfully develop and implement a strategic plan? Who is responsible for monitoring the firm's success in the competitive marketplace to determine whether that plan was well designed and activated? The answer to all of these questions is strategic decision makers. As you saw in Exhibit 1–5, most organizations have multiple levels of strategic decision makers; typically, the larger the firm, the more levels it will have. The strategic managers at the highest level are responsible for decisions that affect the entire firm, commit the firm and its resources for the longest periods, and declare the firm's sense of values. In other words, this group of strategic managers is responsible for overseeing the creation and accomplishment of the company mission. The term that describes the group is *board of directors.*

In overseeing the management of a firm, the board of directors operates as the representatives of the firm's stockholders. Elected by the stockholders, the board has these major responsibilities:

1. To establish and update the company mission.

2. To elect the company's top officers, the foremost of whom is the CEO.

3. To establish the compensation levels of the top officers, including their salaries and bonuses.

4. To determine the amount and timing of the dividends paid to stockholders.

5. To set broad company policy on such matters as labor–management relations, product or service lines of business, and employee benefit packages.

6. To set company objectives and to authorize managers to implement the long-term strategies that the top officers and the board have found agreeable.

7. To mandate company compliance with legal and ethical dictates.

In the current business environment, boards of directors are accepting the challenge of shareholders and other stakeholders to become active in establishing the strategic initiatives of the companies that they serve.

This chapter considers the board of directors because the board's greatest impact on the behavior of a firm results from its determination of the company mission. The philosophy espoused in the mission statement sets the tone by which the firm and all of its employees will be judged. As logical extensions of the mission statement, the firm's objectives and strategies embody the board's view of proper business demeanor. Through its appointment of top executives and its decisions about their compensation, the board reveals its priorities for organizational achievement.

AGENCY THEORY

Whenever there is a separation of the owners (principals) and the managers (agents) of a firm, the potential exists for the wishes of the owners to be ignored. This fact, and the recognition that agents are expensive, established the basis for a set of complex but helpful ideas known as *agency theory.* Whenever owners (or managers) delegate decision-making authority to others, an agency relationship exists between the two parties. Agency relationships, such as those between stockholders and managers, can be very effective as long as managers make investment decisions in ways that are consistent with stockholders' interests. However, when the interests of managers diverge from those of owners, then managers' decisions are more likely to reflect the managers' preferences than the owners' preferences.

In general, owners seek stock value maximization. When managers hold important blocks of company stock, they too prefer strategies that result in stock appreciation. However, when managers better resemble "hired hands" than owner-partners, they often prefer strategies that increase their personal payoffs rather than those of shareholders. Such behavior can result in decreased stock performance (as when high executive bonuses reduce corporate earnings) and in strategic decisions that point the firm in the direction of outcomes that are suboptimal from a stockholder's perspective.

If, as agency theory argues, self-interested managers act in ways that increase their own welfare at the expense of the gain of corporate stockholders, then owners who delegate decision-making authority to their agents will incur both the loss of potential gain that would have resulted from owner-optimal strategies and/or the costs of monitoring and control systems that are designed to minimize the consequences of such self-centered management decisions. In combination, the cost of agency problems and the cost of actions taken to minimize agency problems, are called *agency costs*. These costs can often be identified by their direct benefit for the agents and their negative present value. Agency costs are found when there are differing self-interests between shareholders and managers, superiors and subordinates, or managers of competing departments or branch offices.

How Agency Problems Occur

Because owners have access to only a relatively small portion of the information that is available to executives about the performance of the firm and cannot afford to monitor every executive decision or action, executives are often free to pursue their own interests.[1] This condition is known as the *moral hazard problem* or *shirking*.[2]

As a result of moral hazards, executives may design strategies that provide the greatest possible benefits for themselves, with the welfare of the organization being given only secondary consideration. For example, executives may presell products at year-end to trigger their annual bonuses even though the deep discounts that they must offer will threaten the price stability of their products for the upcoming year. Similarly, unchecked executives may advance their own self-interests by slacking on the job, altering forecasts to maximize their performance bonuses; unrealistically assessing acquisition targets' outlooks in order to increase the probability of increasing organizational size through their acquisition; or manipulating personnel records to keep or acquire key company personnel.

The second major reason that agency costs are incurred is known as *adverse selection*. This refers to the limited ability that stockholders have to precisely determine the competencies and priorities of executives at the time that they are hired. Because principals cannot initially verify an executive's appropriateness as an agent of the owners, unanticipated problems of nonoverlapping priorities between owners and agents are likely to occur.

The most popular solution to moral dilemma and adverse selection problems is for owners to attempt to more closely align their own best interests with those of their agents

---

[1] Substitute the terms *managers* for *owners* and *subordinates* for *executives* for another example of agency theory in operation.
[2] Shirking is described as "self-interest combined with guile."

through the use of executive bonus plans.[3] Foremost among these approaches are stock option plans, which enable executives to benefit directly from the appreciation of the company's stock just as other stockholders do. In most instances, executive bonus plans are unabashed attempts to align the interests of owners and executives and to thereby induce executives to support strategies that increase stockholder wealth. While such schemes are unlikely to eliminate self-interest as a major criterion in executive decision making, they help to reduce the costs associated with moral dilemmas and adverse selections.

Problems That Can Result from Agency

From a strategic management perspective there are five different kinds of problems that can arise because of the agency relationship between corporate stockholders and their company's executives:

1. Executives pursue growth in company size rather than in earnings. Shareholders generally want to maximize earnings, because earnings growth yields stock appreciation. However, because managers are typically more heavily compensated for increases in firm size than for earnings growth, they may recommend strategies that yield company growth such as mergers and acquisitions.

In addition, managers' stature in the business community is commonly associated with company size. Managers gain prominence by directing the growth of an organization, and they benefit in the forms of career advancement and job mobility that are associated with increases in company size.

Finally, executives need an enlarging set of advancement opportunities for subordinates whom they wish to motivate with nonfinancial inducements. Acquisitions can provide the needed positions.

2. Executives attempt to diversify their corporate risk. Whereas stockholders can vary their investment risks through management of their individual stock portfolios, managers' careers and stock incentives are tied to the performance of a single corporation, albeit the one that employs them. Consequently, executives are tempted to diversify their corporation's operation, businesses, and product lines to moderate the risk incurred in any single venture. While this approach serves the executives' personal agendas, it compromises the "pure play" quality of their firm as an investment. In other words, diversifying a corporation reduces the beta associated with the firm's return, which is an undesirable outcome for many stockholders.

3. Executives avoid risk. Even when, or perhaps especially when, executives are willing to restrict the diversification of their companies, they are tempted to minimize the risk that they face. Executives are often fired for failure, but rarely for mediocre corporate performance. Therefore, executives may avoid desirable levels of risk, if they anticipate little reward and opt for conservative strategies that minimize the risk of company failure. If they do, executives will rarely support plans for innovation, diversification, and rapid growth.

However, from an investor's perspective, risk taking is desirable when it is systematic. In other words, when investors can reasonably expect that their company will generate higher long-term returns from assuming greater risk, they may wish to pursue the greater payoff, especially when the company is positioned to perform better than its competitors that face the same nominal risks. Obviously, the agency relationship creates a problem—should executives prioritize their job security or the company's financial returns to stockholders?

[3] An in-depth discussion of executive bonus compensation is provided in Chapter 9.

4. Managers act to optimize their personal payoffs. If executives can gain more from an annual performance bonus by achieving objective 1 than from stock appreciation resulting from the achievement of objective 2, then owners must anticipate that the executives will target objective 1 as their priority, even though objective 2 is clearly in the best interest of the shareholders. Similarly, executives may pursue a range of expensive perquisites that have a net negative effect on shareholder returns. Elegant corner offices, corporate jets, large staffs, golf club memberships, extravagant retirement programs, and limousines for executive benefit are rarely good investments for stockholders.

5. Executives act to protect their status. When their companies expand, executives want to assure that their knowledge, experience, and skills remain relevant and central to the strategic direction of the corporation. They favor doing more of what they already do well. In contrast, investors may prefer revolutionary advancement to incremental improvement. For example, when confronted with Amazon.com, competitor Barnes & Noble initiated a joint venture website with Bertelsmann. In addition, Barnes & Noble used vertical integration with the nation's largest book distributor, which supplies 60 percent of Amazon's books. This type of revolutionary strategy is most likely to occur when executives are given assurances that they will not make themselves obsolete within the changing company that they create.

Solutions to the Agency Problem

In addition to defining an agent's responsibilities in a contract and including elements like bonus incentives that help align executives' and owners' interests, principals can take several other actions to minimize agency problems. The first is for the owners to pay executives a premium for their service. This premium helps executives to see their loyalty to the stockholders as the key to achieving their personal financial targets.

A second solution to agency problems is for executives to receive backloaded compensation. This means that executives are paid a handsome premium for superior future performance. Strategic actions taken in year one, which are to have an impact in year three, become the basis for executive bonuses in year three. This lag time between action and bonus more realistically rewards executives for the consequences of their decision making, ties the executive to the company for the long term, and properly focuses strategic management activities on the future.

Finally, creating teams of executives across different units of a corporation can help to focus performance measures on organizational rather than personal goals. Through the use of executive teams, owner interests often receive the priority that they deserve.

THE STAKEHOLDER APPROACH TO COMPANY RESPONSIBILITY

In defining or redefining the company mission, strategic managers must recognize the legitimate rights of the firm's claimants. These include not only stockholders and employees but also outsiders affected by the firm's actions. Such outsiders commonly include customers, suppliers, governments, unions, competitors, local communities, and the general public. Each of these interest groups has justifiable reasons for expecting (and often for demanding) that the firm satisfy their claims in a responsible manner. In general, stockholders claim appropriate returns on their investment; employees seek broadly defined job satisfactions; customers want what they pay for; suppliers seek dependable buyers; governments want adherence to legislation; unions seek benefits for their members; competitors want fair competition; local communities want the firm to be a responsible citizen; and the general public expects the firm's existence to improve the quality of life.

According to a survey of 2,361 directors in 291 of the largest southeastern U.S. companies:

1. Directors perceived the existence of distinct stakeholder groups.

2. Directors have high stakeholder orientations.

3. Directors view some stakeholders differently, depending on their occupation (CEO directors versus non-CEO directors) and type (inside versus outside directors).

The study also found that the perceived stakeholders were, in the order of their importance, customers and government, stockholders, employees, and society. The results clearly indicated that boards of directors no longer believe that the stockholder is the only constituency to whom they are responsible.

However, when a firm attempts to incorporate the interests of these groups into its mission statement, broad generalizations are insufficient. These steps need to be taken:

1. Identification of the stakeholders.

2. Understanding the stakeholders' specific claims vis-à-vis the firm.

3. Reconciliation of these claims and assignment of priorities to them.

4. Coordination of the claims with other elements of the company mission.

Identification   The left-hand column of Exhibit 2–10 lists the commonly encountered stakeholder groups, to which the executive officer group often is added. Obviously, though, every business faces a slightly different set of stakeholder groups, which vary in number, size, influence, and importance. In defining the company, strategic managers must identify all of the stakeholder groups and weigh their relative rights and their relative ability to affect the firm's success.

Understanding   The concerns of the principal stakeholder groups tend to center on the general claims listed in the right-hand column of Exhibit 2–10. However, strategic decision makers should understand the specific demands of each group. They then will be better able to initiate actions that satisfy these demands.

Reconciliation and Priorities   Unfortunately, the claims of various stakeholder groups often conflict. For example, the claims of governments and the general public tend to limit profitability, which is the central claim of most creditors and stockholders. Thus, claims must be reconciled in a mission statement that resolves the competing, conflicting, and contradicting claims of stakeholders. For objectives and strategies to be internally consistent and precisely focused, the statement must display a single-minded, though multidimensional, approach to the firm's aims.

There are hundreds, if not thousands, of claims on any firm—high wages, pure air, job security, product quality, community service, taxes, occupational health and safety regulations, equal employment opportunity regulations, product variety, wide markets, career opportunities, company growth, investment security, high ROI, and many, many more. Although most, perhaps all, of these claims may be desirable ends, they cannot be pursued with equal emphasis. They must be assigned priorities in accordance with the relative emphasis that the firm will give them. That emphasis is reflected in the criteria that the firm uses in its strategic decision making; in the firm's allocation of its human, financial, and physical resources; and in the firm's long-term objectives and strategies.

EXHIBIT 2–10
A Stakeholder View of Company Responsibility

Source: William R. King and David I. Cleland, *Strategic Planning and Policy.* © 1978 by Litton Educational Publishing, Inc., p. 153. Reprinted by permission of Van Nostrand Reinhold Company.

Stakeholder	Nature of the Claim
Stockholders	Participation in distribution of profits, additional stock offerings, assets on liquidation; vote of stock; inspection of company books; transfer of stock; election of board of directors; and such additional rights as have been established in the contract with the corporation.
Creditors	Legal proportion of interest payments due and return of principal from the investment. Security of pledged assets; relative priority in event of liquidation. Management and owner prerogatives if certain conditions exist with the company (such as default of interest payments).
Employees	Economic, social, and psychological satisfaction in the place of employment. Freedom from arbitrary and capricious behavior on the part of company officials. Share in fringe benefits, freedom to join union and participate in collective bargaining, individual freedom in offering up their services through an employment contract. Adequate working conditions.
Customers	Service provided with the product; technical data to use the product; suitable warranties; spare parts to support the product during use; R&D leading to product improvement; facilitation of credit.
Suppliers	Continuing source of business; timely consummation of trade credit obligations; professional relationship in contracting for, purchasing, and receiving goods and services.
Governments	Taxes (income, property, and so on); adherence to the letter and intent of public policy dealing with the requirements of fair and free competition; discharge of legal obligations of businesspeople (and business organizations); adherence to antitrust laws.
Unions	Recognition as the negotiating agent for employees. Opportunity to perpetuate the union as a participant in the business organization.
Competitors	Observation of the norms for competitive conduct established by society and the industry. Business statesmanship on the part of peers.
Local communities	Place of productive and healthful employment in the community. Participation of company officials in community affairs, provision of regular employment, fair play, reasonable portion of purchases made in the local community, interest in and support of local government, support of cultural and charitable projects.
The general public	Participation in and contribution to society as a whole; creative communications between governmental and business units designed for reciprocal understanding; assumption of fair proportion of the burden of government and society. Fair price for products and advancement of the state-of-the-art technology that the product line involves.

Coordination with Other Elements   The demands of stakeholder groups constitute only one principal set of inputs to the company mission. The other principal sets are the managerial operating philosophy and the determinants of the product-market offering. Those determinants constitute a reality test that the accepted claims must pass. The key question is: How can the firm satisfy its claimants and at the same time optimize its economic success in the marketplace?

EXHIBIT 2–11
Inputs to the Development of the Company Mission

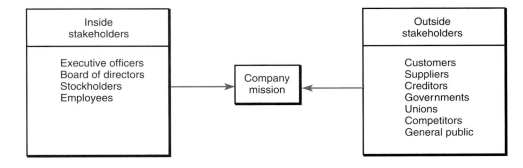

Social Responsibility

As indicated in Exhibit 2–11, the various stakeholders of a firm can be divided into inside stakeholders and outside stakeholders. The insiders are the individuals or groups that are stockholders or employees of the firm. The outsiders are all the other individuals or groups that the firm's actions affect. The extremely large and often amorphous set of outsiders makes the general claim that the firm be socially responsible.

Perhaps the thorniest issues faced in defining a company mission are those that pertain to responsibility. The stakeholder approach offers the clearest perspective on such issues. Broadly stated, outsiders often demand that insiders' claims be subordinated to the greater good of the society; that is, to the greater good of outsiders. They believe that such issues as pollution, the disposal of solid and liquid wastes, and the conservation of natural resources should be principal considerations in strategic decision making. Also broadly stated, insiders tend to believe that the competing claims of outsiders should be balanced against one another in a way that protects the company mission. For example, they tend to believe that the need of consumers for a product should be balanced against the water pollution resulting from its production if the firm cannot eliminate that pollution entirely and still remain profitable. Some insiders also argue that the claims of society, as expressed in government regulation, provide tax money that can be used to eliminate water pollution and the like if the general public wants this to be done.

The issues are numerous, complex, and contingent on specific situations. Thus, rigid rules of business conduct cannot deal with them. Each firm *regardless of size* must decide how to meet its perceived social responsibility. While large, well-capitalized companies may have easy access to environmental consultants, this is not an affordable strategy for smaller companies. However, the experience of many small businesses demonstrates that it is feasible to accomplish significant pollution prevention and waste reduction without big expenditures and without hiring consultants. Once a problem area has been identified, a company's line employees frequently can develop a solution. Other important pollution prevention strategies include changing the materials used or redesigning how operations are bid out. Making pollution prevention a social responsibility can be beneficial to smaller companies. Publicly traded firms also can benefit directly from socially responsible strategies.

Different approaches adopted by different firms reflect differences in competitive position, industry, country, environmental and ecological pressures, and a host of other factors. In other words, they will reflect both situational factors and differing priorities in the acknowledgment of claims. Obviously, winning the loyalty of the growing legions of consumers will require new marketing strategies and new alliances in the 21st century. Many marketers already have discovered these new marketing realities by adopting strategies called the "*4 E's*": (1) make it easy for the consumer to be green, (2) empower

BusinessWeek In Colombia, Los Angeles–based Occidental Petroleum Corp. is clearing the land for an exploratory oil well to be drilled. The government believes the land holds more than half of Colombia's oil reserves and has contracted Occidental to find it. The nature-worshipping U'wa adamantly oppose the exploration. But Occidental emphatically denies that the U'wa will be affected either. The company has held dozens of meetings with community groups and says it is trying to meet all their concerns. Occidental has spent some $140,000 on educational, environmental, agricultural, and basic infrastructure projects in communities closest to the project.

The plight of indigenous groups is penetrating the boardrooms of multinationals, which are being forced to respond as never before to protect their reputations and brand names. Nowhere are the issues more contentious than in investments, such as Occidental's, that involve extracting natural resources in developing nations. Many of these projects have long been marred by corruption, military atrocities, ecological damage, and social upheaval.

Activists and environmental groups have put heavy pressure on multinationals, governments of developing nations, and the World Bank—which funds many such projects—to show there are humane, eco-friendly, and equitable ways to drill and mine in poor nations. On top of this, oil and mining companies now have to answer to institutional investors. And they must meet increasingly stringent environmental and social standards to get financial backing and political-risk guarantees from the World Bank for overseas projects.

The result is shaping up as a new era of corporate responsibility. Multinationals are hiring human-rights advisers, drafting and enforcing codes of conduct, appointing outside monitors, and improving operating practices. They are developing global standards of conduct, such as procedures for security of their installations. They are putting local people on boards of directors and urging government ministers and generals to adhere to international human-rights standards, lest their misdeeds reflect poorly on the investors, too.

Only a handful of multinationals have gotten serious about cleaning up their corporate practices. Even if companies are well-intentioned, the real test is whether the new standards and codes will mean anything in practice.

Source: An excerpt from P. Raeburn and S. Prasso, "Whose Globe?," *BusinessWeek*, November 6, 2000.

consumers with solutions, (3) enlist the support of the consumer, and (4) establish credibility with all publics and help to avoid a backlash.

As presented in Exhibit 2–12, Global Strategy in Action, Occidental Petroleum faces issues of corporate social responsibility in addressing the needs of the many stakeholders involved in the firm's oil exploration in developing countries. The article outlines the many parties that have potential to be impacted by the company's endeavors, including local inhabitants and government, environmental groups, and institutional investors. The article also describes how multinational corporations are acting to benefit the local communities, to restructure their organizations, and to implement codes of conduct to address the needs of the many stakeholders.

British Petroleum' CEO, John Browne, faces the social responsibility questions asked of all leaders of global firms. Global Strategy in Action Exhibit 2–13 presents Browne's view that for his global company to thrive, so must the communities in which his company does business.

Despite differences in their approaches, most American firms now try to assure outsiders that they attempt to conduct business in a socially responsible manner. Many firms, including Abt Associates, Dow Chemical, Eastern Gas and Fuel Associates, Exxon, and the Bank of America, conduct and publish annual social audits. Such audits attempt to evaluate a firm from the perspective of social responsibility. Private consultants often conduct them for the firm and offer minimally biased evaluations on what are inherently highly subjective issues.

BusinessWeek Making globalization work humanely is quickly becoming the dominant issue of our time. From Boston to Bangkok, trade, investment, and information technology are exploding across borders and overwhelming governments' ability to provide social safety nets and public services to cushion the impact on people. A political backlash is building in Asia, Europe, and Latin America. Although international corporations cannot shoulder all the *responsibility*, no challenge is more central to global management than finding a balance between the relentless pressure for short-term profits and broader social *responsibilities*.

What's a chief executive to do? To what degree should companies take on the *responsibility* heretofore shouldered by governments? To what degree can they? One chief executive, John Browne of British Petroleum Co., has a clear philosophy and strategy. Browne believes that for BP to thrive, so must the communities in which it does business. To make that happen, Browne has insisted that the economic and social health of the villages, towns, and cities in which BP does business be a matter of central concern to the company's *board* of directors. He has also made social investment for the long term an important variable in compensating BP employees around the world.

AMBITIOUS GOALS

What to do and how to do it is left to local BP business units. But regular reviews of their activities are held by regional executives. In such areas as job training for local employees and building schools, ambitious goals are set, and performance is measured against them. Involved in the process along with BP employees and *board* directors are local residents whose views are regularly surveyed.

BP's community investments are extensive. In Vietnam, the company is providing computer-based technology to control the damage from recurrent flooding. In Turkey, BP recently financed the replanting of a forest around the Black Sea that had been destroyed by fire. In Zambia, it has supplied 200 solar-powered refrigerators to help doctors store antimalaria vaccines. In South Africa, it has supported the development of small business in urban areas such as Soweto. In Colombia, it is turning its own waste material into bricks for local homebuilding.

In addition, accidents in the workplace, noxious emissions, and oil spills are subject to monitoring and quantification. Ernst & Young verifies company recordkeeping. There is constant pressure to eliminate accidents.

NOT CHARITY

So far, the strategy has not impaired BP's bottom line. To the contrary. "These efforts have nothing to do with charity," says Browne, "and everything to do with our long-term self-interest I see no trade-off between the short term and the long. Twenty years is just 80 quarters. And our shareholders want performance today, and tomorrow, and the day after."

Corporations would do well to take a page out of Browne's playbook: think long-term, invest heavily in the communities that you do business in, be obsessive about achieving profits, and fully integrate social *responsibility* into your policies on governance and compensation.

Source: Jeffrey E. Garten, "Globalism Doesn't Have to Be Cruel," *BusinessWeek*, February 9, 1998.

Corporate Social Responsibility and Profitability

Few trends could so thoroughly undermine the very foundations of our free society as the acceptance by corporate officials of a social responsibility other than to make as much money for their stockholders as possible.

Milton Friedman, Capitalism and Freedom, *1962*

In the four decades since Milton Friedman wrote these words, the issue of *corporate social responsibility* (CSR)—the idea that business has a duty to serve society as well as the financial interest of stockholders—has remained a highly contentious one. Yet managers recognize that deciding to what extent to embrace CSR is an important strategic decision.

There are three principal reasons why managers should be concerned about the socially responsible behavior of their firms. First, a company's right to exist depends on its responsiveness to the external environment. Second, federal, state, and local governments threaten increased regulation if business does not evolve to meet changing social standards. Third, a responsive corporate social policy may enhance a firm's long-term viability. Underscoring the importance of these factors to the firm is the implicit belief that long-run profit maximization is inexorably linked to CSR.

The Debate

Should a company behave in a socially responsible manner? Coming down on one side of the question are those who, like Friedman, believe that a business bears a responsibility only for the financial well-being of its stockholders. Implicit in this statement is the idea that corporate actions motivated by anything other than shareholder wealth maximization threatens that well-being. On the other side, proponents of CSR assert that business does not function in a vacuum; it exists to serve, depends upon its environment, cannot be separated from it, and therefore has a responsibility to ensure its well-being. The environment is represented not only by stockholders/owners and employees, but also by such external stakeholders as customers, unions, suppliers, competitors, government agencies, local communities, and society in general.

The second argument for CSR suggests that stockholders' interests may transcend the financial. Many stockholders expect more from the companies in which they invest than simple appreciation in the economic value of the firm.

The third argument in favor of CSR is that the best way for a company to maximize shareholder wealth is to act in a socially responsible manner. It suggests that when a company behaves responsibly, benefits accrue directly to the bottom line. It also implies that when a company does not behave responsibly, the company and its shareholders suffer financially.

When discussing business ethics, the terms illegal and unethical are often used synonymously. Exhibit 2–14, E-commerce Strategy in Action, presents an argument that eBay is acting unethically by allowing, and profiting from, the sale of "murderabilia" on their website. eBay's lack of prevention is perceived by some critics as "morally reprehensible" and socially irresponsible. Since there are no laws against this type of sale on the Internet, it is not illegal. However, corporate social responsibility is an element of strategic decision making that eBay cannot ignore. If websites are not responsive to society, they increase the odds that people will turn to legislation to discipline corporate behavior.

CSR and the Bottom Line

The goal of every firm is to maintain viability through long-run profitability. Until all costs and benefits are accounted for, however, profits may not be claimed. In the case of CSR, costs and benefits are both economic and social. While economic costs and benefits are easily quantifiable, social costs and benefits are not. Managers therefore risk subordinating social consequences to other performance results that can be more straightforwardly measured.

The dynamic between CSR and success (profit) is complex. While one concept is clearly not mutually exclusive of the other, it is also clear that neither is a prerequisite of the other. Rather than viewing these two concepts as competing, it may be better to view CSR as a component in the decision-making process of business that must determine, among other objectives, how to maximize profits.

Attempts to undertake a cost-benefit analysis of CSR have not been very successful. The process is complicated by several factors. First, some CSR activities incur no dollar costs at all. For example, Second Harvest, the largest nongovernment, charitable food

E-commerce Strategy in Action

eBay's "Murderabilia"?

Exhibit 2–14

BusinessWeek Serial killer Angel Resendez-Ramirez smiles as he sits behind bulletproof glass on Death Row in a maximum-security prison. He has admitted to murdering 12 women across the U.S., yet he jokes and revels in his fame. Locks of his hair and shavings from the callouses on his feet have been sold on Internet auction site eBay for $9.99 a pop. He gets a cut from dealers each time a little piece of him is sold. Tom Konvicka's mother was one of the victims. When Resendez-Ramirez was caught and locked up, Konvicka remembers feeling relief that his mom's murderer was being brought to justice. Now, he's disgusted. Serial killers shouldn't profit from their murders. Their victims are dead and gone and they're still here and making a profit on what they've done.

In Texas, as in most other states, there's nothing to prevent criminals from selling "murderabilia" on the Internet. eBay and other sites don't prevent it, either. In fact, there's little to discourage the sale of a whole range of questionable items online. As the Internet has grown in popularity, it's a ready-made market connecting individuals with a vast audience of potential buyers—all protected by a cloak of semi-anonymity and the hands-off policies of Web auction sites. That wide-open flea market has produced a cornucopia of items for sale that are in bad taste or unethical.

A growing chorus of ethicists, lawmakers, consumer groups, and Internet activists say something needs to be done—either stepped-up monitoring by auction sites themselves, or statutes that police the Netways. By refusing to take responsibility for what is sold on their site, they're cashing in on an overall lack of social accountability the Internet offers. While the sale of murderabilia is not illegal, it's morally reprehensible.

Problem is, when it comes to the Web, it's sometimes difficult to tell what's illegal, what ought to be illegal, and what's just in bad taste. It's clearly against the law to sell things such as endangered species and certain kinds of firearms. But how do you prevent minors from buying alcohol and pornography in a realm where nobody knows their age? Selling body organs online isn't necessarily a crime, but a doctor who participates could breach professional ethics. And how do you prevent the trafficking in items like neo-Nazi paraphernalia that are illegal in some places but not in others?

Given all the confusion, society's first line of defense could be auction site operators—but they're having none of it. eBay has a laissez-faire attitude about what is sold on the site. The company claims it's all part of eBay's philosophy of building a community based on trust. However, by not screening items, eBay skirts potential liability and high monitoring costs.

Now that Net auctions have become such a magnet for potentially dicey items, some states and federal agencies are stepping up their efforts to stop abuses. FBI's Internet Fraud Complaint Center gets more than 1,000 complaints of online auction fraud each month—most of them involving eBay traffic. Agents have begun turning some of these cases over to local law enforcement authorities. In October, state elections officials in Illinois and New York temporarily shut down Voteauction.com, an Internet site where Americans could sell their votes to the highest bidder. Authorities say they are keeping close watch and will nab all who accept money for their votes—and the people who pay them—charging them with violating state and federal election laws. The very nature of the Web makes the unthinkable more possible. Absent the Internet, many people might not have been exposed to the opportunity to revel in Nazi items or bloody murder photos, or be offered an easy chance to buy them without fear of social backlash. eBay is a magnet for people who previously didn't have many outlets because you're immediately linked up to millions of people.

The Web amplifies ethical dilemmas, too. Consider MedicineOnline.com, a site that connects plastic surgery doctors and patients on the Net. The site asks doctors to provide info about their education and experience—including their history of malpractice suits—but takes no responsibility for the veracity of that information. By contrast, a regular hospital is legally bound to take responsibility for the credentials and services of doctors who practice there. That's eBay's answer, too: Since it does not sell anything itself, it's not responsible for what is sold on the site. eBay asks sellers to report any breach of guidelines—in other words, to police the site themselves.

For now, eBay plans to continue to rely on its guidelines—and on its community of members—to blow the whistle on anything beyond the pale. However, with creeps and criminals like Resendez-Ramirez virtually on the loose, eBay's self-monitoring system may not be enough.

Source: An excerpt from Marcia Stepanek, "Making a Killing Online," *BusinessWeek*, November 20, 2000.

distributor in the nation, accepts donations from food manufacturers and food retailers of surplus food that would otherwise be thrown out due to overruns, warehouse damage, or labeling errors. In 10 years, Second Harvest has distributed more than 2 billion pounds of food. Gifts in Kind America is an organization that enables companies to reduce unsold or obsolete inventory by matching a corporation's donated products with a charity's or other nonprofit organization's needs. In addition, a tax break is realized by the company. In the past, corporate donations have included 130,000 pairs of shoes from Nike, 10,000 pairs of gloves from Aris Isotoner, and 480 computer systems from Apple Computer.

In addition, philanthropic activities of a corporation, which have been a traditional mainstay of CSR, are undertaken at a discounted cost to the firm since they are often tax deductible. The benefits of corporate philanthropy can be enormous as is shown by the many national social welfare causes that have been spurred by corporate giving. A few of these causes are described in Exhibit 2–15. While such acts of benevolence often help establish a general perception of the involved companies within society, some philanthropic acts bring specific credit to the firm.

Second, socially responsible behavior does not come at a prohibitive cost. One needs only to look at the problems of A. H. Robbins Company (Dalkon Shield), Beech-Nut Corporation (apple juice), Drexel Burnham (insider trading), and Exxon *(Valdez)* for stark answers on the "cost" of social responsibility (or its absence) in the business environment.

Third, socially responsible practices may create savings and, as a result, increase profits. SET Laboratories uses popcorn to ship software rather than polystyrene peanuts. It is environmentally safer and costs 60 percent less to use. Corporations that offer part-time and adjustable work schedules have realized that this can lead to reduced absenteeism, greater productivity and increased morale. DuPont opted for more flexible schedules for its employees after a survey revealed 50 percent of women and 25 percent of men considered working for another employer with more flexibility for family concerns.

Proponents argue that CSR costs are more than offset in the long run by an improved company image and increased community goodwill. These intangible assets can prove valuable in a crisis, as Johnson & Johnson discovered with the Tylenol cyanide scare in 1982. Because it had established a solid reputation as a socially responsible company before the incident, the public readily accepted the company's assurances of public safety. Consequently, financial damage to Johnson & Johnson was minimized, despite the company's $100 million voluntary recall of potentially tainted capsules. CSR may also head off new regulation, preventing increased compliance costs. It may even attract investors who are themselves socially responsible. Proponents believe that for these reasons, socially responsible behavior increases the financial value of the firm in the long run. The mission statement of Johnson & Johnson is provided as Exhibit 2–16, Strategy in Action.

Performance   To explore the relationship between socially responsible behavior and financial performance, an important question must first be answered: How do managers measure the financial impact of corporate social performance?

Critics of CSR believe that companies that behave in a socially responsible manner, and portfolios comprising these companies' securities, should perform more poorly financially than those that do not. The costs of CSR outweigh the benefits for individual firms, they suggest. In addition, traditional portfolio theory holds that investors minimize risk and maximize return by being able to choose from an infinite universe of investment opportunities. Portfolios based on social criteria should suffer, critics argue, because they are by definition restrictive in nature. This restriction should increase portfolio risk and reduce portfolio return.

Now that U.S. companies are adopting strategic philanthropy, they are assuming an activist stance on social issues. As a result, many causes, including the following, have become national movements.

HUNGER

Before the new approach to corporate philanthropy, the foundations of food companies gave cash donations to antihunger organizations. But when the ranks of the hungry increased tenfold in the 1980s, contributions managers in companies such as General Mills, Grand Metropolitan, Kraft General Foods, and Sara Lee decided to play a larger role *and* establish a rallying point around which disparate units of their companies could come together. Marketers arranged for a portion of product sales to be donated to antihunger programs, human resources staffs deployed volunteers, operating units provided free food, and CEOs joined the board of Chicago-based Second Harvest, the food industry's antihunger voice. As a result of those efforts, a complex infrastructure of food banks and soup kitchens was developed.

COMMUNITY AND ECONOMIC DEVELOPMENT

Major banks such as Bank of America, Chase Manhattan, Citicorp, Morgan Guaranty, and Wells Fargo explored how philanthropy could be tied to marketing, human resources, government affairs, investment, and even trust management. Their business managers were concerned about the Community Reinvestment Act, which requires lenders to be responsive to low-income communities. Philanthropy managers point out that by going beyond the CRA requirements, they develop positive relationships with regulators while scoring public relations points. For example, at least 60 banks in the United States have created community development corporations to assist run-down neighborhoods.

LITERACY

The effort to increase literacy in the United States is the favorite cause of the communications industry. Print media companies such as McGraw-Hill, Prentice Hall, the *Los Angeles Times,* the *Washington Post,* and the *New York Times* are trying to halt the drop in readership, and broadcasters and cable companies are compensating for their role in the decline of literacy. Those companies have mobilized their marketing, human resources, and lobbying power to establish workplace literacy programs. While human resources budgets fund such programs, philanthropy dollars go mostly to volunteer organizations.

SCHOOL REFORM

About 15 percent of the country's cash gifts go to school reform, and a recent study estimated that at least one-third of U.S. school districts have partnership programs with business. The next step toward reform, promoted by the Business Roundtable, is for companies to mobilize their lobbying power at the state level to press for the overhaul of state educational agencies.

AIDS

AIDS is a top cause for insurance companies, who want to reduce claims; pharmaceutical companies, who want public support for the commercialization of AIDS drugs; and design-related companies, who want to support the large number of gays in their work force. Those industries put the first big money into AIDS prevention measures, and they've helped turn the American Foundation for AIDS Research into an advocate for more and better research by the National Institutes of Health.

ENVIRONMENTALISM

Environmental support varies across industries. In high-tech companies, environmentalism is largely a human resources issue because it's the favorite cause of many employees. Among the makers of outdoor apparel, environmentalism is largely a marketing issue, so companies donate a portion of the purchase price to environmental nonprofits. In industries that pollute or extract natural resources, environmentalism is often a government affairs matter.

Several research studies have attempted to determine the relationship between corporate social performance and financial performance. Taken together, these studies fail to establish the nature of the relationship between social and financial performance. There are a number of possible explanations for the findings. One possibility is that there is no meaningful correlation between social and financial performance. A second possibility is

"We believe our first responsibility is to the doctors, nurses and patients, to mothers and fathers and all others who use our products and services. In meeting their needs everything we do must be of high quality. We must constantly strive to reduce our costs in order to maintain reasonable prices. Customers' orders must be serviced promptly and accurately. Our suppliers and distributors must have an opportunity to make a fair profit.

We are responsible to our employees, the men and women who work with us throughout the world. Everyone must be considered as an individual. We must respect their dignity and recognize their merit. They must have a sense of security in their jobs. Compensation must be fair and adequate, and working conditions clean, orderly and safe. Employees must feel free to make suggestions and complaints. There must be equal opportunity for employment, development and advancement for those qualified. We must provide competent management, and their actions must be just and ethical.

We are responsible to the communities in which we live and work and to the world community as well. We must be good citizens—support good works and charities and bear our fair share of taxes. We must encourage civic improvements and better health and education. We must maintain in good order the property we are privileged to use, protecting the environment and natural resources.

Our final responsibility is to our stockholders. Business must make a sound profit. We must experiment with new ideas. Research must be carried on, innovative programs developed and mistakes paid for. New equipment must be purchased, new facilities provided and new products launched. Reserves must be created to provide for adverse times. When we operate according to these principles, the stockholders should realize a fair return."

---

that the benefits of CSR are offset by its negative consequences for the firm, thus producing a nondectectable net financial effect. Other explanations include methodological weaknesses and/or insufficient conceptual models or operational definitions used in the studies. However, among experts, a sense remains that a relationship between CSR and the bottom line does exist, although the exact nature of that relationship is unclear.

CSR Today

A survey of 2,737 senior U.S. managers revealed that 92 percent believed that business should take primary responsibility for, or an active role in, solving environmental problems; 84 percent believed business should do the same for educational concerns.[4] Despite the uncertain impact of CSR on the corporate bottom line, CSR has become a priority with American business. Why? In addition to a commonsense belief that companies should be able to "do well by doing good," at least three broad trends are driving businesses to adopt CSR frameworks: the resurgence of environmentalism, increasing buyer power, and the globalization of business.

The Resurgence of Environmentalism   In March 1989, the Exxon *Valdez* ran aground in Prince William Sound, spilling 11 million gallons of oil, polluting miles of ocean and shore, and helping to revive worldwide concern for the ecological environment. Six months after the *Valdez* incident, the Coalition for Environmentally Responsible Economies (CERES) was formed to establish new goals for environmentally responsible corporate behavior. The group drafted the CERES Principles to "establish an environmental ethic with criteria by which investors and others can assess the environmental performance of companies. Companies that sign these Principles pledge to go voluntarily beyond the requirements of the law."

---

[4] Rosabeth Moss Kanter, "Transcending Business Boundaries: 12,000 World Managers View Change," *Harvard Business Review* 69, no. 3 (May–June 1991), pp. 151–64.

Increasing Buyer Power   The rise of the consumer movement has meant that buyers—consumers and investors—are increasingly flexing their economic muscle. Consumers are becoming more interested in buying products from socially responsible companies. Organizations such as the Council on Economic Priorities (CEP) help consumers make more informed buying decisions through such publications as *Shopping for a Better World,* which provides social performance information on 191 companies making more than 2,000 consumer products. CEP also sponsors the annual Corporate Conscience Awards, which recognize socially responsible companies. One example of consumer power at work is the effective outcry over the deaths of dolphins in tuna fishermen's nets.

Investors represent a second type of influential consumer. There has been a dramatic increase in the number of people interested in supporting socially responsible companies through their investments. Membership in the Social Investment Forum, a trade association serving social investing professionals, has been growing at a rate of about 50 percent annually. As baby boomers achieve their own financial success, the social investing movement has continued its rapid growth.

While social investing wields relatively low power as an individual private act (selling one's shares of Exxon does not affect the company), it can be very powerful as a collective public act. When investors vote their shares in behalf of pro-CSR issues, companies may be pressured to change their social behavior. The South African divestiture movement is one example of how effective this pressure can be.

The Vermont National Bank has added a Socially Responsible Banking Fund to its product line. Investors can designate any of their interest-bearing accounts with a $500 minimum balance to be used by the fund. This fund then lends these monies for purposes such as low-income housing, the environment, education, farming, or small business development. Although it has had a "humble" beginning of approximately 800 people investing about $11 million, the bank has attracted out-of-state depositors and is growing faster than expected.

Social investors comprise both individuals and institutions. Much of the impetus for social investing originated with religious organizations that wanted their investments to mirror their beliefs. At present, the ranks of social investors have expanded to include educational institutions and large pension funds.

Large-scale social investing can be broken down into the two broad areas of guideline portfolio investing and shareholder activism. Guideline portfolio investing is the largest and fastest-growing segment of social investing. Individual and institutional guideline portfolio investors use ethical guidelines as screens to identify possible investments in stocks, bonds, and mutual funds. The investment instruments that survive the social screens are then layered over the investor's financial screens to create the investor's universe of possible investments.

Screens may be negative (e.g., excluding all tobacco companies) or they may combine negative and positive elements (e.g., eliminating companies with bad labor records while seeking out companies with good ones). Most investors rely on screens created by investment firms such as Kinder, Lydenberg Domini & Co. or by industry groups such as the Council on Economic Priorities. In addition to ecology, employee relations, and community development, corporations may be screened on their association with "sin" products (alcohol, tobacco, gambling), defense/weapons production, and nuclear power.

In contrast to guideline portfolio investors, who passively indicate their approval or disapproval of a company's social behavior by simply including or excluding it from their portfolios, shareholder activists seek to directly influence corporate social behavior. Shareholder activists invest in a corporation hoping to improve specific aspects of the company's social performance, typically by seeking a dialogue with upper management.

If this and successive actions fail to achieve the desired results, shareholder activists may introduce proxy resolutions to be voted upon at the corporation's annual meeting. The goal of these resolutions is to achieve change by gaining public exposure for the issue at hand. While the number of shareholder activists is relatively small, they are by no means small in achievement: Shareholder activists, led by such groups as the Interfaith Center on Corporate Responsibility, were the driving force behind the South African divestiture movement. Currently, there are more than 35 socially screened mutual funds available in the United States alone.

The Globalization of Business   Management issues, including CSR, have become more complex as companies increasingly transcend national borders: It is difficult enough to come to a consensus on what constitutes socially responsible behavior within one culture, let alone determine common ethical values across cultures. In addition to different cultural views, the high barriers facing international CSR include differing corporate disclosure practices, inconsistent financial data and reporting methods, and the lack of CSR research organizations within countries. Despite these problems, CSR is growing abroad. The United Kingdom has 30 ethical mutual funds and Canada offers 6 socially responsible funds.

CSR's Effect on the Mission Statement

The mission statement not only identifies what product or service a company produces, how it produces it, and what market it serves, it also embodies what the company believes. As such, it is essential that the mission statement recognize the legitimate claims of its external stakeholders, which may include creditors, customers, suppliers, government, unions, competitors, local communities, and elements of the general public. This stakeholder approach has become widely accepted by U.S. business. For example, a survey of directors in 291 of the largest southeastern U.S. companies found that directors had high stakeholder orientations. Customers, government, stockholders, employees, and society, in that order, were the stakeholders these directors perceived as most important.

In developing mission statements, managers must identify all stakeholder groups and weigh their relative rights and abilities to affect the firm's success. Some companies are proactive in their approach to CSR, making it an integral part of their raison d'être (e.g., Ben & Jerry's ice cream); others are reactive, adopting socially responsible behavior only when they must (e.g., Exxon after the *Valdez* incident).

Social Audit

A *social audit* attempts to measure a company's actual social performance against the social objectives it has set for itself. A social audit may be conducted by the company itself. However, one conducted by an outside consultant who will impose minimal biases may prove more beneficial to the firm. As with a financial audit, an outside auditor brings credibility to the evaluation. This credibility is essential if management is to take the results seriously and if the general public is to believe the company's public relations pronouncements.

Careful, accurate monitoring and evaluation of a company's CSR actions are important not only because the company wants to be sure it is implementing CSR policy as planned, but also because CSR actions by their nature are open to intense public scrutiny. To make sure it is making good on its CSR promises, a company may conduct a social audit of its performance.

Once the social audit is complete, it may be distributed internally or both internally and externally, depending on the firm's goals and situation. Some firms include a section in their annual report devoted to social responsibility activities; others publish a separate periodic report on their social responsiveness. Companies publishing separate social audits include General Motors, Bank of America, Atlantic Richfield, Control Data, and Aetna Life and Casualty Company. Nearly all Fortune 500 corporations disclose social performance information in their annual reports.

Large firms are not the only companies employing the social audit. Boutique ice cream maker Ben & Jerry's, a CSR pioneer, publishes a social audit in its annual report. The audit, conducted by an outside consultant, scores company performance in such areas as employee benefits, plant safety, ecology, community involvement, and customer service. The report is published unedited.

The social audit may be used for more than simply monitoring and evaluating firm social performance. Managers also use social audits to scan the external environment, determine firm vulnerabilities, and institutionalize CSR within the firm. In addition, companies themselves are not the only ones who conduct social audits; public interest groups and the media watch companies who claim to be socially responsible very closely to see if they practice what they preach. These organizations include consumer groups and socially responsible investing firms that construct their own guidelines for evaluating companies.

The Body Shop learned what can happen when a company's behavior falls short of its espoused mission and objectives. The 20-year-old manufacturer and retailer of naturally based hair and skin products had cultivated a socially responsible corporate image based on a reputation for socially responsible behavior. In late 1994, however, *Business Ethics* magazine published an exposé claiming that the company did not "walk the talk." It accused the Body Shop of using nonrenewable petrochemicals in its products, recycling far less than it claimed, using ingredients tested on animals, and making threats against investigative journalists. The Body Shop's contradictions were noteworthy because Anita Roddick, the company's founder, made CSR a centerpiece of the company's strategy.[5]

Summary

Defining the company mission is one of the most often slighted tasks in strategic management. Emphasizing the operational aspects of long-range management activities comes much more easily for most executives. But the critical role of the mission statement repeatedly is demonstrated by failing firms whose short-run actions have been at odds with their long-run purposes.

The principal value of the mission statement is its specification of the firm's ultimate aims. A firm gains a heightened sense of purpose when its board of directors and its top executives address these issues: "What business are we in?" "What customers do we serve?" "Why does this organization exist?" However, the potential contribution of the company mission can be undermined if platitudes or ambiguous generalizations are accepted in response to these questions. It is not enough to say that Lever Brothers is in the business of "making anything that cleans anything" or that Polaroid is committed to businesses that deal with "the interaction of light and matter." Only if a firm clearly articulates its long-term intentions can its goals serve as a basis for shared expectations, planning, and performance evaluation.

A mission statement that is developed from this perspective provides managers with a unity of direction transcending individual, parochial, and temporary needs. It promotes a sense of shared expectations among all levels and generations of employees. It consolidates values over time and across individuals and interest groups. It projects a sense of worth and intent that can be identified and assimilated by outside stakeholders, that is, customers, suppliers, competitors, local committees, and the general public. Finally, it asserts the firm's commitment to responsible action in symbiosis with the preservation and protection of the essential claims of insider stakeholders' survival, growth, and profitability.

[5] Jon Entine, "Shattered Image," *Business Ethics* 8, no. 5 (September/October 1994), pp. 23–28.

Questions for Discussion

1. Reread Nicor, Inc.'s mission statement in Exhibit 2–1, Strategy in Action. List five insights into Nicor that you feel you gained from knowing its mission.

2. Locate the mission statement of a company not mentioned in the chapter. Where did you find it? Was it presented as a consolidated statement, or were you forced to assemble it yourself from various publications of the firm? How many of the mission statement elements outlined in this chapter were discussed or revealed in the statement you found?

3. Prepare a two-page typewritten mission statement for your school of business or for a firm selected by your instructor.

4. List five potentially vulnerable areas of a firm without a stated company mission.

5. Define the term *social responsibility*. Find an example of a company action that was legal but not socially responsible. Defend your example on the basis of your definition.

6. Name five potentially valuable indicators of a firm's social responsibility and describe how company performance in each could be measured.

Chapter 2 Discussion Case

BusinessWeek

Inside a Chinese Sweatshop

1   Liu Zhang (not his real name) was apprehensive about taking a job at the Chun Si Enterprise Handbag Factory in Zhongshan, a booming city in Guangdong Province in southern China, where thousands of factories churn out goods for Western companies. Chun Si, which made Kathie Lee Gifford handbags sold by Wal-Mart Stores Inc. as well as handbags sold by Kansas-based Payless ShoeSource Inc., advertised decent working conditions and a fair salary. But word among migrant workers in the area was that managers there demanded long hours of their workers and sometimes hit them. Still, Liu, a 32–year-old former farmer and construction worker from far-off Henan province, was desperate for work. A factory job would give him living quarters and the temporary-residence permit internal migrants need to avoid being locked up by police in special detention centers. So in late August 1999, he signed up.

2   Liu quickly realized that the factory was even worse than its reputation. Chun Si, owned by Chun Kwan, a Macau businessman, charged workers $15 a month for food and lodging in a crowded dorm—a crushing sum given the $22 Liu cleared his first month. What's more, the factory gave Liu an expired temporary-resident permit; and in return, Liu had to hand over his personal identification card. This left him a virtual captive. Only the local police near the factory knew that Chun Si issued expired cards, Liu says, so workers risked arrest if they ventured out of the immediate neighborhood.

3   HALF A CENT. Liu also found that Chun Si's 900 workers were locked in the walled factory compound for all but a total of 60 minutes a day for meals. Guards regularly punched and hit workers for talking back to managers or even for walking too fast, he says. And they fined them up to $1 for infractions such as taking too long in the bathroom. Liu left the factory for good in December, after he and about 60 other workers descended on the local labor office to protest Chun Si's latest offenses: requiring cash payments for dinner and a phony factory it set up to dupe Wal-Mart's auditors. In his pocket was a total of $6 for three months of 90–hour weeks—an average of about one-half cent an hour. "Workers there face a life of fines and beating," says Liu. Chun Kwan couldn't be reached, but his daughter, Selina Chun, one of the factory managers, says "this is not true, none of this." She concedes that Chun Si did not pay overtime but says few other factories do, either. In a face-to-face interview in August, she also admitted that workers have tried to sue Chun Si.

4   Liu's Dickensian tale stands in stark contrast to the reassurances that Wal-Mart, Payless, and other U.S. companies give American consumers that their goods aren't produced under sweatshop conditions. Since 1992, Wal-Mart has required its suppliers to sign a code of basic labor standards. After exposés in the mid–1990s of abuses in factories making Kathie Lee products, which the chain carries, Wal-Mart and Kathie Lee both began hiring outside auditing firms to inspect supplier factories to ensure their compliance with the code. Many other companies that produce or sell goods made in low-wage countries do similar self-policing, from Toys 'R' Us to Nike and Gap. While no company suggests that its auditing systems are perfect, most say they catch major abuses and either force suppliers to fix them or yank production.

5   What happened at Chun Si suggests that these auditing systems can miss serious problems—and that self-policing allows companies to avoid painful public revelations about them. Allegations about Chun Si first surfaced this May in a report by the National Labor Committee (NLC), a small anti-sweatshop group in New York that in 1997 exposed Kathie Lee's connection to labor violations in Central America. For several months, Wal-Mart repeatedly denied any connection to Chun Si. Wal-Mart and Kathie Lee even went so far as to pass out a press release when the report came out dismissing it as "lies" and insisting that they never had "any relationship with a company or factory by this name anywhere in the world."

6   But in mid-September, after a three-month *BusinessWeek* investigation that involved a visit to the factory, tracking down ex-Chun Si workers, and obtaining copies of records they had smuggled out of the factory, Wal-Mart conceded that it had produced the Kathie Lee bags there until December, 1999. Wal-Mart Vice-President of Corporate Affairs Jay Allen now says that Wal-Mart denied

using Chun Si because it was "defensive" about the sweatshop issue.

7   Wal-Mart Director of Corporate Compliance Denise Fenton says its auditors, Pricewaterhouse Coopers LLP (PWC) and Cal Safety Compliance Corp., had inspected Chun Si five times in 1999 and found that the factory didn't pay the legal overtime rate and had required excessive work hours. Because the factory didn't fix the problems, she says, Wal-Mart stopped making Kathie Lee bags there. Kathie Lee, who licenses her name to Wal-Mart, which handles production, concurred with the chain's action at Chun Si, says her lawyer Richard Hofstetter. Payless also stopped production there after an investigation, a spokesman says.

8   Still, the auditors failed to uncover many of the egregious conditions in the factory despite interviews with dozens of workers, concedes Fenton. Charges NLC Executive Director Charles Kernaghan: "The real issue here is why anyone should believe their audits."

9   A SECOND LOOK. And it's not just Wal-Mart. The NLC's report, entitled Made in China, detailed labor abuses in a dozen factories producing for household-name U.S. companies (www.nlcnet.org). After it came out, bootmaker Timberland Co. asked its auditors to revisit its plant, also in Zhongshan. They found that the factory hadn't fixed most of the violations cited the first time, despite repeated assurances to Timberland that it had. Similarly, in mid-September, Social Accountability International (SAI), a New York group that started a factory monitoring system last year, revoked its certification of a Chinese factory that makes shoes for New Balance Athletic Shoe Inc. after auditors reinspected the plant following the NLC report. "The auditors found that indeed there were many violations they had not picked up the first time," says SAI President Alice Tepper Marlin.

10   Because such efforts to reassure consumers have proven so unsatisfactory, a handful of companies, including Nike Inc. and Reebok International Ltd.—so far, the companies most tarnished by antisweatshop activists—have concluded that self-policing isn't enough. They—along with Kathie Lee—helped form the Fair Labor Assn., created in 1998 after a White House-sponsored initiative. The FLA now has a dozen members and is setting up an independent monitoring system that includes human rights groups.

11   Wal-Mart and many other companies, though, reject such efforts, saying they don't want to tell critics or rivals where their products are made. Yet without independent inspections, such companies leave themselves open to critics' accusations that self-policing doesn't work. "The big retailers, such as Wal-Mart, drive the market today, yet . . . they're not committed to changing the way they do business," says Michael Posner, head of New York-based Lawyers Committee for Human Rights and an FLA board member. Wal-Mart's Allen says that after three years of talks, the company may soon set up independent monitoring with the Interfaith Center on Corporate Responsibility, a religious group in New York City.

12   Certainly, what happened at Chun Si illustrates the inadequacy of many labor-auditing systems in place today. Wal-Mart uses nine auditing firms, including PWC. Like other big accounting firms, PWC has a booming labor-auditing business inspecting many of the thousands of factories making toys and clothes made by Wal-Mart and other companies. After Kathie Lee's drubbing by sweatshop critics, she hired Cal Safety, a Los Angeles-based labor-auditing firm, to do separate audits of the factories that produce the clothing and accessories bearing her name. According to Wal-Mart's Fenton, Cal Safety inspected the factory four times from March to December of last year, and PWC inspected it once, in September. The auditors found that Chun Si had numerous problems, including overtime violations and excessively long hours, says Fenton.

13   But otherwise, concedes Fenton, the audits missed most of the more serious abuses listed in the NLC report and confirmed by *BusinessWeek,* including beatings and confiscated identity papers. (Wal-Mart declined to allow *BusinessWeek* to talk in detail to Cal Safety or PWC, citing confidentiality agreements. Randal H. Rankin, head of PWC's labor practices unit, insists his audit did catch many of the abuses found by the NLC, though he wouldn't provide specifics, also citing Wal-Mart's confidentiality agreement. Cal Safety President Carol Pender says her firm caught some, though not all, of the abuses.)

14   All the while, evidence was piling up at the local labor office in Zhongshan. There, officials received a constant stream of worker complaints—several a month since the factory opened 10 years ago, says Mr. Chen, the head of the local labor office, who declined to give his

full name. "Since they opened their factory, the complaints never stopped," he says. Officials would call or go to the factory once a month or so to mediate disputes, but new complaints kept arising, he says. Neither Wal-Mart's nor Kathie Lee's auditors discovered this history.

15   Chun Si also tried to hoodwink the auditors, according to the workers *BusinessWeek* interviewed. After Cal Safety's initial inspection in March, 1999, Wal-Mart (through its U.S. supplier, which placed the order with the factory) insisted that Chun Si remedy the violations or it would pull the contract. Cal Safety found little improvement when it returned in June, as did PWC in September.

16   DOUBLE STANDARD. Chun Si then took drastic steps, apparently in an effort to pass the final audit upon which its contract depended. In early November, management gave a facelift to the two attached five-story factory buildings, painting walls, cleaning workshops, even putting high-quality toilet paper in the dank bathrooms, according to Liu and Pang Yinguang (also not his real name), another worker employed there at the time whom *BusinessWeek* interviewed in mid-September. Management then split the factory into two groups. The first, with about 200 workers, was assigned to work on the fixed-up second floor, while the remaining 700 or so worked on the fourth floor, leaving the other floors largely vacant. Managers announced that those on the fourth floor were no longer working for Chun Si but for a new factory they called Yecheng. Workers signed new labor contracts with Yecheng, whose name went up outside the fourth floor.

17   The reality soon became clear. Workers on the fourth floor, including Liu and Pang, were still laboring under the old egregious conditions— illegally low pay, 14–hour days, exorbitant fees for meals—and still making the same Kathie Lee handbags. "It felt like being in prison," says Pang, 22. But those on the second floor now received the local minimum wage of $55 a month and no longer had to do mandatory overtime. A new sign went up in the cafeteria used by workers on all floors explaining that the factory was a Wal-Mart supplier and should live up to certain labor standards. Liu says there was even a phone number workers could call with problems: 1-800-WM-ETHIC. "When we saw the Wal-Mart statement, we felt very excited and happy because we thought that now there was a possibility to improve our conditions," says Liu.

18   LAST STRAW. Instead, they got worse. On Nov. 28, a second notice went up stating that starting on Dec. 10, all workers would be required to pay cash for dinner rather than just have money subtracted from their paychecks as before, say Liu and Pang. With up to 80% of workers already skipping breakfast to save money, the upper-floor employees were aghast, says Liu. "If we had left the factory then, we wouldn't have had even enough money for a bus ticket home," he says. "But if we stayed, we knew we wouldn't have enough money to eat."

19   A group of workers, including Liu and Pang, met around a small pond on the factory grounds on one of the following evenings. They knew that workers had fruitlessly complained before to the local labor office. So they decided on a plan to smuggle out documents to prove Chun Si's illegal fees and sub-minimum wages. On Dec. 1, 58 workers overcame their fears of retaliation and marched out the factory gates, down to the labor office.

20   Faced with the throng of workers, local labor officials visited Chun Si and forced the factory to immediately pay the workers and return the illegally collected fees. But the officials also told these workers they would have to give up their jobs at Chun Si. Days later, some 40 labor officials returned, ordered Chun Si to properly register or shut down the so-called Yecheng factory, and fined the company about $8,500. Shortly after the blow-up, Wal-Mart ended production at Chun Si.

21   Kernaghan and other labor activists concede that Chun Si is an extreme example of working conditions in China today. Yet many experts think most factories in China producing for Western companies routinely break China's labor laws. Some Western companies' monitoring efforts do catch and fix some of these problems. But unless companies and governments alike take more serious steps, labor watchdogs will give little credence to company claims that they're doing the best they can.

Source: Dexter Roberts and Aaron Bernstein, "A Life of Fines and Beating: Wal-Mart's self-policing in the Chun Si factory was a disaster. What kind of monitoring system works?" *BusinessWeek*, October 2, 2000.

Chapter **Three**

The External Environment

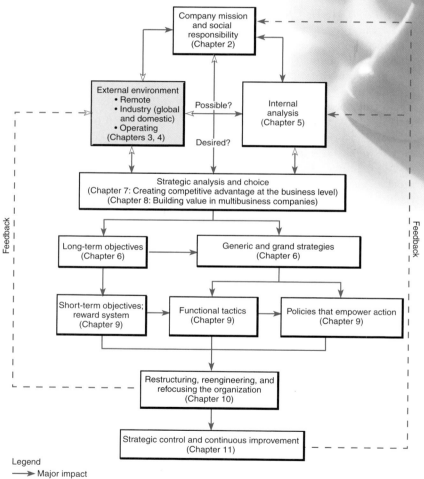

Company mission and social responsibility (Chapter 2)

External environment
- Remote
- Industry (global and domestic)
- Operating (Chapters 3, 4)

Possible?

Desired?

Internal analysis (Chapter 5)

Strategic analysis and choice
(Chapter 7: Creating competitive advantage at the business level)
(Chapter 8: Building value in multibusiness companies)

Long-term objectives (Chapter 6)

Generic and grand strategies (Chapter 6)

Short-term objectives; reward system (Chapter 9)

Functional tactics (Chapter 9)

Policies that empower action (Chapter 9)

Restructuring, reengineering, and refocusing the organization (Chapter 10)

Strategic control and continuous improvement (Chapter 11)

Feedback

Feedback

Legend
⟶ Major impact
⟶▷ Minor impact

A host of external factors influence a firm's choice of direction and action and, ultimately, its organizational structure and internal processes. These factors, which constitute the *external environment,* can be divided into three interrelated subcategories: factors in the *remote* environment, factors in the *industry* environment, and factors in the *operating* environment.[1] This chapter describes the complex necessities involved in formulating strategies that optimize a firm's market opportunities. Exhibit 3–1 suggests the interrelationship between the firm and its remote, its industry, and its operating environments. In combination, these factors form the basis of the opportunities and threats that a firm faces in its competitive environment.

EXHIBIT 3–1
The Firm's External Environment

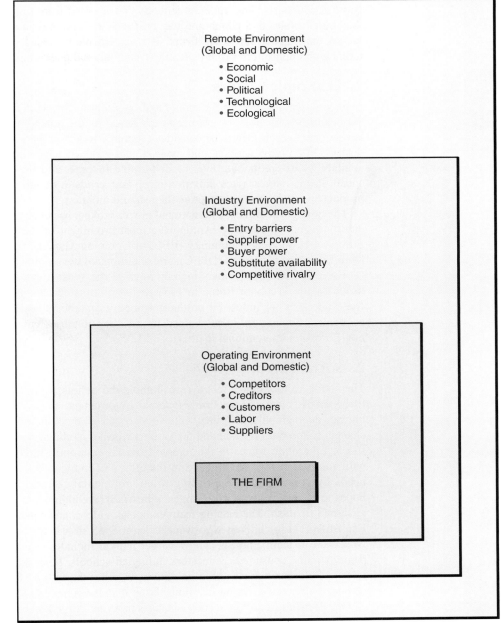

Remote Environment
(Global and Domestic)

- Economic
- Social
- Political
- Technological
- Ecological

Industry Environment
(Global and Domestic)

- Entry barriers
- Supplier power
- Buyer power
- Substitute availability
- Competitive rivalry

Operating Environment
(Global and Domestic)

- Competitors
- Creditors
- Customers
- Labor
- Suppliers

THE FIRM

[1] The operating environment is sometimes referred to as the *task* or *competitive* environment.

REMOTE ENVIRONMENT

The remote environment comprises factors that originate beyond, and usually irrespective of, any single firm's operating situation: (1) economic, (2) social, (3) political, (4) technological, and (5) ecological factors. That environment presents firms with opportunities, threats, and constraints, but rarely does a single firm exert any meaningful reciprocal influence. For example, when the economy slows and construction starts to decrease, an individual contractor is likely to suffer a decline in business, but that contractor's efforts in stimulating local construction activities would be unable to reverse the overall decrease in construction starts. The trade agreements that resulted from improved relations between the United States and China and the United States and Russia are examples of political factors that impact individual firms. The agreements provided individual U.S. manufacturers with opportunities to broaden their international operations.

1. Economic Factors

Economic factors concern the nature and direction of the economy in which a firm operates. Because consumption patterns are affected by the relative affluence of various market segments, each firm must consider economic trends in the segments that affect its industry. On both the national and international level, managers must consider the general availability of credit, the level of disposable income, and the propensity of people to spend. Prime interest rates, inflation rates, and trends in the growth of the gross national product are other economic factors they should monitor.

The emergence of new international power brokers has changed the focus of economic environmental forecasting. Among the most prominent of these power brokers are the European Economic Community (EEC, or Common Market), the Organization of Petroleum Exporting Countries (OPEC), and coalitions of developing countries.

The EEC, whose members include most of the West European countries, was established by the Treaty of Rome in 1957. It has eliminated quotas and established a tariff-free trade area for industrial products among its members. By fostering intra-European economic cooperation, it has helped its member countries compete more effectively in non-European international markets.

2. Social Factors

The social factors that affect a firm involve the beliefs, values, attitudes, opinions, and lifestyles of persons in the firm's external environment, as developed from cultural, ecological, demographic, religious, educational, and ethnic conditioning. As social attitudes change, so too does the demand for various types of clothing, books, leisure activities, and so on. Like other forces in the remote external environment, social forces are dynamic, with constant change resulting from the efforts of individuals to satisfy their desires and needs by controlling and adapting to environmental factors. Teresa Iglesias-Soloman hopes to benefit from social changes with *Ninos,* a children's catalog written in both English and Spanish. The catalog features books, videos, and Spanish cultural offerings for English-speaking children who want to learn Spanish and for Spanish-speaking children who want to learn English. *Ninos'* target market includes middle-to-upper-income Hispanic parents, consumers, educators, bilingual schools, libraries, and purchasing agents. Iglesias-Solomon has reason to be optimistic about the future of *Ninos,* because the Hispanic population is growing five times faster than the general U.S. population.

One of the most profound social changes in recent years has been the entry of large numbers of women into the labor market. This has not only affected the hiring and compensation policies and the resource capabilities of their employers; it has also created or greatly expanded the demand for a wide range of products and services necessitated by their absence from the home. Firms that anticipated or reacted quickly to this social change offered such products and services as convenience foods, microwave ovens, and day care centers.

A second profound social change has been the accelerating interest of consumers and employees in quality-of-life issues. Evidence of this change is seen in recent contract negotiations. In addition to the traditional demand for increased salaries, worker demands such benefits as sabbaticals, flexible hours or four-day workweeks, lump-sum vacation plans, and opportunities for advanced training.

A third profound social change has been the shift in the age distribution of the population. Changing social values and a growing acceptance of improved birth control methods are expected to raise the mean age of the U.S. population, which was 27.9 in 1970, and 34.9 in the year 2000. This trend will have an increasingly unfavorable impact on most producers of predominantly youth-oriented goods and will necessitate a shift in their long-range marketing strategies. Producers of hair and skin care preparations already have begun to adjust their research and development to reflect anticipated changes in demand.

A consequence of the changing age distribution of the population has been a sharp increase in the demands made by a growing number of senior citizens. Constrained by fixed incomes, these citizens have demanded that arbitrary and rigid policies on retirement age be modified and have successfully lobbied for tax exemptions and increases in Social Security benefits. Such changes have significantly altered the opportunity-risk equations of many firms—often to the benefit of firms that anticipated the changes.

The problems of monitoring social changes are multiplied many times as businesses venture into international markets. One simple but poignant example is described in Strategy in Action Exhibit 3–2.

Translating social change into forecasts of business effects is a difficult process, at best. Nevertheless, informed estimates of the impact of such alterations as geographic shifts in populations and changing work values, ethical standards, and religious orientation can only help a strategizing firm in its attempts to prosper.

3. Political Factors

The direction and stability of political factors are a major consideration for managers on formulating company strategy. Political factors define the legal and regulatory parameters within which firms must operate. Political constraints are placed on firms through fair-trade decisions, antitrust laws, tax programs, minimum wage legislation, pollution and pricing policies, administrative jawboning, and many other actions aimed at protecting employees, consumers, the general public, and the environment. Since such laws and regulations are most commonly restrictive, they tend to reduce the potential profits of firms. However, some political actions are designed to benefit and protect firms. Such actions include patent laws, government subsidies, and product research grants. Thus, political factors either may limit or benefit the firms they influence.

As described in Exhibit 3–3, Global Strategy in Action, the direction and stability of political factors are a major consideration when evaluating the remote environment. Specifically, the article addresses the fact that the legal basis of piracy is political. Microsoft's performance in the Chinese market is greatly affected by the lack of legal enforcement of piracy and also by the policies of the Chinese government. Likewise, the government's actions in support of its competitor, Linux, have limited Microsoft's ability to penetrate the Chinese market.

Political activity also has a significant impact on two governmental functions that influence the remote environment of firms: the supplier function and the customer function.

India's sacred cows can stop fretting: McDonald's won't be requiring their services. The burger behemoth announced it will open its first franchises in India early next year—but without Big Macs. Deferring to the country's Hindu tradition, which prohibits the consumption of beef, the company instead will serve chicken and fish, as well as vegetable burgers. It's the first time the fast-food company has excluded beef from its menu. New Delhi consultant Dilip Cherian thinks other multinationals should follow McDonald's culturally sensitive lead: "It's not going to be one grand American burger that sweeps through India," he says.

Source: Keith H. Hammonds, ed., "In India, Beef-Free Mickey D," *BusinessWeek,* April 17, 1995.

Supplier Function

Government decisions regarding the accessibility of private businesses to government-owned natural resources and national stockpiles of agricultural products will affect profoundly the viability of the strategies of some firms.

Customer Function

Government demand for products and services can create, sustain, enhance, or eliminate many market opportunities. For example, in the same way that the Kennedy administration's emphasis on landing a man on the moon spawned a demand for thousands of new products; the Carter administration's emphasis on developing synthetic fuels created a demand for new skills, technologies, and products; the Reagan administration's strategic defense initiative (the "Star Wars" defense) sharply accelerated the development of laser technologies; Clinton's federal block grants to the states for welfare reform led to office rental and lease opportunities; and the war against terrorism during the Bush administration created enormous investment in aviation.

4. Technological Factors

The fourth set of factors in the remote environment involves technological change. To avoid obsolescence and promote innovation, a firm must be aware of technological changes that might influence its industry. Creative technological adaptations can suggest possibilities for new products, for improvements in existing products, or in manufacturing and marketing techniques.

A technological breakthrough can have a sudden and dramatic effect on a firm's environment. It may spawn sophisticated new markets and products or significantly shorten the anticipated life of a manufacturing facility. Thus, all firms, and most particularly those in turbulent growth industries, must strive for an understanding both of the existing technological advances and the probable future advances that can affect their products and services. This quasi-science of attempting to foresee advancements and estimate their impact on an organization's operations is known as *technological forecasting*.

Technological forecasting can help protect and improve the profitability of firms in growing industries. It alerts strategic managers to both impending challenges and promising opportunities. As examples: (1) advances in xerography were a key to Xerox's success but caused major difficulties for carbon paper manufacturers, and (2) the perfection of transistors changed the nature of competition in the radio and television industry, helping such giants as RCA while seriously weakening smaller firms whose resource commitments required that they continue to base their products on vacuum tubes.

BusinessWeek One box that solves two problems. That was Microsoft's hope for Venus, a $240–$360 gadget running Windows CE software that turns Chinese TV sets into Internet appliances. Venus would solve two problems by making it both easier and cheaper for Chinese consumers to access the Web. Venus was the key to penetrating China, because it would make Windows nearly ubiquitous in living rooms from Shenzhen to Shanghai.

Fast-forward to late 2000: Venus seems more like one box containing two disasters. Of the three main Chinese companies that signed up to sell Venus boxes, two have pulled them from the market. Only Legend Computer is still selling the units in China—and it ships most of its supply to Southeast Asia. Why has Venus fizzled? Zhang blames both a lack of online content and the relatively high cost of Internet access. But others say Microsoft misjudged the willingness of Chinese to buy what is essentially low-rent technology. And with PCs selling for as little as $600, there isn't much reason to buy Venus.

The Venus project is not the only misfire in Microsoft's China strategy. Microsoft continues to battle software pirates, a poor image with Chinese authorities and consumers, and a growing threat from local rivals offering inexpensive Linux-based service. Microsoft won't release its China revenues, but analysts say they're probably under $100 million this year—less than the company makes in Hong Kong. "We are much smaller than we expected," says Microsoft General Manager Jack Gao.

Increasingly, Microsoft must contend with companies offering Linux, the open-source operating system. The threat is perhaps more political than anything else. Beijing likes to set one foreign company against another—as it has done with Boeing and Airbus. By playing up the potential of Linux, the government may be telling Microsoft that it had better play by its rules.

But Microsoft faces no greater competitor than the thieves who have elevated software piracy to a fine art. Last year, overall sales of computer hardware in China topped $18 billion. But software sales were a measly $2.1 billion. In other countries, the ratio is closer to even. Blame the shortfall on the pirates. Because of all the counterfeiting, Microsoft sold only 2 million licensed copies of its software in China during the year ending in June.

Chinese aren't ready to give up on counterfeit versions of Windows either. "We have a lot of users," says Jack Gao ruefully. "But we don't have a lot of customers." With Beijing intent on developing a local software industry, he says, cracking down on the pirates is in China's interest, too. That will take time. For now, a more humble Microsoft will have to keep trying to win friends in the emerging market it values most.

Source: An excerpt from B. Einhorn and A. Webb, "Microsoft Misfires in China," *BusinessWeek*, December 18, 2000.

The key to beneficial forecasting of technological advancement lies in accurately predicting future technological capabilities and their probable impacts. A comprehensive analysis of the effect of technological change involves study of the expected impact of new technologies on the remote environment, on the competitive business situation, and on the business-society interface. In recent years, forecasting in the last area has warranted particular attention. For example, as a consequence of increased concern over the environment, firms must carefully investigate the probable effect of technological advances on quality-of-life factors, such as ecology and public safety.

As discussed in Exhibit 3–4, E-commerce Strategy in Action, by combining the powers of Internet technologies with the capability of downloading music in a digital format, Bertelsmann has found a creative technological adaptation for distributing music online to millions of consumers whenever or wherever they might be. The ease and wide availability of Internet technologies is increasing the marketplace for online e-tailers. Bertelsmann's response to the shifts in technological factors enables it to distribute music more rapidly to a growing consumer base.

5. Ecological Factors

The most prominent factor in the remote environment is often the reciprocal relationship between business and the ecology. The term *ecology* refers to the relationships among human beings and other living things and the air, soil, and water that support them.

BusinessWeek On April 2, 2001, Bertelsmann, AOL Time Warner Inc., and London-based EMI Group announced they are teaming up with RealNetworks Inc. on a new online venture called MusicNet. The deal is Middelhoff's latest gambit to ensure that Bertelsmann will play a big role in the digital music business—even if Napster doesn't make it. MusicNet is designed to be a digital music wholesaler. It will act as an intermediary between recording companies and online retailers, providing technology that allows fans to listen to music tracks over the Internet or download songs they can replay and keep. Most important, MusicNet will provide technology allowing recording companies to protect their copyrights and collect royalties. "MusicNet turns into a black box for companies like us that want to offer music services but don't want to have to build all that," says Barry M. Schuler, chairman and CEO of AOL, which plans to use MusicNet as the basis for its own music subscription service.

The MusicNet deal broadens Bertelsmann's digital distribution base. Bertelsmann will own 20% of MusicNet, the same stake as the other recording companies. So Bertelsmann can be sure its music catalog will also be sold on AOL and any other subscription services based on MusicNet. Meanwhile, eCommerce chief Schmidt is making plans for an alternative consumer service called Be Music, which will use MusicNet to make Bertelsmann music available to customers on PCs, mobile phones, and other devices. Bertelsmann's BMG Entertainment, Warner Music Group, and EMI will provide MusicNet with their vast catalogs, accounting for more than 50% of the music market and including artists from Bjork to Madonna. With that kind of critical mass, other record companies will feel pressure to distribute their catalogs via MusicNet. That in turn could push the fragmented music industry toward some kind of technical standard for music sales on the Internet.

If it can overcome the huge technical hurdles, Napster could have enough music from Warner, Bertelsmann, and EMI to convert at least some of its 72 million registered users to paying subscribers. "That's more than enough to build a viable business," says Mark Mulligan, London-based analyst for Jupiter Media Metrix Inc.

Surely many Napster users will bolt to outlaw services if they have to start paying. Even if Napster can get one quarter to pay an average of $5 a month, though, it can generate more than $1 billion a year in revenue. Middelhoff hopes to end the legal challenges, then exercise an option to take a 58% stake and control what is still the media industry's most powerful online draw.

Many in the music industry are still hoping that Napster will die a slow death. Yet none has found an alternative with such powerful popular appeal. "The music business will be transformed by this long-term," says AOL's Schuler.

Source: An excerpt from Jack Ewing, Amy Borrus, Arlene Weintraub, and Jay Greene. "Sold on a Digital Music Dream, An online joint venture could make it come true for Bertelsmann," *BusinessWeek*, April 16, 2001.

Threats to our life-supporting ecology caused principally by human activities in an industrial society are commonly referred to as *pollution*. Specific concerns include global warming, loss of habitat and biodiversity, as well as air, water, and land pollution.

The global climate has been changing for ages; however, it is now evident that humanity's activities are accelerating this tremendously. A change in atmospheric radiation, due in part to ozone depletion, causes global warming. Solar radiation that is normally absorbed into the atmosphere reaches the earth's surface, heating the soil, water, and air.

Another area of great importance is the loss of habitat and biodiversity. Ecologists agree that the extinction of important flora and fauna is occurring at a rapid rate and if this pace is continued, could constitute a global extinction on the scale of those found in fossil records. The earth's life forms are dependent on a well-functioning ecosystem. In addition, immeasurable advances in disease treatment can be attributed to research involving substances found in plants. As species become extinct, the life support system is irreparably harmed. The primary cause of extinction on this scale is a disturbance of natural habitat. For example, current data suggest that the earth's primary tropical forests, a prime source of oxygen and potential plant "cure," could be destroyed in only five decades.

Air pollution is created by dust particles and gaseous discharges that contaminate the air. Acid rain, or rain contaminated by sulfur dioxide, which can destroy aquatic and plant

BusinessWeek Outdoor clothing company Patagonia Inc. has worked hard to be one of the greenest businesses around. It was the first apparel maker to sell synthetic fleece sweaters and warm-up pants made from recycled soda bottles. Last year, it switched to organic cotton for shirts and trousers—and ate half of the 20% markup that organic production added to the garments' cost. Its glossy catalog, printed on recycled paper that is 50% chlorine-free, uses pictures of adventurers in wild places to promote environmental causes.

But Patagonia still has a troubled conscience. In a surprisingly public mea culpa, the company's fall catalog opens with a letter to customers that is a stark critique of Patagonia's reliance on waterproof coatings such as Gore-Tex, which contains chemical toxins, and bright dyes based on strip-mined metals. It is only by using such "dirty" manufacturing processes, the company confesses, that it can offer the "bombproof" outdoor gear and striking colors that customers love. As the letter laments: "The production of our clothing takes a significant toll on the earth."

Turns out it's not easy being green. Patagonia and a handful of other companies that have made protection of the environment a central tenet of their businesses are running into a new wave of polluting problems that require tougher trade-offs than those of the past. Whether it's Ben & Jerry's Home-made coping with massive amounts of high-fat dairy waste, Stonyfield Farm searching for an affordable way to convert to organic fruit for its yogurt, or Orvis, the fishing-gear maker, trying to build a new headquarters that won't threaten bear habitats, green pioneers are struggling for ways to balance *environmental principles* with profit goals.

None are backing off their commitment to the environment. Instead, the greenest companies are testing the limits of what can be done cleanly. "We want it all," Yvon Chouinard, Patagonia's president, told a meeting of the company's suppliers last year. "The best quality and the lowest environmental impact." But it's getting tougher to push the green envelope without compromising business goals. "Our whole system of commerce is not designed to be ecologically sustainable," says Matthew Arnold, director of Washington-based Management Institute for Environment & Business. "These guys are showing the limits of the system to respond."

And customers have made it clear that quality comes first, even if it means passing up the chance to have less impact on the environment. Patagonia surveys show that just 20% of its customers buy from the company because they believe in its environmental mission.

Source: Paul C. Judge in Boston, "It's Not Easy Being Green," *BusinessWeek,* November 24, 1997.

life, is believed to result from coal-burning factories in 70 percent of all cases. A health-threatening "thermal blanket" is created when the atmosphere traps carbon dioxide emitted from smokestacks in factories burning fossil fuels. This "greenhouse effect" can have disastrous consequences, making the climate unpredictable and raising temperatures.

Water pollution occurs principally when industrial toxic wastes are dumped or leak into the nation's waterways. Since fewer than 50 percent of all municipal sewer systems are in compliance with Environmental Protection Agency requirements for water safety, contaminated waters represent a substantial present threat to public welfare. Efforts to keep from contaminating the water supply are a major challenge to even the most conscientious of manufacturing firms. As described in Exhibit 3–5, Strategy in Action, highly reputed "green" supporter Patagonia has judged itself to be guilty of water pollution.

The Patagonia story is especially interesting because of the "green" fervor with which the company pursues its manufacturing objectives. It provides some details on the difficulties that Patagonia faces in its attempts to do what many ecological activists believe should be a national mandate for all corporations.

Land pollution is caused by the need to dispose of ever-increasing amounts of waste. Routine, everyday packaging is a major contributor to this problem. Land pollution is more dauntingly caused by the disposal of industrial toxic wastes in underground sites. With approximately 90 percent of the annual U.S. output of 500 million metric tons of hazardous industrial wastes being placed in underground dumps, it is evident that land pollution and its resulting endangerment of the ecology have become a major item on the political agenda.

EXHIBIT 3–6
Environmental Costs and Competitiveness

Source: Excerpted from Benjamin C. Bonifant, Matthew R. Arnold, and Frederick J. Long, "Gaining Competitive Advantage through Environmental Investments," p. 39. Reprinted from *Business Horizons,* July–August 1995. Copyright 1995 by the Foundation for the School of Business at Indiana University. Used with permission.

Several recent efforts to quantify environmental spending have suggested that enormous costs are being incurred. A 1990 study by the U.S. EPA concluded that environmental spending was approaching 2 percent of GNP. Manufacturers then used this information to support their claim that regulation was harming industrial growth and putting the nation at a competitive disadvantage vis-à-vis foreign suppliers. The claims, however, simply did not hold up to closer inspection. First, only a small share of pollution abatement and control spending was incurred by industrial facilities. By one estimate (one used as a source for the EPA study), manufacturers incurred a total of $31.1 billion in environmental costs in 1990. This amounted to only 1.1 percent of product shipments. The costs identified by the EPA resulted from such areas as the requirement for catalytic converters on all automobiles ($14 billion in 1990), the construction and operation of public sewer systems ($20 billion), and the disposal of household wastes ($10 billion).

Even if environmental spending made up only 1 percent of costs, it would not be unreasonable for manufacturers to claim that these costs had a significant influence on competitiveness if international competitors were not required to meet similar requirements. Comparisons of international spending suggest, however, that manufacturers in important production areas around the world are experiencing costs similar to those faced by U.S. producers. Pollution control's share of capital expenditures in Germany was 12 percent in 1990, matching the costs incurred by American manufacturers. Similarly, recent environmental spending by U.S. pulp and paper manufacturers is closely matched by key competitors in Canada and Sweden.

These comparisons suggest that although pollution abatement expenditures are clearly a material part of total costs, the impact of these costs on competitiveness is mild. In fact, no clear link can be made between environmental regulation and measurably adverse effects on net exports, overall trade flows, or plant location decisions. It appears that little advantage has been gained by foreign firms based on the environmental requirements in the areas of their production.

As a major contributor to ecological pollution, business now is being held responsible for eliminating the toxic by-products of its current manufacturing processes and for cleaning up the environmental damage that it did previously. Increasingly, managers are being required by the government or are being expected by the public to incorporate ecological concerns into their decision making. For example, between 1975 and 1992, 3M cut its pollution in half by reformulating products, modifying processes, redesigning production equipment, and recycling by-products. Similarly, steel companies and public utilities have invested billions of dollars in costlier but cleaner-burning fuels and pollution control equipment. The automobile industry has been required to install expensive emission controls in cars. The gasoline industry has been forced to formulate new low-lead and no-lead products. And thousands of companies have found it necessary to direct their R&D resources into the search for ecologically superior products, such as Sears's phosphate-free laundry detergent and Pepsi-Cola's biodegradable plastic soft-drink bottle.

Environmental legislation impacts corporate strategies worldwide. Many companies fear the consequences of highly restrictive and costly environmental regulations. However, some manufacturers view these new controls as an opportunity, capturing markets with products that help customers satisfy their own regulatory standards. Other manufacturers contend that the costs of environmental spending inhibit the growth and productivity of their operations. Exhibit 3–6 takes a deeper look into the costs of environmental regulations.

The increasing attention by companies to protect the environment is evidenced in the attempts by firms to establish proecology policies. One such approach to environmental activism is described in Global Strategy in Action Exhibit 3–7.

"The ongoing occurrence of environmental incidents has become unacceptable in the public's mind," says George Pilko, president of Houston-based Pilko & Associates, an environmental consulting firm. That's why companies today are taking a proactive stance when it comes to managing environmental issues. The public just won't tolerate any more Love Canals, Bhopals, or major oil spills. "You've got strong public sentiment, increasingly stringent enviromental regulations at the local, state, and federal level, stricter enforcement of existing regulations, and an exponential rise in environmentally oriented lawsuits.

Companies need to make sure they have an environmental policy that clearly explains their commitment to being proactive and is communicated clearly to all employees. Companies also should be aware of the effectiveness of their current programs and when they stand relative to their competitors. In fact, a Pilko & Associates survey of 200 senior executives representing large industrial firms found that 40 percent of the respondents believed their company was doing an excellent job of managing their environmental problems, while only 8 percent thought their competitors were doing an excellent job.

For those CEOs or senior executives interested in getting out the message that they are serious about dealing with the environment. Pilko advises them to ask themselves the following 10 questions:

1. Do you have a clearly articulated environmental policy that has been communicated throughout the company?

2. Have you had an objective, third-party assessment of the effectiveness of your environmental problems?

3. Have you analyzed how your company's environmental performance compares with that of the leading firms in your industry?

4. Does your company view environmental performance not just as a staff function but as the responsibility of all employees?

5. Have you analyzed the potential impact of environmental issues on the future demand for your products and the competitive economics in your industry?

6. Are environmental issues and activities discussed frequently at your board meetings?

7. Do you have a formal system for monitoring proposed regulatory changes and for handling compliance with changing regulations?

8. Do you routinely conduct environmental due-diligence studies on potential acquisitions?

9. Have you successfully budgeted for environmental expenditures, without incurring surprise expenses that materially affected your profitability?

10. Have you identified and quantified environmental liabilities from past operations, and do you have a plan for minimizing those liabilities?

Source: Excerpted from Julie Cohen Mason, "Taking a Step in the Right Direction," p. 23. Reprinted by permission of the publisher from *Management Review*, December 1991, © 1991 American Management Association, New York. All rights reserved.

Despite cleanup efforts to date, the job of protecting the ecology will continue to be a top strategic priority—usually because corporate stockholders and executives choose it, increasingly because the public and the government require it. As evidenced by Exhibit 3–8, the government has made numerous interventions into the conduct of business for the purpose of bettering the ecology.

Benefits of Eco-Efficiency

Many of the world's largest corporations are realizing that business activities must no longer ignore environmental concerns. Every activity is linked to thousands of other transactions and their environmental impact; therefore, corporate environmental responsibility must be taken seriously and environmental policy must be implemented to ensure a comprehensive organizational strategy. Because of increases in government regulations and consumer environmental concerns, the implementation of environmental policy has become a point of competitive advantage. Therefore, the rational goal of business should be to limit its impact on the environment, thus ensuring long-run benefits to both the firm and society. To neglect this responsibility is to ensure the demise of both the firm and our ecosystem.

EXHIBIT 3–8
Federal Ecological
Legislation

Centerpiece Legislation

National Environmental Policy Act, 1969   Established Environmental Protection Agency; consolidated federal environmental activities under it. Established Council on Environmental Quality to advise president on environmental policy and to review environmental impact statements.

Air Pollution

Clean Air Act, 1963   Authorized assistance to state and local governments in formulating control programs. Authorized limited federal action in correcting specific pollution problems.

Clean Air Act, Amendments (Motor Vehicle Air Pollution Control Act), 1965   Authorized federal standards for auto exhaust emission. Standards first set for 1968 models.

Air Quality Act, 1967   Authorized federal government to establish air quality control regions and to set maximum permissible pollution levels. Required states and localities to carry out approved control programs or else give way to federal controls.

Clean Air Act Amendments, 1970   Authorized EPA to establish nationwide air pollution standards and to limit the discharge of six principal pollutants into the lower atmosphere. Authorized citizens to take legal action to require EPA to implement its standards against undiscovered offenders.

Clean Air Act Amendments, 1977   Postponed auto emission requirements. Required use of scrubbers in new coal-fired power plants. Directed EPA to establish a system to prevent deterioration of air quality in clean areas.

Solid Waste Pollution

Solid Waste Disposal Act, 1965   Authorized research and assistance to state and local control programs.

Resource Recovery Act, 1970   Subsidized construction of pilot recycling plants; authorized development of nationwide control programs.

Resource Conservation and Recovery Act, 1976   Directed EPA to regulate hazardous waste management, from generation through disposal.

Surface Mining and Reclamation Act, 1976   Controlled strip mining and restoration of reclaimed land.

Water Pollution

Refuse Act, 1899   Prohibited dumping of debris into navigable waters without a permit. Extended by court decision to industrial discharges.

Federal Water Pollution Control Act, 1956   Authorized grants to states for water pollution control. Gave federal government limited authority to correct specific pollution problems.

Water Quality Act, 1965   Provided for adoption of water quality standards by states, subject to federal approval.

Water Quality Improvement Act, 1970   Provided for federal cleanup of oil spills. Strengthened federal authority over water pollution control.

Federal Water Pollution Control Act Amendments, 1972   Authorized EPA to set water quality and effluent standards; provided for enforcement and research.

Safe Drinking Water Act, 1974   Set standards for drinking water quality.

Clean Water Act, 1977   Ordered control of toxic pollutants by 1984 with best available technology economically feasible.

Stephen Schmidheiny, chairman of the Business Council for Sustainable Development, has coined the term *eco-efficiency* to describe corporations that produce more-useful goods and services while continuously reducing resource consumption and pollution. He cites a number of reasons for corporations to implement environmental policy: customers demand cleaner products, environmental regulations are increasingly more stringent, employees prefer to work for environmentally conscious firms, and financing is more readily available for eco-efficient firms. In addition, the government provides incentives for environmentally responsible companies.

Setting priorities, developing corporate standards, controlling property acquisition and use to preserve habitats, implementing energy-conserving activities, and redesigning products (e.g., minimizing packaging) are a number of measures the firm can implement to enhance an eco-efficient strategy. One of the most important steps a firm can take in achieving a competitive position with regard to the eco-efficient strategy is to fully capitalize on technological developments as a method of gaining efficiency.

Four key characteristics of eco-efficient corporations are:

- Eco-efficient firms are proactive, not reactive. Policy is initiated and promoted by business because it is in their own interests and the interest of their customers, not because it is imposed by one or more external forces.

- Eco-efficiency is designed in, not added on. This characteristic implies that the optimization of eco-efficiency requires every business effort regarding the product and process to internalize the strategy.

- Flexibility is imperative for eco-efficient strategy implementation. Continuous attention must be paid to technological innovation and market evolution.

- Eco-efficiency is encompassing, not insular. In the modern global business environment, efforts must cross not only industrial sectors but national and cultural boundaries as well.

INTERNATIONAL ENVIRONMENT

Monitoring the international environment, perhaps better thought of as the international dimension of the global environment, involves assessing each nondomestic market on the same factors that are used in a domestic assessment. While the importance of factors will differ, the same set of considerations can be used for each country. For example, Exhibit 3–9, Global Strategy in Action, lists the economic, political, legal, and social factors that international expert Arvind Phatak uses to assess international environments. However, there is one complication to this process, namely, that the interplay among international markets must be considered. For example, in recent years, conflicts in the Middle East have made collaborative business strategies among firms in traditionally antagonistic countries especially difficult to implement.

INDUSTRY ENVIRONMENT

Harvard professor Michael E. Porter propelled the concept of industry environment into the foreground of strategic thought and business planning. The cornerstone of his work first appeared in the *Harvard Business Review,* in which Porter explains the five forces that shape competition in an industry. His well-defined analytic framework helps strategic managers to link remote factors to their effects on a firm's operating environment.

Global Strategy in Action
Used to Assess the International Environment

Exhibit 3–9

ECONOMIC ENVIRONMENT

Level of economic development

Population

Gross national product

Per capita income

Literacy level

Social infrastructure

Natural resources

Climate

Membership in regional economic blocs (EU, NAFTA, LAFTA)

Monetary and fiscal policies

Wage and salary levels

Nature of competition

Currency convertibility

Inflation

Taxation system

Interest rates

LEGAL ENVIRONMENT

Legal tradition

Effectiveness of legal system

Treaties with foreign nations

Patent trademark laws

Laws affecting business firms

POLITICAL SYSTEM

Form of government

Political ideology

Stability of government

Strength of opposition parties and groups

Social unrest

Political strife and insurgency

Govermental attitude towards foreign firms

Foreign policy

CULTURAL ENVIRONMENT

Customs, norms, values, beliefs

Language

Attitudes

Motivations

Social institutions

Status symbols

Religious beliefs

Source: Arvind V. Phatak, *International Management* (Cincinnati, OH: South-Western College Publishing, 1997), p. 6.

With the special permission of Professor Porter and the *Harvard Business Review,* we present in this section of the chapter the major portion of his seminal article on the industry environment and its impact on strategic management.[2]

OVERVIEW

The nature and degree of competition in an industry hinge on five forces: the threat of new entrants, the bargaining power of customers, the bargaining power of suppliers, the threat of substitute products or services (where applicable), and the jockeying among

[2] M. E. Porter, "How Competitive Forces Shape Strategy," *Harvard Business Review,* March–April 1979, pp. 137–45.

current contestants. To establish a strategic agenda for dealing with these contending currents and to grow despite them, a company must understand how they work in its industry and how they affect the company in its particular situation. This chapter will detail how these forces operate and suggest ways of adjusting to them, and, where possible, of taking advantage of opportunities that they create.

HOW COMPETITIVE FORCES SHAPE STRATEGY

The essence of strategy formulation is coping with competition. Yet it is easy to view competition too narrowly and too pessimistically. While one sometimes hears executives complaining to the contrary, intense competition in an industry is neither coincidence nor bad luck.

Moreover, in the fight for market share, competition is not manifested only in the other players. Rather, competition in an industry is rooted in its underlying economics, and competitive forces exist that go well beyond the established combatants in a particular industry. Customers, suppliers, potential entrants, and substitute products are all competitors that may be more or less prominent or active depending on the industry.

The state of competition in an industry depends on five basic forces, which are diagrammed in Exhibit 3–10. The collective strength of these forces determines the ultimate profit potential of an industry. It ranges from intense in industries like tires, metal cans, and steel, where no company earns spectacular returns on investment, to mild in industries like oil-field services and equipment, soft drinks, and toiletries, where there is room for quite high returns.

In the economists' "perfectly competitive" industry, jockeying for position is unbridled and entry to the industry very easy. This kind of industry structure, of course, offers the worst prospect for long-run profitability. The weaker the forces collectively, however, the greater the opportunity for superior performance.

Whatever their collective strength, the corporate strategist's goal is to find a position in the industry where his or her company can best defend itself against these forces or can influence them in its favor. The collective strength of the forces may be painfully apparent to all the antagonists; but to cope with them, the strategist must delve below the surface and analyze the sources of competition. For example, what makes the industry vulnerable to entry? What determines the bargaining power of suppliers?

Knowledge of these underlying sources of competitive pressure provides the groundwork for a strategic agenda of action. They highlight the critical strengths and weaknesses of the company, animate the positioning of the company in its industry, clarify the areas where strategic changes may yield the greatest payoff, and highlight the places where industry trends promise to hold the greatest significance as either opportunities or threats.

Understanding these sources also proves to be of help in considering areas for diversification.

CONTENDING FORCES

The strongest competitive force or forces determine the profitability of an industry and so are of greatest importance in strategy formulation. For example, even a company with a strong position in an industry unthreatened by potential entrants will earn low returns if it faces a superior or a lower-cost substitute product—as the leading manufacturers of vacuum tubes and coffee percolators have learned to their sorrow. In such a situation, coping with the substitute product becomes the number one strategic priority.

EXHIBIT 3–10   **Forces Driving Industry Competition**

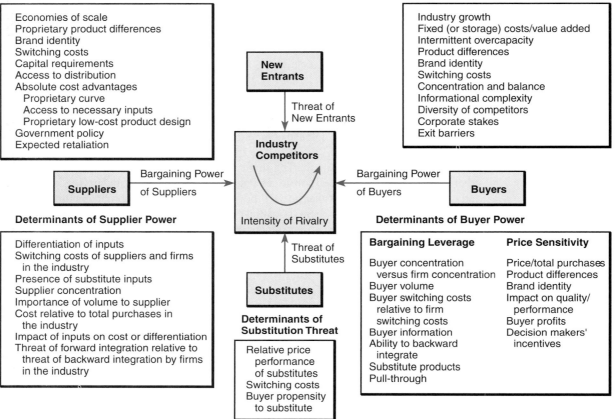

Entry barriers

Economies of scale
Proprietary product differences
Brand identity
Switching costs
Capital requirements
Access to distribution
Absolute cost advantages
    Proprietary curve
    Access to necessary inputs
    Proprietary low-cost product design
Government policy
Expected retaliation

Rivalry Determinants

Industry growth
Fixed (or storage) costs/value added
Intermittent overcapacity
Product differences
Brand identity
Switching costs
Concentration and balance
Informational complexity
Diversity of competitors
Corporate stakes
Exit barriers

New Entrants

Threat of New Entrants

Industry Competitors

Intensity of Rivalry

Bargaining Power of Suppliers

Suppliers

Bargaining Power of Buyers

Buyers

Threat of Substitutes

Substitutes

Determinants of Supplier Power

Differentiation of inputs
Switching costs of suppliers and firms
    in the industry
Presence of substitute inputs
Supplier concentration
Importance of volume to supplier
Cost relative to total purchases in
    the industry
Impact of inputs on cost or differentiation
Threat of forward integration relative to
    threat of backward integration by firms
    in the industry

Determinants of Substitution Threat

Relative price
    performance
    of substitutes
Switching costs
Buyer propensity
    to substitute

Determinants of Buyer Power

Bargaining Leverage	**Price Sensitivity**
Buyer concentration versus firm concentration	Price/total purchases
	Product differences
Buyer volume	Brand identity
Buyer switching costs relative to firm switching costs	Impact on quality/ performance
Buyer information	Buyer profits
Ability to backward integrate	Decision makers' incentives
Substitute products	
Pull-through	

Different forces take on prominence, of course, in shaping competition in each industry. In the oceangoing tanker industry, the key force is probably the buyers (the major oil companies), while in tires it is powerful OEM buyers coupled with tough competitors. In the steel industry the key forces are foreign competitors and substitute materials.

Every industry has an underlying structure, or a set of fundamental economic and technical characteristics, that gives rise to these competitive forces. The strategist, wanting to position his or her company to cope best with its industry environment or to influence that environment in the company's favor, must learn what makes the environment tick.

This view of competition pertains equally to industries dealing in services and to those selling products. To avoid monotony, I refer to both products and services as *products.* The same general principles apply to all types of business.

A few characteristics are critical to the strength of each competitive force. They will be discussed in this section.

A. Threat of Entry

New entrants to an industry bring new capacity, the desire to gain market share, and often substantial resources. Companies diversifying through acquisition into the industry from other markets often leverage their resources to cause a shake-up, as Philip Morris did with Miller beer.

The seriousness of the threat of entry depends on the barriers present and on the reaction from existing competitors that the entrant can expect. If barriers to entry are high and a newcomer can expect sharp retaliation from the entrenched competitors, he or she obviously will not pose a serious threat of entering.

There are six major sources of barriers to entry:

1. Economies of Scale

These economies deter entry by forcing the aspirant either to come in on a large scale or to accept a cost disadvantage. Scale economies in production, research, marketing, and service are probably the key barriers to entry in the mainframe computer industry, as Xerox and GE sadly discovered. Economies of scale also can act as hurdles in distribution, utilization of the sales force, financing, and nearly any other part of a business.

2. Product Differentiation

Brand identification creates a barrier by forcing entrants to spend heavily to overcome customer loyalty. Advertising, customer service, being first in the industry, and product differences are among the factors fostering brand identification. It is perhaps the most important entry barrier in soft drinks, over-the-counter drugs, cosmetics, investment banking, and public accounting. To create high fences around their business, brewers couple brand identification with economies of scale in production, distribution, and marketing.

3. Capital Requirements

The need to invest large financial resources in order to compete creates a barrier to entry, particularly if the capital is required for unrecoverable expenditures in up-front advertising or R&D. Capital is necessary not only for fixed facilities but also for customer credit, inventories, and absorbing start-up losses. While major corporations have the financial resources to invade almost any industry, the huge capital requirements in certain fields, such as computer manufacturing and mineral extraction, limit the pool of likely entrants.

4. Cost Disadvantages Independent of Size

Entrenched companies may have cost advantages not available to potential rivals, no matter what their size and attainable economies of scale. These advantages can stem from the effects of the learning curve (and of its first cousin, the experience curve), proprietary technology, access to the best raw materials sources, assets purchased at preinflation prices, government subsidies, or favorable locations. Sometimes cost advantages are enforceable legally, as they are through patents. (For analysis of the much-discussed experience curve as a barrier to entry, see Exhibit 3–11, Strategy in Action.)

5. Access to Distribution Channels

The new boy or girl on the block must, of course, secure distribution of his or her product or service. A new food product, for example, must displace others from the supermarket shelf via price breaks, promotions, intense selling efforts, or some other means. The more limited the wholesale or retail channels are and the more that existing competitors have these tied up, obviously the tougher that entry into the industry will be. Sometimes this barrier is so high that, to surmount it, a new contestant must create its own distribution channels, as Timex did in the watch industry in the 1950s.

In recent years, the experience curve has become widely discussed as a key element of industry structure. According to this concept, unit costs in many manufacturing industries (some dogmatic adherents say in all manufacturing industries) as well as in some service industries decline with "experience," or a particular company's cumulative volume of production. (The experience curve, which encompasses many factors, is a broader concept than the better-known learning curve, which refers to the efficiency achieved over time by workers through much repetition.)

The causes of the decline in unit costs are a combination of elements, including economies of scale, the learning curve for labor, and capita-labor substitution. The cost decline creates a barrier to entry because new competitors with no "experience" face higher costs than established ones, particularly the producer with the largest market share, and have difficulty catching up with the entrenched competitors.

Adherents of the experience curve concept stress the importance of achieving market leadership to maximize this barrier to entry, and they recommend aggressive action to achieve it, such as price cutting in anticipation of falling costs in order to build volume. For the combatant that cannot achieve a healthy market share, the prescription is usually, "Get out."

Is the experience curve an entry barrier on which strategies should be built? The answer is: not in every industry. In fact, in some industries, building a strategy on the experience curve can be potentially disastrous. That costs decline with experience in some industries is not news to corporate executives. The significance of the experience curve for strategy depends on what factors are causing the decline.

A new entrant may well be more efficient than the more experienced competitors: if it has built the newest plant, it will face no disadvantage in having to catch up. The strategic prescription, "You must have the largest, most efficient plant," is a lot different from "You must produce the greatest cumulative output of the item to get your costs down."

Whether a drop in costs with cumulative (not absolute) volume erects an entry barrier also depends on the sources of the decline. If costs go down because of technical advances known generally in the industry or because of the development of improved equipment that can be copied or purchased from equipment suppliers, the experience curve is not an entry barrier at all–in fact, new or less-experienced competitors may actually enjoy a cost advantage over the leaders. Free of the legacy of heavy past investments, the newcomer or less-experienced competitor can purchase or copy the newest and lowest-cost equipment and technology.

If, however, experience can be kept proprietary, the leaders will maintain a cost advantage. But new entrants may require less experience to reduce their costs than the leaders needed. All this suggests that the experience curve can be a shaky entry barrier on which to build a strategy.

While space does not permit a complete treatment here, I want to mention a few other crucial elements in determining the appropriateness of a strategy built on the entry barrier provided by the experience curve:

The height of the barrier depends on how important costs are to competition compared with other areas like marketing, selling, and innovation.

The barrier can be nullified by product or process innovations leading to a substantially new technology and, thereby, creating an entirely new experience curve. New entrants can leapfrog the industry leaders and alight on the new experience curve, to which those leaders may be poorly positioned to jump.

If more than one strong company is building its strategy on the experience curve, the consequences can be nearly fatal. By the time only one rival is left pursuing such a strategy, industry growth may have stopped and the prospects of reaping the spoils of victory may long since have evaporated.

6. Government Policy

The government can limit or even foreclose entry to industries, with such controls as license requirements and limits on access to raw materials. Regulated industries like trucking, liquor retailing, and freight forwarding are noticeable examples; more subtle government restrictions operate in fields like ski-area development and coal mining. The government also can play a major indirect role by affecting entry barriers through such controls as air and water pollution standards and safety regulations.

The potential rival's expectations about the reaction of existing competitors also will influence its decision on whether to enter. The company is likely to have second thoughts if incumbents have previously lashed out at new entrants, or if:

The incumbents possess substantial resources to fight back, including excess cash and unused borrowing power, productive capacity, or clout with distribution channels and customers.

The incumbents seem likely to cut prices because of a desire to keep market shares or because of industrywide excess capacity.

Industry growth is slow, affecting its ability to absorb the new arrival and probably causing the financial performance of all the parties involved to decline.

B. Powerful Suppliers

Suppliers can exert bargaining power on participants in an industry by raising prices or reducing the quality of purchased goods and services. Powerful suppliers, thereby, can squeeze profitability out of an industry unable to recover cost increases in its own prices. By raising their prices, soft-drink concentrate producers have contributed to the erosion of profitability of bottling companies because the bottlers—facing intense competition from powdered mixes, fruit drinks, and other beverages—have limited freedom to raise their prices accordingly.

The power of each important supplier (or buyer) group depends on a number of characteristics of its market situation and on the relative importance of its sales or purchases to the industry compared with its overall business.

A *supplier* group is powerful if:

1. It is dominated by a few companies and is more concentrated than the industry it sells.

2. Its product is unique or at least differentiated, or if it has built-up switching costs. Switching costs are fixed costs that buyers face in changing suppliers. These arise because, among other things, a buyer's product specifications tie it to particular suppliers, it has invested heavily in specialized ancillary equipment or in learning how to operate a supplier's equipment (as in computer software), or its production lines are connected to the supplier's manufacturing facilities (as in some manufacturing of beverage containers).

3. It is not obliged to contend with other products for sale to the industry. For instance, the competition between the steel companies and the aluminum companies to sell to the can industry checks the power of each supplier.

4. It poses a credible threat of integrating forward into the industry's business. This provides a check against the industry's ability to improve the terms on which it purchases.

5. The industry is not an important customer of the supplier group. If the industry is an important customer, suppliers' fortunes will be tied closely to the industry, and they will want to protect the industry through reasonable pricing and assistance in activities like R&D and lobbying.

C. Powerful Buyers

Customers likewise can force down prices, demand higher quality or more service, and play competitors off against each other—all at the expense of industry profits.

A *buyer* group is powerful if:

1. It is concentrated or purchases in large volumes. Large-volume buyers are particularly potent forces if heavy fixed costs characterize the industry—as they do in metal

containers, corn refining, and bulk chemicals, for example—which raise the stakes to keep capacity filled.

2. The products it purchases from the industry are standard or undifferentiated. The buyers, sure that they always can find alternative suppliers, may play one company against another, as they do in aluminum extrusion.

3. The products it purchases from the industry form a component of its product and represent a significant fraction of its cost. The buyers are likely to shop for a favorable price and purchase selectively. Where the product sold by the industry in question is a small fraction of buyers' costs, buyers are usually much less price sensitive.

4. It earns low profits, which create great incentive to lower its purchasing costs. Highly profitable buyers, however, are generally less price sensitive (i.e., of course, if the item does not represent a large fraction of their costs).

5. The industry's product is unimportant to the quality of the buyers' products or services. Where the quality of the buyers' products is very much affected by the industry's product, buyers are generally less price sensitive. Industries in which this situation exists include oil-field equipment, where a malfunction can lead to large losses and enclosures for electronic medical and test instruments, where the quality of the enclosure can influence the user's impression about the quality of the equipment inside.

6. The industry's product does not save the buyer money. Where the industry's product or service can pay for itself many times over, the buyer is rarely price sensitive; rather, he or she is interested in quality. This is true in services like investment banking and public accounting, where errors in judgment can be costly and embarrassing, and in businesses like the mapping of oil wells, where an accurate survey can save thousands of dollars in drilling costs.

7. The buyers pose a credible threat of integrating backward to make the industry's product. The Big Three auto producers and major buyers of cars often have used the threat of self-manufacture as a bargaining lever. But sometimes an industry so engenders a threat to buyers that its members may integrate forward.

Most of these sources of buyer power can be attributed to consumers as a group as well as to industrial and commercial buyers; only a modification of the frame of reference is necessary. Consumers tend to be more price sensitive if they are purchasing products that are undifferentiated, expensive relative to their incomes, and of a sort where quality is not particularly important.

The buying power of retailers is determined by the same rules, with one important addition. Retailers can gain significant bargaining power over manufacturers when they can influence consumers' purchasing decisions, as they do in audio components, jewelry, appliances, sporting goods, and other goods.

D. Substitute Products

By placing a ceiling on the prices it can charge, substitute products or services limit the potential of an industry. Unless it can upgrade the quality of the product or differentiate it somehow (as via marketing), the industry will suffer in earnings and possibly in growth.

Manifestly, the more attractive the price-performance trade-off offered by substitute products, the firmer the lid placed on the industry's profit potential. Sugar producers confronted with the large-scale commercialization of high-fructose corn syrup, a sugar substitute, learned this lesson.

Substitutes not only limit profits in normal times but also reduce the bonanza an industry can reap in boom times. The producers of fiberglass insulation enjoyed unprecedented demand as a result of high energy costs and severe winter weather. But the industry's ability to raise prices was tempered by the plethora of insulation substitutes, including cellulose, rock wool, and Styrofoam. These substitutes are bound to become an even stronger force once the current round of plant additions by fiberglass insulation producers has boosted capacity enough to meet demand (and then some).

Substitute products that deserve the most attention strategically are those that *(a)* are subject to trends improving their price-performance trade-off with the industry's product or *(b)* are produced by industries earning high profits. Substitutes often come rapidly into play if some development increases competition in their industries and causes price reduction or performance improvement.

E. Jockeying for Position

Rivalry among existing competitors takes the familiar form of jockeying for position—using tactics like price competition, product introduction, and advertising slugfests. This type of intense rivalry is related to the presence of a number of factors:

1. Competitors are numerous or are roughly equal in size and power. In many U.S. industries in recent years, foreign contenders, of course, have become part of the competitive picture.

2. Industry growth is slow, precipitating fights for market share that involve expansion-minded members.

3. The product or service lacks differentiation or switching costs, which lock in buyers and protect one combatant from raids on its customers by another.

4. Fixed costs are high or the product is perishable, creating strong temptation to cut prices. Many basic materials businesses, like paper and aluminum, suffer from this problem when demand slackens.

5. Capacity normally is augmented in large increments. Such additions, as in the chlorine and vinyl chloride businesses, disrupt the industry's supply-demand balance and often lead to periods of overcapacity and price cutting.

6. Exit barriers are high. Exit barriers, like very specialized assets or management's loyalty to a particular business, keep companies competing even though they may be earning low or even negative returns on investment. Excess capacity remains functioning, and the profitability of the healthy competitors suffers as the sick ones hang on. If the entire industry suffers from overcapacity, it may seek government help—particularly if foreign competition is present.

7. The rivals are diverse in strategies, origins, and "personalities." They have different ideas about how to compete and continually run head-on into each other in the process.

As an industry matures, its growth rate changes, resulting in declining profits and (often) a shakeout. In the booming recreational vehicle industry of the early 1970s, nearly every producer did well; but slow growth since then has eliminated the high returns, except for the strongest members, not to mention many of the weaker companies. The same profit story has been played out in industry after industry—snowmobiles, aerosol packaging, and sports equipment are just a few examples.

An acquisition can introduce a very different personality to an industry, as has been the case with Black & Decker's takeover of McCullough, the producer of chain saws.

Technological innovation can boost the level of fixed costs in the production process, as it did in the shift from batch to continuous-line photo finishing in the 1960s.

While a company must live with many of these factors—because they are built into the industry economics—it may have some latitude for improving matters through strategic shifts. For example, it may try to raise buyers' switching costs or increase product differentiation. A focus on selling efforts in the fastest-growing segments of the industry or on market areas with the lowest fixed costs can reduce the impact of industry rivalry. If it is feasible, a company can try to avoid confrontation with competitors having high exit barriers and, thus, can sidestep involvement in bitter price cutting.

INDUSTRY ANALYSIS AND COMPETITIVE ANALYSIS

Designing viable strategies for a firm requires a thorough understanding of the firm's industry and competition. The firm's executives need to address four questions: (1) What are the boundaries of the industry? (2) What is the structure of the industry? (3) Which firms are our competitors? (4) What are the major determinants of competition? The answers to these questions provide a basis for thinking about the appropriate strategies that are open to the firm.

Industry Boundaries

An industry is a collection of firms that offer similar products or services. By "similar products," we mean products that customers perceive to be substitutable for one another. Consider, for example, the brands of personal computers (PCs) that are now being marketed. The firms that produce these PCs, such as AT&T, IBM, Apple, and Compaq, form the nucleus of the microcomputer industry.

Suppose a firm competes in the microcomputer industry. Where do the boundaries of this industry begin and end? Does the industry include desktops? Laptops? These are the kinds of questions that executives face in defining industry boundaries.

Why is a definition of industry boundaries important? First, it helps executives determine the arena in which their firm is competing. A firm competing in the micro-computer industry participates in an environment very different from that of the broader electronics business. The microcomputer industry comprises several related product families, including personal computers, inexpensive computers for home use, and workstations. The unifying characteristic of these product families is the use of a central processing unit (CPU) in a microchip. On the other hand, the electronics industry is far more extensive; it includes computers, radios, supercomputers, superconductors, and many other products.

The microcomputer and electronics industries differ in their volume of sales, their scope (some would consider microcomputers a segment of the electronics industry), their rate of growth, and their competitive makeup. The dominant issues faced by the two industries also are different. Witness, for example, the raging public debate being waged on the future of the "high-definition TV." U.S. policymakers are attempting to ensure domestic control of that segment of the electronics industry. They also are considering ways to stimulate "cutting-edge" research in superconductivity. These efforts are likely to spur innovation and stimulate progress in the electronics industry.

Second, a definition of industry boundaries focuses attention on the firm's competitors. Defining industry boundaries enables the firm to identify its competitors and producers of substitute products. This is critically important to the firm's design of its competitive strategy.

Third, a definition of industry boundaries helps executives determine key factors for success. Survival in the premier segment of the microcomputer industry requires skills that are considerably different from those required in the lower end of the industry. Firms that compete in the premier segment need to be on the cutting edge of technological development and to provide extensive customer support and education. On the other hand, firms that compete in the lower end need to excel in imitating the products introduced by the premier segment, to focus on customer convenience, and to maintain operational efficiency that permits them to charge the lowest market price. Defining industry boundaries enables executives to ask these questions: Do we have the skills it takes to succeed here? If not, what must we do to develop these skills?

Finally, a definition of industry boundaries gives executives another basis on which to evaluate their firm's goals. Executives use that definition to forecast demand for their firm's products and services. Armed with that forecast, they can determine whether those goals are realistic.

Problems in Defining Industry Boundaries

Defining industry boundaries requires both caution and imagination. Caution is necessary because there are no precise rules for this task and because a poor definition will lead to poor planning. Imagination is necessary because industries are dynamic—in every industry, important changes are under way in such key factors as competition, technology, and consumer demand.

Defining industry boundaries is a very difficult task. The difficulty stems from three sources:

1. The evolution of industries over time creates new opportunities and threats. Compare the financial services industry as we know it today with that of the 1990s, and then try to imagine how different the industry will be in the year 2020.

2. Industrial evolution creates industries within industries. The electronics industry of the 1960s has been transformed into many "industries"—TV sets, transistor radios, micro- and macrocomputers, supercomputers, superconductors, and so on. Such transformation allows some firms to specialize and others to compete in different, related industries.

3. Industries are becoming global in scope. Consider the civilian aircraft manufacturing industry. For nearly three decades, U.S. firms dominated world production in that industry. But small and large competitors were challenging their dominance by 1990. At that time, Airbus Industries (a consortium of European firms) and Brazilian, Korean, and Japanese firms were actively competing in the industry.

Developing a Realistic Industry Definition

Given the difficulties outlined above, how do executives draw accurate boundaries for an industry? The starting point is a definition of the industry in global terms; that is, in terms that consider the industry's international components as well as its domestic components.

Having developed a preliminary concept of the industry (e.g., computers), executives flesh out its current components. This can be done by defining its product segments. Executives need to select the scope of their firm's potential market from among these related but distinct areas.

To understand the makeup of the industry, executives adopt a longitudinal perspective. They examine the emergence and evolution of product families. Why did these product families arise? How and why did they change? The answers to such questions provide executives with clues about the factors that drive competition in the industry.

Executives also examine the companies that offer different product families, the overlapping or distinctiveness of customer segments, and the rate of substitutability among product families.

To realistically define their industry, executives need to examine five issues:

1. Which part of the industry corresponds to our firm's goals?

2. What are the key ingredients of success in that part of the industry?

3. Does our firm have the skills needed to compete in that part of the industry? If not, can we build those skills?

4. Will the skills enable us to seize emerging opportunities and deal with future threats?

5. Is our definition of the industry flexible enough to allow necessary adjustments to our business concept as the industry grows?

Industry Structure

Defining an industry's boundaries is incomplete without an understanding of its structural attributes. *Structural attributes* are the enduring characteristics that give an industry its distinctive character. Consider the cable television and financial services industries. Both industries are competitive, and both are important for our quality of life. But these industries have very different requirements for success. To succeed in the cable television industry, firms require vertical integration, which helps them lower their operating costs and ensures their access to quality programs; technological innovation, to enlarge the scope of their services and deliver them in new ways; and extensive marketing, using appropriate segmentation techniques to locate potentially viable niches. To succeed in the financial services industry, firms need to meet very different requirements, among which are extensive orientation of customers and an extensive capital base.

How can we explain such variations among industries? The answer lies in examining the four variables that industry comprises: (1) concentration, (2) economies of scale, (3) product differentiation, and (4) barriers to entry.

Concentration

This variable refers to the extent to which industry sales are dominated by only a few firms. In a highly concentrated industry (i.e., an industry whose sales are dominated by a handful of companies), the intensity of competition declines over time. High concentration serves as a barrier to entry into an industry, because it enables the firms that hold large market shares to achieve significant economies of scale (e.g., savings in production costs due to increased production quantities) and, thus, to lower their prices to stymie attempts of new firms to enter the market.

The U.S. aircraft manufacturing industry is highly concentrated. Its concentration ratio—the percent of market share held by the top four firms in the industry—is 67 percent. Competition in the industry has not been vigorous. Firms in the industry have been able to deter entry through proprietary technologies and the formation of strategic alliances (e.g., joint ventures).

Economies of Scale

This variable refers to the savings that companies within an industry achieve due to increased volume. Simply put, when the volume of production increases, the long-range average cost of a unit produced will decline.

Economies of scale result from technological and nontechnological sources. The technological sources are a higher level of mechanization or automation and a greater up-to-dateness of plant and facilities. The nontechnological sources include better managerial coordination of production functions and processes, long-term contractual agreements with suppliers, and enhanced employee performance arising from specialization.

Economies of scale are an important determinant of the intensity of competition in an industry. Firms that enjoy such economies can charge lower prices than their competitors. They also can create barriers to entry by reducing their prices temporarily or permanently to deter new firms from entering the industry.

Product Differentiation

This variable refers to the extent to which customers perceive products or services offered by firms in the industry as different.

The differentiation of products can be real or perceived. The differentiation between Apple's Macintosh and IBM's PS/2 Personal Computer was a prime example of real differentiation. These products differed significantly in their technology and performance. Similarly, the civilian aircraft models produced by Boeing differed markedly from those produced by Airbus. The differences resulted from the use of different design principles and different construction technologies. For example, the newer Airbus planes followed the principle of "fly by wire," whereas Boeing planes utilized the laws of hydraulics. Thus, in Boeing planes, wings were activated by mechanical handling of different parts of the plane, whereas in the Airbus planes, this was done almost automatically.

Perceived differentiation results from the way in which firms position their products and from their success in persuading customers that their products differ significantly from competing products. Marketing strategies provide the vehicles through which this is done. Witness, for example, the extensive advertising campaigns of the automakers, each of which attempts to convey an image of distinctiveness. BMW ads highlight the excellent engineering of the BMW and its symbolic value as a sign of achievement. Some automakers focus on roominess and durability, which are desirable attributes for the family segment of the automobile market.

Real and perceived differentiations often intensify competition among existing firms. On the other hand, successful differentiation poses a competitive disadvantage for firms that attempt to enter an industry.

Barriers to Entry

As Porter noted earlier in this chapter, barriers to entry are the obstacles that a firm must overcome to enter an industry. The barriers can be tangible or intangible. The tangible barriers include capital requirements, technological know-how, resources, and the laws regulating entry into an industry. The intangible barriers include the reputation of existing firms, the loyalty of consumers to existing brands, and access to the managerial skills required for successful operation in an industry.

Entry barriers both increase and reflect the level of concentration, economies of scale, and product differentiation in an industry, and such increases make it more difficult for new firms to enter the industry. Therefore, when high barriers exist in an industry, competition in that industry declines over time.

In summary, analysis of concentration, economies of scale, product differentiation, and barriers to entry in an industry enables a firm's executives to understand the forces that determine competition in an industry and sets the stage for identifying the firm's competitors and how they position themselves in the marketplace.

Industry regulations are a key element of industry structure and can constitute a significant barrier to entry for corporations. Escalating regulatory standards costs have been a serious concern for corporations for years. As legislative bodies continue their strong hold on corporate activities, businesses feel the impact on their bottom line. In-house counsel departments have been perhaps the most significant additions to corporate structure in the past decade. Legal fees have skyrocketed and managers have learned the hard way about the importance of adhering to regulatory standards. Exhibit 3–12 presents some key principles that enable corporations to abide by the ever-increasing regulations while keeping costs down, maintaining competitiveness, and enhancing creativity.

Competitive Analysis

How to Identify Competitors

In identifying their firm's current and potential competitors, executives consider several important variables:

1. How do other firms define the scope of their market? The more similar the definitions of firms, the more likely the firms will view each other as competitors.

2. How similar are the benefits the customers derive from the products and services that other firms offer? The more similar the benefits of products or services, the higher the level of substitutability between them. High substitutability levels force firms to compete fiercely for customers.

3. How committed are other firms to the industry? Although this question may appear to be far removed from the identification of competitors, it is in fact one of the most important questions that competitive analysis must address, because it sheds light on the long-term intentions and goals. To size up the commitment of potential competitors to the industry, reliable intelligence data are needed. Such data may relate to potential resource commitments (e.g., planned facility expansions).

Common Mistakes in Identifying Competitors

Identifying competitors is a milestone in the development of strategy. But it is a process laden with uncertainty and risk, a process in which executives sometimes make costly mistakes. Examples of these mistakes are:

1. Overemphasizing current and known competitors while giving inadequate attention to potential entrants.

2. Overemphasizing large competitors while ignoring small competitors.

3. Overlooking potential international competitors.

4. Assuming that competitors will continue to behave in the same way they have behaved in the past.

5. Misreading signals that may indicate a shift in the focus of competitors or a refinement of their present strategies or tactics.

6. Overemphasizing competitors' financial resources, market position, and strategies while ignoring their intangible assets, such as a top-management team.

7. Assuming that all of the firms in the industry are subject to the same constraints or are open to the same opportunities.

8. Believing that the purpose of strategy is to outsmart the competition, rather than to satisfy customer needs and expectations.

EXHIBIT 3–12

Innovation-Friendly Regulation

Source: Reprinted by permission of *Harvard Business Review.* An excerpt from "Green and Competitive," by Michael E. Porter and Claas van der Linde, September–October 1995. Copyright © 1995 by the President and Fellows of Harvard University, all rights reserved.

Regulation, properly conceived, need not drive up costs. The following principles of regulatory design will promote innovation, resource productivity, and competitiveness.

Focus on Outcomes, Not Technologies.

Past regulations have often prescribed particular remediation technologies, such as catalysts or scrubbers for air pollution. The phrases "best available technology" (BAT) and "best available control technology" (BACT) are deeply rooted in U.S. practice and imply that one technology is best, thus discouraging innovation.

Enact Strict Rather Than Lax Regulation.

Companies can handle lax regulation incrementally, often with end-of-pipe or secondary treatment solutions. Regulation, therefore, needs to be stringent enough to promote real innovation.

Regulate as Close to the End User as Practical, While Encouraging Upstream Solutions.

This will normally allow more flexibility for innovation in the end product and in all the production and distribution stages. Avoiding pollution entirely or, second best, mitigating it early in the value chain is almost always less costly than late-stage remediation or cleanup.

Employ Phase-In Periods.

Ample but well-defined phase-in periods tied to industry-capital-investment cycles will allow companies to develop innovative resource-saving technologies rather than force them to implement expensive solutions hastily, merely patching over problems.

Use Market Incentives.

Market incentives such as pollution charges and deposit-refund schemes draw attention to resource inefficiencies. In addition, tradable permits provide continuing incentives for innovation and encourage creative use of technologies that exceed current standards.

Harmonize or Converge Regulations in Associated Fields.

Liability exposure in the United States leads companies to stick to safe, BAT approaches, and inconsistent regulation on alternative technologies deters beneficial innovation. For example, one way to eliminate refrigerator cooling agents suspected of damaging the ozone layer involves replacing them with small amounts of propane and butane. But narrowly conceived safety regulations covering these gases seem to have impeded development of the new technology in the United States, while several leading European companies are already marketing the new products.

Develop Regulations in Sync with Other Countries or Slightly Ahead of Them.

It is important to minimize possible competitive disadvantages relative to foreign companies that are not yet subject to the same standard. Developing regulations slightly ahead of other countries will also maximize export potential in the pollution-control sector by raising incentives for innovation.

Make the Regulatory Process More Stable and Predictable.

The regulatory process is as important as the standards. If standards and phase-in periods are set and accepted early enough and if regulators commit to keeping standards in place for, say, five years, industry can lock in and tackle root-cause solutions instead of government philosophy.

Require Industry Participation in Setting Standards from the Beginning.

U.S. regulation differs sharply from European regulation in its adversarial approach. Industry should help in designing phase-in periods, the content of regulations, and the most effective regulatory process.

(continued)

EXHIBIT 3–12
(continued)

> **Develop Strong Technical Capabilities among Regulators.**
>
> Regulators must understand an industry's economics and what drives its competitiveness. Better information exchange will help avoid costly gaming in which ill-informed companies use an array of lawyers and consultants to try to stall the poorly designed regulations of ill-informed regulators.
>
> **Minimize the Time and Resources Consumed in the Regulatory Process Itself.**
>
> Time delays in granting permits are usually costly for companies. Self-regulation with periodic inspections would be more efficient than requiring formal approvals. Potential and actual litigation creates uncertainty and consumes resources. Mandatory arbitration procedures or rigid arbitration steps before litigation would lower costs and encourage innovation.

OPERATING ENVIRONMENT

The operating environment, also called the *competitive* or *task environment,* comprises factors in the competitive situation that affect a firm's success in acquiring needed resources or in profitably marketing its goods and services. Among the most important of these factors are the firm's competitive position, the composition of its customers, its reputation among suppliers and creditors, and its ability to attract capable employees. The operating environment is typically much more subject to the firm's influence or control than the remote environment. Thus, firms can be much more proactive (as opposed to reactive) in dealing with the operating environment than in dealing with the remote environment.

1. Competitive Position

Assessing its competitive position improves a firm's chances of designing strategies that optimize its environmental opportunities. Development of competitor profiles enables a firm to more accurately forecast both its short- and long-term growth and its profit potentials. Although the exact criteria used in constructing a competitor's profile are largely determined by situational factors, the following criteria are often included:

1. Market share.

2. Breadth of product line.

3. Effectiveness of sales distribution.

4. Proprietary and key-account advantages.

5. Price competitiveness.

6. Advertising and promotion effectiveness.

7. Location and age of facility.

8. Capacity and productivity.

9. Experience.

10. Raw materials costs.

11. Financial position.

EXHIBIT 3–13
Competitor Profile

Key Success Factors	Weight	Rating*	Weighted Score
Market share	0.30	4	1.20
Price competitiveness	0.20	3	0.60
Facilities location	0.20	5	1.00
Raw materials costs	0.10	3	0.30
Caliber of personnel	0.20	1	0.20
	1.00†		3.30

*The rating scale suggested is as follows: very strong competitive position (5 points), strong (4), average (3), weak (2), very weak (1).
†The total of the weights must always equal 1.00.

12. Relative product quality.

13. R&D advantages position.

14. Caliber of personnel.

15. General images.

16. Customer profile.

17. Patents and copyrights.

18. Union relations.

19. Technological position.

20. Community reputation.

Once appropriate criteria have been selected, they are weighted to reflect their importance to a firm's success. Then the competitor being evaluated is rated on the criteria, the ratings are multiplied by the weight, and the weighted scores are summed to yield a numerical profile of the competitor, as shown in Exhibit 3–13.

This type of competitor profile is limited by the subjectivity of its criteria selection, weighting, and evaluation approaches. Nevertheless, the process of developing such profiles is of considerable help to a firm in defining its perception of its competitive position. Moreover, comparing the firm's profile with those of its competitors can aid its managers in identifying factors that might make the competitors vulnerable to the strategies the firm might choose to implement.

2. Customer Profiles

Perhaps the most vulnerable result of analyzing the operating environment is the understanding of a firm's customers that this provides. Developing a profile of a firm's present and prospective customers improves the ability of its managers to plan strategic operations, to anticipate changes in the size of markets, and to reallocate resources so as to support forecast shifts in demand patterns. The traditional approach to segmenting customers is based on customer profiles constructed from geographic, demographic, psychographic, and buyer behavior information, as illustrated in Exhibit 3–14.

Enterprising companies have quickly learned the importance of identifying target segments. In recent years, market research has increased tremendously as companies realize the benefits of demographic and psychographic segmentation. Research by American Express showed that competitors were stealing a prime segment of the company's business, affluent business travelers. AMEX's competing companies, including Visa and

EXHIBIT 3–14
Major Segmentation Variables for Consumer Markets

Source: *Marketing Management,* 10/e, by Kotler, © 2000. Adapted by permission of Prentice Hall, Inc., Upper Saddle River, NJ.

Variable	Typical Breakdowns
Geographic	
Region	Pacific, Mountain, West North Central, West South Central, East North Central, East South Central, South Atlantic, Middle Atlantic, New England.
County size	A, B, C, D.
City or SMSA* size	Under 5,000; 5,000–20,000; 20,000–50,000; 50,000–100,000; 100,000–250,000; 250,000–500,000; 500,000–1,000,000; 1,000,000–4,000,000; 4,000,000 or over.
Density	Urban, suburban, rural.
Climate	Northern, southern.
Demographic	
Age	Under 6, 6–11, 12–19, 20–34, 35–49, 50–64, 65+.
Sex	Male, female.
Family size	1–2, 3–4, 5+.
Family life cycle	Young, single; young, married, no children; young, married, youngest child under 6; young, married, youngest child 6 or over; older, married, with children; older, married, no children under 18; older, single; other.
Income	Under $10,000; $10,000–$15,000; $15,000–$20,000; $20,000–$25,000; $25,000–$30,000; $30,000–$50,000; $50,000 and over.
Occupation	Professional and technical; managers, officials, and proprietors; clerical, sales; craftspeople, foremen; operatives; farmers; retired; students; housewives; unemployed.
Education	Grade school or less; some high school; high school graduate; some college; college graduate.
Religion	Catholic, Protestant, Jewish, other.
Race	White, Black, Oriental.
Nationality	American, British, French, German, Scandinavian, Italian, Latin American, Middle Eastern, Japanese.
Psychographic	
Social class	Lower lowers, upper lowers, working class, middle class, upper middles, lower uppers, upper uppers.
Lifestyle	Straights, swingers, longhairs.
Personality	Compulsive, gregarious, authoritarian, ambitious.
Behavioral	
Occasions	Regular occasion, special occasion.
Benefits	Quality, service, economy.
User status	Nonuser, ex-user, potential user, first-time user, regular user.
Usage rate	Light user, medium user, heavy user.
Loyalty status	None, medium, strong, absolute.
Readiness stage	Unaware, aware, informed, interested, desirous, intending to buy.
Attitude toward product	Enthusiastic, positive, indifferent, negative, hostile.

*SMSA stands for standard metropolitan statistical area.

Mastercard, began offering high-spending business travelers frequent flier programs and other rewards including discounts on new cars. In turn, AMEX began to invest heavily in rewards programs, while also focusing on its strongest capabilities, assets, and competitive advantage. Unlike most credit card companies, AMEX cannot rely on charging interest to make money because its customers pay in full each month. Therefore, the company charges higher transaction fees to its merchants. In this way, increases in spending by AMEX customers who pay off their balances each month are more profitable to AMEX than to competing credit card companies.

Assessing consumer behavior is a key element in the process of satisfying your target market needs. Many firms lose market share as a result of assumptions made about target segments. Market research and industry surveys can help to reduce a firm's chances of relying on illusive assumptions. Firms most vulnerable are those that have had success with one or more products in the marketplace and as a result try to base consumer behavior on past data and trends.

Geographic

It is important to define the geographic area from which customers do or could come. Almost every product or service has some quality that makes it variably attractive to buyers from different locations. Obviously, a Wisconsin manufacturer of snow skis should think twice about investing in a wholesale distribution center in South Carolina. On the other hand, advertising in the *Milwaukee Sun-Times* could significantly expand the geographically defined customer market of a major Myrtle Beach hotel in South Carolina.

Demographic

Demographic variables most commonly are used to differentiate groups of present or potential customers. Demographic information (e.g., information on sex, age, marital status, income, and occupation) is comparatively easy to collect, quantify, and use in strategic forecasting, and such information is the minimum basis for a customer profile.

Psychographic

Personality and lifestyle variables often are better predictors of customer purchasing behavior than geographic or demographic variables. In such situations, a psychographic study is an important component of the customer profile. Advertising campaigns by soft-drink producers—Pepsi-Cola ("the Pepsi generation"), Coca-Cola ("the real thing"), and 7UP ("America's turning 7UP")—reflect strategic management's attention to the psychographic characteristics of their largest customer segment—physically active, group-oriented nonprofessionals.

Buyer Behavior

Buyer behavior data also can be a component of the customer profile. Such data are used to explain or predict some aspect of customer behavior with regard to a product or service. As Exhibit 3–14 indicates, information on buyer behavior (e.g., usage rate, benefits sought, and brand loyalty) can provide significant aid in the design of more accurate and profitable strategies.

A second approach to identifying customer groups is by segmenting industrial markets. As shown in Exhibit 3–15, there is considerable overlap between the variables used to segment individual and industrial consumers, but the definition of the customer differs.

EXHIBIT 3–15
Major Segmentation Variables for Industrial Markets

Source: Adapted from Thomas V. Bonoma and Benson P. Shapiro, *Segmenting the Industrial Market* (Lexington, MA: Lexington Books, 1983).

Demographic

Industry: Which industries that buy this product should we focus on?
Company size: What size companies should we focus on?
Location: What geographical areas should we focus on?

Operating Variables

Technology: What customer technologies should we focus on?
User-nonuser status: Should we focus on heavy, medium, light users or nonusers?
Customer capabilities: Should we focus on customers needing many services or few services?

Purchasing Approaches

Purchasing-function organization: Should we focus on companies with highly centralized or decentralized purchasing organizations?
Power structure: Should we focus on companies that are engineering dominated? Financially dominated? Other ways dominated?
Nature of existing relationships: Should we focus on companies with which we have strong existing relationships or simply go after the most desirable companies?
General purchase policies: Should we focus on companies that prefer leasing? Service contracts? Systems purchases? Sealed bidding?
Purchasing criteria: Should we focus on companies that are seeking quality? Service? Price?

Situational Factors

Urgency: Should we focus on companies that need quick and sudden delivery or service?
Specific application: Should we focus on certain applications of our product, rather than all applications?
Size of order: Should we focus on large or small orders?

Perfect Characteristics

Buyer-seller similarity: Should we focus on companies whose people and values are similar to ours?
Attitudes toward risk: Should we focus on risk-taking or risk-avoiding customers?
Loyalty: Should we focus on companies that show high loyalty to their suppliers?

3. Suppliers

Dependable relationships between a firm and its suppliers are essential to the firm's long-term survival and growth. A firm regularly relies on its suppliers for financial support, services, materials, and equipment. In addition, it occasionally is forced to make special requests for such favors as quick delivery, liberal credit terms, or broken-lot orders. Particularly at such times, it is essential for a firm to have had an ongoing relationship with its suppliers.

In the assessment of a firm's relationships with its suppliers, several factors, other than the strength of that relationship, should be considered. With regard to its competitive position with its suppliers, the firm should address the following questions:

Are the suppliers' prices competitive? Do the suppliers offer attractive quantity discounts?

How costly are their shipping charges? Are the suppliers competitive in terms of production standards?

In terms of deficiency rates, are the suppliers' abilities, reputations, and services competitive?

Are the suppliers reciprocally dependent on the firm?

4. Creditors

Because the quantity, quality, price, and accessibility of financial, human, and material resources are rarely ideal, assessment of suppliers and creditors is critical to an accurate evaluation of a firm's operating environment. With regard to its competitive position with its creditors, among the most important questions that the firm should address are the following:

Do the creditors fairly value and willingly accept the firm's stock as collateral?

Do the creditors perceive the firm as having an acceptable record of past payment?

A strong working capital position? Little or no leverage?

Are the creditors' loan terms compatible with the firm's profitability objectives?

Are the creditors able to extend the necessary lines of credit?

The answers to these and related questions help a firm forecast the availability of the resources it will need to implement and sustain its competitive strategies.

5. Human Resources: Nature of the Labor Market

A firm's ability to attract and hold capable employees is essential to its success. However, a firm's personnel recruitment and selection alternatives often are influenced by the nature of its operating environment. A firm's access to needed personnel is affected primarily by three factors: the firm's reputation as an employer, local employment rates, and the ready availability of people with the needed skills.

Reputation

A firm's reputation within its operating environment is a major element of its ability to satisfy its personnel needs. A firm is more likely to attract and retain valuable employees if it is seen as permanent in the community, competitive in its compensation package, and concerned with the welfare of its employees, and if it is respected for its product or service and appreciated for its overall contribution to the general welfare.

Employment Rates

The readily available supply of skilled and experienced personnel may vary considerably with the stage of a community's growth. A new manufacturing firm would find it far more difficult to obtain skilled employees in a vigorous industrialized community than in an economically depressed community in which similar firms had recently cut back operations.

Availability

The skills of some people are so specialized that relocation may be necessary to secure the jobs and the compensation that those skills commonly command. People with such skills include oil drillers, chefs, technical specialists, and industry executives. A firm that seeks to hire such a person is said to have broad labor market boundaries; that is, the geographic area within which the firm might reasonably expect to attract qualified candidates is quite large. On the other hand, people with more common skills are less likely to relocate from a considerable distance to achieve modest economic or career advancements. Thus, the labor market boundaries are fairly limited for such occupational groups as unskilled laborers, clerical personnel, and retail clerks.

EMPHASIS ON ENVIRONMENTAL FACTORS

This chapter has described the remote, industry, and operating environments as encompassing five components each. While that description is generally accurate, it may give the false impression that the components are easily identified, mutually exclusive, and equally applicable in all situations. In fact, the forces in the external environment are so dynamic and interactive that the impact of any single element cannot be wholly disassociated from the impact of other elements. For example, are increases in OPEC oil prices the result of economic, political, social, or technological changes? Or are a manufacturer's surprisingly good relations with suppliers a result of competitors', customers', or creditors' activities or of the supplier's own activities? The answer to both questions is probably that a number of forces in the external environment have combined to create the situation. Such is the case in most studies of the environment.

Strategic managers are frequently frustrated in their attempts to anticipate the environment's changing influences. Different external elements affect different strategies at different times and with varying strengths. The only certainty is that the impact of the remote and operating environments will be uncertain until a strategy is implemented. This leads many managers, particularly in less-powerful or smaller firms to minimize long-term planning, which requires a commitment of resources. Instead, they favor allowing managers to adapt to new pressures from the environment. While such a decision has considerable merit for many firms, there is an associated trade-off, namely that absence of a strong resource and psychological commitment to a proactive strategy effectively bars a firm from assuming a leadership role in its competitive environment.

There is yet another difficulty in assessing the probable impact of remote, industry, and operating environments on the effectiveness of alternative strategies. Assessment of this kind involves collecting information that can be analyzed to disclose predictable effects. Except in rare instances, however, it is virtually impossible for any single firm to anticipate the consequences of a change in the environment; for example, what is the precise effect on alternative strategies of a 2 percent increase in the national inflation rate, a 1 percent decrease in statewide unemployment, or the entry of a new competitor in a regional market?

Still, assessing the potential impact of changes in the external environment offers a real advantage. It enables decision makers to narrow the range of the available options and to eliminate options that are clearly inconsistent with the forecast opportunities. Environmental assessment seldom identifies the best strategy, but it generally leads to the elimination of all but the most promising options.

Exhibit 3–16 provides a set of key strategic forecasting issues for each level of environmental assessment—remote, industry, and operating. While the issues that are presented are not inclusive of all of the questions that are important, they provide an excellent set of questions with which to begin. Appendix 3–A, Sources for Environmental Forecasting, is provided to help identify valuable sources of data and information from which answers and subsequent forecasts can be constructed. It lists governmental and private marketplace intelligence that can be used by a firm to gain a foothold in undertaking a strategic assessment of any level of the competitive environment.

EXHIBIT 3–16
Strategiec
Forecasting Issues

Key Issues in the Remote Environment

Economy

What are the probable future directions of the economies in the firm's regional, national, and international market? What changes in economic growth, inflation, interest rates, capital availability, credit availability, and consumer purchasing power can be expected? What income differences can be expected between the wealthy upper middle class, the working class, and the underclass in various regions? What shifts in relative demand for different categories of goods and services can be expected?

Society and demographics

What effects will changes in social values and attitudes regarding childbearing, marriage, lifestyle, work, ethics, sex roles, racial equality, education, retirement, pollution, and energy have on the firm's development? What effects will population changes have on major social and political expectations—at home and abroad? What constraints or opportunities will develop? What pressure groups will increase in power?

Ecology

What natural or pollution-caused disasters threaten the firm's employees, customers, or facilities? How rigorously will existing environment legislature be enforced? What new federal, state, and local laws will affect the firm, and in what ways?

Politics

What changes in government policy can be expected with regard to industry cooperation, antitrust activites, foreign trade, taxation, depreciation, environmental protection, deregulation, defense, foreign trade barriers, and other important parameters? What success will a new administration have in achieving its stated goals? What effect will that success have on the firm? Will specific international climates be hostile or favorable? Is there a tendency toward instability, corruption, or violence? What is the level of political risk in each foreign market? What other political or legal constraints or supports can be expected in international business (e.g., trade barriers, equity requirements, nationalism, patent protection)?

Techology

What is the current state of the art? How will it change? What pertinent new products or services are likely to become technically feasible in the foreseeable future? What future impact can be expected from technological breakthroughs in related product areas? How will those breakthroughs interface with the other remote considerations, such as economic issues, social values, public safety, regulations, and court interpretations?

Key issues in the Industry Environment

New entrants

Will new technologies or market demands enable competitors to minimize the impact of traditional economies of scale in the industry? Will consumers accept our claims of product or service differentiation? Will potential new entrants be able to match the capital requirements that currently exist? How permanent are the cost disadvantages (independent of size) in our industry? Will conditions change so that all competitors have equal access to marketing channels? Is government policy toward competition in our industry likely to change?

Bargaining power of suppliers

How stable are the size and composition of our supplier group? Are any suppliers likely to attempt forward integration into our business level? How dependent will our suppliers be in the future? Are substitute suppliers likely to become available? Could we become our own supplier?

(continued)

EXHIBIT 3–16
(continued)

Substitute products or services

Are new substitutes likely? Will they be price competitive? Could we fight off substitutes by price competition? By advertising to sharpen product differentation? What actions could we take to reduce the potential for having alternative products seen as legitimate substitutes?

Bargaining power of buyers

Can we break free of overcommitment to a few large buyers? How would our buyers react to attempts by us to differentiate our products? What possibilities exist that our buyers might vertically integrate backward? Should we consider forward integration? How can we make the value of our components greater in the products of our buyers?

Rivalry among existing firms

Are major competitors likely to undo the established balance of power in our industry? Is growth in our industry slowing such that competition will become fiercer? What excess capacity exists in our industry? How capable are our major competitors of withstanding intensified price competition? How unique are the objectives and strategies of our major competitors?

Key Issues in the Operating Environment

Competitive position

What strategic moves are expected by existing rivals—inside and outside the United States? What competitive advantage is necessary in selected foreign markets? What will be our competitors' priorities and ability to change? Is the behavior of our competitors predictable?

Customer profiles and market changes

What will our customer regard as needed value? Is marketing research done, or do managers talk to each other to discover what the customer wants? Which customer needs are not being met by existing products? Why? Are R&D activities under way to develop means for fulfilling these needs? What is the status of these activities? What marketing and distribution channels should we use? What do demographic and population changes portend for the size and sales potential of our market? What new market segments or products might develop as a result of these changes? What will be the buying power of our customer groups?

Supplier relationships

What is the likelihood of major cost increases because of dwindling supplies of a needed natural resource? Will sources of supply, especially of energy, be reliable? Are there reasons to expect major changes in the cost or availability of inputs as a result of money, people, or subassembly problems? Which suppliers can be expected to respond to emergency requests?

Creditors

What lines of credit are available to help finance our growth? What changes may occur in our creditworthiness? Are creditors likely to feel comfortable with our strategic plan and performance? What is the stock market likely to feel about our firm? What flexibility would our creditors show toward us during a downturn? Do we have sufficient cash reserves to protect our creditors and our credit rating?

Labor market

Are potential employees with desired skills and abilities available in the geographic areas in which our facilities are located? Are colleges and vocational-technical schools that can aid in meeting our training needs located near our plant or store sites? Are labor relations in our industry conductive to meeting our expanding needs for employees? Are workers whose skills we need shifting toward or away from the geographic location of our facilities?

Summary

A firm's external environment consists of three interrelated sets of factors that play a principal role in determining the opportunities, threats, and constraints that the firm faces. The remote environment comprises factors originating beyond, and usually irrespective of, any single firm's operating situation—economic, social, political, technological, and ecological factors. Factors that more directly influence a firm's prospects originate in the environment of its industry, including entry barriers, competitor rivalry, the availability of substitutes, and the bargaining power of buyers and suppliers. The operating environment comprises factors that influence a firm's immediate competitive situation—competitive position, customer profiles, suppliers, creditors, and the labor market. These three sets of factors provide many of the challenges that a particular firm faces in its attempts to attract or acquire needed resources and to profitably market its goods and services. Environmental assessment is more complicated for multinational corporations (MNCs) than for domestic firms because multinationals must evaluate several environments simultaneously.

Thus, the design of business strategies is based on the conviction that a firm able to anticipate future business conditions will improve its performance and profitability. Despite the uncertainty and dynamic nature of the business environment, an assessment process that narrows, even if it does not precisely define, future expectations is of substantial value to strategic managers.

Questions for Discussion

1. Briefly describe two important recent changes in the remote environment of U.S. business in each of the following areas:
   a. Economic.
   b. Social.
   c. Political.
   d. Technological.
   e. Ecological.

2. Describe two major environmental changes that you expect to have a major impact on the wholesale food industry in the next 10 years.

3. Develop a competitor profile for your college and for the college geographically closest to yours. Next, prepare a brief strategic plan to improve the competitive position of the weaker of the two colleges.

4. Assume the invention of a competitively priced synthetic fuel that could supply 25 percent of U.S. energy needs within 20 years. In what major ways might this change the external environment of U.S. business?

5. With your instructor's help, identify a local firm that has enjoyed great growth in recent years. To what degree and in what ways do you think this firm's success resulted from taking advantage of favorable conditions in its remote, industry, and operating environments?

6. Choose a specific industry and, relying solely on your impressions, evaluate the impact of the five forces that drive competition in that industry.

7. Choose an industry in which you would like to compete. Use the five-forces method of analysis to explain why you find that industry attractive.

8. Many firms neglect industry analysis. When does this hurt them? When does it not?

9. The model below depicts industry analysis as a funnel that focuses on remote-factor analysis to better understand the impact of factors in the operating environment. Do you find this model satisfactory? If not, how would you improve it?

10. Who in a firm should be responsible for industry analysis? Assume that the firm does not have a strategic planning department.

Chapter 3 Discussion Case

Let's Reinvent the Company

BusinessWeek

1   On a mild New York City afternoon in late October, dozens of employees crowded into theglobe.com Inc.'s 22nd-floor recreation room. The somber mood was a far cry from November 1998, when the popular Internet community site rocketed to fame with the fastest-rising initial public offering ever. The Ping-Pong table was folded up in a corner and the pool table was covered. The executives wore grim faces—and not just because the stock had plummeted 98% from those halcyon days, to 80 cents a share. They faced the monumental task of reinventing the company they had thought was a New Economy star.

2   Using matter-of-fact PowerPoint slides, newly hired Chief Executive Chuck Peck laid out the details of the company's recently launched strategy: moving beyond consumers and providing Net community services to other websites. The massive restructuring, he said, would slash costs and line up more resources behind the new business-to-business push. But the company's third-quarter results—a loss of $16.6 million on revenues of $6.7 million—showed the toughest job was still ahead, including laying off 41% of the staff. "We've had to overhaul the business," Peck says. Now, it's up to him and the 130 remaining employees to pick up the pieces and reassemble them into a sustainable business.

3   It's a scene now playing at dozens of struggling "business-to-consumer" dot-coms. In a bid to survive, they're exclaiming, "B2C? Not me!" Instead of trying to attract advertisers for fickle Webhead consumers, theglobe.com is offering concrete, useful services to real, paying businesses. In recent months, the flow of consumer companies toward B2B has turned from a trickle to a fire hose. The migrants range from Web delivery service Urbanfetch, which recently shuttered its consumer-oriented video-and-munchies service to become a business courier service, to publicly held search engine Ask Jeeves Inc., which is drastically reorganizing its business to focus on providing search services to other sites. Even e-commerce software makers such as Vignette Corp. and InterWorld Corp. are veering away from selling to consumer sites in favor of courting mainstream businesses.

4   Clearly, one big reason for the switch is that some of those business models never worked and probably never will. Indeed, much of the movement appears born of desperation, as wounded dot-coms try to leap on the next hot trend. Problem is, even that doesn't always work: Skeptical investors have pummeled some B2B wannabes, such as software seller Beyond.com, computer reseller Outpost.com, and online auction house Bid.com International—pushing each of those stocks below $3 a share. "Selling Internet ad space is an entirely different ballgame than selling services to businesses," says Bryan Kester, a project leader with venture-capital firm Redleaf Group Inc.

5   GRAND VISIONS. Still, the redemptive power of the Internet is that it's a ready-made place to quickly reach and serve new kinds of customers. With the rapid pace of change on the Net, business-model mutations are not just possible, but virtually required to stay ahead. "Most Internet companies are changing their business models three or four times each year," says Patricia B. Seybold, CEO of market watcher Patricia Seybold Group. In the end, the success or failure of this massive business-model migration may well determine how powerful the Internet is as a tool for corporate change.

6   The toughest challenge for companies trying to make the shift is determining where to jump. It's often difficult to discern between vibrant business opportunities and flavor-of-the-month Internet fads. When AskMe Corp. CEO Udai Shekawat launched his knowledge-sharing software company in August 1999, he was intent on creating great software. But when the AskMe knowledge-sharing website began seeing a significant jump in traffic and resulting advertising revenues, several company insiders—including Shekawat—began harboring grand visions of becoming an online megaportal. "For a brief time, we were going to take on Yahoo!," he says.

7   But after execs hunkered down over spreadsheets of revenue and market projections, they quickly came to their senses. Shekawat pulled in the reins last January and refocused his techies on writing software. Corporations began requesting AskMe's knowledge-sharing program for their corporate intranets. Today, just six months after garnering all of its revenues from online ads, AskMe gets 90% of its sales from corporate customers. The privately held company projects it will turn a profit in six months.

8   Once companies make their decision, they can't waste any time. The penalties for waiting too long are severe. theglobe.com, for one, couldn't decide how fast to move into B2B services, so even as its online ad revenue stalled, the B2B side didn't pick up the slack. Now, with a severely trimmed workforce and less than $24 million in cash, theglobe.com's future looks iffy. Beyond.com also short-circuited its push to sell to businesses, thanks to a management squabble that kept it from running full-bore with the new plan. One camp wanted to move exclusively into B2B, but CEO Mark L. Breier, a consumer brand maven, wanted to stick with consumers. After mounting losses and executive departures last year, the company finally ditched the consumer push, but now the stock languishes at 63 cents a share.

9   By contrast, moving quickly to latch on to B2B opportunities while they're ripe for the picking pays big dividends. Ask Jeeves first began licensing its software to corporations in 1998, two years after it began. Now, about half of its 750 employees are dedicated to supporting its B2B efforts, which pulled in $13.2 million, or 45% of revenues last quarter. The company expects to be profitable overall by mid-2001, with the B2B side turning a profit by the end of 2001.

10   Given the need for speed, it's crucial for companies to get their staff behind the changes fast. When Paula Jagemann decided last February to spin off a company to provide business services such as website hosting from her consumer-focused OnlineOfficeSupplies.com site, she gathered over 120 employees for several all-hands meetings to spell out her plans. That helped prevent a mass exodus of talent, limiting its attrition rate to about 1% annually. Jagemann expects the new business, part of her holding company, E-Commerce Industries Inc., to pull in $15 million, or half its overall revenues, this year. Says Jagemann: "You almost have to behave like a politician, delivering the same message over and over to your employees."

11   Sometimes they have to behave more like the Grim Reaper. Companies that assume their current staff can adequately address an entirely new market are flirting with failure. OpenTable Corp., for example, cut its teeth as an online restaurant-reservation service for consumers. But after tepid results, executives realized there was a much bigger opportunity in providing Net-based reservations systems and customer analysis tools to restaurants and hotels. So last summer, the company overhauled its management team, including a new CEO and several top lieutenants. But a handful of employees didn't like the moves or the ensuing cultural transformation that made the company less cool. So new CEO Jeffrey B. Edwards fired the malcontents. "We couldn't let that negative attitude linger," he says. Brutal, sure, but that helped persuade investors to kick in an additional $42 million last month, a hefty sum in the current dot-com drought.

12   TRICKY MANEUVERS. Since changing business models isn't cheap, it's just as key to get financial backers on board early. For instance, HomePortfolio.com, which boasts a consumer home furnishings site as well as a B2B services business for furniture manufacturers, needed a cash infusion earlier this year. Execs made no bones about the fact that their true moneymaker would be the B2B business, and that their consumer business would fade. Investors bit, helping HomePortfolio.com raise $48 million in May. "This isn't the summer of VC love anymore," says HomePortfolio.com CEO Dale Williams. "You've really got to keep these people in the loop."

13   Jettisoning the old business, however, remains one of the trickiest maneuvers. When you're starving for cash, it's tempting to try to feed from two different troughs. But it's often tough to juggle two divergent business models aimed at both consumers and businesses. Even while starting to court business buyers last year, Beyond.com spent more than $20 million on consumer-

oriented television ads featuring a naked man who was happy he could order from his clothing-optional home. But button-down business buyers may hesitate to make purchases from a company whose icon is a guy with no pants. Says Michael Dunn, CEO of Prophet Brand Strategy, a brand-consulting firm: "Associations with the consumer brand can often be a liability going forward."

14   CROSSING THE CHASM. Indeed, there's no telling which of these transformations will be sustainable and which will prove to be yet another harebrained dot-com scheme. Some companies that have tried to switch have utterly failed: After doing an about-face from a failed strategy to take on Amazon.com Inc., for instance, Value America Inc. tried to offer order-entry and fulfillment services to other businesses after filing for Chapter 11 bankruptcy protection in August. Too late. On Oct. 20, its assets were acquired by technology products distributor Merisel Inc.

15   The companies best prepared to cross the chasm from consumer to B2B e-commerce, say management experts, are those prepared for inevitable change from the beginning. For one, that means building e-commerce systems that can adapt to changing requirements. Timbuk2 Designs of San Francisco, for instance, had a computer system that allowed consumers to design their own backpacks. But analyst Seybold points out that it was flexible enough for retailers to offer the custom-bag service to consumers as well—providing a whole new revenue stream.

16   Mainly, the key is hiring flexible people. Some Net companies ask job candidates questions that focus on how they would react to turmoil and uncertainty. As the rapidly changing Internet economy continues to force fast changes in strategy, companies need to know how to roll with the punches and run with the new opportunities. "This is where a lot of change-management situations fall on their butt," says Ask Jeeves President Adam Klein.

Source: Ben Elgin, "Let's Reinvent the Company. Online consumer sites are embracing a business-to-business model in desperation," *BusinessWeek,* December 11, 2000.

Chapter **Four**

The Global Environment: Strategic Considerations for Multinational Firms

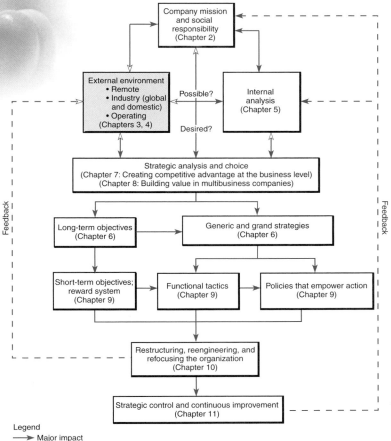

Company mission and social responsibility (Chapter 2)

External environment
• Remote
• Industry (global and domestic)
• Operating
(Chapters 3, 4)

Possible?

Desired?

Internal analysis (Chapter 5)

Strategic analysis and choice
(Chapter 7: Creating competitive advantage at the business level)
(Chapter 8: Building value in multibusiness companies)

Long-term objectives (Chapter 6)

Generic and grand strategies (Chapter 6)

Short-term objectives; reward system (Chapter 9)

Functional tactics (Chapter 9)

Policies that empower action (Chapter 9)

Restructuring, reengineering, and refocusing the organization (Chapter 10)

Strategic control and continuous improvement (Chapter 11)

Feedback

Feedback

Legend
Major impact
Minor impact

Special complications confront a firm involved in the globalization of its operations. *Globalization* refers to the strategy of approaching worldwide markets with standardized products. Such markets are most commonly created by end consumers that prefer lower-priced, standardized products over higher-priced, customized products and by global corporations that use their worldwide operations to compete in local markets. Global corporations headquartered in one country with subsidiaries in other countries experience difficulties that are understandably associated with operating in several distinctly different competitive arenas.

Awareness of the strategic opportunities faced by global corporations and of the threats posed to them is important to planners in almost every domestic U.S. industry. Among corporations headquartered in the United States that receive more than 50 percent of their annual profits from foreign operations are Citicorp, Coca-Cola, Exxon, Gillette, IBM, Otis Elevator, and Texas Instruments. In fact, the 100 largest U.S. globals earn an average of 37 percent of their operating profits abroad. Equally impressive is the impact of foreign-based globals that operate in the United States. Their "direct foreign investment" in the United States now exceeds $90 billion, with Japanese, German, and French firms leading the way.

Understanding the myriad and sometimes subtle nuances of competing in global markets or against global corporations is rapidly becoming a required competence of strategic managers. For example, experts in the advertising community contend that Korean companies only recently recognized the importance of making their names known abroad. In the 1980s, there was very little advertising of Korean brands, and the country had very few recognizable brands abroad. Korean companies tended to emphasize sales and production more than marketing. The opening of the Korean advertising market in the 1990s indicated that Korean firms had acquired a new appreciation for the strategic competencies that are needed to compete globally and created an influx of global firms like Saatchi and Saatchi, J. W. Thompson, Ogilvy and Mather, and Bozell. Many of them established joint ventures or partnerships with Korean agencies. An excellent example of such a strategic approach to globalization by Philip Morris's KGFI is described in Exhibit 4–1, Global Strategy in Action. What is more, the opportunities for corporate growth often seem brightest in global markets. Exhibit 4–2 reports on the growth in national shares of the world's outputs and growth in national economies to the year 2020. While the United States had a commanding lead in the size of its economy in 1992, it was caught by China in the year 2000 and will be far surpassed by 2020. Overall, in less than 20 years, rich industrial countries will be overshadowed by developing countries in their produced share of the world's output.

Because the growth in the number of global firms continues to overshadow other changes in the competitive environment, this section will focus on the nature, outlook, and operations of global corporations.

DEVELOPMENT OF A GLOBAL CORPORATION

The evolution of a global corporation often entails progressively involved strategy levels. The first level, which often entails export-import activity, has minimal effect on the existing management orientation or on existing product lines. The second level, which can involve foreign licensing and technology transfer, requires little change in management or operation. The third level typically is characterized by direct investment in overseas operations, including manufacturing plants. This level requires large capital outlays and the development of global management skills. Although the domestic operations of a firm at

Outside of its core Western markets, Kraft General Foods International's (KGFI) food products have a growing presence in one of the most dynamic business environments in the world—the Asia-Pacific region. Its operations there are expanding rapidly, often aided by links with local manufacturers and distributors.

Japan and Korea, two of the world's fastest-growing economies in the last decade, are important examples. In both countries, local alliances can be crucial to market entry and success. Realizing this fact in the early 1970s, General Foods established joint ventures in both Japan and Korea. These joint ventures, combined with Kraft General Foods International's (KGFI) stand-alone operations, generate more than $1 billion in revenues. In the aggregate, their combined food operations in Japan and Korea are larger than many Fortune 500 companies.

Whereas soluble coffee accounts for just over 25 percent of the coffee consumed in U.S. homes, it fills over 70 percent of the cups consumed in the homes of convenience-minded Japan. Additionally, Japan is the origin of a unique form of packaged coffee—liquid—and a unique channel of distribution—vending machines. Japanese consumers have purchased packaged liquid coffee for years, and it amounts to a $5 billion category. Some 2 million vending machines dispense 9 billion cans of liquid coffee annually—an average of 75 cans per person.

Japan offers a culturally unique distribution channel for coffee products—the gift-set market. Many Japanese exchange specially packaged food or beverage assortments at least twice a year to commemorate holidays as well as special personal or business occasions. The gift-set business has helped Maxim products reinforce their quality image; it also will be a launching pad and support vehicle for Carte Noire coffees.

Outside the Ajinomoto General Foods joint venture, KGFI is developing a freestanding food business under the name Kraft Japan. It is building a cheese business with imported Philadelphia Brand cream cheese, the leading cream cheese in the Tokyo metropolitan market, as well as locally manufactured and licensed Kraft Milk Farm cheese slices. The cheese market is expected to grow approximately 5 percent per year. This is a rapid growth rate for a large food category. In addition to cheese, KGFI also imports Oscar Mayer prepared meats and Jacobs Suchard chocolates.

KGFI's joint venture in Korea, Doug Suh Foods Corporation, is one of the top 10 food companies in the country. Doug Suh manufactures coffees and cereals and has its own distribution network. One of Doug Suh's other businesses in Korea, Post Cereals, is also a strong number two, with a 42 percent category share.

Korea's $400 million coffee market is the fastest-growing major coffee market in the world, expanding at an average annual rate of 14 percent. Growing with the market, Maxim and Maxwell soluble coffees, in both traditional "agglomerate" and freeze-dried forms, account for more than 70 percent of the country's soluble coffee sales. The strength of these brands also brings the company a strong number one position in coffee mix, a mixture of soluble coffee, creamer, and sugar. In addition, its Frima brand leads the market in the nondairy creamer segment.

Beyond Australia, where it has a long-established, wholly owned business, and operations in Japan and Korea, KGFI is targeting many other countries for geographic expansion. In Indonesia, for instance, KGFI has established a rapidly growing cheese business through a licensee and introduced other KGFI products. In Taiwan, the joint venture company, PremierFoods Corporation, holds a 34 percent share of the soluble coffee market and is aggressively developing a Kraft cheese and Jacobs Suchard import business. KGF Philippines, a wholly owned subsidiary, has a leading position in the cheese and powdered soft-drink markets in its country. In the People's Republic of China, the company produces and markets Maxwell House coffees and Tang powdered soft drinks through two successful and rapidly growing joint ventures.

this level continue to dominate its policy, such a firm is commonly categorized as a true multinational corporation (MNC). The most involved strategy level is characterized by a substantial increase in foreign investment, with foreign assets comprising a significant portion of total assets. At this level, the firm begins to emerge as a global enterprise with global approaches to production, sales, finance, and control.

Some firms downplay their global nature (to never appear distracted from their domestic operations), whereas others highlight it. For example, General Electric's formal statement of mission and business philosophy includes the following commitment:

EXHIBIT 4–2   Projected Economic Growth

Source: World Bank, *Global Economic Prospects and the Developing Countries.*

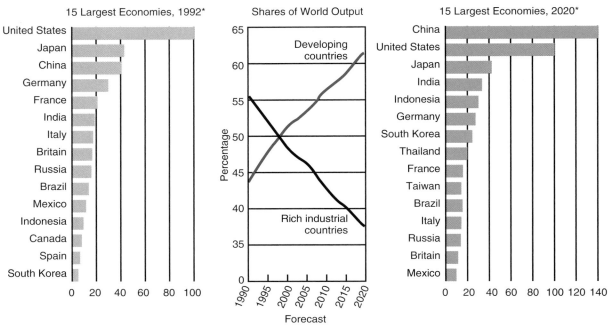

* United States = 100;
Other countries = percentage of U.S.'s GDP

> To carry out a diversified, growing, and profitable worldwide manufacturing business in electrical apparatus, appliances, and supplies, and in related materials, products, systems, and services for industry, commerce, agriculture, government, the community, and the home.

A similar global orientation is evident at IBM, which operates in 125 countries, conducts business in 30 languages and more than 100 currencies, and has 23 major manufacturing facilities in 14 countries.

WHY FIRMS GLOBALIZE

The technological advantage once enjoyed by the United States has declined dramatically during the past 30 years. In the late 1950s, over 80 percent of the world's major technological innovations were first introduced in the United States. By 1990, the figure had declined to less than 50 percent. In contrast, France is making impressive advances in electric traction, nuclear power, and aviation. Germany leads in chemicals and pharmaceuticals, precision and heavy machinery, heavy electrical goods, metallurgy, and surface transport equipment. Japan leads in optics, solid-state physics, engineering, chemistry, and process metallurgy. Eastern Europe and the former Soviet Union, the so-called COMECON (Council for Mutual Economic Assistance) countries, generate 30 percent of annual worldwide patent applications. However, the United States has regained some of its lost technological advantage. Through globalization, U.S. firms often can reap benefits from industries and technologies developed abroad. Even a relatively small service firm that possesses a distinct competitive advantage can capitalize on large overseas operations.

BusinessWeek For most of its 142-year history, Diebold Inc. never worried much about global strategy. As a premier name in bank vaults—and then automated teller machines and security systems—the company focused on U.S. financial institutions, content to let partners hawk what they could abroad. But in 1998, with the U.S. ATM market saturated, Diebold decided it had to be more ambitious. Since then, Diebold has taken off. Sales of security devices, software, and services surged 38% in 2000, to $1.74 billion, led by a 146% jump in overseas sales, to $729 million. The momentum continued in 2001. International sales have gone from 22% of the total to 40% in just two years, and should soon overtake North America.

The ventures overseas have taken Diebold into whole new directions. In China, where it now has half of the fast-growing ATM market, it also is helping the giant International Commercial Bank of China design its self-service branches and data network. In Brazil, Diebold owns and manages a network of 5,000 ATMs—as well as surveillance cameras—for a state-owned bank. In Colombia, it's handling bill collection for a power utility. In Taiwan, where most consumers still prefer to pay bills in cash, Diebold is about to introduce ATMs that both accept and count stacks of up to 100 currency notes and weed out counterfeits. And in South Africa, its ATMs for the techno-illiterate scan fingerprints for identification.

Diebold found it could serve much broader needs in emerging markets than in the United States. Across Latin America, consumers use banks to pay everything from utility bills to taxes. So Diebold ATMs handle these services, 24 hours a day. In Argentina, where filing taxes is a nightmare, citizens now can fill out returns on a PC, store them on a disk, and have their disks scanned on one of 5,000 special Diebold terminals, most of them at banks. Diebold also is landing new contracts across Latin America to manage bank ATM networks.

The $240 million acquisition of Brazil's Procom also gave Diebold an entree into an entirely new line: It landed a huge contract to supply electronic voting machines for Brazil's presidential election last year. Now Diebold is getting into the voting-machine business in the United States, where it expects demand to surge in the wake of the controversial Presidential contest in Florida. Globalization, it seems, can even unveil new opportunities at home.

Source: Excerpt from M. Arndt, P. Engardio, and J. Goodman, "Diebold." *BusinessWeek* (3746), p. 138, August 27, 2001.

As discussed in Exhibit 4–3, Global Strategy in Action, Diebold Inc. once operated solely in the United States, selling ATM machines, bank vaults, and security systems to financial institutions. However, with the U.S. market saturated, Diebold needed to expand internationally to continue its growth. The firm's globalization efforts led to both the development of new technologies in emerging markets and opportunistic entry into entirely new industries that significantly improved Diebold's sales.

In many situations, global development makes sense as a competitive weapon. Direct penetration of foreign markets can drain vital cash flows from a foreign competitor's domestic operations. The resulting lost opportunities, reduced income, and limited production can impair the competitor's ability to invade U.S. markets. A case in point is IBM's move to establish a position of strength in the Japanese mainframe computer industry before two key competitors, Fiyitsue and Hitachi, could dominate it. Once IBM had achieved a substantial share of the Japanese market, it worked to deny its Japanese competitors the vital cash and production experience they needed to invade the U.S. market.

Firms that operate principally in the domestic environment have an important decision to make with regard to their globalization: Should they act before being forced to do so by competitive pressures or after? Should they: (1) be proactive by entering global markets in advance of other firms and thereby enjoy the first-mover advantages often accruing to risk-taker firms that introduce new products or services; or (2) be reactive by taking the more conservative approach and following other companies into global markets once customer demand has been proven and the high costs of new-product or -service introductions have been absorbed by competitors? Although the answers to these questions are determined by the specifics of the company and the context, the issues raised in Exhibit 4–4 are helpful to strategic decision makers faced with the dilemma.

EXHIBIT 4–4
Reasons for Going Global

Source: Betty Jane Punnett and David A. Ricks, *International Business* (Boston: PWS-Kent, 1992), pp. 249–50.

Proactive	
Advantage/Opportunity	**Explanation of Action**
Additional resources	Various inputs—including natural resources, technologies, skilled personnel, and materials—may be obtained more readily outside the home country.
Lowered costs	Various costs—including labor, materials, transportation, and financing—may be lower outside the home country.
Incentives	Various incentives may be available from the host government or the home government to encourage foreign investment in specific locations.
New, expanded markets	New and different markets may be available outside the home country; excess resources—including management, skills, machinery, and money—can be utilized in foreign locations.
Exploitation of firm-specific advantages	Technologies, brands, and recognized names can all provide opportunities in foreign locations.
Taxes	Differing corporate tax rates and tax systems in different locations provide opportunities for companies to maximize their after-tax worldwide profits.
Economies of scale	National markets may be too small to support efficient production, while sales from several combined allow for larger-scale production.
Synergy	Operations in more than one national environment provide opportunities to combine benefits from one location with another, which is impossible without both of them.
Power and prestige	The image of being international may increase a company's power and prestige and improve its domestic sales and relations with various stakeholder groups.
Protect home market through offense in competitor's home	A strong offense in a competitor's market can put pressure on the competitor that results in a pull-back from foreign activities to protect itself at home.

Reactive	
Outside Occurrence	**Explanation of Reaction**
Trade barriers	Tariffs, quotas, buy-local policies, and other restrictive trade practices can make exports to foreign markets less attractive; local operations in foreign locations thus become attractive.
International customers	If a company's customer base becomes international, and the company wants to continue to serve it, then local operations in foreign locations may be necessary.
International competition	If a company's competitors become international, and the company wants to remain competitive, foreign operations may be necessary.
Regulations	Regulations and restrictions imposed by the home government may increase the cost of operating at home; it may be possible to avoid these costs by establishing foreign operations.
Chance	Chance occurrence results in a company deciding to enter foreign locations.

BusinessWeek After a slow start, U.S. e-commerce giants are taking Europe by storm. "The conventional wisdom that Americans couldn't localize their product in Europe has been proved wrong," says Christian Asmussen.

It's a stunning reversal of fortune. Only a year ago, European Net entrepreneurs were giddy with confidence. They planned to beat back U.S. competitors by moving faster into markets they understood better. Initial public offerings were the talk of London, Amsterdam, and Paris. Startups such as Britain's Boo.com, Freeserve, and lastminute.com seemed destined to be tomorrow's cyberstars.

But Boo has gone broke, Freeserve is on the block, and lastminute's stock is sagging—all while American dot-coms soar. Even America Online Inc. (AOL), which had stumbled in a venture with Bertelsmann, has more visitors throughout Europe than T-Online and is ranked No. 2 in both Britain and Germany. The result is a new hierarchy in Europe. At the top are the phone giants, Deutsche Telekom and France Telecom (FTE), which are able to leverage phone systems to build the leading ISPs. But it's the Americans alongside these titans who are the first continental players—a crucial advantage as Europe's industry consolidates.

European e-tailers now face a nasty shakeout. The Americans are buying: Amazon, for example, has bought online booksellers in Britain and Germany.

Although Europe's e-commerce revenues, at $5.4 billion in 2000, are one-sixth of U.S. levels, growth is likely to prove explosive. Forrester Research Inc., the Boston consultancy, predicts that triple-digit expansion will push total e-business in Europe to $1.6 trillion by 2004. Americans know how to exploit such booming markets, thanks to their experience at home.

While U.S. companies have their critics, retailing expertise honed at home is translating well. Amazon's British site features CDs by local singers, but the back office, distribution, and marketing are imported. "We can adopt about 80% of our American business model," says Steve Frazier, managing director in Britain. Amazon added 400,000 British customers in the first quarter of 2000, increasing revenues 210% from the year before, to $45 million. American e-biz stars also benefit from strong brands built up in the United States. In the nine months since eBay opened in Europe, it has already surpassed QXL in audience—in Germany and Britain—and will take on France next.

Source: Excerpted from William Echikson, "American E-Tailers Take Europe by Storm," *BusinessWeek,* August 7, 2000.

Strategic Orientations of Global Firms

Multinational corporations typically display one of four orientations toward their overseas activities. They have a certain set of beliefs about how the management of foreign operations should be handled. A company with an *ethnocentric orientation* believes that the values and priorities of the parent organization should guide the strategic decision making of all its operations. If a corporation has a *polycentric orientation,* then the culture of the country in which a strategy is to be implemented is allowed to dominate the decision-making process. In contrast, a *regiocentric orientation* exists when the parent attempts to blend its own predispositions with those of the region under consideration, thereby arriving at a region-sensitive compromise. Finally, a corporation with a *geocentric orientation* adopts a global systems approach to strategic decision making, thereby emphasizing global integration.

As described in Exhibit 4–5, E-commerce Strategy in Action, American firms have adopted a regiocentric orientation for pursing strategies in Europe. U.S. e-tailers have attempted to blend their own corporate structure and expertise with that of European corporations. For example, Amazon has been able to leverage its experience in the United States while developing regionally and culturally specific strategies overseas. By purchasing European franchises that have had regional success, E*Trade is pursuing a foreign strategy in which they insert their European units into corporate structure. This

EXHIBIT 4–6   **Orientation of a Global Firm**

Source: Adapted from Balaji S. Chakravarthy and Howard V. Perlmutter, "Strategic Planning for a Global Business," *Columbia Journal of World Business,* Summer 1985, pp. 5–6. Copyright 1985, Columbia Journal of World Business. Used with permission.

	Orientation of the Firm			
	Ethnocentric	**Polycentric**	**Regiocentric**	**Geocentric**
Mission	Profitability (viability)	Public acceptance (legitimacy)	Both profitability and public acceptance (viability and legitimacy)	Same as regiocentric
Governance	Top-down	Bottom-up (each subsidiary decides on local objectives)	Mutually negotiated between region and its subsidiaries	Mutually negotiated at all levels of the corporation
Strategy	Global integration	National responsiveness	Regional integration and national responsiveness	Global integration and national responsiveness
Structure	Hierarchical product divisions	Hierarchical area divisions, with autonomous national units	Product and regional organization tied through a matrix	A network of organizations (including some stakeholders and competitor organizations)
Culture	Home country	Host country	Regional	Global
Technology	Mass production	Batch production	Flexible manufacturing	Flexible manufacturing
Marketing	Product development determined primarily by the needs of home-country customers	Local product development based on local needs	Standardize within region, but not across regions	Global product, with local variations
Finance	Repatriation of profits to home country	Retention of profits in host country	Redistribution within region	Redistribution globally
Personnel practices	People of home country developed for key positions everywhere in the world	People of local nationality developed for key positions in their own country	Regional people developed for key positions anywhere in the region	Best people everywhere in the world developed for key positions everywhere in the world

strategy requires the combination and use of culturally different management styles and involves major challenges for upper management.

Exhibit 4–6 shows the impacts of each of the four orientations on key activities of the firm. It is clear from the figure that the strategic orientation of a global firm plays a major role in determining the locus of control and corporate priorities of the firm's decision makers.

AT THE START OF GLOBALIZATION

External and internal assessments are conducted before a firm enters global markets. For example, Japanese investors conduct extensive assessments and analyses before selecting a U.S. site for a Japanese-owned firm. They prefer states with strong markets, low unionization rates, and low taxes. In addition, Japanese manufacturing plants prefer counties characterized by manufacturing conglomeration; low unemployment and poverty rates; and concentrations of educated, productive workers.

External assessment involves careful examination of critical features of the global environment, particular attention being paid to the status of the host nations in such areas as economic progress, political control, and nationalism. Expansion of industrial facilities, favorable balances of payments, and improvements in technological capabilities over the past decade are gauges of the host nation's economic progress. Political status can be gauged by the host nation's power in and impact on global affairs.

Internal assessment involves identification of the basic strengths of a firm's operations. These strengths are particularly important in global operations, because they are often the characteristics of a firm that the host nation values most and, thus, offer significant bargaining leverage. The firm's resource strengths and global capabilities must be analyzed. The resources that should be analyzed include, in particular, technical and managerial skills, capital, labor, and raw materials. The global capabilities that should be analyzed include the firm's product delivery and financial management systems.

A firm that gives serious consideration to internal and external assessment is Business International Corporation, which recommends that seven broad categories of factors be considered. As shown in Exhibit 4–7, Global Strategy in Action, these categories include economic, political, geographic, labor, tax, capital source, and business factors.

COMPLEXITY OF THE GLOBAL ENVIRONMENT

Global strategic planning is more complex than purely domestic planning. There are at least five factors that contribute to this increase in complexity:

1. Globals face multiple political, economic, legal, social, and cultural environments as well as various rates of changes within each of them.

2. Interactions between the national and foreign environments are complex, because of national sovereignty issues and widely differing economic and social conditions.

3. Geographic separation, cultural and national differences, and variations in business practices all tend to make communication and control efforts between headquarters and the overseas affiliates difficult.

4. Globals face extreme competition, because of differences in industry structures.

5. Globals are restricted in their selection of competitive strategies by various regional blocs and economic integrations, such as the European Economic Community, the European Free Trade Area, and the Latin American Free Trade Area. Indications of how these factors contribute to the increased complexity of global strategic management are provided in Exhibit 4–8.

CONTROL PROBLEMS OF THE GLOBAL FIRM

An inherent complicating factor for many global firms is that their financial policies typically are designed to further the goals of the parent company and pay minimal attention to the goals of the host countries. This built-in bias creates conflict between the different parts of the global firm, between the whole firm and its home and host countries, and between the home country and host country themselves. The conflict is accentuated by the

The following considerations were drawn from an 88-point checklist developed by Business International Corporation.

Economic factors:

1. Size of GNP and projected rate of growth.

2. Foreign exchange position.

3. Size of market for the firm's products; rate of growth.

4. Current or prospective membership in a customs union.

Political factors:

5. Form and stability of government.

6. Attitude toward private and foreign investment by government, customers, and competition.

7. Practice of favored versus neutral treatment for state industries.

8. Degree of antiforeign discrimination.

Geographic factors:

9. Efficiency of transport (railways, waterways, highways).

10. Proximity of site to export markets.

11. Availability of local raw materials.

12. Availability of power, water, gas.

Labor factors:

13. Availability of managerial, technical, and office personnel able to speak the language of the parent company.

14. Degree of skill and discipline at all levels.

15. Presence or absence of militant or Communist-dominated unions.

16. Degree and nature of labor voice in management.

Tax factors:

17. Tax-rate trends (corporate and personal income, capital, withholding, turnover, excise, payroll, capital gains, customs, and other indirect and local taxes).

18. Joint tax treaties with home country and others.

19. Duty and tax drawbacks when imported goods are exported.

20. Availability of tariff protection.

Capital source factors:

21. Cost of local borrowing.

22. Local availability of convertible currencies.

23. Modern banking systems.

24. Government credit aids to new businesses.

Business factors:

25. State of marketing and distribution system.

26. Normal profit margins in the firm's industry.

27. Competitive situation in the firm's industry: do cartels exist?

28. Availability of amenities for expatriate executives and their families.

use of various schemes to shift earnings from one country to another in order to avoid taxes, minimize risk, or achieve other objectives.

Moreover, different financial environments make normal standards of company behavior concerning the disposition of earnings, sources of finance, and the structure of capital more problematic. Thus, it becomes increasingly difficult to measure the performance of international divisions.

In addition, important differences in measurement and control systems often exist. Fundamental to the concept of planning is a well-conceived, future-oriented approach to decision making that is based on accepted procedures and methods of analysis. Consistent approaches to planning throughout a firm are needed for effective review and evaluation by corporate headquarters. In the global firm, planning is complicated by differences in national attitudes toward work measurement, and by differences in government requirements about disclosure of information.

EXHIBIT 4–8
Differences between Factors That Affect Strategic Management in the United States and Internationally

Source: Adapted from R. G. Murdick, R. C. Moor, R. H. Eckhouse, and T. W. Zimmerer, *Business Policy: A Framework for Analysis,* 4th ed. (Columbus, OH: Grid, 1984), p. 275.

Factor	U.S. Operations	International Operations
Language	English used almost universally.	Use of local language required in many situations.
Culture	Relatively homogenous.	Quite diverse, both between countries and within countries.
Politics	Stable and relatively unimportant.	Often volatile and of decisive importance.
Economy	Relatively uniform.	Wide variations among countries and among regions within countries.
Government interference	Minimal and reasonably predictable.	Extensive and subject to rapid change.
Labor	Skilled labor available.	Skilled labor often scarce, requiring training or redesign of production methods.
Financing	Well-developed financial markets.	Poorly developed financial markets; capital flows subject to government control.
Media research	Data easy to collect.	Data difficult and expensive to collect.
Advertising	Many media available; few restrictions.	Media limited; many restrictions; low literacy rates rule out print media in some countries.
Money	U.S. dollar used universally.	Must change from one currency to another; problems created by changing exchange rates and government restrictions.
Transportation/ communication	Among the best in the world.	Often inadequate.
Control	Always a problem, but centralized control will work.	A worse problem—centralized control won't work; must walk a tightrope between overcentralizing and losing control through too much decentralizing.
Contracts	Once signed, are binding on both parties even if one party makes a bad deal.	Can be avoided and renegotiated if one party becomes dissatisfied.
Labor relations	Collective bargaining; layoff of workers easy.	Layoff of workers often not possible; may have mandatory worker participation in management; workers may seek change through political process rather than collective bargaining.

Although such problems are an aspect of the global environment, rather than a consequence of poor management, they are often most effectively reduced through increased attention to strategic planning. Such planning will aid in coordinating and integrating the firm's direction, objectives, and policies around the world. It enables the firm to anticipate and prepare for change. It facilitates the creation of programs to deal with worldwide development. Finally, it helps the management of overseas affiliates become more actively involved in setting goals and in developing means to more effectively utilize the firm's total resources.

An example of the need for coordination in global ventures and evidence that firms can successfully plan for global collaboration (e.g., through rationalized production) is the Ford Escort (Europe), the best-selling automobile in the world, which has a component manufacturing network that consists of plants in 15 countries.

GLOBAL STRATEGIC PLANNING

It should be evident from the previous sections that the strategic decisions of a firm competing in the global marketplace become increasingly complex. In such a firm, managers cannot view global operations as a set of independent decisions. These managers are faced with trade-off decisions in which multiple products, country environments, resource sourcing options, corporate and subsidiary capabilities, and strategic options must be considered.

A recent trend toward increased activism of stakeholders has added to the complexity of strategic planning for the global firm. *Stakeholder activism* refers to demands placed on the global firm by the foreign environments in which it operates, principally by foreign governments. This section provides a basic framework for the analysis of strategic decisions in this complex setting.

Multidomestic Industries and Global Industries

Multidomestic Industries

International industries can be ranked along a continuum that ranges from multidomestic to global.

A multidomestic industry is one in which competition is essentially segmented from country to country. Thus, even if global corporations are in the industry, competition in one country is independent of competition in other countries. Examples of such industries include retailing, insurance, and consumer finance.

In a multidomestic industry, a global corporation's subsidiaries should be managed as distinct entities; that is, each subsidiary should be rather autonomous, having the authority to make independent decisions in response to local market conditions. Thus, the global strategy of such an industry is the sum of the strategies developed by subsidiaries operating in different countries. The primary difference between a domestic firm and a global firm competing in a multidomestic industry is that the latter makes decisions related to the countries in which it competes and to how it conducts business abroad.

Factors that increase the degree to which an industry is multidomestic include:[1]

The need for customized products to meet the tastes or preferences of local customers.

Fragmentation of the industry, with many competitors in each national market.

A lack of economies of scale in the functional activities of firms in the industry.

Distribution channels unique to each country.

A low technological dependence of subsidiaries on R&D provided by the global firm.

Global Industries

A global industry is one in which competition crosses national borders. In fact, it occurs on a worldwide basis. In a global industry, a firm's strategic moves in one country can be significantly affected by its competitive position in another country. The very rapidly

[1] Y. Doz and C. K. Prahalad, "Patterns of Strategic Control within Multinational Corporations," *Journal of International Business Studies,* Fall 1984, pp. 55–72.

expanding list of global industries includes commercial aircraft, automobiles, mainframe computers, and electronic consumer equipment. Many authorities are convinced that almost all product-oriented industries soon will be global. As a result, strategic management planning must be global for at least six reasons:

1. *The increased scope of the global management task.* Growth in the size and complexity of global firms made management virtually impossible without a coordinated plan of action detailing what is expected of whom during a given period. The common practice of management by exception is impossible without such a plan.

2. *The increased globalization of firms.* Three aspects of global business make global planning necessary: (1) differences among the environmental forces in different countries, (2) greater distances, and (3) the interrelationships of global operations.

3. *The information explosion.* It has been estimated that the world's stock of knowledge is doubling every 10 years. Without the aid of a formal plan, executives can no longer know all that they must know to solve the complex problems they face. A global planning process provides an ordered means for assembling, analyzing, and distilling the information required for sound decisions.

4. *The increase in global competition.* Because of the rapid increase in global competition, firms must constantly adjust to changing conditions or lose markets to competitors. The increase in global competition also spurs managements to search for methods of increasing efficiency and economy.

5. *The rapid development of technology.* Rapid technological development has shortened product life cycles. Strategic management planning is necessary to ensure the replacement of products that are moving into the maturity stage, with fewer sales and declining profits. Planning gives management greater control of all aspects of new product introduction.

6. *Strategic management planning breeds managerial confidence.* Like the motorist with a road map, managers with a plan for reaching their objectives know where they are going. Such a plan breeds confidence, because it spells out every step along the way and assigns responsibility for every task. The plan simplifies the managerial job.

A firm in a global industry must maximize its capabilities through a worldwide strategy. Such a strategy necessitates a high degree of centralized decision making in corporate headquarters so as to permit trade-off decisions across subsidiaries.

Among the factors that make for the creation of a global industry are:

Economies of scale in the functional activities of firms in the industry.

A high level of R&D expenditures on products that require more than one market to recover development costs.

The presence in the industry of predominantly global firms that expect consistency of products and services across markets.

The presence of homogeneous product needs across markets, which reduces the requirement of customizing the product for each market. The presence of a small group of global competitors.

A low level of trade regulation and of regulation regarding foreign direction investment.[2]

---

[2] G. Harvel and C. K. Prahalad, "Managing Strategic Responsibility in the MNC," *Strategic Management Journal,* October–December 1983, pp. 341–51.

EXHIBIT 4–9
**Factors That Drive
Global Companies**

Source: Robert N. Lussier,
Robert W. Baeder, and Joel
Corman, "Measuring Global
Practices: Global Strategic
Planning through Company
Situational Analysis," p. 57.
Reprinted from *Business
Horizons,* September–October
1994. Copyright 1994 by the
Foundation for the School of
Business at Indiana University.
Used with permission.

1. Global Management Team

Possesses global vision and culture.
Includes foreign nationals.
Leaves management of subsidiaries to foreign nationals.
Frequently travels internationally.
Has cross-cultural training.

2. Global Strategy

Implement strategy as opposed to independent country strategies.
Develop significant cross-country alliances.
Select country targets strategically rather than opportunistically.
Perform business functions where most efficient—no home-country bias.
Emphasize participation in the triad—North America, Europe, and Japan.

3. Global Operations and Products

Use common core operating processes worldwide to ensure quantity and uniformity.
Product globally to obtain best cost and market advantage.

4. Global Technology and R&D

Design global products but take regional differences into account.
Manage development work centrally but carry out globally.
Do not duplicate R&D and product development; gain economies of scale.

5. Global Financing

Finance globally to obtain lowest cost.
Hedge when necessary to protect currency risk.
Price in local currencies.
List shares on foreign exchanges.

6. Global Marketing

Market global products but provide regional discretion if economies of scale are not affected.
Develop global brands.
Use core global marketing practices and themes.
Simultaneously introduce new global products worldwide.

Six factors that drive the success of global companies are listed in Exhibit 4–9. They address key aspects of globalizing a business's operations and provide a framework within which companies can effectively pursue the global marketplace.

The Global Challenge

Although industries can be characterized as global or multidomestic, few "pure" cases of either type exist. A global firm competing in a global industry must be responsive, to some degree, to local market conditions. Similarly, a global firm competing in a multidomestic industry cannot totally ignore opportunities to utilize intracorporate resources in competitive positioning. Thus, each global firm must decide which of its corporate functional activities should be performed where and what degree of coordination should exist among them.

Location and Coordination of Functional Activities

Typical functional activities of a firm include purchases of input resources, operations, research and development, marketing and sales, and after-sales service. A multinational corporation has a wide range of possible location options for each of these activities and

EXHIBIT 4–10
Location and Coordination Issues of Functional Activities

Source: Adapted from Michael E. Porter, "Changing Patterns of International Competition," *California Management Review,* Winter 1986, p. 18.

Functional Activity	Location Issues	Coordination Issues
Operations	Location of production facilities for components.	Networking of international plants.
Marketing	Product line selection. Country (market) selection.	Commonality of brand name worldwide. Coordination of sales to multinational accounts. Similarity of channels and product positioning worldwide. Coordination of pricing in different countries.
Service	Location of service organization.	Similarity of service standards and procedures worldwide.
Research and development	Number and location of R&D centers.	Interchange among dispersed R&D centers. Developing products responsive to market needs in many countries. Sequence of product introductions around the world.
Purchasing	Location of the purchasing function.	Managing suppliers located in different countries. Transferring market knowledge. Coordinating purchases of common items.

must decide which sets of activities will be performed in how many and which locations. A multinational corporation may have each location perform each activity, or it may center an activity in one location to serve the organization worldwide. For example, research and development centered in one facility may serve the entire organization.

A multinational corporation also must determine the degree to which functional activities are to be coordinated across locations. Such coordination can be extremely low, allowing each location to perform each activity autonomously, or extremely high, tightly linking the functional activities of different locations. Coca-Cola tightly links its R&D and marketing functions worldwide to offer a standardized brand name, concentrate formula, market positioning, and advertising theme. However, its operations function is more autonomous, with the artificial sweetener and packaging differing across locations.

Location and Coordination Issues

Exhibit 4–10 presents some of the issues related to the critical dimensions of location and coordination in multinational strategic planning. It also shows the functional activities that the firm performs with regard to each of these dimensions. For example, in connection with the service function, a firm must decide where to perform after-sale service and whether to standardize such service.

How a particular firm should address location and coordination issues depends on the nature of its industry and on the type of international strategy that the firm is pursuing. As discussed earlier, an industry can be ranked along a continuum that ranges between multidomestic at one extreme and global at the other. Little coordination of functional activities across countries may be necessary in a multidomestic industry, since competition occurs within each country in such an industry. However, as its industry becomes

The Model

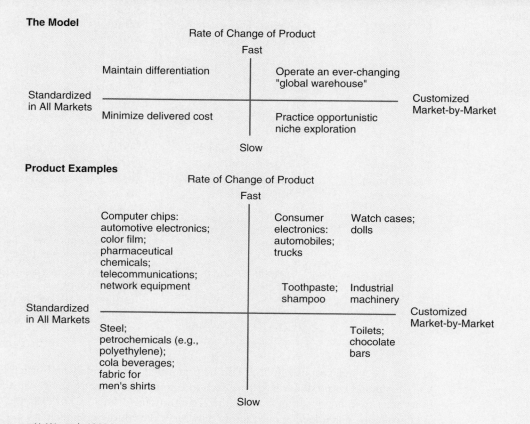

Rate of Change of Product

Fast

Maintain differentiation	Operate an ever-changing "global warehouse"
Minimize delivered cost	Practice opportunistic niche exploration

Standardized in All Markets — Customized Market-by-Market

Slow

Product Examples

Rate of Change of Product

Fast

Computer chips: automotive electronics; color film; pharmaceutical chemicals; telecommunications; network equipment	Consumer electronics: automobiles; trucks Watch cases; dolls
	Toothpaste; shampoo Industrial machinery
Steel; petrochemicals (e.g., polyethylene); cola beverages; fabric for men's shirts	Toilets; chocolate bars

Standardized in All Markets — Customized Market-by-Market

Slow

Source: Lawrence H. Wortzel, *1989 International Business Resource Book* (Strategic Direction Publishers, 1989).

increasingly global, a firm must begin to coordinate an increasing number of functional activities to effectively compete across countries.

Going global impacts every aspect of a company's operations and structure. As firms redefine themselves as global competitors, work forces are becoming increasingly diversified. The most significant challenge for firms, therefore, is the ability to adjust to a work force of varied cultures and lifestyles and the capacity to incorporate cultural differences to the benefit of the company's mission.

Market Requirements and Product Characteristics

Businesses have discovered that being successful in foreign markets often demands much more than simply shipping their well-received domestic products overseas. Firms must assess two key dimensions of customer demand: customers' acceptance of standardized products and the rate of product innovation desired. As shown in the top figure of Exhibit 4–11, Global Strategy in Action, all markets can be arrayed along a continuum from markets in which products are standardized to markets in which products must be

EXHIBIT 4–12
**International
Strategy Options**

Source: Adapted from Michael
E. Porter, "Changing Patterns
of International Competition,"
*California Management
Review,* Winter 1986, p. 19.

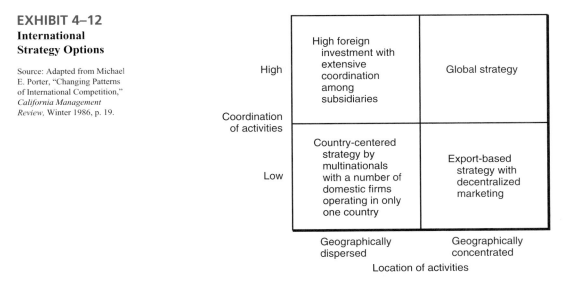

customized for customers from market to market. Standardized products in all markets include color film and petrochemicals, while dolls and toilets are good examples of customized products.

Similarly, products can be arrayed along a continuum from products that are not subject to frequent product innovations to products that are often upgraded. Products with a fast rate of change include computer chips and industrial machinery, while steel and chocolate bars are products that fit in the slow rate of change category.

The bottom figure of Exhibit 4–11 shows that the two dimensions can be combined to enable companies to simultaneously assess both customer need for product standardization and rate of product innovation. The examples listed demonstrate the usefulness of the model in helping firms to determine the degree of customization that they must be willing to accept to become engaged in transnational operations.

International Strategy Options

Exhibit 4–12 presents the basic multinational strategy options that have been derived from a consideration of the location and coordination dimensions. Low coordination and geographic dispersion of functional activities are implied if a firm is operating in a multidomestic industry and has chosen a country-centered strategy. This allows each subsidiary to closely monitor the local market conditions it faces and to respond freely to these conditions.

High coordination and geographic concentration of functional activities result from the choice of a pure global strategy. Although some functional activities, such as aftersale service, may need to be located in each market, tight control of those activities is necessary to ensure standardized performance worldwide. For example, IBM expects the same high level of marketing support and service for all of its customers, regardless of their location.

Two other strategy options are shown in Exhibit 4–12. High foreign investment with extensive coordination among subsidiaries would describe the choice of remaining at a particular growth stage, such as that of an exporter. An export-based strategy with decentralized marketing would describe the choice of moving toward globalization, which a multinational firm might make.

EXHIBIT 4–13
International
Strategy Options

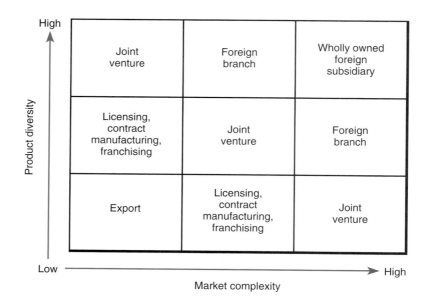

<table>
<tr><td align="center">High ↑
Product diversity</td></tr>
</table>

Joint venture	Foreign branch	Wholly owned foreign subsidiary
Licensing, contract manufacturing, franchising	Joint venture	Foreign branch
Export	Licensing, contract manufacturing, franchising	Joint venture

Low ————————————————→ High
Market complexity

COMPETITIVE STRATEGIES FOR FIRMS IN FOREIGN MARKETS

Strategies for firms that are attempting to move toward globalization can be categorized by the degree of complexity of each foreign market being considered and by the diversity in a company's product line (see Exhibit 4–13). *Complexity* refers to the number of critical success factors that are required to prosper in a given competitive arena. When a firm must consider many such factors, the requirements of success increase in complexity. *Diversity,* the second variable, refers to the breadth of a firm's business lines. When a company offers many product lines, diversity is high.

Together, the complexity and diversity dimensions form a continuum of possible strategic choices. Combining these two dimensions highlights many possible actions.

Niche Market Exporting

The primary niche market approach for the company that wants to export is to modify select product performance or measurement characteristics to meet special foreign demands. Combining product criteria from both the U.S. and the foreign markets can be slow and tedious. There are, however, a number of expansion techniques that provide the U.S. firm with the know-how to exploit opportunities in the new environment. For example, copying product innovations in countries where patent protection is not emphasized and utilizing nonequity contractual arrangements with a foreign partner can assist in rapid product innovation. N. V. Philips and various Japanese competitors, such as Sony and Matsushita, now are working together for common global product standards within their markets. Siemens, with a centralized R&D in electronics, also has been very successful with this approach.

Exporting usually requires minimal capital investment. The organization maintains its quality control standards over production processes and finished goods inventory, and risk to the survival of the firm is typically minimal. Additionally, the U.S. Commerce Department through its Export Now Program and related government agencies lowers the risks to smaller companies by providing export information and marketing advice.

Licensing/Contract Manufacturing

Establishing a contractual arrangement is the next step for U.S. companies that want to venture beyond exporting but are not ready for an equity position on foreign soil. Licensing involves the transfer of some industrial property right from the U.S. licensor to a motivated licensee. Most tend to be patents, trademarks, or technical know-how that are granted to the licensee for a specified time in return for a royalty and for avoiding tariffs or import quotas. Bell South and U.S. West, with various marketing and service competitive advantages valuable to Europe, have extended a number of licenses to create personal computer networks in the United Kingdom.

Another licensing strategy open to U.S. firms is to contract the manufacturing of its product line to a foreign company to exploit local comparative advantages in technology, materials, or labor.

U.S. firms that use either licensing option will benefit from lowering the risk of entry into the foreign markets. Clearly, alliances of this type are not for everyone. They are used best in companies large enough to have a combination of international strategic activities and for firms with standardized products in narrow margin industries.

Two major problems exist with licensing. One is the possibility that the foreign partner will gain the experience and evolve into a major competitor after the contract expires. The experience of some U.S. electronics firms with Japanese companies shows that licensees gain the potential to become powerful rivals. The other potential problem stems from the control that the licensor forfeits on production, marketing, and general distribution of its products. This loss of control minimizes a company's degrees of freedom as it reevaluates its future options.

Franchising

A special form of licensing is franchising, which allows the franchisee to sell a highly publicized product or service, using the parent's brand name or trademark, carefully developed procedures, and marketing strategies. In exchange, the franchisee pays a fee to the parent company, typically based on the volume of sales of the franchisor in its defined market area. The franchise is operated by the local investor who must adhere to the strict policies of the parent.

Franchising is so popular that an estimated 500 U.S. businesses now franchise to over 50,000 local owners in foreign countries. Among the most active franchisees are Avis, Burger King, Canada Dry, Coca-Cola, Hilton, Kentucky Fried Chicken, Manpower, Marriott, Midas, Muzak, Pepsi, and Service Master. However, the acknowledged global champion of franchising is McDonald's, which has 70 percent of its company-owned stores as franchisees in foreign nations.

Joint Ventures

As the multinational strategies of U.S. firms mature, most will include some form of joint venture (JV) with a target nation firm. AT&T followed this option in its strategy to produce its own personal computer by entering into several joint ventures with European producers to acquire the required technology and position itself for European expansion. Because JVs begin with a mutually agreeable pooling of capital, production or marketing equipment, patents, trademarks, or management expertise, they offer more permanent cooperative relationships than export or contract manufacturing.

Compared to full ownership of the foreign entity, JVs provide a variety of benefits to each partner. U.S. firms without the managerial or financial assets to make a profitable independent impact on the integrated foreign markets can share management tasks and cash requirements often at exchange rates that favor the dollar. The coordination of manufacturing and marketing allows ready access to new markets, intelligence data, and reciprocal flows of technical information.

For example, Siemens, the German electronics firm, has a wide range of strategic alliances throughout Europe to share technology and research developments. For years, Siemens grew by acquisitions, but now, to support its horizontal expansion objectives, it is engaged in joint ventures with companies like Groupe Bull of France, International Computers of Britain, General Electric Company of Britain, IBM, Intel, Philips, and Rolm. Another example is Airbus Industries, which produces wide-body passenger planes for the world market as a direct result of JVs among many companies in Britain, France, Spain, and Germany.

JVs speed up the efforts of U.S. firms to integrate into the political, corporate, and cultural infrastructure of the foreign environment, often with a lower financial commitment than acquiring a foreign subsidiary. General Electric's (GE) 3 percent share in the European lighting market was very weak and below expectations. Significant increases in competition throughout many of their American markets by the European giant, Philips Lighting, forced GE to retaliate by expanding in Europe. GE's first strategy was an attempted joint venture with the Siemens lighting subsidiary, Osram, and with the British electronics firm, Thorn EMI. Negotiations failed over control issues. When recent events in Eastern Europe opened the opportunity for a JV with the Hungarian lighting manufacturer, Tungsram, which was receiving 70 percent of revenues from the West, GE capitalized on it.

Although joint ventures can address many of the requirements of complex markets and diverse product lines, U.S. firms considering either equity- or nonequity-based JVs face many challenges. For example, making full use of the native firm's comparative advantage may involve managerial relationships where no single authority exists to make strategic decisions or solve conflicts. Additionally, dealing with host-company management requires the disclosure of proprietary information and the potential loss of control over production and marketing quality standards. Addressing such challenges with well-defined covenants agreeable to all parties is difficult. Equally important is the compatibility of partners and their enduring commitments to mutually supportive goals. Without this compatibility and commitment, a joint venture is critically endangered.

Foreign Branching

A foreign branch is an extension of the company in its foreign market—a separately located strategic business unit directly responsible for fulfilling the operational duties assigned to it by corporate management, including sales, customer service, and physical distribution. Host countries may require that the branch be "domesticated"; that is, have some local managers in middle and upper-level positions. The branch most likely will be outside any U.S. legal jurisdiction, liabilities may not be restricted to the assets of the given branch, and business licenses for operations may be of short duration, requiring the company to renew them during changing business regulations.

Wholly Owned Subsidiaries

Wholly owned foreign subsidiaries are considered by companies that are willing and able to make the highest investment commitment to the foreign market. These companies insist on full ownership for reasons of control and managerial efficiency. Policy decisions about local product lines, expansion, profits, and dividends typically remain with the U.S. senior managers.

Fully owned subsidiaries can be started either from scratch or by acquiring established firms in the host country. U.S. firms can benefit significantly if the acquired company has complementary product lines or an established distribution or service network.

U.S. firms seeking to improve their competitive postures through a foreign subsidiary face a number of risks to their normal mode of operations. First, if the high capital investment is to be rewarded, managers must attain extensive knowledge of the market, the host nation's language, and its business culture. Second, the host country expects both a long-term commitment from the U.S. enterprise and a portion of their nationals to be employed in positions of management or operations. Fortunately, hiring or training foreign managers for leadership positions is commonly a good policy, since they are close to both the market and contacts. This is especially important for smaller firms when markets are regional. Third, changing standards mandated by foreign regulations may eliminate a company's protected market niche. Product design and worker protection liabilities also may extend back to the home office.

The strategies shown in Exhibit 4–13 are not mutually exclusive. For example, a firm may engage in any number of joint ventures while maintaining an export business. Additionally, there are a number of other strategies that a firm should consider before deciding on its long-term approach to foreign markets. These will be discussed in detail in Chapter 6 under the topic of grand strategies. However, the strategies discussed in this chapter provide the most popular starting points for planning the globalization of a firm.

Sample Strategies of Global Competitors

It is interesting and informative to study the actual strategies of companies that have recently chosen to globalize their operations. Exhibit 4–14, Global Strategy in Action, provides examples of six different strategies that are being employed by Asian firms: professionalizing management, remaining entrepreneurial, sticking with the core business, bracing for more open markets, going public, and forging strategic alliances. As the details of their strategies make apparent, foreign firms must design plans that will enable them to generate the best mix of global operations and domestic market shares, exactly as U.S. firms are forced to do.

| Summary | To understand the strategic planning options available to a corporation, its managers need to recognize that different types of industry-based competition exist. Specifically, they must identify the position of their industry along the global versus multidomestic continuum and then consider the implications of that position for their firm. |

To understand the strategic planning options available to a corporation, its managers need to recognize that different types of industry-based competition exist. Specifically, they must identify the position of their industry along the global versus multidomestic continuum and then consider the implications of that position for their firm.

The differences between global and multidomestic industries about the location and coordination of functional corporate activities necessitate differences in strategic emphasis. As an industry becomes global, managers of firms within that industry must increase the coordination and concentration of functional activities.

The appendix at the end of this chapter lists many components of the environment with which global corporations must contend. This list is useful in understanding the issues that confront global corporations and in evaluating the thoroughness of global corporation strategies.

As a starting point for global expansion, the firm's mission statement needs to be reviewed and revised. As global operations fundamentally alter the direction and strategic capabilities of a firm, its mission statement, if originally developed from a domestic perspective, must be globalized.

The globalized mission statement provides the firm with a unity of direction that transcends the divergent perspectives of geographically dispersed managers. It provides a basis for strategic decisions in situations where strategic alternatives may appear to conflict. It promotes corporate values and commitments that extend beyond single cultures and satisfies the demands of the firm's internal and external claimants in different countries. Finally, it ensures the survival of the global corporation by asserting the global corporation's legitimacy with respect to support coalitions in a variety of operating environments.

Movement of a firm toward globalization often follows a systematic pattern of development. Commonly, businesses begin their foreign nation involvements progressively through niche market exporting, license-contract manufacturing, franchising, joint ventures, foreign branching, and foreign subsidiaries.

Global Strategy in Action
Strategies of Asian Competitors

Exhibit 4–14

BusinessWeek

STRATEGY 1: PROFESSIONALIZING MANAGEMENT

A sampling of the best emerging Asian companies and their management strategies

Company	Country	Strategy	Revenue
Johnson Electric	Hong Kong	In the business of micromotors, this family company is bringing in outside executives and investing heavily in training.	$250 million ↑ 29%
Taiwan Semiconductor	Taiwan	This highly successful foundry has an American as president. Under him are a handful of Taiwanese with American MBAs.	$740 million ↑ 57%

STRATEGY 2: REMAINING ENTREPRENEURIAL

Company	Country	Strategy	Revenue
Acer	Taiwan	CEO Stan Shih has broken his PC-making company into small, decentralized units so that each can be highly responsive to the market.	$ 3.2 billion ↑ 71%
San Miguel Corp.	Philippines	This beer and food conglomerate is actively spinning off different divisions into separate companies as a way to gain market share and become more efficient.	$ 190 million ↑ 41%

STRATEGY 3: STICKING WITH THE CORE BUSINESS

Company	Country	Strategy	Revenue
Renong Bernard	Malaysia	This group of eight listed companies is now selling off assets to focus on infrastructure. Its leading executives want the company to specialize rather than be a hodgepodge of investments.	$1.3 billion ↑ 19%
Indofood	Indonesia	This Jakarta-based food company made it big at home with its near monopoly in flour milling. Now, it's exporting its noodles to China, Chile, and Poland with the goal of being a global player.	$6.0 billion ↑ 18.9%

STRATEGY 4: BRACING FOR MORE OPEN MARKETS

Company	Country	Strategy	Revenue
Chinatrust	Taiwan	The country's leading credit-card issuer is finding its niche by providing a wide range of services for Taiwanese executives working abroad and other overseas Chinese.	$12.6 billion* ↑ 20%
Thai Farmers Bank	Thailand	Catching up to Citibank in innovative products, the bank is undergoing a reengineering to become more responsive to customers.	$20 billion* ↑ 15.2%

STRATEGY 5: GOING PUBLIC

Company	Country	Strategy	Revenue
Telkom Indonesia	Indonesia	This state-owned company is raising more than $1 billion of equity in Jakarta, New York, and London as part of the government's privatization drive.	$1.8 billion ↑ 30%
China Steel	Taiwan	Once a sleepy state enterprise, this well-run company has been privatized in a major bid to take on the global competition.	$2.9 billion ↑ 34%

STRATEGY 6: FORGING STRATEGIC PARTNERSHIPS

Company	Country	Strategy	Revenue
Legend	China	This emerging computer distributor and manufacturer in China is a marriage of a Hong Kong software house and Beijing's Academy of Sciences.	$480 million ↑ 50%
Mitac	Taiwan	The island's second-largest PC maker manufactures for Compaq, Apple, and AT&T. It is jointly developing desktop computers with Compaq.	$570 million ↑ 50%

*Assets.

Source: Reprinted from November 27, 1995 issue of *BusinessWeek* by special permission, copyright © 1995 by The McGraw-Hill Companies, Inc.

Questions for Discussion

1. How does environmental analysis at the domestic level differ from global analysis?
2. Which factors complicate environmental analysis at the global level? Which factors are making such analysis easier?
3. Do you agree with the suggestion that soon all industries will need to evaluate global environments?
4. Which industries operate almost devoid of global competition? Which inherent immunities do they enjoy?

Appendix

Components of the Multinational Environment

Multinational firms must operate within an environment that has numerous components. These components include:

1. Government, laws, regulations, and policies of home country (United States, for example).
   a. Monetary and fiscal policies and their effect on price trends, interest rates, economic growth, and stability.
   b. Balance-of-payments policies.
      1. Mandatory controls on direct investment.
      2. Interest equalization tax and other policies.
   c. Commercial policies, especially tariffs, quantitative import restrictions, and voluntary import controls.
   d. Export controls and other restrictions on trade.
   e. Tax policies and their impact on overseas business.
   f. Antitrust regulations, their administration, and their impact on international business.
   g. Investment guarantees, investment surveys, and other programs to encourage private investments in less-developed countries.
   h. Export-import and government export expansion programs.
   i. Other changes in government policy that affect international business.
2. Key political and legal parameters in foreign countries and their projection.
   a. Type of political and economic system, political philosophy, national ideology.
   b. Major political parties, their philosophies, and their policies.
   c. Stability of the government.
      1. Changes in political parties.
      2. Changes in governments.
   d. Assessment of nationalism and its possible impact on political environment and legislation.
   e. Assessment of political vulnerability.
      1. Possibilities of expropriation.
      2. Unfavorable and discriminatory national legislation and tax laws.
      3. Labor laws and problems.
   f. Favorable political aspects.
      1. Tax and other concessions to encourage foreign investments.
      2. Credit and other guarantees.
   g. Differences in legal system and commercial law.
   h. Jurisdiction in legal disputes.
   i. Antitrust laws and rules of competition.
   j. Arbitration clauses and their enforcement.
   k. Protection of patents, trademarks, brand names, and other industrial property rights.
3. Key economic parameters and their projection.
   a. Population and its distribution by age groups, density, annual percentage increase, percentage of working age, percentage of total in agriculture, and percentage in urban centers.

    b. Level of economic development and industrialization.

    c. Gross national product, gross domestic product, or national income in real terms and also on a per capita basis in recent years and projections over future planning period.

    d. Distribution of personal income.

    e. Measures of price stability and inflation, wholesale price index, consumer price index, other price indexes.

    f. Supply of labor, wage rates.

    g. Balance-of-payments equilibrium or disequilibrium, level of international monetary reserves, and balance-of-payments policies.

    h. Trends in exchange rates, currency stability, evaluation of possibility of depreciation of currency.

    i. Tariffs, quantitative restrictions, export controls, border taxes, exchange controls, state trading, and other entry barriers to foreign trade.

    j. Monetary, fiscal, and tax policies.

    k. Exchange controls and other restrictions on capital movements, repatriation of capital, and remission of earnings.

4. Business system and structure.

    a. Prevailing business philosophy: mixed capitalism, planned economy, state socialism.

    b. Major types of industry and economic activities.

    c. Numbers, size, and types of firms, including legal forms of business.

    d. Organization: proprietorships, partnerships, limited companies, corporations, cooperatives, state enterprises.

    e. Local ownership patterns: public and privately held corporations, family-owned enterprises.

    f. Domestic and foreign patterns of ownership in major industries.

    g. Business managers available: their education, training, experience, career patterns, attitudes, and reputations.

    h. Business associations and chambers of commerce and their influence.

    i. Business codes, both formal and informal.

    j. Marketing institutions: distributors, agents, wholesalers, retailers, advertising agencies, advertising media, marketing research, and other consultants.

    k. Financial and other business institutions: commercial and investment banks, other financial institutions, capital markets, money markets, foreign exchange dealers, insurance firms, engineering companies.

    l. Managerial processes and practices with respect to planning, administration, operations, accounting, budgeting, and control.

5. Social and cultural parameters and their projections.

    a. Literacy and educational levels.

    b. Business, economic, technical, and other specialized education available.

    c. Language and cultural characteristics.

    d. Class structure and mobility.

    e. Religious, racial, and national characteristics.

    f. Degree of urbanization and rural-urban shifts.

    g. Strength of nationalistic sentiment.

    h. Rate of social change.

    i. Impact of nationalism on social and institutional change.

Chapter 4 Discussion Case

BusinessWeek

How Well Does Wal-Mart Travel Overseas?

1   In the decade since Wal-Mart Stores Inc. (WMT) began its international exploits with a joint venture in Mexico, its record abroad has been full of merchandising missteps and management upheaval. Such blunders explain why German shopper Claudia Gittel grouses about the meat selection at the Wal-Mart in Esslingen and how the prices were lower when local chain Interspar ran the store. And why rival retailers from Brazil to South Korea scoff at Wal-Mart's product choices and "cookie-cutter" outlets. "We don't see Wal-Mart as a threat anymore," sniffs Hong Sun Sang, assistant manager for E-Mart, a 35-store chain in South Korea.

2   But with its persistence and deep pockets, it would be a mistake to underestimate the world's largest retailer. Just look at the U.S. grocery business, where Wal-Mart is a leader after early stumbles with its huge "supercenters." Likewise, the Bentonville (Ark.) chain has learned some painful lessons about consumers, regulators, and suppliers around the world. Through trial and error, the company has quietly built a powerful force outside the United States. It's now the biggest retailer in Canada and Mexico. Its $32 billion international business equaled 17% of its $191 billion in sales last year, with more than 1,100 stores in nine countries. And its operating profit abroad rose 36% last year, to $1.1 billion, about 12% of total profits. The trend continued in the first half of this year, with international sales rising 9.6% and operating profit jumping 39%.

3   Wal-Mart finally started getting its international act together two years ago after it put then-chief financial officer John B. Menzer in charge of the International Div. The low-key Menzer was credited with tightening financial discipline and boosting return on assets for the parent company. Now he's bringing a similar focus to Wal-Mart's sprawling operations abroad, where he's pushing more authority into the field, working to develop a corps of top managers, and spreading "best practices" from the United States and elsewhere around the world. And for the first time, Wal-Mart is building a global sourcing operation to use its huge sales volumes to command better deals, higher quality, and more innovation from both U.S. and foreign suppliers.

4   The company is backing these efforts with big bucks. Lehman Brothers Inc. estimates that Wal-Mart will devote 26% of its $9 billion in capital expenditures this year to operations abroad, adding about 120 stores. "As a global organization, they've become more savvy," says Ira Kalish, director of global retail intelligence at PricewaterhouseCoopers.

5   Wal-Mart believes that it has no choice but to expand rapidly abroad. Its culture and stock price are built on the expectation of double-digit sales and profit gains year after year. Analysts figure that the company's expanding chain of U.S. supercenters will carry the burden for at least four to eight years. But "someday the United States will slow down, and international will be the growth vehicle for the company," says Menzer.

6   Still, to get there Menzer must clear some high hurdles. The biggest one is Germany, where Wal-Mart bought the 21-store Wertkauf hypermarket chain in 1997 and then 74 unprofitable and often decrepit Interspar stores in 1998. Problems in integrating and upgrading the stores resulted in at least $200 million in losses last year, on roughly $3 billion in sales, estimates analyst Robert Buchanan of A.G. Edwards & Sons Inc. Wal-Mart has stopped predicting when it might make money in Germany. Some analysts believe that it won't break even until at least 2003. "There was a steep learning curve that wasn't expected," says Jim Leach, portfolio manager at shareholder Strong Capital Management.

7   Many of the wounds were self-inflicted. Wal-Mart failed to understand Germany's retail culture, the regulations that can add five years or more to the launch of a new hypermarket, and the stiff competition among some 14 hypermarket chains in a stagnant market. German managers who had been running the Wertkauf and Interspar stores for years didn't always take kindly to American "mentors" who were telling them how to do things when they didn't even speak German. Vendors balked at switching to a new supply system; when Wal-Mart tried to force them to supply its new centralized warehouses, it often found itself with empty shelves.

8   Then, last September, the German Cartel Office compelled Wal-Mart and some rivals to raise prices on milk, butter, and some other staples that they were

found to be selling below cost. Wal-Mart denies that but admits it underestimated the difficulties it would face. "We just walked in and said, 'We're going to lower prices, we're going to add people to the stores, we're going to remodel the stores because inherently that's correct,' and it wasn't," says Wal-Mart CEO H. Lee Scott Jr. "We didn't have the infrastructure to support the kind of things we were doing."

9   FOOD STUFF. Wal-Mart still needs a bigger presence in Germany to compete effectively, many analysts and suppliers contend. They point especially to food, where its market share is put at less than 2%. But Wal-Mart executives insist that they don't need more stores to make the German operation a success. "We have the scale; we just have to operate better," says Menzer.

10   To fix those operational problems, Wal-Mart recently hired a new country head, poaching him from a German tobacco-and-food supplier. Instead of the expensive renovations completed on 24 stores last year, Wal-Mart is carrying out more modest facelifts on 35 outlets this year. And this year it will open its first two new stores since the acquisitions. Wal-Mart is also working more closely with suppliers to boost its centralized distribution effort. About 50% of the products Wal-Mart has targeted for the program now move through central warehouses. Says Menzer: "We set ourselves back a few years, and now we're rebounding."

11   Wal-Mart executives say the German experience helped when they bought the British chain ASDA in 1999. Wal-Mart acquired a strong chain and gave local managers the freedom to run the business. While ASDA is still No. 3 in the grocery market, its share grew from 7.4% in 1995 to 9.6% last year, according to Verdict Research. Wal-Mart gave ASDA better technology for tracking store sales and inventories. And it pulled ASDA into its global buying effort, led by a 40-person unit in Bentonville that helps negotiate prices for products that can be sold in different markets. This enabled ASDA to cut prices on fans and air conditioners, for example, by 50%, boosting sales threefold.

12   Perhaps most important, says ASDA President Paul Mason, "this is still essentially a British business in the way it's run day-to-day." Indeed, one of Menzer's main priorities is to push operational authority to the country chiefs and closer to customers. That has meant cutting the international staff in Bentonville from 450 to 137. Now, Menzer focuses on enforcing certain core Wal-Mart principles, such as "every day low pricing," recently rolled out in Mexico and Argentina. But country managers handle their own buying, logistics, building design, and other operational decisions. "I have the autonomy to do what I need to do to run Wal-Mart Canada," says Mario Pilozzi, president of that business. In contrast, when Wal-Mart entered Canada in 1994, its blueprint specified what to sell and where to sell it—including liquid detergent and Kathie Lee clothing that flopped there. In the past, says CEO Scott, "we could get very specific on what should be on an end cap [a store display at the end of an aisle]. . . . I think we've matured."

13   Still, critics believe that the company retains a headquarters-knows-best mind-set. That raises the question, is Wal-Mart truly a global company, or just a U.S. company with a foreign division? Vijay Govindarajan, a professor of international business at Dartmouth College's Tuck School of Business, says Wal-Mart has few top managers who aren't American and few who speak more than one language and have been posted in several spots abroad. That might be one reason why some competitors scoff at Wal-Mart's claim that it's now sensitive to local tastes. "I get the impression that Wal-Mart is insisting on the American-style layouts and business approach," says Seol Do Won, marketing director at Samsung Tesco Co. in South Korea, which runs seven Home Plus stores. "It's good to introduce global standards, but you also need to adapt to local practice," he says.

14   Menzer insists he's doing just that, and that the lessons are flowing back to Bentonville, too. The U.S. stores and distribution centers, for instance, are now adopting ASDA's system for replenishing fresh food more quickly and in the right quantities. And ASDA's popular line of George brand clothing is being rolled out in the women's department of all U.S. stores this Christmas season. Thomas M. Coughlin, president of the Wal-Mart Stores Div., even removed all the chairs from the room where his managers hold their weekly meeting after he saw ASDA's "air-traffic controllers" room in Leeds. There, managers meet every morning around a high table with no chairs—to keep meetings short and to encourage action—as they pore over figures charted on the walls. As Menzer and Scott have made clear, there's no turning back in Wal-Mart's plan to conquer the world.

Source: Wendy Zellner, "How Well Does Wal-Mart Travel? After early missteps, the retailing giant may finally be getting the hang of selling overseas," *BusinessWeek,* September 3, 2001.

Internal Analysis

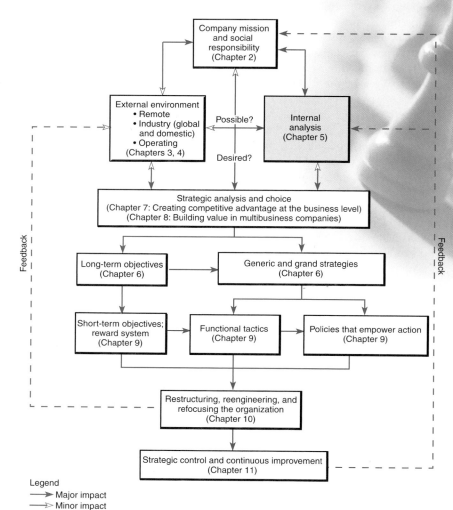

Company mission and social responsibility (Chapter 2)

External environment
- Remote
- Industry (global and domestic)
- Operating
(Chapters 3, 4)

Possible?

Desired?

Internal analysis (Chapter 5)

Strategic analysis and choice
(Chapter 7: Creating competitive advantage at the business level)
(Chapter 8: Building value in multibusiness companies)

Long-term objectives (Chapter 6)

Generic and grand strategies (Chapter 6)

Short-term objectives; reward system (Chapter 9)

Functional tactics (Chapter 9)

Policies that empower action (Chapter 9)

Restructuring, reengineering, and refocusing the organization (Chapter 10)

Strategic control and continuous improvement (Chapter 11)

Feedback

Feedback

Legend
⟶ Major impact
⟶▷ Minor impact

Three ingredients are critical to the success of a strategy. First, the strategy must be *consistent* with conditions in the competitive environment. Specifically, it must take advantage of existing or projected opportunities and minimize the impact of major threats. Second, the strategy must place *realistic* requirements on the firm's resources. In other words, the firm's pursuit of market opportunities must be based not only on the existence of external opportunities but also on competitive advantages that arise from the firm's key resources. Finally, the strategy must be *carefully executed.* The focus of this chapter is on the second ingredient: *realistic analysis of the firm's resources.*

Managers often do this subjectively, based on intuition and "gut feel." Years of seasoned industry experience positions managers to make sound subjective judgments. But just as often, or more often, this may not be the case. In fast-changing environments, reliance on past experiences can cause management myopia or a tendency to accept the status quo and disregard signals that change is needed. And with managers new to strategic decision making, subjective decisions are particularly suspect. A lack of experience is easily replaced by emotion, narrow functional expertise, and the opinions of others creating the foundation on which newer managers build strategic recommendations. So it is that new managers' subjective assessments often come back to haunt them.

Strategy in Action Exhibit 5–1 helps us understand this "subjective" tendency among both new and experienced managers. It looks at what happened a few years ago at Navistar when CEO John R. Horne admonished his management team to join him in buying their rapidly deteriorating (in price) stock as a sign to Wall Street that they had confidence in their company. Most managers declined, as their subjective sense of the company's situation and resources was quite negative. Some were reported to have even shorted the stock. The CEO acted virtually alone based on his view that several Navistar resources provided potential competitive advantages. Two years later, Navistar stock was up 400 percent. Subjective assessment had probably been holding the company back. It undoubtedly hit hard in the pocketbooks of several key managers that saw their own stock as an unwise investment.

Internal analysis has received increased attention in recent years as being a critical underpinning to effective strategic management. Indeed many managers and writers have adopted a new perspective on understanding firm success based on how well the firm uses its internal resources—the *resource-based view* (RBV) of the firm. This chapter will start with a look at the RBV to provide a useful vocabulary for identifying and examining internal *resources.* Next the chapter looks at ways managers achieve greater objectivity and rigor as they analyze their company's resources. Managers often start their internal analysis with questions like: "How well is the current strategy working? What is our current situation? Or what are our strengths and weaknesses?" Traditional *SWOT analysis* is then presented because it remains an approach that managers frequently use to answer these questions. More recently, insightful managers have begun to look at their business as a chain of activities that add value by creating the products or services they sell. Associated with this perspective is a powerful concept for introducing rigor and objectivity into internal analysis, the *value chain,* which this chapter will examine in great detail. Finally, objectivity and realism are enhanced when managers use meaningful standards for comparison regardless of the particular analytical framework they employ in internal analysis. We conclude this chapter by examining how managers do this using *past performance, stages of industry evolution, comparison with competitors* or other *"benchmarks,"* *industry norms,* and traditional *financial analysis.*

Strategy in Action

Navistar: An Objective Internal Analysis Lets It Gun the Engines for the 21st Century

Exhibit 5–1

BusinessWeek As it moved toward a new century, things looked bleak for Navistar International Corp. After decades of crippling labor problems and manufacturing snafus, the $6.4 billion Chicago truck and engine maker had suffered another steep earnings slide last year. Then, in a showdown with United Auto Workers members over costs, CEO John R. Horne had been forced to scrap the company's latest truck introduction. Disheartened investors let the stock drop to $9 a share, just 50¢ above its low.

That's when Horne called his 30 top executives into his office to make a personal plea. Looking for a show of faith in the company, he implored all of them to spend their own money to buy as many shares of Navistar stock as they could. Horne knew it was a lot to ask. Over the previous 10 years, the company—once known as International Harvester—had tallied the worst total return to shareholders of all publicly traded U.S. companies. But he was convinced that if his managers bought, Wall Street would see that as a sign that Navistar's fortunes were turning.

Management's reply was a unanimous no. Many felt that Navistar's shares might drop as low as 6, and all 30 backed away. So Horne bit the bullet alone, buying as much as he could for cash and also turning his 401(k) account entirely into Navistar stock. "I couldn't force them because it was their money," he says. "I laugh at them some now."

All the way to the bank, he might add. By late 2001, Navistar's stock hit 40, a blazing 350% return to shareholders.

What Horne—a 34-year veteran who became president in 1991 and CEO in 1995—convinced himself about was the presence of key resources that were on the verge of becoming distinctive competencies, and key strengths, at Navistar.

TANGIBLE ASSET: CLEANEST BURNING DIESEL ENGINE

Navistar's diesel engine business was the first to be worked over. Horne immediately cut the number of engines in production to two, down from 70 in the mid-80s, for example. And by 1994, with Navistar's balance sheet improving, he introduced a new engine.

Navistar's offering, still the cleanest burning model on the market, quickly attracted major truck manufacturers such as Ford Motor Co. Ford puts the engine in vans and pickups and recently on its hot Expedition sport utility vehicle. Thanks largely to this model, Navistar's share of the diesel engine market rose from 25% in 1990 to 44% in 1998. That's one big reason operating results climbed from a $355 million loss in 1993 to a $349 million profit for the fiscal year ended October 2000.

TANGIBLE ASSET: EXCESS TRUCK AND ENGINE MANUFACTURING CAPACITY

Horne began a wide-ranging overhaul of Navistar's remaining truck and engine manufacturing lines. He started by drastically slicing the number of products Navistar made. Assembly was rationalized too. While Navistar plants used to build multiple trucks for several different markets, today each one specializes in one type of truck with fewer models.

Tackling problems in Navistar's truck and tractor division proved far tougher. Two years ago, for example, Horne laid out a plan to introduce a new generation of trucks. By simplifying the design of components, Horne hoped to bring out a series of truck and trailer models with interchangeable designs and standardized parts, thus cutting costs while reducing errors on the assembly line. Horne's goal: to reduce the 19 heavy-duty and medium truck designs in his main Springfield (Illinois) plant to one or two.

ORGANIZATIONAL CAPABILITY: IMPROVED UNION RELATIONS

Before he got that far, Horne ran smack into the problem that has dogged Navistar for more than a decade: He needed significant concessions from the UAW, which represents almost 80% of Navistar's truck workers. Horne demanded a wage freeze until 2002 and the flexibility to consolidate production. He took a direct approach. "I showed them the books," he says. "They knew survival of the plants depended on the changes."

Union leaders may have known it, but U.S. union members weren't convinced. They rejected the contract outright. Convinced that he could never achieve his profitability goals without the changes, Horne cancelled the new trucks. He took a $35 million charge and made clear his next step would be to look abroad for lower labor costs. By August 1997, the workers folded their cards and approved the plan. Horne's tough stance has paid off. He quickly revived plans for the new truck. And since the new labor contract and other manufacturing changes went into effect last fall, productivity at U.S. plants has already risen 15%.

ORGANIZATIONAL CAPABILITY: NEW PRODUCT DEVELOPMENT PROCESS

Just as important, Horne got Navistar working on new models again for the first time in years. Having brought out few new products during Navistar's long slide, most of the company's models were aging. But to make sure the new products pay off, Horne also introduced tight financial discipline: Today, new projects only win the nod if they can earn a

17.5% return on equity and a 15% return on assets through a business cycle and be available in 2 years or less. *Popular Science* recognized Navistar's revolutionary camless engine technology as "Best of What's New in 2002."

INTANGIBLE ASSET: A VISIONARY LEADER WITH STRONG LEADERSHIP SKILLS

"Horne has done a magnificent job," says David Pedowitz, director of research at New York's David J. Greene & Co. brokerage firm, the largest outside investor with a 5% stake. "For the first time since the breakup of International Harvester, they're in a position to be a world-class competitor."

In the meantime, Horne continues to spread his penny-pinching gospel. Indeed, though he's a big basketball fan, he won't buy courtside seats to see his favorite competitor, Washington Wizards' Michael Jordan, hit the court. When Horne does make it to a home game, it's as a guest. He has other things to do with the fortune he's made in Navistar stock. Like reinvest.

Source: "Navistar: Gunning the Engines," *BusinessWeek,* February 2, 1998; and "Diesels Are the New Thing—Again," *BusinessWeek,* November 13, 2000.

RESOURCE-BASED VIEW OF THE FIRM

Coca-Cola versus Pepsi is a competitive situation virtually all of us recognize. Stock analysts look at the two and frequently conclude that Coke is the clear leader. They cite Coke's superiority in tangible assets (warehouses, bottling facilities, computerization, cash, etc.) and intangible assets (reputation, brand name awareness, tight competitive culture, global business system, etc.). They also mention that Coke leads Pepsi in several capabilities to make use of these assets effectively—managing distribution globally, influencing retailer shelf space allocation, managing franchise bottler relations, marketing savvy, investing in bottling infrastructure, and speed of decision making to take quick advantage of changing global conditions are just a few that are frequently mentioned. The combination of capabilities and assets, most analysts conclude, creates several competencies that give Coke several competitive advantages over Pepsi that are durable and not easily imitated.

The Coke-Pepsi situation provides a useful illustration for understanding several concepts central to the resource-based view (RBV) of the firm. The RBV's underlying premise is that firms differ in fundamental ways because each firm possesses a unique "bundle" of resources—tangible and intangible assets and organizational capabilities to make use of those assets. Each firm develops competencies from these resources and, when developed especially well, these become the source of the firm's competitive advantages. Coke's decision to buy out weak bottling franchisees and regularly invest in or own newer bottling locations worldwide has given Coke a competitive advantage analysts estimate Pepsi will take at least 10 years or longer to match. Coke's strategy for the last 15 years was based in part on the identification of this resource and the development of it into a distinctive competence—a sustained competitive advantage. The RBV is a useful starting point for understanding internal analysis. Let's look at the basic concepts underlying the RBV.

Three Basic Resources: Tangible Assets, Intangible Assets, and Organizational Capabilities

Executives charting the strategy of their businesses historically concentrate their thinking on the notion of a "core competence." Basically, a core competence was seen as a capability or skill running through a firm's businesses that once identified, nurtured, and deployed throughout the firm became the basis for lasting competitive advantage. Executives, enthusiastic about the notion that their job as strategists was to identify and leverage core competencies, encountered difficulty applying the concept because of the generality of its level of analysis. The RBV emerged as a way to make the core competency concept more focused and measurable—creating a more meaningful internal analysis. Central to the RBV's ability to do this is its notion of three basic types of resources that together create the building blocks for distinctive competencies. They are defined below and illustrated in Exhibit 5–2.

Tangible assets are the easiest to identify and are often found on a firm's balance sheet. They include production facilities, raw materials, financial resources, real estate, and computers. Tangible assets are the physical and financial means a company uses to provide value to its customers.

Intangible assets are things like brand names, company reputation, organizational morale, technical knowledge, patents and trademarks, and accumulated experience within an organization. While they are not assets that you can touch or see, they are very often critical in creating competitive advantage.

Organizational capabilities are not specific "inputs" like tangible or intangible assets; rather, they are the skills—the ability and ways of combining assets, people, and processes—that a company uses to transform inputs into outputs. Dell Computer built its first 10 years of unprecedented growth by creating an organization capable of the speedy and inexpensive manufacture and delivery of custom-built PCs. Gateway and Micron have attempted to copy Dell for most of that time but remain far behind Dell's diverse organizational capabilities. Dell subsequently revolutionized its own "system" using the Internet to automate and customize service, creating a whole new level of organizational capability that combines assets, people, and processes throughout and beyond their organization. Concerning this organizational capability, Michael Dell recently said: "Anyone who tries to go direct now will find it very difficult—like trying to jump over the Grand Canyon." Finely developed capabilities, such as Dell's Internet-based customer-friendly system, can be a source of sustained competitive advantage. They enable a firm to take the same input factors as rivals (like Gateway and Micron) and convert them into products and services, either with greater efficiency in the process or greater quality in the output or both.

What Makes a Resource Valuable?

Once managers begin to identify their firm's resources, they face the challenge of determining which of those resources represent strengths or weaknesses—which resources generate core competencies that are sources of sustained competitive advantage. This has been a complex task for managers attempting to conduct a meaningful internal analysis. The RBV has addressed this by setting forth some key guidelines that help determine what constitutes a valuable asset, capability, or competence—that is, what makes a resource valuable.

1. **Competitive superiority: Does the resource help fulfill a customer's need better than those of the firm's competitors?** Two restaurants offer similar food, at similar prices, but one has a location much more convenient to downtown offices than the other. The tangible asset, location, helps fulfill daytime workers' lunch eating needs better than its competitor, resulting in greater profitability and sales volume for the conveniently located restaurant. Wal-Mart redefined discount retailing and outperformed the industry in

EXHIBIT 5–2

**Examples of
Different Resources**

Source R. M. Grant,
*Contemporary Strategy
Analysis* (Oxford: Blackwell,
2001), p. 140.

Tangible Assets	**Intangible Assets**	**Organizational Capabilities**
Hampton Inn's reservation system	Nike's brand name	Dell Computer's customer service
Ford Motor Company's cash reserves	Dell Computer's reputation	Wal-Mart's purchasing and inbound logistics
Georgia Pacific's land holdings	Wendy's advertising with Dave Thomas	Sony's product-development processes
Virgin Airlines' plane fleet	Jack Welch as GE's leader	Coke's global distribution coordination
Coca-Cola's Coke formula	IBM's management team Wal-Mart's culture	3M's innovation process

Classifying and Assessing the Firm's Resources

Resource	**Relevant Characteristics**	**Key Indicators**
Tangible Resources Financial Resources	The firm's borrowing capacity and its internal funds generation determine its resilience and capacity for investment.	• Debt/equity ratio • Operating cash flow/free cash flow • Credit rating
Physical Resources	Physical resources constrain the firm's set of production possibilities and impact its cost position. Key characteristics include: • The size, location, technical sophistication, and flexibility of plant and equipment • Location and alternative uses for land and buildings • Reserves of raw materials	• Market values of fixed assets • Vintage of capital equipment • Scale of plants • Flexibility of fixed assets
Intangible Resources Technological Resources	Intellectual property: patent portfolio, copyright, trade secrets Resources for innovation: research facilities, technical and scientific employees	• Number and significance of patents • Revenue from licensing patents and copyrights • R&D staff as a percent of total employment • Number and location of research facilities
Reputation	Reputation with customers through the ownership of brands and trademarks; established relationships with customers; the reputation of the firm's products and services for quality and reliability. The reputation of the company with suppliers (including component suppliers, banks and financiers, employees and potential employees), with government and government agencies, and with the community.	• Brand recognition • Brand equity • Percent of repeat buying • Objective measures of comparative product performance (e.g., Consumers' Association ratings, J. D. Power ratings) • Surveys of corporate reputation (e.g., *BusinessWeek*)

EXHIBIT 5–3
Wal-Mart's Resource-Based Competitive Advantage

Source: Pankaj Ghemawat, "Wal-Mart Stores' Discount Operations," Harvard Business School case number 9-387-018.

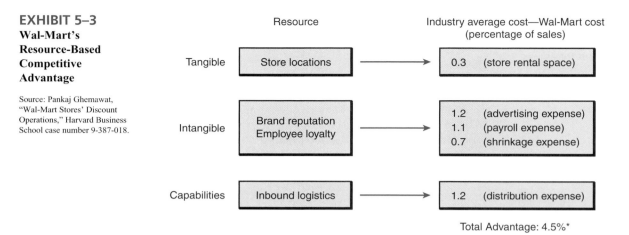

Resource

Industry average cost—Wal-Mart cost (percentage of sales)

Tangible — Store locations → 0.3   (store rental space)

Intangible — Brand reputation / Employee loyalty → 1.2   (advertising expense) / 1.1   (payroll expense) / 0.7   (shrinkage expense)

Capabilities — Inbound logistics → 1.2   (distribution expense)

Total Advantage: 4.5%*

*Wal-Mart's cost advantage as a percent of sales. Each percentage point advantage is worth $500 million in net income to Wal-Mart.

profitability by 4.5 percent of sales—a 200 percent improvement. Four resources—store locations, brand recognition, employee loyalty, and sophisticated inbound logistics—allowed Wal-Mart to fulfill customer needs much better and more cost effectively than Kmart and other discount retailers, as shown in Exhibit 5–3. In both of these examples, *it is important to recognize that only resources that contributed to competitive superiority were valuable.* At the same time, other resources such as the restaurant's menu and specific products or parking space at Wal-Mart were essential to doing business but contributed little to competitive advantage because they did not distinguish how the firm fulfilled customer needs.

2. **Resource scarcity: Is the resource in short supply?** When it is, it is more valuable. When a firm possesses a resource and few if any others do, and it is central to fulfilling customers' needs, then it becomes a distinctive competence for the firm. The real way resource scarcity contributes value is when it can be sustained over time. To really answer this very basic question we must explore the following questions.

3. **Inimitability: Is the resource easily copied or acquired?** A resource that competitors can readily copy can only generate temporary value. It cannot generate a long-term competitive advantage. When Wendy's first emerged, it was the only major hamburger chain with a drive-through window. This unique organizational capability was part of a "bundle" of resources that allowed Wendy's to provide unique value to its target customers, young adults seeking convenient food service. But once this resource, or organizational capability, proved valuable to fast-food customers, every fast-food chain copied the feature. Then Wendy's continued success was built on other resources that generated other distinctive competencies.

Inimitability doesn't last forever, as the Wendy's example illustrates. Competitors will match or better any resource as soon as they can. It should be obvious, then, that the firm's ability to forestall this eventuality is very important The RBV identifies four characteristics, called *isolating mechanisms,* that make resources difficult to imitate:

- **Physically unique resources** are virtually impossible to imitate. A one-of-a-kind real estate location, mineral rights, and patents are examples of resources that cannot be imitated. Disney's Mickey Mouse copyright or Winter Park, Colorado's Iron Horse resort possess physical uniqueness. While many strategists claim that resources are physically unique, this is seldom true. Rather, other characteristics are typically what make most resources difficult to imitate.

- **Path-dependent resources** are very difficult to imitate because of the difficult "path" another firm must follow to create the resource. These are resources that cannot be instantaneously acquired but rather must be created over time in a manner that is frequently very expensive and always difficult to accelerate. When Michael Dell said that "anyone who tries to go direct now will find it very difficult—like trying to jump over the Grand Canyon" (see page 128), he was asserting that Dell's system of selling customized PCs direct via the Internet and Dell's unmatched customer service is in effect a path-dependent organizational capability. It would take any competitor years to develop the expertise, infrastructure, reputation, and capabilities necessary to compete effectively with Dell. Coca-Cola's brand name, Gerber Baby Food's reputation for quality, and Steinway's expertise in piano manufacture would take competitors many years and millions of dollars to match. Consumers' many years of experience drinking Coke or using Gerber or playing a Steinway would also need to be matched.

- **Causal ambiguity** is a third way resources can be very difficult to imitate. This refers to situations where it is difficult for competitors to understand exactly how a firm has created the advantage it enjoys. Competitors can't figure out exactly what the uniquely valuable resource is, or how resources are combined to create the competitive advantage. Causally ambiguous resources are often organizational capabilities that arise from subtle combinations of tangible and intangible assets and culture, processes, and organizational attributes the firm possesses. Southwest Airlines has regularly faced competition from major and regional airlines, with some like United and Continental eschewing their traditional approach and attempting to compete by using their own version of the Southwest approach—same planes, routes, gate procedures, number of attendants, and so on. They have yet to succeed. The most difficult thing to replicate is Southwest's "personality," or culture of fun, family, and frugal yet focused services and attitude. Just how that works is hard for United and Continental to figure out.

- **Economic deterrence** is a fourth source of inimitability. This usually involves large capital investments in capacity to provide products or services in a given market that are scale sensitive. It occurs when a competitor understands the resource that provides a competitive advantage and may even have the capacity to imitate, but chooses not to because of the limited market size that realistically would not support two players the size of the first mover.

While we may be inclined to think of a resource's inimitability as a yes-or-no situation, inimitability is more accurately measured on a continuum that reflects difficulty and time. Exhibit 5–4 illustrates such a continuum. Some resources may have multiple imitation deterrents. For example, 3M's reputation for innovativeness may involve path dependencies and causal ambiguity.

   4. **Appropriability: Who actually gets the profit created by a resource?** Warren Buffet is known worldwide as one of the most successful investors of the last 25 years. One of his legendary investments was the Walt Disney Company, which he once said he liked "because the Mouse does not have an agent."[1] What he was really saying was that Disney owned the Mickey Mouse copyright, and all profits from that valuable resource went directly to Disney. Other competitors in the "entertainment" industry generated similar profits from their competing offerings, for example, movies, but they often "captured" substantially less of those profits because of the amounts that had to be paid to well-known actors or directors or other entertainment contributors seen as the real creators of the movie's value.

[1] *The Harbus,* March 25, 1996, p. 12.

EXHIBIT 5–4
Resource
Inimitability

Source: Cynthia A.
Montgomery, "Resources:
The Essence of Corporate
Advantage:" Harvard Business
School Case N1-792-064.

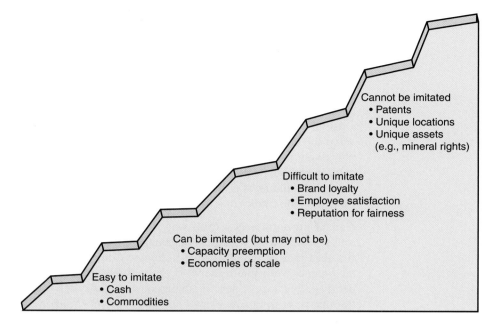

Cannot be imitated
• Patents
• Unique locations
• Unique assets
  (e.g., mineral rights)

Difficult to imitate
• Brand loyalty
• Employee satisfaction
• Reputation for fairness

Can be imitated (but may not be)
• Capacity preemption
• Economies of scale

Easy to imitate
• Cash
• Commodities

Sports teams, investment services, and consulting businesses are other examples of companies that generate sizable profits based on resources (key people, skills, contacts, for example) that are not inextricably linked to the company and therefore do not allow the company to easily capture the profits. Superstar sports players can move from one team to another, or command excessively high salaries, and this circumstance could arise in other personal services business situations. It could also occur when one firm joint ventures with another, sharing resources and capabilities and the profits that result. Sometimes restaurants or lodging facilities that are franchisees of a national organization are frustrated by the fees they pay the franchisor each month and decide to leave the organization and go "independent." They often find, to their dismay, that the business declines significantly. The value of the franchise name, reservation system, and brand recognition is critical in generating the profits of the business.

Bottom line: resources that one develops and controls—where ownership of the resource and its role in value creation is obvious—are more valuable than resources that can be easily bought, sold, or moved from one firm to another.

5. **Durability: How rapidly will the resource depreciate?** The slower a resource depreciates, the more valuable it is. Tangible assets, like commodities or capital, can have their depletion measured. Intangible resources, like brand names or organizational capabilities, present a much more difficult depreciation challenge. The Coca-Cola brand has continued to appreciate, whereas technical know-how in various computer technologies depreciates rapidly. In the increasingly hypercompetitive global economy of the 21st century, distinctive competencies and competitive advantages can fade quickly, making the notion of durability a critical test of the value of key resources and capabilities. Some believe that this reality makes well-articulated visions and associated cultures within organizations potentially the most important contributor to long-term survival.[2]

[2] James C. Collins, *Good to Great: Why Some Companies Make the Leap . . . and Others Don't* (New York: HarperCollins, 2001).

6. **Substitutability: Are other alternatives available?** We discussed the threat of substitute products in Chapter 3 as part of the five forces model for examining industry profitability. This basic idea can be taken further and used to gauge the value of particular resources. DeLite's of America was once a hot IPO as a new fast-food restaurant chain focused exclusively on selling lite food—salads, lean sandwiches, and so on. The basic idea was to offer, in a fast-food format, food low in calories and saturated fat. Investors were very excited about this concept because of the high-calorie, high-fat content of the foods offered by virtually every existing chain. Unfortunately for these investors, several key fast-food players, like Wendy's and later McDonald's, Burger King, and Hardees, adapted their operations to offer salad bars or premade salads and other "lean" sandwich offerings without disrupting their more well known fare. With little change and adaptation of their existing facility and operational resources, these chains quickly created alternatives to DeLite's offerings and the initial excitement about those offerings faded. DeLite's was driven out of business by substitute resources and capabilities rather than substitute products.

Using the Resource-Based View in Internal Analysis

To use the RBV in internal analysis, a firm must first identify and evaluate its resources to find those that provide the basis for future competitive advantage. This process involves defining the various resources the firm possesses, and examining them based on the above discussion to gauge which resources truly have strategic value. Four final guidelines have proven helpful in this undertaking:

- *Disaggregate resources*—break them down into more specific competencies—rather than stay with broad categorizations. Saying that Domino's Pizza has better marketing skills than Pizza Hut conveys little information. But dividing that into subcategories such as advertising that, in turn, can be divided into national advertising, local promotions, and couponing allows for a more measurable assessment. Exhibit 5–5 provides a useful illustration of this at Whitbread's Restaurant.

- *Utilize a functional perspective.* Looking at different functional areas of the firm, disaggregating tangible and intangible assets as well as organizational capabilities that are present, can begin to uncover important value-building resources and activities that deserve further analysis. Exhibit 5–6 lists a variety of functional area resources and activities that deserve consideration.

- *Look at organizational processes* and combinations of resources and not only at isolated assets or capabilities. While disaggregation is critical, you must also take a creative, gestalt look at what competencies the firm possesses or has the potential to possess that might generate competitive advantage.

- *Use the value chain approach* to uncover organizational capabilities, activities, and processes that are valuable potential sources of competitive advantage. Value chain analysis is discussed starting on page 137.

Although the RBV enables a systematic assessment of internal resources, it is important to stress that a meaningful analysis of those resources best takes place in the context of the firm's competitive environment. Possessing valuable resources will not generate commensurate profits unless resources are applied in an effective product market strategy; they must be deployed in an optimum way and align related activities for the firm to pursue its chosen sources of competitive advantage. Traditional strategy

Source: Andrew Campbell and
Kathleen Sommers-Luchs, *Core
Competency-Based Strategy*
(London: International
Thomson, 1997).

EXHIBIT 5–5
Disaggregating Whitbread Restaurant's Customer Service Resource

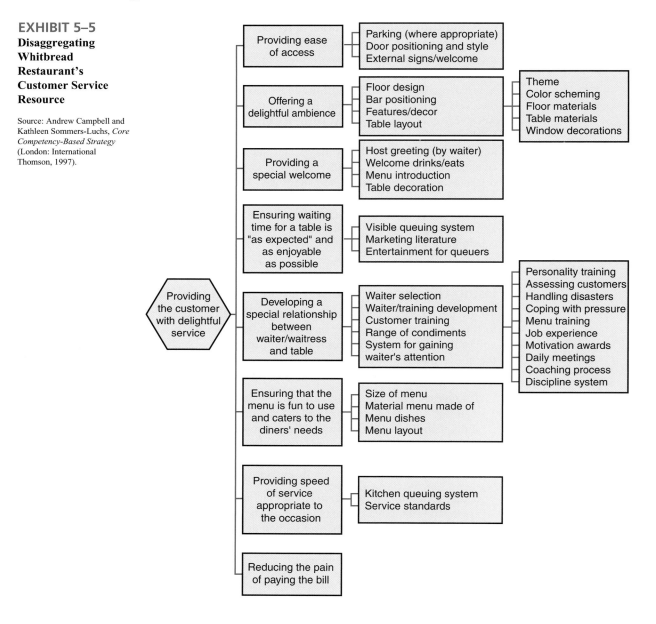

formulation—externally positioning a firm to capitalize on its strengths and opportunities and to minimize its threats and weaknesses—remains essential to realizing the competitive advantage envisioned from an RBV of the firm.[3] The next section examines this traditional approach, often called *SWOT analysis,* as a conceptual framework that may complement the RBV in conducting a sound internal analysis.

[3] Jay B. Barney and Asli M. Arikan, "The Resource-Based View: Origins and Implications," in *Handbook of Strategic Management,* Michael A. Hitt, R. Edward Freeman, and Jeffrey S. Harrison, editors (Oxford, UK: Blackwell Publishers, 2001).

EXHIBIT 5–6
Key Resources across Functional Areas

Marketing

Firm's products-services: breadth of product line.
Concentration of sales in a few products or to a few customers.
Ability to gather needed information about markets.
Market share or submarket shares.
Product-service mix and expansion potential: life cycle of key products; profit-sales balance in product-service.
Channels of distribution: number, coverage, and control.
Effective sales organization: knowledge of customer needs.
Internet usage.
Product-service image, reputation, and quality.
Imaginativeness, efficiency, and effectiveness of sales promotion and advertising.
Pricing strategy and pricing flexibility.
Procedures for digesting market feedback and developing new products, services, or markets.
After-sale service and follow-up.
Goodwill—brand loyalty.

Financial and Accounting

Ability to raise short-term capital.
Ability to raise long-term capital; debt-equity.
Corporate-level resources (multibusiness firm).
Cost of capital relative to that of industry and competitors.
Tax considerations.
Relations with owners, investors, and stockholders.
Leverage position; capacity to utilize alternative financial strategies, such as lease or sale and leaseback.
Cost of entry and barriers to entry.
Price-earnings ratio.
Working capital; flexibility of capital structure.
Effective cost control; ability to reduce cost.
Financial size.
Efficiency and effectiveness of accounting system for cost, budget, and profit planning.

Production, Operations, Technical

Raw materials cost and availability, supplier relationships.
Inventory control systems; inventory turnover.
Location of facilities; layout and utilization of facilities.
Economies of scale.
Technical efficiency of facilities and utilization of capacity.
Effectiveness of subcontracting use.
Degree of vertical integration; value added and profit margin.
Efficiency and cost-benefit of equipment.
Effectiveness of operation control procedures: design, scheduling, purchasing, quality control, and efficiency.
Costs and technological competencies relative to those of industry and competitors.
Research and development—technology—innovation.
Patents, trademarks, and similar legal protection.

(continued)

EXHIBIT 5–6
continued

Personnel

Management personnel.
Employees' skill and morale.
Labor relations costs compared to those of industry and competitors.
Efficiency and effectiveness of personnel policies.
Effectiveness of incentives used to motivate performance.
Ability to level peaks and valleys of employment.
Employee turnover and absenteeism.
Specialized skills.
Experience.

Quality Management

Relationship with suppliers, customers.
Internal practices to enhance quality of products and services.
Procedures for monitoring quality.

Information Systems

Timeliness and accuracy of information about sales, operations, cash, and suppliers.
Relevance of information for tactical decisions.
Information to manage quality issues: customer service.
Ability of people to use the information that is provided.
Linkages to suppliers and customers.

Organization and General Management

Organizational structure.
Firm's image and prestige.
Firm's record in achieving objectives.
Organization of communication system.
Overall organizational control system (effectiveness and utilization).
Organizational climate; organizational culture.
Use of systematic procedures and techniques in decision making.
Top-management skill, capabilities, and interest.
Strategic planning system.
Intraorganizational synergy (multibusiness firms).

SWOT ANALYSIS

SWOT is an acronym for the internal Strengths and Weaknesses of a firm and the environmental Opportunities and Threats facing that firm. SWOT analysis is a widely used technique through which managers create a quick overview of a company's strategic situation. It is based on the assumption that an effective strategy derives from a sound "fit" between a firm's internal resources (strengths and weaknesses) and its external situation (opportunities and threats). A good fit maximizes a firm's strengths and opportunities and minimizes its weaknesses and threats. Accurately applied, this simple assumption has powerful implications for the design of a successful strategy.

Environmental industry analysis in Chapters 3 and 4 provides the information needed to identify opportunities and threats in a firm's environment, the first fundamental focus in SWOT analysis.

Opportunities

An *opportunity* is a major favorable situation in a firm's environment. Key trends are one source of opportunities. Identification of a previously overlooked market segment, changes in competitive or regulatory circumstances, technological changes, and improved buyer or supplier relationships could represent opportunities for the firm.

Threats

A *threat* is a major unfavorable situation in a firm's environment. Threats are key impediments to the firm's current or desired position. The entrance of new competitors, slow market growth, increased bargaining power of key buyers or suppliers, technological changes, and new or revised regulations could represent threats to a firm's success.

Understanding the key opportunities and threats facing a firm helps its managers identify realistic options from which to choose an appropriate strategy and clarifies the most effective niche for the firm. The second fundamental focus in SWOT analysis is the identification of internal strengths and weaknesses.

Strengths

A *strength* is a resource advantage relative to competitors and the needs of the markets a firm serves or expects to serve. It is a *distinctive competence* when it gives the firm a comparative advantage in the marketplace. Strengths arise from the resources and competencies available to the firm.

Weaknesses

A *weakness* is a limitation or deficiency in one or more resources or competencies relative to competitors that impedes a firm's effective performance.

The sheer size and level of Microsoft's user base have proven to be a key strength on which it built its aggressive entry into Internet services. Limited financial capacity was a weakness recognized by Southwest Airlines, which charted a selective route expansion strategy to build the best profit record in a deregulated airline industry.

SWOT analysis can be used in many ways to aid strategic analysis. The most common way is to use it as a logical framework guiding systematic discussion of a firm's resources and the basic alternatives that emerge from this resource-based view. What one manager sees as an opportunity, another may see as a potential threat. Likewise, a strength to one manager may be a weakness to another. Different assessments may reflect underlying power considerations within the firm or differing factual perspectives. Systematic analysis of these issues facilitates objective internal analysis.

The diagram in Exhibit 5–7 illustrates how SWOT analysis builds on the results of an RBV of a firm to aid strategic analysis. Key external opportunities and threats are systematically compared with internal resources and competencies—that is, strengths and weaknesses—in a structured approach. The objective is identification of one of four distinct patterns in the match between a firm's internal resources and external situation. Cell 1 is the most favorable situation; the firm faces several environmental opportunities and has numerous strengths that encourage pursuit of those opportunities. This situation suggests growth-oriented strategies to exploit the favorable match. America OnLine's intensive market development strategy in the online services market is the result of a favorable match of its strong technical expertise, early entry, and reputation resources with an opportunity for impressive market growth as millions of people joined the information highway in the last decade. Its continued strength in interactivity with Net-delivered media is currently a key component of AOL-Time Warner's new growth-oriented strategy in 2004.

EXHIBIT 5–7
SWOT Analysis
Diagram

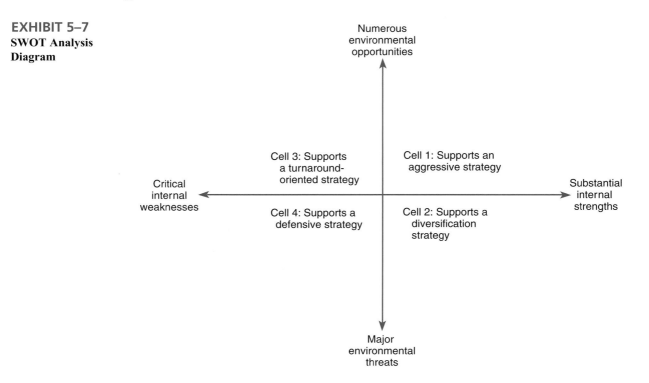

Cell 4 is the least favorable situation, with the firm facing major environmental threats from a weak resource position. This situation clearly calls for strategies that reduce or redirect involvement in the products or markets examined by means of SWOT analysis. Texas Instruments offers a good example of a Cell 4 firm. It was a sprawling maker of chips, calculators, laptop PCs, military electronics, and engineering software on a sickening slid toward oblivion just ten years ago. Its young CEO, Tom Engibous, reinvigorated the ailing electronics giant and turned it into one of the hottest plays in semiconductors by betting the company on an emerging class of chips known as digital signal processors (DSPs). The chips crunch vast streams of data for an array of digital gadgets, including modems and cellular phones. Engibous shed billions of dollars worth of assets to focus on DSPs, which he calls "the most important silicon technology of the next decade." TI now commands nearly half of the $4.4 billion global market for the most advanced DSPs, and it's the No. 1 chip supplier to the sizzling digital wireless phone market.

In Cell 2, a firm whose RBV has identified several key strengths, faces an unfavorable environment. In this situation, strategies would seek to redeploy those strong resources and competencies to build long-term opportunities in more opportunistic product markets. IBM, a dominant manufacturer of mainframes, servers, and PCs worldwide, has nurtured many strengths in computer-related and software-related markets for many years. Increasingly, however, it has had to address major threats that include product commoditization, pricing pressures, accelerated pace of innovation, and the like. Fortunately, Sam Palmisano's determined development of ISSC, better known now as IBM Global Services, has allowed IBM to build a long-term opportunity in more profitable growing markets of the next decade. In the last ten years since Palmisano ran it, Global Services has become the fastest-growing division of the company, its largest employer, and the keystone of IBM's strategic future. The group does everything from running a customer's IT department to consulting on legacy system upgrades to building custom supply-chain management applications. As IBM's hardware divisions struggle against price wars and commoditization and its software units fight to gain share beyond mainframes, it is Global Services that drives the company's growth.

A firm in Cell 3 faces impressive market opportunity but is constrained by weak internal resources. The focus of strategy for such a firm is eliminating the internal weaknesses so as to more effectively pursue the market opportunity. The AOL-Time Warner merger may well have afforded both companies a way to overcome key weaknesses keeping them from pursuing vast 21st-century, Internet-based opportunities. AOL lacks programming content and the ability to sell programming profitably over time. Time Warner is at a loss in managing the complexities of interactive media services.

SWOT analysis has been a framework of choice among many managers for a long time because of its simplicity and its portrayal of the essence of sound strategy formulation—matching a firm's opportunities and threats with its strengths and weaknesses. Central to making SWOT analysis effective is accurate internal analysis—the identification of specific strengths and weaknesses around which sound strategy can be built. One of the historical deficiencies of SWOT analysis was the tendency to rely on a very general, categorical assessment of internal capabilities. The resource-based view came to exist in part as a remedy to this void in the strategic management field. It is an excellent way to identify internal strengths and weaknesses and use that information to enhance the quality of a SWOT analysis. The RBV perspective was presented earlier in this chapter. While the conceptual appeal of the RBV is compelling, many managers remain comfortable with a functional approach to isolate and evaluate internal strengths and weaknesses. The next section describes the functional approach so that you will be aware of how management teams that don't use the RBV identify internal strengths and weaknesses.

While SWOT analysis offers simple, logical approaches to guide internal analysis, managers that endured the downsizing and reengineering of the last decade found the need for an approach that focused them even more narrowly on how work actually took place within their companies as they sought to meet customer needs. What these managers were responding to was the reality that producing goods or services and handling customers often necessitated the simultaneous involvement of multiple functions to be effective. They needed a way to look at their business as a series of activities that took place to create value for a customer—and to use this view as the framework to guide internal analysis. The value chain concept is one such framework.

VALUE CHAIN ANALYSIS

The term *value chain* describes a way of looking at a business as a chain of activities that transform inputs into outputs that customers value. Customer value derives from three basic sources: activities that differentiate the product, activities that lower its cost, and activities that meet the customer's need quickly. *Value chain analysis* (VCA) attempts to understand how a business creates customer value by examining the contributions of different activities within the business to that value.

VCA takes a process point of view: It divides (sometimes called disaggregates) the business into sets of activities that occur *within the business,* starting with the inputs a firm receives and finishing with the firm's products (or services) and after-sales service to customers. VCA attempts to look at its costs across the series of activities the business performs to determine where low-cost advantages or cost disadvantages exist. It looks at the attributes of each of these different activities to determine in what ways each activity that occurs between purchasing inputs and after-sales service helps differentiate the company's products and services. Proponents of VCA believe VCA allows managers to better

EXHIBIT 5–8
The Value Chain

Source: *Harvard Business School on Managing the Value Chain* (Cambridge: HBS Press, 2000).

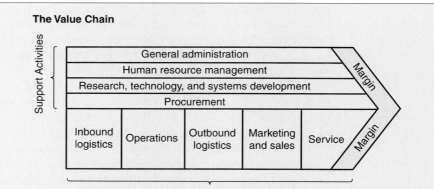

The Value Chain

Primary Activities

- **Inbound Logistics**—Activities, costs, and assets associated with obtaining fuel, energy, raw materials, parts components, merchandise, and consumable items from vendors; receiving, storing, and disseminating inputs from suppliers; inspection; and inventory management.
- **Operations**—Activities, costs, and assets associated with converting inputs into final product form (production, assembly, packaging, equipment maintenance, facilities, operations, quality assurance, environmental protection).
- **Outbound Logistics**—Activities, costs, and assets dealing with physically distributing the product to buyers (finished goods warehousing, order processing, order picking and packing, shipping, delivery vehicle operations).
- **Marketing and Sales**—Activities, costs, and assets related to sales force efforts, advertising and promotion, market research and planning, and dealer/distributor support.
- **Service**—Activities, costs, and assets associated with providing assistance to buyers, such as installation, spare parts delivery, maintenance and repair, technical assistance, buyer inquiries, and complaints.

Support Activities

- **General Administration**—Activities, costs, and assets relating to general management, accounting and finance, legal and regulatory affairs, safety and security, management information systems, and other "overhead" functions.
- **Human Resources Management**—Activities, costs, and assets associated with the recruitment, hiring, training, development, and compensation of all types of personnel; labor relations activities; development of knowledge-based skills.
- **Research, Technology, and Systems Development**—Activities, costs, and assets relating to product R&D, process R&D, process design improvement, equipment design, computer software development, telecommunications systems, computer-assisted design and engineering, new database capabilities, and development of computerized support systems.
- **Procurement**—Activities, costs, and assets associated with purchasing and providing raw materials, supplies, services, and outsourcing necessary to support the firm and its activities. Sometimes this activity is assigned as part of a firm's inbound logistic purchasing activities.

identify their firm's strengths and weaknesses by looking at the business as a process—a chain of activities—of what actually happens in the business rather than simply looking at it based on arbitrary organizational dividing lines or historical accounting protocol.

Exhibit 5–8 shows a typical value chain framework. It divides activities within the firm into two broad categories: primary activities and support activities. *Primary activities*

BusinessWeek Founder Fred Smith and executives running companies controlled by FedEx say they are planning a monumental shift in the FedEx mission. They are accelerating plans to focus on information systems that track and coordinate packages. They are seeking to "morph" themselves from being a transportation company into an information company.

FedEx already has one of the most heavily used websites on the Internet. Company management claims to have 1,500 in-house programmers writing more software code than almost any other non-software company. To complement package delivery, FedEx designs and operates high-tech warehouses and distribution systems for big manufacturers and retailers around the world. For almost two decades, FedEx has been investing massive amounts to develop software and create a giant digital network. FedEx has built corporate technology campuses around the world, and its electronic systems are directly linked via the Internet or otherwise to over 1 million customers worldwide. That system now allows FedEx to track packages on an hourly basis, but it also allows FedEx to predict future flow of goods and then rapidly refigure the information and logistical network to handle those flows.

"Moving an item from point A to point B is no longer a big deal," say James Barksdale, CEO of Netscape and early architect of FedEx's information strategies. "Having the information about that item, and where it is, and the best way to use it. . . . That is value. The companies that will be big winners will be the ones who can best maximize the value of these information systems." Where FedEx's value has long been built on giant airplanes and big trucks, founder Smith sees a time when it will be built on information, computers, and the allure of the FedEx brand name.

If it works, FedEx's value chain will shrink in areas involved with inbound and outbound operations—taking off and landing on the tarmac—and will expand in areas involved with zapping around the pristine and pilot-free world of cyberspace to manage a client's supply chain and its distribution network.

Source: "UPS vs. FedEx: Ground Wars," *BusinessWeek*, May 21, 2001.

(sometimes called *line* functions) are those involved in the physical creation of the product, marketing and transfer to the buyer, and after-sale support. *Support activities* (sometimes called *staff* or *overhead* functions) assist the firm as a whole by providing infrastructure or inputs that allow the primary activities to take place on an ongoing basis. The value chain includes a *profit margin* since a markup above the cost of providing a firm's value-adding activities is normally part of the price paid by the buyer—creating value that exceeds cost so as to generate a return for the effort.

Judgment is required across individual firms and different industries because what may be seen as a support activity in one firm or industry may be a primary activity in another. Computer operations might typically be seen as infrastructure support, for example, but may be seen as a primary activity in airlines, newspapers, or banks. Exhibit 5–9, Strategy in Action, describes how Federal Express reconceptualized its company using a value chain analysis that ultimately saw its information support become its primary activity and source of customer value.

Conducting a Value Chain Analysis

Identify Activities

The initial step in value chain analysis is to divide a company's operations into specific activities or business processes, usually grouping them similarly to the primary and support activity categories shown in Exhibit 5–9. Within each category, a firm typically performs a number of discrete activities that may represent key strengths or weaknesses. Service activities, for example, may include such discrete activities as installation, repair, parts distribution, and upgrading—any of which could be a major source of competitive

EXHIBIT 5–10   **The Difference between Traditional Cost Accounting and Activity-Based Cost Accounting**

Traditional Cost Accounting in a Purchasing Department		Activity-Based Cost Accounting in the Same Purchasing Department for Its "Procurement" Activities	
Wages and salaries	$175,000	Evaluate supplier capabilities	$ 67,875
Employee benefits	57,500	Process purchase orders	41,050
Supplies	3,250	Expedite supplier deliveries	11,750
Travel	1,200	Expedite internal processing	7,920
Depreciation	8,500	Check quality of items purchased	47,150
Other fixed charges	62,000	Check incoming deliveries against purchase orders	24,225
Miscellaneous operating expenses	12,625	Resolve problems	55,000
	$320,075	Internal administration	65,105
			$320,075

advantage or disadvantage. The manager's challenge at this point is to be very detailed attempting to "disaggregate" what actually goes on into numerous distinct, analyzable activities rather than settling for a broad, general categorization.

Allocate Costs

The next step is to attempt to attach costs to each discrete activity. Each activity in the value chain incurs costs and ties up time and assets. Value chain analysis requires managers to assign costs and assets to each activity, thereby providing a very different way of viewing costs than traditional cost accounting methods would produce. Exhibit 5–10 helps illustrate this distinction. Both approaches in Exhibit 5–10 tell us that the purchasing department (procurement activities) cost $320,150. The traditional method lets us see that payroll expenses are 73 percent [(175 + 57.5)/320] of our costs with "other fixed charges" the second largest cost, 19 percent [62/320] of the total procurement costs. VCA proponents would argue that the benefit of this information is limited. Their argument might be the following:

> With this information we could compare our procurement costs to key competitors, budgets, or industry averages, and conclude that we are better, worse, or equal. We could then ascertain that our "people" costs and "other fixed charges" cost are advantages, disadvantages, or "in line" with competitors. Managers could then argue to cut people, add people, or debate fixed overhead charges. However, they would get lost in what is really a budgetary debate without ever examining what it is those people do in accomplishing the procurement function, what value that provides, and how cost effective each activity is.

VCA proponents hold that the activity-based VCA approach would provide a more meaningful analysis of the procurement function's costs and consequent value-added. The activity-based side of Exhibit 5–10 shows that approximately 21 percent of the procurement cost or value-added involves evaluating supplier capabilities. A rather sizable cost, 20 percent, involves internal administration, with an additional 17 percent spent resolving problems and almost 15 percent spent on quality control efforts. VCA advocates see this information as being much more useful than traditional cost accounting information, especially when compared to the cost information of key competitors or other "benchmark" companies. VCA supporters might assert the following argument that the benefit of this activity-based information is substantial:

> Rather than analyzing just "people" and "other charges," we are now looking at meaningful categorizations of the work that procurement actually does. We see, for example, that a key value-added activity (and cost) involves "evaluating supplier capabilities." The amount spent on "internal administration" and "resolving problems" seems high, and may indicate a

weakness or area for improvement if the other activities' costs are in line and outcomes favorable. The bottom line is that this approach lets us look at what we actually "do" in the business—the specific activities—to create customer value, and that in turn allows more specific internal analysis than traditional, accounting-based cost categories.

Recognize the Difficulty in Activity-Based Cost Accounting   It is important to note that existing financial management and accounting systems in many firms are not set up to easily provide activity-based cost breakdowns. Likewise, in virtually all firms, the information requirements to support activity-based cost accounting can create redundant work because of the financial reporting requirements that may force firms to retain the traditional approach for financial statement purposes. The time and energy to change to an activity-based approach can be formidable, and still typically involves arbitrary cost allocation decisions trying to allocate selected asset or people costs across multiple activities in which they are involved. Challenges dealing with a cost-based use of VCA have not deterred use of the framework to identify sources of differentiation. Indeed, conducting a VCA to analyze competitive advantages that differentiate the firm is compatible with the RBV's examination of intangible assets and capabilities as sources of distinctive competence.

Identify the Activities That Differentiate the Firm

Scrutinizing a firm's value chain may not only reveal cost advantages or disadvantages, it may also bring attention to several sources of differentiation advantage relative to competitors. Dell Computer considers its Internet-based after-sales service (activities) to be far superior to any competitor's. Dell knows it has cost advantage because of the time and expense replicating this activity would take. But Dell considers it an even more important source of value to the customer because of the importance customers place on this activity, which differentiates Dell from many similarly priced competitors. Likewise Federal Express, as we noted earlier, considers its information management skills to have become the core competence and essence of the company because of the value these skills allow FedEx to provide its customers and the importance they in turn place on such skills. Exhibit 5–11 suggests some factors for assessing primary and support activities' differentiation and contribution.

Examine the Value Chain

Once the value chain has been documented, managers need to identify the activities that are critical to buyer satisfaction and market success. It is those activities that deserve major scrutiny in an internal analysis. Three considerations are essential at this stage in the value chain analysis. First, the company's basic mission needs to influence managers' choice of the activities they examine in detail. If the company is focused on being a low-cost provider, then management attention to lower costs should be very visible; and missions built around commitment to differentiation should find managers spending more on activities that are differentiation cornerstones. Retailer Wal-Mart focuses intensely on costs related to inbound logistics, advertising, and loyalty to build its competitive advantage (see Exhibit 5–3), while Nordstrom builds its distinct position in retailing by emphasizing sales and support activities on which they spend twice the retail industry average. The application of value chain analysis to explore Volkswagen's strategic situation in 2003–2004 is described in Exhibit 5–12, Strategy in Action.

Second, the nature of value chains and the relative importance of the activities within them vary by industry. Lodging firms like Holiday Inn's major costs and concerns involve operational activities—it provides its service instantaneously at each location—and marketing activities, while having minimal concern for outbound

EXHIBIT 5–11   Possible Factors for Assessing Sources of Differentiation in Primary and Support Activities

Source: Adapted from *Harvard Business School on Managing the Value Chain* (Cambridge: HBS Press, 2000).

Support Activities

- Capability to identify new-product market opportunities and potential environmental threats
- Quality of the strategic planning system to achieve corporate objectives
- Coordination and integration of all value chain activities among organizational subunits
- Ability to obtain relatively low-cost funds for capital expenditures and working capital
- Level of information systems support in making strategic and routine decisions
- Timely and accurate management information on general and competitive environments
- Relationships with public policymakers and interest groups
- Public image and corporate citizenship

General Administration

- Effectiveness of procedures for recruiting, training, and promoting all levels of employees
- Appropriateness of reward systems for motivating and challenging employees
- A work environment that minimizes absenteeism and keeps turnover at desirable levels
- Relations with trade unions
- Active participation by managers and technical personnel in professional organizations
- Levels of employee motivation and job satisfaction

Human Resource Management

- Success of research and development activities in leading to product and process innovations
- Quality of working relationships between R&D personnel and other departments
- Timeliness of technology development activities in meeting critical deadlines
- Quality of laboratories and other facilities
- Qualification and experience of laboratory technicians and scientists
- Ability of work environment to encourage creativity and innovation

Technology Development

- Development of alternate sources for inputs to minimize dependence on a single supplier
- Procurement of raw materials (1) on a timely basis, (2) at lowest possible cost, (3) at acceptable levels of quality
- Procedures for procurement of plant, machinery, and buildings
- Development of criteria for lease-versus-purchase decisions
- Good, long-term relationships with reliable suppliers

Procurement

Profit Margin

Inbound Logistics	Operations	Outbound Logistics	Marketing and Sales	Service
■ Soundness of material and inventory control systems ■ Efficiency of raw material warehousing activities	■ Productivity of equipment compared to that of key competitors ■ Appropriate automation of production processes ■ Effectiveness of production control systems to improve quality and reduce costs ■ Efficiency of plant layout and work-flow design	■ Timeliness and efficiency of delivery of finished goods and services ■ Efficiency of finished goods warehousing activities	■ Effectiveness of market research to identify customer segments and needs ■ Innovation in sales promotion and advertising ■ Evaluation of alternate distribution channels ■ Motivation and competence of sales force ■ Development of an image of quality and a favorable reputation ■ Extent of brand loyalty among customers ■ Extent of market dominance within the market segment or overall market	■ Means to solicit customer input for product improvements ■ Promptness of attention to customer complaints ■ Appropriateness of warranty and guarantee policies ■ Quality of customer education and training ■ Ability to provide replacement parts and repair services

Profit Margin

Primary Activities

Strategy in Action
Value Chain Analysis Explains Volkswagen's Reasons for Success and Concern

Exhibit 5–12

BusinessWeek Volkswagen CEO Ferdinand Piëch had every reason to feel satisfied. The Austrian engineer and scion of one of Europe's most noted automotive dynasties was less than a year from retirement as chief of the German carmaker. As he looked back, Piëch could boast of one of the great turnarounds in automotive history. Since taking the top job at the Wolfsburg headquarters in 1993, his engineering brilliance had helped resurrect Volkswagen quality and turn models such as the Golf and Passat into all-time best-sellers. Piëch's relaunch of the Beetle cemented VW's hold in the U.S. market. Only VW had successfully revived a communist-era carmaker, Skoda of the Czech Republic. In 2001, as the global car industry lurches through a stressful year, VW saw profits grow above 2000 levels, when they more than doubled, to $1.8 billion, on sales of $76 billion.

Yet Piëch was stressed. Value chain analysis suggested two key value activities had driven his success—product development and operations. It also suggested that two other activities were becoming serious potential drains on the value chain and value he had so meticulously driven—human resource management and marketing and sales.

PRODUCT DEVELOPMENT

Piëch was driven. Unlike many other auto chiefs, he called the shots on product design and engineering. And if you worked for Dr. Piëch, you had better get it right. In Wolfsburg, executives joked that PEP, the acronym for the product development process (*Produktentwicklungsprozess*) really stands for *Piëch entscheidet persönlich*—Piëch decides himself. And he did so fast. He is said to have sketched out the Audi's all-wheel-drive system on the back of an envelope.

Without question, those achievements have been considerable. Volkswagen's four main brands—VW, Audi, Seat, and Skoda—have taken 19% of the European auto market, a gain of some three points in eight years, mostly at the expense of General Motors Corp. and Ford. Not bad for a company that eight years ago suffered from quality problems and a paucity of hit models. In South America, VW vehicles account for one-quarter of car sales, and in China, one-half. The top VW brands in the United States are the Jetta, Passat, and the new Beetle, a remake of the humble bug so beloved of 60s youth. Part of VW success lies in its quirky features. At night, the dashboard instruments the driver looks at, such as the speedometer and clock, light up in red, while those the driver touches, such as the radio, are backlit in blue. "It gives the vehicle some soul, which many of VW's competitors lack horribly," says Wes Brown, a consultant at Nextrend Inc., a Thousand Oaks (Calif.) auto-research firm.

OPERATIONS

When Piëch wasn't drawing up the plans, he was examining them with a gimlet eye. No screaming, of course: That was not the way for Piëch, an Austrian blueblood. One former transmission-plant manager said Piëch would tour the factory quietly, reviewing production data sheets and zeroing in instantly on any numbers suggesting something was amiss in the manufacturing process. "He's the only person whose very presence on the floor would make my stomach begin to hurt," says this manager.

Terrifying, yet inspiring. Under Piëch's tutelage, VW sweated the small stuff. Check this out, says one rival exec: On VW models, the gap between body panels—say between the front fender and wheel panel—had been cut to 1 millimeter. That puts them in a league with the industry's best.

HUMAN RESOURCE MANAGEMENT

In 1993, to buy labor peace, Piëch cut the workweek at VW's German plants from 35 hours to 28.8. That saved 30,000 jobs. But now VW workers can make upwards of $34 an hour. Piëch tried to push through a plan to lower the base wages of new German workers and link them to output instead of hours as this story was published. If this doesn't succeed, VW threatens to put new projects in places such as the Czech Republic, where wages are less than one-third German levels. Cutting such a deal is turning into a hard slog. The unions concede they need to be more flexible. But they are resisting management's demands to increase the workweek to more than 40 hours during peak production without paying overtime.

And investors frustrated with a low stock-PE ratio cannot expect a swift boost to the stock price. The government of Lower Saxony, the biggest investor, worries more about jobs than shareholder value. Five of VW's seven German factories are located in Lower Saxony, and they're among the least productive in Europe. According to World Markets Research Center in London, production at the Wolfsburg plant runs at 46 cars per worker per year, compared with 101 at Nissan Motor Co.'s British factory in Sunderland.

(continued)

MARKETING AND SALES

VW also had gaps in its product lineup. It had nothing to offer in the category of compact minivans—the scaled-down versions of minivans that are popular in Europe. A sport utility vehicle was not scheduled to come out until 2003. "We're [also] missing some niche models—sports car, roadster, another convertible," says Jürgen Lehmann, manager of the Autohaus Moltke dealership in Stuttgart. VW had to sort out these issues while the competition gets tougher.

Bottomline, VW's value chain presents interesting challenges for Piëch's successor, Bernd Pischetsrieder. He inherits extraordinary strengths in product development and manufacturing operations. But for all of the success of the last decade, and an impressive market presence worldwide, he faces emerging value chain weaknesses in human resource management cost considerations and product line gaps in marketing and sales.

Source: "Volkswagen," *BusinessWeek,* July 23, 2001.

logistics. Yet for a distributor, such as the food distributor PYA, inbound and outbound logistics are the most critical area. Major retailers like Wal-Mart have built value advantages focusing on purchasing and inbound logistics while the most successful personal computer companies have built via sales, outbound logistics, and service through the mail order process.

Third, the relative importance of value activities can vary by a company's position in a broader value system that includes the value chains of its upstream suppliers and downstream customers or partners involved in providing products or services to end users. A producer of roofing shingles depends heavily on the downstream activities of wholesale distributors and building supply retailers to reach roofing contractors and do-it-yourselfers. Maytag manufactures its own appliances, sells them through independent distributors, and provides warranty service to the buyer. Sears outsources the manufacture of its appliances while it promotes its brand name—Kenmore—and handles all sales and service.

As these examples suggest, it is important that managers take into account their level of vertical integration when comparing their cost structure for activities on their value chain to those of key competitors. Comparing a fully integrated rival with a partially integrated one requires adjusting for the scope of activities performed to achieve meaningful comparison. It also suggests the need for examining costs associated with activities provided by upstream or downstream companies; these activities ultimately determine comparable, final costs to end users. Said another way, one company's comparative cost disadvantage (or advantage) may emanate more from activities undertaken by upstream or downstream "partners" than from activities under the direct control of that company—therefore suggesting less of a relative advantage or disadvantage within the company's direct value chain.

Compare to Competitors

The final basic consideration when applying value chain analysis is the need to have a meaningful comparison to use when evaluating a value activity as a strength or weakness. Value chain analysis is most effective when comparing the value chains or activities of key competitors. Whether using the value chain approach or an examination of functional areas, or both approaches, the strategist's next step in a systematic internal analysis is to compare the firm's status with meaningful standards to determine which of its value activities are strengths or weaknesses. Four sources of meaningful standards for evaluating internal factors and value activities are discussed in the next section.

INTERNAL ANALYSIS: MAKING MEANINGFUL COMPARISONS

Managers need objective standards to use when examining internal resources and value-building activities. Whether applying the RBV, SWOT analysis, or the value chain approach, strategists rely on four basic perspectives to evaluate where their firm stacks up on its internal capabilities. These four perspectives are discussed in this section.

Comparison with Past Performance

Strategists use the firm's historical experience as a basis for evaluating internal factors. Managers are most familiar with the internal capabilities and problems of their firm because they have been immersed in its financial, marketing, production, and R&D activities. Not surprisingly, a manager's assessment of whether a certain internal factor—such as production facilities, sales organization, financial capacity, control systems, or key personnel—is a strength or a weakness will be strongly influenced by his or her experience in connection with that factor. In the capital-intensive airline industry, for example, debt capacity is a strategic internal factor. Delta Airlines managers view Delta's debt-equity ratio of less than 1.9 brought on by its acquisition of PanAm's international operations as a real weakness limiting its flexibility to invest in facilities because it maintained a ratio less than 0.6 for over 20 years. Continental Airlines managers, on the other hand, view Continental's much higher 3.5 debt-equity ratio as a growing strength, because it is down 50 percent from its 7.0 level five years earlier.

Although historical experience can provide a relevant evaluation framework, strategists must avoid tunnel vision in making use of it. NEC, Japan's IBM, initially dominated Japan's PC market with a 70 percent market share using a proprietary hardware system, much higher screen resolution, powerful distribution channels, and a large software library from third-party vendors. Far from worried, Hajime Ikeda, manager of NEC's planning division at the time, was quoted as saying: "We don't hear complaints from our users." By 2001, IBM, Apple, and Compaq filled the shelves in Japan's famous consumer electronics district, Akihabara. Hiroki Kamata, president of a Japanese computer research firm, reported that Japan's PC market, worth over $25 billion in 2001, saw Apple and IBM compatibles each having more market share than NEC because of better technology, software, and the restrictions created by NEC's proprietary technology. Clearly, using only historical experience as a basis for identifying strengths and weaknesses can prove dangerously inaccurate.

Stages of Industry Evolution

The requirements for success in industry segments change over time. Strategists can use these changing requirements, which are associated with different stages of industry evolution, as a framework for identifying and evaluating the firm's strengths and weaknesses.

Exhibit 5–13 depicts four stages of industry evolution and the typical changes in functional capabilities that are often associated with business success at each of these stages. The early development of a product market, for example, entails minimal growth in sales, major R&D emphasis, rapid technological change in the product, operating losses, and a need for sufficient resources or slack to support a temporarily unprofitable operation. Success at this introduction stage may be associated with technical skill, with being first in new markets, or with having a marketing advantage that creates widespread awareness. Radio Shack's initial success with its TRS–80 home computer was based in part on its ability to gain widespread exposure and acceptance in the ill-defined home computer market via the large number of existing Radio Shack outlets throughout the country.

EXHIBIT 5–13   **Sources of Distinctive Competence at Different Stages of Industry Evolution**

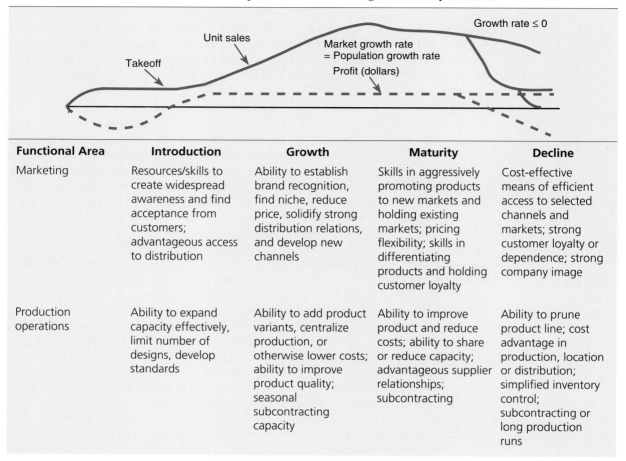

Functional Area	Introduction	Growth	Maturity	Decline
Marketing	Resources/skills to create widespread awareness and find acceptance from customers; advantageous access to distribution	Ability to establish brand recognition, find niche, reduce price, solidify strong distribution relations, and develop new channels	Skills in aggressively promoting products to new markets and holding existing markets; pricing flexibility; skills in differentiating products and holding customer loyalty	Cost-effective means of efficient access to selected channels and markets; strong customer loyalty or dependence; strong company image
Production operations	Ability to expand capacity effectively, limit number of designs, develop standards	Ability to add product variants, centralize production, or otherwise lower costs; ability to improve product quality; seasonal subcontracting capacity	Ability to improve product and reduce costs; ability to share or reduce capacity; advantageous supplier relationships; subcontracting	Ability to prune product line; cost advantage in production, location or distribution; simplified inventory control; subcontracting or long production runs

The strengths necessary for success change in the growth stage. Rapid growth brings new competitors into the product market. At this stage, such factors as brand recognition, product differentiation, and the financial resources to support both heavy marketing expenses and the effect of price competition on cash flow can be key strengths. IBM entered the personal computer market in the growth stage and was able to rapidly become the market leader with a strategy based on its key strengths in brand awareness and possession of the financial resources needed to support consumer advertising. Radio Shack discontinued its TRS–80 due to IBM's strength. Within a few years, however, IBM lost that lead in the next stage as speed in distribution and cost structures became the key success factors—strengths for Dell and several mail order–oriented computer assemblers.

As the industry moves through a shakeout phase and into the maturity stage, industry growth continues, but at a decreasing rate. The number of industry segments expands, but technological change in product design slows considerably. As a result, competition usually becomes more intense, and promotional or pricing advantages and differentiation become key internal strengths. Technological change in process design becomes intense as the many competitors seek to provide the product in the most efficient manner. Where R&D was critical in the introduction stage, efficient production is now crucial to

EXHIBIT 5–13 *continued*

Functional Area	Introduction	Growth	Maturity	Decline
Finance	Resources to support high net cash overflow and initial losses; ability to use leverage effectively	Ability to finance rapid expansion, to have net cash outflows but increasing profits; resources to support product improvements	Ability to generate and redistribute increasing net cash inflows; effective cost control systems	Ability to reuse or liquidate unneeded equipment; advantage in cost of facilities; control system accuracy; streamlined management control
Personnel	Flexibility in staffing and training new management; existence of employees with key skills in new products or markets	Existence of an ability to add skilled personnel; motivated and loyal workforce	Ability to cost effectively, reduce workforce, increase efficiency	Capacity to reduce and reallocate personnel; cost advantage
Engineering and research and development	Ability to make engineering changes, have technical bugs in product and process resolved	Skill in quality and new feature development; ability to start developing successor product	Ability to reduce costs, develop variants, differentiate products	Ability to support other grown areas or to apply product to unique customer needs
Key functional area and strategy focus	Engineering: market penetration	Sales: consumer loyalty; market share	Production efficiency; successor products	Finance; maximum investment recovery

continued success in the broader industry segments. Ford's emphasis on quality control and modern, efficient production has helped it prosper in the maturing U.S. auto industry, while General Motors, which pays almost 50 percent more than Ford to produce a comparable car, continues to decline.

When the industry moves into the decline stage, strengths and weaknesses center on cost advantages, superior supplier or customer relationships, and financial control. Competitive advantage can exist at this stage, at least temporarily, if a firm serves gradually shrinking markets that competitors are choosing to leave.

Exhibit 5–13 is a rather simple model of the stages of industry evolution. These stages can and do vary from the model. What should be borne in mind is that the relative importance of various determinants of success differs across the stages of industry evolution. Thus, the state of that evolution must be considered in internal analysis. Exhibit 5–13 suggests dimensions that are particularly deserving of in-depth consideration when a company profile is being developed.

Benchmarking—Comparison with Competitors

A major focus in determining a firm's resources and competencies is comparison with existing (and potential) competitors. Firms in the same industry often have different marketing skills, financial resources, operating facilities and locations, technical know-how, brand images, levels of integration, managerial talent, and so on. These different internal resources can become relative strengths (or weaknesses) depending on the strategy a firm chooses. In choosing a strategy, managers should compare the firm's key internal capabilities with those of its rivals, thereby isolating its key strengths and weaknesses.

In the home appliance industry, for example, Sears and General Electric are major rivals. Sears's principal strength is its retail network. For GE, distribution—through independent franchised dealers—has traditionally been a relative weakness. GE's possession of the financial resources needed to support modernized mass production has enabled it to maintain both cost and technological advantages over its rivals, particularly Sears. This major strength for GE is a relative weakness for Sears, which depends solely on subcontracting to produce its Kenmore appliances. On the other hand, maintenance and repair service are important in the appliance industry. Historically, Sears has had strength in this area because it maintains fully staffed service components and spreads the costs of components over numerous departments at each retail location. GE, on the other hand, has had to depend on regional service centers and on local contracting with independent service firms by its independent local dealers. Among the internal factors that Sears and GE must consider in developing a strategy are distribution networks, technological capabilities, operating costs, and service facilities. Managers in both organizations have built successful strategies yet those strategies are quite different. Benchmarking each other, they have identified ways to build on relative strengths while avoiding dependence on capabilities at which the other firm excels.

Benchmarking, comparing the way "our" company performs a specific activity with a competitor or other company doing the same thing, has become a central concern of managers in quality commitment companies worldwide. Particularly as the value chain framework has taken hold in structuring internal analysis, managers seek to systematically benchmark the costs and results of the smallest value activities against relevant competitors or other useful standards because it has proven to be an effective way to continuously improve that activity. The ultimate objective in benchmarking is to identify the "best practices" in performing an activity, to learn how lower costs, fewer defects, or other outcomes linked to excellence are achieved. Companies committed to benchmarking attempt to isolate and identify where their costs or outcomes are out of line with what the best practicers of a particular activity experience (competitors and noncompetitors) and then attempt to change their activities to achieve the new best practices standard.

Comparison with key competitors can prove useful in ascertaining whether their internal capabilities on these and other factors are strengths or weaknesses. Significant favorable differences (existing or expected) from competitors are potential cornerstones of a firm's strategy. Moreover, through comparison with major competitors, a firm may avoid strategic commitments that it cannot competitively support. Exhibit 5–14, Strategy in Action, shows how UPS used competitor comparison to assess its strengths and weaknesses in the package transportation industry.

Comparison with Success Factors in the Industry

Industry analysis (see Chapter 3) involves identifying the factors associated with successful participation in a given industry. As was true for the evaluation methods discussed above, the key determinants of success in an industry may be used to identify a firm's internal strengths and weaknesses. By scrutinizing industry competitors, as well as customer needs, vertical industry structure, channels of distribution, costs, barriers

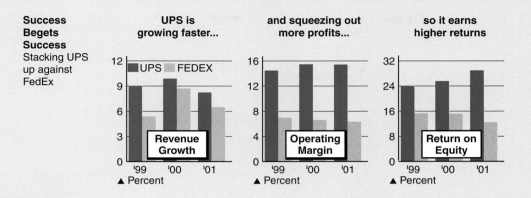

Success Begets Success Stacking UPS up against FedEx

UPS is growing faster...

and squeezing out more profits...

so it earns higher returns

Revenue Growth — ▲ Percent

Operating Margin — ▲ Percent

Return on Equity — ▲ Percent

Data: Banc of America Securities ©BW

BusinessWeek Over the past two years, the company has quietly shed its image as the slowpoke of shipping. Be it e-tailing frenzy or dot-com crash, UPS has captured customers by bombarding them with choices: fast flights versus cheap ground delivery, simple shipping or a panoply of manufacturing, warehousing, and supply-chain services. In the United States and several foreign markets, UPS has grabbed a commanding lead over FedEx—and not just in everyday package delivery but in the New Economy services such as logistics. In North America, UPS has even snagged the distinction of preferred carrier to the Web generation: The company handles 36% of all online purchases, versus 13% for FedEx. "UPS is doing things in e-commerce that other companies are just starting to talk about," says Jack R. Staff, chief economist at Zona Research in Redwood City, Calif.

The ascent of UPS charts a reversal of fortune in one of the fiercest rivalries in Corporate America. It was FedEx, after all, that pioneered both overnight delivery of packages and the ability to track their journey using computers. These 1970s' era innovations rocked the shipping industry and helped set the stage for the Internet Revolution of the 1990s. Even now, FedEx rules in certain areas of air freight. Its carefully burnished brand still says "absolutely, positively" to thousands of loyal customers—and not without reason. FedEx is one of America's great success stories, extolled for its customer service.

In the view of many analysts and industry execs, however, UPS now has a pronounced advantage in several hotly contested areas. In addition to its overwhelming lead in ground shipping and its online triumphs, UPS can point to a logistics business that is growing by 40% a year. FedEx is struggling to reverse a decline in this area.

Even in sectors where FedEx still rules, UPS is catching up quickly. FedEx has a commanding lead in the profitable overnight service, for example, delivering more than 3 million such packages daily in 200-plus countries and accounting for 39% of the market. UPS is No. 2, with 2.2 million overnight packages—but its volume has been growing faster than FedEx's for at least three years. In 2000, UPS's overnight business grew at 8%, compared with FedEx's 3.6%. And UPS's operating margin on its domestic air-express service is higher—24% versus 6%—according to Gary H. Yablon, a transportation analyst at Credit Suisse First Boston.

So what accounts for UPS's growth in overnight? The company trumpets its decision in 1999 to integrate overnight delivery into its vast ground-transportation network. UPS, like FedEx, still uses planes to make most such deliveries. But in the past two years, its logisticians have also figured out how to make quick mid-distance deliveries—as far as 500 miles in one night—by truck, which is much less expensive than by air. As a result, UPS's overall cost per package is $6.65, compared with FedEx's $11.89, according to CSFB. Even though FedEx also uses trucks for short hauls, "UPS has a real cost advantage," says John D. Kasarda, director of the University of North Carolina's Frank Hawkins Kenan Institute of Private Enterprise and a former FedEx consultant.

UPS's core strength is its fleet of 152,000 brown trucks, which reach virtually every address in the United States—and increasingly, the world. FedEx has belatedly begun to build its own home-delivery system. But the cost of duplicating a system UPS has spent nearly 100 years building could prove prohibitive. And with $3 billion in cash on

(continued)

hand, UPS could easily wage a price war against FedEx, which isn't generating any spare cash. "This is a game FedEx can't win," says Peter V. Coleman, a transportation analyst at Bank of America Securities. That leaves FedEx dependent on an air-delivery system that is increasingly expensive to operate.

	UPS	FedEx
Founded	1907	1971
Chairman	James P. Kelly	Frederick W. Smith
Headquarters	Atlanta, Ga.	Memphis, Tenn.
2000 Revenue	$29.77 billion	$18.3 billion
Net Income	$2.93 billion	$688 million
Employees	359,000	215,000
Daily Package Volume	13.2 million	5 million
Fleet	152,500 trucks, 560 planes	43,500 trucks, 662 planes

	Unit Cost	Unit Profit	Operating Margin	Avg Daily Volume
Air Deliveries, U.S.				
FedEx	$15.27	$0.93	6%	2,924,000
UPS	$14.60	$3.76	22%	2,162,000
Ground Deliveries, U.S.				
FedEx	$4.77	$0.68	13%	1,541,000
UPS	$4.95	$0.61	11%	10,945,000
Overall Average, including International				
FedEx	$11.89	$0.85	7%	4,788,000
UPS	$6.65	$1.17	15%	14,236,000

Data: Credit Suisse First Boston

to entry, availability of substitutes, and suppliers, a strategist seeks to determine whether a firm's current internal capabilities represent strengths or weaknesses in new competitive arenas. The discussion in Chapter 3 provides a useful framework—five industry forces—against which to examine a firm's potential strengths and weaknesses. General Cinema Corporation, the largest U.S. movie theater operator, determined that its internal skills in marketing, site analysis, creative financing, and management of geographically dispersed operations were key strengths relative to major success factors in the soft-drink bottling industry. This assessment proved accurate. Within 10 years after it entered the soft-drink bottling industry, General Cinema became the largest franchised bottler of soft drinks in the United States, handling Pepsi, 7UP, Dr Pepper, and Sunkist. Exhibit 5–15, Strategy in Action, describes how Avery Dennison used industry evolution benchmarking versus 3M to create a new, successful strategy.

Summary

This chapter looked at several ways managers achieve greater objectivity and rigor as they analyze their company's internal capabilities. Managers often start their internal analysis with questions like: "How well is the current strategy working? What is our current situation? Or what are our strengths and weaknesses?" The resource-based view provides a key, fundamental framework for analyzing firm success based on the firm's internal resources and competencies. *SWOT analysis,* a widely used approach to internal analysis, provides a logical way to apply the results of an RBV. Managers frequently use RBV and SWOT analysis to introduce realism and greater objectivity into their internal analysis. This chapter also described how insightful managers look at their business as a chain of activities that add value creating the products or services they sell—this is called *value chain analysis.* Managers who use value chain analysis to understand the value structure within

Strategy in Action
Avery Dennison Uses Benchmarking and Stage of Industry Evaluation
to Turn Weakness into Strength

Exhibit 5–15

BusinessWeek Avery Dennison has long made adhesives and what it calls "sticky papers" for business customers. Ten years ago, AD decided to take on 3M with its own version of 3M's highly successful Post-It notes and Scotch transparent tape.

How frequently did you buy Avery Notes and Avery Tape? You probably have never heard of them, right? That is because Avery was beat up in that market by 3M and AD exited the business after just a few years. Key strengths, distribution and brand name, that 3M used to build those products were major weaknesses at AD. Plus, in President Charles Miller's way of viewing it, 3M remained aggressive and true to an innovative culture to back its products while AD had grown rusty and "me too" rather than being the innovator it had traditionally been with pressure-sensitive

papers. So faced with considerable weakness competing against a major threat, Miller refocused AD on getting innovative in areas of traditional technical strength.

Today, AD has 30 percent of its sales from products introduced in the past five years. It has half the market for adhesive paper stock and 40 percent of the market for coated paper films for package labels. Says Miller, "We believe in market evolution. The best way to control a market is to invent it. With innovative products, superstores aren't able to squeeze margins, as they can in commodity products." New products now pour out of AD labs to position AD strengths against early life cycle stage opportunities.

Source: "The Business Week 50," *BusinessWeek,* March 23, 2001.

their firm's activities and look at the value system, which also includes upstream suppliers and downstream partners and buyers, often gain very meaningful insights into their company's strategic resources, competencies, and options. Finally, this chapter covered four ways objectivity and realism are enhanced when managers use meaningful standards for comparison regardless of the particular analytical framework they employ in internal analysis. This chapter is followed by an appendix covering traditional financial analysis to serve as a refresher and reminder about this basic internal analysis tool.

When matched with management's environmental analyses and mission priorities, the process of internal analysis provides the critical foundation for strategy formulation. Armed with an accurate, thorough, and timely internal analysis, managers are in a better position to formulate effective strategies. The next chapter describes basic strategy alternatives that any firm may consider.

Questions for Discussion

1. Describe SWOT analysis as a way to guide internal analysis. How does this approach reflect the basic strategic management process?

2. What is the resource-based view of the firm? Give examples of three different types of resources.

3. What are three characteristics that make resources more, or less, valuable? Provide an example of each.

4. Apply SWOT analysis to yourself and your career aspirations. What are your major strengths and weaknesses? How might you use your knowledge of these strengths and weaknesses to develop your future career plans?

5. Why do you think value chain analysis has become a preferred approach to guide internal analysis? What are its strengths? Its weaknesses?

Chapter 5 Discussion Case

BusinessWeek

Gap's Internal Analysis: 2002

1 "Give a little bit. Give a little bit of your love to me." So goes the holiday jingle featured in Gap's latest ubiquitous ad campaign. How apt. The fast-growth retailer that Wall Street loved in the 1990s is trying awfully hard to rekindle the old flame.

2 Things sure have changed. Today, "it's awfully easy to hate this company," says Richard Jaffe, an analyst at UBS Warburg. Harsh words. But for the past 18 months, San Francisco-based Gap (GPS) has been disappointing the Street, mainly because it faltered on the most critical piece of the apparel-retail puzzle—fashion. With so many competitors selling the kind of snappy casual clothes that Gap and its Banana Republic and Old Navy offshoots were famous for, the retailer decided it was time for a new approach. But the trendier offerings seemed to turn off mainstream shoppers. Now, the majority of some 29 analysts who cover the company have hold or sell ratings on the stock.

3 However, patient investors might want to look past the dismal news in the next several months and instead focus on how Gap will do next year, say a handful of analysts who recommend its stock. These Gap followers believe that the worst may be over for the retailer because the company is getting a handle on costs and inventory—and has some appealing new fashions for fall 2002. The stock look cheap enough, trading around $13 a share—the lowest since late 1997.

4 BRIGHTER FALL? Over the next 12 months, the clothing retailer will likely have to pull back even more on expansion plans, close underperforming stores, and shrink the size of its larger stores. Gap's management team, headed by retailing guru Mickey Drexler, has publicly acknowledged these weaknesses and the necessity to make changes. Even as many lament the company's recent decline, some analysts still have faith in Drexler's ability to turn Gap around.

5 "I believe in the viability of the brands and the opportunity in the next 12 to 18 months to demonstrate incremental improvement in results," says UBS Warburg's Jaffe. He expects the company's fall 2002 lines to show significant improvement from the too-trendy offerings that will still litter the shelves for most of next year. Jaffe says Gap's ability to tweak offerings to appeal to a broader population is probably still intact.

6 The past several quarters of fashion misfires have been hard lessons for Drexler. But Gap appears to have become more disciplined in ways that will help it get through a few more quarters of disappointing sales. "Into the late '90s, Gap didn't have much use for operational controls. But now that product is falling off, they do," says Kindra Devaney, an analyst with Fulcrum Global Partners.

7 TRIMMING GROWTH. Gap declined to comment for this article. The company, which operates more than 4,000 stores nationwide, used to stuff its shelves with inventory, but it has been paring back over the past year, Devaney says. Its balance sheet has become stronger, as cash flow has increased as less is spent on inventory. "Gap is healthier today than it was 12 to 18 months ago," she says. By sometime in mid-2002, she expects the stock to rise to her price target of $16 a share, a 23% jump from where it trades now, as sales at comparable stores (same Gap-owned stores open at least a year) improve and margins start picking up.

8 Gap also is addressing criticism that it has opened too many new stores. It's pulling back substantially—to 5% to 7% store growth in 2001, from a previously promised 17%. The company expects similar growth in 2002. "They've been taking a look at the big stores and trying to maximize production and downsize their selling footage," Devaney says. Capital expenditures, mainly used for new-store growth, have also come down—to about $1.1 billion this year, from $1.8 billion last year. Gap projects a $650 million capital-spending budget for 2002.

9 If Gap follows through on these plans, momentum in the stock could build quickly. As Gap is the biggest specialty-apparel retailer, with a market cap of $11 billion-plus, a lot of investors are waiting to jump back into it. "Obviously we're keeping an eye on it. I think it has the potential to be a really interesting story," says Angela Auchey Kohler, portfolio manager at Federated Investors.

10   HUGE DISAPPOINTMENT. She's not ready to buy Gap stock just yet, but she's encouraged by the company's ability to control inventory and its brand identities. Kohler says she's waiting to see one month of improved comparable-store sales: "That's all it takes for the stock to shoot up."

11   The going could still be rough in the near term. Gap's fiscal third-quarter sales, ended Nov. 3, were a huge disappointment, declining 17% at stores open at least one year, versus an 8% decrease during the same period last year. The company's reported net loss for the quarter of $46 million before a special charge of $131 million was driven by a decline in gross margins and weaker sales. Compare that to last year's third quarter, when the Gap earned $186 million or 21 cents a share.

12   The fourth quarter, the most important for most retailers, will likely be ugly too, if November is any indication. Total sales for the month fell 14%, to $1.2 billion, compared with last year's $1.4 billion. On average, analysts are expecting Gap to lose 11 cents per share in the fourth quarter.

13   FOREIGN INVASION. Eric Jemetz, senior equity analyst at New Amsterdam Partners, wants to see a turnaround at Old Navy, the Gap unit that has slipped the most in sales, before he considers buying Gap stock again. He also wants to see that Gap can compete abroad and against international retailers moving into the U.S. For one, Swedish-based H&M, which has opened stores in the Northeast, will increase its presence in the states substantially in 2002. "We want to see [Gap] acknowledge that they have this competition coming," Jemetz says.

14   Will Gap be able to reverse its course? Some analysts think the jeans and casual-wear giant is on the right track to reclaiming its place in mass-market apparel. No, it's not a sure bet—far from it. UBS Warburg's Jaffe, who rates the shares a buy, still cautions that the company is in a precarious position. "It's a high-risk gamble," he says.

15   But if Gap gets its fashion knack back and keeps costs under control, investors with a horizon of several years could be rewarded as the retailer gets back on its feet.

Source: Amy Tsao, "How Gap Could Climb Out of Its Hole, *BusinessWeek*, December 17, 2001.

Chapter Six

Formulating Long-Term Objectives and Grand Strategies

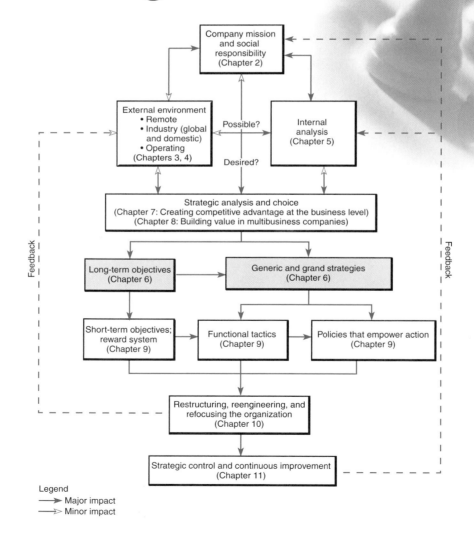

```
                          ┌──────────────────┐
                          │ Company mission  │◄─────────────────┐
                          │    and social    │                  │
                          │  responsibility  │◄────┐            │
                          │   (Chapter 2)    │     │            │
                          └──────────────────┘     │            │
                                                    │            │
    ┌──────────────────┐    Possible?    ┌──────────────────┐   │
    │External environment│◄────────────►│     Internal     │◄──┤
    │ • Remote          │                │     analysis     │   │
    │ • Industry (global│                │   (Chapter 5)    │◄──┤
    │   and domestic)   │                │                  │   │
    │ • Operating       │    Desired?    └──────────────────┘   │
    │  (Chapters 3, 4)  │                                       │
    └──────────────────┘                                       │
                                                               │
    ┌──────────────────────────────────────────────────────┐  │
    │        Strategic analysis and choice                   │  │
    │ (Chapter 7: Creating competitive advantage at the      │  │
    │              business level)                           │  │
    │ (Chapter 8: Building value in multibusiness companies) │  │
    └──────────────────────────────────────────────────────┘  │
```

(flowchart)

- Company mission and social responsibility (Chapter 2)
- External environment • Remote • Industry (global and domestic) • Operating (Chapters 3, 4)
- Possible?
- Desired?
- Internal analysis (Chapter 5)
- Strategic analysis and choice (Chapter 7: Creating competitive advantage at the business level) (Chapter 8: Building value in multibusiness companies)
- Long-term objectives (Chapter 6)
- Generic and grand strategies (Chapter 6)
- Short-term objectives; reward system (Chapter 9)
- Functional tactics (Chapter 9)
- Policies that empower action (Chapter 9)
- Restructuring, reengineering, and refocusing the organization (Chapter 10)
- Strategic control and continuous improvement (Chapter 11)
- Feedback

Legend
→ Major impact
--▷ Minor impact

The company mission was described in Chapter 2 as encompassing the broad aims of the firm. The most specific statement of aims presented in that chapter appeared as the goals of the firm. However, these goals, which commonly dealt with profitability, growth, and survival, were stated without specific targets or time frames. They were always to be pursued but could never be fully attained. They gave a general sense of direction but were not intended to provide specific benchmarks for evaluating the firm's progress in achieving its aims. Providing such benchmarks is the function of objectives.[1]

The first part of this chapter will focus on long-term objectives. These are statements of the results a firm seeks to achieve over a specified period, typically three to five years. The second part will focus on the formulation of grand strategies. These provide a comprehensive general approach in guiding major actions designed to accomplish the firm's long-term objectives.

The chapter has two major aims: (1) to discuss in detail the concept of long-term objectives, the topics they cover, and the qualities they should exhibit; and (2) to discuss the concept of grand strategies and to describe the 15 principal grand strategy options that are available to firms singly or in combination, including three newly popularized options that are being used to provide the basis for global competitiveness.

LONG-TERM OBJECTIVES

Strategic managers recognize that short-run profit maximization is rarely the best approach to achieving sustained corporate growth and profitability. An often repeated adage states that if impoverished people are given food, they will eat it and remain impoverished; however, if they are given seeds and tools and shown how to grow crops, they will be able to improve their condition permanently. A parallel choice confronts strategic decision makers:

1. Should they eat the seeds to improve the near-term profit picture and make large dividend payments through cost-saving measures such as laying off workers during periods of slack demand, selling off inventories, or cutting back on research and development?

2. Or should they sow the seeds in the effort to reap long-term rewards by reinvesting profits in growth opportunities, committing resources to employee training, or increasing advertising expenditures?

For most strategic managers, the solution is clear—distribute a small amount of profit now but sow most of it to increase the likelihood of a long-term supply. This is the most frequently used rationale in selecting objectives.

To achieve long-term prosperity, strategic planners commonly establish long-term objectives in seven areas:

Profitability   The ability of any firm to operate in the long run depends on attaining an acceptable level of profits. Strategically managed firms characteristically have a profit objective, usually expressed in earnings per share or return on equity.

Productivity   Strategic managers constantly try to increase the productivity of their systems. Firms that can improve the input-output relationship normally increase profitability. Thus, firms almost always state an objective for productivity. Commonly used productivity objectives are the number of items produced or the number of services rendered per unit of

---

[1] The terms *goals* and *objectives* are each used to convey a special meaning, with goals being the less specific and more encompassing concept. Most authors follow this usage; however, some use the two words interchangeably, while others reverse the usage.

input. However, productivity objectives sometimes are stated in terms of desired cost decreases. For example, objectives may be set for reducing defective items, customer complaints leading to litigation, or overtime. Achieving such objectives increases profitability if unit output is maintained.

Competitive Position   One measure of corporate success is relative dominance in the marketplace. Larger firms commonly establish an objective in terms of competitive position, often using total sales or market share as measures of their competitive position. An objective with regard to competitive position may indicate a firm's long-term priorities. For example, Gulf Oil set a five-year objective of moving from third to second place as a producer of high-density polypropylene. Total sales were the measure.

Employee Development   Employees value education and training, in part because they lead to increased compensation and job security. Providing such opportunities often increases productivity and decreases turnover. Therefore, strategic decision makers frequently include an employee development objective in their long-range plans. For example, PPG has declared an objective of developing highly skilled and flexible employees and, thus, providing steady employment for a reduced number of workers.

Employee Relations   Whether or not they are bound by union contracts, firms actively seek good employee relations. In fact, proactive steps in anticipation of employee needs and expectations are characteristic of strategic managers. Strategic managers believe that productivity is linked to employee loyalty and to appreciation of managers' interest in employee welfare. They, therefore, set objectives to improve employee relations. Among the outgrowths of such objectives are safety programs, worker representation on management committees, and employee stock option plans.

Technological Leadership   Firms must decide whether to lead or follow in the marketplace. Either approach can be successful, but each requires a different strategic posture. Therefore, many firms state an objective with regard to technological leadership. For example, Caterpillar Tractor Company established its early reputation and dominant position in its industry by being in the forefront of technological innovation in the manufacture of large earthmovers. Exhibit 6–1, E-commerce Strategy in Action, explains that e-commerce technology officers will have more of a strategic role in the management hierarchy of the future, demonstrating that the Internet has become an integral aspect of corporate long-term objective setting. In offering an e-technology manager higher-level responsibilities, a firm is pursuing a leadership position in terms of innovation in computer networks and systems. Officers of e-commerce technology at GE and Delta Air have shown their ability to increase profits by driving down transaction-related costs with Web-based technologies that seamlessly integrate their firms' supply chains. These technologies have the potential to "lock in" certain suppliers and customers and heighten competitive position through supply chain efficiency.

Public Responsibility   Managers recognize their responsibilities to their customers and to society at large. In fact, many firms seek to exceed government requirements. They work not only to develop reputations for fairly priced products and services but also to establish themselves as responsible corporate citizens. For example, they may establish objectives for charitable and educational contributions, minority training, public or political activity, community welfare, or urban revitalization. In an attempt to exhibit their public responsibility in the United States, Japanese companies, such as Toyota, Hitachi, and Matsushita, contribute more than $500 million annually to American educational projects, charities, and nonprofit organizations.

Now, in the Internet era, a new type of tech exec is needed. Corporations will need an executive who can harness the latest technology to reach out to customers on one end and suppliers on the other with seamless, up-to-the-minute data communications. In the 21st-century corporation, all managers will have to be tech experts, but the grand high pooh-bah will be somebody we're calling the chief Web officer.

This executive could emerge as the CEO's most important lieutenant, working hand in hand to retool companies into e-businesses. Like today's CIO, the chief Web officer will oversee information systems and strategies—which, by definition, will be based on Internet technology. But, in addition, he or she will create and manage an interwoven web of business relationships made possible by communications technology. Forging flexible e-links between an organization and its partners, suppliers, and customers. Technology and partnerships can't work well without each other—and leaving them in separate hands risks failing to exploit the Net's potential for radically transforming business processes.

For companies that recognize the strategic importance of the Net and appoint leaders to exploit it, the payoff can be enormous. At GE a customer inquiry that used to cost $80 to handle over the phone costs just 50 cents via the Web. With savings like that, analysts figure GE will slash expenses by hundreds of millions this year, while pushing more than $5 billion worth of purchases through the electronic systems. The same goes for Delta Air Lines, where selling a ticket online costs one-quarter as much as a travel agent sale. Delta saved more than $100 million last year thanks to e-commerce, says CFO Edward H. West, who manages the company's online initiatives.

Achieving such results relies on making the Net a strategic priority. But the transition to chief Web officer isn't always easy. Even though CIOs entered the upper ranks of executives in the 90s, the departments they ran were "still the servant of the business," says Harvard Business School professor Robert Austin. Indeed, many CIOs still focus on running internal computer systems, he says, even though "the more exciting stuff is being done elsewhere."

That stuff—websites, e-commerce, online customer support—often bubbles up from skunkworks scattered around a company. Or, it falls under an "e-czar" who bypasses the CIO to report directly to the chief executive. In the coming years, the CIO and e-czar should morph into one. Companies that fail to move in this direction run the risk of turf wars between execs or between line managers launching their own e-commerce initiatives and IT departments charged with keeping corporate digital systems in prime condition.

Source: An excerpt from Andy Reinhardt, "From Gearhead to Grand High Pooh-Bah," *BusinessWeek*, August 28, 2000.

Qualities of Long-Term Objectives

What distinguishes a good objective from a bad one? What qualities of an objective improve its chances of being attained? These questions are best answered in relation to seven criteria that should be used in preparing long-term objectives: acceptable, flexible, measurable over time, motivating, suitable, understandable, and achievable.

Acceptable Managers are most likely to pursue objectives that are consistent with their preferences. They may ignore or even obstruct the achievement of objectives that offend them (e.g., promoting a high-sodium food product) or that they believe to be inappropriate or unfair (e.g., reducing spoilage to offset a disproportionate allocation of fixed overhead). In addition, long-term corporate objectives frequently are designed to be acceptable to groups external to the firm. An example is efforts to abate air pollution that are undertaken at the insistence of the Environmental Protection Agency.

Flexible Objectives should be adaptable to unforeseen or extraordinary changes in the firm's competitive or environmental forecasts. Unfortunately, such flexibility usually is increased at the expense of specificity. One way of providing flexibility while minimizing its negative effects is to allow for adjustments in the level, rather than in the nature, of objectives. For example, the personnel department objective of providing managerial development training for 15 supervisors per year over the next five-year period might be adjusted by changing the number of people to be trained. In contrast, changing the personnel department's objective of "assisting production supervisors in reducing job-related injuries by 10 percent per year" after three months had gone by would understandably create dissatisfaction.

Measurable   Objectives must clearly and concretely state what will be achieved and when it will be achieved. Thus, objectives should be measurable over time. For example, the objective of "substantially improving our return on investment" would be better stated as "increasing the return on investment on our line of paper products by a minimum of 1 percent a year and a total of 5 percent over the next three years."

Motivating   People are most productive when objectives are set at a motivating level— one high enough to challenge but not so high as to frustrate or so low as to be easily attained. The problem is that individuals and groups differ in their perceptions of what is high enough. A broad objective that challenges one group frustrates another and minimally interests a third. One valuable recommendation is that objectives be tailored to specific groups. Developing such objectives requires time and effort, but objectives of this kind are more likely to motivate.

Suitable   Objectives must be suited to the broad aims of the firm, which are expressed in its mission statement. Each objective should be a step toward the attainment of overall goals. In fact, objectives that are inconsistent with the company mission can subvert the firm's aims. For example, if the mission is growth oriented, the objective of reducing the debt-to-equity ratio to 1.00 would probably be unsuitable and counterproductive.

Understandable   Strategic managers at all levels must understand what is to be achieved. They also must understand the major criteria by which their performance will be evaluated. Thus, objectives must be so stated that they are as understandable to the recipient as they are to the giver. Consider the misunderstandings that might arise over the objective of "increasing the productivity of the credit card department by 20 percent within two years." What does this objective mean? Increase the number of outstanding cards? Increase the use of outstanding cards? Increase the employee workload? Make productivity gains each year? Or hope that the new computer-assisted system, which should improve productivity, is approved by year 2? As this simple example illustrates, objectives must be clear, meaningful, and unambiguous.

Achievable   Finally, objectives must be possible to achieve. This is easier said than done. Turbulence in the remote and operating environments affects a firm's internal operations, creating uncertainty and limiting the accuracy of the objectives set by strategic management. To illustrate, the rapidly declining U.S. economy in 2000–2001 made objective setting extremely difficult, particularly in such areas as sales projections.

The Balanced Scorecard

The Balanced Scorecard is a set of measures that are directly linked to the company's strategy. Developed by Robert S. Kaplan and David P. Norton, it directs a company to link its own long-term strategy with tangible goals and actions. The scorecard allows managers to evaluate the company from four perspectives: financial performance, customer knowledge, internal business processes, and learning and growth.

EXHIBIT 6–2
The Balanced Scorecard

Source: Robert S. Kaplan and David P. Norton, "Using the Balanced Scorecard as a Strategic Management System," *Harvard Business Review,* January–February 1996, p. 76. Reprinted with permission.

The balanced scorecard provides a framework to translate a strategy into operational terms

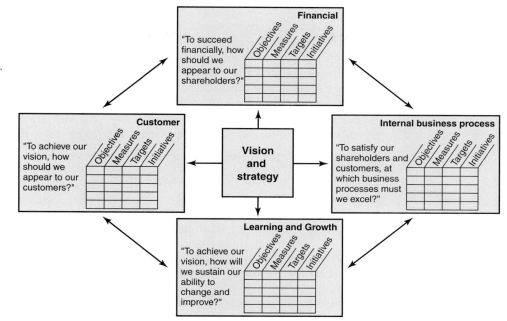

The Balanced Scorecard, as shown in Exhibit 6–2, contains a concise definition of the company's vision and strategy. Surrounding the vision and strategy are four additional boxes; each box contains the objectives, measures, targets, and initiatives for one of the four perspectives:

- The box at the top of Exhibit 6–2 represents the financial perspective, and answers the question "To succeed financially, how should we appear to our shareholders?"

- The box to the right represents the internal business process perspective and addresses the question "To satisfy our shareholders and customers, what business processes must we excel at?"

- The learning and growth box at the bottom of Exhibit 6–2 answers the question "To achieve our vision, how will we sustain our ability to change and improve?"

- The box at the left reflects the customer perspective, and responds to the question "To achieve our vision, how should we appear to our customers?"

All of the boxes are connected by arrows to illustrate that the objectives and measures of the four perspectives are linked by cause-and-effect relationships that lead to the successful implementation of the strategy. Achieving one perspective's targets should lead to desired improvements in the next perspective, and so on, until the company's performance increases overall.

A properly constructed scorecard is balanced between short- and long-term measures; financial and nonfinancial measures; and internal and external performance perspectives.

The Balanced Scorecard is a management system that can be used as the central organizing framework for key managerial processes. Chemical Bank, Mobil Corporation's US Marketing and Refining Division, and CIGNA Property and Casualty Insurance have used the Balanced Scorecard approach to assist in individual and team goal setting, compensation, resource allocation, budgeting and planning, and strategic feedback and learning.

GENERIC STRATEGIES

Many planning experts believe that the general philosophy of doing business declared by the firm in the mission statement must be translated into a holistic statement of the firm's strategic orientation before it can be further defined in terms of a specific long-term strategy. In other words, a long-term or grand strategy must be based on a core idea about how the firm can best compete in the marketplace.

The popular term for this core idea is *generic strategy.* From a scheme developed by Michael Porter, many planners believe that any long-term strategy should derive from a firm's attempt to seek a competitive advantage based on one of three generic strategies:

1. Striving for overall low-cost leadership in the industry.

2. Striving to create and market unique products for varied customer groups through *differentiation.*

3. Striving to have special appeal to one or more groups of consumer or industrial buyers, *focusing* on their cost or differentiation concerns.

Advocates of generic strategies believe that each of these options can produce above-average returns for a firm in an industry. However, they are successful for very different reasons.

Low-cost leaders depend on some fairly unique capabilities to achieve and sustain their low-cost position. Examples of such capabilities are: having secured suppliers of scarce raw materials, being in a dominant market share position, or having a high degree of capitalization. Low-cost producers usually excel at cost reductions and efficiencies. They maximize economies of scale, implement cost-cutting technologies, stress reductions in overhead and in administrative expenses, and use volume sales techniques to propel themselves up the earning curve. The commonly accepted requirements for successful implementation of the low-cost and the other two generic strategies are overviewed in Exhibit 6–3.

A low-cost leader is able to use its cost advantage to charge lower prices or to enjoy higher profit margins. By so doing, the firm effectively can defend itself in price wars, attack competitors on price to gain market share, or, if already dominant in the industry, simply benefit from exceptional returns. As an extreme case, it has been argued that National Can Company, a corporation in an essentially stagnant industry, is able to generate attractive and improving profits by being the low-cost producer.

Strategies dependent on differentiation are designed to appeal to customers with a special sensitivity for a particular product attribute. By stressing the attribute above other product qualities, the firm attempts to build customer loyalty. Often such loyalty translates into a firm's ability to charge a premium price for its product. Cross-brand pens, Brooks Brothers suits, Porsche automobiles, and Chivas Regal Scotch whiskey are all examples.

The product attribute also can be the marketing channels through which it is delivered, its image for excellence, the features it includes, and the service network that supports it. As a result of the importance of these attributes, competitors often face "perceptual" barriers to entry when customers of a successfully differentiated firm fail to see largely identical products as being interchangeable. For example, General Motors hopes that customers will accept "only genuine GM replacement parts."

A focus strategy, whether anchored in a low-cost base or a differentiation base, attempts to attend to the needs of a particular market segment. Likely segments are those that are ignored by marketing appeals to easily accessible markets, to the "typical" customer, or to customers with common applications for the product. A firm pursuing a

EXHIBIT 6–3
Requirements for Generic Competitive Strategies

Source: Free Press *COMPETITIVE STRATEGY: Techniques for Analyzing Industries and Competitors,* pp. 40–41. Reprinted with permission of the Free Press, a division of Simon & Schuster, from *Competitive Strategy: Techniques for Analyzing Industries and Competitors,* by Michael E. Porter. Copyright © 1980 by Michael E. Porter.

Generic Strategy	Commonly Required Skills and Resources	Common Organizational Requirements
Overall cost leadership	Sustained capital investment and access to capital. Process engineering skills. Intense supervision of labor. Products designed for ease in manufacture. Low-cost distribution system.	Tight cost control. Frequent, detailed control reports. Structured organization and responsibilities. Incentives based on meeting strict quantitative targets.
Differentiation	Strong marketing abilities. Product engineering. Creative flare. Strong capability in basic research. Corporate reputation for quality or technological leadership. Long tradition in the industry or unique combination of skills drawn from other businesses. Strong cooperation from channels.	Strong coordination among functions in R&D, product development, and marketing. Subjective measurement and incentives instead of quantitative measures. Amenities to attract highly skilled labor scientists, or creative people.
Focus	Combination of the above policies directed at the particular strategic target.	Combination of the above policies directed at the regular strategic target.

focus strategy is willing to service isolated geographic areas; to satisfy the needs of customers with special financing, inventory, or servicing problems; or to tailor the product to the somewhat unique demands of the small-to-medium-sized customer. The focusing firms profit from their willingness to serve otherwise ignored or underappreciated customer segments. The classic example is cable television. An entire industry was born because of a willingness of cable firms to serve isolated rural locations that were ignored by traditional television services. Brick producers that typically service a radius of less than 100 miles and commuter airlines that serve regional geographic areas are other examples of industries where a focus strategy frequently yields above-average industry profits.

While each of the generic strategies enables a firm to maximize certain competitive advantages, each one also exposes the firm to a number of competitive risks. For example, a low-cost leader fears a new low-cost technology that is being developed by a competitor; a differentiating firm fears imitators; and a focused firm fears invasion by a firm that largely targets customers. As Exhibit 6–4 suggests, each generic strategy presents the firm with a number of risks.

GRAND STRATEGIES

While the need for firms to develop generic strategies remains an unresolved debate, designers of planning systems agree about the critical role of grand strategies. *Grand strategies,* often called master or business strategies, provide basic direction for strategic actions. They are the basis of coordinated and sustained efforts directed toward achieving long-term business objectives.

The purpose of this section is twofold: (1) to list, describe, and discuss 15 grand strategies that strategic managers should consider and (2) to present approaches to the selection of an optimal grand strategy from the available alternatives.

EXHIBIT 6–4
Risks of the Generic Strategies

Source: Free Press *Competitive Advantage: Creating and Sustaining Superior Performance*, p. 21. Adapted with the permission of the Free Press, a division of Simon & Schuster, from *Competitive Strategy: Creating and Sustaining Superior Performance*, by Michael E. Porter. Copyright © 1985 by Michael E. Porter.

Risks of Cost Leadership	Risks of Differentiation	Risks of Focus
Cost of leadership is not sustained: • Competitors imitate. • Technology changes. • Other bases for cost leadership erode.	Differentiation is not sustained: • Competitors imitate. • Bases for differentiation become less important to buyers.	The focus strategy is imitated. The target segment becomes structurally unattractive: • Structure erodes. • Demand disappears.
Proximity in differentiation is lost.	Cost proximity is lost.	Broadly targeted competitors overwhelm the segment: • The segment's differences from other segments narrow. • The advantages of a broad line increase.
Cost focusers achieve even lower cost in segments.	Differentiation focusers achieve even greater differentiation in segments.	New focusers subsegment the industry.

Grand strategies indicate the time period over which long-range objectives are to be achieved. Thus, a grand strategy can be defined as a comprehensive general approach that guides a firm's major actions.

The 15 principal grand strategies are: concentrated growth, market development, product development, innovation, horizontal integration, vertical integration, concentric diversification, conglomerate diversification, turnaround, divestiture, liquidation, bankruptcy, joint ventures, strategic alliances, and consortia. Any one of these strategies could serve as the basis for achieving the major long-term objectives of a single firm. But a firm involved with multiple industries, businesses, product lines, or customer groups—as many firms are—usually combines several grand strategies. For clarity, however, each of the principal grand strategies is described independently in this section, with examples to indicate some of its relative strengths and weaknesses.

Concentrated Growth

Many of the firms that fell victim to merger mania were once mistakenly convinced that the best way to achieve their objectives was to pursue unrelated diversification in the search for financial opportunity and synergy. By rejecting that "conventional wisdom," such firms as Martin-Marietta, KFC, Compaq, Avon, Hyatt Legal Services, and Tenant have demonstrated the advantages of what is increasingly proving to be sound business strategy. A firm that has enjoyed special success through a strategic emphasis on increasing market share through concentration is Chemlawn. With headquarters in Columbus, Ohio, Chemlawn is the North American leader in professional lawn care. Like others in the lawn-care industry, Chemlawn is experiencing a steadily declining customer base. Market analysis shows that the decline is fueled by negative environmental publicity, perceptions of poor customer service, and concern about the price versus the value of the company's services, given the wide array of do-it-yourself alternatives. Chemlawn's approach to increasing market share hinges on addressing quality, price, and value issues; discontinuing products that the public or environmental authorities perceive as unsafe; and improving the quality of its workforce.

These firms are just a few of the majority of American firms that pursue a concentrated growth strategy by focusing on a specific product and market combination. *Concentrated growth* is the strategy of the firm that directs its resources to the profitable growth of a single product, in a single market, with a single dominant technology. The main rationale for this approach, sometimes called a market penetration or concentration strategy, is that the firm thoroughly develops and exploits its expertise in a delimited competitive arena.

Rationale for Superior Performance

Concentrated growth strategies lead to enhanced performance. The ability to assess market needs, knowledge of buyer behavior, customer price sensitivity, and effectiveness of promotion are characteristics of a concentrated growth strategy. Such core capabilities are a more important determinant of competitive market success than are the environmental forces faced by the firm. The high success rates of new products also are tied to avoiding situations that require undeveloped skills, such as serving new customers and markets, acquiring new technology, building new channels, developing new promotional abilities, and facing new competition.

A major misconception about the concentrated growth strategy is that the firm practicing it will settle for little or no growth. This is certainly not true for a firm that correctly utilizes the strategy. A firm employing concentrated growth grows by building on its competences, and it achieves a competitive edge by concentrating in the product-market segment it knows best. A firm employing this strategy is aiming for the growth that results from increased productivity, better coverage of its actual product-market segment, and more efficient use of its technology.

Conditions That Favor Concentrated Growth

Specific conditions in the firm's environment are favorable to the concentrated growth strategy. The first is a condition in which the firm's industry is resistant to major technological advancements. This is usually the case in the late growth and maturity stages of the product life cycle and in product markets where product demand is stable and industry barriers, such as capitalization, are high. Machinery for the paper manufacturing industry, in which the basic technology has not changed for more than a century, is a good example.

An especially favorable condition is one in which the firm's targeted markets are not product saturated. Markets with competitive gaps leave the firm with alternatives for growth, other than taking market share away from competitors. The successful introduction of traveler services by Allstate and Amoco demonstrates that even an organization as entrenched and powerful as the AAA could not build a defensible presence in all segments of the automobile club market.

A third condition that favors concentrated growth exists when the firm's product markets are sufficiently distinctive to dissuade competitors in adjacent product markets from trying to invade the firm's segment. John Deere scrapped its plans for growth in the construction machinery business when mighty Caterpillar threatened to enter Deere's mainstay, the farm machinery business, in retaliation. Rather than risk a costly price war on its own turf, Deere scrapped these plans.

A fourth favorable condition exists when the firm's inputs are stable in price and quantity and are available in the amounts and at the times needed. Maryland-based Giant Foods is able to concentrate in the grocery business largely due to its stable long-term arrangements with suppliers of its private-label products. Most of these suppliers are makers of the national brands that compete against the Giant labels. With a high market share and aggressive retail distribution, Giant controls the access of these brands to the consumer. Consequently, its suppliers have considerable incentive to honor verbal agreements, called *bookings,* in which they commit themselves for a one-year period with regard to the price, quality, and timing of their shipments to Giant.

The pursuit of concentrated growth also is favored by a stable market—a market without the seasonal or cyclical swings that would encourage a firm to diversify. Night Owl Security, the District of Columbia market leader in home security services, commits its customers to initial four-year contracts. In a city where affluent consumers tend to be quite transient, the length of this relationship is remarkable. Night Owl's concentrated growth strategy has been reinforced by its success in getting subsequent owners of its customers' homes to extend and renew the security service contracts. In a similar way, Lands' End reinforced its growth strategy by asking customers for names and addresses of friends and relatives living overseas who would like to receive Lands' End catalogs.

A firm also can grow while concentrating, if it enjoys competitive advantages based on efficient production or distribution channels. These advantages enable the firm to formulate advantageous pricing policies. More efficient production methods and better handling of distribution also enable the firm to achieve greater economies of scale or, in conjunction with marketing, result in a product that is differentiated in the mind of the consumer. Graniteville Company, a large South Carolina textile manufacturer, enjoyed decades of growth and profitability by adopting a "follower" tactic as part of its concentrated growth strategy. By producing fabrics only after market demand had been well established, and by featuring products that reflected its expertise in adopting manufacturing innovations and in maintaining highly efficient long production runs, Graniteville prospered through concentrated growth.

Finally, the success of market generalists creates conditions favorable to concentrated growth. When generalists succeed by using universal appeals, they avoid making special appeals to particular groups of customers. The net result is that many small pockets are left open in the markets dominated by generalists, and that specialists emerge and thrive in these pockets. For example, hardware store chains, such as Home Depot, focus primarily on routine household repair problems and offer solutions that can be easily sold on a self-service, do-it-yourself basis. This approach leaves gaps at both the "semiprofessional" and "neophyte" ends of the market—in terms of the purchaser's skill at household repairs and the extent to which available merchandise matches the requirements of individual homeowners.

Risk and Rewards of Concentrated Growth

Under stable conditions, concentrated growth poses lower risk than any other grand strategy; but, in a changing environment, a firm committed to concentrated growth faces high risks. The greatest risk is that concentrating in a single product market makes a firm particularly vulnerable to changes in that segment. Slowed growth in the segment would jeopardize the firm because its investment, competitive edge, and technology are deeply entrenched in a specific offering. It is difficult for the firm to attempt sudden changes if its product is threatened by near-term obsolescence, a faltering market, new substitutes, or changes in technology or customer needs. For example, the manufacturers of IBM clones faced such a problem when IBM adopted the OS/2 operating system for its personal computer line. That change made existing clones out of date.

The concentrating firm's entrenchment in a specific industry makes it particularly susceptible to changes in the economic environment of that industry. For example, Mack Truck, the second-largest truck maker in America, lost $20 million as a result of an 18-month slump in the truck industry.

Entrenchment in a specific product market tends to make a concentrating firm more adept than competitors at detecting new trends. However, any failure of such a firm to properly forecast major changes in its industry can result in extraordinary losses. Numerous makers of inexpensive digital watches were forced to declare bankruptcy because they failed to anticipate the competition posed by Swatch, Guess, and other trendy watches that emerged from the fashion industry.

A firm pursuing a concentrated growth strategy is vulnerable also to the high opportunity costs that result from remaining in a specific product market and ignoring other options that could employ the firm's resources more profitably. Overcommitment to a specific technology and product market can hinder a firm's ability to enter a new or growing product market that offers more attractive cost-benefit trade-offs. Had Apple Computers maintained its policy of making equipment that did not interface with IBM equipment, it would have missed out on what have proved to be its most profitable strategic options.

Concentrated Growth Is Often the Most Viable Option

Examples abound of firms that have enjoyed exceptional returns on the concentrated growth strategy. Such firms as McDonald's, Goodyear, and Apple Computers have used firsthand knowledge and deep involvement with specific product segments to become powerful competitors in their markets. The strategy is associated even more often with successful smaller firms that have steadily and doggedly improved their market position.

The limited additional resources necessary to implement concentrated growth, coupled with the limited risk involved, also make this strategy desirable for a firm with limited funds. For example, through a carefully devised concentrated growth strategy, medium-sized John Deere & Company was able to become a major force in the agricultural machinery business even when competing with such firms as Ford Motor Company. While other firms were trying to exit or diversify from the farm machinery business, Deere spent $2 billion in upgrading its machinery, boosting its efficiency, and engaging in a program to strengthen its dealership system. This concentrated growth strategy enabled it to become the leader in the farm machinery business despite the fact that Ford was more than 10 times its size.

The firm that chooses a concentrated growth strategy directs its resources to the profitable growth of a narrowly defined product and market, focusing on a dominant technology. Firms that remain within their chosen product market are able to extract the most from their technology and market knowledge and, thus, are able to minimize the risk associated with unrelated diversification. The success of a concentration strategy is founded on the firm's use of superior insights into its technology, product, and customer to obtain a sustainable competitive advantage. Superior performance on these aspects of corporate strategy has been shown to have a substantial positive effect on market success.

A grand strategy of concentrated growth allows for a considerable range of action. Broadly speaking, the firm can attempt to capture a larger market share by increasing the usage rates of present customers, by attracting competitors' customers, or by selling to nonusers. In turn, each of these options suggests more specific options, some of which are listed in the top section of Exhibit 6–5.

When strategic managers forecast that their current products and their markets will not provide the basis for achieving the company mission, they have two options that involve moderate costs and risk: market development and product development.

Market Development

Market development commonly ranks second only to concentration as the least costly and least risky of the 15 grand strategies. It consists of marketing present products, often with only cosmetic modifications, to customers in related market areas by adding channels of

EXHIBIT 6–5
Specific Options under the Grand Strategies of Concentration, Market Development, and Product Development

Source: Adapted from Philip Kotler, *Marketing Management Analysis, Planning, and Control,* 11th ed., 2002. Reprinted by permission of Prentice Hall, Inc., Upper Saddle River, NJ.

Concentration (increasing use of present products in present markets):

1. Increasing present customers' rate of use:
    a. Increasing the size of purchase.
    b. Increasing the rate of product obsolescence.
    c. Advertising other uses.
    d. Giving price incentives for increased use.
2. Attracting competitors' customers:
    a. Establishing sharper brand differentiation.
    b. Increasing promotional effort.
    c. Initiating price cuts.
3. Attracting nonusers to buy the product:
    a. Inducing trial use through sampling, price incentives, and so on.
    b. Pricing up or down.
    c. Advertising new uses.

Market development (selling present products in new markets):

1. Opening additional geographic markets:
    a. Regional expansion.
    b. National expansion.
    c. International expansion.
2. Attracting other market segments:
    a. Developing product versions to appeal to other segments.
    b. Entering other channels of distribution.
    c. Advertising in other media.

Product development (developing new products for present markets):

1. Developing new product features:
    a. Adapt (to other ideas, developments).
    b. Modify (change color, motion, sound, odor, form, shape).
    c. Magnify (stronger, longer, thicker, extra value).
    d. Minify (smaller, shorter, lighter).
    e. Substitute (other ingredients, process, power).
    f. Rearrange (other patterns, layout, sequence, components).
    g. Reverse (inside out).
    h. Combine (blend, alloy, assortment, ensemble; combine units, purposes, appeals, ideas).
2. Developing quality variations.
3. Developing additional models and sizes (product proliferation).

distribution or by changing the content of advertising or promotion. Several specific market development approaches are listed in Exhibit 6–5. Thus, as suggested by the figure, firms that open branch offices in new cities, states, or countries are practicing market development. Likewise, firms are practicing market development if they switch from advertising in trade publications to advertising in newspapers or if they add jobbers to supplement their mail-order sales efforts.

Market development allows firms to practice a form of concentrated growth by identifying new uses for existing products and new demographically, psychographically, or geographically defined markets. Frequently, changes in media selection, promotional appeals, and distribution are used to initiate this approach. Du Pont used market development when it found a new application for Kevlar, an organic material that police, security, and military personnel had used primarily for bulletproofing. Kevlar now is being used to refit and maintain wooden-hulled boats, since it is lighter and stronger than glass fibers and has 11 times the strength of steel.

The medical industry provides other examples of new markets for existing products. The National Institutes of Health's report of a study showing that the use of aspirin may lower the incidence of heart attacks was expected to boost sales in the $2.2 billion analgesic market. It was predicted that the expansion of this market would lower the market share of nonaspirin brands, such as industry leaders Tylenol and Advil. Product extensions currently planned include Bayer Calendar Pack, 28-day packaging to fit the once-a-day prescription for the prevention of a second heart attack.

Another example is Chesebrough-Ponds, a major producer of health and beauty aids, which decided several years ago to expand its market by repacking its Vaseline Petroleum Jelly in pocket-size squeeze tubes as Vaseline "Lip Therapy." The corporation decided to place a strategic emphasis on market development, because it knew from market studies that its petroleum-jelly customers already were using the product to prevent chapped lips. Company leaders reasoned that their market could be expanded significantly if the product were repackaged to fit conveniently in consumers' pockets and purses.

Product Development

Product development involves the substantial modification of existing products or the creation of new but related products that can be marketed to current customers through established channels. The product development strategy often is adopted either to prolong the life cycle of current products or to take advantage of a favorite reputation or brand name. The idea is to attract satisfied customers to new products as a result of their positive experience with the firm's initial offering. The bottom section in Exhibit 6–5 lists some of the options available to firms undertaking product development. A revised edition of a college textbook, a new car style, and a second formula of shampoo for oily hair are examples of the product development strategy.

The product development strategy is based on the penetration of existing markets by incorporating product modifications into existing items or by developing new products with a clear connection to the existing product line. The telecommunications industry provides an example of product extension based on product modification. To increase its estimated 8–10 percent share of the $5–$6 billion corporate user market, MCI Communication Corporation extended its direct-dial service to 146 countries, the same as those serviced by AT&T, at lower average rates than those of AT&T. MCI's addition of 79 countries to its network underscores its belief in this market, which it expects to grow 15–20 percent annually. Another example of expansions linked to existing lines is Gerber's decision to engage in general merchandise marketing. Gerber's recent introduction included 52 items that ranged from feeding accessories to toys and children's wear. Likewise, Nabisco Brands seeks competitive advantage by placing its strategic emphasis on product development. With headquarters in Parsippany, New Jersey, the company is one of three operating units of RJR Nabisco. It is the leading producer of biscuits, confections, snacks, shredded cereals, and processed fruits and vegetables. To maintain its position as leader, Nabisco pursues a strategy of developing and introducing new products and expanding its existing product line. Spoon Size Shredded Wheat and Ritz Bits crackers are two examples of new products that are variations on existing products.

Innovation

In many industries, it has become increasingly risky not to innovate. Both consumer and industrial markets have come to expect periodic changes and improvements in the products offered. As a result, some firms find it profitable to make *innovation* their grand strategy. They seek to reap the initially high profits associated with customer acceptance of a new or greatly improved product. Then, rather than face stiffening competition as the basis of profitability shifts from innovation to production or marketing competence, they search for other original or novel ideas. The underlying rationale of the grand strategy of innovation is to create a new product life cycle and thereby make similar existing products obsolete. Thus, this strategy differs from the product development strategy of extending an existing product's life cycle. For example, Intel, a leader in the semiconductor industry, pursues expansion through a strategic emphasis on innovation. With headquarters in California, the company is a designer and manufacturer of semiconductor components and related computers, of microcomputer systems, and of software. Its Pentium microprocessor gives a desktop computer the capability of a mainframe.

While most growth-oriented firms appreciate the need to be innovative occasionally, a few firms use it as their fundamental way of relating to their markets. An outstanding example is Polaroid, which heavily promotes each of its new cameras until competitors are able to match its technological innovation; by this time, Polaroid normally is prepared to introduce a dramatically new or improved product. For example, it introduced consumers in quick succession to the Swinger, the SX-70, the One Step, and the Sun Camera 660.

Few innovative ideas prove profitable because the research, development, and premarketing costs of converting a promising idea into a profitable product are extremely high. A study by the Booz Allen & Hamilton management research department provides some understanding of the risks. As shown in Exhibit 6–6, Booz Allen & Hamilton found that less than 2 percent of the innovative projects initially considered by 51 companies eventually reached the marketplace. Specifically, out of every 58 new product ideas, only 12 pass an initial screening test that finds them compatible with the firm's mission and long-term objectives, only 7 remain after an evaluation of their potential, and only 3 survive development attempts. Of the three survivors, two appear to have profit potential after test marketing and only one is commercially successful.

Horizontal Integration

When a firm's long-term strategy is based on growth through the acquisition of one or more similar firms operating at the same stage of the production-marketing chain, its grand strategy is called *horizontal integration.* Such acquisitions eliminate competitors and provide the acquiring firm with access to new markets. One example is Warner-Lambert's acquisition of Parke Davis, which reduced competition in the ethical drugs field for Chilcott Laboratories, a firm that Warner-Lambert previously had acquired. Another example is the long-range acquisition pattern of White Consolidated Industries, which expanded in the refrigerator and freezer market through a grand strategy of horizontal integration, by acquiring Kelvinator Appliance, the Refrigerator Products Division of Bendix Westinghouse Automotive Air Brake, and Frigidaire Appliance from General Motors. Nike's acquisition in the dress shoes business and N. V. Homes's purchase of Ryan Homes have vividly exemplified the success that horizontal integration strategies can bring.

Exhibit 6–7, Global Strategy in Action, describes Deutsche Telekom growth strategy of horizontal acquisition. Deutsche Telekom was a dominant player in the European wireless services market, but without a presence in the fast-growing U.S. market. To correct this limitation, Deutsche Telekom horizontally integrated by purchasing the American firm VoiceStream Wireless, a company that was growing faster than most domestic rivals and that owned spectrum licenses providing access to 220 million potential customers.

EXHIBIT 6–6
Decay of New Product Ideas (51 Companies)

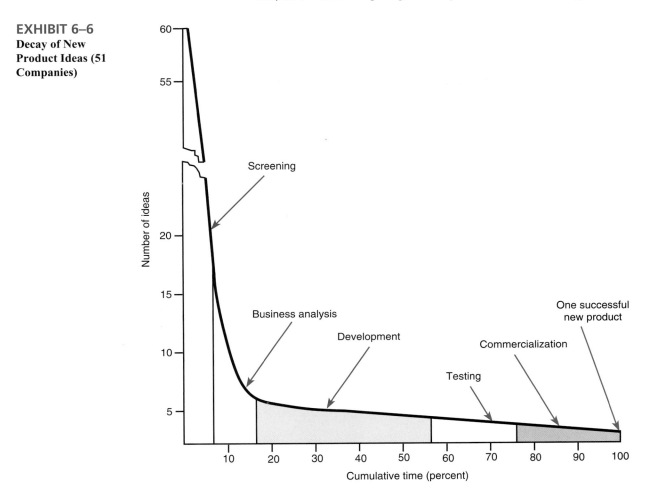

Vertical Integration

When a firm's grand strategy is to acquire firms that supply it with inputs (such as raw materials) or are customers for its outputs (such as warehousers for finished products), *vertical integration* is involved. To illustrate, if a shirt manufacturer acquires a textile producer—by purchasing its common stock, buying its assets, or exchanging ownership interests—the strategy is vertical integration. In this case, it is *backward* vertical integration, since the acquired firm operates at an earlier stage of the production-marketing process. If the shirt manufacturer had merged with a clothing store, it would have been *forward* vertical integration—the acquisition of a firm nearer to the ultimate consumer.

Amoco emerged as North America's leader in natural gas reserves and products as a result of its acquisition of Dome Petroleum. This backward integration by Amoco was made in support of its downstream businesses in refining and in gas stations, whose profits made the acquisition possible.

Exhibit 6–8 depicts both horizontal and vertical integration. The principal attractions of a horizontal integration grand strategy are readily apparent. The acquiring firm is able to greatly expand its operations, thereby achieving greater market share, improving economies of scale, and increasing the efficiency of capital use. In addition, these

BusinessWeek Measured against the nation's wireless giants, VoiceStream Wireless Corp. has been a bit of a pipsqueak. So why would Germany's Deutsche Telekom pay an eye-popping $21,639 per subscriber for the little Bellevue, Washington, cell phone company? Simply put, Deutsche Telekom is not buying subscribers in the United States. It's buying potential—in this case, the potential to become a dominant player—not just in the United States, but globally. By the end of 2000, only about 32.5% of the U.S. population will be using some form of wireless compared with 52% in Europe and 60% in Japan. Growth prospects in such a relatively undeveloped market, the German executives reckon, are so high that their company will emerge almost immediately as a formidable rival. U.S. telecom execs say a DT-VoiceStream link will force U.S. players to step up efforts to provide wireless Net service to a broader market, including overseas.

To gain this kind of sway over the lucrative U.S. market and the global market, Deutsche Telekom felt it was worth significantly besting the $4,390 per subscriber Britain's Vodafone paid for AirTouch in 1999 or the estimated $12,400 that the combined Vodafone-AirTouch paid for Mannesmann earlier this year. That has set off a torrent of criticism that it has wildly overpaid for its position. However, Deutsche Telekom's CEO Sommer is confident. Here's what he considered when he agreed to the price: VoiceStream owns licenses in 23 of the top 25 U.S. markets. In wireless lingo, its licenses cover areas with a 220 million subscriber base. Though it has relatively few subscribers signed up and currently does not actually provide service to many of the locales where it holds licenses, it is adding subscribers at a sizzling pace—an 18.5% growth rate that is among the top in the industry.

Wireless companies across the country are taking note, given DT's deep pockets and promise to make a starting investment of at least $5 billion in VoiceStream. With the $5 billion, VoiceStream can accelerate construction of wireless systems in places like California and Ohio. Stanton estimates that the cash infusion will help him push up the roll-out of his service by 6 to 18 months. Also, Deutsche Telekom's cash is expected to allow Voicestream to participate in a major way in the upcoming auction of more spectrum licenses by the FCC.

Source: Excerpted from R. O. Crockett and D. Fairlamb, August 7, 2000, "Deutsche Telekom's Wireless Wager," *BusinessWeek* (3693), pp. 30–32.

benefits are achieved with only moderately increased risk, since the success of the expansion is principally dependent on proven abilities.

The reasons for choosing a vertical integration grand strategy are more varied and sometimes less obvious. The main reason for backward integration is the desire to increase the dependability of the supply or quality of the raw materials used as production inputs. That desire is particularly great when the number of suppliers is small and the number of competitors is large. In this situation, the vertically integrating firm can better control its costs and, thereby, improve the profit margin of the expanded production-marketing system. Forward integration is a preferred grand strategy if great advantages accrue to stable production. A firm can increase the predictability of demand for its output through forward integration; that is, through ownership of the next stage of its production-marketing chain.

Some increased risks are associated with both types of integration. For horizontally integrated firms, the risks stem from increased commitment to one type of business. For vertically integrated firms, the risks result from the firm's expansion into areas requiring strategic managers to broaden the base of their competences and to assume additional responsibilities.

Concentric Diversification

Grand strategies involving diversification represent distinctive departures from a firm's existing base of operations, typically the acquisition or internal generation (spin-off) of a separate business with synergistic possibilities counterbalancing the strengths and

EXHIBIT 6–8
Vertical and Horizontal Integrations

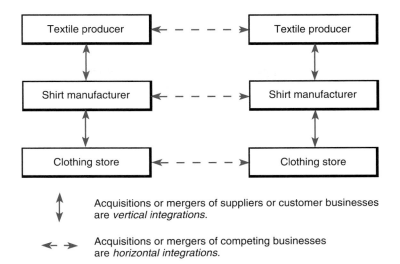

Acquisitions or mergers of suppliers or customer businesses are *vertical integrations*.

Acquisitions or mergers of competing businesses are *horizontal integrations*.

weaknesses of the two businesses. For example, Head Ski initially sought to diversify into summer sporting goods and clothing to offset the seasonality of its "snow" business. However, diversifications occasionally are undertaken as unrelated investments, because of their high profit potential and their otherwise minimal resource demands.

Regardless of the approach taken, the motivations of the acquiring firms are the same:

- Increase the firm's stock value. In the past, mergers often have led to increases in the stock price or the price-earnings ratio.

- Increase the growth rate of the firm.

- Make an investment that represents better use of funds than plowing them into internal growth.

- Improve the stability of earnings and sales by acquiring firms whose earnings and sales complement the firm's peaks and valleys.

- Balance or fill out the product line.

- Diversify the product line when the life cycle of current products has peaked.

- Acquire a needed resource quickly (e.g., high-quality technology or highly innovative management).

- Achieve tax savings by purchasing a firm whose tax losses will offset current or future earnings.

- Increase efficiency and profitability, especially if there is synergy between the acquiring firm and the acquired firm.[2]

Concentric diversification involves the acquisition of businesses that are related to the acquiring firm in terms of technology, markets, or products. With this grand strategy, the selected new businesses possess a high degree of compatibility with the firm's current businesses. The ideal concentric diversification occurs when the combined company

[2] Godfrey Devlin and Mark Bleackley, "Strategic Alliances—Guidelines for Success," *Long Range Planning,* October 1988, pp. 18–23.

profits increase the strengths and opportunities and decrease the weaknesses and exposure to risk. Thus, the acquiring firm searches for new businesses whose products, markets, distribution channels, technologies, and resource requirements are similar to but not identical with its own, whose acquisition results in synergies but not complete interdependence.

Conglomerate Diversification

Occasionally a firm, particularly a very large one, plans to acquire a business because it represents the most promising investment opportunity available. This grand strategy is commonly known as *conglomerate diversification*. The principal concern, and often the sole concern, of the acquiring firm is the profit pattern of the venture. Unlike concentric diversification, conglomerate diversification gives little concern to creating product-market synergy with existing businesses. What such conglomerate diversifiers as ITT, Textron, American Brands, Litton, U.S. Industries, Fuqua, and I. C. Industries seek is financial synergy. For example, they may seek a balance in their portfolios between current businesses with cyclical sales and acquired businesses with countercyclical sales, between high-cash/low-opportunity and low-cash/high-opportunity businesses, or between debt-free and highly leveraged businesses.

The principal difference between the two types of diversification is that concentric diversification emphasizes some commonality in markets, products, or technology, whereas conglomerate diversification is based principally on profit considerations.

Several of the grand strategies discussed above, including concentric and conglomerate diversification and horizontal and vertical integration, often involve the purchase or acquisition of one firm by another. It is important to know that the majority of such acquisitions fail to produce the desired results for the companies involved. Exhibit 6–9, Strategy in Action, provides seven guidelines that can improve a company's chances of a successful acquisition.

Turnaround

For any one of a large number of reasons, a firm can find itself with declining profits. Among these reasons are economic recessions, production inefficiencies, and innovative breakthroughs by competitors. In many cases, strategic managers believe that such a firm can survive and eventually recover if a concerted effort is made over a period of a few years to fortify its distinctive competences. This grand strategy is known as *turnaround*. It typically is begun through one of two forms of retrenchment, employed singly or in combination:

1. *Cost reduction.* Examples include decreasing the workforce through employee attrition, leasing rather than purchasing equipment, extending the life of machinery, eliminating elaborate promotional activities, laying off employees, dropping items from a production line, and discontinuing low-margin customers.

2. *Asset reduction.* Examples include the sale of land, buildings, and equipment not essential to the basic activity of the firm and the elimination of "perks," such as the company airplane and executives' cars.

Interestingly, the turnaround most commonly associated with this approach is in management positions. In a study of 58 large firms, researchers Shendel, Patton, and Riggs found that turnaround almost always was associated with changes in top management.[3]

---

[3] Other forms of joint ventures (such as leasing, contract manufacturing, and management contracting) offer valuable support strategies. They are not included in the categorization, however, because they seldom are employed as grand strategies.

1. *The wrong target.* This error becomes increasingly visible as time passes after the acquisition, when the acquiror may realize that anticipated synergies just don't exist, that the expanded market just isn't there, or that the acquiror's and target's technologies simply were not complementary.

   The first step to avoid such a mistake is for the acquiror and its financial advisors to determine the strategic goals and identify the mission. The product of this strategic review will be specifically identified criteria for the target.

   The second step required to identify the right target is to design and carry out an effective due diligence process to ascertain whether the target indeed has the identified set of qualities selected in the strategic review.

2. *The wrong price.* Even in a strategic acquisition, paying too much will lead to failure. For a patient strategic acquiror with long-term objectives, overpaying may be less of a problem than for a financial acquiror looking for a quick profit. Nevertheless, overpaying may divert needed acquiror resources and adversely affect the firm's borrowing capacity. In the extreme case, it can lead to continued operating losses and business failure.

   The key to avoiding this problem lies in the acquiror's valuation model. The model will incorporate assumptions concerning industry trends and growth patterns developed in the strategic review.

3. *The wrong structure.* Both financial and strategic acquisitions benefit by the structure chosen. This may include the legal structure chosen for the entities, the geographic jurisdiction chosen for newly created entities, and the capitalization structure selected for the business after the acquisition. The wrong structure may lead to an inability to repatriate earnings (or an ability to do so only at a prohibitive tax cost), regulatory problems that delay or prevent realization of the anticipated benefits, and inefficient pricing of debt and equity securities or a bar to chosen exit strategies due to inflexibility in the chosen legal structure.

   The two principal aspects of the acquisition process that can prevent this problem are a comprehensive regulatory compliance review and tax and legal analysis.

4. *The lost deal.* Lost deals often can be traced to poor communication. A successful strategic acquisition requires agreement upon the strategic vision, both with the acquiring company and between the acquiror and the continuing elements of the target. This should be established in the preliminary negotiations that lead to the letter of intent.

   The letter must spell out not only the price to be paid but also many of the relational aspects that will make the strategic acquisition successful. Although an acquiror may justifiably focus on expenses, indemnification, and other logical concerns in the letter of intent, relationship and operational concerns are also important.

5. *Management difficulties.* Lack of attention to management issues may lead to a lost deal. These problems can range from a failure to provide management continuity or clear lines of authority after a merger to incentives that cause management to steer the company in the wrong direction.

   The remedy for this problem must be extracted from the initial strategic review. The management compensation structure must be designed with legal and business advisors to help achieve those goals. The financial rewards to management must depend upon the financial and strategic success of the combined entity.

6. *The closing crisis.* Closing crises may stem from unavoidable changed conditions, but most often they result from poor communication. Negotiators sometimes believe that problems swept under the table maintain a deal's momentum and ultimately allow for its consummation. They are sometimes right—and often wrong. Charting a course through an acquisition requires carefully developed skills for every kind of professional—business, accounting, and legal.

7. *The operating transition crisis.* Even the best conceived and executed acquisition will prevent significant transition and postclosing operation issues. Strategic goals cannot be achieved by quick asset sales or other accelerated exit strategies. Management time and energy must be spent to assure that the benefits identified in the strategic review are achieved.

   The principal constraints on smooth implementation are usually human: poor interaction of personnel between the two preexisting management structures and resistance to new systems. Problems also may arise from too much attention to the by now well-communicated strategic vision and too little attention to the nuts and bolts of continuing business operations.

Source: Excerpted from D. A. Tanner, "Seven Deadly Sins of Strategic Acquisition," *Management Review:* June 1991, pp. 50–53. Reprinted by permission of publisher, from MANAGEMENT REVIEW, June 1991, © 1991. American Management Association, New York, All rights reserved.

EXHIBIT 6–10   A Model of the Turnaround Process

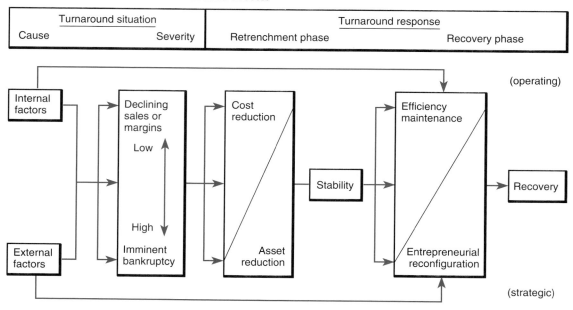

Bringing in new managers was believed to introduce needed new perspectives on the firm's situation, to raise employee morale, and to facilitate drastic actions, such as deep budgetary cuts in established programs.

Strategic management research provides evidence that the firms that have used a *turnaround strategy* have successfully confronted decline. The research findings have been assimilated and used as the building blocks for a model of the turnaround process shown in Exhibit 6–10.

The model begins with a depiction of external and internal factors as causes of a firm's performance downturn. When these factors continue to detrimentally impact the firm, its financial health is threatened. Unchecked decline places the firm in a turnaround situation.

A *turnaround situation* represents absolute and relative-to-industry declining performance of a sufficient magnitude to warrant explicit turnaround actions. Turnaround situations may be the result of years of gradual slowdown or months of sharp decline. In either case, the recovery phase of the turnaround process is likely to be more successful in accomplishing turnaround when it is preceded by planned retrenchment that results in the achievement of near-term financial stabilization. For a declining firm, stabilizing operations and restoring profitability almost always entail strict cost reduction followed by a shrinking back to those segments of the business that have the best prospects of attractive profit margins. The need for retrenchment was reflected in unemployment figures during the 2000–2001 recession. More layoffs of American workers were announced in 2001 than in any of the previous eight years. U.S. companies announced nearly 2 million layoffs in 2001 as the economy sunk into its first recession in a decade.

The immediacy of the resulting threat to company survival posed by the turnaround situation is known as *situation severity*. Severity is the governing factor in estimating the speed with which the retrenchment response will be formulated and activated. When severity is low, a firm has some financial cushion. Stability may be achieved through cost retrenchment alone. When turnaround situation severity is high, a firm must immediately stabilize the decline or bankruptcy is imminent. Cost reductions must be supplemented with more drastic asset reduction measures. Assets targeted for divestiture are those determined to be underproductive. In contrast, more productive resources are protected from cuts and represent critical elements of the future core business plan of the company (i.e., the intended recovery response).

Turnaround responses among successful firms typically include two stages of strategic activities: retrenchment and the recovery response. *Retrenchment* consists of cost-cutting and asset-reducing activities. The primary objective of the retrenchment phase is to stabilize the firm's financial condition. Situation severity has been associated with retrenchment responses among successful turnaround firms. Firms in danger of bankruptcy or failure (i.e., severe situations) attempt to halt decline through cost and asset reductions. Firms in less severe situations have achieved stability merely through cost retrenchment. However, in either case, for firms facing declining financial performance, the key to successful turnaround rests in the effective and efficient management of the retrenchment process.

The primary causes of the turnaround situation have been associated with the second phase of the turnaround process, the *recovery response*. For firms that declined primarily as a result of external problems, turnaround most often has been achieved through creative new entrepreneurial strategies. For firms that declined primarily as a result of internal problems, turnaround has been most frequently achieved through efficiency strategies. *Recovery* is achieved when economic measures indicate that the firm has regained its predownturn levels of performance.

Divestiture

A *divestiture strategy* involves the sale of a firm or a major component of a firm. Sara Lee Corp. (SLE) provides a good example. It sells everything from Wonderbras and Kiwi shoe polish to Endust furniture polish and Chock full o'Nuts coffee. In the 1990s, the company used a conglomerate diversification strategy to build Sara Lee into a huge portfolio of disparate brands. A new president in 1998, C. Steven McMillan, faced stagnant revenues and earnings. So he consolidated, streamlined, and focused the company on its core categories—food, underwear, and household products. He divested 15 businesses, including Coach leather goods in 2000, which together equaled over 20 percent of the company's revenue, and laid off 13,200 employees, nearly 10 percent of the workforce. McMillan used the cash from asset sales to snap up brands that enhanced Sara Lee's clout in key categories, like the $2.8 billion purchase of St. Louis-based breadmaker Earthgrains Co. in 2001 to quadruple Sara Lee's bakery operations.

When retrenchment fails to accomplish the desired turnaround, as in the Goodyear situation, or when a nonintegrated business activity achieves an unusually high market value, strategic managers often decide to sell the firm. However, because the intent is to find a buyer willing to pay a premium above the value of a going concern's fixed assets, the term *marketing for sale* is often more appropriate. Prospective buyers must be convinced that because of their skills and resources or because of the firm's synergy with their existing businesses, they will be able to profit from the acquisition.

The reasons for divestiture vary. They often arise because of partial mismatches between the acquired firm and the parent corporation. Some of the mismatched parts cannot be integrated into the corporation's mainstream activities and, thus, must be spun off. A second reason is corporate financial needs. Sometimes the cash flow or financial stability of the corporation as a whole can be greatly improved if businesses with high market value can be sacrificed. The result can be a balancing of equity with long-term risks or of long-term debt payments to optimize the cost of capital. A third, less frequent reason for divestiture is government antitrust action when a firm is believed to monopolize or unfairly dominate a particular market.

Although examples of the divestiture grand strategy are numerous, CBS, Inc., provides an outstanding example. In a two-year period, the once diverse entertainment and publishing giant sold its Records Division to Sony, its magazine publishing business to Diamandis Communications, its book publishing operations to Harcourt Brace Jovanovich, and its music publishing operations to SBK Entertainment World. Other firms that have pursued this type of grand strategy include Esmark, which divested Swift & Company, and White Motors, which divested White Farm.

Liquidation

When liquidation is the grand strategy, the firm typically is sold in parts, only occasionally as a whole—but for its tangible asset value and not as a going concern. In selecting liquidation, the owners and strategic managers of a firm are admitting failure and recognize that this action is likely to result in great hardships to themselves and their employees. For these reasons, liquidation usually is seen as the least attractive of the grand strategies. As a long-term strategy, however, it minimizes the losses of all the firm's stockholders. Faced with bankruptcy, the liquidating firm usually tries to develop a planned and orderly system that will result in the greatest possible return and cash conversion as the firm slowly relinquishes its market share.

Planned liquidation can be worthwhile. For example, Columbia Corporation, a $130 million diversified firm, liquidated its assets for more cash per share than the market value of its stock.

Bankruptcy

Business failures are playing an increasingly important role in the American economy. In an average week, more than 300 companies fail. More than 75 percent of these financially desperate firms file for a *liquidation bankruptcy*—they agree to a complete distribution of their assets to creditors, most of whom receive a small fraction of the amount they are owed. Liquidation is what the layperson views as bankruptcy: The business cannot pay its debts, so it must close its doors. Investors lose their money, employees lose their jobs, and managers lose their credibility. In owner-managed firms, company and personal bankruptcy commonly go hand in hand.

The other 25 percent of these firms refuse to surrender until one final option is exhausted. Choosing a strategy to recapture its viability, such a company asks the courts for a *reorganization bankruptcy*. The firm attempts to persuade its creditors to temporarily freeze their claims while it undertakes to reorganize and rebuild the company's operations more profitably. The appeal of a reorganization bankruptcy is based on the company's ability to convince creditors that it can succeed in the marketplace by implementing a new strategic plan, and that when the plan produces profits, the firm will be able to repay its creditors, perhaps in full. In other words, the company offers its creditors a carefully designed alternative to forcing an immediate, but fractional, repayment of its financial obligations. The option of reorganization bankruptcy offers maximum repayment of debt at some specified future time if a new strategic plan is successful.

The Bankruptcy Situation

Imagine that your firm's financial reports have shown an unabated decline in revenue for seven quarters. Expenses have increased rapidly, and it is becoming difficult, and at times not possible, to pay bills as they become due. Suppliers are concerned about shipping goods without first receiving payment, and some have refused to ship without advanced payment in cash. Customers are requiring assurances that future orders will be delivered and some are beginning to buy from competitors. Employees are listening seriously to rumors of financial problems and a higher than normal number have accepted other employment. What can be done? What strategy can be initiated to protect the company and resolve the financial problems in the short term?

The Harshest Resolution

If the judgment of the owners of a business is that its decline cannot be reversed, and the business cannot be sold as a going concern, then the alternative that is in the best interest of all may be a liquidation bankruptcy, also known as Chapter 7 of the Bankruptcy Code. The court appoints a trustee, who collects the property of the company, reduces it to cash, and distributes the proceeds proportionally to creditors on a pro rata basis as expeditiously as possible. Since all assets are sold to pay outstanding debt, a liquidation bankruptcy terminates a business. This type of filing is critically important to sole proprietors or partnerships. Their owners are personally liable for all business debts not covered by the sale of the business assets unless they can secure a Chapter 7 bankruptcy, which will allow them to cancel any debt in excess of exempt assets. Although they will be left with little personal property, the liquidated debtor is discharged from paying the remaining debt.

The shareholders of corporations are not liable for corporate debt and any debt existing after corporate assets are liquidated is absorbed by creditors. Corporate shareholders may simply terminate operations and walk away without liability to remaining creditors. However, filing a Chapter 7 proceeding will provide for an orderly and fair distribution of assets to creditors and thereby may reduce the negative impact of the business failure.

A Conditional Second Chance

A proactive alternative for the endangered company is reorganization bankruptcy. Chosen for the right reasons, and implemented in the right way, reorganization bankruptcy can provide a financially, strategically, and ethically sound basis on which to advance the interests of all of the firm's stakeholders.

A thorough and objective analysis of the company may support the idea of its continuing operations if excessive debt can be reduced and new strategic initiatives can be undertaken. If the realistic possibility of long-term survival exists, a reorganization under Chapter 11 of the Bankruptcy Code can provide the opportunity. Reorganization allows a business debtor to restructure its debts and, with the agreement of creditors and approval of the court, to continue as a viable business. Creditors involved in Chapter 11 actions often receive less than the total debt due to them but far more than would be available from liquidation.

A Chapter 11 bankruptcy can provide time and protection to the debtor firm (which we will call the *Company*) to reorganize and use future earnings to pay creditors. The Company may restructure debts, close unprofitable divisions or stores, renegotiate labor contracts, reduce its work force, or propose other actions that could create a profitable business. If the plan is accepted by creditors, the Company will be given another chance to avoid liquidation and emerge from the bankruptcy proceedings rehabilitated.

Seeking Protection of the Bankruptcy Court

If creditors file lawsuits or schedule judicial sales to enforce liens, the Company will need to seek the protection of the Bankruptcy Court. Filing a bankruptcy petition will invoke the protection of the court to provide sufficient time to work out a reorganization that was not achievable voluntarily. If reorganization is not possible, a Chapter 7 proceeding will allow for the fair and orderly dissolution of the business.

If a Chapter 11 proceeding is the required course of action, the Company must determine what the reorganized business will look like, if such a structure can be achieved, and how it will be accomplished while maintaining operations during the bankruptcy proceeding. Will sufficient cash be available to pay for the proceedings and reorganization? Will customers continue to do business with the Company or seek other more secure businesses with which to deal? Will key personnel stay on or look for more secure employment? Which operations should be discontinued or reduced?

Emerging from Bankruptcy

Bankruptcy is only the first step toward recovery for a firm. Many questions should be answered: How did the business get to the point at which the extreme action of bankruptcy was necessary? Were warning signs overlooked? Was the competitive environment understood? Did pride or fear prevent objective analysis? Did the business have the people and resources to succeed? Was the strategic plan well designed and implemented? Did financial problems result from unforeseen and unforeseeable problems or from bad management decisions?

Commitments to "try harder," "listen more carefully to the customer," and "be more efficient" are important but insufficient grounds to inspire stakeholder confidence. A recovery strategy must be developed to delineate how the company will compete more successfully in the future.

An assessment of the bankruptcy situation requires executives to consider the causes of the Company's decline and the severity of the problem it now faces. Investors must decide whether the management team that governed the company's operations during the downturn can return the firm to a position of success. Creditors must believe that the company's managers have learned how to prevent a recurrence of the observed and similar problems. Alternatively, they must have faith that the company's competencies can be sufficiently augmented by key substitutions to the management team, with strong support in decision making from a board of directors and consultants, to restore the firm's competitive strength.

CORPORATE COMBINATIONS

The 15 grand strategies discussed above, used singly and much more often in combinations, represent the traditional alternatives used by firms in the United States. Recently, three new grand types have gained in popularity; all fit under the broad category of corporate combinations. Although they do not fit the criterion by which executives retain a high degree of control over their operations, these grand strategies deserve special attention and consideration especially by companies that operate in global, dynamic, and technologically driven industries. These three newly popularized grand strategies are joint ventures, strategic alliances, and consortia.

Joint Ventures

Occasionally two or more capable firms lack a necessary component for success in a particular competitive environment. For example, no single petroleum firm controlled sufficient resources to construct the Alaskan pipeline. Nor was any single firm capable of processing and marketing all of the oil that would flow through the pipeline. The solution was a set of *joint ventures,* which are commercial companies (children) created and operated for the benefit of the co-owners (parents). These cooperative arrangements provided both the funds needed to build the pipeline and the processing and marketing capacities needed to profitably handle the oil flow.

The particular form of joint ventures discussed above is *joint ownership*. In recent years, it has become increasingly appealing for domestic firms to join foreign firms by means of this form. For example, Diamond-Star Motors is the result of a joint venture between a U.S. company, Chrysler Corporation, and Japan's Mitsubishi Motors corporation. Located in Normal, Illinois, Diamond-Star was launched because it offered Chrysler and Mitsubishi a chance to expand on their long-standing relationship in which subcompact cars (as well as Mitsubishi engines and other automotive parts) are imported to the United States and sold under the Dodge and Plymouth names.

The joint venture extends the supplier-consumer relationship and has strategic advantages for both partners. For Chrysler, it presents an opportunity to produce a high-quality car using expertise brought to the venture by Mitsubishi. It also gives Chrysler the chance to try new production techniques and to realize efficiencies by using the workforce that was not included under Chrysler's collective bargaining agreement with the United Auto Workers. The agreement offers Mitsubishi the opportunity to produce cars for sale in the United States without being subjected to the tariffs and restrictions placed on Japanese imports.

As a second example, Bethlehem Steel acquired an interest in a Brazilian mining venture to secure a raw material source. The stimulus for this joint ownership venture was grand strategy, but such is not always the case. Certain countries virtually mandate that foreign firms entering their markets do so on a joint ownership basis. India and Mexico are good examples. The rationale of these countries is that joint ventures minimize the threat of foreign domination and enhance the skills, employment, growth, and profits of local firms.

It should be noted that strategic managers understandably are wary of joint ventures. Admittedly, joint ventures present new opportunities with risks that can be shared. On the other hand, joint ventures often limit the discretion, control, and profit potential of partners, while demanding managerial attention and other resources that might be directed toward the firm's mainstream activities. Nevertheless, increasing globalization in many industries may require greater consideration of the joint venture approach, if historically national firms are to remain viable.

Strategic Alliances

Strategic alliances are distinguished from joint ventures because the companies involved do not take an equity position in one another. In many instances, strategic alliances are partnerships that exist for a defined period during which partners contribute their skills and expertise to a cooperative project. For example, one partner provides manufacturing capabilities while a second partner provides marketing expertise. Many times, such alliances are undertaken because the partners want to learn from one another with the intention to be able to develop in-house capabilities to supplant the partner when the contractual arrangement between them reaches its termination date. Such relationships are tricky since in a sense the partners are attempting to "steal" each other's know-how. Exhibit 6–11, Global Strategy in Action, lists many important questions about their learning intentions that prospective partners should ask themselves before entering into a strategic alliance.

In other instances, strategic alliances are synonymous with licensing agreements. Licensing involves the transfer of some industrial property right from the U.S. licensor to a motivated licensee in a foreign country. Most tend to be patents, trademarks, or technical know-how that are granted to the licensee for a specified time in return for a royalty and for avoiding tariffs or import quotas. Bell South and U.S. West, with various marketing and service competitive advantages valuable to Europe, have extended a number of licenses to create personal computer networks in the United Kingdom (U.K.).

Objective	Major Questions
1. Assess and value partner knowledge.	• What were the strategic objectives in forming the alliance? • What are the core competencies of our alliance partner? • Which partner contributes key alliance inputs? • What specific knowledge does the partner have that could enhance our competitive strategy? Is that knowledge or some of the knowledge embodied in the alliance? • What are the core partner skills relevant for our product/markets? • Are we realistic about partner skills and capabilities relevant to our strategy and capabilities?
2. Determine knowledge accessibility.	• Have learning issues been discussed in the alliance negotiations? • How have key alliance responsibilities been allocated to the partners? Which partner controls key managerial responsibilities? • Do we have easy geographic access to the alliance operations? • Does the alliance agreement specify restrictions on our access to the alliance operations? • Has our partner taken explicit steps to restrict our access? If yes, can we eliminate these restrictions through negotiation or assignment of managers to the alliance?
3. Evaluate knowledge tacitness and ease of transfer.	• Is our learning objective focused on explicit operational knowledge? • Where in the alliance does the knowledge reside? • Is the knowledge strategic or operational? • Reality check: Do we understand what we are trying to learn and how we can use the knowledge?
4. Establish knowledge connections between the alliance and the partner.	• Do parent managers visit the alliance on a regular basis? • Has a systematic plan been established for managers to rotate between the alliance and the parent? • Are parent managers in regular contact with senior alliance managers? • Has the alliance been incorporated into parent strategic plans and do alliance managers participate in parent strategic planning discussions? • What is the level of trust between parent and alliance managers? • Do alliance financial issues dominate meetings between alliance and parent managers?
5. Draw on existing knowledge to facilitate learning.	• Have the partner firms worked together in the past? • In the learning process, have efforts been made to involve managers with prior experience in either/both alliance management and partner ties? • Are experiences with other alliances being used as the basis for managing the current alliance? • Are we realistic about our partner's learning objectives? • Are we open-minded about knowledge without immediate short-term applicability?
6. Ensure that partner and alliance managerial cultures are in alignment.	• Is the alliance viewed as a threat or an asset by parent managers? • In the parent, is there agreement on the strategic rationale for the alliance? • In the alliance, do managers understand the importance of the parent's learning objective?

Source: Andrew C. Inkpen. "Learning and Knowledge Acquisition through International Strategic Alliances," *Academy of Management Executive* 12, no. 4 (1998), p. 78.

1. **Improve Business Focus.**
   For many companies, the single most compelling reason for outsourcing is that several "how" issues are siphoning off huge amounts of management's resources and attention.
2. **Access to World-Class Capabilities.**
   By the very nature of their specialization, outsourcing providers bring extensive worldwide, world-class resources to meeting the needs of their customers. According to Norris Overton, vice president of reengineering, AMTRAK, partnering with an organization with world-class capabilities, can offer access to new technology, tools, and techniques that the organization may not currently possess; better career opportunities for personnel who transition to the outsourcing provider; more structured methodologies, procedures, and documentation; and competitive advantage through expanded skills.
3. **Accelerated Reengineering Benefits.**
   Outsourcing is often a byproduct of another powerful management tool—business process reengineering. It allows an organization to immediately realize the anticipated benefits of reengineering by having an outside organization—one that is already reengineered to world-class standards—take over the process.
4. **Shared Risks.**
   There are tremendous risks associated with the investments an organization makes. When companies outsource they become more flexible, more dynamic, and better able to adapt to changing opportunities.
5. **Free Resources for Other Purposes.**
   Every organization has limits on the resources available to it. Outsourcing permits an organization to redirect its resources from noncore activities toward activities that have the greater return in serving the customer.

Another licensing strategy open to U.S. firms is to contract the manufacturing of its product line to a foreign company to exploit local comparative advantages in technology, materials, or labor. For example, MIPS Computer Systems has licensed Digital Equipment Corporation, Texas Instruments, Cypress Semiconductor, and Bipolar Integrated Technology in the United States, and Fujitsu, NEC, and Kubota in Japan to market computers based on its designs in the partner's country.

Service and franchise-based firms—including Anheuser-Busch, Avis, Coca-Cola, Hilton, Hyatt, Holiday Inns, Kentucky Fried Chicken, McDonald's, and Pepsi—have long engaged in licensing arrangements with foreign distributors as a way to enter new markets with standardized products that can benefit from marketing economies.

Outsourcing is a rudimentary approach to strategic alliances that enables firms to gain a competitive advantage. Significant changes within many segments of American business continue to encourage the use of outsourcing practices. Within the health care arena, an industry survey recorded 67 percent of hospitals using provider outsourcing for at least one department within their organization. Services such as information systems, reimbursement, and risk and physician practice management are outsourced by 51 percent of the hospitals that use outsourcing.

Another successful application of outsourcing is found in human resources. A survey of human resource executives revealed 85 percent have personal experience leading an outsourcing effort within their organization. In addition, it was found that two-thirds of pension departments have outsourced at least one human resource function.

Within customer service and sales departments, outsourcing increased productivity in such areas as product information, sales and order taking, sample fulfillment, and complaint handling. Exhibit 6–12 presents the top five strategic and tactical reasons for exploiting the benefits of outsourcing.

Consortia, Keiretsus, and Chaebols

Consortia are defined as large interlocking relationships between businesses of an industry. In Japan such consortia are known as *keiretsus,* in South Korea as *chaebols.*

In Europe, consortia projects are increasing in number and in success rates. Examples include the Junior Engineers' and Scientists' Summer Institute, which underwrites cooperative learning and research; the European Strategic Program for Research and Development in Information Technologies, which seeks to enhance European competitiveness in fields related to computer electronics and component manufacturing; and EUREKA, which is a joint program involving scientists and engineers from several European countries to coordinate joint research projects.

A Japanese *keiretsu* is an undertaking involving up to 50 different firms that are joined around a large trading company or bank and are coordinated through interlocking directories and stock exchanges. It is designed to use industry coordination to minimize risks of competition, in part through cost sharing and increased economies of scale. Examples include Sumitomo, Mitsubishi, Mitsui, and Sanwa. Exhibit 6–13, Global Strategy in Action, presents a new side to *keiretsus,* namely, that they are adding global partners, including several from the United States. Their cooperative nature is growing in evidence as is their market success.

A South Korean chaebol resembles a consortium or keiretsu except that they are typically financed through government banking groups and largely are run by professional managers trained by participating firms expressly for the job.

SELECTION OF LONG-TERM OBJECTIVES AND GRAND STRATEGY SETS

At first glance, the strategic management model, which provides the framework for study throughout this book, seems to suggest that strategic choice decision making leads to the sequential selection of long-term objectives and grand strategies. In fact, however, strategic choice is the simultaneous selection of long-range objectives and grand strategies. When strategic planners study their opportunities, they try to determine which are most likely to result in achieving various long-range objectives. Almost simultaneously, they try to forecast whether an available grand strategy can take advantage of preferred opportunities so the tentative objectives can be met. In essence, then, three distinct but highly interdependent choices are being made at one time. Several triads, or sets, of possible decisions are usually considered.

A simplified example of this process is shown in Exhibit 6–14. In this example, the firm has determined that six strategic choice options are available. These options stem from three interactive opportunities (e.g., West Coast markets that present little competition.) Because each of these interactive opportunities can be approached through different grand strategies—for options 1 and 2, the grand strategies are horizontal integration and market development—each offers the potential for achieving long-range objectives to varying degrees. Thus, a firm rarely can make a strategic choice only on the basis of its preferred opportunities, long-range objectives, or grand strategy. Instead, these three elements must be considered simultaneously, because only in combination do they constitute a strategic choice.

In an actual decision situation, the strategic choice would be complicated by a wider variety of interactive opportunities, feasible company objectives, promising grand strategy options, and evaluative criteria. Nevertheless, Exhibit 6–14 does partially reflect the nature and complexity of the process by which long-term objectives and grand strategies are selected.

BusinessWeek Amid rolling hills outside Nagoya, Toshiba Corp. recently took the wraps off a new $1 billion chipmaking facility that uses ultraviolet lithography to etch circuits less than one micron wide—a tiny fraction of the width of a human hair.

The Toshiba chip site owes much to a strategic alliance with IBM and Siemens of Germany. In fact, IBM's know how in chemical mechanical polishing, essential to smoothing the tiny surfaces of multilayered chips, played a critical role. "We had little expertise here," concedes Toshiba's Koichi Suzuki.

QUIET CHANGE

What's more, about 20 IBM engineers will show up shortly to transfer the technology back to an IBM-Toshiba facility in Manassas, Virginia. In addition to the semiconductor cooperation, IBM and Toshiba jointly make liquid-crystal display panels—even though they use the LCDs in their fiercely competitive lines of laptop computers. "It's no longer considered a loss of corporate manhood to let others help out," says IBM Asia Pacific President Robert C. Timpson.

For years, many U.S. tie-ups with Japanese companies tended to be defensive in nature, poorly managed, and far removed from core businesses. Now, the alliances are deepening, taking on increasingly important products, and expanding their geographic reach in terms of sales. U.S.-Japanese partnerships are, for example, popping up in Asia's emerging but tricky markets, reducing the risks each company faces.

This deepening web of relationships reflects a quiet change in thinking by Japanese and U.S. multinationals in an era when keeping pace with technological change and competing globally have stretched the resources of even the richest companies. "The scale and technology are so great that neither can do it alone," says Jordan D. Lewis, author of *The Connected Corporation*.

Overall, instances of joint investments in research, products, and distribution by Japanese companies and foreign counterparts, mostly American, have jumped 26%, to 155, in the first quarter of 1996—on top of a 33% increase between 1993 and 1995—according to the Sakura Institute of Research.

ENVY

And while Uncle Sam and U.S. companies with grievances have attacked Japan's system of big industrial groups, called keiretsu, as exclusionary, other chieftains of Corporate America have quietly become *stakeholders* of sorts. The list includes companies as diverse as IBM, General Motors, TRW, Boeing, and Caterpillar.

Many American executives who have established these alliances say they appreciate the attributes of Japan's big industrial groups. U.S. managers have always envied the keiretsu edge in spreading risk over a cluster of companies when betting on a new technology or blitzing emerging markets.

In one industry after another, U.S. and Japanese partners are breaking new ground in their level of cooperation. The impact is felt far beyond the U.S. and Japanese home markets. Take the 50-50 venture between Caterpillar Inc. and Mitsubishi Heavy Industries LTD., part of Japan's $200 billion keiretsu of the same name. Early on, Cat wanted a way to sell its construction equipment in Japan and compete with rival Komatsu Ltd. on its home turf. Mitsubishi wanted to play catch-up with Komatsu, too, and expand its export markets.

Their alliance played a key role in taming Komatsu. But the partners have broader ambitions. Since Cat shifted all design work for its "300" series of excavators to the partnership back in 1987, the venture's two Japanese factories have emerged as Cat's primary source of production for sales to fast-growing Asia. The alliance's products reach the world market through Cat's network of 186 independent dealers in 197 countries.

Source: Brian Bemner in Tokyo, with Zachary Schiller in Cleveland, Tim Smart in Fairfield, William J. Holstein in New York, and bureau reports, "Keiretsu Connections," *BusinessWeek*, July 22, 1996.

In the next chapter, the strategic choice process will be fully explained. However, knowledge of long-term objectives and grand strategies is essential to understanding that process.

SEQUENCE OF OBJECTIVES AND STRATEGY SELECTION

The selection of long-range objectives and grand strategies involves simultaneous, rather than sequential, decisions. While it is true that objectives are needed to prevent the firm's direction and progress from being determined by random forces, it is equally true that objectives can be achieved only if strategies are implemented. In fact, long-term objectives and grand strategies are so interdependent that some business consultants do not distinguish between them. Long-term objectives and grand strategies are still combined

EXHIBIT 6–14   A Profile of Strategic Choice Options

	Six Strategic Choice Options					
	1	**2**	**3**	**4**	**5**	**6**
Interactive opportunities	West Coast markets present little competition		Current markets sensitive to price competition		Current industry product lines offer too narrow a range of markets	
Appropriate long-range objectives (limited sample):						
Average 5-year ROI.	15%	19%	13%	17%	23%	15%
Company sales by year 5.	+50%	+40%	+20%	+0%	+35%	+25%
Risk of negative profits.	.30	.25	.10	.15	.20	.05
Grand strategies	Horizontal integration	Market development	Concentration	Selective retrenchment	Product development	Concentration

under the heading of company strategy in most of the popular business literature and in the thinking of most practicing executives.

However, the distinction has merit. Objectives indicate what strategic managers want but provide few insights about how they will be achieved. Conversely, strategies indicate what types of actions will be taken but do not define what ends will be pursued or what criteria will serve as constraints in refining the strategic plan.

Does it matter whether strategic decisions are made to achieve objectives or to satisfy constraints? No, because constraints are themselves objectives. The constraint of increased inventory capacity is a desire (an objective), not a certainty. Likewise, the constraint of an increase in the sales force does not assure that the increase will be achieved, given such factors as other company priorities, labor market conditions, and the firm's profit performance.

Summary

Before we learn how strategic decisions are made, it is important to understand the two principal components of any strategic choice; namely, long-term objectives and the grand strategy. The purpose of this chapter was to convey that understanding.

Long-term objectives were defined as the results a firm seeks to achieve over a specified period, typically five years. Seven common long-term objectives were discussed: profitability, productivity, competitive position, employee development, employee relations, technological leadership, and public responsibility. These, or any other long-term objectives, should be acceptable, flexible, measurable over time, motivating, suitable, understandable, and achievable.

Grand strategies were defined as comprehensive approaches guiding the major actions designed to achieve long-term objectives. Fifteen grand strategy options were discussed: concentrated growth, market development, product development, innovation, horizontal integration, vertical integration, concentric diversification, conglomerate diversification, turnaround, divestiture, liquidation, bankruptcy, joint ventures, strategic alliances, and consortia.

Questions for Discussion

1. Identify firms in the business community nearest to your college or university that you believe are using each of the 15 grand strategies discussed in this chapter.

2. Identify firms in your business community that appear to rely principally on 1 of the 15 grand strategies. What kind of information did you use to classify the firms?

3. Write a long-term objective for your school of business that exhibits the seven qualities of long-term objectives described in this chapter.

4. Distinguish between the following pairs of grand strategies:
   a. Horizontal and vertical integration.
   b. Conglomerate and concentric diversification.
   c. Product development and innovation.
   d. Joint venture and strategic alliance.

5. Rank each of the 15 grand strategy options discussed in this chapter on the following three scales:

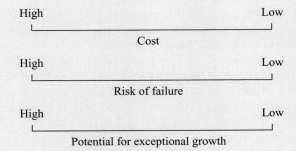

High   Low

Cost

High   Low

Risk of failure

High   Low

Potential for exceptional growth

6. Identify firms that use one of the eight specific options shown in Exhibit 6–5 under the grand strategies of concentration, market development, and product development.

Chapter 6 Discussion Case

BusinessWeek

GM's Strategy of Piecemeal Alliances

1 For Fiat, General Motors' purchase of 20% of its auto business on March 13 is just the breather it was seeking. The Italian carmaker gets a deep-pocketed partner with a reputation as an easygoing, hands-off minority stakeholder, leaving Fiat's managers in charge. And GM's prize? It gets small Fiat diesel engines and a chance to trim its costs in Europe and Latin America—not to mention the pleasure of thwarting rival DaimlerChrysler's effort to swallow Fiat whole. Yet GM's minority stake gives it little clout to force the tough cost-cutting Fiat needs, and it leaves GM competing fiercely with its new partner in key European auto segments. Laments one large GM institutional investor: "It looks like a huge victory for Fiat, but it doesn't do very much for GM."

2 In short, it looks like most of GM's growing network of global auto tie-ups: a puzzling mix of missed opportunities and timid half steps. As the global auto industry has consolidated rapidly—with DaimlerChrysler and Ford moving boldly to acquire key players—GM has tiptoed into a series of minority stakes and ad-hoc alliances with rivals. GM hopes to reap the benefits of partnership without the messy culture clash, nationalist backlash, and red ink that a full buyout often entails. Says GM Chief Executive G. Richard Wagoner Jr.: "We think we've hit on the right formula."

3 But its track record suggests a different lesson: little ventured, little gained. Consider GM's stake in struggling Isuzu Motors Ltd. After 29 years as a minority shareholder, GM has gotten some diesel truck engines and co-designed pickup trucks. But Isuzu racked up a $200 million operating loss last year and amassed $8.3 billion in debt. In 1999, GM raised its holdings to 49% from 38%. Grouses the GM investor: "GM never exercised the management due diligence it should have, but it was probably unable to."

4 Even where it has taken control, GM's kid-glove style has brought limited benefit. When it bought half of Saab in 1990, the Swedish carmaker was a money-losing seller of 93,000 cars a year. Cash-strapped itself at first, GM shared major components between Saab and other GM divisions, improved Saab quality, and eventually rolled out new models. But while Saab's small U.S. sales are rising smartly, it barely ekes out a profit on the 131,000 cars it sells annually worldwide.

5 Still, Wagoner is stepping up GM's efforts to forge alliances. In December, the No. 1 automaker agreed to buy 20% of Fuji Heavy Industries Ltd., maker of Subaru cars, after tripling its holdings in Suzuki Motor Corp., to 10%, in 1998. In 1999, GM bought the remaining half of Saab. It is also negotiating to buy Korea's Daewoo Motor and has inked a technology-sharing deal with Toyota and an engine pact with Honda Motor.

6 GM's strategy has some advantages. Buying a small chunk of a company allows the auto giant inside for a closer look before deciding whether to take a bigger plunge. And taking a small stake in a healthy rival to share the costs of developing new technology or gain access to distribution in another region can help meet a strategic need cheaply.

7 But like elsewhere in life, you get what you pay for. If the partnership isn't a two-way exchange of expertise and capital, the value can be limited. Subaru and Suzuki, for instance, bring GM some small cars without bolstering its know-how. Says Brandies University international marketing professor Shih-Fen Chen: "GM's reliance on Japanese alliances prevents the company from developing its own small cars."

8 Acting as a silent partner is weak medicine indeed when buying into a company that urgently needs fixing. Only a full merger will let GM and Fiat tackle their biggest headache in the European market: overcapacity. To make their alliance pay off, they must quickly ax overlapping models and overhead to cut costs. Since Fiat factories run at just 60% of capacity, some must close. But GM can't make any of that happen—which is just fine with Fiat's managers and the Italian government. DaimlerChrysler execs say privately that they refused to accept such terms.

9   LOPSIDED DEAL. While GM's partial ownership may ultimately lead to a merger, that's at least several years away. By then, both carmakers will have lost the opportunity to fix their European operations while the market was strong. Moreover, the deal gives Fiat the upper hand: It can compel GM to buy the rest of Fiat any time from 2004 to 2009 at a fair-market price. "How do they know where Fiat will be five years from now, especially since they won't have a hand in running it?" says Deutsche Bank Securities Inc. analyst Rod Lache. "That's a pretty big leap of faith." What's more, Fiat can sell its 80% stake to anyone after a year as long as GM has a chance to match terms.

10   In the short run, GM and Fiat plan to gain efficiency by sharing chassis and key components, analysts say. While that's a good idea, getting engineers from different companies and cultures to collaborate is extremely tricky. GM has repeatedly stumbled at the far less complex task of fostering in-house cooperation between its North American and European engineers. The task could be far tougher for GM and Fiat, which will continue to battle in the small and midsize car segments. "If you're competing on 40% of your product [lineup], how willing are you going to be to share product information?" notes Lache.

11   Despite the messy details, merger mania in the auto industry continues at fever pitch. The field of remaining candidates is down to a handful: Daewoo, Mitsubishi Motors, PSA Peugeot Citroen, Volvo truck. That leaves only holdouts BMW and Honda, which are not on the block. But BMW may toss Rover Cars back on the market after trying fruitlessly since 1994 to fix it. Daimler is busily trying to cement a deal with Mitsubishi, and Ford has joined the fray. GM may now seek a partner in its Daewoo buyout attempt. Not everyone has a good economic reason for doing these deals, warns Brandeis' Chen. But until almost everything is snapped up, they're likely to proceed apace.

Source: Kathleen Kerwin, David Welch, and Joann Muller, "For GM, Once Again, Little Ventured, Little Gained. Its small Fiat stake continues a strategy of piecemeal alliances," *BusinessWeek,* March 27, 2000.

Chapter **Seven**

Strategic Analysis and Choice in Single- or Dominant-Product Businesses: Building Sustainable Competitive Advantages

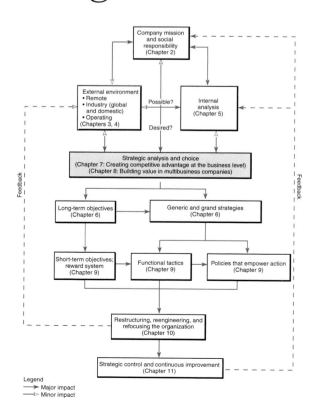

Company mission and social responsibility (Chapter 2)

External environment
• Remote
• Industry (global and domestic)
• Operating
(Chapters 3, 4)

Possible?

Desired?

Internal analysis (Chapter 5)

Strategic analysis and choice
(Chapter 7: Creating competitive advantage at the business level)
(Chapter 8: Building value in multibusiness companies)

Long-term objectives (Chapter 6)

Generic and grand strategies (Chapter 6)

Short-term objectives; reward system (Chapter 9)

Functional tactics (Chapter 9)

Policies that empower action (Chapter 9)

Restructuring, reengineering, and refocusing the organization (Chapter 10)

Strategic control and continuous improvement (Chapter 11)

Feedback

Legend
→ Major impact
⇢ Minor impact

Strategic analysis and choice is the phase of the strategic management process when business managers examine and choose a business strategy that allows their business to maintain or create a sustainable competitive advantage. Their starting point is to evaluate and determine which value chain activities provide the basis for distinguishing the firm in the customer's mind from other reasonable alternatives. Businesses with a dominant product or service line must also choose among alternate grand strategies to guide the firm's activities, particularly when they are trying to decide about broadening the scope of the firm's activities beyond its core business.

This chapter examines strategic analysis and choice in single- or dominant-product/service businesses by addressing two basic issues:

1. **What strategies are most effective at building sustainable competitive advantages for single business units?** What competitive strategy positions a business most effectively in its industry? For example, Scania, the most productive truck manufacturer in the world, joins its major rival Volvo as two anchors of Sweden's economy. Scania's return on sales of 9.9 percent far exceeds Mercedes (2.6 percent) and Volvo (2.5 percent), a level it has achieved most of the last 60 years. Scania has built a sustainable competitive advantage with a strategy of focusing solely on heavy trucks, in a limited geographic area—Europe—and by providing customized trucks with standardized components (20,000 components per truck versus 25,000 for Volvo and 40,000 for Mercedes). Scania is a low-cost producer of a differentiated truck that can be custom-manufactured quickly and sold to a regionally focused market.

2. **Should dominant-product/service businesses diversify** to build value and competitive advantage? What grand strategies are most appropriate? For example, Compaq Computers and Coca-Cola managers have examined the question of diversification and apparently concluded that continued concentration on their core products and services and development of new markets for those same core products and services are best. IBM and Pepsi examined the same question and concluded that related diversification and vertical integration were best. Why?

EVALUATING AND CHOOSING BUSINESS STRATEGIES: SEEKING SUSTAINED COMPETITIVE ADVANTAGE

Business managers evaluate and choose strategies that they think will make their business successful. Businesses become successful because they possess some advantage relative to their competitors. The two most prominent sources of competitive advantage can be found in the business's cost structure and its ability to differentiate the business from competitors. Disney World in Orlando offers theme park patrons several unique, distinct features that differentiate it from other entertainment options. Wal-Mart offers retail customers the lowest prices on popular consumer items because they have created a low-cost structure resulting in a competitive advantage over most competitors.

Businesses that create competitive advantages from one or both of these sources usually experience above-average profitability within their industry. Businesses that lack a cost or differentiation advantage usually experience average or below-average profitability. Two recent studies found that businesses that do not have either form of competitive advantage perform the poorest among their peers while businesses that possess both forms of competitive advantage enjoy the highest levels of profitability within their industry.[1] The average return on investment for over 2,500 businesses across seven industries looked as follows:

[1] R. B. Robinson and J. A. Pearce, "Planned Patterns of Strategic Behavior and Their Relationship to Business Unit Performance," *Strategic Management Journal* 9, no. 1 (1988), pp. 43–60; G. G. Dess and G. T. Lumpkin, "Emerging Issues in Strategy Process Research," in *Handbook of Strategic Management,* Hitt et. al., 2002.

Differentiation Advantage	Cost Advantage	Overall Average ROI across Seven Industries
High	High	35.0%
Low	High	26.0
High	Low	22.0
Low	Low	9.5

Initially, managers were advised to evaluate and choose strategies that emphasized one type of competitive advantage. Often referred to as *generic strategies,* firms were encouraged to become either a differentiation-oriented or low-cost-oriented company. In so doing, it was logical that organizational members would develop a clear understanding of company priorities and, as these studies suggest, likely experience profitability superior to competitors without either a differentiation or low-cost orientation.

The studies mentioned above, and the experience of many other businesses, indicate that the highest profitability levels are found in businesses that possess both types of competitive advantage at the same time. In other words, businesses that have one or more value chain activities that truly differentiate them from key competitors and also have value chain activities that let them operate at a lower cost will consistently outperform their rivals that don't. So the challenge for today's business managers is to evaluate and choose business strategies based on core competencies and value chain activities that sustain both types of competitive advantage simultaneously. Exhibit 7–1, Global Strategy in Action, shows Honda Motor Company attempting to do just this in Europe.

Evaluating Cost Leadership Opportunities

Business success built on cost leadership requires the business to be able to provide its product or service at a cost below what its competitors can achieve. And it must be a sustainable cost advantage. Through the skills and resources identified in Exhibit 7–2, a business must be able to accomplish one or more activities in its value chain activities—procuring materials, processing them into products, marketing the products, and distributing the products or support activities—in a more cost-effective manner than that of its competitors or it must be able to reconfigure its value chain so as to achieve a cost advantage. Exhibit 7–2 provides examples of ways this might be done.

Strategists examining their business's value chain for low-cost leadership advantages evaluate the sustainability of those advantages by *benchmarking* (refer to Chapter 5 for a discussion of this comparison technique) their business against key competitors and by considering the impact of any cost advantage on the five forces in their business's competitive environment. Low-cost activities that are sustainable and that provide one or more of these advantages relative to key industry forces should become the basis for the business's competitive strategy.

Low-Cost Advantages That Reduce the Likelihood of Pricing Pressure from Buyers   When key competitors cannot match prices from the low-cost leader, customers pressuring the leader risk establishing a price level that drives alternate sources out of business.

Truly Sustained Low-Cost Advantages May Push Rivals into Other Areas, Lessening Price Competition   Intense, continued price competition may be ruinous for all rivals, as seen occasionally in the airline industry.

Global Strategy in Action
Honda Pursues Low-Cost Leadership and Differentiation Strategies in Europe

Exhibit 7–1

BusinessWeek Honda is hot. In the United States, the Tokyo company can barely keep up with demand for models like the Acura MDX sport utility vehicle and the Odysssey minivan. Four of the top 10 best-selling cars in Japan are Hondas. Honda recently passed rival Nissan to become Japan's second-largest automaker after Toyota.

But the road is not entirely smooth for the Japanese carmaker. Honda Motor Co. has suffered a serious breakdown in Europe. Honda's operations in the Old World reported a loss of nearly half a billion dollars in Britain and the Continent for the year ended March 31. "Our biggest worry is weak sales in Europe," says CEO Hiroyuki Yoshino.

So Yoshino's managers have gone into overdrive to repair the European business. Their game plan includes cost leadership initiatives: boosting capacity at two plants in Britain, heeding European calls for cars with diesel engines, and implementing a hard-nosed cost-cutting program that targets parts suppliers . . . and differentiation opportunities: launching an all-new car for the subcompact market.

Honda has a reputation for tackling all of its challenges head-on. But the European problem, even against the background of record results in the United States, underscores Honda's fragility. Although less than 10% of Honda's global volume—and far less revenue—comes from Europe, the region has outsized importance to Yoshino and his deputies. Why? Because Honda has no safe harbor if its sales in the United States begin to flag, as some analysts expect. The company earns some 90% of its profits in America, a far higher percentage than other Japanese carmakers. "Honda is the least globally diverse Japanese automobile manufacturer," says Chris Redl, director of equity research at UBS Warburg's office in Tokyo. "It's a minor problem for now, but with the U.S. market heading down, it could become a major problem." So a closer look at the cost leadership and differentiation approach at Honda Europe, their confident answer, is as follows.

COST LEADERSHIP

Honda's struggles in Europe today are partly the result of a key strategic error it made when it started making cars in Britain 10 years ago. Company officials didn't foresee the huge runup in the value of the British pound against Europe's single currency, the euro, which made its cars more expensive than competing models manufactured on the Continent. Subpar sales cut output in Britain last year to levels near 50% of capacity: It's impossible to make money at that production level. "Europe is definitely an Achilles' heel for Honda," says Toru Shimano, an analyst at Okasan Securities Co. in Tokyo.

So Honda is increasing purchases of cheaper parts from suppliers outside Britain and moving swiftly to freshen its lineup. Earlier this year, a remodeled and roomier five-door Civic hatchback with improved fuel efficiency rolled off production lines in Britain. To goose output at its British operations, Honda will start exporting perky three-door Civic sedans built at its newest plant to the United States and Japan this year. It also plans to export its British-made CR-V compact SUV to America to augment the Japan-made CR-Vs now being sold there.

DIFFERENTIATION

All of that will help, but Honda's big issue is the hole in its lineup: subcompacts. While 1-liter-engine cars sell poorly in the United States, Europeans and Japanese can't get enough of them. "Honda does not have a product for Europe yet," says UBS Warburg's Redl. It missed out with its 1-liter Logo. "It didn't stand out from the crowd," Yoshino admits.

So the Logo is history, and Honda's new salvation in Europe, due to launch first in Japan on June 21, is an all-new five-door hatchback called the Fit. At 1.3 liters, its engine outpowers Toyota's competing Vitz-class line of cars. Honda says the sporty Fit also boasts a number of nifty features. The only one it would confirm, however, is that owners will be able to flatten all four seats, including the driver's, at the flick of a switch—a selling point for youths keen to load bikes or sleep in it on long road trips.

Source: "Honda's Weak Spot: Europe," *BusinessWeek,* June 11, 2001.

New Entrants Competing on Price Must Face an Entrenched Cost Leader without the Experience to Replicate Every Cost Advantage EasyJet, a British startup with a Southwest Airlines copycat strategy, entered the European airline market with much fanfare in 2000 with low priced, city-to-city, no frills flights.

EXHIBIT 7–2 **Evaluating a Business's Cost Leadership Opportunities**

Source: Adapted with permission of *Harvard Business School on Managing the Value Chain* (Cambridge: HBS Press, 2000).

A. Skills and Resources That Foster Cost Leadership

Sustained capital investment and access to capital.
Process engineering skills.
Intense supervision of labor or core technical operations.
Products or services designed for ease of manufacture or delivery.
Low-cost distribution system.

B. Organizational Requirements to Support and Sustain Cost Leadership Activities

Tight cost control.
Frequent, detailed control reports.
Continuous improvement and benchmarking orientation.
Structured organization and responsibilities.
Incentives based on meeting strict, usually quantitative targets.

C. Examples of Ways Businesses Achieve Competitive Advantage via Cost Leadership

Technology Development	Process innovations that lower production costs.		Product redesign to reduce the number of components.		
Human Resource Management	Safety training for all employees reduces absenteeism, downtime, and accidents.				
General Administration	Reduced levels of management cuts corporate overhead.		Computerized, integrated information system reduces errors and administrative costs.		
Procurement	Favorable long-term contracts; captive suppliers or key customer for supplier.				
	Global, online suppliers provide automatic restocking of orders based on our sales.	Economy of scale in plant reduces equipment costs and depreciation.	Computerized routing lowers transportation expense.	Cooperative advertising with distributors creates local cost advantage in buying media space and time.	Subcontracted service technicians repair product correctly the first time or they bear all costs.
	Inbound logistics	Operations	Outbound logistics	Marketing and Sales	Service

Profit margin

Analysts caution that by the time you read this, British Airways, KLM's no-frills offshoot, Buzz, and Virgin Express will simply match fares on EasyJet's key routes and let high landing fees and flight delays take their toll on the British upstart.

Low-Cost Advantages Should Lessen the Attractiveness of Substitute Products A serious concern of any business is the threat of a substitute product in which buyers can meet their original need. Low-cost advantages allow the holder to resist this happening because it allows them to remain competitive even against desirable substitutes and it allows them to lessen concerns about price facing an inferior, lower priced substitute.

Higher Margins Allow Low-Cost Producers to Withstand Supplier Cost Increases and Often Gain Supplier Loyalty over Time Sudden, particularly uncontrollable increases in the costs suppliers face can be more easily absorbed by low-cost, higher margin producers. Severe droughts in California quadrupled the price of lettuce—a key restaurant demand. Some chains absorbed the cost; others had to confuse customers with a "lettuce tax." Furthermore, chains that worked well with produce suppliers gained a loyal, cooperative "partner" for possible assistance in a future, competitive situation.

Once managers identify opportunities to create cost advantage–based strategies, they must consider whether key risks inherent in cost leadership are present in a way that may mediate sustained success. The key risks with which they must be concerned are discussed next.

Many Cost-Saving Activities Are Easily Duplicated   Computerizing certain order entry functions among hazardous waste companies gave early adopters lower sales costs and better customer service for a brief time. Rivals quickly adapted, adding similar capabilities with similar impacts on their costs.

Exclusive Cost Leadership Can Become a Trap   Firms that emphasize lowest price and can offer it via cost advantages where product differentiation is increasingly not considered must truly be convinced of the sustainability of those advantages. Particularly with commodity-type products, the low-cost leader seeking to sustain a margin superior to lesser rivals may encounter increasing customer pressure for lower prices with great damage to both leader and lesser players.

Obsessive Cost Cutting Can Shrink Other Competitive Advantages Involving Key Product Attributes   Intense cost scrutiny can build margin, but it can reduce opportunities for or investment in innovation—processes and products. Similarly, such scrutiny can lead to the use of inferior raw materials, processes, or activities that were previously viewed by customers as a key attribute of the original products. Some mail-order computer companies that sought to maintain or enhance cost advantages found reductions in telephone service personnel and automation of that function backfiring with a drop in demand for their products even though their low prices were maintained.

Cost Differences Often Decline over Time   As products age, competitors learn how to match cost advantages. Absolute volumes sold often decline. Market channels and suppliers mature. Buyers become more knowledgeable. All of these factors present opportunities to lessen the value or presence of earlier cost advantages. Said another way, cost advantages that are not sustainable over a period of time are risky.

Once business managers have evaluated the cost structure of their value chain, determined activities that provide competitive cost advantages, and considered their inherent risks, they start choosing the business's strategy. Those managers concerned with differentiation-based strategies, or those seeking optimum performance incorporating both sources of competitive advantage, move to evaluating their business's sources of differentiation.

Evaluating Differentiation Opportunities

Differentiation requires that the business have sustainable advantages that allow it to provide buyers with something uniquely valuable to them. A successful differentiation strategy allows the business to provide a product or service of perceived higher value to buyers at a "differentiation cost" below the "value premium" to the buyers. In other words, the buyer feels the additional cost to buy the product or service is well below what the product or service is worth compared to other available alternatives.

Differentiation usually arises from one or more activities in the value chain that create a unique value important to buyers. Perrier's control of a carbonated water spring in France, Stouffer's frozen food packaging and sauce technology, Apple's highly integrated chip designs in its Mac computers, American Greeting Card's automated inventory

EXHIBIT 7–3 Evaluating a Business's Differentiation Opportunities

Source: Adapted with permission of *Harvard Business School on Managing the Value Chain* (Cambridge; HBS Press, 2000).

A. Skills and Resources That Foster Differentiation

Strong marketing abilities.
Product engineering.
Creative talent and flair.
Strong capabilities in basic research.
Corporate reputation for quality or technical leadership.
Long tradition in an industry or unique combination of skills drawn from other businesses.
Strong cooperation from channels.
Strong cooperation from suppliers of major components of the product or service.

B. Organizational Requirements to Support and Sustain Differentiation Activities

Strong coordination among functions in R&D, product development, and marketing.
Subjective measurement and incentives instead of quantitative measures.
Amenities to attract highly skilled labor, scientists, and creative people.
Tradition of closeness to key customers.
Some personnel skilled in sales and operations—technical and marketing.

C. Examples of Ways Businesses Achieve Competitive Advantage via Differentiation

Technology Development	Cutting-edge production technology and product features to maintain a "distinct" image and actual product.			
Human Resource Management	Programs to ensure technical competence of sales staff and a marketing orientation of service personnel.			
General Administration	Comprehensive, personalized database to build knowledge of groups of customers and individual buyers to be used in "customizing" how products are sold, serviced, and replaced.			
Procurement	Quality control presence at key supplier facilities; work with suppliers' new product development activities			
Purchase superior quality, well-known components, raising the quality and image of final products.	Careful inspection of products at each step in production to improve product performance and lower defect rate.	JIT coordination with buyers; use of own or captive transportation service to ensure timeliness.	Expensive, informative advertising and promotion to build brand image.	Allowing service personnel considerable discretion to credit customers for repairs.
Inbound logistics	Operations	Outbound logistics	Marketing and Sales	Service

Profit margin

system for retailers, and Federal Express's customer service capabilities are all examples of sustainable advantages around which successful differentiation strategies have been built. A business can achieve differentiation by performing its existing value activities or reconfiguring in some unique way. And the sustainability of that differentiation will depend on two things—a continuation of its high perceived value to buyers and a lack of imitation by competitors.

Exhibit 7–3 suggests key skills that managers should ensure are present to support an emphasis on differentiation. Examples of value chain activities that provide a differentiation advantage are also provided.

Strategists examining their business's value chain for differentiation advantages evaluate the sustainability of those advantages by *benchmarking* (refer to Chapter 5 for a discussion of this comparison technique) their business against key competitors and by considering the impact of any differentiation advantage on the five forces in their business's competitive environment. Sustainable activities that provide one or more of the following opportunities relative to key industry forces should become the basis for differentiation aspects of the business's competitive strategy:

Rivalry Is Reduced When a Business Successfully Differentiates Itself BMW's new Z23, made in Greer, South Carolina, does not compete with Saturns made in central Tennessee. A Harvard education does not compete with a local technical school. Both situations involve the same basic needs, transportation or education. However, one rival has clearly differentiated itself from others in the minds of certain buyers. In so doing, they do not have to respond competitively to that competitor.

Buyers Are Less Sensitive to Prices for Effectively Differentiated Products The Highlands Inn in Carmel, California, and the Ventana Inn along the Big Sur charge a minimum of $600 and 900, respectively, per night for a room with a kitchen, fireplace, hot tub, and view. Other places are available along this beautiful stretch of California's spectacular coastline, but occupancy rates at these two locations remain over 90 percent. Why? You can't get a better view and a more relaxed, spectacular setting to spend a few days on the Pacific Coast. Similarly, buyers of differentiated products tolerate price increases low-cost–oriented buyers would not accept. The former become very loyal to certain brands.

Brand Loyalty Is Hard for New Entrants to Overcome Many new beers are brought to market in the United States, but Budweiser continues to gain market share. Why? Brand loyalty is hard to overcome! And Anheuser-Busch has been clever to extend its brand loyalty from its core brand into newer niches, like nonalcohol brews, that other potential entrants have pioneered.

Managers examining differentiation-based advantages must take potential risks into account as they commit their business to these advantages. Some of the more common ways risks arise are discussed next.

Imitation Narrows Perceived Differentiation, Rendering Differentiation Meaningless AMC pioneered the Jeep passenger version of a truck 40 years ago. Ford created the Explorer, or luxury utility vehicle, in 1990. It took luxury car features and put them inside a jeep. Ford's payoff was substantial. The Explorer has become Ford's most popular domestic vehicle. However, virtually every vehicle manufacturer offered a luxury utility in 2003, with customers beginning to be hard pressed to identify clear distinctions between lead models. Ford's Explorer managers were looking for a new business strategy for the next decade that relied on new sources of differentiation and placed greater emphasis on low-cost components in their value chain.

Technological Changes That Nullify Past Investments or Learning The Swiss controlled over 95 percent of the world's watch market into the 1970s. The bulk of the craftspeople, technology, and infrastructure resided in Switzerland. U.S.-based Texas Instruments decided to experiment with the use of its digital technology in watches. Swiss producers were not interested, but Japan's SEIKO and others were. In 2005, the Swiss will make less than 5 percent of the world's watches.

The Cost Difference between Low-Cost Competitors and the Differentiated Business Becomes Too Great for Differentiation to Hold Brand Loyalty.   Buyers may begin to choose to sacrifice some of the features, services, or image possessed by the differentiated business for large cost savings. The rising cost of a college education, particularly at several "premier" institutions, has caused many students to opt for lower-cost destinations that offer very similar courses without image, frills, and professors that seldom teach undergraduate students anyway.

Evaluating Speed as a Competitive Advantage

While most telecommunication companies have used the last decade to leap aboard the information superhighway, GTE continued its impressive turnaround focusing on its core business—providing local telephone services. Long lagging behind the Baby Bells in profitability and efficiency, GTE has emphasized improving its poor customer service throughout the decade. The service was so bad in Santa Monica, California, that officials once tried to remove GTE as the local phone company. Candidly saying "we were the pits," new CEO Chuck Lee largely did away with its old system of taking customer service requests by writing them down and passing them along for resolution. Now, using personal communication services and specially designed software, service reps can solve 70 percent of all problems on the initial call—triple the success rate at the beginning of the last decade. Repair workers meanwhile plan their schedules on laptops, cutting downtime and speeding responses. CEO Lee has spent $1.5 billion on reengineering that slashed 17,000 jobs, replaced people with technology, and prioritized *speed* as the defining feature of GTE's business practices.

Speed, or rapid response to customer requests or market and technological changes, has become a major source of competitive advantage for numerous firms in today's intensely competitive global economy. Speed is certainly a form of differentiation, but it is more than that. Speed involves the *availability of a rapid response* to a customer by providing current products quicker, accelerating new product development or improvement, quickly adjusting production processes, and making decisions quickly. While low cost and differentiation may provide important competitive advantages, managers in tomorrow's successful companies will base their strategies on creating speed-based competitive advantages. Exhibit 7–4 describes and illustrates key skills and organizational requirements that are associated with speed-based competitive advantage. Jack Welch, now retired, the CEO who transformed General Electric from a fading company into one of Wall Street's best performers over the last 20 years, had this to say about speed:

> Speed is really the driving force that everyone is after. Faster products, faster product cycles to market. Better response time to customers. . . . Satisfying customers, getting faster communications, moving with more agility, all these things are easier when one is small. And these are all characteristics one needs in a fast-moving global environment.[2]

Speed-based competitive advantages can be created around several activities:

Customer Responsiveness   All consumers have encountered hassles, delays, and frustration dealing with various businesses from time to time. The same holds true when dealing business to business. Quick response with answers, information, and solutions to mistakes can become the basis for competitive advantage . . . one that builds customer loyalty quickly.

---

[2] "Jack Welch: A CEO Who Can't Be Cloned," *BusinessWeek,* September 17, 2001.

EXHIBIT 7–4 Evaluating a Business's Rapid Response (Speed) Opportunities

A. Skills and Resources That Foster Speed

Process engineering skills.
Excellent inbound and outbound logistics.
Technical people in sales and customer service.
High levels of automation.
Corporate reputation for quality or technical leadership.
Flexible manufacturing capabilities.
Strong downstream partners.
Strong cooperation from suppliers of major components of the product or service.

B. Organizational Requirements to Support and Sustain Rapid Response Activities

Strong coordination among functions in R&D, product development, and marketing.
Major emphasis on customer satisfaction in incentive programs.
Strong delegation to operating personnel.
Tradition of closeness to key customers.
Some personnel skilled in sales and operations—technical and marketing.
Empowered customer service personnel.

C. Examples of Ways Businesses Achieve Competitive Advantage via Speed

Technology Development	Use of companywide technology sharing activities and autonomous product development teams to speed new product development.
Human Resource Management	Develop self-managed work teams and decision making at the lowest levels to increase responsiveness.
General Administration	Highly automated and integrated information processing system. Include major buyers in the "system" on a real-time basis.
Procurement	Preapproved, online suppliers integrated into production.

Inbound logistics	Operations	Outbound logistics	Marketing and Sales	Service
Working very closely with suppliers to include their choice of warehouse location to minimize delivery time.	Standardize dies, components, and production equipment to allow quick changeover to new or special orders.	JIT delivery plus partnering with express mail services to ensure very rapid delivery.	Use of laptops linked directly to operations to speed the order process and shorten the sales cycle.	Locate service technicians at customer facilities that are geographically close.

Profit margin

Product Development Cycles   Japanese car makers have focused intensely on the time it takes to create a new model because several experienced disappointing sales growth in the last decade in Europe and North America competing against new vehicles like Ford's Explorer and Renault's Megane. VW had recently conceived, prototyped, produced, and marketed a totally new 4-wheel-drive car in Europe within 12 months. Honda, Toyota, and Nissan lowered their product development cycle from 24 months to 9 months from conception to production. This capability is old hat to 3M Corporation, which is so successful at speedy product development that one-fourth of its sales and profits each year are from products that didn't exist five years earlier.

Product or Service Improvements   Like development time, companies that can rapidly adapt their products or services and do so in a way that benefits their customers or creates new customers have a major competitive advantage over rivals that cannot do this.

Speed in Delivery or Distribution   Firms that can get you what you need when you need it, even when that is tomorrow, realize that buyers have come to expect that level of responsiveness. Federal Express's success reflects the importance customers place on speed in inbound and outbound logistics.

Information Sharing and Technology   Speed in sharing information that becomes the basis for decisions, actions, or other important activities taken by a customer, supplier, or partner has become a major source of competitive advantage for many businesses. Telecommunications, the Internet, and networks are but a part of a vast infrastructure that is being used by knowledgeable managers to rebuild or create value in their businesses via information sharing.

These rapid response capabilities create competitive advantages in several ways. They create a way to lessen rivalry because they have *availability* of something that a rival may not have. It can allow the business to charge buyers more, engender loyalty, or otherwise enhance the business's position relative to its buyers. Particularly where impressive customer response is involved, businesses can generate supplier cooperation and concessions since their business ultimately benefits from increased revenue. Finally, substitute products and new entrants find themselves trying to keep up with the rapid changes rather than introducing them. Exhibit 7–5, Strategy in Action, provides examples of how "speed" has become a source of competitive advantage for several well-known companies around the world.

While the notion of speed-based competitive advantage is exciting, it has risks managers must consider. First, speeding up activities that haven't been conducted in a fashion that prioritizes rapid response should only be done after considerable attention to training, reorganization, and/or reengineering. Second, some industries—stable, mature ones that have very minimal levels of change—may not offer much advantage to the firm that introduces some forms of rapid response. Customers in such settings may prefer the slower pace or the lower costs currently available or they may have long time frames in purchasing such that speed is not that important to them.

Evaluating Market Focus as a Way to Competitive Advantage

Small companies, at least the better ones, usually thrive because they serve narrow market niches. This is usually called *focus,* the extent to which a business concentrates on a narrowly defined market. Take the example of Soho Beverages, a business former Pepsi manager Tom Cox bought from Seagram after Seagram had acquired it and was unable to make it thrive. The tiny brand, once a healthy niche product in New York and a few other east coast locations, muddled within Seagrams because its sales force was unused to selling in delis. Cox was able to double sales in one year. He did this on a lean marketing budget that didn't include advertising or database marketing. He hired Korean- and Arabic-speaking college students and had his people walk into practically every deli in Manhattan in order to reacquaint owners with the brand, spot consumption trends, and take orders. He provided rapid stocking services to all Manhattan-area delis, regardless of size. The business has continued sales growth at over 50 percent per year. Why? Cox says "It is attributable to focusing on a niche market, delis; differentiating the product and its sales force; achieving low costs in promotion and delivery; and making rapid, immediate response to any deli owner request its normal practice."

Two things are important in this example. First, this business focused on a narrow niche market in which to build a strong competitive advantage. But focus alone was

BusinessWeek

SPEED IN DISTRIBUTION AND DELIVERY

Clad in a blue lab coat, a technician in Singapore waves a scanner like a wand over a box of newly minted computer chips. With that simple act, he sets in motion a delivery process that is efficient and automated, almost to the point of magic. This cavernous National Semiconductor Corp. (NSM) warehouse was designed and built by shipping wizards at United Parcel Service Inc. (UPS). It is UPS's computers that speed the box of chips to a loading dock, then to truck, to plane, and to truck once again. In just 12 hours, the chips will reach one of National's customers, a PC maker half a world away in Silicon Valley. Throughout the journey, electronic tags embedded in the chips will let the customer track the order with accuracy down to about three feet. In the two years since UPS and National starting this relationship, the team in brown has slashed National Semiconductor's inventory and shipment costs by 15% while reducing the time from factory floor to customer site by 60%.

INFORMATION SHARING AND TECHNOLOGY

Meanwhile, in the Old Economy, UPS is winning giant customers such as Ford Motor Co., which uses UPS's computerized logistics to route cars more efficiently to its dealerships. In a year, Ford has reduced delivery times by 26% and saved $240 million, says Frank M. Taylor, Ford's vice president for material planning and logistics. "Speed is the mindset at UPS. They'll meet a deadline at any cost," Taylor says. UPS Chairman James P. Kelly chalks it up to the company's slow-and-steady work ethic. "We've spent the past seven years studying where we should be long-term," he says.

While FedEx backpedals in logistics, UPS is in growth mode. And it has figured out how to manage distribution for many companies at one central location—a massive warehouse in Louisville, Ky. Here, UPS handles storage, tracking, repair, and shipping for clients such as Sprint, Hewlett-Packard (HWP), and Nike (NKE) using a mix of high- and low-tech methods. Computerized forklifts scan in new inventory while people in sneakers dash across the vast warehouse to pluck products, box them, and ship them out. In short, UPS uses expensive technology only where it cuts costs.

SPEED IN NEW PRODUCT DEVELOPMENT AND MANAGEMENT DECISION MAKING

Recently retired Volkswagen CEO Ferdinand Piëch has every reason to feel satisfied. The Austrian engineer and scion of one of Europe's most noted automotive dynasties can boast of one of the great turnarounds in automotive history, based on his attention to new product development combined with speed of decision making. Unlike many other auto chiefs, he called the shots on product design and engineering. And if you worked for Dr. Piëch, you had better get it right. In Wolfsburg, executives used to joke that PEP, the acronym for the product development process (Produkt entwicklungsprozess) really stood for Piëch entscheidet persönlich—Piëch decides himself. And he did it fast. He is said to have sketched out the Audi's all-wheel-drive system on the back of an envelope.

Obsession with detail and speed are key reasons VW has succeeded so brilliantly reviving its fortunes in the United States, where the VW brand was road kill a decade ago. Last year, VW and Audi sales in the United States jumped 14%, to 437,000 units, for a combined 2.5% market share. That's up from a microscopic 0.5% in 1995. Although VW trails its Japanese rivals, it's the only European mass-market carmaker in the United States. Volkswagen's four main brands—VW (VLKAY), Audi, Seat, and Skoda—have taken 19% of the European auto market, a gain of some three points in eight years, mostly at the expense of General Motors Corp. (GM) and Ford. Not bad for a company that eight years ago suffered from quality problems and a paucity of hit models. In South America, VW vehicles account for one-quarter of car sales, and in China, one-half.

CUSTOMER RESPONSIVENESS

Vodafone seemed to be losing ground to aggressive newcomers when Chris Gent, who had been developing Vodafone's international portfolio, took over as CEO in early 1997. He immediately canned the old ad agency and set about building a network of 250 company stores in towns and villages throughout Britain. The idea: to build brand recognition and neighborhood service that would keep customers, especially business users, loyal to Vodafone. Gent's timing couldn't have been better. He had Vodafone ready just as Britain's market was taking off. In the last two years, the combination of lower prices and a booming economy have fueled cell-phone mania in Britain—a phenomenon that Gent and others expect to hit the U.S. soon. In one year, British subscriptions grew by 53%, to 13 million, or 22.4% of the population. Vodafone became an instantly established cell phone provider due to its speed of customer responsiveness through its 250+ company-owned stores.

Source: "UPS vs. FedEx: Ground Wars," *BusinessWeek,* May 21, 2001; "Vodaphone's Wireless Warrior," *BusinessWeek,* May 21, 2001; "Volkswagen," *BusinessWeek,* July 23, 2001.

not enough to build competitive advantage. Rather, Cox created several value chain activities that achieved differentiation, low-cost, and rapid response competitive advantages within this niche market that would be hard for other firms, particularly mass market-oriented firms, to replicate.

Focus allows some businesses to compete on the basis of low cost, differentiation, and rapid response against much larger businesses with greater resources. Focus lets a business "learn" its target customers—their needs, special considerations they want accommodated—and establish personal relationships in ways that "differentiate" the smaller firm or make it more valuable to the target customer. Low costs can also be achieved filling niche needs in a buyer's operations that larger rivals either do not want to bother with or cannot do as cost effectively. Cost advantage often centers around the high level of customized service the focused, smaller business can provide. And perhaps the greatest competitive weapon that can arise is rapid response. With enhanced knowledge of its customers and intricacies of their operations, the small, focused company builds up organizational knowledge about timing sensitive ways to work with a customer. Often the needs of that narrow set of customers represent a large part of the small, focused business's revenues. Exhibit 7–6, Strategy in Action, illustrates how Sweden's Scania has become the global leader in heavy trucks via the focused application of low cost, differentiation, and speed.

The risk of focus is that you attract major competitors that have waited for your business to "prove" the market. Domino's proved that a huge market for pizza delivery existed and now faces serious challenges. Likewise, publicly traded focused companies become takeover targets for large firms seeking to fill out a product portfolio. And perhaps the greatest risk of all is slipping into the illusion that it is focus itself, and not some special form of low cost, differentiation, or rapid response, that is creating the business's success.

Managers evaluating opportunities to build competitive advantage should link strategies to value chain activities that exploit low cost, differentiation, and rapid response competitive advantages. When advantageous, they should consider ways to use focus to leverage these advantages. One way business managers can enhance their likelihood of identifying these opportunities is to consider several different "generic" industry environments from the perspective of the typical value chain activities most often linked to sustained competitive advantages in those unique industry situations. The next section discusses five key generic industry environments and the value chain activities most associated with success.

SELECTED INDUSTRY ENVIRONMENTS AND BUSINESS STRATEGY CHOICES

The analysis and choice of the ways a business will seek to build competitive advantage can be enhanced when managers take industry conditions into account. Chapter 3 discussed ways to examine industry conditions, so we do not repeat that here. Likewise, Chapter 5 showed how the market life cycle concept can be used to examine business strengths. What is important to recognize as managers evaluate opportunities to emphasize a narrow set of core competencies and potential competitive advantages is that different sets appear to be more useful in different, unique industry environments. We examine five "typical" industry settings and opportunities for generating competitive advantages that strategists should look for in their deliberations. Three of these five settings relate to industry life cycle. Managers use these as ways to evaluate their value

Global Strategy in Action
Sweden's Scania Combines Low Cost, Speed, Differentiation, and Focus to Consistently Beat Other Global Truck Manufacturers

Exhibit 7–6

BusinessWeek The preeminent consulting firm McKinsey and Company recently studied the global truck industry to understand which producers had the strongest competitive advantages and why they did. It quickly became a study of the Swedish firm, Scania, and its long time rival, Volvo. On an index that measured value added per hour worked, Scania scored 100 with Volvo close behind. The best Japanese, U.S., and German truck makers trailed by more than 25 points.

Leif Ostling, Scania's burly CEO, attributes the business's success to a determination to stick to its strategy of concentrating on heavy trucks, and rely on its own resources to deliver quality products commanding market-leading prices. McKinsey's analysis broadens the explanation as it sought an answer to how Scania had arrived at its enviable position and what its prospects were for remaining a world leader. McKinsey concluded:

1. Benchmarking: Intense competition between Scania and Volvo in tiny Sweden prepared them both to compete better than other rivals in the global market because the truck industry is much less international than the car industry, leaving newer rivals less competitive even on their home turf. Scania and Volvo have been benchmarking each other for years.

2. Low cost: Scania uses a building principle of maximization of standardization of parts across many brands while also leading the industry in responding to the demand for customization of each vehicle that is sold. How? While every truck is a unique order, Scania uses less than 20,000 components to build their truck compared to 25,000 for Volvo and 40,000 for Mercedes. Fewer parts mean lower development costs, lower manufacturing costs, and lower distribution costs.

3. Speed: Scania produces all main components in house, which allows them to maximize integration of design, development, and production, thus saving time, allowing for greater customization, and fewer parts.

4. Differentiation: There is strong emphasis on customization of each vehicle: "We have to supply a specific truck to a customer's specific needs," said Kaj Holmelius, head of chassis development, pointing to a production line, "Each of these is for a specific order and almost every one will be different in some way when they come off the end of the line. At the same time we want to get as large volumes as possible for individual components."

5. Focus: Scania will not expand into lighter trucks because it would dilute the efficiencies it has wrung out of its modular system. It has no plans to enter the North American market because of very different truck specifications and lower margins. The intention is to grow chiefly in Central and Eastern Europe and in the Pacific region. "We will stick to what we know how to do in limited, margin favorable markets," said Ostling.

The bottom line is, Scania has built a variety of sustainable competitive advantages that promise to keep it on top the world heavy truck market for a long time.

Sources: By Stanley Reed, with Ariane Sains, in Stockholm, "The Young Wallenbergs," *Business Week* International Edition: October 20, 1997; "Scania Pulls Ahead of the Crowd," *Financial Times,* October 16, 1995.

chain activities and then select the ones around which it is most critical to build competitive advantage.[3]

Competitive Advantage in Emerging Industries

Emerging industries are newly formed or re-formed industries that typically are created by technological innovation, newly emerging customer needs, or other economic or sociological changes. Emerging industries of the last decade have been the Internet browser, fiber optics, solar heating, cellular telephone, and on-line services industries.

From the standpoint of strategy formulation, the essential characteristic of an emerging industry is that there are no "rules of the game." The absence of rules presents both a risk and an opportunity—a wise strategy positions the firm to favorably shape the emerging industry's rules.

[3] These industry characterizations draw heavily on the work of Michael E. Porter, *Competitive Advantage: Creating and Sustaining Superior Performance* (New York: Free Press, 1985).

Business strategies must be shaped to accommodate the following characteristics of markets in emerging industries.

Technologies that are mostly proprietary to the pioneering firms and technological uncertainty about how product standardization will unfold.

Competitor uncertainty because of inadequate information about competitors, buyers, and the timing of demand.

High initial costs but steep cost declines as the experience curve takes effect.

Few entry barriers, which often spurs the formation of many new firms.

First-time buyers requiring initial inducement to purchase and customers confused by the availability of a number of nonstandard products.

Inability to obtain raw materials and components until suppliers gear up to meet the industry's needs.

Need for high-risk capital because of the industry's uncertainty prospects.

For success in this industry setting, business strategies require one or more of these features:

1. The ability to *shape the industry's structure* based on the timing of entry, reputation, success in related industries or technologies, and role in industry associations.

2. The ability to *rapidly improve product quality* and performance features.

3. *Advantageous relationships* with key suppliers and promising distribution channels.

4. The ability to *establish the firm's technology as the dominant one* before technological uncertainty decreases.

5. The early acquisition of *a core group of loyal customers* and then the expansion of that customer base through model changes, alternative pricing, and advertising.

6. The ability to *forecast future competitors* and the strategies they are likely to employ.

A firm that has had repeated successes with business in emerging industries is 3M Corporation. In each of the last 20 years, over 25 percent of 3M's annual sales have come from products that did not exist 5 years earlier. Start-up companies enhance their success by having experienced entrepreneurs at the helm, a knowledgeable management team and board of directors, and patient sources of venture capital. Amazon.com's dramatic debut on Wall Street symbolically ushering in the emerging E-commerce industry era for investors will certainly lead to questions about the lasting competitive advantage at Amazon.com. Exhibit 7–7, Strategy in Action, examines whether Amazon.com has the capacity to prevail in this emerging industry.

Competitive Advantage in the Transition to Industry Maturity

As an industry evolves, its rate of growth eventually declines. This "transition to maturity" is accompanied by several changes in its competitive environment:

Competition for market share becomes more intense as firms in the industry are forced to achieve sales growth at one another's expense.

Firms in the industry sell increasingly to experienced, repeat buyers that are now making choices among known alternatives.

Strategy in Action
Does Amazon.com Have a Sustainable Competitive Advantage in the Emerging "E-Commerce" Industry?

Exhibit 7–7

BusinessWeek When giant retailer Wal-Mart Stores Inc. sued upstart Internet bookseller Amazon.com Inc. in late 1998, jaws dropped. Wal-Mart accused Amazon of raiding its executives to steal its computerized merchandising and distribution trade secrets. The amazing part: Wal-Mart said tiny, money-losing Amazon had caused it "economic damage" and continues to do so. Regardless of the outcome, this case may well signal a watershed in the history of the Internet: the moment when cyberspace retailers began to turn the tables on earthly ones. Indeed, Amazon is blazing a trail in the world of commerce where no merchant has gone before.

Can it shape the E-commerce industry structure? By pioneering—and possibly perfecting—the art of selling online, it is forcing the titans of retail to scramble onto the Net. More than that it's jolting them into rethinking whether their traditional advantages—physical size, mass-media branding, and even the sensory appeal of shopping in stores—will be enough to thrive in the New Economy. Says Duke University marketing professor Martha Rogers: "Amazon is an example of how an upstart can redefine its whole industry."

Can it rapidly improve product quality & features? Consider this: Amazon offers an easily searchable trove of 3.1 million titles—15 times more than any bookstore on the planet and without the costly overhead of multimillion-dollar buildings and scads of store clerks. That paves the way for each of its 1,600 employees to generate, on average, $375,000 in annual revenues—almost four times that of No. 1 bricks-and-mortar bookseller Barnes & Noble Inc.'s 27,000 employees. It has 24 inventory turns per year versus 3 for Barnes & Noble, and high cash flow versus low cash flow at B&N.

Can its technology become the dominant one? Amazon's cutting-edge technology gives it a leg up, too, by automatically analyzing past purchases to make recommendations customized to each buyer—a trick that confounds 20th century mass marketing. And with a single mouse click, an order can be placed on its Web site, making shopping a friendly, frictionless, even fun experience that can take less time than finding a parking space at the mall.

Does it have a core group of loyal customers that might buy other things? It has a two-year head start, unheard of in the software industry, on key software that handles millions of transactions and personalizes the customers' experience. It gathers instant information on customer preferences to help understand what else [books and other things] they might want to buy. "We want Amazon.com to be the right store for you as an individual," says founder Jeffrey Bezos. "If we have 4.5 million customers, we should have 4.5 million stores."

While these observations seemed favorable, Merrill Lynch analyst Jonathan Cohen was not. "The company has been able to show it can sell lots of books for less without making money," he said, "and now it has shown it can sell lots of music without making money." Forrester Research CEO George Colony, pointing out entrenched rivals in every sector Amazon.com seeks to enter/redefine, declared that it would soon become known as "Amazon.toast."

Fast forward to late 2001. On any other day, it would've been big news. Pressured to show a path to profits after years of losses, Amazon.com Inc. was to announce that discounter Target Corp. would open an online store on Amazon's home page this fall. Target would pay the e-tailer to sell products such as apparel and jewelry, and would hire it to run the Target Web site. For Amazon, the timing seemed perfect since the deal promised millions in high-margin business. Just one problem: The news crossed the wires at 8:39 A.M. September 11, six minutes before the first hijacked jet crashed into the World Trade Center.

Far from getting a boost from the scarcely noticed deal, Amazon found itself deeper in the soup on concern that Amazon would run out of cash by early 2002. Says Safa Rashtchy, an analyst with U.S. Bancorp Piper Jaffray: "They have to show the Street they can make money." So, Amazon increasingly aims to get other retailers to sell their wares on the Amazon site. "We want to be the place for people to find and discover anything they want to buy online," says Bezos. "But we've never said we had to do it all."

Maybe so. Still, it's a big comedown: Amazon is attempting to become less of an online department store and more a retailing back office. The upstart many people thought would knock off brick-and-mortar giants now aims to be their best friend. What a surprise that one of its major clients would be Wal-Mart. These days, servicing other retailers using its existing logistics, customer service, and Web site operations looks like a surer route to profits than selling lawn furniture. Says Jupiter Media Metrix Inc. analyst Ken Cassar: "Amazon has come to the realization it can't be the dominant force in retail it once hoped."

Source: "Amazon.com: The Wild World of E-commerce," *BusinessWeek,* December 14, 1998. p. 106; "Amazon.com," December 28, 2001.

Competition becomes more oriented to cost and service as knowledgeable buyers expect similar price and product features.

Industry capacity "tops out" as sales growth ceases to cover up poorly planned expansions.

New products and new applications are harder to come by.

International competition increases as cost pressures lead to overseas production advantages.

Profitability falls, often permanently, as a result of pressure to lower prices and the increased costs of holding or building market share.

These changes necessitate a fundamental strategic reassessment. Strategy elements of successful firms in maturing industries often include:

1. *Pruning the product line* by dropping unprofitable product models, sizes, and options from the firm's product mix.

2. *Emphasis on process innovation* that permits low-cost product design, manufacturing methods, and distribution synergy.

3. *Emphasis on cost reduction* through exerting pressure on suppliers for lower prices, switching to cheaper components, introducing operational efficiencies, and lowering administrative and sales overhead.

4. *Careful buyer selection* to focus on buyers that are less aggressive, more closely tied to the firm, and able to buy more from the firm.

5. *Horizontal integration* to acquire rival firms whose weaknesses can be used to gain a bargain price and are correctable by the acquiring firms.

6. *International expansion* to markets where attractive growth and limited competition still exist and the opportunity for lower-cost manufacturing can influence both domestic and international costs.

Business strategists in maturing industries must avoid several pitfalls. First, they must make a clear choice among the three generic strategies and avoid a middle-ground approach, which would confuse both knowledgeable buyers and the firm's personnel. Second, they must avoid sacrificing market share too quickly for short-term profit. Finally, they must avoid waiting too long to respond to price reductions, retaining unneeded excess capacity, engaging in sporadic or irrational efforts to boost sales, and placing their hopes on "new" products, rather than aggressively selling existing products.

Competitive Advantage in Mature and Declining Industries

Declining industries are those that make products or services for which demand is growing slower than demand in the economy as a whole or is actually declining. This slow growth or decline in demand is caused by technological substitution (such as the substitution of electronic calculators for slide rules), demographic shifts (such as the increase in the number of older people and the decrease in the number of children), and shifts in needs (such as the decreased need for red meat).

Firms in a declining industry should choose strategies that emphasize one or more of the following themes:

Strategy in Action

Penn Racquet Sports Seeks Concentric Diversification as the Answer to Declining Sales in a Declining Industry—Tennis Balls

Exhibit 7–8

Tennis ball bust

Sales

▲ Millions of dollars

BusinessWeek Suppose your industry were in free fall. Yet you were the leader in that industry . . . the strongest! What would you do to find more customers? Would you go global in search of sales? Try the Internet? Refocus your business? How about switching species?

That's the drastic move made by Penn Racquet Sports, the nation's No. 1 maker of tennis balls. Penn recently began marketing its fuzzy orbs to some undeniably loyal customers: dogs. *R. P. Fetchem's* is a traditional tennis ball that has been gussied up as a "natural felt fetch toy" for pooches. "Ten times more people own pets than play tennis," explains Penn President Gregg R. Weida. Tennis may be stalled, but pet-pampering is booming. Human beings will shell out $5.95 a box for doggie pasta and will pay $59.95 for a pet canopy bed. Most important to Penn, they buy toys: Last year, owners lavished $41.7 million on dog toys sold in pet stores. While $5 a can might make tennis players gasp, it's no barrier for dog lovers in search of the perfect treat. New York dog owner Joel Katz didn't balk at the Fetchem's price tag. "This guy will do anything for a ball," he said of his cocker spaniel, Max. "He loves them more than food."

Source: "Now, Tennis Balls Are Chasing the Dogs," *BusinessWeek*, July 13, 1998, p. 138.

1. *Focus* on segments within the industry that offer a chance for higher growth or a higher return.

2. *Emphasize product innovation and quality improvement,* where this can be done cost effectively, to differentiate the firm from rivals and to spur growth.

3. *Emphasize production and distribution efficiency* by streamlining production, closing marginal productions facilities and costly distribution outlets, and adding effective new facilities and outlets.

4. *Gradually harvest the business*—generate cash by cutting down on maintenance, reducing models, and shrinking channels and make no new investment.

Strategists who incorporate one or more of these themes into the strategy of their business can anticipate relative success, particularly where the industry's decline is slow and smooth and some profitable niches remain. Exhibit 7–8, Strategy in Action, describes how Penn Racquet Sports went from "humans to dogs" to reenergize the declining tennis ball market. At the same time, three pitfalls must be avoided: (1) being overly optimistic about the prospects for a revival of the industry, (2) getting trapped in a profitless war of attrition, and (3) harvesting from a weak position.

Competitive Advantage in Fragmented Industries

A fragmented industry is one in which no firm has a significant market share and can strongly influence industry outcomes. Fragmented industries are found in many areas of the economy and are common in such areas as professional services, retailing, distribution, wood and metal fabrication, and agricultural products. The funeral industry is an example of a highly fragmented industry. Business strategists in fragmented industries pursue low-cost, differentiation, or focus competitive advantages in one of five ways.

Tightly Managed Decentralization

Fragmented industries are characterized by a need for intense local coordination, a local management orientation, high personal service, and local autonomy. Recently, however, successful firms in such industries have introduced a high degree of professionalism into the operations of local managers.

"Formula" Facilities

This alternative, related to the previous one, introduces standardized, efficient, low-cost facilities at multiple locations. Thus, the firm gradually builds a low-cost advantage over localized competitors. Fast-food and motel chains have applied this approach with considerable success.

Increased Value-Added

The products or services of some fragmented industries are difficult to differentiate. In this case, an effective strategy may be to add value by providing more service with the sale or by engaging in some product assembly that is of additional value to the customer.

Specialization

Focus strategies that creatively segment the market can enable firms to cope with fragmentation. Specialization can be pursued by:

1. *Product type.* The firm builds expertise focusing on a narrow range of products or services.

2. *Customer type.* The firm becomes intimately familiar with and serves the needs of a narrow customer segment.

3. *Type of order.* The firm handles only certain kinds of orders, such as small orders, custom orders, or quick turnaround orders.

4. *Geographic area.* The firm blankets or concentrates on a single area.

Although specialization in one or more of these ways can be the basis for a sound focus strategy in a fragmented industry, each of these types of specialization risks limiting the firm's potential sales volume.

Bare Bones/No Frills

Given the intense competition and low margins in fragmented industries, a "bare bones" posture—low overhead, minimum wage employees, tight cost control—may build a sustainable cost advantage in such industries.

Competitive Advantage in Global Industries

A global industry is one that comprises firms whose competitive positions in major geographic or national markets are fundamentally affected by their overall global competitive positions. To avoid strategic disadvantages, firms in global industries are virtually required to compete on a worldwide basis. Oil, steel, automobiles, apparel, motorcycles, televisions, and computers are examples of global industries.

Global industries have four unique strategy-shaping features:

Differences in prices and costs from country to country due to currency exchange fluctuations, differences in wage and inflation rates, and other economic factors.

Differences in buyer needs across different countries.

Differences in competitors and ways of competing from country to country.

Differences in trade rules and governmental regulations across different countries.

These unique features and the global competition of global industries require that two fundamental components be addressed in the business strategy: (1) the approach used to gain global market coverage and (2) the generic competitive strategy.

Three basic options can be used to pursue global market coverage:

1. *License* foreign firms to produce and distribute the firm's products.

2. *Maintain a domestic production base* and export products to foreign countries.

3. *Establish foreign-based plants and distribution* to compete directly in the markets of one or more foreign countries.

Along with the market coverage decision, strategists must scrutinize the condition of the global industry features identified earlier to choose among four generic global competitive strategies:

1. *Broad-line global competition*—directed at competing worldwide in the full product line of the industry, often with plants in many countries, to achieve differentiation or an overall low-cost position.

2. *Global focus* strategy—targeting a particular segment of the industry for competition on a worldwide basis.

3. *National focus* strategy—taking advantage of differences in national markets that give the firm an edge over global competitors on a nation-by-nation basis.

4. *Protected niche* strategy—seeking out countries in which governmental restraints exclude or inhibit global competitors or allow concessions, or both, that are advantageous to localized firms.

Competing in global industries is an increasing reality for many U.S. firms. Strategists must carefully match their skills and resources with global industry structure and conditions in selecting the most appropriate strategy option.

In conclusion, the analysis and choice of business strategy involves three basic considerations. First, strategists must recognize that their overall choice revolves around three sources of competitive advantage that require total, consistent commitment. Second, strategists must carefully weigh the skills, resources, organizational requirements, and risks associated with each source of competitive advantage. Finally, strategists must consider the unique influence that the generic industry environment most similar to the firm's situation will have on the set of value chain activities they choose to build competitive advantage.

EXHIBIT 7–9
Grand Strategy
Selection Matrix

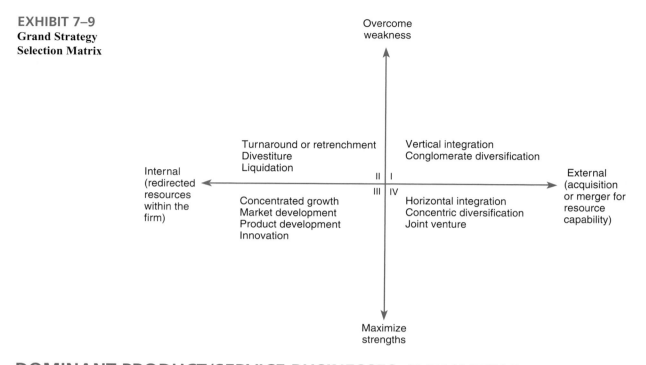

DOMINANT PRODUCT/SERVICE BUSINESSES: EVALUATING AND CHOOSING TO DIVERSIFY TO BUILD VALUE

McDonald's has frequently looked at numerous opportunities to diversify into related businesses or to acquire key suppliers. Its decision has consistently been to focus on its core business using the grand strategies of concentration, market development, and product development. Rival Pepsi, on the other hand, has chosen to diversify into related businesses and vertical integration as the best grand strategies for it to build long-term value. Both firms experienced unprecedented success during the last 20 years.

Many dominant product businesses face this question as their core business proves successful: What grand strategies are best suited to continue to build value? Under what circumstances should they choose an expanded focus (diversification, vertical integration); steady continued focus (concentration, market or product development); or a narrowed focus (turnaround or divestiture)? This section examines two ways you can analyze a dominant product company's situation and choose among the 15 grand strategies identified in Chapter 6.

Grand Strategy Selection Matrix

One valuable guide to the selection of a promising grand strategy is the matrix shown in Exhibit 7–9. The basic idea underlying the matrix is that two variables are of central concern in the selection process: (1) the principal purpose of the grand strategy and (2) the choice of an internal or external emphasis for growth or profitability.

In the past, planners were advised to follow certain rules or prescriptions in their choice of strategies. Now, most experts agree that strategy selection is better guided by the conditions of the planning period and by the company strengths and weaknesses. It should be noted, however, that even the early approaches to strategy selection sought to match a concern over internal versus external growth with a desire to overcome weaknesses or maximize strengths.

The same considerations led to the development of the grand strategy selection matrix. A firm in quadrant I, with "all its eggs in one basket," often views itself as over-committed to a particular business with limited growth opportunities or high risks. One reasonable solution is *vertical integration,* which enables the firm to reduce risk by reducing uncertainty about inputs or access to customers. Another is *conglomerate diversification,* which provides a profitable investment alternative with diverting management attention from the original business. However, the external approaches to overcoming weaknesses usually result in the most costly grand strategies. Acquiring a second business demands large investments of time and sizable financial resources. Thus, strategic managers considering these approaches must guard against exchanging one set of weaknesses for another.

More conservative approaches to overcoming weaknesses are found in quadrant II. Firms often choose to redirect resources from one internal business activity to another. This approach maintains the firm's commitment to its basic mission, rewards success, and enables further development of proven competitive advantages. The least disruptive of the quadrant II strategies is *retrenchment,* pruning the current activities of a business. If the weaknesses of the business arose from inefficiencies, retrenchment can actually serve as a *turnaround* strategy—that is, the business gains new strength from the streamlining of its operations and the elimination of waste. However, if those weaknesses are a major obstruction to success in the industry and the costs of overcoming them are unaffordable or are not justified by a cost-benefit analysis, then eliminating the business must be considered. *Divestiture* offers the best possibility for recouping the firm's investment, but even *liquidation* can be an attractive option if the alternatives are bankruptcy or an unwarranted drain on the firm's resources.

A common business adage states that a firm should build from strength. The premise of this adage is that growth and survival depend on an ability to capture a market share that is large enough for essential economies of scale. If a firm believes that this approach will be profitable and prefers an internal emphasis for maximizing strengths, four grand strategies hold considerable promise. As shown in quadrant III, the most common approach is *concentrated growth,* that is, market penetration. The firm that selects this strategy is strongly committed to its current products and markets. It strives to solidify its position by reinvesting resources to fortify its strengths.

Two alternative approaches are *market development* and *product development.* With these strategies, the firm attempts to broaden its operations. Market development is chosen if the firm's strategic managers feel that its existing products would be well received by new customer groups. Product development is chosen if they feel that the firm's existing customers would be interested in products related to its current lines. Product development also may be based on technological or other competitive advantages. The final alternative for quadrant III firms is *innovation.* When the firm's strengths are in creative product design or unique production technologies, sales can be stimulated by accelerating perceived obsolescence. This is the principle underlying the innovative grand strategy.

Maximizing a firm's strengths by aggressively expanding its base of operations usually requires an external emphasis. The preferred options in such cases are shown in quadrant IV. *Horizontal integration* is attractive because it makes possible a quick increase in output capability. Moreover, in horizontal integration, the skills of the managers of the original business often are critical in converting newly acquired facilities into profitable contributors to the parent firm; this expands a fundamental competitive advantage of the firm—its management.

Concentric diversification is a good second choice for similar reasons. Because the original and newly acquired businesses are related, the distinctive competencies of the diversifying firm are likely to facilitate a smooth, synergistic, and profitable expansion.

The final alternative for increasing resource capability through external emphasis is a *joint venture* or *strategic alliance.* This alternative allows a firm to extend its strengths into competitive arenas that it would be hesitant to enter alone. A partner's production, technological, financial, or marketing capabilities can reduce the firm's financial investment significantly and increase its probability of success.

EXHIBIT 7–10
Model of Grand
Strategy Clusters

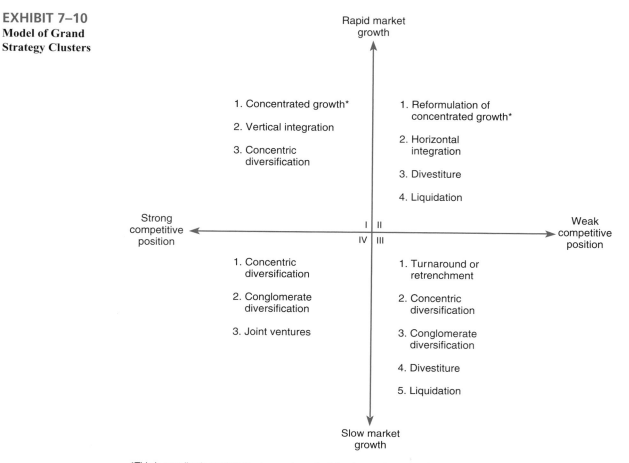

*This is usually via market development, product development, or a combination of both.

Model of Grand Strategy Clusters

A second guide to selecting a promising grand strategy is shown in Exhibit 7–10. The figure is based on the idea that the situation of a business is defined in terms of the growth rate of the general market and the firm's competitive position in that market. When these factors are considered simultaneously, a business can be broadly categorized in one of four quadrants: (I) strong competitive position in a rapidly growing market, (II) weak position in a rapidly growing market, (III) weak position in a slow-growth market, or (IV) strong position in a slow-growth market. Each of these quadrants suggests a set of promising possibilities for the selection of a grand strategy.

Firms in quadrant I are in an excellent strategic position. One obvious grand strategy for such firms is continued concentration on their current business as it is currently defined. Because consumers seem satisfied with the firm's current strategy, shifting notably from it would endanger the firm's established competitive advantages. McDonald's Corporation has followed this approach for 25 years. However, if the firm has resources that exceed the demands of a concentrated growth strategy, it should consider vertical integration. Either forward or backward integration helps a firm protect its profit margins and market share by ensuring better access to consumers or material inputs. Finally, to diminish the risks associated with a narrow product or service line, a quadrant I firm might be wise to consider concentric diversification; with this strategy, the firm continues to invest heavily in its basic area of proven ability.

Firms in quadrant II must seriously evaluate their present approach to the marketplace. If a firm has competed long enough to accurately assess the merits of its current grand strategy, it must determine (1) why that strategy is ineffectual and (2) whether it is capable of competing effectively. Depending on the answers to these questions, the firm should choose one of four grand strategy options: formulation or reformulation of a concentrated growth strategy, horizontal integration, divestiture, or liquidation.

In a rapidly growing market, even a small or relatively weak business often is able to find a profitable niche. Thus, formulation or reformulation of a concentrated growth strategy is usually the first option that should be considered. However, if the firm lacks either a critical competitive element or sufficient economies of scale to achieve competitive cost efficiencies, then a grand strategy that directs its efforts toward horizontal integration is often a desirable alternative. A final pair of options involve deciding to stop competing in the market or product area of the business. A multiproduct firm may conclude that it is most likely to achieve the goals of its mission if the business is dropped through divestiture. This grand strategy not only eliminates a drain on resources but also may provide funds to promote other business activities. As an option of last resort, a firm may decide to liquidate the business. This means that the business cannot be sold as a going concern and is at best worth only the value of its tangible assets. The decision to liquidate is an undeniable admission of failure by a firm's strategic management and, thus, often is delayed—to the further detriment of the firm.

Strategic managers tend to resist divestiture because it is likely to jeopardize their control of the firm and perhaps even their jobs. Thus, by the time the desirability of divestiture is acknowledged, businesses often deteriorate to the point of failing to attract potential buyers. The consequences of such delays are financially disastrous for firm owners because the value of a going concern is many times greater than the value of its assets.

Strategic managers who have a business in quadrant III and expect a continuation of slow market growth and a relatively weak competitive position will usually attempt to decrease their resource commitment to that business. Minimal withdrawal is accomplished through retrenchment; this strategy has the side benefits of making resources available for other investments and of motivating employees to increase their operating efficiency. An alternative approach is to divert resources for expansion through investment in other businesses. This approach typically involves either concentric or conglomerate diversification because the firm usually wants to enter more promising arenas of competition than integration or concentrated growth strategies would allow. The final options for quadrant III businesses are divestiture, if an optimistic buyer can be found, and liquidation.

Quadrant IV businesses (strong competitive position in a slow-growth market) have a basis of strength from which to diversify into more promising growth areas. These businesses have characteristically high cash flow levels and limited internal growth needs. Thus, they are in an excellent position for concentric diversification into ventures that utilize their proven acumen. Exhibit 7–8, Strategy in Action, (on p. 205), describes how the number-one tennis ball maker, Penn Racquet Sports, chose concentric diversification from humans to dogs as their best option. A second option is conglomerate diversification, which spreads investment risk and does not divert managerial attention from the present business. The final option is joint ventures, which are especially attractive to multinational firms. Through joint ventures, a domestic business can gain competitive advantages in promising new fields while exposing itself to limited risks.

Opportunities for Building Value as a Basis for Choosing Diversification or Integration

The grand strategy selection matrix and model of grand strategy clusters are useful tools to help dominant product company managers evaluate and narrow their choices among alternative grand strategies. When considering grand strategies that would broaden the scope of their company's business activities through integration, diversification, or joint venture strategies, managers must examine whether opportunities to build value are present. Opportunities to build value via diversification, integration, or joint venture strategies are usually found in market-related, operating-related, and management activities. Such opportunities center around reducing costs, improving margins, or providing access to new revenue sources more cost effectively than traditional internal growth options via concentration, market development, or product development. Major opportunities for sharing and value building as well as ways to capitalize on core competencies are outlined in the next chapter, which covers strategic analysis and choice in diversified companies.

Dominant product company managers who choose diversification or integration eventually create another management challenge. That challenge is charting the future of a company that becomes a collection of several distinct businesses. These distinct businesses often encounter different competitive environments, challenges, and opportunities. The next chapter examines ways managers of such diversified companies attempt to evaluate and choose corporate strategy. Central to their challenge is the continued desire to build value, particularly shareholder value.

Summary

This chapter examined how managers in businesses that have a single or dominant product or service evaluate and choose their company's strategy. Two critical areas deserve their attention: first, their business's value chain; second, the appropriateness of 12 different grand strategies based on matching environmental factors with internal capabilities.

Managers in single-product-line business units examine their business's value chain to identify existing or potential activities around which they can create sustainable competitive advantages. As managers scrutinize their value chain activities, they are looking for three sources of competitive advantage: low cost, differentiation, and rapid response capabilities. They also examine whether focusing on a narrow market niche provides a more effective, sustainable way to build or leverage these three sources of competitive advantage.

Managers in single or dominant product/service businesses face two interrelated issues. First, they must choose which grand strategies make best use of their competitive advantages. Second, they must ultimately decide whether to diversify their business activity. Twelve grand strategies were identified in this chapter along with three frameworks that aid managers in choosing which grand strategies should work best and when diversification or integration should be the best strategy for the business. The next chapter expands the coverage of diversification to look at how multi-business companies evaluate continued diversification and how they construct corporate strategy.

Questions for Discussion

1. What are three activities or capabilities a firm should possess to support a low-cost leadership strategy? Use Exhibit 7–2 to help you answer this question. Can you give an example of a company that has done this?

2. What are three activities or capabilities a firm should possess to support a differentiation-based strategy? Use Exhibit 7–3 to help you answer this question. Can you give an example of a company that has done this?

3. What are three ways a firm can incorporate the advantage of speed in its business? Use Exhibit 7–4 to help you answer this question. Can you give an example of a company that has done this?

4. Do you think is it better to concentrate on one source of competitive advantage (cost versus differentiation versus speed) or to nurture all three in a firm's operation? What did Caterpillar do in the *BusinessWeek* Discussion Case?

5. How does market focus help a business create competitive advantage? What risks accompany such a posture? How did market focus come into play at Caterpillar?

6. Using Exhibits 7–9 and 7–10, describe situations or conditions under which horizontal integration and concentric diversification would be preferred strategic choices.

Chapter 7 Discussion Case

BusinessWeek

Strategic Analysis and Choice in the 1990s at Caterpillar, Inc.

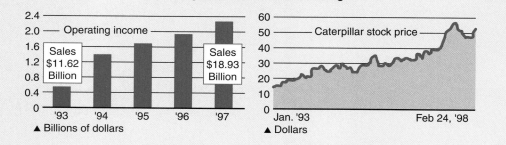

**Cat in the 1990s:
fast growth has the stock climbing**

Caterpillar, long the global standard in heavy-duty construction equipment was almost destroyed by the painful industry collapse in the 1980s and subsequent union difficulties. Global demand was dropping fast, and the weak yen allowed Cat's biggest rival, Japan's Komatsu Ltd., to undercut prices by 40%. When Komatsu began to gain share, Cat's CEO Donald Fites—and Cat—got the scare of their lives. And a lengthy, debilitating strike with the United Auto Workers in 1990–91 made matters even more difficult. Fites, who became CEO coming from Caterpillar's marketing organization, took an aggressive stance toward the UAW and sought to craft a strategy for the 1990s that would rebuild Caterpillar as the industry leader. *BusinessWeek*'s De'Ann Weimer visited Caterpillar to report on the strategic analysis and choices Fites made during that time that led to the outstanding turnaround she summarized for you in the chart above. Her findings from mid-1998 illustrate how one company analyzed and chose to build a strategy around key cost, differentiation, and speed competitive advantages in existing markets and eventually new, growth markets.

1   STRATEGIC ANALYSIS. Core operations were too costly—old equipment; slow production processes; numerous dedicated production lines for individual truck and tractor models; product design activities for each model, again quite costly; Problematic union agreement.

2   STRATEGIC CHOICE. **Seek low-cost and speed-enhancing leadership advantages** by integrating production activities across multiple models

to gain economies of scale; speeding up production processes with newer technology; and reducing inventory costs with increased JIT accommodated with speedier production activities:

Fites began by overhauling manufacturing in Cat's core truck and tractor operations. He invested almost $2 billion to modernize his U.S. plants. New state-of-the-art machinery helped Cat **slash time** *out of such mundane tasks as painting, for example, and* **vastly simplified production.** *Today, Cat can build 20 different models from the same basic design. The changes—together with the increased use of temporary workers in its nonunion plants—have also greatly* **improved Cat's flexibility.** *The company can now* **change production levels with a week's notice**—*down from six months at the height of its 1980s crisis. Altogether, Cat's manufacturing time has fallen 75%—one key reason operating margins have exploded, from 5.2% in 1993, to 12.6% in 1997.* **Faster production** *has also allowed Fites to* **slash inventories.** *Gone are the long order backlogs and dealer inventories that weighed heavily on Cat's books; today, it* **refuses orders more than three months in advance.**

3   STRATEGIC ANALYSIS. Caterpillar was getting hurt not only on price, but because many models had changed very little compared to key Japanese competitors. Newer competitors had begun to differentiate themselves based on providing product line extensions with varying product features.

4   STRATEGIC CHOICE. **Seek to differentiate Caterpillar's products** by introducing products that enhance construction efficiency while repre-

senting basic product line extensions or adaptations of Caterpillar's manufacturing and design capabilities.

*While aggressively redesigning its manufacturing system, **Cat broadened its products.** In the last two years, it has introduced 90 offerings—**some all-new, some well-targeted fine extensions** that enhance construction site efficiency and capabilities in very specific construction tasks. In 1997, for example, Cat introduced a telescopic handler—essentially a tractor with an arm on it that allows masons to work their way up the side of a building eliminating the need for scaffolding so expensive in traditional construction methods.*

5 STRATEGIC ANALYSIS. Caterpillar is a global business. It is affected significantly by currency fluctuations, by development opportunities outside the United States and cyclical downturns, and labor costs in the U.S. versus overseas markets.

6 STRATEGIC CHOICE. **Focus on selected national markets** where establishing **incountry plants** and distribution provide cost advantages while allowing potential synergy across global markets in selected product offerings.

Good timing helped with the turnaround, too. As the combination of reduced costs and the end of recession restored the company's financial health, Fites pushed into new markets. He focused on Asia, where infrastructure development created huge demand. Markets in Latin America, Central Europe, Russia, and other former Soviet states.

7 STRATEGIC ANALYSIS. The heavy construction industry is very cyclical. The global nature of the industry heightens the potential cyclical impact and adds currency risks from fluctuating currency values. Restrictive UAW contracts in the United States add to the cost impact of these risks when demand, and sales, decrease due to global cyclical pressures yet higher labor costs remain built into Cat's cost structure.

8 STRATEGIC CHOICE. **Concentric diversification** into related product-markets that leverage key strengths making engines **into less cyclical markets** than trucks and tractors; and into product-markets that leverage sales and distribution strengths. **Use acquisitions** to accelerate this effort. **Increase global presence of facilities over time** to decrease currency fluctuation impact and reliance on UAW labor.

Some 51% of Cat sales come from overseas—though Fites wants to hit 75% by 2008. To cut the risk of fluctuating currencies—and trim labor costs—Fites has also pushed much manufacturing abroad. Today, roughly half of Cat's 74 plants are abroad, versus just 39% of its 38 plants a decade ago. In the wake of the UAW's rejection of the labor contract—which will prevent Cat from hiring new workers at lower wages or demanding more flexible scheduling in union plants—analysts say the percentage of foreign production could go even higher.

Fites also bulked up in less-cyclical businesses like electric power generation. An offshoot of its long-standing engine business, the move into power gained steam in 1996 when Fites purchased a German maker of engines for generators. Driven by demand for power in developing countries—where governments often don't want to build big power plants—generation has helped boost engines to more than 25% of Cat sales. "They are trending toward smaller, easier-to-operate generators," said Siegfried R. Ramseyer, vice-president of Cat Asia. "This we can do very, very well." He predicted sales could triple in a few years.

The company's largest acquisition to date—the $1.3 billion purchase of Britain's Perkins Engines, which closed in February—was directed at another target altogether: the fast-growing $3.6 billion market for compact construction machinery. These machines, typically operated by one person, are the industry's hottest segment. The star of the category: skid-steer loaders, which break up asphalt, move dirt, and do such a variety of useful things that sales are growing a red-hot 11% a year.

Cat was all but absent in the lucrative small-equipment market, but Fites targeted a 20% share by 2003. He counted on big gains from Perkins, which makes engines for skid-steers. Since engines account for 25% of the costs of a skid-steer, Cat figures that trimming those expenses will allow it to undercut rivals while maintaining margins. Elsewhere, Fites has tapped other new markets by focusing dealers on rental equipment. Initially unpopular with dealers, who must keep rental gear on their books as assets, the change drew lots of smaller customers. The added demand also helped keep prices strong. In 1997, for example, when few companies could do so, Cat raised prices.

WHAT WAS THE RESULT OF CATERPILLAR'S STRATEGIC ANALYSIS AND CHOICE?

9   The reborn company skyrocketed through the upturn with flying colors. Since 1993, when Cat completed its manufacturing overhaul amid soaring demand for construction equipment in the United States and developing nations, sales leaped from $11.6 billion to $18.9 billion, an average of 13% a year. Meanwhile, earnings rose a stunning 45% annually, jumping from just $626 million to $2.3 billion in 1997. Investors won big: In five years, Cat's stock more than tripled.

10   The U.S. market, where Cat sells 49% of its goods, started to slow by 1999. And Asia, Cat's fastest-growing market suffered a headline-grabbing downturn. American dealers quickly started seeing barely used, heavily discounted Cat equipment begin to trickle into the United States from Asia, as customers dumped equipment to raise cash. The slowdown promised the biggest test yet of the "New Cat."

11   The global slowdown in 2000 and recession in 2001 saw Caterpillar's earnings plummet to 1993 levels. The slowdown could hardly have come at a worse time for CEO Gleb Barton, a Caterpillar lifer who moved up to the top job in 2000 with the retirement of Chairman and CEO Donald V. Fites. Under Fites, Caterpillar tallied six consecutive years of record sales and five years in a row of record earnings in the 1990s. But as Barton, 61, wrapped up his second year as boss in 2001 and his 40th year with Cat, it's clear he has his hands full. On Jan. 21, the company said profits fell for the second year in a row, and sales slipped 6% both years. The outsized drop in earnings reflects Cat's increased dependence on engines and other lower-margin products.

12   When it comes to earnings, however, smaller may not be better. Compact gear generally has modest markups. Also, buyers of such gear typically care more about price than service. "At the end of the day, it's the fastest-growing business, and Cat has to be there," says David Raso of Lehman Brothers Inc. in New York. "But it doesn't quite leverage Cat's strength." Lately, Cat's U.S. sales have been driven by the rise of a new distribution channel—equipment-rental companies. Some analysts fear these companies are in for a shakeout, and that could crush demand—and prices—if they are forced to liquidate. And as Cat introduces scaled-down products, competitors are bulldozing their way into its core heavy-equipment business. Moline (Ill.)-based Deere recently came out with its first 55-ton and 75-ton excavators. CNH, which now has global reach and ambitions, also will expand its line of large construction equipment, vows Jean-Pierre Rosso, chief executive of the Dutch company, which has its head office in Racine, Wis. Despite harder times, Cat still dominates, outselling Komatsu and CNH roughly 3 to 1 in heavy equipment. And sooner or later, the North American market will revive. But down cycles can be stubborn. With all of the company's problems, Barton cannot afford a sophomore slump.

Source: "A New Cat on the Hot Seat," *BusinessWeek,* March 9, 1998; "Don't Count Caterpillar Out," *BusinessWeek,* March 20, 2000; and "This Cat Isn't So Nimble," *BusinessWeek,* February 20, 2001.

Chapter Eight

Strategic Analysis and Choice in the Multibusiness Company: Rationalizing Diversification and Building Shareholder Value

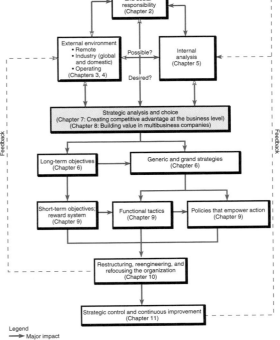

Company mission
and social
responsibility
(Chapter 2)

External environment
• Remote
• Industry (global
and domestic)
• Operating
(Chapters 3, 4)

Possible?

Internal
analysis
(Chapter 5)

Desired?

Strategic analysis and choice
(Chapter 7: Creating competitive advantage at the business level)
(Chapter 8: Building value in multibusiness companies)

Long-term objectives
(Chapter 6)

Generic and grand strategies
(Chapter 6)

Short-term objectives;
reward system
(Chapter 9)

Functional tactics
(Chapter 9)

Policies that empower action
(Chapter 9)

Restructuring, reengineering, and
refocusing the organization
(Chapter 10)

Strategic control and continuous improvement
(Chapter 11)

Feedback

Feedback

Legend
→ Major impact
→ Minor impact

Strategic analysis and choice is more complicated for corporate-level managers because they must create a strategy to guide a company that contains numerous businesses. They must examine and choose which businesses to own and which ones to forgo or divest. They must consider business managers' plans to capture competitive advantage, and then decide how to allocate resources among businesses as part of this phase. This chapter will first examine diversified, multibusiness companies. Specifically, how should the diversified business build shareholder value? For example, MCI has decided to pursue an aggressive diversification program to expand its presence in a variety of different industries; AT&T has recently decided to split into several separate companies while divesting itself of other businesses on three dramatic occasions in the last decade. Why?

A final topic that is important to an understanding of strategic analysis and choice in business organization is the "nonbusiness," behavioral factors that often exert a major influence on strategic decisions. This is true in the single-product business as well as the multibusiness company. What behavioral considerations often influence how managers analyze strategic options and make strategic choices? For example, J. E. Schrempp became CEO of Germany's Daimler Benz as planned, having taken over from his mentor, Edzard Reuter, with whom he had charted a steady 10-year diversification to build a $74 billion company. Three months later, Schrempp reversed the strategy to break up the company, focus on core businesses, and reconstruct a new management team. How could such a dramatic, sudden shift take place? Answering that question requires you to consider behavioral factors as well as strategic issues at Daimler Benz.

RATIONALIZING DIVERSIFICATION AND INTEGRATION

When a single or dominant-business company is transformed into a collection of numerous businesses across several industries, strategic analysis becomes more complex. Managers must deal not only with each business's strategic situation, they must set forth a corporate strategy that rationalizes the collection of businesses they have amassed. Two key audiences are listening. First, managers within the organization want to understand their role and access to resources relative to other businesses within the company. Second, and of greatest importance, stockholders deserve to understand how this collection of businesses is expected to build shareholder value over the long term more effectively than simply investing in separate businesses. In a sense the question is: "Are there compelling reasons why corporate management is better able to invest shareholder value in a variety of other businesses versus allowing shareholders to make that decision themselves?"

Stockholder value in a diversified company is ultimately determined by how well its various businesses perform and/or how compelling potential synergies and opportunities appear to be. Business-level performance is enhanced by sustained competitive advantages. Wise diversification has at its core the search for ways to build value and sustained competitive advantage across multiple business units. We saw several ways opportunities for sharing and building value may be present across different businesses. The bottom line is that diversification that shares skills and core competencies across multiple businesses to strengthen value chains and build competitive advantage enhances shareholder value. And so it is that strategic analysis and choice for corporate managers overseeing multibusiness companies involves determining whether their portfolio of business units is capturing the synergies they intended, how to respond accordingly, and choosing among future diversification or divestiture options. Managers address the following four basic questions to do this.

Are Opportunities for Sharing Infrastructure and Capabilities Forthcoming?

Opportunities to build value via diversification, integration, or joint venture strategies are usually found in market-related, operating-related, and management activities. Each business's basic value chain activities or infrastructure becomes a source of potential synergy and competitive advantage for another business in the corporate portfolio. Morrison's Cafeteria, long a mainstay in U.S. food services markets, rapidly accelerated its diversification into other restaurant concepts like Ruby Tuesdays. Numerous opportunities for shared operating capabilities and management capabilities drove this decision and, upon repeated strategic analysis, accelerated corporate managers' decision to move Morrison's totally out of the cafeteria segment by 2000. Some of the more common opportunities to share value chain activities and build value are identified in Exhibit 8–1.

Strategic analysis is concerned with whether or not the potential competitive advantages expected to arise from each value opportunity have materialized. Where advantage has not materialized, corporate strategists must take care to scrutinize possible impediments to achieving the synergy or competitive advantage. We have identified in Exhibit 8–1 several impediments associated with each opportunity, which strategists are well advised to examine. Good strategists assure themselves that their organization has ways to avoid or minimize the impact of any impediments or they recommend against further integration or diversification and consider divestiture options.

Two elements are critical in meaningful shared opportunities. First, the shared opportunities must be a significant portion of the value chain of the businesses involved. Returning to Morrison's Cafeteria, its purchasing and inbound logistics infrastructure give Ruby Tuesday's operators an immediate cost-effective purchasing and inventory management capability that lowered its cost in a significant cost activity. Second, the businesses involved must truly have shared needs—need for the same activity—or there is no basis for synergy in the first place. Novell, the U.S.-based networking software giant, paid $900 million for WordPerfect, envisioning numerous synergies serving offices globally not to mention 15 million WordPerfect users. Little more than a year later, Novell would sell WordPerfect for less than $300 million, because, as CEO Bob Frankenberg said, "It is not because WordPerfect is not a business without a future, but for Novell it represented a distraction from our strategy." Corporate strategies have repeatedly rushed into diversification only to find perceived opportunities for sharing were nonexistent because the businesses did not really have shared needs. Exhibit 8–2, Strategy in Action, examines just this dilemma at several well-known U.S. companies that have botched their synergy searches.

Are We Capitalizing on Our Core Competencies?

Perhaps the most compelling reason companies should diversify can be found in situations where core competencies—key value-building skills—can be leveraged with other products or into markets that are not a part of where they were created. Where this works well, extraordinary value can be built. Managers undertaking diversification strategies should dedicate a significant portion of their strategic analysis to this question.

General Cinema was a company that grew from drive-in theaters to eventually dominate the multicinema, movie exhibition industry. Next, they entered soft-drink bottling and became the largest bottler of soft drinks (Pepsi) in North America. Their stock value rose 2,000 percent in 10 years. They found that core competencies in movie exhibition—managing many small, localized businesses; dealing with a few large suppliers; applying central marketing skills locally; and acquiring or crafting a "franchise"—were virtually the

EXHIBIT 8–1   **Value Building in Multibusiness Companies**

Source: Adapted with the permission of *Harvard Business School on Managing the Value Chain* (Cambridge: HBS Press, 2000).

Opportunities to Build Value or Sharing	Potential Competitive Advantage	Impediments to Achieving Enhanced Value
Market-Related Opportunities:		
Shared sales force activities or shared sales office, or both.	Lower selling costs. Better market coverage. Stronger technical advice to buyers. Enhanced convenience for buyers (can buy from single source). Improved access to buyers (have more products to sell).	• Buyers have different purchasing habits toward the products. • Different salespersons are more effective in representing the product. • Some products get more attention than others. • Buyers prefer to multiple-source rather than single-source their purchases.
Shared after-sale service and repair work.	Lower servicing costs. Better utilization of service personnel (less idle time). Faster servicing of customer calls.	• Different equipment or different labor skills, or both, are needed to handle repairs. • Buyers may do some in-house repairs.
Shared brand name.	Stronger brand image and company reputation. Increased buyer confidence in the brand.	• Company reputation is hurt if quality of one product is lower.
Shared advertising and promotional activities.	Lower costs. Greater clout in purchasing ads.	• Appropriate forms of messages are different. • Appropriate timing of promotions is different.
Common distribution channels.	Lower distribution costs. Enhanced bargaining power with distributors and retailers to gain shelf space, shelf positioning, stronger push and more dealer attention, and better profit margins.	• Dealers resist being dominated by a single supplier and turn to multiple sources and lines. • Heavy use of the shared channel erodes willingness of other channels to carry or push the firm's products.
Shared order processing.	Lower order processing costs. One-stop shopping for buyer enhances service and, thus, differentiation.	• Differences in ordering cycles disrupt order processing economies.

EXHIBIT 8–1   *continued*

Opportunities to Build Value or Sharing	Potential Competitive Advantage	Impediments to Achieving Enhanced Value
Operating Opportunities:		
Joint procurement of purchased inputs.	Lower input costs. Improved input quality. Improved service from suppliers.	• Input needs are different in terms of quality or other specifications. • Inputs are needed at different plant locations, and centralized purchasing is not responsive to separate needs of each plant.
Shared manufacturing and assembly facilities.	Lower manufacturing/assembly costs. Better capacity utilization, because peak demand for one product correlates with valley demand for other. Bigger scale of operation improves access to better technology and results in better quality.	• Higher changeover costs in shifting from one product to another. • High-cost special tooling or equipment is required to accommodate quality differences or design differences.
Shared inbound or outbound shipping and materials handling.	Lower freight and handling costs. Better delivery reliability. More frequent deliveries, such that inventory costs are reduced.	• Input sources or plant locations, or both, are in different geographic areas. • Needs for frequency and reliability of inbound/outbound delivery differ among the business units.
Shared product and process technologies or technology development or both.	Lower product or process design costs, or both, because of shorter design times and transfers of knowledge from area to area. More innovative ability, owing to scale of effort and attraction of better R&D personnel.	• Technologies are the same, but the applications in different business units are different enough to prevent much sharing of real value.
Shared administrative support activities.	Lower administrative and operating overhead costs.	• Support activities are not a large proportion of cost, and sharing has little cost impact (and virtually no differentiation impact).
Management Opportunities:		
Shared management know-how, operating skills, and proprietary information.	Efficient transfer of a distinctive competence—can create cost savings or enhance differentiation. More effective management as concerns strategy formulation, strategy implementation, and understanding of key success factors.	• Actual transfer of know-how is costly or stretches the key skill personnel too thinly, or both. • Increased risks that proprietary information will leak out.

BusinessWeek AT&T shelled out $7 billion for NCR Corp. early in the 1990s and finally staked out the strategic beachhead in computers that it had failed, despite billions of dollars spent, to achieve on its own. When AT&T succeeded in taking over computer maker NCR, it figured it had won a major victory in its dream of linking computers and telecommunications. As things turned out, the dream proved to be wishful thinking. Four years and $4 billion in net NCR losses later, AT&T was ready to cut its losses and spin off NCR. AT&T had also invested an additional $3.2 billion into NCR by the time it was spun off to the public. And after its initial emotional IPO market reception in early 1997, NCR stock quickly nosedived as its long-term prospects became more obvious, and unattractive. Analysts and competitors say NCR's computer problems are a lingering result of neglect under AT&T. For starters, NCR's computer sales force was allowed to shrink too much. And though it boasted customers such as H&R Block Inc. and J.C. Penney Co., outsiders say NCR was far too dependent on sales to AT&T. Worse, the phone giant failed to invest enough in the business or expand NCR's computer product lines, especially its Unix-based servers. "What NCR found, because of the AT&T screwup, is that their critical mass in the Unix business is not that big," says Nick Earle, worldwide marketing manager for Hewlett-Packard Co.'s enterprise systems group, a strong NCR rival in both servers and data warehousing.

Although consolidation of health-care providers has made sense for some, it certainly didn't for Dallas-based Medical Care International Inc. and Critical Care America, based in Westborough, Massachusetts. If ever there was a marriage made in hell, this combination of the nation's largest surgery-center chain and largest independent operator of home intravenous services was it. The concept—to create a hospital without walls and enable Medical Care America to profit from the rising demand for low-cost outpatient services—certainly sounded good. But virtually everything that could go wrong in a merger went wrong in this one. Poor timing, faulty due diligence, culture clashes, and big egos doomed the deal from the start. The merger took place just as intensified competition began driving down prices for home infusion services. Critical Care's problems were masked by slow insurer payments and infrequent internal reporting, which made it difficult to spot trends. Less than three weeks after the merger, Chairman and CEO Donald E. Steen announced that third-quarter results would fall below expectations, triggering a free fall in Medical Care America's shares. Management responded by slashing Critical Care's staff, which, in turn, caused it to lose customers. Shareholder lawsuits followed. "The Critical Care merger was bad, really bad," says Steen. "It's something I'm trying to forget." Soon thereafter Medical Care America sold off Critical Care to Caremark International Inc. and six months later sold out to Colurnbia/HCA Healthcare Corp. for $850 million. "This has been a very good merger," Steen says, largely because its broad geographic coverage and supply contracts have enabled it to lower prices.

same in soft-drink bottling. Disney and ABC saw shared core competencies as central in the entertainment industry of the 21st century. AT&T and TCI saw shared core competencies as central to telecommunications success. These and many more companies look to three basic considerations to evaluate whether they are capitalizing on core competencies.

Is Each Core Competency Providing a Relevant Competitive Advantage to the Intended Businesses?

The core competency must assist the intended business in creating strength relative to key competition. This could occur at any step in the business's value chain. But it must represent a major source of value to be a basis for competitive advantage—and the core competence must be transferrable. Honda of Japan viewed itself as having a core competence in manufacturing small, internal combustion engines. It diversified into small garden tools, perceiving that traditional electric tools would be much more attractive if powered by a lightweight, mobile, gas combustion motor. Their core competency created a major competitive advantage in a market void of gas-driven hand tools. When Coca-Cola added bottled water to its portfolio of products, it expected its extraordinary core competencies in marketing and distribution to rapidly build value in this business. Ten years later, Coke sold its water assets concluding that the product did not have enough margin to interest its

Other attempts at expanding by acquiring closely related companies have also bombed. Take, for example, Kmart Corp.'s 1990s acquisitions strategy. Instead of focusing on its core discount business, it lost more ground to Wal-Mart Stores Inc. when it diverted its attention and capital to buying up fast-growing specialized retailers, sometimes paying top dollar. Before long, Kmart had become a $30 billion-sales retail conglomerate with seven specialty store chains and 2,300 Kmart stores. But overhead was higher than rival Wal-Mart and sales per square foot lower. "The Kmart stores were totally neglected," says Trish Reopelle, an analyst with the State of Wisconsin Investment Board. Mid-decade, Kmart was forced to begin selling its specialty stores and CEO Joseph Antonini was out of a job. Kmart has continued to try to avoid bankruptcy protection as it seeks to survive its mistaken pursuit of synergy and diversification.

Few deals made more sense on paper yet so little sense culturally than the merger of Price Club and Costco Wholesale to create Price/Costco Inc., which became the second-largest operator of warehouse clubs after Wal-Mart's Sam's Club. "The economies of the two companies coming together to compete with Sam's Club were compelling," says Jeffrey Atkin, principal of the Seattle money-management firm of Kunath Karren Rinne & Atkin.

The deal had many problems, but the worst were cultural. The Price and Costco people just didn't seem to hit it off. Says analyst Michael J. Shea of Charter Investment Group: "The Price guys had much more of a real estate strip-mall mentality. The Costco guys were the type who started working at grocery stores bagging groceries when they were 10 years old and worked their way up the ladder." In one of the shortest corporate marriages ever, Price and Costco broke up after less than a year. Says analyst Mark Byl, of Laird Norton Trust Co.: "The best thing to happen to that marriage was the divorce."

All this indicates that many large-company CEOs are making multibillion-dollar decisions about the future of their companies, employees, and shareholders in part by the seat of their pants. When things go wrong, as the evidence demonstrates that they often do, these decisions create unnecessary tumult, losses, and heartache. While there clearly is a role for thoughtful and well-conceived mergers in American business, all too many don't meet that description. Moreover, in merging and acquiring mindlessly and flamboyantly, dealmakers may be eroding the nation's growth prospects and global competitiveness. Dollars that are wasted needlessly on mergers that don't work might better be spent on research and new-product development. And in view of the growing number of corporate divorces, it's clear that the best strategy for most would-be marriage partners is never to march to the altar at all.

Sources: "The Case against Mergers," *BusinessWeek,* October 30, 1995; "Is NCR Ready to Ring Up Some Cash?" *BusinessWeek,* October 14, 1996; and "Still Waiting for the New NCR," *BusinessWeek,* December 15, 1997.

franchised bottlers and that marketing was not a significant value-building activity among many small suppliers competing primarily on the cost of "producing" and shipping water. In the last few years, however, Coke has reversed its decision and added the Danske water brand because a rapidly increasing consumer demand has made the value of its extensive distribution network a relevant competitive advantage to the Danske water product line.

Are Businesses in the Portfolio Related in Ways That Make the Company's Core Competence(s) Beneficial?

Related versus unrelated diversification is an important distinction to understand as you evaluate the diversification question. "Related" businesses are those that rely on the same or similar capabilities to be successful and attain competitive advantage in their respective product markets. The discussion case at the end of Chapter 7 described how Caterpillar pursued related diversification into the portable power generation business from its core truck and tractor focus. This related move was very successful in part because Caterpillar's expertise in diesel engine manufacturing, indeed its same engines, could be used to strategic advantage in small scale, portable power generation. Earlier, we described General Cinema's spectacular success in both movie exhibition and soft-drink bottling. Seemingly unrelated, they were actually very related businesses in terms of key core competencies that shaped success—managing a network of diverse business locations, localized competition, reliance on a few large suppliers, and centralized marketing advantages. Thus, the products of various businesses do not necessarily have to be similar to leverage core competencies. While their products may not be related, it is essential that some activities in their value chains require similar skills to create competitive advantage if the company is going to leverage its core competence(s) in a value-creating way.

Situations that involve "unrelated" diversification occur when no real overlapping capabilities or products exist other than financial resources. We refer to this as *conglomerate diversification* in Chapter 6. Recent research indicates that the most profitable firms are those that have diversified around a set of resources and capabilities that are specialized enough to confer a meaningful competitive advantage in an attractive industry, yet adaptable enough to be advantageously applied across several others. The least profitable are broadly diversified firms whose strategies are built around very general resources (e.g., money) that are applied in a wide variety of industries, but are seldom instrumental to competitive advantage in those settings.[1]

Are Our Combination of Competencies Unique or Difficult to Re-create?

Skills that corporate strategists expect to transfer from one business to another, or from corporate to various businesses, may be transferrable. They may also be easily replicated by competitors. When this is the case, no sustainable competitive advantage is created. Sometimes strategists look for a combination of competencies, a package of various interrelated skills, as another way to create a situation where seemingly easily replicated competencies become unique, sustainable competitive advantages. 3M Corporation has the enviable record of having 25 percent of its earnings always coming from products introduced within the last five years. 3M has been able to "bundle" the skills necessary to accelerate the introduction of new products so that it consistently extracts early life cycle value from adhesive-related products that hundreds of competitors with similar technical or marketing competencies cannot touch.

All too often companies envision a combination of competencies that make sense conceptually. This vision of synergy develops an energy of its own leading CEOs to relentlessly push the merger of the firms involved. But what makes sense conceptually and is seen as difficult for competitors to re-create often proves difficult if not impossible to create in the first place. Exhibit 8–3, Strategy in Action, discusses this dilemma, making a case against merger and diversification.

Does the Company's Business Portfolio Balance Financial Resources?

Multibusiness companies usually find that their various businesses generate and consume very different levels of cash. Some generate more cash than they can use to maintain or expand their business while others consume more than they generate. Corporate managers face the very important challenge of determining the best way to generate and use financial resources among the businesses within their company. Faced with this challenge, managers historically looked to balance cash generators and cash users so that, along with outside capital sources, they can efficiently manage the cash flows across their business portfolio.

---

[1] David J. Collis and Cynthia A. Montgomery, *Corporate Strategy* (Chicago: Irwin), 1997, p. 88. "Why Mergers Fail," *McKinsey Quarterly Report*, 2001, vol. 4. "Deals That Create Value," *McKinsey Quarterly Report,* 2001, vol. 1.

BusinessWeek American companies are in the grip of full-blown merger mania. Each of the last ten years has topped the previous year's merger and acquisition activity. This historic surge of consolidations and combinations is occurring in the face of strong evidence that mergers and acquisitions, at least over the past 35 years or so, have hurt more than helped companies and shareholders. The conglomerate deals of the 1960s and 1970s that gave rise to such unwieldy companies as ITT Corp. and Litton Industries have since been thoroughly discredited, and most of these behemoths have been broken up. The debt-laden leveraged buyouts and bust-ups of the 1980s didn't fare any better, and many surely did a whole lot worse. That era ended not with a whimper but with a bang: In October 1989, when bankers couldn't raise the money for the ill-conceived buyout of UAL Corp., the deal collapsed, dragging the stock market down with it.

During the last decade, chief executives and investment bankers figured that they had finally gotten it right. If UAL marked the end of the 1980s crazy season, then the July, 1991, announcement by Chemical Bank Corp. and Manufacturers Hanover Corp. that they would join in a $2.3 billion stock swap to create the nation's second-largest banking company and produce $650 million in annual expense savings by 1994, seemed to signal that the Age of Reason in mergers and acquisitions had begun. This was to be the era of strategic deals—friendly, intelligent, and relatively debt-free transactions done mostly as stock swaps, which were supposed to enrich shareholders by producing synergies in which two plus two would equal five or more. These synergies would take the form of economies of scale, improved channels of distribution, greater market clout, and ultimately higher profits for surviving companies. Although Harvard University's Michael Porter in a seminal *Harvard Business Review* article argued persuasively that most would-be deal synergies are never realized, the new strategic transactions, Wall Street promised, would be different.

It turns out they're not. Indeed, with investment bankers singing their new, improved siren song, many big company CEOs are demonstrating that they still are as vulnerable to the latest fad as the most naive individual investor. An exhaustive analysis by *BusinessWeek* and Mercer Management Consulting Inc., a leading management consulting firm, of

hundreds of deals in this decade indicates that their performance has fallen far short of their promise. Deals that were announced with much fanfare such as AT&T's acquisition of NCR and Matsushita's acquisition of MCA, have since unraveled. Acquisitions by big pharmaceutical manufacturers of drug wholesalers, as well as software and entertainment deals aren't producing the results the acquirers had hoped for. Some recent megadeals like AOL-Time Warner, and Disney's acquisition of Capital Cities/ABC leave many media-industry observers scratching their heads over where the gains are going to come from. "For all these deals to work out, you have to believe that the American public is under-entertained," says Wilbur L. Ross, senior managing director at Rothschild Inc.

These anecdotal findings are supported statistically. The *BusinessWeek*/Mercer analysis indicates that companies performed better in the wake of '90s deals, most of which have been done ostensibly for business reasons, than they did after '80s transactions, a high proportion of which were financially driven. But the analysis also concluded that most of the '90s deals still haven't worked. Of 150 deals valued at $500 million or more, about half destroyed shareholder wealth, judged by stock performance in relation to Standard & Poor's industry indexes. Another third contributed only marginally to it. Further, says James Quella, director of Mercer Management Consulting, "many deals destroy a lot of value." Mergers and acquisitions, he declares, "are still a slippery slope." Key reasons mergers fail were:

Deal performance has been poor because melding two companies is enormously difficult and only a few companies are very good at it. One reason is that buyers often stack the odds against success by rushing headlong into mergers and acquisitions for the wrong reasons in search of synergies that don't exist. To make matters worse, they often pay outlandish premiums that can't be recovered even if everything goes right. And finally—and this is the real deal-killer—they fail to effectively integrate the two companies after the toasts have been exchanged. Good postmerger integration rarely makes a really bad deal work, but bad execution almost always wrecks one that might have had a shot. Says Kenneth W. Smith, a Mercer vice-president based in Toronto: "The deal is won or lost after it's done."

(continued)

Most transactions fall below expectations, but an even greater percentage of companies lose in the M&A game. That's because **a few large, proficient acquirers,** such as General Electric Co. and Dover Corp. (BW—Jan. 23), tend to **do a lot of successful deals while a much larger number of less adept companies execute one or two unsuccessful mergers.** In the 51/2 years ending July 31, 72% of companies that completed six or more deals valued over $5 million each yielded returns above the industry average, compared with 54% of companies that closed just one to five transactions.

Nonacquirers are more likely to outperform their respective industry indices than are **active acquirers.** Only about a fourth of the nation's 500 largest companies have not yet made a single acquisition larger than $5 million in this decade. But over 70% of companies that made no acquisitions larger than $5 million outperformed their respective Standard & Poor's industry indices. Only 50% of all acquirers did better than their industry indices. Many companies—notably Andrew Corp. and Coca Cola Co.—whose industry rivals are bent on growing through acquisition, have delivered superior returns by keeping investment bankers at bay and sticking to their knitting.

Many deals are poorly thought out, founded on dubious assumptions about the potential benefits by CEOs with questionable motivations. "There's tremendous allure to mergers and acquisitions," says Porter. "It's the big play, the dramatic gesture. With the stroke of a pen you can add billions to size, get a front-page story, and create excitement in the markets." Numerous companies have blundered lately when they tried to engineer a major redefinition of their businesses through merger and acquisition—often in response to sea changes in regulation, technology, and even geopolitics. If the spate of copycat deals in computers, telecommunications, media, and technology are any indication, these companies seem to fear they will be left behind forever if they don't do something and do it fast. "Nobody wants to be marooned," says David A. Nadler, chairman of Delta Consulting Group.

Optimism is bolstered by a variety of rationales. One is that vertical integration—linking manufacturing with distribution—will yield vast synergies. On that theory, Merck, Eli Lilly, and SmithKline paid handsomely for drug wholesalers, but the prospects for those deals are looking bleaker and bleaker. Such linkages are behind the Hollywood deals, such as Disney's acquisition of Capital Cities/ABC. "I hate to use the 's' word," says Disney Chairman Michael Eisner, "but that's synergy at work." Others are skeptical. Says Tele-Communications Inc. CEO John C. Malone: "It's an industry that's as certain as betting on a race horse."

Many experts say that the deal-breaker is usually **bad postmerger planning and integration.** If a deal is to stand any chance of success, companies must move quickly and decisively to appoint the new management team, cut costs, reassure customers, and resolve cultural conflicts.

To be sure, some strategic transactions have worked well. The Chemical-Manny Hanny merger; Primerica's acquisition of Travelers Corp.; Toymaker Mattel Corp.'s acquisition of Fisher-Price; and Campbell Soup–Pace Foods have worked. But the kinds of mergers and acquisitions with a better-than-even shot at success are limited indeed. Small and midsize deals—notably leveraged "buildups" in such fragmented industries as funeral homes and health clubs—frequently work. The best acquisitions, says Harvard's Porter, involve "gap-filling," including those in which one company buys another to strengthen its product line or expand its territory. "Globalizing" acquisitions, such as those that enable companies to expand their core business into other countries, may make sense, though culture and language problems undermine many of these deals. Mergers of direct competitors aimed at dominating a market, such as marriages of big banks with overlapping branches, often have worked out.

Source: Phillip L. Zweig in New York, with Judy Perlman Kline in Pittsburgh, Stephanie Anderson Forest in Dallas, and Kevin Gudridge, "The Case against Mergers," *BusinessWeek,* October 30, 1995.

Responding to this challenge during the diversification explosion of the 1970s, the Boston Consulting Group pioneered an approach called *portfolio techniques* that attempted to help managers "balance" the flow of cash resources among their various businesses while also identifying their basic strategic purpose within the overall portfolio. Three of these techniques are reviewed here. Once reviewed, we will identify some of the problems with the portfolio approach that you should keep in mind when considering its use.

EXHIBIT 8–4
The BCG Growth-
Share Matrix

Source: The growth-share
matrix was originally developed
by the Boston Consulting
Group.

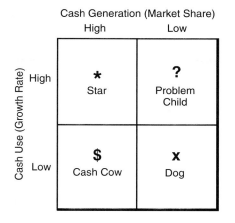

Cash Generation (Market Share)

Description of Dimensions

Market Share: Sales relative to those of other competitors in the market
(dividing point is usually selected to have only the two–three largest
competitors in any market fall into the high market share region)

Growth Rate: Industry growth rate in constant dollars
(dividing point is typically the GNP's growth rate)

The BCG Growth-Share Matrix

Managers using the BCG matrix plotted each of the company's businesses according to market growth rate and relative competitive position. *Market growth rate* is the projected rate of sales growth for the market being served by a particular business. Usually measured as the percentage increase in a market's sales or unit volume over the two most recent years, this rate serves as an indicator of the relative attractiveness of the markets served by each business in the firm's portfolio of businesses. *Relative competitive position* usually is expressed as the market share of a business divided by the market share of its largest competitor. Thus, relative competitive position provides a basis for comparing the relative strengths of the businesses in the firm's portfolio in terms of their positions in their respective markets. Exhibit 8–4 illustrates the growth-share matrix.

The *stars* are businesses in rapidly growing markets with large market shares. These businesses represent the best long-run opportunities (growth and profitability) in the firm's portfolio. They require substantial investment to maintain (and expand) their dominant position in a growing market. This investment requirement is often in excess of the funds that they can generate internally. Therefore, these businesses are often short-term, priority consumers of corporate resources.

Cash cows are businesses with a high market share in low-growth markets or industries. Because of their strong positions and their minimal reinvestment requirements, these businesses often generate cash in excess of their needs. Therefore, they are selectively "milked" as a source of corporate resources for deployment elsewhere (to stars and question marks). Cash cows are yesterday's stars and the current foundation of corporate portfolios. They provide the cash needed to pay corporate overhead and dividends and provide debt capacity. They are managed to maintain their strong market share while generating excess resources for corporatewide use.

Low market share and low market growth businesses are the *dogs* in the firm's portfolio. Facing mature markets with intense competition and low profit margins, they are managed for short-term cash flow (through ruthless cost cutting, for example) to supplement corporate-level resource needs. According to the original BCG prescription, they are divested or liquidated once this short-term harvesting has been maximized.

Question marks are businesses whose high growth rate gives them considerable appeal but whose low market share makes their profit potential uncertain. Question marks are cash guzzlers because their rapid growth results in high cash needs, while their small market share results in low cash generation. At the corporate level, the concern is to identify the question marks that would increase their market share and move into the star group if extra corporate resources were devoted to them. Where this long-run shift from question mark to star is unlikely, the BCG matrix suggests divesting the question mark and repositioning its resources more effectively in the remainder of the corporate portfolio.

The Industry Attractiveness–Business Strength Matrix

Corporate strategists found the growth-share matrix's singular axes limiting in their ability to reflect the complexity of a business's situation. Therefore, some companies adopted a matrix with a much broader focus. This matrix, developed by McKinsey & Company at General Electric, is called the Industry Attractiveness–Business Strength Matrix. This matrix uses multiple factors to assess industry attractiveness and business strength rather than the single measures (market share and market growth, respectively) employed in the BCG matrix. It also has nine cells as opposed to four—replacing the high/low axes with high/medium/low axes to make finer distinctions among business portfolio positions.

The company's businesses are rated on multiple strategic factors within each axis, such as the factors described in Exhibit 8–5. The position of a business is then calculated by "subjectively" quantifying its rating along the two dimensions of the matrix. Depending on the location of a business within the matrix as shown in Exhibit 8–6, one of the following strategic approaches is suggested: (1) invest to grow, (2) invest selectively and manage for earnings, or (3) harvest or divest for resources. The resource allocation decisions remain quite similar to those of the BCG approach.

Although the strategic recommendations generated by the Industry Attractiveness–Business Strength Matrix are similar to those generated by the BCG matrix, the Industry Attractiveness–Business Strength Matrix improves on the BCG matrix in three fundamental ways. First, the terminology associated with the Industry Attractiveness–Business Strength Matrix is preferable because it is less offensive and more understandable. Second, the multiple measures associated with each dimension of the business strength matrix tap many factors relevant to business strength and market attractiveness besides market share and market growth. And this, in turn, makes for broader assessment during the planning process, bringing to light considerations of importance in both strategy formulation and strategy implementation.

The Life Cycle–Competitive Strength Matrix

One criticism of the first two portfolio methods was their static quality—their portrayal of businesses as they exist at one point in time, rather than as they evolve over time. A third portfolio approach was introduced that attempted to overcome these deficiencies and better identify "developing winners" or potential "losers."[2] This approach uses the multiple-factor approach to assess competitive strength as one dimension and stage of the market life cycle as the other dimension.

---

[2] Attributed to Arthur D. Little, a consulting firm, and to Charles W. Hofer in "Conceptual Constructs for Formulating Corporate and Business Strategies" (Boston: Harvard Case Services, #9-378-754, 1977).

EXHIBIT 8–5
Factors Considered in Constructing an Industry Attractiveness–Business Strength Matrix

Industry Attractiveness	Business Strength

Industry Attractiveness

Nature of Competitive Rivalry

Number of competitors
Size of competitors
Strength of competitors' corporate parents
Price wars
Competition on multiple dimensions

Bargaining Power of Suppliers/Customers

Relative size of typical players
Numbers of each
Importance of purchases from or sales to
Ability to vertically integrate

Threat of Substitute Products/ New Entrants

Technological maturity/stability
Diversity of the market
Barriers to entry
Flexibility of distribution system

Economic Factors

Sales volatility
Cyclicality of demand
Market growth
Capital intensity

Financial Norms

Average profitability
Typical leverage
Credit practices

Sociopolitical Considerations

Government regulation
Community support
Ethical standards

Business Strength

Cost Position

Economies of scale
Manufacturing costs
Overhead
Scrap/waste/rework
Experience effects
Labor rates
Proprietary processes

Level of Differentiation

Promotion effectiveness
Product quality
Company image
Patented products
Brand awareness

Response Time

Manufacturing flexibility
Time needed to introduce new products
Delivery times
Organizational flexibility

Financial Strength

Solvency
Liquidity
Break-even point
Cash flows
Profitability
Growth in revenues

Human Assets

Turnover
Skill level
Relative wage/salary
Morale
Managerial commitment
Unionization

Public Approval

Goodwill
Reputation
Image

The life cycle dimension allows users to consider multiple strategic issues associated with each life cycle stage (refer to the discussion in Chapter 5), thereby enriching the discussion of strategic options. It also gives a "moving indication" of both issues—those strategy needs to address currently and those that could arise next. Exhibit 8–7 provides an illustration of this matrix. It includes basic strategic investment parameters recommended for different positions in the matrix. While this approach seems valuable, its recommendations are virtually identical to the previous two portfolio matrices.

EXHIBIT 8–6
The Industry Attractiveness– Business Strength Matrix

Source: McKinsey & Company and General Electric.

	High	Medium	Low
High	Invest	Selective Growth	Grow or Let Go
Medium	Selective Growth	Grow or Let Go	Harvest
Low	Grow or Let Go	Harvest	Divest

Business Strength (vertical axis)

Description of Dimensions

Industry Attractiveness: Subjective assessment based on broadest possible range of external opportunities and threats beyond the strict control of management

Business Strength: Subjective assessment of how strong a competitive advantage is created by a broad range of the firm's internal strengths and weaknesses

BCG's Strategic Environments Matrix

BCG's latest matrix offering (see Exhibit 8–8) took a different approach using the idea that it was the nature of competitive advantage in an industry that determined the strategies available to a companies businesses, which in turn determined the structured of the industry. Their idea was that such a framework could help ensure that individual business' strategies were consistent with strategies appropriate to their strategic environment. Furthermore, for corporate managers in multiple business companies, this matrix offered one way to rationalize which businesses they are in—business that share core competencies and associated competitive advantages because of similar strategic environments.

The matrix has two dimensions. The number of sources of competitive advantage could be many with complex products and services (e.g. automobiles, financial services) and few with commodities (chemicals, microprocessors). Complex products offer multiple opportunities for differentiation as well as cost, while commodities must seek opportunities for cost advantages to survive.

The second dimension is size of competitive advantage. How big is the advantage available to the industry leader? The two dimensions then define four industry environments as follows:

EXHIBIT 8–7
The Market Life Cycle–Competitive Strength Matrix

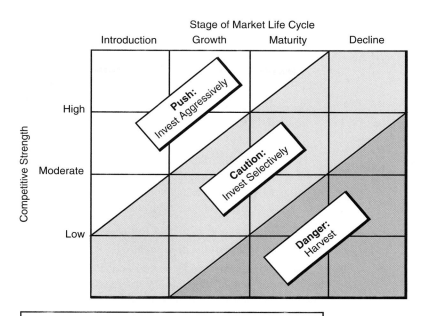

Description of Dimensions

Stage of Market Life Cycle: See page 146.

Competitive Strength: Overall subjective rating, based on a wide range of factors regarding the likelihood of gaining and maintaining a competitive advantage

EXHIBIT 8–8
BCG's Strategic Environments Matrix

Source: R. M. Grant, *Contemporary Strategy Analysis* (Oxford: Blackwell, 2002), p. 327.

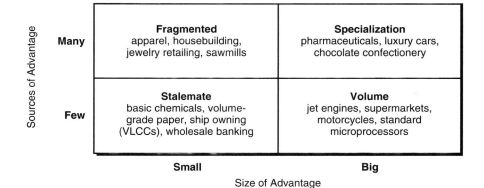

Volume businesses are those that have few sources of advantage, but the size is large—typically the result of scale economies. Advantages established in one such business may be transferable to another as Honda has done with its scale and expertise with small gasoline engines.

Stalemate businesses have few sources of advantage, with most of those small. This results in very competitive situations. Skills in operational efficiency, low overhead, and cost management are critical to profitability.

Fragmented businesses have many sources of advantage, but they are all small. This typically involves differentiated products with low brand loyalty, easily replicated technology, and scale economies minimal. Skills in focused market segments, typically geographic, the ability to respond quickly to changes and low costs are critical in this environment.

Specialization businesses have many sources of advantage, and find those advantages potentially sizable. Skills in achieving differentiation—product design, branding expertise, innovation, first-mover, and perhaps scale—characterize winners here.

BCG viewed this matrix as providing guidance to multibusiness managers to determine whether they possessed the sources and size of advantage associated with the type of industry facing each business; and allow them a framework to realistically explore the nature of the strategic environments in which they competed or were interested in entering.

Limitations of Portfolio Approaches

Portfolio approaches made several contributions to strategic analysis by corporate managers convinced of their ability to transfer the competitive advantage of professional management across a broad array of businesses. They helped convey large amounts of information about diverse business units and corporate plans in a greatly simplified format. They illuminated similarities and differences between business units and helped convey the logic behind corporate strategies for each business with a common vocabulary. They simplified priorities for sharing corporate resources across diverse business units that generated and used those resources. They provided a simple prescription that gave corporate managers a sense of what they should accomplish—a balanced portfolio of businesses—and a way to control and allocate resources among them. While these approaches offered meaningful contributions, they had several critical limitations and shortcomings:

- A key problem with the portfolio matrix was that it did not address how value was being created across business units—the only relationship between them was cash. Because of this, its valued simplicity encouraged a tendency to trivialize strategic thinking among users that did not take proper time for thorough underlying analysis.

- Truly accurate measurement for matrix classification was not as easy as the matrices portrayed. Identifying individual businesses, or distinct markets, was not often as precise as underlying assumptions required.

- The underlying assumption about the relationship between market share and profitability—the experience curve effect—varied across different industries and market segments. Some have no such link. Some find that firms with low market share can generate superior profitability with differentiation advantages.

- The limited strategic options, intended to describe the flow of resources in a company, came to be seen more as basic strategic missions. Doing this creates a false sense of what strategies were when none really existed. This becomes more acute when attempting to use the matrices to conceive strategies for average businesses in average growth markets.

- The portfolio approach portrayed the notion that firms needed to be self-sufficient in capital. This ignored capital raised in capital markets.

- The portfolio approach typically failed to compare the competitive advantage a business received from being owned by a particular company with the costs of owning it. The 1980s saw many companies build enormous corporate infrastructures that created only small gains at the business level. The deconstruction in the 1990s of some "model" portfolio companies reflects this important omission.

Constructing business portfolio matrices must be undertaken with these limitations in mind. Perhaps it is best to say that they provide one form of input to corporate managers seeking to balance financial resources. They should be used merely to provide a basis for further discussion of corporate strategy and the allocation of corporate resources, and to provide a picture of the "balance" of resource generators and users to test underlying assumptions about these issues in more involved corporate planning efforts to leverage core competencies to build sustained competitive advantages. For while the portfolio approaches have serious limitations, the challenge for corporate managers overseeing the allocation of resources among a variety of business units is still to maintain a balanced use of the company's financial resources.

Does Our Business Portfolio Achieve Appropriate Levels of Risk and Growth?

Diversification has traditionally been recommended as a way to manage, or diversify, risk. Said another way, "not having all your eggs in one basket" allows corporate managers to potentially reduce risk to company stockholders. Balancing cyclical revenue streams to reduce earnings volatility is one way diversification may reduce risk. So managers need to ask this question as a part of their strategic analysis and subsequent choice. Likewise, revenue growth can be enhanced by diversification. Many companies in the hazardous waste industry maintained the steady growth investors had come to expect by continuously making acquisitions of other businesses to gain immediate sales growth. Indeed, Exhibit 8–9, Strategy in Action, reports that Generation X managers are much more comfortable with "M&A" diversification growth than their elderly counterparts, with the exception of GE legend Jack Welch.

Both risk and growth are assumptions or priorities corporate managers should carefully examine as they undertake strategic analysis and choice. Is growth always desirable? Can risks truly be managed most effectively by corporate management? Many companies have pursued growth to gain market share without accompanying attention to profitability. Similarly, companies have built diverse business portfolios in part to manage overall risk. In both instances, the outcome is often a later time when subsequent management must "look in the bag" of businesses and aggressively divest and downsize the company until true value-adding activities and synergies linked to sustained competitive advantages are uncovered. Exhibit 8–10, Strategy in Action, shows Finland's Nokia outdistancing Motorola and Ericsson due to the advantage Nokia's focus provides over the others' portfolio problems.

BEHAVIORAL CONSIDERATIONS AFFECTING STRATEGIC CHOICE

After alternative strategies have been analyzed, managers choose one of those strategies. If the analysis identified a clearly superior strategy or if the current strategy will clearly meet future company objectives, then the decision is relatively simple. Such clarity is the exception, however, and strategic decision makers often are confronted with several

Strategy in Action
Generation Xers and Jack Welch Say Mergers and Acquisitions
Can Be OK!

Exhibit 8–9

BusinessWeek

FOR GEN X, M&A IS A-OK

Twenty somethings strongly support the mergers-and-acquisitions trend. The young tend to be optimistic, as opposed to those over 65, who grew up in an era when bigger was often not seen as better.

Some have argued that single-product businesses have a focus that gives them an advantage over multibusiness companies like our own—and perhaps they would have, but only if we neglect our own overriding advantage: the ability to share the ideas that are the result of wide and rich input from a multitude of global sources.

GE businesses share technology, design, compensation and personnel evaluation systems, manufacturing practices, and customer and country knowledge. Gas Turbines shares manufacturing technology with Aircraft Engines; Motors and Transportation Systems work together on new propulsion systems; Lighting and Medical Systems collaborate to improve x-ray tube processes; and GE Capital provides innovative financing packages that help all our businesses around the globe. Supporting all this is a management system that fosters and rewards this sharing and teamwork, and, increasingly, a culture that

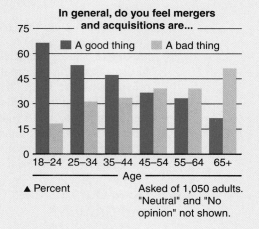

In general, do you feel mergers and acquisitions are...

■ A good thing   ▨ A bad thing

▲ Percent

Asked of 1,050 adults. "Neutral" and "No opinion" not shown.

makes it reflexive and natural at every level and corner of our Company.

—Jack Welch, Chairman, General Electric Company, 1981–2001

Source: "Up-Front Section," *BusinessWeek,* August 10, 1998, p. 6; Letters to Shareholders, General Electric Company.

viable alternatives rather than the luxury of a clear-cut choice. Under these circumstances, several factors influence the strategic choice. Some of the more important are:

1. Role of the current strategy.

2. Degree of the firm's external dependence.

3. Attitudes toward risk.

4. Managerial priorities different from stockholder interests.

5. Internal political considerations.

6. Competitive reaction.

Role of the Current Strategy

Current strategists are often the architects of past strategies. If they have invested substantial time, resources, and interest in those strategies, they logically would be more comfortable with a choice that closely parallels or involves only incremental alterations to the current strategy.

Such familiarity with and commitment to past strategy permeates the entire firm. Thus, lower-level managers reinforce the top managers' inclination toward continuity with past strategy during the choice process. Research in several companies found lower-level

BusinessWeek Focused growth in new geographic cell phone markets and related products, rather than product and technology diversification, is Finland's Nokia's impressive secret.

Six years ago, as an untested CEO, Jorma Ollila bet Nokia, the 133-year-old Finnish conglomerate, on cellular phones, challenging rivals Motorola Inc. and L. M. Ericsson. In the struggle that ensued, Ollila's Finns outdid themselves. Fast and focused, with a canny eye for design, Nokia wrested market share from entrenched competitors and emerged as the most profitable player in the industry.

All told, Nokia is providing troubled Motorola Inc., the leader in old-fashioned analog phones, with a humiliating tutorial on digital communications. Motorola CEO Christopher B. Galvin glumly concedes that "the analog business is trending down." Ollila, for his part, predicts that Nokia will be "No. 1 in the world in the number of phones sold, in growth, and return on capital employed." Rapid growth should about double the worldwide number of cellular subscribers, now equally divided among Europe, Asia, and the Americas, to 550 million by 2001. This benefits the big three—Motorola, Ericsson, and, of course, Nokia—which rule three-quarters of the cellular market with nearly equal shares. Motorola, though, is struggling to escape from dying analog, where prices are collapsing. And Ericsson, while fully in stride with Nokia in digital sets, is far larger and more diverse and is burdened with less profitable old-line businesses.

Source: "Can CEO Ollila Keep the Cellular Superstar Flying High?" *BusinessWeek*, August 10, 1998, p. 55.

Nokia is battling two Goliaths...

	Motorola	Ericsson	**Nokia**
1997 Sales	$29.8	$21.17	**$9.64**
% Increase	+6.5%	+35%	**+34%**
Operating profits*	$1.95	$2.37	**$1.58**
% Increase	Flat	75%	**+98%**

*Billions of dollars

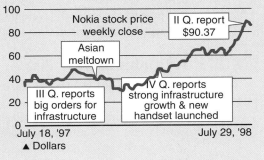

...But its laserlike focus on cell phones...

Cell phones and infrastructure as percent of sales**

** Includes infrastructure

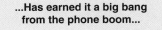

...Has earned it a big bang from the phone boom...

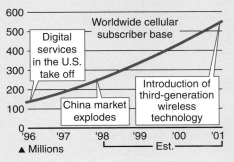

Worldwide cellular subscriber base

Digital services in the U.S. take off

China market explodes

Introduction of third-generation wireless technology

▲ Millions — Est. —

...And investors appreciate the difference

Nokia stock price weekly close

II Q. report $90.37

Asian meltdown

III Q. reports big orders for infrastructure

IV Q. reports strong infrastructure growth & new handset launched

July 18, '97   July 29, '98
▲ Dollars

managers suggested strategic choices that were consistent with current strategy and likely to be accepted while withholding suggestions with less probability of approval. Research by Henry Mintzberg suggests that past strategy strongly influences current strategic choice. The older and more successful a strategy has been, the harder it is to replace. Similarly, once a strategy has been initiated, it is very difficult to change because organizational momentum keeps it going. Even as a strategy begins to fail due to changing conditions, strategists often increase their commitment to it. Thus, firms may replace top executives when performance has been inadequate for an extended period because replacing these executives lessens the influence of unsuccessful past strategy on future strategic choice.

Degree of the Firm's External Dependence

If a firm is highly dependent on one or more environmental elements, its strategic alternatives and its ultimate strategic choice must accommodate that dependence. The greater a firm's external dependence, the lower its range and flexibility in strategic choice.

Bama Pies is a great family business success story. It makes excellent pies—apple turnovers. For many years, Bama Pies sold most of its pie output to one customer—McDonald's. With its massive retail coverage and its access to alternative suppliers. McDonald's was a major external dependence for Bama Pies. Bama Pies' strategic alternatives and ultimate choice of strategy were limited and strongly influenced by McDonald's demands.

Numerous small software companies and even many larger computer, software, and Internet-related businesses have considerable external dependence on Microsoft's operating system for their main products and services. Decisions to pursue options that put that relationship at risk are weighed with much hesitation because of the impact a negative Microsoft reaction could have on their company's survival. Or consider Amazon.com, the Internet bookseller and e-commerce bellwether company. As Amazon began to build momentum, arch rival Barnes & Noble acquired the leading book distributor Ingram Book Group, which supplied 60 percent of Amazon.com's books. Barnes & Noble promised "no favoritism," but Amazon's high external dependence on Ingram would no doubt be reevaluated and other sources considered even at a higher cost.

While external dependence can restrict options, it isn't necessarily a strategic threat. The last decade has seen firms' efforts to enhance quality and cost include decisions to "sole-source" certain supplies or services, even ones central to the firm's strategic capabilities. This increases "external dependence," but it is seen as a way to "strategically partner" that allows both firms to share information, and improve and integrate product and process design and development, to mention a few benefits that may accrue to both partners. More on this in Chapter 10.

Attitudes toward Risk

Attitudes toward risk exert considerable influence on strategic choice. Where attitudes favor risk, the range of the strategic choices expands and high-risk strategies are acceptable and desirable. Where management is risk averse, the range of strategic choices is limited and risky alternatives are eliminated before strategic choices are made. Past strategy exerts far more influence on the strategic choices of risk-averse managers. Exhibit 8–10, Strategy in Action, shows how the highly focused, risk-tolerant Nokia has flown past risk-averse Motorola in cell phones.

Industry volatility influences the propensity of managers toward risk. Top managers in highly volatile industries absorb and operate with greater amounts of risk than do their counterparts in stable industries. Therefore, top managers in volatile industries consider a broader, more diverse range of strategies in the strategic choice process.

Industry evolution is another determinant of managerial propensity toward risk. A firm in the early stages of the product-market cycle must operate with considerably greater risk and uncertainty than a firm in the later stages of that cycle.

In making a strategic choice, risk-oriented managers lean toward opportunistic strategies with higher payoffs. They are drawn to offensive strategies based on innovation, company strengths, and operating potential. Risk-averse managers lean toward safe, conservative strategies with reasonable, highly probable returns. They are drawn to defensive strategies that minimize a firm's weaknesses, external threats, and the uncertainty associated with innovation-based strategies.

Managerial Priorities Different from Stockholder Interests

Corporate managers are hired, theoretically, to act as agents of shareholders and to make decisions that are in shareholders' best interests. An increasing area of research known as *agency theory* suggests that managers frequently place their own interests above those of their shareholders.[3] This appears to be particularly true when the strategic decisions involve diversification. While stockholder value may be maximized by selling a company, for example, managers in the acquired company may lose their jobs—a potential conflict of interests. In these circumstances, several of the benefits sought through diversification give rise to potential manager-stockholder conflicts. The idea of "sharing core competencies" may encounter resistance from managers suspicious about diluting their valued capability. "Shared infrastructure" usually means fewer managers are needed. "Balancing financial resources" realistically means resources controlled by one management group become shared or diluted to support other businesses.

Similarly, some managers may seek diversification to accelerate sales growth, although continued focus in a narrow market area ensures increased competitive advantage to sustain long-term shareholder value. "Growth" achieved by combining two companies increases the basis on which some managers are compensated, regardless of whether the combination is truly advantageous to stockholders. The bottom line is, particularly where diversification decisions are being made, managerial self-interests can result in strategic choices that benefit managers to the detriment of stockholders. In these situations, strategic decision making can take on a political context like that described in the next section and Exhibit 8–11.

Internal Political Considerations

Power/political factors influence strategic choice. The use of power to further individual or group interest is common in organizational life. A major source of power in most firms is the chief executive officer (CEO). In smaller firms, the CEO is consistently the dominant force in strategic choice. Regardless of firm size, when the CEO begins to favor a particular choice, it is often selected unanimously.

Coalitions are power sources that influence strategic choice. In large firms, subunits and individuals (particularly key managers) have reason to support some alternatives and oppose others. Mutual interest draws certain groups together in coalitions to enhance their position on major strategic issues. These coalitions, particularly the more powerful ones (often called *dominant coalitions*), exert considerable influence on the strategic choice process. Numerous studies confirm the frequent use of power and coalitions in strategic decision making.

[3] K. M. Eisenhardt, "Agency Theory: An Assessment and Review," *Academy of Management Review* 14 (1989), pp. 57–74; B. M. Oviatt, "Agency and Transaction Cost Perspectives on the Manager-Shareholder Relationship: Incentives for Congruent Interests," *Academy of Management Review* 13 (1988), pp. 214–25.

EXHIBIT 8–11   **Political Activities in Phases of Strategic Decision Making**

Source: Adapted from Liam Fahey and V. K. Naroyanan, "The Politics of Strategic Decision Making," in The Strategic Management Handbook, ed. Kenneth J. Albert (New York: McGraw-Hill, 1983), pp. 20–21.

Phases of Strategic Decision Making	Focus of Political Action	Examples of Political Activity
Identification and diagnosis of strategic issues.	Control of: Issues to be discussed. Cause-and-effect relationships to be examined.	Control agenda. Interpretation of past events and future trends.
Narrowing the alternative strategies for serious consideration.	Control of alternatives.	Mobilization: Coalition formation. Resource commitment for information search.
Examining and choosing the strategy.	Control of choice.	Selective advocacy of criteria. Search and representation of information to justify choice.
Initiating implementation of the strategy.	Interaction between winners and losers.	Winners attempt to "sell" or co-opt losers. Losers attempt to thwart decisions and trigger fresh strategic issues.
Designing procedures for the evaluation of results.	Representing oneself as successful.	Selective advocacy of criteria.

Exhibit 8–11 shows that the *content* of strategic decisions and the *processes* of arriving at such decisions are politically charged. Each phase in the process of strategic choice presents an opportunity for political action intended to influence the outcome. The challenge for strategists lies in recognizing and managing this political influence. For example, selecting the criteria used to compare alternative strategies or collecting and appraising information regarding those criteria may be particularly susceptible to political influence. This possibility must be recognized and, where necessary, "managed" to avoid dysfunctional political bias. Relying on different sources to collect and appraise information might serve this purpose.

Organizational politics must be viewed as an inevitable dimension of organizational decision making that strategic management must accommodate. Some authors argue that politics is a key ingredient in the "glue" that holds an organization together. Formal and informal negotiating and bargaining between individuals, subunits, and coalitions are indispensable mechanisms for organizational coordination. Accommodating these mechanisms in the choice of strategy will result in greater commitment and more realistic strategy. The costs of doing so, however, are likely to be increased time spent on decision making and incremental (as opposed to drastic) change.

Competitive Reaction

In weighing strategic choices, top management frequently incorporates perceptions of likely competitor reactions to those choices. For example, if it chooses an aggressive strategy directly challenging a key competitor, that competitor can be expected to mount an aggressive counterstrategy. In weighing strategic choices, top management must consider the probable impact of such reactions on the success of the chosen strategy.

The beer industry provides a good illustration. Anheuser-Busch dominated the industry, and Miller Brewing Company, recently acquired by Philip Morris, was a weak and declining competitor. Miller's management decided to adopt an expensive advertising-oriented strategy that challenged the big three (Anheuser-Busch, Pabst, and Schlitz) head-on because it assumed that their reaction would be delayed due to Miller's current declining status in the industry. This assumption proved correct, and Miller was able to reverse its trend in market share before Anheuser-Busch countered with an equally intense advertising strategy.

Miller's management took another approach in its next major strategic decision. It introduced (and heavily advertised) a low-calorie beer—Miller Lite. Other industry members had introduced such products without much success. Miller chose a strategy that did not directly challenge its key competitors and was not expected to elicit immediate counterattacks from them. This choice proved highly successful, because Miller was able to establish a dominant share of the low-calorie beer market before those competitors decided to react. In this case, as in the preceding case, expectations regarding the reactions of competitors were a key determinant in the strategic choice made by Miller's management.

Summary

This chapter examined how managers evaluate and choose their company's strategy in multibusiness settings. They look to rationalize their efforts to diversify and their current or anticipated collection of businesses. Doing this means identifying opportunities to share skills and core competencies across businesses or from corporate capabilities to business operational needs. Such opportunities usually arise in marketing, operations, management, or a combination of these activities when a capability in one area contributes to a competitive advantage in another.

Diversified, multibusiness companies face yet another, more complicated process of strategy analysis and choice. This chapter looked at the evolution of this challenge from portfolio approaches to value-based ways to decide which set of businesses maximizes opportunities to build shareholder value.

Critical, often overlooked in the process of strategic analysis and choice, are behavioral considerations that may well determine a company's choice of strategy as much or more so than solely rational analysis. Commitment to the current strategy, external dependence, managerial self-interests, political considerations, and competitive considerations combine to exercise a major influence on how managers eventually evaluate and choose strategies.

Questions for Discussion

1. How does strategic analysis at the corporate level differ from strategic analysis at the business unit level? How are they related?

2. When would multi-industry companies find the portfolio approach to strategic analysis and choice useful?

3. What are three types of opportunities for sharing that form a sound basis for diversification or vertical integration? Give an example of each from companies you have read about.

4. What role might power and politics play in strategic analysis within a multibusiness company? Strategic choice within that same company? Would you expect these issues to be more prominent in a diversified company or in a single–product line company? Why or why not?

5. Several behavioral considerations discussed in this chapter appear to influence strategic analysis and choice within many companies as they seek to chart future direction. From your reading of current business publications, select and explain an example of a company in which one of these behavioral considerations influenced strategic analysis and choice.

Chapter 8 Discussion Case

BusinessWeek

Daimler's Diversification Dance

Chapter 8 has helped you look at companies' decisions to become more diversified, to become multi-business companies, or to narrow their scope to fewer businesses.

Daimler Benz is an interesting company for you to examine in the *BusinessWeek* Discussion Case because it has had such a varied diversification experience in the decade just ended. You might say that this last decade has been Daimler Benz's *decade-long dance with the diversification devil.*

So *BusinessWeek* reporters take you through *Daimler's Diversification Dance* to illustrate some of the concepts about strategic analysis and choice involving multibusiness companies. They examine it in three phases, or dance steps, ending with the Daimler-Chrysler waltz, which they examined in the greatest detail when it was first consummated. Then, they return three years later to re-examine Daimler's DD at the end of this discussion case.

1   Daimler Benz has "danced" an incredible and varied dance with diversification in the 1990s. You could say there were three segments, steps, or eras to the dance:

• **Obsession with Diversification—Be all we can possibly be—in the decade's first half**

• **Revulsion with Diversification—Be only what we have to be—in the mid-decade**

• **Simple related Diversification—Be the global car company we have to be—decade's end**

OBSESSION WITH DIVERSIFICATION—BE ALL WE CAN POSSIBLY BE—IN THE DECADE'S FIRST HALF

2   Daimler Benz spent billions of dollars on acquisitions in the early 1990s to try to transform itself from an auto maker into a high-tech conglomerate excelling at everything from telecommunications to jet planes. In perhaps the most critical step toward that goal, CEO Edzard Reuter laid out an additional

$1.9 billion—and even billions more later—in a bid to succeed in an industry where his European rivals have failed and become a global heavyweight in microelectronics.

3   Reuter thought he didn't have much choice. Whether in aerospace or autos, Daimler needs to become a leader in microelectronics if it hopes to stay competitive with the United States and Japan. Daimler's new venture would steer clear of standard memory chips, which have led to huge losses. Instead, it will make specialized chips that are custom-designed to control everything from automobile engines to computerized production lines. Daimler executives worried that if they don't make their own chips they will be increasingly dependent on Japanese and American technology for their next generation of products. It would mean sharing sensitive product knowhow with outsiders who design the chips. That's a risk the Germans didn't want to take. One way or another, microelectronics influences two-thirds of Germany's gross national product, said Frank Dieter Maier, head of the new Daimler chip unit. Daimler wasn't alone. Other German industrial giants, such as Siemens and Robert Bosch, also ramped up production of application-specific chips, called ASICs, and other logic products. In fact, the Germans moved toward Japanese-style integration, where systems manufacturers and electronics companies often share space under the same keiretsu roof. Without a competitive chip operation, "Daimler's engineers will lose touch with fast-paced semiconductor developments that have a huge impact on their automotive electronics," said Tomihiro Matsumura, the senior executive vice-president who heads chip operations at NEC Corp.

4   Despite Daimler's deep pockets, Reuter's bet was a risky one. Competition in the multibillion dollar ASIC business gets hotter every day as well-heeled memory-chip makers from South Korea to Tokyo to the Silicon Valley seek to step up production of custom chips. That means learning the hard way. Early in its efforts, when Daimler sold bipolar chips to Mitsubishi Electric, Mitsubishi rejected them, saying they weren't good enough. Daimler engineers redoubled their efforts, revamping test

procedures from start to finish on the production line. Said a hopeful Maier: "It's a learning experience. It will pay off."

5   By the mid-1990s Edzard Reuter was ready to retire at 66 years old having returned Daimler to profitability ($750 million on $74 billion in sales versus a $1.3 billion loss the previous year). He was still passing out copies of his glossy document called The New Age in which Reuter boasted that he had transformed Daimler from a luxury car maker into an "integrated technology group" involved in aerospace, microelectronics, and many kinds of transportation. His heir apparent Jürgen E. Schrempp, had been the leading CEO candidate ever since Reuter appointed him CEO of Deutsche Aerospace (DASA). His mission there was to weld a grab bag of outfits making engines, rockets, planes, and helicopters into a coherent company. That job was a small-scale version of what Reuter has been trying to do with all of Daimler—pool the technical know-how of its autos to avionics units into an integrated high-technology concern, a sort of Teutonic General Electric Co. The effort included pouring $6.25 billion into acquisitions over five years. Reuter left saying the strategy was working. There was little evidence it would pay off soon.

REVULSION WITH DIVERSIFICATION—BE ONLY WHAT WE HAVE TO BE—IN THE MID-DECADE

6   It could have been the smoothest of handovers. When Jürgen E. Schrempp became chief executive of Germany's Daimler Benz, he was expected to inherit a $74 billion industrial empire restored to financial health. His predecessor and mentor, Edzard Reuter, boasted of a return to profitability and promised another boost the next year. But less than three months later, the empire was in disarray. Hit by the soaring German mark, management disputes, and losses from Reuter's own diversification strategy, Daimler was faced with another dangerous slide in profits. Brokers have stamped "sell" recommendations on the stock. In a fight to restore the company's credibility, Schrempp, 50, reversed Reuter's forecast and warned of "severe losses" in his first full year.

7   It turned out that Schrempp, while learning under diversification champion Reuter, had been spending his final year of grooming to become CEO preparing a very different, anti-diversification strategy for Daimler. All that year, Schrempp prepared his strategy, and once in power, he executed it with exacting swiftness. The goal: to reverse his former mentor's grand scheme of building an integrated technology company. First, he streamlined head-office hierarchy, cutting staff by more than 75%. "You have to sweep the stairs from the top down," he says. Then he examined each business unit, grilling frightened managers nearly to tears and set a 12% return-on-capital target for each unit. When the dust had settled, Daimler was down to 23 units from 35 and carried 63,000 fewer people on the payroll within six months after Schrempp became CEO.

8   That year observers described his long-term strategy as:

- Make a decisive break with failed diversification strategy

- Focus on core automotive and truck businesses, which provide most of the group's profits

- Close the money-losing Daimler Benz Industrie unit with sell-offs and transfers of profitable operations to other divisions

- Slim down DASA Daimler Benz Aerospace, reducing its workforce of 40,000 by up to 50%, and step up sourcing of parts from dollar and other weak-currency areas

- Speed up globalization of manufacturing by locating big-ticket plant investments outside Germany

9   By 1997, focus had started to pay off and the "swagger" was back at Mercedes. Take the U.S. market for example. It has been a remarkable turnaround for the German company, whose U.S. sales hit rock bottom in 1991 in the face of a successful onslaught by Japanese luxury brands. But they have since left rivals behind in the slow lane. Bolstered by a stable of new products and aggressive marketing campaigns, Mercedes (and BMW) again rank as the hottest luxury brands in the U.S. They ended 1997 in a dead heat for preeminence among luxury import brands, with BMW's sales of 122,500 vehicles edging out Mercedes' 122,417. And in a luxury-car market that grew just 6% from 1991 to

1997, BMW sales soared 130%, while Mercedes rose 83%. That has allowed the German brands to leapfrog past their top two Japanese rivals, Lexus and Acura. If BMW and Mercedes keep accelerating, they could roar past the faltering U.S. market leaders, General Motors' Cadillac Div. and Ford's Lincoln unit, within the next five years.

10   Competitors now hold Mercedes and BMW up as the standard to beat. "They have clearly reframed the luxury market," says John F. Smith, general manager of GM's Cadillac Div. "I think they've been much more responsive to a variety of consumer tastes." That's just the opposite of the reputations BMW and Mercedes carried at their low point in 1991. Back then, the pair admittedly lost touch with consumers. They paid the price: Sales bottomed out at 53,343 vehicles for BMW and 58,869 for Mercedes—down 45% and 41%, respectively, from their high five years earlier. "The key issue then was to survive," says Michael Jackson, president of Mercedes-Benz of North America.

11   The bottom line was a resounding rejection of the prior diversification strategy choosing instead to focus on stablizing the business around core competencies and capabilities relative to automotive and key transportation products, and to globalize its operations where cost benefits were derived.

SIMPLE RELATED DIVERSIFICATION—BE THE GLOBAL CAR COMPANY WE HAVE TO BE—DECADE'S END

12   CEO Schrempp led an aggressive effort to refocus and simplify Daimler Benz. It worked. But as he looked toward the 21st century's global automotive industry, he had some concerns. Daimler Benz had a limited, upper-scale product line with an industry becoming truly global with overcapacity and increasing full product line competitors. Globally, in 1998 there was plant capacity to build at least 15 million more vehicles each year than could realistically be sold. And overcapacity was expected to balloon to 18.2 million vehicles by 2002. So while he was dismantling Daimler Benz and refocusing it around the automotive industry, Schrempp was thinking about eventually seeking a partner for Daimler that would diversify its product line and

geographic presence in the global automotive industry. He had decided that a carmaker can't compete without a full range of products, and he couldn't stretch the Mercedes brand any further downmarket.

13   But first he had to get Daimler in shape for a merger. Mercedes-Benz was a separate operating company with its own board, run by Helmut Werner, who was a hero in Germany for reviving the Mercedes lineup. Schrempp wanted to give Daimler direct operating control of Mercedes. "We had steps and steps, and layers and layers," Schrempp explains, moving Marlboros around the table to illustrate. "It took months to make a decision." In 1995 and early 1996, talks between Chrysler CEO Eaton and Mercedes CEO Werner about a joint venture for all their international businesses outside Europe and North America had bogged down because of this structure. That failure helped spur Schrempp's reorganization. Although Werner fought to keep Mercedes independent, Schrempp prevailed with the supervisory board. By early 1997, Mercedes was folded into Daimler, Werner was out, and Schrempp was running a car business. A year later the lean, chainsmoking 54-year-old chief executive of Daimler Benz approached Chrysler CEO Robert J. Eaton in his office in Auburn Hills, Michigan with a scheme to merge their two companies. In a steak house with Daimler colleagues after the 17-minute chat, Schrempp worried that he may have been too bold. His fears were unfounded. America's scrappy No. 3 car company and Germany's most revered brand name quickly decided to combine to become the world's fifth-largest carmaker when shares in DaimlerChrysler first traded in November, 1998.

14   Schrempp and Eaton are entering into an unprecedented business experiment. The auto industry has long been among the world's most international. But the DaimlerChrysler merger ushers in a new phase of global competitiveness when the very biggest players in the world's main regions unite as industrial powerhouses of tremendous scope. Schrempp will be judged both on his ability to run this ungainly giant and on whether he can emerge as Europe's most forceful business leader.

15   The megadeal unites two of the world's most profitable auto companies—with combined 1997 net earnings of $4.6 billion. And if ever a merger had the potential for that elusive quality—

synergy—this could be the one. Mercedes-Benz passenger cars are synonymous with luxury and sterling engineering. Chrysler is renowned for its low-cost production of trucks, minivans, and sport-utility vehicles. Chrysler is almost wholly domestic, and Mercedes is increasing global sales—albeit within the confines of the luxury-car market. By spreading Chrysler's production expertise to Daimler operations and merging both product-development forces, the new company could cut costs by up to $3 billion annually—including $1.1 billion in purchasing costs, analysts say. And fundamental synergies are as follows:

Product Synergies: There is almost no product overlap. Mercedes-Benz luxury cars compete in a market beyond Chrysler's mainstream offerings. Chrysler brings strength in minivans, profitable pickups, and sport-utility vehicles. Mercedes has hot-sellers like the E-class sedan and SLK roadster. The only overlapping model: Mercedes M-class, which goes against Jeep Grand Cherokee.

Geographic Synergies: Each company is strong where the other is weak. Chrysler derives 93% of its sales from North America. Mercedes-Benz depends on Europe for 63% of its business. Each company is looking to strengthen its position in its partner's home market and conquer emerging markets together.

One of the biggest opportunities is for the paired company to plunge into new markets that neither could assay alone. Neither has much of a presence in Latin America or Asia, although Daimler does sell heavy trucks there. Chrysler's inexpensive small cars will give Daimler a vehicle to drive into emerging markets. "With our [upscale] product portfolio, we will never be a mass marketer," says a source close to Daimler. "There are some markets where [Mercedes] will never be able to have an impact."

Operational Synergies: Chrysler's slowly improving quality could take a quantum leap forward with help from Daimler engineers. And Daimler's diesel engines, for example, could help Chrysler in its efforts to sell subcompacts and minivans in Europe and elsewhere. Chrysler, for its part, has the industry's best supplier relations, while Daimler still relies on strong-arm techniques to get lower prices from its suppliers. Together, they can save on warehousing and logistics for cars and spare parts in both Europe and the U.S. They also can jointly make internal components like air-conditioning systems and door latches and pool their resources in developing basic technology.

COMBINING DIVERGENT CORPORATE CULTURES: THE KEY CHALLENGE

16   Most rivals were too stunned to react when the merger was first announced. Both Ford and GM declined to comment in the U.S. as did BMW in Germany. On the other hand, many industry watchers immediately questioned whether the enormously divergent cultures of Auburn Hills and Stuttgart won't get in the way of all that synergy. "I can't imagine two more different cultures," says Furman Selz auto analyst Maryann N. Keller. Chrysler's brushes with bankruptcy forged a culture dedicated to speedy product development, lean operations, and flashy design. Daimler remains a buttoned-down, engineering-driven bureaucracy known for conservatively styled products. "The reaction here is shock, excitement, enthusiasm, and concern," said one Chrysler exec.

17   Indeed, most observers feel that Daimler-Chrysler's success hinges on melding two starkly different corporate cultures. Daimler's methodical decision making could squelch Chrysler's famed creativity. Mercedes' reputation for luxury and quality could be tarnished by Chrysler's downmarket image. If they can't create a climate of learning from each other, warns Ulrich Steger, a management professor at IMD, the Lausanne business school, "they could be heading for unbelievable catastrophe."

18   If that happens, it won't be the first time. Big cross-border mergers have a poor track record. In most cases, the hoped-for savings are not realized, the weaker partner is stripped of its best assets, and margins plunge. For instance, BMW's merger with Rover floundered because BMW lacked a clear strategy, and the companies' models cannibalized each other. BMW has asked the British government for aid. Another deal involving a high-profile takeover by an admired foreign company of prized American assets: Sony Corp.'s acquisition of both CBS Records Inc. and Columbia Pictures saw Sony start off mistakenly thinking that it could oversee its freewheeling American companies from afar and with a light touch. It failed to put its own

strong management structure in the U.S. It neglected to build links between Sony's American subsidiaries on the two coasts. It lost control of expenses, and by 1994, Sony was forced to take a $2.7 billion write-off.

19   Sony and Daimler are in different businesses, of course, and no one blueprint applies to all big international mergers. But the most successful global companies, such as Nestlé, ABB Asea Brown Boveri, and General Electric, have put their unambiguous imprint on all their operations by imposing one strong corporate culture with central management for the most critical functions. Someone must articulate overall philosophy and values and establish companywide investment priorities. Someone must set financial and operational performance requirements, compensation policies, and development paths for senior executives. Unless Daimler takes charge of these kinds of tasks immediately, don't be surprised if the deal comes unwound.

20   To avoid a similar fate, Schrempp and Eaton analyzed 50 large-scale mergers from many industries before launching their own. They found that 70% had stumbled, most for lack of clear targets and speed. "What you don't do in the first 12 to 24 months will be very difficult to do later," Schrempp said.

21   That's especially true for two industrial icons from business cultures that couldn't be more different. Chrysler is the very symbol of American adaptability and resilience. Having survived a near-death experience that required a 1979 government bailout, it scrambled under legendary CEO Lee A. Iacocca, and then Eaton, to become one of the world's leanest and nimblest car companies.

22   Daimler Benz, meanwhile, has long represented the epitome of German industrial might, its Mercedes cars the purest examples of German quality and engineering. But despite Schrempp's shakeup at the top, its middle ranks exemplify the hierarchical, procedure-driven German management style that could smother an agile company like Chrysler.

23   He was certainly the dominant player in forging the merger. "I wasn't going to sit passively and be the object of someone else's decision," Schrempp told 1,000 of Munich's glitterati as he introduced the new Mercedes S-Class sedan last month. Schrempp had talked to Ford Motor Co. in 1997, but the U.S. company's family-ownership structure would have complicated a merger. Sources close to Daimler say that Schrempp also approached Honda Motor Co., but found the cultural differences too great.

24   Investors immediately applauded—pushing Chrysler shares up $7\frac{3}{8}$ to $48\frac{13}{16}$ on May 6. "Chrysler has the trucks, vans, and SUVs, and Daimler has the luxury cars," says Seth M. Glickenhaus of Glickenhaus & Co., an investment firm that holds 8 million Chrysler shares. "There are enormous synergies in product." Amid the initial euphoria, *BusinessWeek*'s Jeffrey E. Garten offered perhaps the most objective summary of the cultural challenge to make the DaimlerChrysler merger work: The new company will face massive challenges. DaimlerChrysler will still be only the fifth-largest car company, behind General Motors, Ford, Toyota, and Volkswagen. Its product line, ranging from an $11,000 Dodge to a $130,000 Mercedes, could foster a confused image and culture. The German corporate governance system in which labor and banks hold board seats in order to take a longer-term view could collide with the obsession of American shareholders with immediate returns. Compensation philosophies could be irreconcilable: Just compare Chrysler Chairman and CEO Robert J. Eaton's 1997 pay package of $16 million with that of Daimler chief Jürgen E. Schrempp's $1.9 million. And politically explosive decisions are sure to arise about how to apportion layoffs between America and Germany when downsizing occurs because of the overcapacity in the global auto industry.

25   One final likely outcome from this merger, well before anyone knows if DaimlerChrysler is a success—its very existence could reshape the industry. Look for automakers to scramble for partners to ensure survival as one of the 21st century 20. How that plays out is anybody's guess. "The odd man out here seems to be the Japanese," says Phillippi of Lehman Brothers. "Nissan and Honda in particular have only two legs to stand on: North America and Japan." That won't be enough in this race.

DAIMLERCHRYSLER—2001

26   MARCH 2001. It has been a disastrous run for DaimlerChrysler CEO Jürgen E. Schrempp: expected losses in the billions at Chrysler, a huge

recall at DaimlerChrysler's partner, Mitsubishi Motors Corp., savage attacks in the usually respectful German press. Wrote a commentator recently in the weekly *Die Zeit:* "Should Daimler get rid of Chrysler—or Schrempp?"

27 Schrempp's not going anywhere for now. If anything, he plans to tighten his grip on his global auto empire in a bold attempt to turn this company around for good. The really interesting moves involve the executive suite and Schrempp's own tortured relationship with Chrysler headquarters in Auburn Hills, Michigan. He plans to scrap the automotive and sales councils that Daimler Benz and Chrysler Corp. decided to set up after they merged in 1998. Instead, Schrempp will create a tightly knit executive auto committee headed by him and by Mercedes-Benz chief Jürgen Hubbert. The new committee will make all key strategic decisions and coordinate production and marketing across the group's divisions.

28 It will be an all-German club. Other members will include Daimler hands who helped Schrempp consolidate his power six years ago: Chrysler CEO Dieter Zetsche, commercial vehicles director Eckhard Cordes, Mitsubishi board member Manfred Bischoff, and corporate strategy director Rudiger Grube. The idea is to speed up decision making on everything from overhauling assembly lines and laying off workers to sharing technologies and parts among Chrysler, Mercedes, and Mitsubishi.

29 Another power grab by the *uber*-boss? This time, it makes sense. True, the American absence in the inner circle will be painful to what's left of Chrysler's executive corps. But the only way to boost morale at Chrysler is to get it back on its feet. If the streamlined structured can turn Chrysler around, hurt feelings will fade. While Germans like Schrempp are portrayed as terribly aggressive, their problem to date has been in waiting too long to interfere with foreign subsidiaries. BMW left management of its Rover acquisition in British hands until the brand's value had deteriorated alarmingly. Similarly, if investors want to fault Schrempp for anything, it should be for not stepping in and taking control of Chrysler much earlier. He even left an inexperienced North American executive in charge for nearly a year before bringing in Zetsche. So to analysts, setting up this committee is part of the same take-charge approach Schrempp has shown by sending Zetsche to fix Chrysler, and it's welcome.

30 Of course, Schremmp has yet to find the answer to the most perplexing question: Can anyone run a monster like DaimlerChrysler? No car merger of this kind has ever been tried, so there's no blueprint on the best way to run it. Diffuse decision making certainly didn't do the trick. But Schremmp's central committee risks misreading certain markets and their special demands by making the decisions from too far away. The committee will certainly have to get results fast. Schremmp has agreed to meet six-month performance targets, which could include anything from operating profit to productivity goals. If he misses those targets, the pressure will mount for his removal.

31 NOVEMBER 2001. Just eight months ago, DaimlerChrysler (DCX) CEO Jürgen Schrempp was in the hot seat. Chrysler was expected to lose billions, and some shareholders and commentators were calling for his ouster. But Schrempp dug in his heels, centralized decision making, and agreed to meet tough performance targets: at least $1.1 billion in operating profit this year.

32 Chrysler indeed is losing billions. But thanks to draconian cost-cutting at Chrysler and the consistent strength of the Mercedes-Benz luxury car business, Schrempp still expects the company to meet his 2001 target. Investors were pleased that Chrysler's third-quarter losses, bad as they were, weren't worse. In the meantime, Schrempp has expanded his grip on power. On Sept. 27, DaimlerChrysler's supervisory board extended his mandate by two more years, to 2005

33 September 11 has thrown all these calculations off. Schrempp has already told division chiefs to rethink their numbers in light of the deteriorating economy and get back to him in December—the first sign he may have trouble meeting the 2002 target. Next year will test all of Schrempp's management skills. The company estimates that industry sales will decline by 5% to 8% in the United States and 2% to 3% in Europe. With incentives surging in the U.S. market, Chrysler may have to cut costs even more next year than planned. It already had eliminated 26,000 jobs, slashed procurement costs and cut capacity by 15%. "Like Ford and General Motors, we might have to idle additional plants for two or three weeks, depending on the market," says Schrempp.

34   Schrempp is sticking to his vision of turning DaimlerChrysler into a mighty global group offering a full range of vehicles, from subcompacts to heavy trucks in all major markets. But with Chrysler's outlook deteriorating by the day, balancing long- and short-term goals—especially the interest of Mercedes and Chrysler—will keep getting harder and harder. The survivor still has to learn how to thrive.

Sources: "Schrempp, the Survivor?" *BusinessWeek,* March 5, 2001; "Downshifting Ambitions at DaimlerChrysler," *BusinessWeek,* November 12, 2001.

Strategy Implementation

The last section of this book examines what is often called the *action phase* of the strategic management process: implementation of the chosen strategy. Up to this point, three phases of that process have been covered—strategy formulation, analysis of alternative strategies, and strategic choice. Although important, these phases alone cannot ensure success. To ensure success, the strategy must be translated into carefully implemented action. This means that:

1. The strategy must be translated into guidelines for the daily activities of the firm's members.

2. The strategy and the firm must become one—that is, the strategy must be reflected in the way the firm organizes its activities and in the firm's values, beliefs, and tone.

3. In implementing the strategy, the firm's managers must direct and control actions and outcomes and adjust to change.

Chapter 9 explains how organizational action is successfully initiated in four interrelated steps:

1. Creation of clear *short-term objectives* and *action plans*.

2. Development of specific *functional tactics* that create competitive advantage.

3. Empowerment of operating personnel through *policies* to guide decisions.

4. Implementation of effective *reward system*.

Short-term objectives and action plans guide implementation by converting long-term objectives into short-term actions and targets. Functional tactics translate the business strategy into activities that build advantage. Policies empower operating personnel by defining guidelines for making decisions. Reward systems encourage effective results.

Today's competitive environment often necessitates restructuring and reengineering the organization to sustain competitive advantage. Chapter 10 examines how restructuring and reengineering are pursued in three organizational elements that provide fundamental, long-term means for institutionalizing the firm's strategy:

1. The firm's *structure.*

2. The *leadership* provided by the firm's CEO and key managers.

3. The fit between the strategy and the firm's *culture.*

Since the firm's strategy is implemented in a changing environment, successful implementation requires that execution be controlled and continuously improved. The control and improvement process must include at least these dimensions:

1. *Strategic controls* that "steer" execution of the strategy.

2. *Operations control systems* that monitor performance, evaluate deviations, and initiate corrective action.

3. *Continuous improvement* through total quality initiatives a balanced scorecard perspective.

Chapter 11 examines the dimensions of the control and improvement process. It explains the essence of change as an ever-present force driving the need for strategic control. The chapter concludes with a look at the global "quality imperative," which is redefining the essence of control into the 21st century.

Implementation is "where the action is." It is the arena that most students enter at the start of their business careers. It is the strategic phase in which staying close to the customer, achieving competitive advantage, and pursuing excellence become realities. The chapters in this part will help you understand how this is done.

Chapter **Nine**

Implementing Strategy through Short-Term Objectives, Functional Tactics, Reward System, and Employee Empowerment

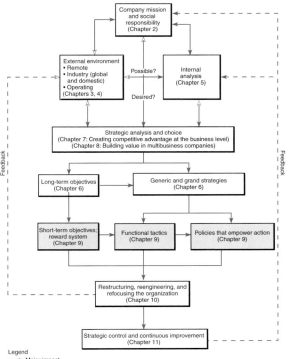

Company mission
and social
responsibility
(Chapter 2)

External environment
• Remote
• Industry (global
and domestic)
• Operating
(Chapters 3, 4)

Possible?

Desired?

Internal
analysis
(Chapter 5)

Strategic analysis and choice
(Chapter 7: Creating competitive advantage at the business level)
(Chapter 8: Building value in multibusiness companies)

Long-term objectives
(Chapter 6)

Generic and grand strategies
(Chapter 6)

Short-term objectives;
reward system
(Chapter 9)

Functional tactics
(Chapter 9)

Policies that empower action
(Chapter 9)

Restructuring, reengineering, and
refocusing the organization
(Chapter 10)

Strategic control and continuous improvement
(Chapter 11)

Feedback

Feedback

Legend
⟶ Major impact
⟶ Minor impact

Once corporate and business strategies have been agreed upon and long-term objectives set, the strategic management process moves into a critical new phase—translating strategic thought into organizational action. In the words of two well-worn phrases, they move from "planning their work" to "working their plan" as they shift their focus from strategy formulation to strategy implementation. Managers successfully make this shift when they do four things well:

1. Identify short-term objectives.

2. Initiate specific functional tactics.

3. Communicate policies that empower people in the organization.

4. Design effective rewards.

Short-term objectives translate long-range aspirations into this year's targets for action. If well developed, these objectives provide clarity, a powerful motivator and facilitator of effective strategy implementation.

Functional tactics translate business strategy into daily activities people need to execute. Functional managers participate in the development of these tactics, and their participation, in turn, helps clarify what their units are expected to do in implementing the business's strategy.

Policies are empowerment tools that simplify decision making by empowering operating managers and their subordinates. Policies can empower the "doers" in an organization by reducing the time required to decide and act.

A powerful part of getting things done in any organization can be found in the way its reward system rewards desired action and results. Rewards that align manager and employee priorities with organizational objectives and shareholder value provide very effective direction in strategy implementation.

SHORT-TERM OBJECTIVES

Chapter 6 described business strategies, grand strategies, and long-term objectives that are critically important in crafting a successful future. To make them become a reality, however, the people in an organization that actually "do the work" of the business need guidance in exactly what needs to be done today and tomorrow to make those long-term strategies become reality. Short-term objectives help do this. They provide much more specific guidance for what is to be done, a clear delineation of impending actions needed, which helps translate vision into action.

Short-term objectives help implement strategy in at least three ways. First, short-term objectives "operationalize" long-term objectives. If we commit to a 20 percent gain in revenue over five years, what is our specific target or objective in revenue during the current year, month, or week to indicate we are making appropriate progress? Second, discussion about and agreement on short-term objectives help raise issues and potential conflicts within an organization that usually require coordination to avoid otherwise dysfunctional consequences. Exhibit 9–1 illustrates how objectives within marketing, manufacturing, and accounting units within the same firm can be very different even when created to pursue the same firm objective (e.g., increased sales, lower costs). The third way short-term objectives assist strategy implementation is to identify measurable outcomes of action plans or functional activities, which can be used to make feedback, correction, and evaluation more relevant and acceptable.

EXHIBIT 9–1
Potential Conflicting Objectives and Priorities

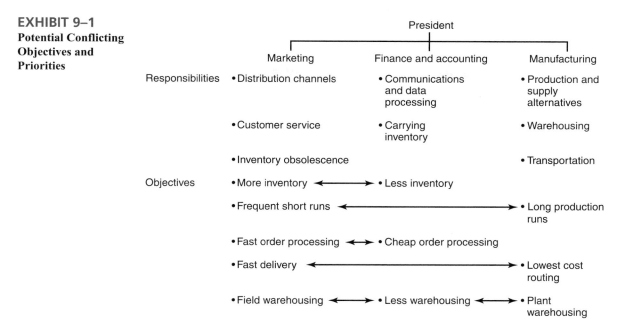

Short-term objectives are usually accompanied by action plans, which enhance these objectives in three ways. First, action plans usually identify functional tactics and activities that will be undertaken in the next week, month, or quarter as part of the business's effort to build competitive advantage. The important point here is *specificity*—what exactly is to be done. We will examine functional tactics in a subsequent section of this chapter. The second element of an action plan is a clear *time frame for completion*—when the effort will begin and when its results will be accomplished. A third element action plans contain is identification of *who is responsible* for each action in the plan. This accountability is very important to ensure action plans are acted upon. Exhibit 9–2, Strategy in Action, illustrates the use of short-term objectives, action plans, and accountability by Kmart's CEO Charles Conaway as he attempted to turn around the dying retailer.

Because of the particular importance of short-term objectives in strategy implementation, the next section addresses how to develop meaningful short-term objectives.

Qualities of Effective Short-Term Objectives

Measurable
Short-term objectives are more consistent when they clearly state *what* is to be accomplished, *when* it will be accomplished, and *how* its accomplishment will be *measured*. Such objectives can be used to monitor both the effectiveness of each activity and the collective progress across several interrelated activities. Exhibit 9–3 illustrates several effective and ineffective short-term objectives. Measurable objectives make misunderstanding less likely among interdependent managers who must implement action plans. It is far easier to quantify the objectives of *line* units (e.g., production) than of certain *staff* areas (e.g., personnel). Difficulties in quantifying objectives often can be overcome by initially focusing on *measurable activity* and then identifying *measurable outcomes*.

When Charles C. Conaway became Kmart Corp. CEO, he brought along a mania for performance-based analysis. Today, it's hard to miss the point: Conaway's office is dominated by a 20-foot-long mural upon which the CEO tracks quarterly progress on nearly 100 restructuring initiatives, from replenishing shelves to implementing price changes within 48 hours. Beside each project is the cost and benefit to date, plus the name—and phone number—of the manager in charge. "It's the ultimate accountability," Conaway says.

Accountability has been in short supply for years at the foundering discounter, which has seen one turnaround effort after another sputter out as its chronically under-stocked shelves, tacky merchandise, and poor service drove shoppers to rivals like Wal-Mart Stores Inc. But Conaway, a 40-year-old operations whiz recruited from drug retailer CVS Corp., where he was president and COO, says he's the one to change all that. Since his arrival, Conaway and his band of young management recruits from Wal-Mart, Target, and Coca-Cola (KO) have been attacking the structural problems that led to Kmart's decline. Now that they claim to be making progress on those fronts, they're ready to issue a blue-edged invitation to consumers to try the stores again.

Conaway unveiled a new marketing strategy that draws heavily on the one icon of Kmart's past that still resonates with consumers: the Blue Light Special which was discontinued in 1991. Store managers used the flashing blue police light in the 1960s, 70s and 80s to direct shoppers to unadvertised bargains. By offering a contemporary take on that old device, company officials hope to restore a sense of excitement and reward to shopping at Kmart. "There's a funness to it that, frankly, Kmart didn't have [recently],"

says Steve Feuling, chief marketing officer for Kmart's Blue Light efforts.

The return of the Blue Light via a $25 million advertising blitz, the biggest such initiative in Kmart history, is just a piece of Conaway's overall strategy. After all, the marketing come-on will be wasted if consumers enticed into the stores suffer the same old frustrations. So Conaway has been taking sweeping—and costly—steps to raise service levels, ensure that popular items are in stock, and brighten up the stores.

Conaway's elaborate chart notwithstanding, the payoff still isn't clear. That't why all the resuscitation efforts are overshadowed by a big question: Is there still a role for Kmart between Wal-Mart and Target? "I'm not sure there's room for them," bluntly says the CEO of a major supplier to all three. But Conaway vows it's not too late—as long as Kmart does a better job of staking out its turf between low-price leader Wal-Mart and cheap-chic purveyor Target. Conaway insists the middle ground is wide open for a retailer that relentlessly focuses on moms and two of their key priorities: their kids and their homes. Kmart can meet those priorities with exclusive brands like Martha Stewart and Sesame Street and new licensing and promotional tie-ins with everyone from Walt Disney Co. (DIS) to World Wrestling Federation Entertainment Inc. (WWF) creating a buzz. With research showing that shoppers still have fond memories of the Blue Light Special, the discounter is putting the blue hue at the center of its effort to entice them into the stores more often. TBWA\Chiat\Day, the ad agency best known for its cutting-edge work for Apple Computer, will herald that "The Blue Light Is Back" with ads that place a blue glow in such unexpected settings as the Statue of Liberty's torch or fireflies buzzing in a kid's jar. Kmart's BlueLight.com e-commerce effort

Priorities

Although all annual objectives are important, some deserve priority because of a timing consideration or their particular impact on a strategy's success. If such priorities are not established, conflicting assumptions about the relative importance of annual objectives may inhibit progress toward strategic effectiveness. Facing the most rapid, dramatic decline in profitability of any major computer manufacturer as it confronted relentless lower pricing by Dell Computer and AST, Compaq Computer formulated a retrenchment strategy with several important annual objectives in pricing, product design, distribution, and financial condition. But its highest priority was to dramatically lower overhead and production costs so as to satisfy the difficult challenge of dramatically lowering prices while also restoring profitability.

Exhibit 9–2

already has shown that the theme can click even with more cutting-edge consumers.

Consumers intrigued enough to pay a visit will find that once-dreary stores have been splashed with blue and animated by "celebrity" announcers—Homer Simpson is a possibility—directing shoppers to a central "Blue Light Zone" for the deals. This time around, they're not junky clearance items but coveted products like Sony Playstations, TVs, and Coca-Cola. Also new: a "Blue Light Always" pricing strategy that will slash tags on everyday basics like shampoo, diapers, medicines, and groceries by 2% to 5% to make them competitive with Wal-Mart prices. "Now we're saying we're there for everything you need," says Conaway.

ATTENTION KMART SKEPTICS

Here's how Kmart hopes to get customers into its stores more often

- *Brighter marketing.* It will bathe stores in blue and debut an updated "Blue Light Special" with a $25 million ad blitz.

- *Lower price.* Kmart is matching Wal-Mart (WMT) prices on thousands of basic items.

- *More stock.* It is spending $2 billion to overhaul inventory controls and increase the items it has on hand.

- *Better service.* Employee incentives are helping to raise customer-satisfaction ratings.

Just getting Kmart's best customers to increase their visits from 3.2 per month to 4, as Wal-Mart's core shoppers do, would add $2.8 billion to the top line, says Kmart's chief marketing officer Brent Willis, a recruit from Coke's Latin American unit. "We don't have to take a single customer from Wal-Mart," he says.

To make sure shelves are kept fully stocked, Kmart is spending nearly $2 billion on technology to overhaul its inventory controls. Since October, it's also taken an unusual tack to upgrade service by entering all shoppers willing to dial a hotline in a $10,000 sweepstakes to rate their overall shopping experience. Some 20 million already have responded, generating a database that enables managers to pinpoint performance at the store level and reward cashiers at popular units with as much as $1,200 in quarterly bonuses. Since the program began, Kmart says its satisfaction rating has climbed from 40% to 55%. Conaway's goal is 70%.

Shoppers like Dolores Ronzani, who still smiles at the recollection of booty scored from Blue Light Specials of decades ago, seem receptive to the idea. These days, the 70-year-old widow from Highland Park, Ill., frequents Target, Marshalls, and T.J. Maxx but finds they don't measure up to Kmart in its heyday: "The excitement of the Blue Light Special is missing." If it's excitement she craves, Conaway and Co. aim to provide it in spades.

Source: "Kmart's Bright Idea," *BusinessWeek,* April 9, 2001.

Priorities are established in various ways. A simple *ranking* may be based on discussion and negotiation during the planning process. However, this does not necessarily communicate the real difference in the importance of objectives, so such terms as *primary, top,* and *secondary* may be used to indicate priority. Some firms assign *weights* (e.g., 0 to 100 percent) to establish and communicate the relative priority of objectives. Whatever the method, recognizing priorities is an important dimension in the implementation value of short-term objectives.

Linked to Long-Term Objectives

Short-term objectives can add breadth and specificity in identifying *what* must be accomplished to achieve long-term objectives. For example, Wal-Mart's top management recently set out "to obtain 45 percent market share in five years" as a long-term objective. Achieving that objective can be greatly enhanced if a series of specific short-term objectives identify what must be accomplished each year in order to do so. If Wal-Mart's market share is now 25 percent, then one likely annual objective might be "to have each regional office achieve a minimum 4 percent increase in market share in the next year." "Open two regional distribution centers in the Southwest in 2005" might be an annual objective that Wal-Mart's marketing and distribution managers consider essential if the firm

EXHIBIT 9–3
Creating Measurable Objectives

Examples of Deficient Objectives	Examples of Objectives with Measurable Criteria for Performance
To improve morale in the division (plant, department, etc.)	To reduce turnover (absenteeism, number of rejects, etc.) among sales managers by 10 percent by January 1, 2004. *Assumption:* Morale is related to measurable outcomes (i.e., high and low morale are associated with different results).
To improve support of the sales effort	To reduce the time lapse between order data and delivery by 8 percent (two days) by June 1, 2004. To reduce the cost of goods produced by 6 percent to support a product price decrease of 2 percent by December 1, 2004. To increase the rate of before- or on-schedule delivery by 5 percent by June 1, 2004.
To improve the firm's image	To conduct a public opinion poll using random samples in the five largest U.S. metropolitan markets to determine average scores on 10 dimensions of corporate responsibility by May 15, 2004. To increase our score on those dimensions by an average of 7.5 percent by May 1, 2005.

is to achieve a 45 percent market share in five years. "Conclude arrangements for a $1 billion line of credit at 0.25 percent above prime in 2004" might be an annual objective of Wal-Mart's financial managers to support the operation of new distribution centers and the purchase of increased inventory in reaching the firm's long-term objective.

The link between short-term and long-term objectives should resemble cascades through the firm from basic long-term objectives to specific short-term objectives in key operation areas. The cascading effect has the added advantage of providing a clear reference for communication and negotiation, which may be necessary to integrate and coordinate objectives and activities at the operating level.

The qualities of good objectives discussed in Chapter 6—acceptable, flexible, suitable, motivating, understandable, and achievable—also apply to short-term objectives. They will not be discussed again here, but you should review the discussion in Chapter 6 to appreciate these qualities, common to all good objectives.

The Value-Added Benefits of Short-Term Objectives and Action Plans

One benefit of short-term objectives and action plans is that they give operating personnel a better understanding of their role in the firm's mission. "Achieve $2.5 million in 2005 sales in the Chicago territory," "Develop an OSHA-approved safety program for handling acids at all Georgia Pacific plants in 2005," and "Reduce Ryder Truck's average age of accounts receivable to 31 days by the end of 2005" are examples of how short-term objectives clarify the role of particular personnel in their firm's broader mission. Such *clarity of purpose* can be a major force in helping use a firm's "people assets" more effectively, which may add tangible value.

A second benefit of short-term objectives and action plans comes from the process of developing them. If the managers responsible for this accomplishment have participated in their development, short-term objectives and action plans provide valid bases for addressing and accommodating conflicting concerns that might interfere with strategic effectiveness (see Exhibit 9–1). Meetings to set short-term objectives and action plans become the forum for raising and resolving conflicts between strategic intentions and operating realities.

A third benefit of short-term objectives and action plans is that they provide *a basis for strategic control.* The control of strategy will be examined in detail in Chapter 11. However, it is important to recognize here that short-term objectives and action plans provide a clear, measurable basis for developing budgets, schedules, trigger points, and other mechanisms for controlling the implementation of strategy. Exhibit 9–2, Strategy in Action, describes how new Kmart CEO Charles Conaway used short-term objectives as a key basis for strategic control.

A fourth benefit is often a *motivational payoff.* Short-term objectives and action plans that clarify personal and group roles in a firm's strategies and are also measurable, realistic, and challenging can be powerful motivators of managerial performance—particularly when these objectives are linked to the firm's reward structure.

FUNCTIONAL TACTICS THAT IMPLEMENT BUSINESS STRATEGIES

Functional tactics are the key, routine activities that must be undertaken in each functional area—marketing, finance, production/operations, R&D, and human resource management—to provide the business's products and services. In a sense, functional tactics translate thought (grand strategy) into action designed to accomplish specific short-term objectives. Every value chain activity in a company executes functional tactics that support the business's strategy and help accomplish strategic objectives.

Exhibit 9–4 illustrates the difference between functional tactics and corporate and business strategy. It also shows that functional tactics are essential to implement business strategy. The corporate strategy defined General Cinema Corporation's general posture in the broad economy. The business strategy outlined the competitive posture of its operations in the movie theater industry. To increase the likelihood that these strategies would be successful, specific functional tactics were needed for the firm's operating components. These functional tactics clarified the business strategy, giving specific, short-term guidance to operating managers in the areas of marketing, operations, and finance.

Differences between Business Strategies and Functional Tactics

Functional tactics are different from business or corporate strategies in three fundamental ways:

1. Time horizon.

2. Specificity.

3. Participants who develop them.

Time Horizon

Functional tactics identify activities to be undertaken "now" or in the immediate future. Business strategies focus on the firm's posture three to five years out. Delta Air lines is committed to a concentration/market development business strategy that seeks competitive advantage via differentiation in its level of service and focus on the business traveler. Its pricing tactics are often to price above industry averages, but it often lowers fares on

EXHIBIT 9–4
**Functional Tactics
at General Cinema
Corporation**

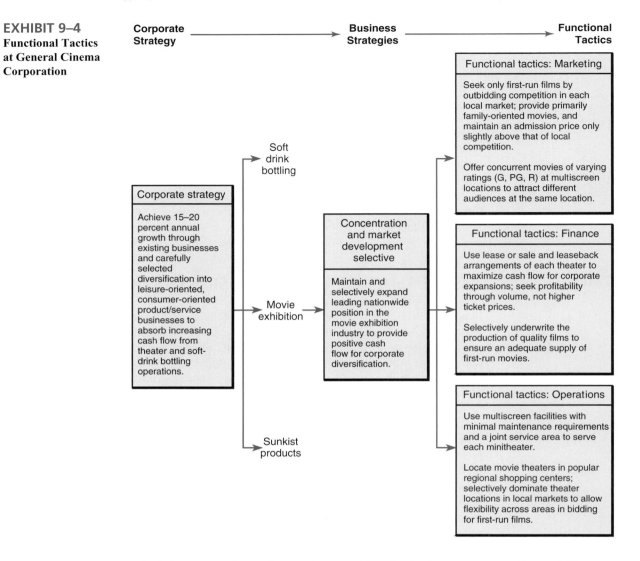

selected routes to thwart low-cost competition. Its business strategy is focused 10 years out; its pricing tactics change weekly.

The shorter time horizon of functional tactics is critical to the successful implementation of a business strategy for two reasons. First, it focuses the attention of functional managers on what needs to be done *now* to make the business strategy work. Second, it allows functional managers like those at Delta to adjust to changing current conditions.

Specificity

Functional tactics are more specific than business strategies. Business strategies provide general direction. Functional tactics identify the specific activities that are to be undertaken in each functional area and thus allow operating managers to work out *how* their unit is expected to pursue short-term objectives. General Cinema's business strategy gave its movie theater division broad direction on how to pursue a concentration and selective market development strategy. Two functional tactics in the marketing area gave managers specific direction on what types of movies (first-run, primarily family-oriented, G, PG, R) should be shown and what pricing strategy (competitive in the local area) should be followed.

Specificity in functional tactics contributes to successful implementation by:

- Helping ensure that functional managers know what needs to be done and can focus on accomplishing results.

- Clarifying for top management how functional managers intend to accomplish the business strategy, which increases top management's confidence in and sense of control over the business strategy.

- Facilitating coordination among operating units *within* the firm by clarifying areas of interdependence and potential conflict.

Exhibit 9–5, Strategy in Action, illustrates the nature and value of specificity in functional tactics versus business strategy in an upscale pizza restaurant chain.

Participants

Different people participate in strategy development at the functional and business levels. Business strategy is the responsibility of the general manager of a business unit. That manager typically delegates the development of functional tactics to subordinates charged with running the operating areas of the business. The manager of a business unit must establish long-term objectives and a strategy that corporate management feels contributes to corporate-level goals. Similarly, key operating managers must establish short-term objectives and operating strategies that contribute to business-level goals. Just as business strategies and objectives are approved through negotiation between corporate managers and business managers, so, too, are short-term objectives and functional tactics approved through negotiation between business managers and operating managers.

Involving operating managers in the development of functional tactics improves their understanding of what must be done to achieve long-term objectives and, thus, contributes to successful implementation. It also helps ensure that functional tactics reflect the reality of the day-to-day operating situation. And perhaps most important, it can increase the commitment of operating managers to the strategies developed.

EMPOWERING OPERATING PERSONNEL: THE ROLE OF POLICIES

Specific functional tactics provide guidance and initiate action implementing a business's strategy, but more is needed. Supervisors and personnel in the field have been charged in today's competitive environment with being responsible for customer value—for being the "front line" of the company's effort to truly meet customers' needs. Meeting customer needs, becoming obsessed with quality service, was the buzzword that started organizational revolutions in the 1980s. Efforts to do so often failed because employees that were the real contact point between the business and its customers were not *empowered* to make decisions or act to fulfill customer needs. One solution has been to empower operating personnel by pushing down decision making to their level. General Electric allows appliance repair personnel to decide about warranty credits on the spot, a decision that used to take several days and multiple organizational levels. Delta Air Lines allows customer service personnel and their supervisors wide range in resolving customer ticket pricing decisions. Federal Express couriers make decisions and handle package routing information that involves five management levels in the U.S. Postal Service.

BusinessWeek A restaurant business was encountering problems. Although its management had agreed unanimously that it was committed to a business strategy to differentiate itself from other competitors based on concept and customer service rather than price, it continued to encounter inconsistencies across different store locations in how well it did this. Consultants indicated that the customer experience varied greatly from store to store. The conclusion was that while the management understood the "business strategy," and the employees did too in general terms, the implementation was inadequate because of a lack of specificity in the functional tactics—what everyone should do every day in the restaurant—to make the vision a reality in terms of the customers' dining experience. The following breakdown of part of their business strategy into specific functional tactics just in the area of customer service helps illustrate the value specificity in functional tactics brings to strategy implementation.

Source: Adapted from "How to Have Your Pizza and Eat It, Too," *BusinessWeek,* November 16, 1998; and A. Campbell and K. Luchs, *Strategic Synergy* (London: Butterworth-Heineman, 1992).

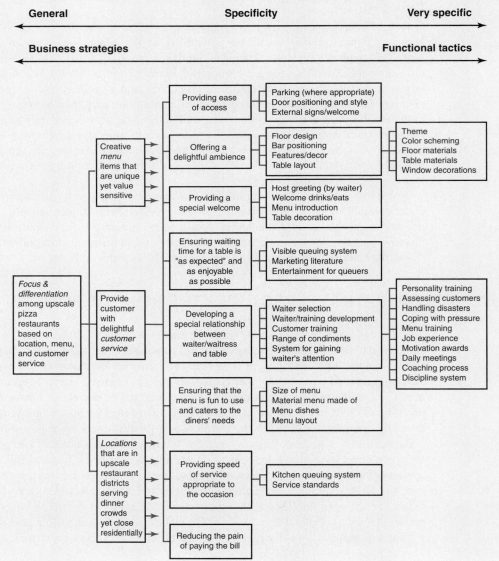

Empowerment is being created in many ways. Training, self-managed work groups, eliminating whole levels of management in organizations, and aggressive use of automation are some of the ways and ramifications of this fundamental change in the way business organizations function. At the heart of the effort is the need to ensure that decision making is consistent with the mission, strategy, and tactics of the business while at the same time allowing considerable latitude to operating personnel. One way operating managers do this is through the use of policies.

Policies are directives designed to guide the thinking, decisions, and actions of managers and their subordinates in implementing a firm's strategy. Previously referred to as *standard operating procedures,* policies increase managerial effectiveness by standardizing many routine decisions and clarifying the discretion managers and subordinates can exercise in implementing functional tactics. Logically, policies should be derived from functional tactics (and, in some instances, from corporate or business strategies) with the key purpose of aiding strategy execution.[1] Exhibit 9–6, Strategy in Action, illustrates selected policies of several well-known firms.

Creating Policies That Empower

Policies communicate guidelines to decisions. They are designed to control decisions while defining allowable discretion within which operational personnel can execute business activities. They do this in several ways:

1. *Policies establish indirect control over independent action* by clearly stating how things are to be done *now.* By defining discretion, policies in effect control decisions yet empower employees to conduct activities without direct intervention by top management.

2. *Policies promote uniform handling of similar activities.* This facilitates the coordination of work tasks and helps reduce friction arising from favoritism, discrimination, and the disparate handling of common functions—something that often hampers operating personnel.

3. *Policies ensure quicker decisions* by standardizing answers to previously answered questions that otherwise would recur and be pushed up the management hierarchy again and again—something that required unnecessary levels of management between senior decision makers and field personnel.

4. *Policies institutionalize basic aspects of organization behavior.* This minimizes conflicting practices and establishes consistent patterns of action in attempts to make the strategy work—again, freeing operating personnel to act.

5. *Policies reduce uncertainty in repetitive and day-to-day decision making,* thereby providing a necessary foundation for coordinated, efficient efforts and freeing operating personnel to act.

---

[1] The term *policy* has various definitions in management literature. Some authors and practitioners equate policy with strategy. Others do this inadvertently by using *policy* as a synonym for company mission, purpose, or culture. Still other authors and practitioners differentiate policy in terms of "levels" associated respectively with purpose, mission, and strategy. "Our policy is to make a positive contribution to the communities and societies we live in" and "our policy is not to diversify out of the hamburger business" are two examples of the breadth of what some call policies. This book defines *policy* much more narrowly as specific guides to managerial action and decisions in the implementation of strategy. This definition permits a sharper distinction between the formulation and implementation of functional strategies. And, of even greater importance, it focuses the tangible value of the policy concept where it can be most useful—as a key administrative tool to enhance effective implementation and execution of strategy.

3M Corporation has a *personnel policy,* called the *15 percent rule,* that allows virtually any employee to spend up to 15 percent of the workweek on anything that he or she wants to, as long as it's product related.

(This policy supports 3M's corporate strategy of being a highly innovative manufacturer, with each division required to have a quarter of its annual sales come from products introduced within the past five years.)

Wendy's has a *purchasing policy* that gives local store managers the authority to buy fresh meat and produce locally, rather than from regionally designated or company-owned sources.

(This policy supports Wendy's functional strategy of having fresh, unfrozen hamburgers daily.)

General Cinema has a *financial policy* that requires annual capital investment in movie theaters not to exceed annual depreciation.

(By seeing that capital investment is no greater than depreciation, this policy supports General Cinema's financial strategy of maximizing cash flow—in this case, all profit—to its growth areas. The policy also reinforces General Cinema's financial strategy of leasing as much as possible.)

IBM had a *marketing policy* of not giving free IBM personal computers (PCs) to any person or organization.

(This policy attempted to support IBM's image strategy by maintaining its image as a professional, high-value, service business as it sought to dominate the PC market.)

Crown, Cork, and Seal Company has an *R&D policy* of not investing any financial or people resources in basic research.

(This policy supports Crown, Cork, and Seal's functional strategy, which emphasizes customer services, not technical leadership.)

Bank of America has an *operating policy* that requires annual renewal of the financial statement of all personal borrowers.

(This policy supports Bank of America's financial strategy, which seeks to maintain a loan-to-loss ratio below the industry norm.)

6. *Policies counteract resistance to or rejection of chosen strategies by organization members.* When major strategic change is undertaken, unambiguous operating policies clarify what is expected and facilitate acceptance, particularly when operating managers participate in policy development.

7. *Policies offer predetermined answers to routine problems.* This greatly expedites dealing with both ordinary and extraordinary problems—with the former, by referring to these answers; with the latter, by giving operating personnel more time to cope with them.

8. *Policies afford managers a mechanism for avoiding hasty and ill-conceived decisions in changing operations.* Prevailing policy can always be used as a reason for not yielding to emotion-based, expedient, or temporarily valid arguments for altering procedures and practices.

Policies may be written and formal or unwritten and informal. Informal, unwritten policies are usually associated with a strategic need for competitive secrecy. Some policies of this kind, such as promotion from within, are widely known (or expected) by employees and implicitly sanctioned by management. Managers and employees often like the latitude granted by unwritten and informal policies. However, such policies may detract from the long-term success of a strategy. Formal, written policies have at least seven advantages:

1. They require managers to think through the policy's meaning, content, and intended use.

2. They reduce misunderstanding.

3. They make equitable and consistent treatment of problems more likely.

4. They ensure unalterable transmission of policies.

5. They communicate the authorization or sanction of policies more clearly.

6. They supply a convenient and authoritative reference.

7. They systematically enhance indirect control and organizationwide coordination of the key purposes of policies.

The strategic significance of policies can vary. At one extreme are such policies as travel reimbursement procedures, which are really work rules and may not be linked to the implementation of a strategy. At the other extreme are organizationwide policies that are virtually functional strategies, such as Wendy's requirement that every location invest 1 percent of its gross revenue in local advertising.

Policies can be externally imposed or internally derived. Policies regarding equal employment practices are often developed in compliance with external (government) requirements, and policies regarding leasing or depreciation may be strongly influenced by current tax regulations.

Regardless of the origin, formality, and nature of policies, the key point to bear in mind is that they can play an important role in strategy implementation. Communicating specific policies will help overcome resistance to strategic change, empower people to act, and foster commitment to successful strategy implementation.

Policies empower people to act. Compensation, at least theoretically, rewards their action. The last decade has seen many firms realize that the link between compensation, particularly executive management compensation, and value-building strategic outcomes within their firms was uncertain. The recognition of this uncertainty has brought about increased recognition of the need to link management compensation with the successful implementation of strategies that build long-term shareholder value. The next section examines this development and major types of executive bonus compensation plans.

EXECUTIVE BONUS COMPENSATION PLANS[2]

Major Plan Types

The goal of an executive bonus compensation plan is to motivate executives to achieve maximization of shareholder wealth—the underlying goal of most firms. Since shareholders are both owners and investors of the firm, they desire a reasonable return on their investment. Because they are absentee landlords, shareholders want the decision-making logic of their firm's executives to be concurrent with their own primary motivation.

However, agency theory instructs us that the goal of shareholder wealth maximization is not the only goal that executives may pursue. Alternatively, executives may choose actions that increase their personal compensation, power, and control. Therefore, an executive compensation plan that contains a bonus component can be used to orient management's decision making toward the owners' goals. The success of bonus compensation as an incentive hinges on a proper match between an executive bonus plan and the firm's strategic objectives. As one author has written: "Companies can succeed by clarifying their business vision or strategy and aligning company pay programs with its strategic direction."[3]

---

[2] We wish to thank Roy Hossler for his assistance on this section.
[3] James E. Nelson, "Linking Compensation to Business Strategy," *The Journal of Business Strategy* 19, no. 2 (1998), pp. 25–27.

Strategy in Action
Microsoft Stock Options and Bill Gates's Booking Wealth

Exhibit 9–7

Microsoft has issued 807 million stock options to employees since 1990—worth $80 billion if they were exercised in late 1998.

Analysts estimate several thousand of Microsoft's 28,000 employees are stock-option millionaires. Even relatively low-level managers can tuck away a small fortune.

The option plan has made some veteran executives fabulously wealthy, including Michel Lacombe, president, Microsoft Europe, $152 million; Paul Maritz, group vice-president, $176 million; Nathan Myrhvold, chief technology officer, $179 million; Jeffrey Raikes, group vice-president, $237 million.

But the biggest winner is Bill Gates, whose 20.8% stake in Microsoft was worth a staggering $50 billion in 1998.

Source: Table: "The Microsoft Money Machine," *BusinessWeek,* October 26, 1998.

Stock Options

A common measure of shareholder wealth creation is appreciation of company stock price. Therefore, a popular form of bonus compensation is stock options. Stock options currently represent 55 percent of a chief executive officer's average pay package.[4] Stock options provide the executive with the right to purchase company stock at a fixed price in the future. The precise amount of compensation is based on the difference, or "spread," between the option's initial price and its selling, or exercised, price. As a result, the executive receives a bonus only if the firm's share price appreciates. If the share price drops below the option price, the options become worthless. Exhibit 9–7, Strategy in Action, summarizes the Microsoft stock option story.

The largest single option sale of all time occurred on December 3, 1997. Disney Chief Executive Officer Michael D. Eisner exercised more than 7 million options on Disney stock that he had been given in 1989 as part of his bonus plan. Eisner sold his shares for more than $400 million.

Although stock options only compensate an executive when wealth is created for shareholders, some critics question whether options truly gauge executive performance. Those doubting the accuracy of options as performance measures question why an executive should profit by merely riding a bull market where virtually every blue-chip firm's stock appreciates. In essence, they argue that the stock market may lack a correlation with firm operational performance, thus the movement of a company's stock price may be mostly outside the influence of most executives.[5] The case involving Michael King of King World Productions is noteworthy.

Chief Executive Officer Michael King was granted options on December 20, 1995, at the then-market price of $39.50. In about two years the stock rose about 40 percent to $5513/16. Over the same period, the Standard & Poor's 500 stock index gained 61 percent. Although King World shareholders realized wealth creation over this period, the level was mediocre compared to what an average blue-chip stock achieved. While King's wealth increased $24 million, other shareholders would have profited more by investing in a security that mirrored the stock market.

Although the indexing of stock option plans is rare in bull markets, indexing these plans in bear markets is not uncommon. During a bear market, stock prices will decline due to outside factors such as investor uncertainty resulting from volatile international

---

[4] Gary McWilliams, Richard A. Melcher, and Jennifer Reingold, "Executive Pay," *BusinessWeek,* April 20, 1998, pp. 64–70.
[5] William Franklin, "Making the Fat Cats Earn Their Cream," *Accountancy,* July 1998, pp. 38–39.

markets. In this market environment, some firms will re-price their executives' options at the lower current market value. In truth, the credibility of options may be strengthened at any time by indexing firm stock performance against a peer group of stocks, or against a popular market barometer. "Indexing some of the Chief Executive Officer's options to general stock market measures, such as the Standard & Poor's 500 index, will neither reward them for bull markets, nor penalize them for bear markets; such indexing can help mitigate the effect of overall market moves on executives' pay."[6]

Research suggests that stock option plans lack the benefits of plans that include true stock ownership. Stock option plans provide unlimited upside potential for executives, but limited downside risk since executives incur only opportunity costs. Because of the tremendous advantages to the executive of stock price appreciation, there is an incentive for the executive to take undue risk. Thus, supporters of stock ownership plans argue that direct ownership instills a much stronger behavioral commitment, even when the stock price falls, since it binds executives to their firms more than do options.[7] Additionally, "Executive stock options may be an efficient means to induce management to undertake more risky projects."[8]

By providing stock option plans with a so-called reload feature, firms may reap the previously mentioned benefits of direct executive stock ownership. A *reload* is a bonus of stock options given to executives when options are exercised.[9] In other words, when the executive converts her options into shares, thereby making a very sizable personal investment in the stock of the company, she receives a second bonus grant of stock options to continue to incentivize her to perform. The reload feature allows executives to realize present-day profits, while being rewarded with new options with the potential for future share price appreciation. Because the executive can take advantage of the reload feature only when she is willing to invest her own money into the company, the reload feature achieves the firm's goal of more tightly linking shareholders' and executives' wealth.

Restricted Stock

A restricted stock plan is designed to provide benefits of direct executive stock ownership. In a typical restricted stock plan, an executive is given a specific number of company stock shares. The executive is prohibited from selling the shares for a specified time period. Should the executive leave the firm voluntarily before the restricted period ends, the shares are forfeited. Therefore, restricted stock plans are a form of deferred compensation that promotes longer executive tenure than other types of plans.

In addition to being contingent on a vesting period, restricted stock plans may also require the achievement of predetermined performance goals. Price-vesting restricted stock plans tie vesting to the firm's stock price in comparison to an index, or to reaching a predetermined goal or annual growth rate. If the executive falls short on some of the restrictions, a certain amount of shares are forfeited. The design of these plans motivates the executive to increase shareholder wealth while promoting a long-term commitment to stay with the firm.

[6] Nicholas Carr, "Compensation: Refining CEO Stock Options," *Harvard Business Review* 76, no. 5 (September–October 1998), pp. 15–18.

[7] Jeffrey Pfeffer, "Seven Practices of Successful Organizations," *California Management Review*, Winter 1998.

[8] Richard A. DeFusco, Robert R. Johnson, and Thomas S. Zorn, "The Effect of Executive Stock Option Plans on Stockholders and Bondholders," *Journal of Finance* 45, no. 2 (1990), pp. 617–35.

[9] Jennifer Reingold and Leah Nathans Spiro, "Nice Option If You Can Get It," *BusinessWeek*, May 4, 1998, pp. 111–14.

If the restricted stock plan lacks performance goal provisions, the executive needs only to remain employed with the firm over the vesting period to cash in on the stock. Performance provisions make sure executives are not compensated without achieving some level of shareholder wealth creation. Like stock options, restricted stock plans offer no downside risk to executives, since the shares were initially gifted to the executive. Shareholders, on the other hand, do suffer a loss in personal wealth resulting from a share price drop.

Investment bank Lehman Brothers has a restricted stock plan in place for hundreds of managing directors and senior vice presidents. The plan vests with time and does not include stock price performance provisions. It is a two-tiered plan consisting of a principal stock grant and a discounted share plan. For managing directors, the discount is 30 percent. For senior vice presidents, the discount is 25 percent. The principal stock grant is a block of shares given to the executive. The discounted share plan allows executives to purchase shares with their own money at a discount to current market prices.

Managing directors at Lehman are able to cash in on one-half the principal portion of their stock grant three years after the grant is awarded. The rest of the principal and any shares bought at a discount must vest for five years. Senior vice presidents receive the entire principal after two years and any discounted shares after five years. Provisions also exist for resignation. If managing directors leave Lehman for a competitor within three years of the award, all stock compensation is forfeited. For senior vice presidents, the period is two years, and the penalties for jumping to a noncompetitor of Lehman's are not as severe.

Golden Handcuffs

The rationale behind plans that defer compensation forms the basis for another type of executive compensation called *golden handcuffs*. Golden handcuffs refer to either a restricted stock plan, where the stock compensation is deferred until vesting time provisions are met, or to bonus income deferred in a series of annual installments. This type of plan may also involve compensating an executive a significant amount upon retirement or at some predetermined age. In most cases, compensation is forfeited if the executive voluntarily resigns or is discharged before certain time restrictions.

Many boards consider their executives' skills and talents to be their firm's most valuable assets. These "assets" create and sustain the professional relationships that generate revenue and control expenses for the firm. Research suggests that the departure of key executives is unsettling for companies and often disrupts long-range plans when new key executives adopt a different management strategy.[10] Thus, the golden handcuffs approach to executive compensation is more congruent with long-term strategies than short-term performance plans, which offer little staying-power incentive.

Firms may turn to golden handcuffs if they believe stability of management is critical to sustain growth. Jupiter Asset Management tied 10 fund managers to the firm with golden handcuffs in 1995. The compensation scheme calls for a cash payment in addition to base salaries if the managers remain at the firm for five years. From 1995 to 1996, the firm's pretax profits more than doubled, and their assets under management increased 85 percent. The firm's chairman has also signed a new incentive deal that will keep him at Jupiter for four years.

Deferred compensation is worrisome to some executives. In cases where the compensation is payable when the executives are retired and no longer in control, as when the

---

[10] William E. Hall, Brian J. Lake, Charles T. Morse, and Charles T. Morse, Jr., "More Than Golden Handcuffs," *Journal of Accountancy* 184, no. 5 (1997), pp. 37–42.

firm is acquired by another firm or a new management hierarchy is installed, the golden handcuff plans are considerably less attractive to executives.

Golden handcuffs may promote risk averseness in executive decision making due to the huge downside risk borne by executives. This risk averseness could lead to mediocre performance results from executives' decisions. When executives lose deferred compensation if the firm discharges them voluntarily or involuntarily, the executive is less likely to make bold and aggressive decisions. Rather, the executive will choose safe, conservative decisions to reduce the downside risk of bold decision making.

Golden Parachutes

Golden parachutes are a form of bonus compensation that is designed to retain talented executives. A *golden parachute* is an executive perquisite that calls for a substantial cash payment if the executive quits, is fired, or simply retires. In addition, the golden parachute may also contain covenants that allow the executive to cash in on noninvested stock compensation.

The popularity of golden parachutes grew during the last decade, when abundant hostile takeovers would often oust the acquired firm's top executives. In these cases, the golden parachutes encouraged executives to take an objective look at takeover offers. The executives could decide which move was in the best interests of the shareholders, having been personally protected in the event of a merger. The "parachute" helps soften the fall of the ousted executive. It is "golden" because the size of the cash payment often varies from several to tens of millions of dollars.

AMP Incorporated, the world's largest producer of electronic connectors, has golden parachutes for several executives. On August 4, 1998, Allied Signal proclaimed itself an unsolicited suitor for AMP. The action focused attention on the AMP parachutes for its three top executives.

Robert Ripp became AMP's chief executive officer in August 1998. If Allied Signal ousted him, he stood to receive a cash payment of three times the amount of his salary as well as his highest annual bonus from the previous three years. His current salary in 1998 was $600,000 and his 1997 bonus was almost $200,000. The cash payment to Ripp would therefore exceed $2 million. Parachutes would also open for William Hudson, the former chief executive officer, and James Marley, the former chairman. Hudson and Marley were slated to officially retire on June 1, 1999, and August 1, 2000, respectively. Since they remain on the payroll, they stand to receive their parachutes if they are ousted before their respective retirement dates. Hudson and Marley's parachutes are both valued at more than $1 million.

In addition to cash payments, these three executives' parachutes also protect existing blocks of restricted stock grants and nonvested stock options. The restricted stock grants were scheduled to become available within three years. Should the takeover come to fruition, the executives would receive the total value of the restricted stock even if it was not yet vested. The stock options would also become available immediately. Some of the restricted stock was performance restricted. Under normal conditions this stock would not be available without the firm reaching certain performance levels. However, the golden parachutes allow the executives to receive double the value of the performance-restricted stock.

Golden parachutes are designed in part to anticipate hostile takeovers like this. In AMP's case, Ripp's position is to lead the firm's board of directors in deciding if Allied Signal's offer is in the long-term interests of shareholders. Since Ripp is compensated heavily whether AMP is taken over or not, the golden parachute has helped remove the temptation that Ripp could have of not acting in the best interests of shareholders.

By design, golden parachutes benefit top executives whether or not there is evidence that value is created for shareholders. In fact, research has suggested that since high-performing firms are rarely taken over, golden parachutes often compensate top executives for abysmal performance.[11] For example, in 1998, AMP went through a troubled period that included plant closings and layoffs, which depressed its stock price.

Cash

Executive bonus compensation plans that focus on accounting measures of performance are designed to offset the limitations of market-based measures of performance. This type of plan is most usually associated with the payment of periodic (quarterly or annual) cash bonuses. Market factors beyond the control of management, such as pending legislation, can keep a firm's share price repressed even though a top executive is exceeding the performance expectations of the board. In this situation, a highly performing executive loses bonus compensation due to the undervalued stock. However, accounting measures of performance correct for this problem by tying executive bonuses to improvements in internally measured performance.

Traditional accounting measures, such as net income, earnings per share, return on equity and return on assets, are used because they are easily understood, are familiar to senior management, and are already tracked by firm data systems.[12]

Sears, Roebuck and Company bases annual bonus payments on such performance criteria, given an executive's business unit and level with the firm. The measures used by Sears include return on equity, revenue growth, net sales growth, and profit growth.

Critics argue that due to inherent flaws in accounting systems, basing compensation on these figures may not result in an accurate gauge of managerial performance. Return on equity estimates, for example, are skewed by inflation distortions and arbitrary cost allocations.[13] Accounting measures are also subject to manipulation by firm personnel to artificially inflate key performance figures. Firm performance schemes, critics believe, need to be based on a financial measure that has a true link to shareholder value creation.[14] This issue led to the creation of the Balanced Scorecard, which emphasizes not only financial measures, but also such measures as new product development, market share, and safety.

Matching Bonus Plans and Corporate Goals

Exhibit 9–8 provides a summary of the five types of executive bonus compensation plans. The figure includes a brief description, a rationale for implementation, and the identification of possible shortcomings for each of the compensation plans. Not only do compensation plans differ in the method through which compensation is rewarded to the executive, but they also provide the executive with different incentives.

Exhibit 9–9 matches a company's strategic goal with the most likely compensation plan. On the vertical axis are common strategic goals. The horizontal axis lists the main compensation types that serve as incentives for executives to reach the firm's goals. A rationale is provided to explain the logic behind the connection between the firm's goal and the suggested method of executive compensation.

[11] Graef S. Crystal, *In Search of Excess* (New York: W. W. Norton & Company, 1991).

[12] Francine C. McKenzie and Matthew D. Shilling, "Avoiding Performance Measurement Traps: Ensuring Effective Incentive Design and Implementation," *Compensation and Benefits Review,* July–August 1998, pp. 57–65.

[13] Fred K. Foulkes, *Executive Compensation: A Strategic Guide for the 1990s* (Boston: Harvard Business School, 1985).

[14] William Franklin, "Making the Fat Cats Earn Their Cream," *Accountancy,* July 1998, pp. 38–39.

EXHIBIT 9–8   **Types of Executive Bonus Compensation**

Bonus Type	Description	Rationale	Shortcomings
Stock option grants	Right to purchase stock in the future at a price set now. Compensation is determined by "spread" between option price and exercise price.	Provides incentive for executive to create wealth for shareholders as measured by increase in firm's share price.	Movement in share price does not explain all dimensions of managerial performance.
Restricted stock plan	Shares given to executive who is prohibited from selling them for a specific time period. May also include performance restrictions.	Promotes longer executive tenure than other forms of compensation.	No downside risk to executive, who always profits unlike other shareholders.
Golden handcuffs	Bonus income deferred in a series of annual installments. Deferred amounts not yet paid are forfeited with executive resignation.	Offers an incentive for executive to remain with the firm.	May promote risk-averse decision making due to downside risk borne by executive.
Golden parachute	Executives have right to collect the bonus if they lose position due to takeover, firing, retirement, or resignation.	Offers an incentive for executive to remain with the firm.	Compensation is achieved whether or not wealth is created for shareholders. Rewards either success or failure.
Cash based on internal business performance using financial measures	Bonus compensation based on accounting performance measures such as return on equity.	Offsets the limitations of focusing on market-based measures of performance.	Weak correlation between earnings measures and shareholder wealth creation. Annual earnings do not capture future impact of current decisions.

Researchers emphasize that fundamental to these relationships is the importance of incorporating the level of strategic risk of the firm into the design of the executive's compensation plan. Incorporating an appropriate level of executive risk can create a desired behavioral change commensurate with the risk level of strategies shareholders and their firms want.[15] To help motivate an executive to pursue goals of a certain risk-return level, the compensation plan can quantify that risk-return level and reward the executive accordingly.

The links we show between bonus compensation plans and strategic goals were derived from the results of prior research. The basic principle underlying Exhibit 9–9 is that different types of bonus compensation plans are intended to accomplish different purposes; one element may serve to attract and retain executives, another may serve as an incentive to encourage behavior that accomplishes firm goals.[16] Although every strategy option has probably been linked to each compensation plan at some time, experience shows that there may be scenarios where a plan type best fits a strategy option. Exhibit 9–9 attempts to display the "best matches."

[15] Ira T. Kay, *Value at the Top* (New York: HarperCollins, 1992).
[16] James E. Nelson, "Linking Compensation to Business Strategy," *The Journal of Business Strategy* 19, no. 2 (1998), pp. 25–27.

EXHIBIT 9–9 **Compensation Plan Selection Matrix**

Strategic Goal	Type of Bonus Compensation					Rationale
	Cash	Golden Handcuffs	Golden Parachutes	Restricted Stock Plans	Stock Options	
Achieve corporate turnaround					X	Executive profits only if turnaround is successful in returning wealth to shareholders.
Create and support growth opportunities					X	Risk associated with growth strategies warrants the use of this high-reward incentive.
Defend against unfriendly takeover			X			Parachute helps remove temptation for executive to evaluate takeover based on personal benefits.
Evaluate suitors objectively			X			Parachute compensates executive if job is lost due to a merger favorable to the firm.
Globalize operations					X	Risk of expanding overseas requires a plan that compensates only for achieved success.
Grow share price incrementally	X					Accounting measures can identify periodic performance benchmarks.
Improve operational efficiency	X					Accounting measures represent observable and agreed-upon measures of performance.
Increase assets under management				X		Executive profits proportionally as asset growth leads to long-term growth in share price.
Reduce executive turnover		X				Handcuffs provide executive tenure incentive.
Restructure organization					X	Risk associated with major change in firm's assets warrant the use of this high-reward incentive.
Streamline operations				X		Rewards long-term focus on efficiency and cost control.

Once the firm has identified strategic goals that will best serve shareholders' interests, an executive bonus compensation plan can be structured in such a way as to provide the executive with an incentive to work toward achieving these goals.

Summary

The first concern in the implementation of business strategy is to translate that strategy into action throughout the organization. This chapter discussed four important tools for accomplishing this.

Short-term objectives are derived from long-term objectives, which are then translated into current actions and targets. They differ from long-term objectives in time frame, specificity, and measurement. To be effective in strategy implementation, they must be integrated and coordinated. They also must be consistent, measurable, and prioritized.

Functional tactics are derived from the business strategy. They identify the specific, immediate actions that must be taken in key functional areas to implement the business strategy.

Employee empowerment through policies provides another means for guiding behavior, decisions, and actions at the firm's operating levels in a manner consistent with its business and functional strategies. Policies empower operating personnel to make decisions and take action quickly.

Compensation rewards action and results. Once the firm has identified strategic objectives that will best serve stockholder interests, there are five bonus compensation plans that can be structured to provide the executive with an incentive to work toward achieving those goals.

Objectives, functional tactics, policies, and compensation represent only the start of the strategy implementation. The strategy must be institutionalized—it must permeate the firm. The next chapter examines this phase of strategy implementation.

Questions for Discussion

1. How does the concept "translate thought into action" bear on the relationship between business strategy and operating strategy? Between long-term and short-term objectives?

2. How do functional tactics differ from corporate and business strategies?

3. What key concerns must functional tactics address in marketing? Finance? POM? Personnel?

4. How do policies aid strategy implementation? Illustrate your answer.

5. Use Exhibits 9–8 and 9–9 to explain five executive bonus compensation plans.

6. Illustrate a policy, an objective, and a functional tactic in your personal career strategy.

7. Why are short-term objectives needed when long-term objectives are already available?

Chapter 9 Discussion Case

BusinessWeek

Amazing Amazon.com

Who would believe that you could start a company in your garage and three years later have it worth over $17 billion as a public company with only about $500 million in annual sales and a sizable loss? Jeff Bezos did just that at Amazon.com!

A few stock analysts think Amazon.com is way overvalued; that investors are "nuts" to pay an amount equal to five times Barnes & Noble for this company. You can examine that valuation today as you read this discussion case and see whether they, or the "nutty" investors, were wisest.

Regardless, the value of the Amazon.com story for you is to see why those E-commerce- and Internet-savvy people, many somewhat ahead of the curve in the Internet world of online purchasing, liked the company. And what you will see is that they liked Amazon.com because of the functional tactics and activities—how Amazon.com conducted its business each day.

Those functional activities allowed Amazon.com's strategy to be the first true E-commerce company to become a reality such that these "nutty" investors invested because they could get on the Net and experience those tactics working every day! Amazon.com is a company that *BusinessWeek* journalists Robert Hof, Ellen Neuborne, and Heather Green found to have pioneered and perfected the simple idea of selling online to anyone anywhere in mass before any other business did.

1   Amazon offers an easily searchable trove of 3.1 million titles—15 times more than any bookstore on the planet and without the costly overhead of multimillion-dollar buildings and scads of store clerks. That paves the way for each of its 1,600 employees to generate, on average, $375,000 in annual revenues—more than triple that of No. 1 bricks-and-mortar bookseller Barnes & Noble Inc.'s 27,000 employees.

2   Amazon's cutting-edge technology gives it a leg up, too, by automatically analyzing past purchases to make recommendations customized to each buyer—a trick that confounds 20th century mass marketing. And with a single mouse click, an order can be placed on its Web site, making shopping a friendly, frictionless, even fun experience that can take less time than finding a parking space at the mall.

3   Amazon is extending its warm and fuzzy formula far beyond the bibliophile set. In 1999 Amazon debuted a video store, as well as an expanded gift shop—a clear sign that founder Jeff Bezos aimed to make Amazon the Net's premier shopping destination. Buyers who visit the Web site can now find everything from Pictionary games and Holiday Barbies to Sony Walkmen and watches. And Amazon isn't apt to stop there. Not surprisingly, Bezos, who abruptly left a cushy job as a Wall Street hedge-fund manager in 1994 to race across the country and launch Amazon in his Seattle garage, keeps his plans close to the vest. But experts say he's eyeing everything from software and apparel to flowers and travel packages—markets that could pit the upstart against more heavyweights, such as Microsoft Corp. and Nordstrom Inc., as early as next year.

4   Can Bezos, a 34-year-old computer whiz with no previous experience in retail, pull it off? Don't bet against him: In Amazon's first full quarter selling music CDs, it drew $14.4 million in sales, quickly edging out two-year-old cyberleader CDnow Inc. Says analyst Lauren Cooks Levitan of BancBoston Robertson Stephens: "When you think of Web shopping, you think of Amazon first." But as Bezos moves into new markets, he will run smack into traditional retailers that are starting to wield their brands online. A new study by Boston Consulting Group found that 59% of consumer E-commerce revenues—including retail sites and online financial and travel services—are generated by companies such as Eddie Bauer and 1-800-FLOWERS that also sell through traditional channels. Says Carol Sanger, a vice-president at Macy's parent Federated Department Stores Inc.: "We think the brand of Macy's is far more meaningful to the consumer who is looking for traditional department-store goods than any Internet brand name."

5   As if all the rivals aren't scary enough, Amazon faces an even more fundamental uncertainty: Retailing is a business with razor-thin margins,

prompting some analysts to question whether the company will ever be profitable. The theory: Its ambitious growth plans will keep it on the fast track for entering new markets, propelling costs ever upward—and earnings out of reach. Analysts estimate that Amazon will spend nearly $200 million on marketing next year, up 50% over a year ago. "The company has been able to show it can sell lots of books for less without making money, and now it has shown it can sell lots of music for less without making money," says Merrill Lynch & Co. analyst Jonathan Cohen, one of only two analysts with a sell rating on the stock.

6   For every Cohen, though, there are seven analysts who think Amazon ultimately will fulfill investors' seemingly outsized expectations. For one thing, it has an almost unheard-of two-year head start on key software that handles millions of transactions and personalizes the customers' experience. Amazon, for instance, was the first commerce site to use so-called collaborative-filtering technology, which analyzes a customer's purchases and suggests other books that people with similar purchase histories bought: the ultimate in targeted marketing.

7   Besides spurring more purchases, there's another huge bonus for Amazon: It can gather instant feedback on customer preferences to divine what else they might want to buy. Such valuable information has proven forbiddingly effective in capturing new markets online. While it may appear as though the company is careening willy-nilly into new terrain, Amazon is in fact targeting areas its customers have already requested. "We want Amazon.com to be the right store for you as an individual," says Bezos. "If we have 4.5 million customers, we should have 4.5 million stores."

8   Not since superstores and mail-order catalogers came along in the 1980s have merchants faced such a wrenching shift to a new way of doing business. It's a lot like what Wal-Mart did in the past decade: It used computers to transform the entire process of getting products to customers, all the way from the warehouse to Wal-Mart's welcome mats. Now Bezos is using Net technologies to shatter the perennial retail trade-off—he can offer a rich selection and personalized service, while still reaching millions of customers.

9   But technology is just one way Amazon is trying to rewrite the rules of retail. Bookstore and other retail chains largely depend on opening new stores to boost revenues—a huge cost that Amazon completely avoids. In the reverse of traditional retailers, Amazon has relatively high initial costs for things such as computer systems and editorial staff—which partly explain its red ink today. But unlike retailers, who must continually invest in new stores to hike revenues, Amazon can boost sales by simply getting more people to come to its single online store. Says Chief Financial Officer Joy Covey: "I don't think we could have grown a physical store base four times in one year."

10   Of course, for now, Amazon has to spend millions on marketing to bring in new customers—about 24 cents per dollar of revenue last quarter, compared with 4 cents for traditional retailers. But it's little understood just how much leverage Amazon's low capital costs provide to support that spending. Here's how it works: Physical bookstores must stock up to 160 days' worth of inventory to provide the kind of in-store selection people want. Yet they must pay distributors and publishers 45 to 90 days after they buy the books—so on average, they carry the costs of those books for up to four months. Amazon, by contrast, carries only 15 days' worth of inventory and is paid immediately by credit card. So it gets about a month's use of interest-free money.

11   That float—amounting to well over $25 million so far this year—actually provides a large chunk of the cash Amazon needs to cover its operating expenses. In its latest quarter, Amazon used a mere $600,000 in operating cash while jacking up its customer base by 37%, or 1.4 million customers.

12   Even though Amazon is still a long way from making a profit, its basic economics suggest the upstart will someday look more like a fat-cat software company than a scrambling-for-profits retailer. Once Amazon gets enough customers and sales to pay off its initial marketing and technology investments—and as that technology pays off in falling labor costs—additional revenue drops to the bottom line. "Amazon's changing the business model of retailing," says Ann Winblad, a principal at Hummer Winblad Venture Partners.

13   It's no accident that Bezos named Amazon after the river that carries the greatest volume of water. "He wants Amazon to be a $10 billion [in revenues] company," says early investor and board member Tom A. Alberg. To look at Amazon's crowded, grubby Seattle headquarters, you'd never suspect such grand ambitions: It's an unmarked building across from Wigland, the Holy Ghost Revivals mission, and the Seattle–King County needle-exchange program. Unlike most of his Silicon Valley colleagues, Bezos is so cheap that the desks are made of doors and four-by-fours, while computer monitors sit on stacks of phone books. Of course, there's one big bonus: Everyone gets stock options, which have made dozens of Amazonians millionaires. But the usual Valley perks such as free neck massages? Yeah, right.

14   And it's only natural that in a company where everything is being created from whole cloth, the people don't exactly fit either the Silicon Valley or the Microsoft mold. Dogs, sometimes including Bezos' golden retriever, Kamala (named after a minor Star Trek character), and green-haired twentysomethings with multiple piercings run loose, often around the clock. Says Acting Customer Service Director Jane Slade: "We tell the temp agencies, 'Send us your freaks.'"

15   Bezos' executive staff is nearly as eclectic. It's a motley, though whip-smart, band of executives ranging from Microsoft refugees to liberal-arts majors and rock musicians. Ryan Sawyer, for instance, the vice-president for strategic growth, was a Rhodes scholar who studied poetry at Oxford. "They don't care what has been done in the past," says Anne Martin, a principal at BT Alex. Brown Inc., who was on Amazon's IPO road show.

16   And that includes Bezos. What he understood before most people was that the ability of the Web to connect almost anyone with almost any product meant that he could do things that couldn't be done in the physical world—such as sell 3 million books in a single store. Starting the company in his suburban Bellevue (Washington) garage, Bezos interviewed suppliers and prospective employees at, ironically, a nearby cafe inside a Barnes & Noble superstore. Launching Amazon.com quietly in July, 1995, Bezos quickly set out to make the customer's experience as appealing as sipping a latte in a bookstore cafe.

17   Besides the huge selection and simple web pages that load fast, he created a sense of online community. He invited people to post their own reviews of books; some 800,000 are now up. He brought in authors for chats and more: John Updike started a short story, and 400,000 people sent in contributions to finish it.

18   Most important, Bezos made it irresistibly easy to buy a book. After the first purchase, a customer's shipping and credit-card information are stored securely, so the next time, all it takes is a single click to send the books winging their way to a mailbox. And to assure people that their purchase went through, Amazon sent e-mail confirmations of orders—which were often upgraded to priority shipping for free.

19   Rivals have since copied those tactics, but Amazon continues to give customers the red-carpet treatment. This month, it introduced GiftClick, which lets customers choose a gift and simply type in the recipient's e-mail address—Amazon takes care of the rest. The result: Some 64% of orders are from repeat customers, and that's rising steadily. For many, Amazon's a lifeline to literature. Marcia Ellis, an American attorney working in Hong Kong, used to drag home a suitcase full of books when she visited the United States. Now, she orders two books a month online. "Most of the people we know here get books from Amazon," she says.

20   Bezos also was one of the first merchants to leverage the Web's power in unique ways to spread the Amazon brand. Early on, he offered other Web sites the chance to sell books related to their visitors' interests through a link to Amazon. Their inducement: a cut of up to 15% of sales. Now, he has 140,000 sites in the so-called Associates Program.

21   That's what has kept even the online arm of Barnes & Noble at bay. Certainly the No. 1 bookseller, which built its first store 125 years ago, is a savvy merchant, but it proved vulnerable when it came to the ways of the Web. For one thing, it was late in arriving, and its store-trained executives took longer to learn the new rules of e-commerce than Amazon's Net-centric staff. "In the early days, there's a big advantage in not having that baggage," says William McKiernan, chairman of e-commerce services provider CyberSource Corp.

22   Even after Barnes & Noble went online, it was slower to take advantage of the Net's ability to customize its site to each shopper. That allowed Amazon to use its appealing customer experience as a branding tool far more powerful than conventional advertising. And Barnes & Noble? Despite its well-known name and huge online marketing campaign, only 37% of Internet users recognized the brand without prompting, versus 50% that knew Amazon, according to Intelliquest Information Group.

23   The result: 18 months after Barnes & Noble went online, Amazon.com's $153.6 million in third-quarter sales, up 306% from a year ago, still overwhelm the book giant's online sales by 11 times. And Barnes & Noble's online customer base rose 29%, to 930,000—still less than a quarter of Amazon's.

24   Still, the bottom line is that Amazon needs to get customers to buy more. Indeed, with the bruising price wars that are sure to come, getting each customer to spend a tad extra may be critical for survival. It's just that the next step—the first beyond entertainment media—is a doozy. For one thing, it's unclear that the Amazon brand will extend into, say, toys or consumer electronics. "I get the combination of books and music and videos," says Robert Kagle, a venture capitalist who invests in Internet startups for Benchmark Capital. "Beyond that, I don't know how far their brand goes."

25   Even if the brand does travel well, it's almost guaranteed that other products won't be as profitable. Take CDs: They have lower margins than books. Same for videos. Toys have the disadvantage of not having as established a distribution network as books and music. So Amazon may have to stock more on its own, increasing its inventory costs and skimming off some of that nice float.

26   Already, established competitors are forcing it to do just that. Reel. com says 96% of the 20,000 titles it stocks are on the backlist. Those videos constitute most of its sales—and by far the most profitable portion. "If Amazon wants to ship them in a reasonable time, they'll have to stock them," says Reel.com CEO Julie Wainwright. And some

products, such as cars, real estate, or office products, are simply too cumbersome or expensive to ship. Or they may require too much aftersale support—which makes software a dicey product for Amazon to sell.

27   That's why Bezos will likely branch out beyond retail. In August, he spent $270 million for two companies that steer Amazon even more firmly toward becoming a shopping service rather than just a retailer. One of them, Junglee, has technology that makes it easy to scour the Web for products and compare prices or other features. "We don't even necessarily have to be selling all those things," says Bezos. "We just help people find things that are being sold elsewhere on the Web." Amazon might take a cut of revenues from other retailers if its customers buy their products. Says marketing prof Rogers, who is a partner in consultancy Peppers & Rogers: "Their next mission is to be a service agent."

TENUOUS ADVANTAGE

28   It's a tricky mission. Why? It will be tough to guarantee that the entire customer experience will measure up to Amazon's standard. Any glitches could quickly damage the company's carefully crafted brand name. "In three or four years, they'll be known for 'big,' " says CDnow CEO Jason Olim. "Well, whoop-di-do."

29   In the end, Amazon's success or failure will ride on maintaining a delightful experience for all of those new customers. Indeed, satisfied Amazon customers may well be helping more than most people realize: Analysts say one key to the sky-high stock price, which underwrites so much of its coming opportunity, is that investors can get a personal feel for Amazon's prospects by trying it out—something that's tough to do with most technology companies. Says Halsey Minor, CEO of online network CNET Inc.: "His [Bezos'] greatest advantage is a lot of people who buy his stock buy his books."

Source: Robert Hof, Ellen Neuborne, and Heather Green, "Amazon.com: The Wild World of E-Commerce," *BusinessWeek*, December 14, 1998.

Chapter Ten

Implementing Strategy: Structure, Leadership, and Culture

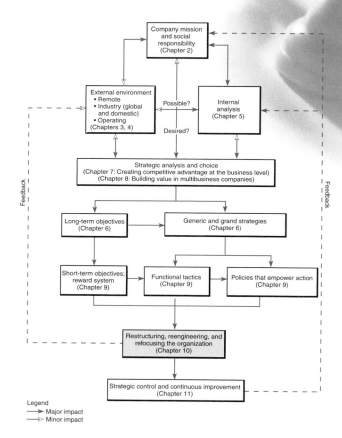

Company mission and social responsibility (Chapter 2)

External environment
• Remote
• Industry (global and domestic)
• Operating (Chapters 3, 4)

Possible?

Desired?

Internal analysis (Chapter 5)

Strategic analysis and choice
(Chapter 7: Creating competitive advantage at the business level)
(Chapter 8: Building value in multibusiness companies)

Long-term objectives (Chapter 6)

Generic and grand strategies (Chapter 6)

Short-term objectives; reward system (Chapter 9)

Functional tactics (Chapter 9)

Policies that empower action (Chapter 9)

Restructuring, reengineering, and refocusing the organization (Chapter 10)

Strategic control and continuous improvement (Chapter 11)

Feedback

Feedback

Legend
→ Major impact
⇢ Minor impact

Until this point in the strategic management process, managers have maintained a decidedly market-oriented focus as they formulate strategies and begin implementation through action plans detailing the tactics and actions that will be taken in each functional activity. Now the process takes an organizational focus—getting the work of the business done efficiently and effectively so as to make the strategy work. What is the best way to organize ourselves to accomplish the mission? Where should leadership come from? What values should guide our activities each day? What should this organization and its people be like? These are some of the fundamental issues managers face as they turn to the heart of strategy implementation.

While the focus is internal, the firm must still consider external factors as well. The intense competition in today's global marketplace has led most companies to consider their structure, or how the activities within their business are conducted, with an unprecedented attentiveness to what that marketplace—customers, competitors, suppliers, distribution partners—suggests or needs from the "internal" organization. This chapter explores three basic "levers" through which managers can implement strategy. The first lever is structure—the basic way the firm's different activities are organized. Second is leadership, encompassing the need to establish direction, embrace change and build a team to execute the strategy. The third lever is culture—the shared values that create the norms of individual behavior and the tone of the organization.

Consider the situation facing new Hewlett-Packard CEO Carly Fiorina in 2001. The unfortunate reality for her: HP's lumbering organization was losing touch with its global customers. Her response: As illustrated in Exhibit 10–1, Strategy in Action, Fiorina immediately dismantled the decentralized structure honed throughout HP's 64-year history. Pre-Fiorina, HP was a collection of 83 independently run units, each focused on a product such as scanners or security software. Fiorina collapsed those into four sprawling organizations. One so-called back-end unit develops and builds computers, and another focuses on printers and imaging equipment. The back-end divisions hand products off to two "front-end" sales and marketing groups that peddle the wares—one to consumers, the other to corporations. The theory: The new structure would boost collaboration, giving sales and marketing execs a direct pipeline to engineers so products are developed from the ground up to solve customer problems. This was the first time a company with thousands of product lines and scores of businesses has attempted a front-back approach, a structure that requires laser focus and superb coordination.

Fiorina believed she had little choice lest the company experience a near-death experience like Xerox or, ten years earlier, IBM. The conundrum: how to put the full force of the company behind winning in its immediate fiercely competitive technology business when they must also cook up brand-new megamarkets? It's a riddle Fiorina said she could solve only by sweeping structural change that would ready HP for the next stage of the technology revolution, when companies latch on to the Internet to transform their operations. At its core lay a conviction that HP must become "ambidextrous" excelling at short-term execution while pursuing long-term visions that create new markets. In addition to changing HP's structure, Fiorina also sought to revamp its culture of creativity. Her plan for unleashing a new culture of creativity was what she called "inventing at the intersection." Until 2001, HP made stand-alone products and innovations from $20 ink cartridges to $3 million servers. To revolutionize HP's culture and approach, she launched three "cross-company iniatives"—wireless services, digital imaging, and commercial printing—the first formal effort to get all of HP's separate and sometimes warring "tribes" working together.

Will it work? You are in the position of using hindsight to find out. Regardless, she earned high marks for zeroing in on HP's core problems and for having the courage to

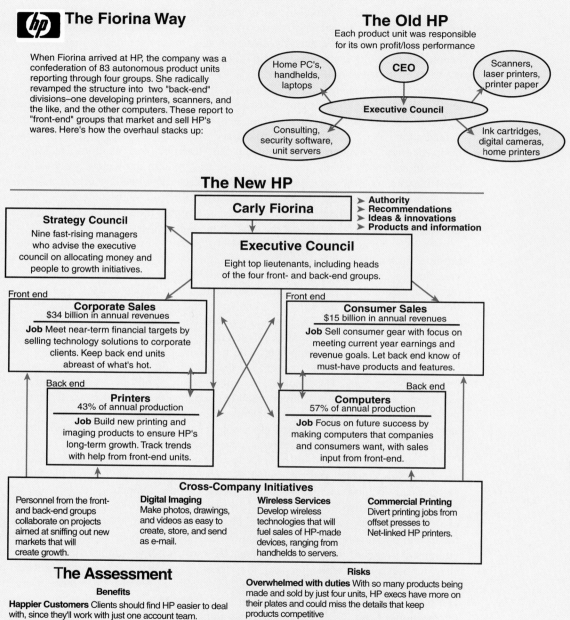

The Fiorina Way

When Fiorina arrived at HP, the company was a confederation of 83 autonomous product units reporting through four groups. She radically revamped the structure into two "back-end" divisions—one developing printers, scanners, and the like, and the other computers. These report to "front-end" groups that market and sell HP's wares. Here's how the overhaul stacks up:

The Old HP
Each product unit was responsible for its own profit/loss performance

- Home PC's, handhelds, laptops
- CEO
- Scanners, laser printers, printer paper
- Executive Council
- Consulting, security software, unit servers
- Ink cartridges, digital cameras, home printers

The New HP

Carly Fiorina

- ➤ Authority
- ➤ Recommendations
- ➤ Ideas & innovations
- ➤ Products and information

Strategy Council
Nine fast-rising managers who advise the executive council on allocating money and people to growth initiatives.

Executive Council
Eight top lieutenants, including heads of the four front- and back-end groups.

Front end

Corporate Sales
$34 billion in annual revenues
Job Meet near-term financial targets by selling technology solutions to corporate clients. Keep back end units abreast of what's hot.

Front end

Consumer Sales
$15 billion in annual revenues
Job Sell consumer gear with focus on meeting current year earnings and revenue goals. Let back end know of must-have products and features.

Back end

Printers
43% of annual production
Job Build new printing and imaging products to ensure HP's long-term growth. Track trends with help from front-end units.

Back end

Computers
57% of annual production
Job Focus on future success by making computers that companies and consumers want, with sales input from front-end.

Cross-Company Initiatives

Personnel from the front- and back-end groups collaborate on projects aimed at sniffing out new markets that will create growth.

Digital Imaging
Make photos, drawings, and videos as easy to create, store, and send as e-mail.

Wireless Services
Develop wireless technologies that will fuel sales of HP-made devices, ranging from handhelds to servers.

Commercial Printing
Divert printing jobs from offset presses to Net-linked HP printers.

The Assessment

Benefits

Happier Customers Clients should find HP easier to deal with, since they'll work with just one account team.

Sales Boost HP should maximize its selling opportunities because account reps will sell all HP products, not just those from one division.

Real Solutions HP can sell its products in combination as "solutions"—instead of just PCs or printers—to companies facing e-business problems.

Financial Flexibility With all corporate sales under one roof, HP can measure the total value of a customer, allowing reps to discount some products and still maximize profits on the overall contract.

Risks

Overwhelmed with duties With so many products being made and sold by just four units, HP execs have more on their plates and could miss the details that keep products competitive

Poorer Execution When product managers oversaw everything from manufacturing to sales, they could respond quickly to changes. That will be harder with front- and back-end groups synching their plans only every few weeks.

Less Accountability Profit-and-loss responsibility is shared between the front- and back-end groups so no one person is on the hot seat. Finger-pointing and foot-dragging could replace HP's collegial cooperation.

Fewer Spending Controls With powerful division chiefs keeping a tight rein on the purse strings, spending rarely got out of hand in the old HP. In the fourth quarter, expenses soared as those lines of command broke down.

EXHIBIT 10–2
What a Difference a Century Can Make

Contrasting views of the corporation:		
Characteristic	**20th Century**	**21st Century**
ORGANIZATION	The Pyramid	The Web or Network
FOCUS	Internal	External
STYLE	Structured	Flexible
SOURCE OF STRENGTH	Stability	Change
STRUCTURE	Self-sufficiency	Interdependencies
RESOURCES	Atoms—physical assets	Bits—information
OPERATIONS	Vertical integration	Virtual integration
PRODUCTS	Mass production	Mass customization
REACH	Domestic	Global
FINANCIALS	Quarterly	Real-time
INVENTORIES	Months	Hours
STRATEGY	Top-down	Bottom-up
LEADERSHIP	Dogmatic	Inspirational
WORKERS	Employees	Employees and free agents
JOB EXPECTATIONS	Security	Personal growth
MOTIVATION	To compete	To build
IMPROVEMENTS	Incremental	Revolutionary
QUALITY	Affordable best	No compromise

DATA: *BusinessWeek,* August 28, 2000.

tackle them head-on. And, if it did, the then 46-year-old CEO would become a 21st century management hero for a reinvigorated HP becoming a blueprint for others trying to transform major technology companies into 21st century dynamos. Said Stanford professor Robert Burgelman at the time, "there isn't a major technology company in the world that has solved the problem she's trying to address, and we're all going to learn from her experience."[1]

What CEO Fiorina faced, and Professor Burgelman recognizes, is the vast difference between business organizations of the 20th century and those of today. Exhibit 10–2 compares both on 18 different characteristics. The contrasts are striking, perhaps most so for leaders and managers faced with implementing strategies within them.

Fiorina offers a courageous example of a leader who recognized these compelling differences in the HP of the 20th century and what the HP of the 21st century needed to be. And her decision to adopt a laserlike focus on three key "levers" within HP to attempt to make HP's strategy successful are reflected in the focus of this chapter. Her first lever was HP's *organizational structure,* which was so important from her point of view that, without major change, would mean a partial or complete failure of HP. Her second concern was *leadership,* both from herself and key managers throughout HP. Finally, she knew that the HP *culture,* in this case birth of a new one, was the third critical lever with which to make the new HP vision and strategy have a chance for success.

STRUCTURING AN EFFECTIVE ORGANIZATION

Exhibit 10–2 offers a useful starting point in examining effective organizational structure. In contrasting 20th century and 21st century corporations on different characteristics, it offers a historical or evolutionary perspective on organizational attributes associated with

[1] "The Radical," *BusinessWeek,* February 19, 2001.

successful strategy execution today and just a few years ago. Successful organization once required an internal focus, structured interaction, self-sufficiency, a top-down approach. Today and tomorrow, organizational structure reflects an external focus, flexible interaction, interdependency, and a bottom-up approach, just to mention a few characteristics associated with strategy execution and success. Three fundamental trends are driving decisions about effective organizational structures in the 21st century: globalization, the Internet, and speed of decision making.

Globalization   The earlier example at Hewlett-Packard showed CEO Fiorina facing a desperate truth: HP's cumbersome organization was losing touch with its global customers. So she radically reorganized HP in part so multinational clients could go to just one sales and marketing group to buy everything from ink cartridges to supercomputers, in Buffalo or Bangkok. Over two-thirds of all industry either operates globally (e.g., computers, aerospace) or will soon do so. In the last half of the last decade, the percentage of sales from outside the home market for these five companies grew dramatically:

	1995	2000
General Electric	16.5%	35.1%
Wal-Mart	0.0	18.8
McDonald's	46.9	65.5
Nokia	85.0	98.6
Toyota	44.6	53.5

The need for global coordination and innovation is forcing constant experimentation and adjustment to get the right mix of local initiative, information flow, leadership, and corporate culture. At Swedish-based Ericsson, top managers scrutinize compensation schemes to make managers pay attention to global performance and avoid turf battles, while also attending to their local operations. Companies like Dutch electronics giant Philips regularly move headquarters for different businesses to the hottest regions for new trends—the "high voltage" markets. Its digital set-top box is now in California, its audio business moved from Europe to Hong Kong.[2]

Global once meant selling goods in overseas markets. Next was locating operations in numerous countries. Today it will call on talents and resources wherever they can be found around the globe, just as it now sells worldwide. It may be based in the United States, do its software programming in New Delhi, its engineering in Germany, and its manufacturing in Indonesia. The ramifications for organizational structures are revolutionary.

The Internet   The Net gives everyone in the organization, or working with it, from the lowest clerk to the CEO to any supplier or customer, the ability to access a vast array of information—instantaneously, from anywhere. Ideas, requests, instructions zap around the globe in the blink of an eye. It allows the global enterprise with different functions, offices, and activities dispersed around the world to be seamlessly connected so that far-flung customers, employees, and suppliers can work together in real time. The result—coordination, communication and decision-making functions accomplished through and the purpose for traditional organizational structures become slow, inefficient, noncompetitive weights on today's organization.

[2] "See the World, Erase Its Borders," *BusinessWeek,* August 28, 2000.

Speed   Technology, or digitization, means removing human minds and hands from an organization's most routine tasks and replacing them with computers and networks. Digitizing everything from employee benefits to accounts receivable to product design cuts cost, time, and payroll resulting in cost savings and vast improvements in speed. "Combined with the Internet, the speed of actions, deliberations, and information will increase dramatically," says Intel's Andy Grove. "You are going to see unbelievable speed and efficiencies," says Cisco's John Chambers, "with many companies about to increase productivity 20 percent to 40 percent per year." Leading-edge technologies will enable employees throughout the organization to seize opportunity as it arises. These technologies will allow employees, suppliers, and freelancers anywhere in the world to converse in numerous languages online without need for a translator to develop markets, new products, new processes. Again, the ramifications for organizational structures are revolutionary.

Whether technology assisted or not, globalization of business activity creates a potential sheer velocity of decisions that must be made which challenges traditional hierarchial organizational structures. A company like Cisco, for example, may be negotiating 50–60 alliances at one time due to the nature of its diverse operations. The speed at which these negotiations must be conducted and decisions made require a simple and accommodating organizational structure lest the opportunities may be lost.

Faced with these and other major trends, how should managers structure effective organizations? Consider these recent observations by *BusinessWeek* editors at the end of a year-long research effort asking just the same question:

> The management of multinationals used to be a neat discipline with comforting rules and knowable best practices. But globalization and the arrival of the information economy have rapidly demolished all the old precepts. The management of global companies, which must innovate simultaneously and speed information through horizontal, global-spanning networks, has become a daunting challenge. Old, rigid hierarchies are out—and flat, speedy, virtual organizations are in. Teamwork is a must and compensation schemes have to be redesigned to reward team players. But aside from that bit of wisdom, you can throw out the textbooks.
>
> CEOs will have to custom-design their organizations based on their industry, their own corporate legacy, and their key global customers—and they may have to revamp more than once to get it right. Highly admired companies such as General Electric, Hewlett-Packard, ABB Ltd., and Ericsson have already been through several organizational reincarnations in the past decade to boost global competitiveness.[3]

Our research concurs with these findings by *BusinessWeek* editors—there is no one best organizational structure. At the same time, there are several useful guidelines and approaches that help answer this question which we will now cover in the next several sections.

Match Structure to Strategy

The recent changes at Hewlett-Packard in Exhibit 10–1, Strategy in Action, illustrate this fundamental guideline. CEO Fiorina adopted the difficult, career-risking path of creating a major new structure at HP because that new structure reflected the needs of HP's strategy for the 21st century. An easier alternative would have been to create a strategy compatible with the existing decentralized structure of 83 semi-autonomous business units that had been in place for over half a century. While easier, however, the result would have been damaging to HP in the long run, perhaps even fatal, because strategic priorities and initiatives would have been guided by structural considerations, rather than the other way around.

[3] "The 21st Century Corporation," *BusinessWeek,* August 28, 2000.

The origins of this maxim come from a historical body of strategic management research[4] that examined how the evolution of a business over time and the degree of diversification from a firm's core business affected its choice of organizational structure. The primary organizational structures associated with this important research are still prevalent today—simple functional structures, geographical structures, multidivisional structures, and strategic business units.[5] Four basic conclusions were derived from this research:

1. *A single-product firm or single dominant business firm should employ a functional structure.* This structure allows for strong task focus through an emphasis on specialization and efficiency, while providing opportunity for adequate controls through centralized review and decision making.

2. *A firm in several lines of business that are somehow related should employ a multidivisional structure.* Closely related divisions should be combined into groups within this structure. When synergies (i.e., shared or linked activities) are possible within such a group, the appropriate location for staff influence and decision making is at the group level, with a lesser role for corporate-level staff. The greater the degree of diversity across the firm's businesses, the greater should be the extent to which the power of staff and decision-making authority is lodged within the divisions.

3. *A firm in several unrelated lines of business should be organized into strategic business units.* Although the strategic business unit structure resembles the multidivisional structure, there are significant differences between the two. With a strategic business unit structure, finance, accounting, planning, legal, and related activities should be centralized at the corporate office. Since there are no synergies across the firm's businesses, the corporate office serves largely as a capital allocation and control mechanism. Otherwise, its major decisions involve acquisitions and diverstitures. All operational and business-level strategic plans are delegated to the strategic business units.

4. *Early achievement of a strategy-structure fit can be a competitive advantage.* A competitive advantage is obtained by the first firm among competitors to achieve appropriate strategy-structure fit. That advantage will disappear as the firm's competitors also attain such a fit. Moreover, if the firm alters its strategy, its structure must obviously change as well. Otherwise, a loss of fit will lead to a competitive disadvantage for the firm.

These research-based guidelines were derived from 20th century companies not yet facing the complex, dynamically changing environments we see today. So an easy conclusion would be to consider them of little use. That is not the case, however. First, the admonition to let strategy guide structure rather than the other way around is very important today. While seemingly simple and obvious, resistance to changing existing structures—"the way we do things around here"—continues to be a major challenge to new

[4] Alfred D. Chandler, *Strategy and Structure* (Cambridge: MIT Press, 1962); Larry Wrigley, *Divisional Autonomy and Diversification,* doctoral dissertation, Harvard Business School, 1970; Richard Rumelt, "Diversification Strategy and Performance," *Strategic Management Journal* 3 (January–February 1982), pp. 359–69; Richard Rumelt, *Strategy, Structure and Economic Performance* (Boston: HBS Press, 1986). Rumelt used a similar, but more detailed classification scheme; D. A. Nathanson and J. S. Cassano, "Organization, Diversity, and Performance," *Wharton's Magazine* 6 (1982), pp. 19–26; and Christopher A. Bartlett and Sumantra Ghoshal, "Matrix Management: Not a Structure, a Frame of Mind," *Harvard Business Review* 68, no. 4 (1990), pp. 138–45; V. R. Galbraith and R. K. Kazanjian, *Strategy Implementation: Structure, Systems & Processes* (St. Paul, MN: West Publishing, 1986).
[5] Each primary structure is diagrammed and described in detail along with the advantages and disadvantages historically associated with each in an appendix to this chapter.

strategies in many organizations even today as HP again illustrates. Second, the notion that firms evolve over time from a single product/service focus to multiple products/services and markets requiring different structures is an important reality to accommodate when implementing growth strategies. Finally, many firms today have found value in multiple structures operating simultaneously in their company. People may be assigned within the company as part of a functional structure, but they work on teams or other groupings that operate outside the primary functional structure. We will explore this practice in a subsequent section, but the important point here is that while new and important hybrid organizational structures have proven essential to strategy implementation in the 21st century, these same "innovative" firms incorporate these "older" primary organizational structures in the fabric of their contemporary organizational structure.

Balance the Demands for Control/Differentiation with the Need for Coordination/Integration

Specialization of work and effort allows a unit to develop greater expertise, focus, and efficiency. So it is that some organizations adopt functional, or similar structures. Their strategy depends on dividing different activities within the firm into logical, common groupings—sales, operations, administration, or geography—so that each set of activity can be done most efficiently. Control of sets of activities is at a premium. Dividing activities in this manner, sometimes called "differentiation," is an important structural decision. At the same time, these separate activities, however they are differentiated, need to be coordinated and integrated back together as a whole so the business functions effectively. Demands for control and the coordination needs differ across different types of businesses and strategic situations.

The rise of a consumer culture around the world has led brand marketers to realize they need to be more responsive to local preferences. Coca-Cola, for example, used to control its products rigidly from its Atlanta headquarters. But managers have found in some markets consumers thirst for more than Coke, Diet Coke, and Sprite. So Coke has altered its structure to reduce the need for control in favor of greater coordination/integration in local markets where local managers independently launch new flavored drinks. At the same time, GE, the paragon of new age organization, had altered its GE Medical Systems organization structure to allow local product managers to handle everything from product design to marketing. This emphasis on local coordination and reduced central control of product design led managers obsessed with local rivalries to design and manufacture similar products for different markets—a costly and wasteful duplication of effort. So GE reintroduced centralized control of product design, with input from a worldwide base of global managers, and their customers, resulting in the design of several single global products produced quite cost competitively to sell worldwide. GE's need for control of product design outweighed the coordination needs of locally focused product managers.[6] At the same time, GE obtained input from virtually every customer or potential customer worldwide before finalizing the product design of several initial products, suggesting that it rebalanced in favor of more control, but organizationally coordinated input from global managers and customers so as to ensure a better potential series of medical scanner for hospitals worldwide.

Restructure to Emphasize and Support Strategically Critical Activities

Restructuring has been the buzzword of global enterprise for the last 10 years. Its contemporary meaning is multifaceted. At the heart of the restructuring trend is the notion that some activities within a business's value chain are more critical to the success of the

[6] "See the World, Erase Its Borders," *BusinessWeek,* August 28, 2000.

business's strategy than others. Wal-Mart's organizational structure is designed to ensure that its impressive logistics and purchasing competitive advantages operate flawlessly. Coordinating daily logistical and purchasing efficiencies among separate stores lets Wal-Mart lead the industry in profitability yet sell retail for less than many competitors buy the same merchandise at wholesale. Motorola's organizational structure is designed to protect and nurture its legendary R&D and new product development capabilities—spending over twice the industry average in R&D alone each year. Motorola's R&D emphasis continually spawns proprietary technologies that support its technology-based competitive advantage. Coca-Cola emphasizes the importance of distribution activities, advertising, and retail support to its bottlers in its organizational structure. All three of these companies emphasize very different parts of the value chain process, but they are extraordinarily successful in part because they have designed their organizational structures to emphasize and support strategically critical activities. Exhibit 10–3, Strategy in Action, provides some guidelines that should influence how an organization is structured depending on which among five different sources of competitive advantage are emphasized in its strategy.

Two critical considerations arise when restructuring the organization to emphasize and support strategically critical activities. First, managers need to make the strategically critical activities the central building blocks for designing organization structure. Those activities should be identified and separated as much as possible into self-contained parts of the organization. Then the remaining structure must be designed so as to ensure timely integration with other parts of the organization.

While this is easily proposed, managers need to recognize that strategically relevant activities may still reside in different parts of the organization, particularly in functionally organized structures. Support activities like finance, engineering, or information processing are usually self-contained units, often outside the unit around which core competencies are built. This often results in an emphasis on departments obsessed with performing their own tasks more than emphasizing the key results (customer satisfaction, differentiation, low costs, speed) the business as a whole seeks. So the second consideration is to design the organizational structure so that it helps coordinate and integrate these support activities to (1) maximize their support of strategy-critical primary activities in the firm's value chain and (2) does so in a way to minimize the costs for support activities and the time spent on internal coordination. Managerial efforts to do this in the 1990s have placed reengineering, downsizing, and outsourcing as prominent tools for strategists restructuring their organizations.

Reengineer Strategic Business Processes

Business process reengineering (BPR), popularized by consultants Michael Hammer and James Champy,[7] is one of the more popular methods by which organizations worldwide are undergoing restructuring efforts to remain competitive in the 21st century. BPR is intended to reorganize a company so that it can best create value for the customer by eliminating barriers that create distance between employees and customers. It involves fundamental rethinking and radical redesign of a business process. It is characterized as radical because it strives to structure organizational efforts and activities around results and value creation by focusing on the processes that are undertaken to meet customer needs, not specific tasks and functional areas such as marketing and sales.

---

[7] Michael Hammer and James Champy, *Reengineering the Corporation* (New York: HarperBusiness, 1993).

BusinessWeek One of the key things business managers should keep in mind when restructuring their organizations is to devise the new structure so that it emphasizes strategically critical activities within the business's value chain. This means that the structure should allow those activities to have considerable autonomy over issues that influence their operating excellence and timeliness; they should be in a position to easily coordinate with other parts of the business—to get decisions made fast.

Below are five different types of critical activities that may be at the heart of a business's effort to build and sustain competitive advantage. Beside each one are typical conditions that will affect and shape the nature of the organization's structure:

Potential Strategic Priority and Critical Activities	Concomitant Conditions That May Affect or Place Demands on the Organizational Structure and Operating Activities to Build Competitive Advantage
1. Compete as low-cost provider of goods or services.	Broadens market. Requires longer production runs and fewer product changes. Requires special-purpose equipment and facilities.
2. Compete as high-quality provider.	Often possible to obtain more profit per unit, and perhaps more total profit from a smaller volume of sales. Requires more quality-assurance effort and higher operating cost. Requires more precise equipment, which is more expensive. Requires highly skilled workers, necessitating higher wages and greater training efforts.
3. Stress customer service.	Requires broader development of servicepeople and service parts and equipment. Requires rapid response to customer needs or changes in customer tastes, rapid and accurate information system, careful coordination. Requires a higher inventory investment.
4. Provide rapid and frequent introduction of new products.	Requires versatile equipment and people. Has higher research and development costs. Has high retraining costs and high tooling and changeover costs. Provides lower volumes for each product and fewer opportunities for improvements due to the learning curve.
5. Seek vertical integration.	Enables firm to control more of the process. May not have economies of scale at some stages of process. May require high capital investment as well as technology and skills beyond those currently available within the firm.

Business reengineering reduces fragmentation by crossing traditional departmental lines and reducing overhead to compress formerly separate steps and tasks that are strate-
gically intertwined in the process of meeting customer needs. This "process orientation," rather than a traditional functional orientation, becomes the perspective around which various activities and tasks are then grouped to create the building blocks of the organization's structure. This is usually accomplished by assembling a multifunctional, multilevel team that begins by identifying customer needs and how the customer wants to deal with

the firm. Customer focus must permeate all phases. Companies that have successfully reengineered their operations around strategically critical business processes have pursued the following steps:[8]

- Develop a flowchart of the total business process, including its interfaces with other value chain activities.

- Try to simplify the process first, eliminating tasks and steps where possible and analyzing how to streamline the performance of what remains.

- Determine which parts of the process can be automated (usually those that are repetitive, time-consuming, and require little thought or decision); consider introducing advanced technologies that can be upgraded to achieve next-generation capability and provide a basis for further productivity gains down the road.

- Evaluate each activity in the process to determine whether it is strategy-critical or not. Strategy-critical activities are candidates for benchmarking to achieve best-in-industry or best-in-world performance status.

- Weigh the pros and cons of outsourcing activities that are noncritical or that contribute little to organizational capabilities and core competencies.

- Design a structure for performing the activities that remain; reorganize the personnel and groups who perform these activities into the new structure.

When asked recently about his new networking-oriented direction for IBM, IBM CEO Gerstner responded: "It's called *reengineering*. It's called *getting competitive*. It's called *reducing cycle time and cost, flattening organizations, increasing customer responsiveness*. All of these require a collaboration with the customer and with suppliers and with vendors."

Downsize and Self-Manage: Force Decisions to Operating Level

Reengineering and a value orientation have led managers to scrutinize even further the way their organizational structures are crucial to strategy implementation. That scrutiny has led to downsizing, outsourcing, and self-management as three important themes influencing the organizational structures into the 21st century. *Downsizing* is eliminating the number of employees, particularly middle management, in a company. The arrival of a global marketplace, information technology, and intense competition caused many companies to reevaluate middle management activities to determine just what value was really being added to the company's products and services. The result of this scrutiny, along with continuous improvements in information processing technology, has been widespread downsizing in the number of management personnel in thousands of companies worldwide. These companies often eliminate whole levels of management. General Electric went from 400,000 to 280,000 employees in this decade while its sales have almost tripled and its profit risen fivefold. Jack Welch's observations about GE's downsizing and the results of *BusinessWeek*'s survey of companies worldwide that have been actively downsizing (which attempts to extract guidelines for downsizing) are shown in Strategy in Action 10–4.

One of the outcomes of downsizing was increased *self-management* at operating levels of the company. Cutbacks in the number of management people left those that remained

[8] Judy Wade, "How to Make Reengineering Really Work," *Harvard Business Review* 71, no. 6 (November–December 1993), pp. 119–31.

BusinessWeek

GE used to have things like department managers, subsection managers, unit managers, supervisors. We're driving those titles out . . . We used to go from the CEO to sectors, to groups, to businesses. We now go from the CEO to businesses. Nothing else.

—Jack Welch

It's hard to find a major corporation that hasn't downsized in recent years. But simple reductions in staffing don't make for lean management. Here's a checklist, developed by *BusinessWeek* from interviews with executives and consultants, that may tell you if your company needs a diet.

Company Characteristic	Analysis
1. Layers of management between CEO and the shop floor.	Some companies, such as Ameritech, now have as few as four or five where as many as 12 had been common. More than six is most likely too many.
2. Number of employees managed by the typical executive.	At lean companies, spans of control range up to one manager to 30 staffers. A ratio of lower than 1:10 is a warning of arterial sclerosis.
3. Amount of work cut out by your downsizing.	Eliminating jobs without cutting out work can bring disaster. A downsizing should be accompanied by at least a 25% reduction in the number of tasks performed. Some lean companies have hit 50%.
4. Skill levels of the surviving management group.	Managers must learn to accept more responsibility and to eliminate unneeded work. Have you taught them how?
5. Size of your largest profit center by number of employees.	Break down large operating units into smaller profit centers—less than 500 employees is a popular cutoff—to gain the economies of entrepreneurship and offset the burdens of scale.
6. Post-downsizing size of staff at corporate headquarters.	The largest layoffs, on a percentage basis, should be at corporate headquarters. It is often the most overstaffed—and the most removed from customers.

Source: "The 21st Century Corporation," *BusinessWeek,* August 28, 2000.

with more work to do. The result was that they had to give up a good measure of control to workers, and they had to rely on those workers to help out. Spans of control, traditionally thought to maximize under 10 people, have become much larger due to information technology, running "lean and mean," and delegation to lower levels. Ameritech, one of the Baby Bells, has seen its spans of control rise to as much as 30 to 1 in some divisions because most of the people that did staff work—financial analysts, assistant managers, and so on—have disappeared. This delegation, also known as empowerment, is accomplished through concepts like self-managed work groups, reengineering, and automation. It is also seen through efforts to create distinct businesses within a business—conceiving a business as a confederation of many "small" businesses, rather than one large, interconnected business. Whatever the terminology, the idea is to push decision making down in the organization by allowing major management decisions to be made at operating levels. The result is often the elimination of up to half the levels of management previously existing in an organizational structure.

EXHIBIT 10–5
The Product-Team
Structure

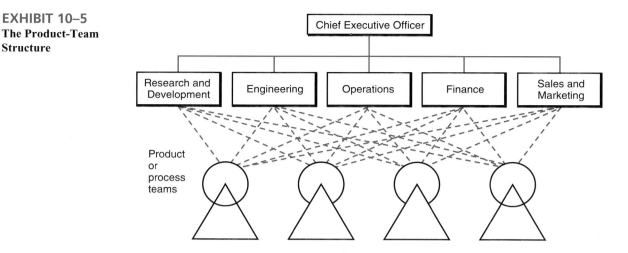

Allow Multiple Structures to Operate Simultaneously within the Organization to Accommodate Products, Geography, Innovation and Customers

The *matrix organization* described in this chapter's Appendix A was one of the early structural attempts to do this so that skills and resources could be better assigned and used within a large company. People typically had a permanent assignment to a certain organizational unit, usually a functional or staff department, yet they were also frequently assigned to work in another project or activity at the same time. For example, a product development project may need a market research specialist for several months and a financial analyst for a week. It was tried by many companies, and is still in use today. The dual chains of command, particularly given a temporary assignment approach, proved problematic for some organizations, particularly in an international context complicated by distance, language, time, and culture.

The *product-team structure* emerged as an alternative to the matrix approach to simplify and amplify the focus of resources on a narrow but strategically important product, project, market, customer or innovation. Exhibit 10–5 illustrates how the product-team structure looks.

The product-team structure assigns functional managers and specialists (e.g., engineering, marketing, financial, R&D, operations) to a new product, project, or process team that is empowered to make major decisions about their product. The team is usually created at the inception of the new product idea, and they stay with it indefinitely if it becomes a viable business. Instead of being assigned on a temporary basis, as in the matrix structure, team members are assigned permanently to that team in most cases. This results in much lower coordination costs and, since every function is represented, usually reduces the number of management levels above the team level needed to approve team decisions.

It appears that product teams formed at the beginning of product-development processes generate cross-functional understanding that irons out early product or process design problems. They also reduce costs associated with design, manufacturing, and marketing, while typically speeding up innovation and customer responsiveness because authority rests with the team allowing decisions to be made more quickly. That ability to make speedier, cost-saving decisions has the added advantage of eliminating the need for one or more management layers above the team level, which would traditionally have been in place to review and control these types of decisions. While seemingly obvious, it has only recently become apparent that those additional management layers were also

BusinessWeek Building teams is a new organization art form for Corporate America. Getting people to work together successfully has become a critical managerial skill. Those companies that learn the secrets of creating cross-functional teams are winning the battle for global market share and profits. Those that don't are losing out.

Take General Motors. Both Ford and Chrysler are picking up market share in the U.S. because each in its own way has discovered how to build product-development teams that generate successful new models. Their method: Bring together people from engineering, design, purchasing, manufacturing, and marketing, and make them responsible as a group for the new car. Then destroy all bureaucracy above them, except for service support. GM has yet to do this. Its team members remain tied to their old structures—the engineers to engineering, purchasing agents to the purchasing department. Decisions aren't made for the good of the new product but to satisfy atavistic requirements of ancient bureaucracies.

Consider Modicon Inc., a North Andover (Massachusetts) maker of automation-control equipment with annual revenues of $300 million. Instead of viewing product development as a task of the engineering function, President Paul White defined it more broadly as a process that would involve a team of 15 managers from engineering, manufacturing, marketing, sales, and finance. By working together, Modicon's team avoided costly delays from disagreements and misunderstandings. "In the past," says White, "an engineering team would have worked on this alone with some dialogue from marketing. Manufacturing wouldn't get involved until the design was brought into the factory. Now, all the business issues are right on the table from the beginning." The change allowed Modicon to bring six software products to market in one-third the time it would normally take. The company still has a management structure organized by function. But many of the company's 900 employees are involved in up to 30 teams that span several functions and departments. Predicts White: "In five years, we'll still have some formal functional structure, but people will probably feel free enough to spend the majority of their time outside their functions."

Eastman Chemical Co., the $3.5 billion unit of Eastman Kodak Co. recently spun off as a stand-alone company, replaced several of its senior vice-presidents in charge of the key functions with "self-directed work teams." Instead of having a head of manufacturing, for example, the company uses a team consisting of all its plant managers. "It was the most dramatic change in the company's 70-year history," maintains Ernest W. Deavenport Jr., president of Eastman Chemical. "It makes people take off their organizational hats and put on their team hats. It gives people a much broader perspective and forces decision-making down at least another level." In creating the new organization, the 500 senior managers agreed that the primary role of the functions was to support Eastman's business in chemicals, plastics, fibers, and polymers. "A function does not and should not have a mission of its own," insists Deavenport. Common sense? Of course. But over the years, the functional departments had grown strong and powerful, as they have in many organizations, often at the expense of the overall company as they fought to protect and build turf. Now, virtually all of the company's managers work on at least one cross-functional team, and most work on two or more on a daily basis. For example, Tom O. Nethery, a group vice-president, runs an industrial-business group. But he also serves on three other teams that deal with such diverse issues as human resources, cellulose technology, and product-support services.

Source: John A. Byrne, "The Horizontal Corporation," *BusinessWeek,* December 20, 1993; and "What GM Needs to Do," *BusinessWeek,* November 1, 1993.

making these decisions with less firsthand understanding of the issues involved than the cross-functional team members brought to the product or process in the first place. Exhibit 10–6, Strategy in Action, gives examples of a product-team approach at several well-known companies and some of the advantages that appear to have accrued.

Take Advantage of Being a Virtual Organization

True 21st century corporations will increasingly see their structure become an elaborate network of external and internal relationships. This organizational phenomenon has been termed the *virtual organization,* which is defined as a temporary network of independent companies—suppliers, customers, subcontractors, even competitors—linked primarily by

EXHIBIT 10–7
**General Motors:
alliances with
competitors**

Source: General Motors
Corporation Annual Reports;
"Carmakers Take Two Routes
to Global Growth," *Financial
Times* (July 11, 2000), p. 19.

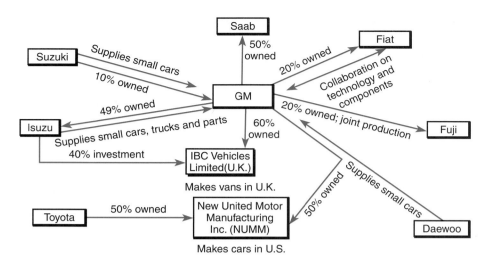

information technology to share skills, access to markets, and costs.[9] Outsourcing along with strategic alliances are integral in making a virtual organization work. Globalization has accelerated the use of and need for the virtual organization.

Outsourcing was an early driving force for the virtual organization trend. Dell does not make PCs. Cisco doesn't make its world renowned routers. Motorola doesn't make cell phones. Sony makes Apple's low-end PowerBook computers. *Outsourcing* is simply obtaining work previously done by employees inside the companies from sources outside the company. Managers have found that as they attempt to restructure their organizations, particularly if they do so from a business process orientation, numerous activities can often be found in their company that are not "strategically critical activities." This has particularly been the case of numerous staff activities and administrative control processes previously the domain of various middle management levels in an organization. But it can also refer to primary activities that are steps in their business's value chain—purchasing, shipping, making certain parts, and so on. Further scrutiny has led managers to conclude that these activities not only add little or no value to the product or services, but that they can be done much more cost effectively (and competently) by other businesses specializing in these activities. If this is so, then the business can enhance its competitive advantage by outsourcing the activities. Many organizations have outsourced information processing, various personnel activities, and production of parts that can be done better outside the company. Outsourcing, then, can be a source of competitive advantage and result in a leaner, flatter organizational structure.

Strategic alliances, some long-term and others for very short periods, with suppliers, partners, contractors, and other providers of world class capabilities allow partners to the alliance to focus on what they do best, farm out everything else, and quickly provide value to the customer. Engaging in alliances, whether long-term or one-time, let each participant take advantage of fleeting opportunities quickly, usually without tying up vast amounts of capital. FedEx and the U.S. Postal Service have formed an alliance—FedEx planes carry USPS next-day letters and USPS delivers FedEx ground packages—to allow both to challenge their common rival, UPS. Exhibit 10–7 shows how General Motors, in its effort to become more competitive globally, has entered into numerous alliances with competitors. Cisco owns only two of

---

[9] W. H. Davidow and M. S. Malone, *The Virtual Corporation* (New York: Harper, 1992).

EXHIBIT 10–8
From Traditional Structure to B-Web Structure

Source: Adapted from Don Tapscott, David Ticoll, and Alex Lowry, *Digital Capital: Harnessing the Power of Business Webs* (Boston: Harvard Business School Press, 2000).

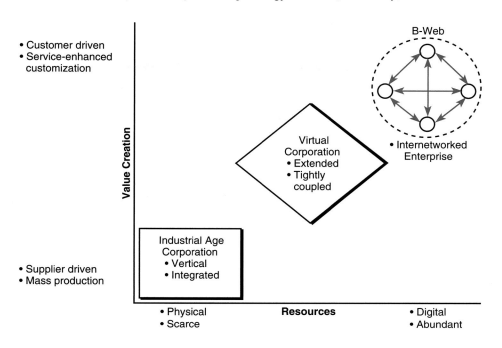

34 plants that produce its routers, and over 50 percent of all orders fulfilled by Cisco are done without a Cisco employee being involved.

Web-Based Organizations   As we noted at the beginning of this section, globalization has accelerated many changes in the way organizations structure, and that is certainly the case in driving the need to become part of a virtual organization or make use of one. Technology, particularly driven by the Internet, has and will be a major driver of the virtual organization. Commenting on technology's impact on Cisco, John Chambers observed that with all its outsourcing and strategic alliances, roughly 90 percent of all orders come into Cisco without ever being touched by human hands. "To my customers, it looks like one big virtual plant where my suppliers and inventory systems are directly tied into our virtual organization," he said. "That will be the norm in the future. Everything will be completely connected, both within a company and between companies. The people who get that will have a huge competitive advantage."

The Web's contribution electronically has simultaneously become the best analogy in explaining the future virtual organization. So it is not just the Web as in the Internet, but a weblike shape of successful organizational structures in the future. If there are a pair of images that symbolize the vast changes at work, they are the pyramid and the web. The organizational chart of large-scale enterprise had long been defined as a pyramid of ever-shrinking layers leading to an omnipotent CEO at its apex. The 21st century corporation, in contrast, is far more likely to look like a web: a flat, intricately woven form that links partners, employees, external contractors, suppliers, and customers in various collaborations. The players will grow more and more interdependent. Fewer companies will try to master all the disciplines necessary to produce and market their goods but will instead outsource skills—from research and development to manufacturing—to outsiders who can perform those functions with greater efficiency.[10] Exhibit 10–8 illustrates this

---

[10] "The 21st Century Organization," *BusinessWeek,* August 28, 2000.

evolution in organization structure to what it calls the B-Web, a truly Internet driven form of organization designed to deliver speed, customized service-enhanced products to savvy customers from an integrated virtual B-Web organization pulling together abundant, world class resources digitally.

Managing this intricate network of partners, spin-off enterprises, contractors, and free-lancers will be as important as managing internal operations. Indeed, it will be hard to tell the difference. All of these constituents will be directly linked in ways that will make it nearly impossible for outsiders to know where an individual firm begins and where it ends. "Companies will be much more molecular and fluid," predicts Don Tapscott, co-author of *Digital Capital.* "They will be autonomous business units connected not necessarily by a big building but across geographies all based on networks. The boundaries of the firm will be not only fluid or blurred but in some cases hard to define."[11]

Remove Structural Barriers and Create a Boundaryless, Ambidextrous Learning Organization

The evolution of the virtual organizational structure as an integral mechanism managers use to implement strategy has brought with it recognition of the central role knowledge plays in this process. *Knowledge* may be in terms of operating know-how, relationships with and knowledge of customer networks, technical knowledge upon which products or processes are based or will be, relationships with key people or a certain person than can get things done quickly, and so forth. Exhibit 10–9, Strategy in Action, shares how McKinsey organizational expert Lowell Bryan sees this shaping future organizational structure with managers becoming knowledge "nodes" through which intricate networks of personal relationships—inside and outside the formal organization—are constantly co-ordinated to bring together relevant know-how and successful action.

Management icon Jack Welch coined the term *boundaryless* organization, to charac-terize what he attempted to make GE become in order for it to be able to generate knowl-edge, share knowledge and get knowledge to the places it could be best used to provide superior value. A key component of this concept was erasing internal divisions so the people in GE could work across functional, business, and geographic boundaries to achieve an integrated diversity—the ability to transfer the best ideas, the most developed knowledge, and the most valuable people quickly, easily and freely throughout GE. Here is his description:

> Boundaryless behavior is the soul of today's GE . . . Simply put, people seem compelled to build layers and walls between themselves and others, and that human tendency tends to be magnified in large, old institutions like ours. These walls cramp people, inhibit creativity, waste time, restrict vision, smother dreams and above all, slow things down . . . Boundary-less behavior shows up in actions of a woman from our Appliances Business in Hong Kong helping NBC with contacts needed to develop satellite television service in Asia . . . And finally, boundaryless behavior means exploiting one of the unmatchable advantages a multibusiness GE has over almost any other company in the world. Boundaryless behavior combines 12 huge global businesses—each number one or number two in its markets—into a vast laboratory whose principal product is new ideas, coupled with a common commitment to spread them throughout the Company.
>
> —Letter to Shareholders, Jack Welch
> Chairman, General Electric Company, 1981–2001

A shift from what Subramanian Rangan calls *exploitation to exploration* indicates the growing importance of organizational structures that enable a *learning organization*

---

[11] Ibid.

BusinessWeek Lowell Bryan, a senior partner and director at consultancy McKinsey & Co., leads McKinsey's global industries practice and is the author of *Race for the World: Strategies to Build a Great Global Firm* and *Market Unbound: Unleashing Global Capitalism*.

Q: How will global companies be managed in the 21st century?

A: Describing it is hard because the language of management is based on command-and-control structures and "who reports to whom." Now, the manager is more of a network operator. He is part of a country team and part of a business unit. Some companies don't even have country managers anymore.

Q: What is the toughest challenge in managing global companies today?

A: Management structures are now three-dimensional. You have to manage by geography, products, and global customers. The real issue is building networked structures between those three dimensions. That is the state of the art. It's getting away from classic power issues. Managers are becoming nodes, which are part of geographical structures and part of a business unit.

Q: What are the telltale questions that reflect whether a company is truly global?

A: CEOs should ask themselves four questions: First, how do people interact with each other: Do employees around the world know each other and communicate regularly? Second, do management processes reflect a network or an old-style hierarchy? Third, is information provided to everyone simultaneously? And fourth, is the company led from the bottom up, not the top down?

Q: Why do multinationals that have operated for decades in foreign markets need to overhaul their management structures?

A: The sheer velocity of decisions that must be made is impossible in a company depending on an old-style vertical hierarchy. Think of a company [like] Cisco that is negotiating 50 to 60 alliances at one time. The old corporate structures [can't] integrate these decisions fast enough. The CEO used to be involved in every acquisition, every alliance. Now, the role of the corporate center is different. Real business decisions move down to the level of business units.

Q: If there is not clear hierarchy, and managers have conflicting opinions, how does top management know when to take a decision? Doesn't that raise the risk of delay and inaction?

A: In the old centralized model, there was no communication. If you have multiple minds at work on a problem, the feedback is much quicker. If five managers or "nodes" in the network say something is not working right, management better sit up and take notice.

Q: Are there any secrets to designing a new management architecture?

A: Many structures will work. [H]aving the talent and capabilities you need to make a more fluid structure work [is key]. [But] it's much harder to do. The key is to create horizontal flow across silos to meet customers needs. The question is how you network across these silos. [G]etting people to work together [is paramount]. That's the revolution that is going on now.

Q: What is the role of the CEO?

A: The CEO is the architect. He puts in place the conditions to let the organization innovate. No one is smart enough to do it alone anymore. Corporate restructuring should liberate the company from the past. As you break down old formal structures, knowledge workers are the nodes or the glue that hold different parts of the company together. They are the network. Nodes are what it is all about.

Q: How do you evaluate performance in such a squishy system?

A: The role of the corporate center is to worry about talent and how people do relative to each other. Workers build a set of intangibles around who they are. If they are not compensated for their value-added, they will go somewhere else.

Source: *BusinessWeek*, August 28, 2000.

---

to allow global companies the chance to build competitive advantage.[12] Rather than going to markets to exploit brands or for inexpensive resources, in Rangan's view, the smart ones are going global to learn. This shift in the intent of the structure, then, is to seek information, to create new competences. Demand in another part of the world could be a

[12] Subramanian Rangan, *A Prism on Globalization* (Fountainebleau, FR.: INSEAD, 1999).

new product trendsetter at home. So a firm's structure needs to be organized to enable learning, to share knowledge, to create opportunities to create it. Others look to companies like 3M or Procter & Gamble that allow slack time, new product champions, manager mentors—all put in place in the structure to provide resources, support, and advocacy for cross-functional collaboration leading to innovation new product development, the generation and use of new ideas. This perspective is similar to the boundaryless notion— accommodate the speed of change and therefore opportunity by freeing up historical constraints found in traditional organizational approaches. So having structures that emphasize coordination over control, that allow flexibility (are *ambidextrous*) emphasize the value and importance of informal relationships and interaction over formal systems, techniques and controls are all characteristics associated with what are seen as effective structures for the 21st century.

Redefine the Role of Corporate Headquarters from Control to Support and Coordination

The role of corporate management is multibusiness, and multinational companies increasingly face a common dilemma—how can the resource advantages of a large company be exploited, while ensuring the responsiveness and creativity found in the small companies against which each of their businesses compete? This dilemma constantly presents managers with conflicting priorities or adjustments as corporate managers:[13]

- Rigorous financial controls and reporting enable cost efficiency, resource deployment, and autonomy across different units; flexible controls are conductive to responsiveness, innovation and "boundary spanning."

- Multibusiness companies historically gain advantage by exploiting resources and capabilities across different business and markets, yet competitive advantage in the future increasingly depends on the creation of new resources and capabilities.

- Aggressive portfolio management seeking maximum shareholder value is often best achieved through independent businesses; the creation of competitive advantage increasingly requires the management—recognition and coordination—of business interdependencies.

Increasingly, globally engaged multibusiness companies are changing the role of corporate headquarters from a control, resource allocation, and performance monitoring to one of coordinator of linkages across multiple business, supporter and enabler of innovation and synergy. One way this has been done is to create an executive council comprised of top managers from each business, usually including four to five of their key managers, with the council then serving as the critical forum for corporate decision, discussions, and analysis. Exhibit 10–1, Strategy in Action, at the beginning of this chapter showed this type of forum as central to HP's radical restructuring. GE created this approach over 20 years ago in its rise to top corporate success. These councils replace the traditional corporate staff function of overseeing and evaluating various business units, replacing it instead with a forum to share business unit plans, to discuss problems and issues, to seek assistance and expertise, and to foster cooperation and innovation.

Welch's experience at GE provides a useful example. Upon becoming chairman, he viewed GE headquarters as interfering too much in GE's various businesses, generating too much paperwork, and offering minimal value added. He sought to "turn their role 180 degrees from checker, inquisitor, and authority figure to facilitator, helper, and supporter

[13] Robert M. Grant, *Contemporary Strategy Analysis* (Oxford: Blackwell, 2001), p. 503.

of GE's 13 businesses." He said, "What we do here at headquarters . . . is to multiply the resources we have, the human resources, the financial resources, and the best practices . . . Our job is to help, it's to assist, it's to make these businesses stronger, to help them grow and be more powerful." GE's Corporate Executive Council was reconstituted from predominantly a corporate level group of sector managers (which was eliminated) into a group comprised of the leaders of GE's 13 businesses and a few corporate executives. They met formally two days each quarter to discuss problems and issues and to enable cooperation and resource sharing. This has expanded to other councils throughout GE intent on greater coordination, synergy, and idea sharing.

ORGANIZATIONAL LEADERSHIP

The job of leading a company has never been more demanding, and it will only get tougher in the 21st century. The CEO will retain ultimate authority, but the corporation will depend increasingly on the skills of the CEO and a host of subordinate leaders. The accelerated pace and complexity of business will continue to force corporations to push authority down through increasingly horizontal management structures. In the future, every line manager will have to exercise leadership's prerogatives—and bear its burdens—to an extent unthinkable 20 years ago.[14]

John Kotter, a widely recognized leadership expert, predicted this evolving role of leadership in an organization when he distinguished between management and leadership:[15]

> Management is about coping with complexity. Its practices and procedures are largely a response to one of the most significant developments of the 20th century: the emergence of large organizations. Without good management, complex enterprises tend to become chaotic in ways that threaten their very existence. Good management brings a degree of order and consistency to key dimensions like the quality and profitability of products.
>
> Leadership, by contrast, is about coping with change. Part of the reason it has become so important in recent years is that the business world has become more competitive and more volatile. . . . The net result is that doing what was done yesterday, or doing it 5 percent better, is no longer a formula for success. Major changes are more and more necessary to survive and compete effectively in this new environment. More change always demands more leadership.

Organizational leadership, then, involves action on two fronts. The first is in guiding the organization to deal with constant change. This requires CEOs that embrace change, and that do so by clarifying strategic intent, that build their organization and shape their culture to fit with opportunities and challenges change affords. The second is in providing the management skill to cope with the ramifications of constant change. This means identifying and supplying the organization with operating managers prepared to provide operational leadership and vision as never before. Let's explore each of these five aspects to organization leadership.

Strategic Leadership: Embracing Change

The blending of telecommunications, computers, the Internet, and one global marketplace has increased the pace of change exponentially during the last 10 years. All business organizations are affected. Change has become an integral part of what leaders and managers deal with daily.

[14] Anthony Bianco, "The New Leadership," *BusinessWeek,* August 28, 2000.
[15] John P. Kotter, "What Leaders Really Do," *Harvard Business Review,* May–June, 1990, p. 104.

The leadership challenge is to galvanize commitment among people within an organization as well as stakeholders outside the organization to embrace change and implement strategies intended to position the organization to do so. Leaders galvanize commitment to embrace change through three interrelated activities: clarifying strategic intent, building an organization, and shaping organizational culture.

Clarifying Strategic Intent

Leaders help stakeholders embrace change by setting forth a clear vision of where the business's strategy needs to take the organization. Traditionally, the concept of vision has been a description or picture of what the company could be that accommodates the needs of all its stakeholders. The intensely competitive, rapidly changing global marketplace has refined this to be targeting a very narrowly defined strategic intent—*an articulation of a simple criterion or characterization of what the company must become to establish and sustain global leadership.* Lou Gerstner is a good example of a leader in the middle of trying to shape strategic intent. "One of the great things about this industry is that every decade or so, you get a chance to redefine the playing field," said Gerstner. "We're in that phase of redefinition right now, and winners or losers are going to emerge from it. We've got to become *the leader in 'network-centric computing.'*" It's an opportunity brought about by telecommunications-based change that will change IBM more than semiconductors did in the 1980s. Says Gerstner, "I sensed there were too many people inside IBM who wanted to fight the war we lost," referring to PCs and PC software, so now he is aggressively trying to shape network-centric computing as the strategic intent for IBM in the next century.

Clarifying strategic intent can come in many different forms. Coca-Cola's legendary former CEO and Chairman Roberto Goizueta said, "Our company is a global business system for which we raise capital to make concentrate and sell it at an operating profit. Then we pay the cost of that capital. Shareholders pocket the difference." Coke averaged 27 percent annual return on stockholder equity for 18 years under his leadership. Travelers Insurance lost $200 million in 1992. Sanford Weill assumed leadership, focusing on a short-term turnaround. Recalling that time, he said, "We sent letters to all suppliers saying: Dear Supplier, either we rebid your business or you lower your costs 15 percent." Within two years, nonpersonnel costs were cut 49 percent in addition to 15,000 jobs. Travelers made $700 million in 1996. Mr. Weill was effective in setting forth strategic intent for Travelers' turnaround. While Coke and Travelers are very different situations, their leaders were both very effective in shaping and clarifying strategic intent in a way that helped stakeholders understand what needed to be done.

Building an Organization

The previous section examined alternative structures to use in designing the organization necessary to implement strategy. Leaders spend considerable time shaping and refining their organizational structure and making it function effectively to accomplish strategic intent. Since leaders are attempting to embrace change, they are often rebuilding or remaking their organization to align it with the ever-changing environment and needs of the strategy. And since embracing change often involves overcoming resistance to change, leaders find themselves addressing problems like the following as they attempt to build or rebuild their organization:

- Ensuring a common understanding about organizational priorities.
- Clarifying responsibilities among managers and organizational units.
- Empowering newer managers and pushing authority lower in the organization.

- Uncovering and remedying problems in coordination and communication across the organization.

- Gaining the personal commitment to a shared vision from managers throughout the organization.

- Keeping closely connected with "what's going on in the organization and with its customers."

Leaders do this in many ways. Larry Bossidy, the CEO who had quadrupled Allied Signal's stock price in the last four years, spends 50 percent of his time each year flying to Allied Signal's various operations around the world meeting with managers and discussing decisions, results, and progress. Bill Gates at Microsoft spends two hours each day reading and sending E-mail to any of Microsoft's 16,000 employees that want to contact him. All managers adapt structures, create teams, implement systems, and otherwise generate ways to coordinate, integrate, and share information about what their organization is doing and might do. Others create customer advisory groups, supplier partnerships, R&D joint ventures, and other adjustments to build an adaptable, learning organization that embraces the leader's vision and strategic intent and the change driving the future opportunities facing the business. These, in addition to the fundamental structural guidelines described in the previous section for restructuring to support strategically critical activities, are the issues leaders constantly address as they attempt to build a supportive organization.

Shaping Organization Culture

Leaders know well that the values and beliefs shared throughout their organization will shape how the work of the organization is done. And when attempting to embrace accelerated change, reshaping their organization's culture is an activity that occupies considerable time for most leaders. Listen to these observations by and about MCI and its CEO Bert Roberts about competing in the rapidly changing telecommunications industry prior to its merger with WorldCom:[16]

> Says Roberts: "We run like mad and then we change directions." Indeed, the ever-changing wireless initiative (reselling wireless services rather than creating its own capacity) illustrates a trait that sets apart MCI from its competitors—a willingness to try new things, and if they don't work, to try something else. "Over at AT&T, people are afraid to make mistakes," says Jeff Kagan, president of Kagan Telecom in Atlanta, Ga. "At MCI, people are afraid not to make mistakes."

It appears that MCI CEO Bert Roberts wanted an organizational culture that was risk taking and somewhat free wheeling in order to take advantage of change in the telecommunications industry. He did this by example, by expectations felt by his managers, and in the way decision making is approached within MCI.

Leaders use reward systems, symbols, and structure among other means to shape the organization's culture. Travelers' turnaround was accomplished in part by changing its "hidebound" culture through a change in its agent reward system. Employees previously on salary with occasional bonuses were given rewards that involved substantial cash bonuses and stock options. Observed a customer and risk management director at drugmaker Becton Dickinson, "They're hungrier now. They want to make deals. They're different than the old, hidebound Travelers' culture."

[16] Alison Sprout, "MCI: Can It Become the Communications Company of the Next Century?" *Fortune,* October 2, 1995, p. 110.

BusinessWeek EXPERIENCE

- Multinational Corp.—Worked with top-notch mentors in an established company with global operations. Managed a talented and fickle staff and helped tap new markets.

- Foreign Operation LLC—A stint at a subsidiary of a U.S. company, or at a foreign operation in a local market. Exposure to different cultures, conditions, and ways of doing business.

- Startup Inc.—Helped to build a business from the ground up, assisting with everything from product development to market research. Honed entrepreneurial skills.

- Major Competitor Ltd.—Scooped up by the competition and exposed to more than one corporate culture.

EDUCATION

- Liberal Arts University—Majored in economics, but took courses in psychology (how to motivate customers and employees), foreign language (the world is a lot bigger than the 50 states), and philosophy (to seek vision and meaning in your work).

- Graduate Studies—The subject almost doesn't matter, so long as you developed your thinking and analytical skills.

EXTRACURRICULAR

- Debating (where you learned to market ideas and think on your feet).

- Sports (where you learned discipline and team work).

- Volunteer work (where you learned to step outside your own narrow world to help others).

- Travel (where you learned about different cultures).

Source: "A Résumé for the 21st Century," *BusinessWeek*, August 28, 2000.

As leaders clarify strategic intent, build an organization, and shape their organization's culture, they look to one key element to help—their management team throughout their organization. As Allied Signal's visible CEO Larry Bossidy candidly observed when asked about how after 38 years at General Electric and now at Allied Signal with seemingly drab businesses he could expect exciting growth: "There's no such thing as a mature market. What we need is mature executives who can find ways to grow." Leaders look to managers they need to execute strategy as another source of leadership to accept risk and cope with the complexity that change brings about. So assignment of key managers becomes a leadership tool.

Recruiting and Developing Talented Operational Leadership

As we noted at the beginning of this section on Organizational Leadership, the accelerated pace and complexity of business will increase pressure on corporations to push authority down in their organizations ultimately meaning that every line manager will have to exercise leadership's prerogatives to an extent unthinkable a generation earlier. They will each be global managers, change agents, strategists, motivators, strategic decision-makers, innovators, and collaborators if the business is to survive and prosper. Exhibit 10–10, Strategy in Action, provides an interesting perspective on this reality showing *BusinessWeek*'s version of a résumé for the typical 21st century operating manager every company will be looking for in today's fast-paced, global marketplace.

Today's need for fluid, learning organizations capable of rapid response, sharing, and cross-cultural synergy place incredible demands on young managers to bring important competencies to the organization. Exhibit 10–11 looks at the needs organizations look to managers to meet, and then identifies the corresponding competencies

EXHIBIT 10–11
What Competencies Should Managers Possess?

Source: Ruth L. Williams and Joseph P. Cothrel, "Building Tomorrow's Leaders Today," *Strategy and Leadership* 26 (September–October 1997), pp. 17–23.

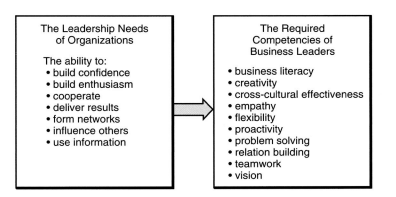

The Leadership Needs of Organizations

The ability to:
• build confidence
• build enthusiasm
• cooperate
• deliver results
• form networks
• influence others
• use information

The Required Competencies of Business Leaders

• business literacy
• creativity
• cross-cultural effectiveness
• empathy
• flexibility
• proactivity
• problem solving
• relation building
• teamwork
• vision

managers would need to do so. Ruth Williams and Joseph Cothrel drew this conclusion in their research about competencies needed from managers in today's fast changing business environment:[17]

> Today's competitive environment requires a different set of management competencies than we traditionally associate with the role. The balance has clearly shifted from attributes traditionally thought of as masculine (strong decision making, leading the troops, driving strategy, waging competitive battle) to more feminine qualities (listening, relationship-building, and nurturing). The model today is not so much "take it on your shoulders" as it is to "create the environment that will enable others to carry part of the burden." The focus is on unlocking the organization's human asset potential.

Researcher David Goleman addressed the question of what types of personality attributes generate the type of competencies described in Exhibit 10–11. His research suggested that a set of four characteristics commonly referred to as emotional intelligence play a key role in bringing the competencies needed from today's desirable manager:[18]

• *Self-awareness* in terms of the ability to read and understand one's emotions and assess one's strengths and weaknesses, underlain by the confidence that stems from positive self-worth.

• *Self-management* in terms of control, integrity, conscientiousness, initiative, and achievement orientation.

• *Social awareness* in relation to sensing others' emotions (empathy), reading the organization (organizational awareness), and recognizing customers' needs (service orientation).

• *Social skills* in relation to influencing and inspiring others; communicating, collaborating, and building relationships with others; and managing change and conflict.

One additional perspective on the role of organizational leadership and management selection is found in the work of Bartlett and Ghoshal. Their study of several of the most successful global companies in the last decade suggests that combining flexible responsiveness with integration and innovation requires rethinking the management role and the distribution of management roles within a 21st century company. They see three critical

[17] Ruth Williams and Joseph Cothrel, "Building Tomorrow's Leaders Today," *Strategy and Leadership* 26 (September–October 1997), p. 21.
[18] D. Goleman, "What Makes a Leader?," *Harvard Business Review* (November–December 1998), pp. 93–102.

EXHIBIT 10–12
Management Processes and Levels of Management

Source: C. A. Bartlett and S. Ghoshal, "The Myth of the General Manager: New Personal Competencies for New Management Roles," *California Management Review* 40 (Fall 1997); R. M. Grant, *Contemporary Strategy Analysis* (Oxford: Blackwell, 2001), p. 529.

Front-Line Management	Middle Management	Top Management
Attracting resources and capabilities and developing the business	**RENEWAL PROCESS** Developing operating managers and supporting their activities. Maintaining organizational trust	Providing institutional leadership through shaping and embedding corporate purpose and challenging embedded assumptions
Managing operational interdependencies and personal networks	**INTEGRATION PROCESS** Linking skills, knowledge, and resources across units. Reconciling short-term performance and long-term ambition	Creating corporate direction. Developing and nurturing organizational values
Creating and pursuing opportunities. Managing continuous performance improvement	**ENTREPRENEURIAL PROCESS** Reviewing, developing, and supporting initiatives	Establishing performance standards

management roles: the *entrepreneurial process* (decisions about opportunities to pursue and resource deployment), the *integration process* (building and deploying organizational capabilities), and the *renewal process* (shaping organizational purpose and enabling change). Traditionally viewed as the domain of top management, their research suggests that these functions need to be shared and distributed across three management levels as suggested in Exhibit 10–12.[19]

ORGANIZATIONAL CULTURE

Organizational culture is the set of important assumptions (often unstated) that members of an organization share in common. Every organization has its own culture. An organization's culture is similar to an individual's personality—an intangible yet ever-present theme that provides meaning, direction, and the basis for action. In much the same way as personality influences the behavior of an individual, the shared assumptions (beliefs and values) among a firm's members influence opinions and actions within that firm.

A member of an organization can simply be aware of the organization's beliefs and values without sharing them in a personally significant way. Those beliefs and values have more personal meaning if the member views them as a guide to appropriate behavior in the organization and, therefore, complies with them. The member becomes fundamentally committed to the beliefs and values when he or she internalizes them; that is, comes to hold them as personal beliefs and values. In this case, the corresponding behavior is *intrinsically rewarding* for the member—the member derives personal satisfaction from his or her actions in the organization because those actions are congruent with corresponding personal beliefs and values. *Assumptions become shared assumptions through internalization among an organization's individual members.* And those shared, internalized beliefs and values shape the content and account for the strength of an organization's culture.

[19] C. A. Barlett and S. Ghoshal, "The Myth of the General Manager: New Personal Competencies for New Management Roles," *California Management Review* 40 (Fall 1997), pp. 92–116; and "Beyond Structure to Process," *Harvard Business Review* (January–February 1995).

Leaders typically attempt to manage and create distinct cultures through a variety of ways. Some of the most common ways are as follows:

Emphasize Key Themes or Dominant Values   Businesses build strategies around distinct competitive advantages they possess or seek. Quality, differentiation, cost advantages, and speed are four key sources of competitive advantage. So insightful leaders nurture key themes or dominant values within their organization that reinforce competitive advantages they seek to maintain or build. Key themes or dominant values may center around wording in an advertisement. They are often found in internal company communications. They are most often found as a new vocabulary used by company personnel to explain "who we are." At Xerox, the key themes include respect for the individual and services to the customer. At Procter & Gamble (P&G), the overarching value is product quality; McDonald's uncompromising emphasis on QSCV—quality, service, cleanliness, and value—through meticulous attention to detail is legendary; Delta Airlines is driven by the "family feeling" theme, which builds a team spirit and nurtures each employee's cooperative attitude toward others, cheerful outlook toward life, and pride in a job well done. Du Pont's safety orientation—a report of every accident must be on the chairman's desk within 24 hours—has resulted in a safety record that was 17 times better than the chemical industry average and 68 times better than the all-manufacturing average.

Encourage Dissemination of Stories and Legends about Core Values   Companies with strong cultures are enthusiastic collectors and tellers of stories, anecdotes, and legends in support of basic beliefs. Frito-Lay's zealous emphasis on customer service is reflected in frequent stories about potato chip route salespeople who have slogged through sleet, mud, hail, snow, and rain to uphold the 99.5 percent service level to customers in which the entire company takes great pride. Milliken (a textile leader) holds "sharing" rallies once every quarter at which teams from all over the company swap success stories and ideas. Typically, more than 100 teams make five-minute presentations over a two-day period. Every rally is designed around a major theme, such as quality, cost reduction, or customer service. No criticisms are allowed, and awards are given to reinforce this institutionalized approach to storytelling. L. L. Bean tells customer service stories; 3M tells innovation stories; P&G, Johnson & Johnson, IBM, and Maytag tell quality stories. These stories are very important in developing an organizational culture, because organization members identify strongly with them and come to share the beliefs and values they support.

Institutionalize Practices That Systematically Reinforce Desired Beliefs and Values   Companies with strong cultures are clear on what their beliefs and values need to be and take the process of shaping those beliefs and values very seriously. Most important, the values these companies espouse undergird the strategies they employ. For example, McDonald's has a yearly contest to determine the best hamburger cooker in its chain. First, there is a competition to determine the best hamburger cooker in each store; next, the store winners compete in regional championships; finally, the regional winners compete in the "All-American" contest. The winners, who are widely publicized throughout the company, get trophies and All-American patches to wear on their McDonald's uniforms.

Adapt Some Very Common Themes in Their Own Unique Ways   The most typical beliefs that shape organizational culture include (1) a belief in being the best (or, as at GE, "better than the best"); (2) a belief in superior quality and service; (3) a belief in the importance of people as individuals and a faith in their ability to make a strong contribution; (4) a belief in the importance of the details of execution, the nuts and bolts of doing the job well; (5) a belief that customers should reign supreme; (6) a belief in inspiring people to do their best, whatever their ability; (7) a belief in the importance of informal communication; and (8) a belief that growth and profits are essential to a company's well-being. Every company implements these beliefs differently (to fit its particular situation), and every company's values are the handiwork of one or two legendary figures in leadership positions. Accordingly, every company has a distinct culture that it believes no other company can copy successfully. And in companies with strong cultures, managers and workers either accept the norms of the culture or opt out from the culture and leave the company.

The stronger a company's culture and the more that culture is directed toward customers and markets, the less the company uses policy manuals, organization charts, and detailed rules and procedures to enforce discipline and norms. The reason is that the guiding values inherent in the culture convey in crystal-clear fashion what everybody is supposed to do in most situations. Poorly performing companies often have strong cultures. However, their cultures are dysfunctional, being focused on internal politics or operating by the numbers as opposed to emphasizing customers and the people who make and sell the product.

Managing Organizational Culture in a Global Organization[20]

The reality of today's global organizations is that organizational culture must recognize cultural diversity. *Social norms* create differences across national boundaries that influence how people interact, read personal cues, and otherwise interrelate socially. *Values* and *attitudes* about similar circumstances also vary from country to country. Where individualism is central to a North American's value structure, the needs of the group dominate the value structure of their Japanese counterparts. *Religion* is yet another source of cultural differences. Holidays, practices, and belief structures differ in very fundamental ways that must be taken into account as one attempts to shape organizational culture in a global setting. Finally, *education,* or ways people are accustomed to learning, differ across national borders. Formal classroom learning in the United States may teach things that are only learned via apprenticeship in other cultures. Since the process of shaping an organizational culture often involves considerable "education," leaders should be sensitive to global differences in approaches to education to make sure their cultural education efforts are effective. The discussion case on Hewlett-Packard at the end of this chapter provides some relevant examples of how CEO Carly Fiorina was trying to radically alter HP's organization's culture in 2001.

Managing the Strategy-Culture Relationship

Managers find it difficult to think through the relationship between a firm's culture and the critical factors on which strategy depends. They quickly recognize, however, that key components of the firm—structure, staff, systems, people, style—influence the ways in which key managerial tasks are executed and how critical management relationships are formed. And implementation of a new strategy is largely concerned with adjustments in these components to accommodate the perceived needs of the strategy. Consequently, managing the strategy-culture relationship requires sensitivity to the interaction between the changes necessary to implement the new strategy and

---

[20] Differing backgrounds, often referred to as *cultural diversity,* is something that most managers will certainly see more of, both because of the growing cultural diversity domestically and the obvious diversification of cultural backgrounds that result from global acquisitions and mergers. For example, Harold Epps, manager of DEC's computer keyboard plant in Boston, manages 350 employees representing 44 countries of origin and 19 languages.

EXHIBIT 10–13
Managing the Strategy-Culture Relationship

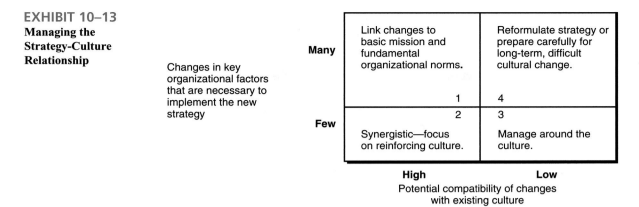

		High	Low
Changes in key organizational factors that are necessary to implement the new strategy	**Many**	Link changes to basic mission and fundamental organizational norms. 1	Reformulate strategy or prepare carefully for long-term, difficult cultural change. 4
	Few	2 Synergistic—focus on reinforcing culture.	3 Manage around the culture.

Potential compatibility of changes with existing culture

the compatibility or "fit" between those changes and the firm's culture. Exhibit 10–13 provides a simple framework for managing the strategy-culture relationship by identifying four basic situations a firm might face.

Link to Mission

A firm in cell 1 is faced with a situation in which implementing a new strategy requires several changes in structure, systems, managerial assignments, operating procedures, or other fundamental aspects of the firm. However, most of the changes are potentially compatible with the existing organizational culture. Firms in this situation usually have a tradition of effective performance and are either seeking to take advantage of a major opportunity or are attempting to redirect major product-market operations consistent with proven core capabilities. Such firms are in a very promising position: they can pursue a strategy requiring major changes but still benefit from the power of cultural reinforcement.

Four basic considerations should be emphasized by firms seeking to manage a strategy-culture relationship in this context. First, *key changes should be visibly linked to the basic company mission.* Since the company mission provides a broad official foundation for the organizational culture, top executives should use all available internal and external forums to reinforce the message that the changes are inextricably linked to it. Second, *emphasis should be placed on the use of existing personnel* where possible to fill positions created to implement the new strategy. Existing personnel embody the shared values and norms that help ensure cultural compatibility as major changes are implemented. Third, *care should be taken if adjustments in the reward system are needed.* These adjustments should be consistent with the current reward system. If, for example, a new product-market thrust requires significant changes in the way sales are made, and, therefore, in incentive compensation, common themes (e.g., incentive oriented) should be emphasized. In this way, current and future reward approaches are related and the changes in the reward system are justified (encourage development of less familiar markets). Fourth, *key attention should be paid to the changes that are least compatible with the current culture,* so current norms are not disrupted. For example, a firm may choose to subcontract an important step in a production process because that step would be incompatible with the current culture.

IBM's strategy in entering the Internet-based market is an illustration. Serving this radically different market required numerous organizational changes. To maintain maximum compatibility with its existing culture while doing so, IBM went to considerable public and internal effort to link its new Internet focus with its long-standing mission. Numerous messages relating the network-centric computing to IBM's tradition of top-quality service appeared on television and in magazines, and every IBM manager was encouraged to go online. Where feasible, IBM personnel were used to fill the new positions created to implement the strategy. But because the software requirements were not compatible with IBM's current operations, virtually all of its initial efforts were linked to newly acquired Lotus Notes.

Maximize Synergy

A firm in cell 2 needs only a few organizational changes to implement its new strategy, and those changes are potentially quite compatible with its current culture. A firm in this situation should emphasize two broad themes: (1) *take advantage of the situation to reinforce and solidify the current culture* and (2) *use this time of relative stability to remove organizational roadblocks to the desired culture.* Holiday Inns' move into casino gambling required a few major organizational changes. Holiday Inns saw casinos as resort locations requiring lodging, dining, and gambling/entertainment services. It only had to incorporate gambling/entertainment expertise into its management team, which was already capable of managing the lodging and dining requirements of casino (or any other) resort locations. It successfully inculcated this single major change by selling the change internally as completely compatible with its mission of providing high-quality accommodations for business and leisure travelers. The resignation of Roy Clymer, its CEO, removed an organizational roadblock, legitimizing a culture that placed its highest priority on quality service to the middle-to-upper-income business traveler, rather than a culture that placed its highest priority on family-oriented service. The latter priority was fast disappearing from Holiday Inns' culture, with the encouragement of most of the firm's top management, but its disappearance had not yet been fully sanctioned because of Clymer's personal beliefs. His voluntary departure helped solidify the new values that top management wanted.

Manage around the Culture

A firm in cell 3 must make a few major organizational changes to implement its new strategy, but these changes are potentially inconsistent with the firm's current organizational culture. The critical question for a firm in this situation is whether it can make the changes with a reasonable chance of success.

A firm can manage around the culture in various ways: create a separate firm or division; use task forces, teams, or program coordinators; subcontract; bring in an outsider; or sell out. These are a few of the available options, but the key idea is to create a method of achieving the change desired that avoids confronting the incompatible cultural norms. As cultural resistance diminishes, the change may be absorbed into the firm.

In the Southeast, Rich's was a highly successful, quality-oriented department store chain that served higher income customers in several southeastern locations. With Wal-Mart and Kmart experiencing rapid growth in the sale of mid- to low-priced merchandise, Rich's decided to serve this market as well. Finding such merchandise inconsistent with the successful values and norms of its traditional business, it created a separate business called Richway to tap this growth area in retailing. Through a new store network, it was able to *manage around its culture.* Both Rich's and Richway experienced solid regional success, though their cultures are radically different in some respects.

BusinessWeek Behind his gentlemanly demeanor, Jorma Ollila, CEO of Nokia Corp., is a man of extremes. As his wife, Liisa Annikki, tells it, her husband fires up the Finnish sauna a good 15 degrees warmer than she likes it, all the way to 212F—hot enough to boil a pot of tea. It was late March, ice was still floating on Lake Pukala north of Helsinki, and the kids challenged their father to dive in. Emerging from the sauna, Ollila paused, then plunged naked into the icy lake.

Ollila, a 47-year-old former banker, lives by the plunge. He believes people get comfy and complacent and that it takes a dive into the unknown, or a push, to tap into their strongest instincts—those that guide survival. Six years ago, as an untested CEO, he bet the 133-year-old Finnish conglomerate on cellular phones, challenging rivals Motorola Inc. and L. M. Ericsson. In the struggle that ensued, Ollila's Finns outdid themselves. Fast and focused, with a canny eye for design, Nokia wrested market share from entrenched competitors and emerged as the most profitable player in the industry.

The company's startling climb has provided the Continent with something it was sorely lacking: a new high-tech superstar. What's more, that triumph is in a crucial technology—mobile communications. That's the next frontier for the Internet, and one of the few areas where Europe is racing ahead of the U.S.

Smack in the middle of Nokia's success stands Ollila, whose name is accented on the "O." He's a self-avowed nontechie who hasn't even put plumbing in his lakeside cabin. But it's Ollila who is improvising a brand-new style of high-tech management. Refuting the common "slip-and-you-die" thinking, Ollila sticks with slip and you grow.

In a sense, this model is a variation on the man's freezing plunge at the lake. Ollila views disasters as education, and he fires almost no one. While others rush to the world's high-tech hot spots, Ollila created one of his own in an underpopulated stretch between Russia and the Arctic Circle. From

there, he nurtures a network of suppliers around the globe. And just when Nokia seems to be performing in top gear, as it is now, Ollila risks disarray by switching the jobs of all his top managers.

Trouble is, Nokia isn't the only one searching for a digital El Dorado in the form of convergence. While Ollila's sharp and nimble Finns ambushed Ericsson and Motorola in the telephone market, they're now converging right into a Silicon Valley traffic jam. To sell pocket-size Net devices, Ollila must maneuver his way among the brightest stars of America's high-tech economy, where everyone from Microsoft Corp. to 3Com Corp. wants to own a piece of the same business.

And few of them are convinced that this next revolution is going to be conducted through mobile telephones. Who's to say, after all, that mobile Web surfers won't use palmtop computers equipped with telephone chips? And there's always the chance the public will shrug at the entire selection of these tiny devices. "You have to think hard," says Richard Howard, director of the wireless research lab at Lucent Technologies Inc.'s Bell Labs. "Do you really need full-motion video in a car phone?"

So despite his laid-back manner, Ollila has no time to catch his breath. He must prepare Nokia for a metamorphosis. Like a snake growing out of its skin, the company has to emerge sleek and strong in the next generation, when simple handsets are stocking stuffers and mobile phones molt into powerful new be-alls. Ollila's tried-and-true motivator is the plunge. In the past, there have been plenty of crises around which to rally the team. Ollila recalls them with great fondness.

So how does Ollila conjure up a sense of fear and urgency? For starters, on July 1, he reached into Nokia's sparkling glass-and-steel headquarters on the shore of the Baltic, took the inner circle of four fortysomething Finns who

(continued)

Reformulate the Strategy or Culture

A firm in cell 4 faces the most difficult challenge in managing the strategy-culture relationship. To implement its new strategy, such a firm must make organizational changes that are incompatible with its current, usually entrenched, values and norms. A firm in this situation faces the complex, expensive, and often long-term challenge of changing its culture; it is a challenge that borders on impossible. Exhibit 10–14, Strategy in Action, describes the exciting success at Finland's Nokia where CEO Jorma Ollila transformed a 133-year-old company into a world technology leader.

When a strategy requires massive organizational change and engenders cultural resistance, a firm should determine whether reformulation of the strategy is appropriate. Are all of the organizational changes really necessary? Is there any real expectation that the run the company's main divisions, and switched all their jobs. His infrastructure executive, Matti Alahuhta, was rotated from his customer-schmoozing position into the marketing vortex of handsets. Asia-Pacific chief Sari Baldauf was told to head up infrastructure, as well as development on Third Generation. Handset chief Pekka Ala-Pietila, who oversaw the spectacular development of the 6100s, became vice-chairman, charged with exploring new ventures. Later this year, Ollila will bring back his chief executive for U.S. operations, Olli-Pekka Kallasvuo, to be chief financial officer. In short, except for Ollila, every top person at the company is getting ready for a brand-new job—all in the name of "removing people from their comfort areas," as Ollila puts it.

Despite the upheaval, Ollila is determined to preserve a corporate culture in Helsinki dominated by Finns. He jokes about this, explaining that the best brains in Silicon Valley, London, or Hong Kong recoil from moving to icy Helsinki, where it's dark all winter. The trick is to give his new recruits autonomy and let them pursue their careers in Nokia's big markets, where taxes are far lower and the lakes thaw by Easter. But Ollila also believes that Nokia draws strength from its understated collegiality, which he associates with the Finnish character. "We don't snap our suspenders," he says in his fluent British English.

The culture Ollila struggles to preserve goes back a ways. Founded in 1865 in a mill town 100 miles north of Helsinki, Nokia has made just about everything at one time or another. Many Finns still associate the name with the rubber snow boots they wore as children. A hundred years later, Nokia had grown into a regional conglomerate.

While Nokia, Ericsson, and Motorola are all preparing to battle one another with Internet phones and intelligent base stations, they've been forced to join forces on the Third Generation. Their worst nightmare: All the new features arrive on schedule—on palmtop computers instead of cell phones. To avoid that scenario, in June the three companies formed a London joint venture with British computer maker Psion PLC. The deal establishes a common software platform—Psion's operating system—for the coming generation of mobile Net devices.

In linking up with tiny Psion, Ollila and his competitors jilted none other than William H. Gates III. Earlier in the year, the Microsoft chairman toured Europe, plugging Microsoft's Windows CE software for Third Generation machines. He lost out. His software, phonemakers complained, was wrenched from the PC and not created for next-generation machines. Gates's loss, though, means that cellular phones could eventually be battling a slew of Microsoft-powered handheld devices in the same mobile market.

Ollila claims not to be worried. "The market will be big enough for all of us," he says. But don't misread the man. He's plenty competitive: He can recite the exact ages of his two sons when they finally beat him in tennis. When it comes time to plunge, Ollila is extreme—a man of fire and ice, leading Nokia into cyberspace.

Source: "Nokia," *BusinessWeek,* August 10, 1998.

changes will be acceptable and successful? If these answers are yes, then massive changes in management personnel are often necessary. AT&T offered early retirement to over 20,000 managers as part of a massive recreation of its culture to go along with major strategic changes in recent years. If the answer to these questions is no, the firm might reformulate its strategic plan so as to make it more consistent with established organizational norms and practices.

Merrill Lynch faced the challenge of strategy-culture incompatibility in the last decade. Seeking to remain number one in the newly deregulated financial services industry, it chose to pursue a product development strategy in its brokerage business. Under this strategy, Merrill Lynch would sell a broader range of investment products to a more diverse customer base and would integrate other financial services, such as real estate sales, into the Merrill Lynch organization. The new strategy could succeed only if Merrill Lynch's traditionally service-oriented brokerage network became sales and marketing oriented. Initial efforts to implement the strategy generated substantial resistance from Merrill Lynch's highly successful brokerage network. The strategy was fundamentally inconsistent with long-standing cultural norms at Merrill Lynch that emphasized personalized service and very close broker-client relationships. Merrill Lynch ultimately divested its real estate operation, reintroduced specialists that supported broker/retailers, and refocused its brokers more narrowly on basic client investment needs.

Summary

This chapter examined the idea that a key aspect of implementing a strategy is the *institutionalization* of the strategy so it permeates daily decisions and actions in a manner consistent with long-term strategic success. The "recipe" that binds strategy and organization involves three key ingredients: *organizational structure, leadership,* and *culture.*

Five fundamental organizational structures were examined, and the advantages and disadvantages of each were identified. Institutionalizing a strategy requires a good strategy-structure fit. This chapter dealt with how this requirement often is overlooked until performance becomes inadequate and then indicated the conditions under which the various structures would be appropriate.

Organizational leadership is essential to effective strategy implementation. The CEO plays a critical role in this regard. Assignment of key managers, particularly within the top-management team, is an important aspect of organizational leadership. Deciding whether to promote insiders or hire outsiders is often a central leadership issue in strategy implementation. This chapter showed how this decision could be made in a manner that would best institutionalize the new strategy.

Organizational culture has been recognized as a pervasive influence on organizational life. Organizational culture, which is the shared beliefs and values of an organization's members, may be a major help or hindrance to strategy implementation. This chapter discussed an approach to managing the strategy-culture fit. It identified four fundamentally different strategy-culture situations and provided recommendations for managing the strategy-culture fit in each of these situations.

The chapter concluded with an examination of structure, leadership, and culture for 21st century companies. Networked organizations, with intense customer focus, and alliances are keys to success. Talent-focused acquisitions, success sharing, and leaders as coaches round out the future success scenario.

Questions for Discussion

1. What key structural considerations must be incorporated into strategy implementation? Why does structural change often lag a change in strategy?

2. Which organizational structure is most appropriate for successful strategy implementation? Explain how state of development affects your answer.

3. Why is leadership an important element in strategy implementation? Find an example in a major business periodical of the CEO's key role in strategy implementation.

4. Under what conditions would it be more appropriate to fill a key management position with someone from outside the firm when a qualified insider is available?

5. What is organizational culture? Why is it important? Explain two different situations a firm might face in managing the strategy-culture relationship.

Chapter 10 Discussion Case

BusinessWeek

Carly Fiorina's Bold Management Experiment at HP

1   Since taking over as chief executive of Hewlett-Packard Co., Carleton S. "Carly" Fiorina has pushed the company to the limit to recapture the form that made it a management icon for six decades. Last November, it looked like she might have pushed too hard. After weeks of promising that HP would meet its quarterly numbers, Fiorina got grim news from the finance department. While sales growth beat expectations, profits had fallen $230 million short. The culprit, in large part, was Fiorina's aggressive management makeover. With HP's 88,000 staffers adjusting to the biggest reorganization in the company's history, expenses had risen out of control. And since new computer systems to track the changes weren't yet in place, HP's bean counters didn't detect the problem until 10 days after the quarter was over. "It was frantic. The financial folks were running all around looking for more dollars," says one HP manager.

2   One might expect a CEO in this spot to dial down on such a massive overhaul. Not Fiorina. After crunching numbers in an all-day session on Saturday and offering apologies for missing the forecast to HP's board at an emergency meeting Sunday, Fiorina told analysts she was raising HP's sales growth target for fiscal 2001 from 15% to as much as 17%. "We hit a speed bump—a big speed bump—this quarter," she said in a speech broadcast to employees a few days later. "But does it mean, 'Gee, this is too hard?' No way. In blackjack, you double down when you have an increasing probability of winning. And we're going to double down."

3   The stakes couldn't be higher—both for Fiorina and for the Silicon Valley pioneer started in a Palo Alto garage in 1938. Just as founders Bill Hewlett and David Packard broke the mold back then by eliminating hierarchies and introducing innovations such as profit-sharing and cubicles, Fiorina is betting on an approach so radical that experts say it has never been tried before at a company of HP's size and complexity. What's more, management gurus haven't a clue as to whether it will work—though the early signs suggest it may be too much, too fast. Not content to tackle one problem at a time, Fiorina

is out to transform all aspects of HP at once, current economic slowdown be damned. That means strategy, structure, culture, compensation—everything from how to spark innovation to how to streamline internal processes. Such sweeping change is tough anywhere, and doubly so at tradition-bound HP. The reorganization will be "hard to do—and there's not much DNA for it at HP," says Jay R. Galbraith, professor at the Institute for Management Development in Lausanne, Switzerland.

4   Fiorina believes she has little choice. Her goal is to mix up a powerful cocktail of changes that will lift HP from its slow-growth funk of recent years before the company suffers a near-death experience similar to the one IBM endured 10 years ago and that Xerox and others are going through now. The conundrum for these behemoths: how to put the full force of the company behind winning in today's fiercely competitive technology business when they must also cook up brand-new megamarkets? It's a riddle, says Fiorina, that she can solve only by sweeping action that will ready HP for the next stage of the technology revolution, when companies latch on to the Internet to transform their operations. "We looked in the mirror and saw a great company that was becoming a failure," Fiorina told employees. "This is the vision Bill and Dave would have had if they were sitting here today."

5   At its core lies a conviction that HP must become "ambidextrous." Like a constantly mutating organism, the new HP is supposed to strike a balance: It should excel at short-term execution while pursuing long-term visions that create new markets. It should increase sales and profits in harmony rather than sacrifice one to gain the other. And HP will emphasize it all—technology, software, and consulting in every corner of computing, combining the product excellence of a Sun Microsystems Inc. with IBM's services strength.

6   To achieve this, Fiorina has dismantled the decentralized approach honed throughout HP's 64-year history. Until last year, HP was a collection of 83 independently run units, each focused on a product such as scanners or security software. Fiorina has collapsed those into four sprawling

organizations. See Exhibit 10–1, Strategy in Action, for a diagram showing Fiorina's structural changes at HP). One so-called back-end unit develops and builds computers, and another focuses on printers and imaging equipment. The back-end divisions hand products off to two "front-end" sales and marketing groups that peddle the wares—one to consumers, the other to corporations. The theory: The new structure will boost collaboration, giving sales and marketing execs a direct pipeline to engineers so products are developed from the ground up to solve customer problems. This is the first time a company with thousands of product lines and scores of businesses has attempted a front-back approach, a strategy that requires laser focus and superb coordination.

7   Just as radical is Fiorina's plan for unleashing creativity. She calls it "inventing at the intersection." Until now, HP has made stand-alone products, from $20 ink cartridges to $3 million Internet servers. By tying them all together, HP hopes to sniff out new markets at the junctions where the products meet. The new HP, she says, will excel at dreaming up new e-services and then making the gear to deliver them. By yearend, for example, HP customers should be able to call up a photo stored on the Net using a handheld gizmo and then wirelessly zap it to a nearby printer. To create such opportunities, HP has launched three "cross-company initiatives"—wireless services, digital imaging, and commercial printing—that are the first formal effort to get all of HP's warring tribes working together.

8   Will her grand plan work? It's still the petri-dish phase of the experiment, so it's too soon to say. But the initial results are troubling. While she had early success, the reorganization started to run aground nine months ago. Cushy commissions intended to light a fire under HP's sales force boosted sales, but mostly for low-margin products that did little for corporate profits. A more fundamental problem stems directly from the front-back structure: It doesn't clearly assign responsibility for profits and losses, meaning it's tough to diagnose and fix earnings screwups—especially since no individual manager will take the heat for missed numbers. And with staffers in 120 countries, redrawing the lines of communication and getting veterans of rival divisions to work together is proving nettlesome.

"The people who deal with Carly directly feel very empowered, but everyone else is running around saying, 'What do we do now?'" says one HP manager. Another problem: Much of the burden of running HP lands squarely on Fiorina's shoulders. Some insiders and analysts say she needs a second-in-command to manage day-to-day operations. "She's playing CEO, visionary, and COO, and that's too hard to do," says Sanford C. Bernstein analyst Toni Sacconaghi.

9   Fiorina gets frosty at the notion that her restructuring is hitting snags. "This is a multiyear effort," she says. "I always would have characterized Year Two as harder than Year One because this is when the change really gets binding. I actually think our fourth-quarter miss and the current slowing economy are galvanizing us. When things are going well, you can convince yourself that change isn't as necessary as you thought." Fiorina also dismisses the need for a COO: "I'm running the business the way I think it ought to be run."

10   If Fiorina pulls this off, she'll be tech's newest hero. The 46-year-old CEO already has earned top marks for zeroing in on HP's core problems—and for having the courage to tackle them head-on. And she did raise HP's growth to 15% in fiscal 2000 from 7% in 1999. If she keeps it up, a reinvigorated HP could become a blueprint for others trying to transform technology dinosaurs into dynamos. "There isn't a major technology company in the world that has solved the problem she's trying to address, and we're all going to learn from her experience," says Stanford Business School professor Robert Burgelman.

11   Fiorina needs results—and fast. For all its internal changes, HP today is more dependent than ever on maturing markets. While PCs and printers contributed 69% of HP's sales and three-fourths of its earnings last year, those businesses are expected to slow to single-digit growth in coming years, with falling profitability. Last year, HP was tied with Compaq as the leading U.S. maker of home PCs and sold 60% of home printers, according to IDC. Those numbers make it hard to boost market share. In corporate computing—where the company is banking on huge growth—HP has made only minor strides toward capturing lucrative business such as consulting services, storage, and software. And the failure of Fiorina's $16 billion bid to buy the

consulting arm of PricewaterhouseCoopers LLP leaves her without a strong services division to help transform HP from high-tech's old reliable box-maker into a Net powerhouse, offering e-business solutions.

12   CAREENING. With the tech sector slowing in 2001, this may be the wrong time to make a miracle. In January, HP said its revenue and earnings would fall short of targets for the first quarter, and Fiorina cut her sales-growth estimates to about 5%—a far cry from the mid-teens she had been promising. In late January, the company announced it was laying off 1,700 marketing workers. HP's stock, which has dropped from a split-adjusted $67 in July to less than $40, is 19% below its level when Fiorina took the helm.

13   It's not just Fiorina's lofty goals that are so radical, but the way she's trying to achieve them. She's careening along at Net speed, ordering changes she hopes are right—but which may need adjustment later. That goes even for the front-back management structure. "When you sail, you don't get there in a straight line," Fiorina argues. "You adjust your course to fit the times and the current conditions." Insiders say that before the current slowdown, she expected HP to clock sales growth of 20% in 2002 and thereafter—a record clip for a $50 billion company. Fiorina won't confirm specific growth goals but says the downturn doesn't change her long-term plan.

14   Her overambitious targets have cost her credibility with Wall Street, too. While she earned kudos for increasing sales growth and meeting expectations early on, she has damaged her reputation by trying to put a positive spin on more troubled recent quarters. Hewlett Packard insiders say that while former CEO Lewis E. Platt spent a few hours reviewing the results at the end of each quarter, Fiorina holds marathon, multiday sessions to figure out how to cast financials in the best light. Not everyone is impressed. "I grew up with HP calculators, but they don't work right anymore," jokes Edward J. Zander, president of rival Sun Microsystems. "Everything they mention seems to be growing 50%, but the company as a whole only grows 10%." Fiorina says HP has accurately reported all segments of its business and that she makes no special effort to spin the results. "The calculators still work fine," she says.

15   Fiorina was well aware of the challenges when she joined HP, but she also saw the huge untapped potential. She had grown to admire the company while working as an HP intern during her years studying medieval history at Stanford University. Later, as president of the largest division of telecommunications equipment maker Lucent Technologies Inc., she learned the frustrations of buying products from highly decentralized HP. When HP's board asked her to take over, she jumped at the chance to show off her management chops. While she had spearheaded the company's spin-off from AT&T in 1996, then CEO Richard A. McGinn got all the credit.

16   "PERFECTLY POSITIONED." Soon after signing on, Fiorina decided the front-back structure was the salve for HP's ills. With the help of consultants, she tailored the framework to HP's needs and developed a multiyear plan for rejuvenating the company. Step One would be to shake up complacent troops. Next, Fiorina set out to refine a strategy and "reinvent" HP from the ground up, a task she expected would take most of 2000. Only then—meaning about now—would HP be ready to unleash its potential as a top supplier of technology for companies revamping their businesses around the Web.

17   That's where the cross-company initiatives come in. So far, HP has identified three. There's the digital-imaging effort to make photos, drawings, and videos as easy to create, store, and send as e-mail. A commercial-printing thrust aims to capture business that now goes to offset presses. And a wireless services effort might, say, turn a wristwatch into a full-function Net device that tracks the wearer's heart rate and transmits that info to a hospital. "All the great technology companies got great by seeing trends and getting there first—and they're always misunderstood initially," says Fiorina. "We think we see where the market is going and that we're perfectly positioned."

18   The first chapters of Fiorina's plan came off as scripted. When she replaced 33-year HP veteran Platt on a balmy July day in 1999, Fiorina swept in with a rush of fresh thinking and made headway—for a time. She ordered unit chiefs to justify why HP should continue in that line of business. And she gave her marketers just six weeks to revamp advertising and relaunch the brand. After a few

days on the job, she met with researchers who feared that Fiorina—a career salesperson—would move HP away from its engineering roots. She wowed them. In sharp contrast to the phlegmatic Platt, Fiorina moved through the crowd, microphone in hand, exhorting them to change the world. "There was a lot of skepticism about her," says Stan Williams, director of HP's quantum science research program. "But she was fantastic."

19   If she was a hit with engineers, it took a bit longer to win over HP's executive council. For years, these top execs had measured HP's performance against its ability to meet internal goals, but rarely compared its growth rates to those of rivals. In August, Fiorina rocked their cozy world when she shared details of her reorganization—and of her sky-high growth targets. She went to a whiteboard and compared HP with better-performing competitors: Dell Computer in PCs, Sun in servers, and IBM in services. She issued a challenge: If the executives could show her another way to hit her 20% growth target by 2002, she would postpone the restructuring, insiders say. Five weeks later, the best alternative was a plan for just 16% growth. The restructuring would start by year end.

20   She dove into the details. While Platt ran HP like a holding company, Fiorina demanded weekly updates on key units and peppered mid-level managers with 3 A.M. voice mails on product details. She injected much needed discipline into HP's computer sales force, which had long gotten away with lowering quotas at the end of each quarter. To raise the stakes, she tied more sales compensation to performance and changed the bonus period from once a year to every six months to prevent salespeople from coasting until the fourth quarter. While some commissions were tied to the number of orders rather than the sales amount and contributed to the earnings miss, Fiorina has fixed the problem and accomplished her larger goal of kick-starting sales. "You can feel the stress her changes are causing," says Kevin P. McManus, a vice-president of Premier Systems Integrators, which installs HP equipment. "These guys know they have to perform."

21   This play-to-win attitude has started to take root in other areas. Take HP Labs. In recent years, the once proud research and development center made too many incremental improvements to existing

products, in part because engineers' bonuses were tied to the number, rather than the impact, of their inventions. Now, Fiorina is focusing HP's R&D dollars on "big bang" projects. Consider Bob Rau's PICO software, which helps automate the design of chips used in electronic gear. Rau had worked for years on the project, but the technology languished. Last spring, Rau told Fiorina that the market for such systems was projected to grow to $300 billion as appliance makers built all sorts of Net-enabled gadgets. Within days, Fiorina created a separate division that operates alongside the two back-end groups and has grown to 250 people. Besides Rau's software, it will sell other HP technologies such as new disk drives to manufacturers. "It was like we'd been smothered for four years and someone was finally kind enough to lift the pillow off our face," says Rau.

22   ROUGH EDGES. With Phase One of her transformation behind her, Fiorina launched a formal reinvention process last spring. First up: cutting expenses. Over nine days, a 12-person team came up with ways to slash $1 billion by fiscal 2002. HP could save $100 million by outsourcing procurement. It could trim $10 million by letting employees log their hours online rather than on cardboard time cards. And the company could revamp its stodgy marketing by consolidating advertising from 43 agencies into two. That would save money and, better yet, focus HP's campaigns on Fiorina's big Web plans rather than on its various stand-alone products.

23   But when the big changes really started to kick in, Fiorina's plan started to bog down. In the past, HP's product chieftains ran their own operations, from design to sales and support. Today, they're folded into the two back-end units, leaving product chiefs with a far more limited role. They're still responsible for keeping HP competitive with rivals, hitting cost goals, and getting products to market on time. But they hand those products to the front-end organizations responsible for marketing and selling them.

24   The arrangement solves a number of long-standing HP problems. For one, it makes HP far easier to do business with. Rather than getting mobbed by salespeople from various divisions, now customers deal with one person. It lets HP's expert product designers focus on what they do best and

gives the front-end marketers authority to make the deals that are most profitable for HP as a whole— say, to sell a server at a lower margin to customers who commit to long-term consulting services. "You couldn't miss how silly it was the old way if you were part of the wide-awake club," says Scott Stallard, a vice-president in HP's computing group. "A parade of HP salesmen in Tauruses would pull up and meet for the first time outside of the customer's building."

25   These advantages, though, aren't enough to convince management experts or many HP veterans that a front-back approach will work at such a complex company. How do back-end product designers stay close enough to customers to know when a new feature becomes a must-have? Will executives, now saddled with thousands of HP products under their supervision, give sufficient attention to each of them to stay competitive? And with shared profit-and-loss responsibility between front- and back-ends, who has the final say when an engineer wants to take a flier on expensive research? "You just diffuse responsibility and authority," says Sara L. Beckman, a former HP manager who teaches at the Haas Business School at the University of California at Berkeley. "It makes it easier to say, 'Hey, that wasn't my problem.'"

26   Indeed, the front-back plan is showing some rough edges. While HP cited many reasons for its troubling fourth-quarter results, the reorganization is probably front and center. Freed from decades-old lines of command, employees spent as if they had already hit hypergrowth. In October alone, the company hired 1,200 people. Even dinner and postage expenses ran far over the norm. Such profligate spending was rare under the old structure where powerful division chiefs kept a tight rein on the purse strings. "They spent too much money on high-fives and setting themselves up to grow the following quarter," says Salomon Smith Barney analyst John B. Jones.

27   That situation could improve over time. Fiorina rushed the reorganization into place before the company's information systems were revamped to reflect the changes. Before Fiorina arrived, each product division had its own financial reporting system. It was only on November 1 that HP rolled out a new *uber*-system so staffers could work off the same books. Although it's too soon to say

whether it's a winner, HP claims the system will let it watch earnings in powerful new ways. Rather than just see sales for a product line, managers will be able to track profits from a given customer companywide or by region. That way they can cut deals on some products to boost other sales and wind up with a more lucrative relationship.

28   Another restructuring red flag is the way Fiorina now sets strategy, a big departure from "The HP Way"—the principles laid out by the founders in 1957. Based on the belief that smart people will make the right choices if given the right tools and authority, "Bill and Dave" pushed strategy down to the managers most involved in each business. The approach worked. Not only did HP dominate most of its markets, but low-level employees unearthed new opportunities for the company. "HP was always the exact opposite of a command-and-control environment," says former CEO Platt. Although Platt wouldn't comment on Fiorina directly, he says, "Bill and Dave did not feel they had to make every decision." Hewlett Packard's $10 billion inkjet printer business, for example, got its start in a broom closet at HP's Corvallis (Ore.) campus, where its inventors had to set up because they had no budget.

29   EYES ON THE PRIZES. Fiorina isn't waiting for another broom-closet miracle. Since the halcyon mid-90s, the old HP way hasn't worked quite as well. The last mega-breakthrough product HP introduced was the inkjet printer, in 1984. Growth had slowed to just 4% in the six months before Fiorina took over. To give HP better direction, Fiorina has created a nine-person Strategy Council that meets every month to allocate resources, set priorities, and advise her on acquisitions and partnerships. "This is a company that can do anything," Fiorina says. "But it can't do everything."

30   Again, the move makes sense on paper. By steering the entire company, the council can focus HP on a few big Internet prizes rather than myriad underfunded pet projects. But this top-down engine could backfire. Experts point out that except for visionaries like Apple Computer's Steve Jobs or IBM's Thomas J. Watson Jr., it's rare for the suits in the corner office to be able to predict the future— especially in a market as fast-changing as the Net. "If we were to go too far toward top-down, it would not be right for this company," acknowledges Debra L. Dunn, HP's vice-president of strategy.

31   To be sure, Fiorina is quick to embrace ideas from below if she thinks they'll solve a problem. This spring, Sam Mancuso, HP's vice-president of corporate accounts, proposed a team-based plan that advances the front-back approach. Time was, PC salespeople weren't allowed to sell, say, printers. Mancuso has fixed that by pulling together 20-person teams to concentrate on the top 75 corporate customers. The teams create an "opportunity map" for each customer, tracking the total amount of business HP could possibly book. Then the team analyzes what deal would maximize earnings for HP. Mancuso says his operation has boosted sales to top customers by more than 30% since May. "We're taking the handcuffs off, so now we can be more aggressive," Mancuso says.

32   The shackles may be off, but HP still lags its competitors in many areas. For all HP's talk of becoming a Net power, in the fourth quarter, Sun held 39% of the market for Unix servers preferred by e-businesses, according to IDC. HP is in second place with 23% share, a slight improvement over the year before. But it faces growing competition from third-place IBM, which just introduced a product line that many analysts say handily outperforms HP's servers. "HP is just not making much headway," says Ellen M. Hancock, CEO of Exodus Communications Inc. Her company uses 62,000 servers in its Web hosting centers, virtually none of them from HP. And most of HP's Net schemes, such as Cartogra, a service that lets consumers post pictures on the Web, have failed to catch on.

33   Even fans of Fiorina acknowledge she has a ways to go. While wireless juggernaut Nokia Corp. just signed a deal to use HP software, Chairman Jorma Ollila questions how successful Fiorina's turnaround is likely to be. "Carly is very impressive," he says. "But the jury is still out on HP." Says Cisco Systems Inc. CEO John T. Chambers, who named Fiorina to his board on January 10: "I'd bet that Carly will be one of the top 5 or 10 CEOs in the nation. But she has still got to get them running faster." Fiorina wouldn't disagree and says she plans to keep upping her bets. "The greatest risk is standing still," she says. She should hope she has picked the right cards, because she's gambling with Silicon Valley's proudest legacy.

Source: "The Radical," *BusinessWeek,* February 19, 2001.

Primary Organizational Structures and Their Strategy-Related Pros and Cons

Matching the structure to the strategy is a fundamental task of company strategists. To understand how that task is handled, we first must review the five basic primary structures. We will then turn to guidelines for matching structure to strategy.

The five basic primary structures are: (1) functional, (2) geographic, (3) divisional, or strategic business unit, (4) matrix, and (5) product team. Each structure has advantages and disadvantages that strategists must consider when choosing an organization form.

FUNCTIONAL ORGANIZATIONAL STRUCTURE

Functional structures predominate in firms with a single or narrow product focus. Such firms require well-defined skills and areas of specialization to build competitive advantages in providing their products or services. Dividing tasks into functional specialties enables the personnel of these firms to concentrate on only one aspect of the necessary work. This allows use of the latest technical skills and develops a high level of efficiency.

Product, customer, or technology considerations determine the identity of the parts in a functional structure. A hotel business might be organized around housekeeping (maids), the front desk, maintenance, restaurant operations, reservations and sales, accounting, and personnel. An equipment manufacturer might be organized around production, engineering/quality control, purchasing, marketing, personnel, and finance/accounting. Two examples of functional organizations are illustrated in Exhibit 10–A.

The strategic challenge presented by the functional structure is effective coordination of the functional units. The narrow technical expertise achieved through specialization can lead to limited perspectives and to differences in the priorities of the functional units. Specialists may see the firm's strategic issues primarily as "marketing" problems or "production" problems. The potential conflict among functional units makes the coordinating role of the chief executive critical. Integrating devices (such as project teams or planning committees) are frequently used in functionally organized firms to enhance coordination and to facilitate understanding across functional areas.

GEOGRAPHIC ORGANIZATIONAL STRUCTURE

Firms often grow by expanding the sale of their products or services to new geographic areas. In these areas, they frequently encounter differences that necessitate different approaches in producing, providing, or selling their products or services. Structuring by geographic areas is usually required to accommodate these differences. Thus, Holiday Inns is organized by regions of the world because of differences among nations in the laws, customs, and economies affecting the lodging industry. And even within its U.S. organization, Holiday Inns is organized geographically because of regional differences in traveling requirements, lodging regulations, and customer mix.

EXHIBIT 10–A
Functional Organization Structures

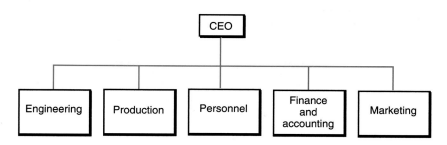

A process-oriented functional structure (an electronics distributor):

Strategic Advantages	Strategic Disadvantages
1. Achieves efficiency through specialization.	1. Promotes narrow specialization and functional rivalry or conflict.
2. Develops functional expertise.	2. Creates difficulties in functional coordination and interfunctional decision making.
3. Differentiates and delegates day-to-day operating decisions.	3. Limits development of general managers.
4. Retains centralized control of strategic decisions.	4. Has a strong potential for interfunctional conflict—priority placed on functional areas, not the entire business.
5. Tightly links structure to strategy by designating key activities as separate units.	

The key strategic advantage of geographic organizational structures is responsiveness to local market conditions. Exhibit 10–B illustrates a typical geographic organizational structure and itemizes the strategic advantages and disadvantages of such structures.

DIVISIONAL OR STRATEGIC BUSINESS UNIT STRUCTURE

When a firm diversifies its product/service lines, utilizes unrelated market channels, or begins to serve heterogeneous customer groups, a functional structure rapidly becomes inadequate. If a functional structure is retained under these circumstances, production managers may have to oversee the production of numerous and varied products or services, marketing managers may have to create sales programs for vastly different products or sell through vastly different distribution channels, and top management may be confronted with excessive coordination demands. A new organizational structure is often necessary to meet the increased coordination and decision-making requirements that

EXHIBIT 10–B
A Geographic Organizational Structure

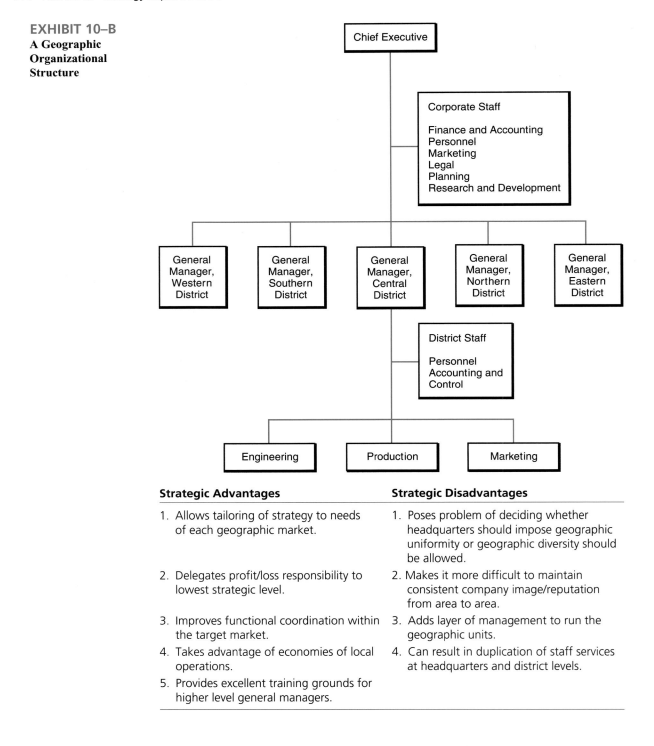

Strategic Advantages	Strategic Disadvantages
1. Allows tailoring of strategy to needs of each geographic market.	1. Poses problem of deciding whether headquarters should impose geographic uniformity or geographic diversity should be allowed.
2. Delegates profit/loss responsibility to lowest strategic level.	2. Makes it more difficult to maintain consistent company image/reputation from area to area.
3. Improves functional coordination within the target market.	3. Adds layer of management to run the geographic units.
4. Takes advantage of economies of local operations.	4. Can result in duplication of staff services at headquarters and district levels.
5. Provides excellent training grounds for higher level general managers.	

result from increased diversity and size, and the divisional or strategic business unit (SBU) organizational structure is the form often chosen.

For many years, Ford and General Motors have used divisional/SBU structures organized by product groups. Manufacturers often organize sales into divisions based on differences in distribution channels.

A divisional/SBU structure allows corporate management to delegate authority for the strategic management of distinct business entities—the division/SBU. This expedites decision making in response to varied competitive environments and enables corporate management to concentrate on corporate-level strategic decisions. The division/SBU usually is given profit responsibility, which facilitates accurate assessment of profit and loss.

Exhibit 10–C illustrates a divisional/SBU organizational structure and specifies the strategic advantages and disadvantages of such structures.

MATRIX ORGANIZATIONAL STRUCTURE

In large companies, increased diversity leads to numerous product and project efforts of major strategic significance. The result is a need for an organizational form that provides skills and resources where and when they are most vital. For example, a product development project needs a market research specialist for two months and a financial analyst one day per week. A customer site application needs a software engineer for one month and a customer service trainer one day per month for six weeks. Each of these situations is an example of a matrix organization that has been used to temporarily put people and resources where they are most needed. Among the firms that now use some form of matrix organization are Citicorp, Matsushita, DaimlerChrysler, Microsoft, Dow Chemical, and Texas Instruments.

The matrix organization provides dual channels of authority, performance responsibility, evaluation, and control, as shown in Exhibit 10–D. Essentially, subordinates are assigned both to a basic functional area and to a project or product manager. The matrix form is intended to make the best use of talented people within a firm by combining the advantages of functional specialization and product-project specialization.

The matrix structure also increases the number of middle managers who exercise general management responsibilities (through the project manager role) and, thus, broaden their exposure to organizationwide strategic concerns. In this way, the matrix structure overcomes a key deficiency of functional organizations while retaining the advantages of functional specialization.

Although the matrix structure is easy to design, it is difficult to implement. Dual chains of command challenge fundamental organizational orientations. Negotiating shared responsibilities, the use of resources, and priorities can create misunderstanding or confusion among subordinates. These problems are heightened in an international context with the complications introduced by distance, language, time, and culture.

To avoid the deficiencies that might arise from a permanent matrix structure, some firms are accomplishing particular strategic tasks, by means of a "temporary" or "flexible" *overlay structure*. This approach, used recently by such firms as NEC, Matsushita, Philips, and Unilever, is meant to take *temporary* advantage of a matrix-type team while preserving an underlying divisional structure. Thus, the basic idea of the matrix structure—*to simplify and amplify the focus of resources on a narrow but strategically important product, project, or market*—appears to be an important structural alternative for large, diverse organizations.

EXHIBIT 10–C
Divisional or
Strategic Business
Unit Structure

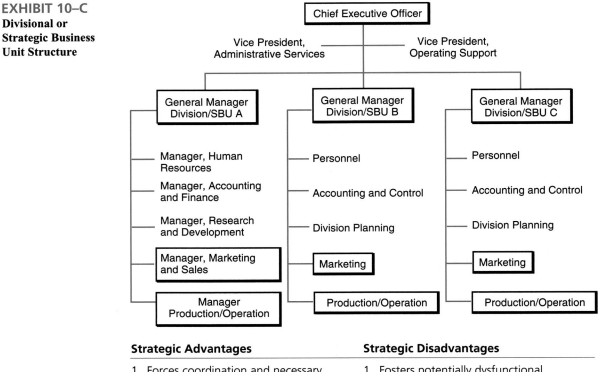

Strategic Advantages

1. Forces coordination and necessary authority down to the appropriate level for rapid response.
2. Places strategy development and implementation in closer proximity to the unique environments of the divisions/SBUs.
3. Frees chief executive officer for broader strategic decision making.
4. Sharply focuses accountability for performance.
5. Retains functional specialization within each division/SBU.
6. Provides good training grounds for strategic managers.
7. Increases focus on products, markets, and quick response to change.

Strategic Disadvantages

1. Fosters potentially dysfunctional competition for corporate-level resources.
2. Presents the problem of determining how much authority should be given to division/SBU managers.
3. Creates a potential for policy inconsistencies among divisions/SBUs.
4. Presents the problem of distributing corporate overhead costs in a way that's acceptable to division managers with profit responsibility.
5. Increases costs incurred through duplication of functions.
6. Creates difficulty maintaining overall corporate image.

EXHIBIT 10–D
Matrix
Organizational
Structure

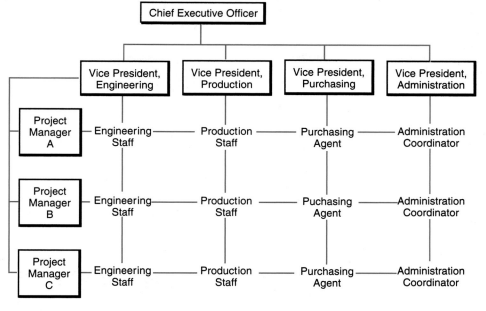

Strategic Advantages

1. Accomodates a wide variety of project-oriented business activity.
2. Provides good training grounds for strategic managers.
3. Maximizes efficient use of functional managers.
4. Fosters creativity and multiple sources of diversity.
5. Gives middle management broader exposure to strategic issues.

Strategic Disadvantages

1. May result in confusion and contradictory policies.
2. Necessitates tremendous horizontal and vertical coordination.
3. Can proliferate information logjams and excess reporting.
4. Can trigger turf battles and loss of accountability.

Chapter **Eleven**

Strategic Control and Continuous Improvement

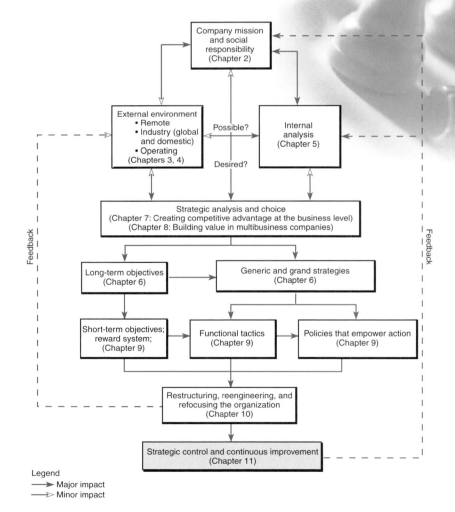

Strategies are forward looking, designed to be accomplished several years into the future, and based on management assumptions about numerous events that have not yet occurred. How should managers control a strategy?

Strategic control is concerned with tracking a strategy as it is being implemented, detecting problems or changes in its underlying premises, and making necessary adjustments. In contrast to postaction control, strategic control is concerned with guiding action in behalf of the strategy as that action is taking place and when the end result is still several years off. Managers responsible for the success of a strategy typically are concerned with two sets of questions:

1. Are we moving in the proper direction? Are key things falling into place? Are our assumptions about major trends and changes correct? Are we doing the critical things that need to be done? Should we adjust or abort the strategy?

2. How are we performing? Are objectives and schedules being met? Are costs, revenues, and cash flows matching projections? Do we need to make operational changes?

The rapid, accelerating change of the global marketplace of the last 10 years has made *continuous improvement* another aspect of strategic control in many business organizations. Synonymous with the total quality movement, continuous improvement provides a way for organizations to provide strategic control that allows an organization to respond more proactively and timely to rapid developments in hundreds of areas that influence a business's success. This chapter discusses traditional strategic controls and then explains ways that the *continuous improvement quality imperative* and the balanced scoreboard methodology can be key vehicles for strategic control.

ESTABLISHING STRATEGIC CONTROLS

The control of strategy can be characterized as a form of "steering control." Ordinarily, a good deal of time elapses between the initial implementation of a strategy and achievement of its intended results. During that time, investments are made and numerous projects and actions are undertaken to implement the strategy. Also, during that time, changes are taking place in both the environmental situation and the firm's internal situation. Strategic controls are necessary to steer the firm through these events. They must provide the basis for adapting the firm's strategic actions and directions in response to these developments and changes.

The four basic types of strategic control are:

1. Premise control.

2. Special alert control.

3. Strategic surveillance.

4. Implementation control.

The nature of these four types is summarized in Exhibit 11–1.

Premise Control

Every strategy is based on certain planning premises—assumptions or predictions. *Premise control is designed to check systematically and continuously whether the premises on which the strategy is based are still valid.* If a vital premise is no longer valid, the strategy may have to be changed. The sooner an invalid premise can be recognized and

EXHIBIT 11–1   Four Types of Strategic Control

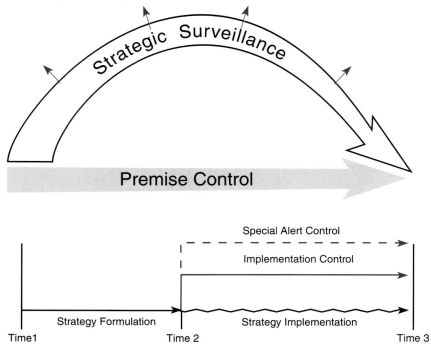

Characteristics of the Four Types of Strategic Control

	Types of Strategic Control			
Basic Characteristics	Premise Control	Implementation Control	Strategic Surveillance	Special Alert Control
Objects of control	Planning premises and projections	Key strategic thrusts and milestones	Potential threats and opportunities related to the strategy	Occurrence of recognizable but unlikely events
Degree of focusing	High	High	Low	High
Data acquisition:				
Formalization	Medium	High	Low	High
Centralization	Low	Medium	Low	High
Use with:				
Environmental factors	Yes	Seldom	Yes	Yes
Industry factors	Yes	Seldom	Yes	Yes
Strategy-specific factors	No	Yes	Seldom	Yes
Company-specific factors	No	Yes	Seldom	Seldom

Source: Adapted from G. Schreyogg and H. Steinmann, "Strategic Control: A New Perspective," *Academy of Management Review* 12, no. 1 (1987).

rejected, the better are the chances that an acceptable shift in the strategy can be devised. Planning premises are primarily concerned with environmental and industry factors.

Environmental Factors

Although a firm has little or no control over environmental factors, these factors exercise considerable influence over the success of its strategy, and strategies usually are based on key premises about them. Inflation, technology, interest rates, regulation, and demographic/social changes are examples of such factors.

EPA regulations and federal laws concerning the handling, use, and disposal of toxic chemicals have a major effect on the strategy of Velsicol Chemical Company, a market leader in pesticide chemicals sold to farmers and exterminators. So Velsicol's management makes and constantly updates premises about future regulatory actions.

Industry Factors

The performance of the firms in a given industry is affected by industry factors. These differ among industries, and a firm should be aware of the factors that influence success in its particular industry. Competitors, suppliers, product substitutes, and barriers to entry are a few of the industry factors about which strategic assumptions are made.

Rubbermaid has long been held up as a model of predictable growth, creative management, and rapid innovation in the plastic housewares and toy industry. Its premise going into the 21st century was that large retail chains would continue to prefer its products over competitors' because of this core competence. This premise included continued receptivity to regular price increases when necessitated by raw materials costs. Retailers, most notably Wal-Mart, recently balked at Rubbermaid's attempt to raise prices to offset the doubling of resin costs. Furthermore, traditionally overlooked competitors have begun to make inroads with computerized stocking services. Rubbermaid is moving aggressively to adjust its strategy because of the response of Wal-Mart and other key retailers.

Strategies are often based on numerous premises, some major and some minor, about environmental and industry variables. Tracking all of these premises is unnecessarily expensive and time consuming. Managers must select premises whose change (1) is likely and (2) would have a major impact on the firm and its strategy.

Strategic Surveillance

By their nature, premise controls are focused controls; strategic surveillance, however, is unfocused. *Strategic surveillance is designed to monitor a broad range of events inside and outside the firm that are likely to affect the course of its strategy.*[1] The basic idea behind strategic surveillance is that important yet unanticipated information may be uncovered by a general monitoring of multiple information sources.

Strategic surveillance must be kept as unfocused as possible. It should be a loose "environmental scanning" activity. Trade magazines, *The Wall Street Journal,* trade conferences, conversations, and intended and unintended observations are all subjects of strategic surveillance. Despite its looseness, strategic surveillance provides an ongoing, broad-based vigilance in all daily operations that may uncover information relevant to the firm's strategy. Citicorp benefited significantly from an Argentine manager's strategic surveillance of political speeches by Argentina's former president, as discussed in Exhibit 11–2, Strategy in Action.

Special Alert Control

Another type of strategic control, really a subset of the other three, is special alert control. *A special alert control is the thorough, and often rapid, reconsideration of the firm's strategy because of a sudden, unexpected event.* The tragic events of September 11, 2001, an outside firm's sudden acquisition of a leading competitor, an unexpected product difficulty, such as the poisoned Tylenol capsules—events of these kinds can drastically alter the firm's strategy.

[1] G. Schreyogg and H. Steinmann, "Strategic Control: A New Perspective," *Academy of Management Review* 12, no. 1 (1987), p. 101.

BusinessWeek IMPLEMENTATION CONTROL AT DAYS INN

When Days Inn pioneered the budget segment of the lodging industry, its strategy placed primary emphasis on company-owned facilities and it insisted on maintaining a roughly 3-to-1 company-owned/franchise ratio. This ratio ensured the parent company's total control over standards, rates, and so forth.

As other firms moved into the budget segment, Days Inn saw the need to expand rapidly throughout the United States and, therefore, reversed its conservative franchise posture. This reversal would rapidly accelerate its ability to open new locations. Longtime executives, concerned about potential loss of control over local standards, instituted *implementation controls* requiring both franchise evaluation and annual milestone reviews. Two years into the program, Days Inn executives were convinced that a high franchise-to-company ratio was manageable, and so they accelerated the growth of franchising by doubling the franchise sales department.

STRATEGIC SURVEILLANCE AT CITICORP

Citicorp has been pursuing an aggressive product development strategy intended to achieve an annual earnings growth of 15 percent while it becomes an institution capable of supplying clients with any kind of financial service anywhere in the world. A major obstacle to the achievement of this earnings growth is Citicorp's exposure to default because of its extensive earlier loans to troubled developing countries. Citicorp is sensitive to the wide variety of predictions about impending defaults.

Citicorp's long-range plan assumes an annual 10 percent default on its developing economy loans over any five-year period. Yet it maintains active *strategic surveillance control*

by having each of its international branches monitor daily announcements from key governments and from inside contacts for signs of changes in a host country's financial environment. When that surveillance detects a potential problem, management attempts to adjust Citicorp's posture. For example, when a former Argentine president, stated that his country may not pay interest on its debt as scheduled, Citicorp raised its annual default charge to 20 percent of its $500 million Argentine exposure.

SPECIAL ALERT CONTROL AT UNITED AIRLINES

The sudden impact of an airline crash can be devastating to a major airline. United Airlines has made elaborate preparations to deal with this contingency. Its executive vice president, James M. Guyette, heads a crisis team that is permanently prepared to respond. Members of the team carry beepers and are always on call. When United's Chicago headquarters received word of the September 11th hijacking and crash, they were in a "war room" within an hour to direct the response. Beds are set up nearby so team members can catch a few winks; while they sleep, alternates take their places.

Members of the team have been carefully screened through simulated crisis drills. "The point is to weed out those who don't hold up well under stress," says Guyette. Although the team was established to handle flight disasters, it has since assumed an expanded role. The crisis team was activated when American Airlines launched a fare war. And according to Guyette, "We're brainstorming about how we would be affected by everything from a competitor who had a serious problem to a crisis involving a hijacking or taking a United employee hostage."

Such an event should trigger an immediate and intense reassessment of the firm's strategy and its current strategic situation. In many firms, crisis teams handle the firm's initial response to unforeseen events that may have an immediate effect on its strategy. Increasingly, firms have developed contingency plans along with crisis teams to respond to circumstances such as United Airlines did on September 11, 2001 as summarized in Strategy in Action 11–2.

Implementation Control

Strategy implementation takes place as series of steps, programs, investments, and moves that occur over an extended time. Special programs are undertaken. Functional areas initiate strategy-related activities. Key people are added or reassigned. Resources are mobilized. In other words, managers implement strategy by converting broad plans into the concrete, incremental actions and results of specific units and individuals.

Implementation control is the type of strategic control that must be exercised as those events unfold. *Implementation control is designed to assess whether the overall strategy should be changed in light of the results associated with the incremental actions that implement the overall strategy.* The two basic types of implementation control are (1) monitoring strategic thrusts and (2) milestone reviews.

Monitoring Strategic Thrusts or Projects

As a means of implementing broad strategies, narrow strategic projects often are undertaken—projects that represent part of what needs to be done if the overall strategy is to be accomplished. These strategic thrusts provide managers with information that helps them determine whether the overall strategy is progressing as planned or needs to be adjusted.

Although the utility of strategic thrusts seems readily apparent, it is not always easy to use them for control purposes. It may be difficult to interpret early experience or to evaluate the overall strategy in light of such experience. One approach is to agree early in the planning process on which thrusts or which phases of thrusts are critical factors in the success of the strategy. Managers responsible for these implementation controls will single them out from other activities and observe them frequently. Another approach is to use stop/go assessments that are linked to a series of meaningful thresholds (time, costs, research and development, success, and so forth) associated with particular thrusts. A program of regional development via company-owned inns in the Rocky Mountain area was a monitoring thrust that Days Inn used to test its strategy of becoming a nationwide motel chain. Problems in meeting time targets and unexpectedly large capital needs led Days Inn's executives to abandon the overall strategy and eventually sell the firm.

Milestone Reviews

Managers often attempt to identify significant milestones that will be reached during strategy implementation. These milestones may be critical events, major resource allocations, or simply the passage of a certain amount of time. The milestone reviews that then take place usually involve a full-scale reassessment of the strategy and of the advisability of continuing or refocusing the firm's direction.

A useful example of implementation control based on milestone review is offered by Boeing's product-development strategy of entering the supersonic transport (SST) airplane market. Boeing had invested millions of dollars and years of scarce engineering talent during the first phase of its SST venture, and competition from the British/French Concorde effort was intense. Since the next phase represented a billion-dollar decision, Boeing's management established the initiation of the phase as a milestone. The milestone reviews greatly increased the estimates of production costs; predicted relatively few passengers and rising fuel costs, thus raising the estimated operating costs; and noted that the Concorde, unlike Boeing, had the benefit of massive government subsidies. These factors led Boeing's management to scrap its SST strategy in spite of high sunk costs, pride, and patriotism. Only an objective, full-scale strategy reassessment could have led to such a decision.

In this example, a milestone review occurred at a major resource allocation decision point. Milestone reviews may also occur concurrently when a major step in a strategy's implementation is being taken or when a key uncertainty is resolved. Managers even may set an arbitrary period, say two years, as a milestone review point. Whatever the basis for selecting that point, the critical purpose of a milestone review is to thoroughly scrutinize the firm's strategy so as to control the strategy's future.

Implementation control is also enabled through operational control systems like budgets, schedules and key success factors. While strategic controls attempt to steer the company over an extended period (usually five years of more), operational controls provide postaction evaluation and control over short periods—usually from one month to one year. To be effective, operational control systems must take four steps common to all postaction controls:

1. Set standards of performance.

2. Measure actual performance.

3. Identify deviations from standards set.

4. Initiate corrective action.

Exhibit 11–3 illustrates a typical operational control system. These indicators represent progress after two years of a five-year strategy intended to differentiate the firm as a customer-service-oriented provider of high-quality products. Management's concern is to compare *progress to date* with *expected progress*. The *current deviation* is of particular interest, because it provides a basis for examining *suggested actions* (usually suggested by subordinate managers) and for finalizing decisions on changes or adjustments in the firm's operations.

From Exhibit 11–3, it appears that the firm is maintaining control of its cost structure. Indeed, it is ahead of schedule on reducing overhead. The firm is well ahead of its delivery cycle target, while slightly below its target service-to-sales personnel ratio. Its product returns look OK, although product performance versus specification is below standard. Sales per employee and expansion of the product line are ahead of schedule. The absenteeism rate in the service area is on target, but the turnover rate is higher than that targeted. Competitors appear to be introducing products more rapidly than expected.

After deviations and their causes have been identified, the implications of the deviations for the ultimate success of the strategy must be considered. For example, the rapid product-line expansion indicated in Exhibit 11–3 may have been a response to the increased rate of competitors' product expansion. At the same time, product performance is still low; and, while the installation cycle is slightly above standard (improving customer service), the ratio of service to sales personnel is below the targeted ratio. Contributing to this substandard ratio (and perhaps reflecting a lack of organizational commitment to customer service) is the exceptionally high turnover in customer service personnel. The rapid reduction in indirect overhead costs might mean that administration integration of customer service and product development requirements has been cut back too quickly.

This information presents operations managers with several options. They may attribute the deviations primarily to internal discrepancies. In that case, they can scale priorities up or down. For example, they might place more emphasis on retaining customer service personnel and less emphasis on overhead reduction and new product development. On the other hand, they might decide to continue as planned in the face of increasing competition and to accept or gradually improve the customer service situation. Another possibility is reformulating the strategy or a component of the strategy in the face of rapidly increasing competition. For example, the firm might decide to emphasize more standardized or lower-priced products to overcome customer service problems and take advantage of an apparently ambitious sales force.

This is but one of many possible interpretations of Exhibit 11–3. The important point here is the critical need to monitor progress against standards and to give serious in-depth attention to both the causes of observed deviations and the most appropriate responses to them. After the deviations have been evaluated, slight adjustments may be made to keep progress, expenditure, or other factors in line with the strategy's programmed needs. In the unusual event of extreme deviations—generally because of unforeseen changes—management is alerted to the possible need for revising the budget, reconsidering certain functional plans related to budgeted expenditures, or examining the units concerned and the effectiveness of their managers.

EXHIBIT 11–3 **Monitoring and Evaluating Performance Deviations**

Key Success Factors	Objective, Assumption, or Budget	Forecast Performance at This Time	Current Performance	Current Deviation	Analysis
Cost control: Ratio of indirect overhead cost to direct field and labor costs	10%	15%	12%	+3 (ahead)	Are we moving too fast, or is there more unnecessary overhead than was originally thought?
Gross profit	39%	40%	40%	0%	
Customer service: Installation cycle in days	2.5 days	3.2 days	2.7 days	+0.5 (ahead)	Can this progress be maintained?
Ratio of service to sales personnel	3.2	2.7	2.1	−0.6 (behind)	Why are we behind here? How can we maintain the installation-cycle progress?
Product quality: Percentage of products returned	1.0%	2.0%	2.1%	−0.1% (behind)	Why are we behind here? What are the ramifications for other operations?
Product performance versus specification	100%	92%	80%	−12% (behind)	
Marketing: Monthly sales per employee	$12,500	$11,500	$12,100	+$600 (ahead)	Good progress. Is it creating any problems to support?
Expansion of product line	6	3	5	+2 products (ahead)	Are the products ready? Are the perfect standards met?
Employee morale in service area: Absenteeism rate	2.5%	3.0%	3.0%	(on target)	
Turnover rate	5%	10%	15%	−8% (behind)	Looks like a problem! Why are we so far behind?
Competition: New product introductions (average number)	6	3	6	−3 (behind)	Did we underestimate timing? What are the implications for our basic assumptions?

Correcting deviations in performance brings the entire management task into focus. Managers can correct such deviations by changing measures or plans. They also can eliminate poor performance by changing how things are done, by hiring or retraining workers, by changing job assignments, and so on. Correcting deviations, therefore, can involve all of the functions, tasks, and responsibilities of operations managers. Managers in other cultures, most notably Japan, have for some time achieved operational control by seeking their unit's continuous improvement. Companies worldwide have adapted this point of view that operational control is best achieved through a pervasive commitment to quality, originally called *total quality management* (TQM), which is seen as essential to strategic success into the 21st century.

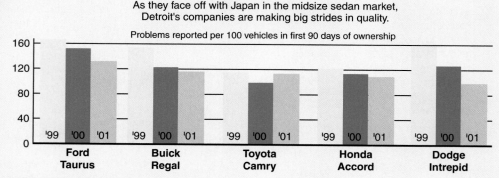

BusinessWeek

Quality Quotients

As they face off with Japan in the midsize sedan market,
Detroit's companies are making big strides in quality.

Problems reported per 100 vehicles in first 90 days of ownership

Ford Taurus	Buick Regal	Toyota Camry	Honda Accord	Dodge Intrepid
'99 '00 '01	'99 '00 '01	'99 '00 '01	'99 '00 '01	'99 '00 '01

Data: J. D. Power & Associates ©BW

You'd think Ford Motor Co. would learn a lesson about keeping an eye on quality from the $3.5 billion Explorer tire debacle. And, indeed, the automaker went to extraordinary lengths to ensure that its revised 2002 Explorer launched without a hiccup. It even took the unprecedented step of holding up vehicles in the factory for engineers to pore over them for defects. But that wasn't enough. Last May, the new Explorer had to be recalled. It turned out that while redesigning the car, engineers forgot to adjust a rail used to guide the vehicle along an assembly line. The oversight meant that some Explorers limped off the line with nine-inch-long gashes in their tires.

Try as it might, the U.S. auto industry can't shake its karma for shaky quality—even though its cars and trucks are better than ever. *Consumer Reports* recently found that the average number of problems per 100 new vehicles built by General Motors, Ford, and Chrysler dropped from 105 in 1980 to just 23 in 2000. But as the Explorer Redux episode highlights, U.S. cars still are not up to snuff. Despite the improvement, *Consumer Reports* pegs the quality of American vehicles at Japanese levels circa 1985. And the Big Three currently spend about $125 more per vehicle in warranty costs than their Japanese rivals.

Why the gap? It's not that American factory workers are sloppier than their Japanese counterparts. In fact, fewer than 15% of quality problems can be traced to shoddy workmanship or other factory errors, says Sandy Munro, president of Munro & Associates Inc., a Troy (Mich.)-based manufacturing consultant. The real problem, he says, is at the front end of the development process. "It has more to do with who designed it, how they designed it, and what processes and materials they used," Munro contends.

Raiding Toyota

Now, in a drive to reduce costs and boost quality, U.S. carmakers are revamping their approach, trying to root out problems before assembly lines start rolling. They're borrowing strategies invented by the Japanese, or—in the case of Chrysler Corp—raiding Toyota Motor Corp. for quality expertise. And they're bringing suppliers into the design process earlier and treating them like partners, in hopes of spotting problems with components as early as possible.

Detroit is finding, as it did back in the 1970s, that there is no better way to begin than with a close look at Japan. There, top car builders take an evolutionary approach to design, stressing continuous improvement. From year to year, if

THE QUALITY IMPERATIVE: CONTINUOUS IMPROVEMENT TO BUILD CUSTOMER VALUE

The initials TQM have become the most popular abbreviation in business management literature since MBO (management by objectives). TQM Stands for *total quality management*, an umbrella term for the quality programs that have been implemented in many businesses worldwide in the last two decades. TQM was first implemented in several large U.S. manufacturers in the face of the overwhelming success of Japanese and German competitors. Japanese manufacturers embraced the quality messages of Americans

parts are working well, they are kept, not replaced. And by using common components across a range of vehicles, Japanese designs cut down on variability—the old, familiar foe of quality.

In stark contrast, U.S. automakers tend to start with a clean sheet of paper whenever they redesign a vehicle. And this can lead to trouble. When Chrysler introduced the redesigned 1999 Jeep Grand Cherokee, former CEO Robert J. Eaton bragged that there were so few shared bits between the new and old models, they'd all fit in a bag in his hand. He should have kept mum: *Consumer Reports* says the Grand Cherokee's "reliability has been among the worst we've seen."

Another nagging problem at U.S. car shops is an overly narrow focus on component design without enough regard for the larger task of integrating parts on the factory floor. The trouble, points out Jay Baron, director of manufacturing systems group at the Center for Automotive Research in Ann Arbor, Mich., is that good components that don't fit together demand costly last-minute design changes. "This is one area where the Japanese are way ahead of us," says Baron. Instead of striving for perfection in the design of each component, the Japanese fast-forward to the manufacturing phase to make sure the parts fit, and then back up to make necessary adjustments, he says. Now, all three Detroit automakers are beginning to follow suit.

Tricky Problems

Ford, by any calculation, needs the most work. Last year alone, recalls and other quality gaffes cost the company at least $1 billion. Now, Ford is pinning its quality hopes on Six Sigma, a data-driven method pioneered by industrial giants such as AlliedSignal Inc. and Motorola Inc. It's an approach that depends on rigorous statistical analysis to unearth tough problems. And it's already helping crack some tricky ones at Ford. Ill-fitting doors on Ford's top-selling F-150 pickup truck, for example, were blamed for chronic wind noise and leaks. So, after studying the installation of hundreds of such

doors, a Six Sigma team working at Ford's Norforlk (Va.) truck factory discovered that door-fit varied according to the order in which bolts attaching the door to the frame were driven in. The problem implied its own solution. Experimenting with various sequences, the team reduced the defects rate by two-thirds—without changing a single part. The change immediately saved $35,000 on the plant floor by eliminating the refitting of bad doors. Larger savings in warranty haven't yet been tallied.

Of the Big Three, GM has made the most progress on quality. This year, it climbed to No. 4 on J. D. Power & Associates' annual overall quality rankings, just a notch behind Nissan Motor Co. Now, GM is looking to close in on the leaders, Toyota and Honda, by working more closely with its suppliers, says GM manufacturing chief Gary Cowger. On some vehicles, GM is even handing over complete design responsibility for its interiors to large suppliers, such as Lear Corp. and Johnson Controls Inc. The subcontractors, GM figures, can better monitor quality by designing and building fully integrated systems—complete seats or dashboards as opposed to just seat frames or speedometers.

At Chrysler, the struggling U.S. unit of Germany's DaimlerChrysler, improving quality is an even more urgent mission. The company's new CEO, former Mercedes chief engineer Dieter Zetsche, has made it a cornerstone of his $3.9-billion turnaround plan. He's overhauling Chrysler's vehicle development processes by pulling together teams from all areas of the company—design, engineering, marketing, manufacturing, and purchasing—in a bid to drive out waste. By involving everyone up front, his goal is to avoid the kinds of last-minute design changes that lead to errors later on. Even before Zetsche arrived, Chrysler quality was improving: Its Dodge Intrepid beat out the Toyota Camry and the Honda Accord—long-time leaders in the midsize sedan segment—in J. D. Power's 2001 new car quality survey.

Source: "Detroit Is Cruising for Quality," *BusinessWeek,* September 3, 2001.

W. Edwards Deming and J. M. Juran following World War II, and by the 1970s Japanese products had acquired unquestioned reputations for superior high quality.

Growing numbers of U.S. manufacturers have attempted to change this imbalance with their own quality programs, and the practice has spread to large retail and service companies as well. Increasingly, smaller companies that supply big TQM companies have adopted quality programs, often because big companies have required small suppliers to adopt quality programs of their own. Exhibit 11–4, Strategy in Action, describes the aggressive quality imperative thrusted on Detroit automakers in the new century.

TQM is viewed as virtually a new organizational culture and way of thinking. It is built around an intense focus on customer satisfaction; on accurate measurement of every critical variable in a business's operation; on continuous improvement of products, services, and processes; and on work relationships based on trust and teamwork. One useful explanation of the quality imperative suggests 10 essential elements of implementing total quality management, as follows:

1. **Define *quality* and *customer value.*** Rather than be left to individual interpretation, company personnel should have a clear definition of what *quality* means in the job, department, and throughout the company. It should be developed from your customer's perspective and communicated as a written policy.

Thinking in terms of customer value broadens the definition of *quality* to include efficiency and responsiveness. Said another way, quality to your customer often means that the product performs well; that it is priced competitively (efficiency); and that you provide it quickly and adapt it when needed (responsiveness). Customer value is found in the combination of all three—quality, price, and speed.

2. **Develop a customer orientation.** Customer value is what the customer says it is. Don't rely on secondary information—talk to your customers directly. Also recognize your "internal" customers. Usually less than 20 percent of company employees come into contact with external customers, while the other 80 percent serve internal customers—other units with real performance expectations.

The value chain provides an important way to think about customer orientation, particularly to recognize *internal* as well as external (ultimate) customers. Operating personnel are *internal* customers of the accounting department for useful information and also the purchasing department for quality, timely supplies. When they are "served" with quality, efficiency, and responsiveness, value is added to their efforts, and is passed on to their internal customers and, eventually, external (ultimate) customers.

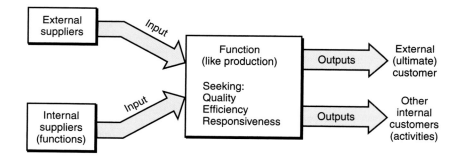

3. **Focus on the company's business processes.** Break down every minute step in the process of providing the company's product or service and look at ways to improve it, rather than focusing simply on the finished product or service. Each process contributes value in some way, which can be improved or adapted to help other processes (internal customers) improve. Examples of ways customer value is enhanced across business processes in several functions are:

	Quality	Efficiency	Responsiveness
Marketing	Provides accurate assessment of customer's product preferences to R&D	Targets advertising campaign at customers, using cost-effective medium	Quickly uncovers and reacts to changing market trends
Operations	Consistently produces goods matching engineering design	Minimizes scrap and rework through high-production yield	Quickly adapts to latest demands with production flexibility
Research and development	Designs products that combine customer demand and production capabilities	Uses computers to test feasibility of idea before going to more expensive full-scale prototype	Carries out parallel product/process designs to speed up overall innovation
Accounting	Provides the information that managers in other functions need to make decisions	Simplifies and computerizes to decrease the cost of gathering information	Provides information in "real time" (as the events described are still happening)
Purchasing	Selects vendors for their ability to join in an effective "partnership"	Given the required vendor quality, negotiates prices to provide good value	Schedules inbound deliveries efficiently, avoiding both extensive inventories and stock-outs
Personnel	Trains workforce to perform required tasks	Minimizes employee turnover, reducing hiring and training expenses	In response to strong growth in sales, finds large numbers of employees and quickly teaches needed skills

4. **Develop customer and supplier partnerships.** Organizations have a destructive tendency to view suppliers and even customers adversarily. It is better to understand the horizontal flow of a business—outside suppliers to internal suppliers/customers (a company's various departments) to external customers. This view suggests suppliers are partners in meeting customer needs, and customers are partners by providing input so the company and suppliers can meet and exceed those expectations.

Ford Motor Company's Dearborn, Michigan, plant is linked electronically with supplier Allied Signal's Kansas City, Missouri, plant. A Ford computer recently sent the design for a car's connecting rod to an Allied Signal factory computer, which transformed the design into instructions that it fed to a machine tool on the shop floor. The result: quality, efficiency, and responsiveness.

5. **Take a preventive approach.** Many organizations reward "fire fighters," not "fire preventers," and identify errors after the work is done. Management, instead, should be rewarded for being prevention oriented and seeking to eliminate nonvalue-added work.

6. **Adopt an error-free attitude.** Instill an attitude that "good enough" is not good enough anymore. "Error free" should become each individual's performance standard, with managers taking every opportunity to demonstrate and communicate the importance of this imperative.

7. **Get the facts first.** Continuous improvement–oriented companies make decisions based on facts, not on opinions. Accurate measurement, often using readily available statistical techniques, of every critical variable in a business's operation—and using those measurements to trace problems to their roots and eliminate their causes—is a better way.

8. **Encourage every manager and employee to participate.** Employee participation, empowerment, participative decision making, and extensive training in quality techniques, in statistical techniques, and in measurement tools are the ingredients continuous improvement companies employ to support and instill a commitment to customer value.

9. **Create an atmosphere of total involvement.** Quality management cannot be the job of a few managers or of one department. Maximum customer value cannot be achieved unless all areas of the organization apply quality concepts simultaneously.

10. **Strive for continuous improvement.** Stephen Yearout, director of Ernst & Young's Quality Management Center, recently observed that "Historically, meeting your customers' expectations would distinguish you from your competitors. The 21st century will require you to anticipate customer expectations and deliver quality service faster than the competition." Quality, efficiency, and responsiveness are not one-time programs of competitive response, for they create a new standard to measure up to. Organizations quickly find that continually improving quality, efficiency, and responsiveness in their processes, products, and services is not just good business; it's a necessity for long-term survival.

Six-Sigma Approach to Continuous Improvement

Sometimes referred to as the "new TQM," Six-Sigma is a highly rigorous and analytical approach to quality and continuous improvement with an objective to improve profits through defect reduction, yield improvement, improved consumer satisfaction and best-in-class performance. Six-Sigma complements TQM philosophies such as management leadership, continuous education and customer focus while deploying a disciplined and structured approach of hard-nosed statistics. Critics of TQM see key success factors differentiating Six-Sigma from TQM.

- Acute understanding of customers and the product or service provided

- Emphasis on the science of statistics and measurement

- Meticulous and structured training development

- Strict and project-focused methodologies

- Reinforcement of the doctrine advocated by Juran such as top management support and continuous education

Companies such as Honeywell (1994), Motorola (1987), GE (1995), Polaroid (1998) and Texas Instruments (1988) have adopted the Six-Sigma discipline as a major business initiative. Many of these companies invested heavily in and pursued this model initially in order to create products and services that were of equal and higher quality than those of its competitors and to improve relationships with customers. Much like TQM, the technique implies a whole culture of strategies, tools, and statistical methodologies to improve the bottom line resulting in tremendous savings, subsequent improvement initiatives, and management action.

A Six-Sigma program at many organizations simply means a measure of quality that strives for near perfection in every facet of the business including every product, process, and transaction. The approach was introduced and established at Motorola in 1987 becoming the key factor in Motorola winning the 1988 Malcolm Baldrige Award for Quality, and has had impressive and undisputed results for many companies who have undertaken it. Allied Signal reported an estimated savings of $1.5 billion in its 1997 annual report while GE's savings in a 1998 annual letter to its shareholders reported benefits exceeding $750 million a year.

How the Six-Sigma Statistical Concept Works

Six-Sigma means a failure rate of 3.4 parts per million or 99.9997%. At the six standard deviation from the mean under a normal distribution, 99.9996% of the population is under the curve with not more than 3.4 parts per million defective. The higher the sigma value, the less likely a process will produce defects as excellence is approached.

If you played 100 rounds of golf per year and played at:
2 Sigma: You'd miss 6 putts per round.
3 Sigma: You'd miss 1 putt per round.
4 Sigma: You'd miss 1 putt every 9 rounds.
5 Sigma: You'd miss 1 putt every 2.33 years.
6 Sigma: You'd miss 1 putt every 163 years!

Source: "When Near Is Not Good Enough," *The Australian CPA,* August 2000.

Many frameworks, management philosophies, and specific statistical tools exist for implementing the Six-Sigma methodology and its objective to create a near perfect process or service. One such method for improving a system for existing processes falling below specification while looking for incremental improvement is the DMAIC process (define, measure, analyze, improve, control).

Define

- Project Definition
- Project Charter
- Gathering Voice of the Customer
- Translating Customer Needs into Specific Requirements

Measure

- Process Mapping (As-Is Process)
- Data Attributes (Continuous vs. Discrete)
- Measurement System Analysis
- Gage Repeatability and Reproducibility
- Measuring Process Capability
- Calculating Process Sigma Level
- Visually Displaying Baseline Performance

THE BIG PICTURE

In 1997 Citibank set about to apply this technique to its non-manufacturing environment by contracting with Motorola University Consulting and Training Services for extensive Six-Sigma training. The goal was to improve Citibank operations globally through defect reduction and process timeline improvement while increasing customer loyalty and satisfaction.

Citibank's mission focused on becoming the premier international financial company in the next millennium requiring excellence in every facet of the business and action on the part of every Citibank employee. This quality initiative began with training 650 senior managers by October 1997 and over 92,000 employees trained worldwide by early 1999.

SIX SIGMA TO THE RESCUE

The initial phase of the Six-Sigma process involved Motorola University training Citibank employees on both Cycle Time Reduction (CTR) and Cross Functional Process Mapping (CFPM). These methodologies essentially set the stage for Six-Sigma by mapping and eliminating wasteful and nonvalue added processing steps from the business. In a nonmanufacturing company, 90 percent of activities may fall into this category. A sigma is a statistical term which measures to what degree a process varies from perfection. A rating of three sigma equals 66,807 defects per million opportunities; a rating of Six-Sigma equals 3.4 defects per million opportunities, or virtual perfection.

Six-Sigma is accomplished using simple tools, including the Pareto chart. The data on the chart identify which problems occur with the greatest frequency or incur the highest cost. It provides the direct evidence of what would be analyzed and corrected first. Typically 20 percent of the possible causes are responsible for 80 percent of any problem.

Citibank undertook the Six-Sigma process to investigate why it was not achieving complete customer satisfaction with a goal to have 10 times reduction in defects and cycle time by December 2000 and 10 times again every two years. Six-Sigma classifies a defect as anything that results in customer dissatisfaction and unhappiness. Indicators of less than optimal status are customer opinions such as:

- You're difficult to do business with;

- You don't fix my problems;

- You're not staying innovative and your systems are not state-of-the-art;

- You are slow and complicated.

Analyze

- Visually Displaying Data (Histogram, Run Chart, Pareto Chart, Scatter Diagram)
- Value-Added Analysis
- Cause and Effect Analysis (a.k.a. Fishbone, Ishikawa)
- Verification of Root Causes
- Determining Opportunity (Defects and Financial) for Improvement
- Project Charter Review and Revision

Improve

- Brainstorming
- Quality Function Deployment (House of Quality)
- Failure Modes and Effects Analysis (FMEA)
- Piloting Your Solution
- Implementation Planning
- Culture Modification Planning for Your Organization

Control

- Statistical Process Control (SPC) Overview
- Developing a Process Control Plan
- Documenting the Process

continued

Exhibit 11–5

TEAM APPROACH

A team composed of bankers and operations people identified the entire funds transfer process, tabulating defects and analyzing them using Pareto charts. Highest on the list of defects for this process was the internal callback procedure, which required a staffer to phone back the requester to make sure that the instructions were correct, or had not been altered. "We cut monthly callbacks from 8,000 to 1,000 and we eliminated callbacks for 73 percent of the transactions coming in," says Cherylann Munoz, compliance director of Citibank's Private Bank in the United States and Western Hemisphere.

In Citibank's Global Cash and Trade Organization (GCTO), MU's Six-Sigma methodology helped track defects and documented the results by teaching team members to identify appropriate metrics, determine a baseline, establish appropriate standards, and monitor execution. The employees formed teams to solve any issues they discovered during this analysis.

To reduce the time for opening an account, Citibank formed a cross-functional global team of 80 people. The team first identified sponsors and formed a steering committee to champion the effort. Employees were invited to participate based on their subject matter know-how and ability to assist with the solution. The biggest hurdle for Citibank employees was allocating the time to participate while juggling their daily job responsibilities. Sue Andros, a global process owner in the GCTO responsible for the end-to-end customer experience says process mapping "lets people get to know one another."

"Team members worked well together, since achieving the objectives would make their professional responsibilities easier and would benefit their customers—a win/win situation for everyone," Andros says. "The focus on cycle time and deficiencies has made an impact on how we serve customers. It's not just a matter of doing things faster, it's doing things better. This means eliminating redundancy, minimizing hand-offs, and establishing metrics that reflect performance in the eyes of the customer."

Dipak Rastogi, executive vice president for Citibank's Eastern European/Central Asia and Africa region headquartered in London, agrees with those sentiments. "Introducing quality as a core strategy was viewed as a unique opportunity and differentiating feature not only with regard to our customers, but also our employees," says Rastogi. "When implemented correctly, quality increases customer satisfaction and leads to shorter reaction time and faster introduction of new products—providing a sustainable competitive advantage."

MANAGEMENT COMMITMENT

Teams involved in the Citibank quality initiative needed to have full autonomy to make decisions about changes to the established processes. Senior management sponsored these initiatives or served on steering committees to champion the work and there was an "open door" policy so that teams could gain access to them as needed. According to Peter Klimes, quality director for Citibank in the Czech Republic, the involvement of senior support is a continuous process all the way from setting critical business issues and objectives, to the final improvement implementation. "We have had a well-balanced split between projects initiated by senior management and those initiated by employees," Klimes says. "Our senior operations officer and our corporate bank head were our most active supporters of Six-Sigma projects. Their commitment helps balance back and front office aspects of projects."

Source: "Citibank Increases Loyalty with Defect-Free Processes," *The Journal for Quality & Participation,* Fall 2000, pp. 32–36.

Six-Sigma programs promote an uncompromising orientation of all business processes toward the customer. The first step is always achieving an understanding of customer expectations so that suitable tools can be employed to improve both the internal and external processes. This program does not come fast and cheap, however, management commitment is crucial to the success, and employees must be trained in Six-Sigma methodologies. Exhibit 11–5, Strategy in Action, describes the use of Six-Sigma at Citibank.

ISO 9001 and the Era of International Standards

The ISO 9001 quality management system standard, introduced in 1987, is international in both scope and impact. In early 2000 there were almost 300,000 firms registered in over 143 countries, almost 25,000 of those registered firms in the United States. The trend towards ISO 9001 registration and the creation of additional management system

333

standards such as ISO 14001 (environmental), ISO 18001 (health and safety) and sector-specific standards such as QS-9001 (automotive) and AS-9001 (aerospace) has continued to grow and develop internationally. The standards are voluntary and apply to many kinds of businesses including manufacturers, distributors, services, software developers, public utilities, government TQM agencies, and financial and educational institutions.

The *ISO 9001 standard* focuses on achieving customer satisfaction through continuous measurement, documentation, assessment, and adjustment. A diagram of the approach is provided below. The standard specifies requirements for a quality management system where an organization:

1. Needs to demonstrate its ability to consistently provide product and services that meet customer requirements, and

2. Aims to enhance customer satisfaction through the effective application of the system, including processes for continual improvement of the system and the assurance of conformity to customer requirements.

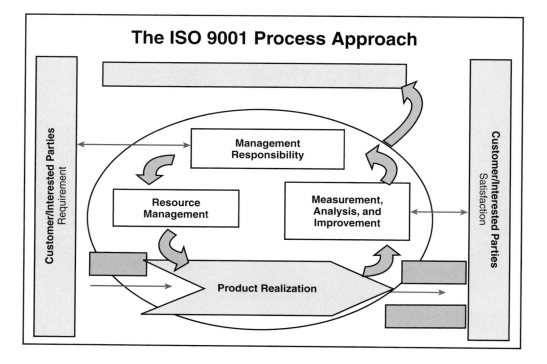

The ISO 9001 Process Approach

ISO 9001 has strong commonalities with other quality schemes such as Mil-Q, Deming's 14 points, TQM and the Malcolm Baldrige National Quality Award Criteria. The four focus areas of the ISO 9001 process approach are 1) management responsibility, 2) resource management, 3) product realization, and 4) measurement, analysis, and improvement. ISO 9001 differs from other quality approaches in that it involves formal certification by a sanctioned ISO certification source before a company can claim to meet the standard. Exhibit 11–6, Strategy in Action, describes how well-known golf club maker Ping chose to become ISO 9001 certified.

Upon introduction of the ISO 9001 series of standards, many American and multinational firms not only foresaw the competitive advantage possible by adopting ISO 9001, but also

When John Solheim took the helm at golf equipment maker Ping in 1995, he had a legacy to protect and improve—that of his father, Karsten Solheim. When the employee handbook was written in 1993, Karsten wrote: "It is the customer who keeps us in business, and we must always be sure to give each one first-class treatment. The role of each employee is also very important because dedication to quality assures the success of the company."

The family business was founded over 42 years ago and is based in Phoenix. Today Ping is best known for its custom fit, custom-built golf clubs and competes in a highly innovative and competitive $4 billion golf equipment industry. John wasn't satisfied with the existing standard of quality and set about to find a way to measure the company business against an internationally accepted standard, ISO 9001. "By embarking on this journey, we hoped to measure ourselves against recognized criteria that would reassure us we were doing business appropriately," says Solheim. "We also believed such an accomplishment might help identify areas where we could advance." Both of Solheim's hopes were fulfilled.

THE IMPLEMENTATION AND REGISTRATION PROCESS

After conducting some research, John Solheim decided to pursue registration to both ISO 9001 (quality management system standard) and ISO 14001 (environmental management system standard). This decision was based on several factors:

1. The ISO (International Organization for Standardization) standards are internationally recognized.

2. Attaining registration would provide Ping with a competitive advantage in the marketplace. Ping would be the first competitor in the golf industry to be registered to both ISO 9001 and ISO 14001 standards.

3. Ping wanted the benefits of implementing the management systems such as improved quality, increased environmental awareness, customer satisfaction, and continuous improvement.

Ping began the implementation process in November 1999. The first step was to develop documentation, identify and improve processes and provide training to all personnel involved in the implementation. A preassessment audit acted as a dress rehearsal for employees and heightened their understanding of the requirements as well as identified opportunities for improvement in the existing system.

During this process Ping faced many challenges. First, its workforce consisted of over 1,000 employees who spoke at least six different languages. Additionally, company processes, documentation, and policies were very informal.

Many hours were spent training and developing valuable manuals that are used as reference resources. "The registration process helped me see how everything in the company ties together and our processes really interrelate," said Solheim. "I thought I was fairly well-organized, but the registration audit taught me to dot my I's and cross my T's."

BENEFITS

Ping's steering committee identified many benefits of the ISO 9001 and ISO 14001 registration.

1. Enhanced internal communication and increased focus on customer requirements throughout the organization.

2. The generation of useful information to allow more strategic decision making by all levels of management.

3. Better measurement of the processes that are responsible for quality and the ability to continually improve product quality.

4. Improved customer satisfaction and the continued reputation for quality, innovation, and service in the golf equipment market.

5. Development of a new customer service call system that improved reduced customer response time.

6. Improved environmental performance resulting in reduced emissions.

7. Improved cycle times to meet our customers' demands.

Ping officially achieved registration on October 17, 2000. Ping is now in the process of implementing ISO 9001 and ISO 14001 in its sister company, Ping Europe Ltd., in Gainsborough, United Kingdom. This registration will include the Gainsborough Golf Club, a private 36-hole facility with a driving range and modern clubhouse. Ping believes this will be the first country club to ever be registered to international standards.

Now registered, the company is continuing to focus intensely on continuous improvement of the quality of its systems, operations, service and products in a highly competitive worldwide market. "We continuously hone our ISO 9001 and 14001 systems, strengthening our quality and environmental objectives while looking for improvement opportunities. No one asked us to become ISO registered," Solheim says. "We raised our standards because golfers ultimately decide the fate of our products. Customer satisfaction will be the program's greatest benefit."

Source: Robert T. Driescher, *Quality Progress,* August 2001, pp. 37–41.

saw the value of quality management system implementation in achieving customer satisfaction. As a result, many of these larger firms subsequently imposed the requirements of ISO 9001 on suppliers as a condition to do business and as a way to reduce the supply base to only those suppliers committed to quality and service. It is believed by many that eventually ISO 9001 would reduce and possibly eliminate the need for customer-sponsored audits. In the ISO 9001 registration scheme, third-party auditors employed by registrars conduct ISO 9001 registration audits. National and international accreditation bodies accredit the registrars to certify and publish that the company has met the requirements of ISO 9001.

Customer mandates initially served as an incentive for suppliers desiring to retain existing levels of business with their customers to jump on the ISO 9001 bandwagon and pursue registration. In many cases registration to ISO 9001 gave these suppliers a clear competitive advantage in the marketplace. However in 2001, as many companies continue to pursue and maintain registration, ISO 9001 functions as a way of life for many companies and has become ingrained in daily processes, no longer thought of as a unique or identifiable program. Other companies, who were not pressured to implement ISO 9001, chose to put it into practice as a methodology by which to systematize their operations and to focus on and improve both daily operations and quality levels throughout their organizations.

Nevertheless, along with the establishment of ISO 9001 standards came many misperceptions. Here are just a few of the criticisms targeted at ISO 9001.

- ***ISO 9001 is a European standard and cannot be applicable to American firms.***
  ISO 9001 has traceable American ancestry to military quality systems. The United States is a member of International Organization for Standardization (ISO) and participates in the formulation and continuing committee reviews of ISO 9001.

- ***Implementing ISO 9001 is mandatory if you plan to do business in Europe.***
  This is true for a small number of firms manufacturing a relative handful of products—a list that may continue to grow in the coming years. But the doors to Europe did not slam shut on non-ISO 9001 registered companies in January 1993. Rather, ISO 9001 registration has increasingly become desired, expected and even required in certain markets and industries (i.e., Automotive QS-9001), but growth was driven primarily by customer requirements and competitive pressures.

- ***ISO 9001 is all about paperwork.***
  Ironically, ISO 9001 had in most cases reduced the redundancy and massive manuals and shelves of procedures and books that already exist. Documentation is central to ISO 9001 requirements for the purposes of planning, controlling, training and providing objective evidence of conformance. The goal is to make the documentation support the value-added activity clearly and concisely, eliminating redundancy while supporting usefulness. The standard does not prescribe specific solutions, tactics, strategies or procedures which gives ISO 9001 enormous flexibility.

- ***ISO 9001 is inspection-based as opposed to prevention-based.***
  ISO 9001 requires the quality management system monitor conformance to requirements. This is just one part of the measurement, analysis, and continuous improvement cycle at the heart of the standard. Implementation of the standard alone will not guarantee quality. Management commitment and employee involvement are instrumental in the implementation process.

Since its introduction, international participation in ISO 9001 continues to climb and offers organizations a framework for quality system management. It is no longer new or radical, yet it provides a common language for quality that is easily translatable and applicable across many countries, cultures, and businesses. The focus is not on products and services but rather on the organization's network of activities designed and operated to ensure that output meets the ultimate business objective: satisfying the customer.

The Balanced Scorecard Methodology

A new approach to strategic control was developed in the last decade by Harvard Business School professors Robert Kaplan and David Norton. They named this system the *balanced scorecard.* Recognizing some of the weaknesses and vagueness of previous implementation and control approaches, the balanced scorecard approach was intended to provide a clear prescription as to what companies should measure in order to "balance" the financial perspective in implementation and control of strategic plans.[2]

The balanced scorecard was viewed as a *management system* (not only a measurement system) that enables companies to clarify their strategies, translate them into action, and provide meaningful feedback. It provides feedback around both the internal business processes and external outcomes in order to continuously improve strategic performance and results. When fully deployed, the balanced scorecard is intended to transform strategic planning from a separate top management exercise into the nerve center of an enterprise. Kaplan and Norton describe the innovation of the balanced scorecard as follows:

> The balanced scorecard retains traditional financial measures. But financial measures tell the story of past events, an adequate story for industrial age companies for which investments in long-term capabilities and customer relationships were not critical for success. These financial measures are inadequate, however, for guiding and evaluating the journey that information age companies must make to create future value through investment in customers, suppliers, employees, processes, technology, and innovation.[3]

The balanced scorecard methodology adapts the TQM ideas of customer-defined quality, continuous improvement, employee empowerment, and measurement-based management/feedback into an expanded methodology that includes traditional financial data and results. The balanced scorecard incorporates feedback around internal business process *outputs,* as in TQM, but also adds a feedback loop around the *outcomes* of business strategies. This creates a "double-loop feedback" process in the balanced scorecard. In doing so, it links together two areas of concern in strategy execution—quality operations and financial outcomes—that are typically addressed separately yet are obviously critically intertwined as any company executes its strategy. A system that links shareholder interests in return on capital with a system of performance management that is linked to ongoing, operational activities and processes within the company is what the balanced scorecard attempts to achieve.

Exhibit 11–7 illustrates the balanced scorecard approach drawing on the traditional DuPont formula discussed in Chapter 5 and historically used to examine drivers of stockholder-related financial performance across different company activities. The balanced scorecard seeks to "balance" shareholder goals with customer goals and operational performance goals, and Exhibit 11–7 shows that they are interconnected—

---

[2] This methodology is covered in great detail in a number of books and articles by R. S. Kaplan and D. P. Norton. It is also the subject of frequent special publications by the Harvard Business Review that provided updated treatment of uses and improvements in the balanced scorecard methodology. Some useful books include *Balanced Scorecard: Translating Strategies into Action* (Boston: Harvard Business School Press, 1996); *The Strategy-Focused Organization* (Boston: Harvard Business School Press, 2001). And, in HBR, "Using the Balanced Scorecard as a Strategic Management System," *Harvard Business Review* (January–February, 1996). Numerous useful websites also exist such as www.bscol.com.

[3] Another useful treatment of various aspects of the Balanced Scoreboard to include further learning opportunities you may wish to explore, especially with regard to the use of this approach with governmental organizations, may be found at www.balancedscorecard.org.

EXHIBIT 11–7
Integrating Shareholder Value and Organizational Activities across Organizational Levels

Source: R. M. Grant, *Contemporary Strategy Analysis* (Oxford, UK: Blackwell, 2002), p. 56.

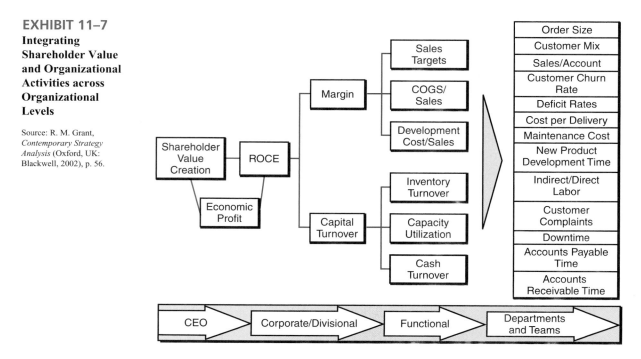

shareholder value creation are linked to divisional concerns for return on capital employed which in turn are driven by functional outcomes in sales, inventory, capacity utilization that in turn come about through the results of departments and teams daily activities throughtout the company. The balanced scorecard suggests that we view the organization from *four* perspectives, and to develop metrics, collect data and analyze it relative to each of these perspectives:

1. *The Learning and Growth Perspective: How well are we continuously improving and creating value?* The scorecard insists on measures related to innovation and organizational learning to gauge performance on this dimension—technological leadership, product development cycle times, operational process improvement, and so on.

2. *The Business Process Perspective: What are our core competencies and areas of operational excellence?* Internal business processes and their effective execution as measured by productivity, cycle time, quality measures, downtime, various cost measures among others provide scorecard input here.

3. *The Customer Perspective: How satisfied are our customers?* A customer satisfaction perspective typically adds measures related to defect levels, on-time delivery, warranty support, product development among others that come from direct customer input and are linked to specific company activities.

4. *The Financial Perspective: How are we doing for our shareholders?* A financial perspective typically using measures like cash flow, return on equity, sales and income growth.

Through the integration of goals from each of these four perspectives, the balanced scorecard approach enables the strategy of the business to be linked with shareholder value creation while providing several measurable short-term outcomes that guide and

EXHIBIT 11–8
Balanced Scorecard for Mobil Corporation's NAM&R

Source: "How Mobil Became a Strategy-Focused Organization," Chapter 2 in R. Kaplan and D. Norton, *The Strategy-Focused Organization* (Boston: Harvard Business School Press, 2001).

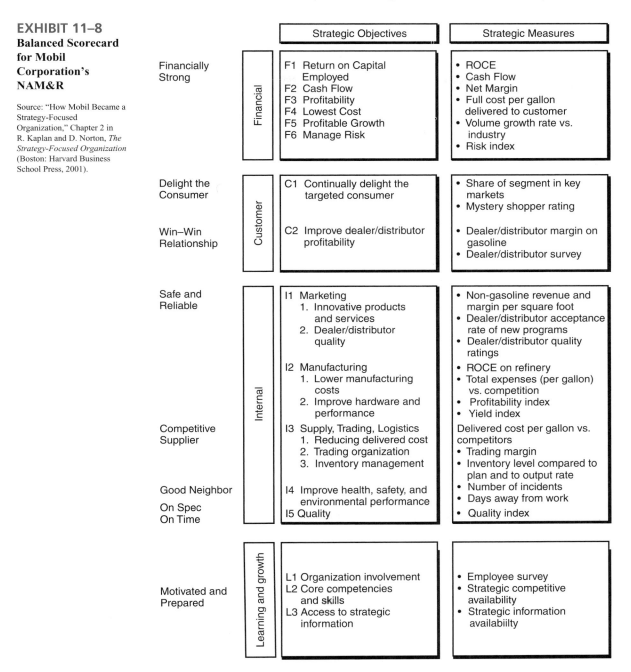

		Strategic Objectives	Strategic Measures
Financially Strong	Financial	F1 Return on Capital Employed F2 Cash Flow F3 Profitability F4 Lowest Cost F5 Profitable Growth F6 Manage Risk	• ROCE • Cash Flow • Net Margin • Full cost per gallon delivered to customer • Volume growth rate vs. industry • Risk index
Delight the Consumer Win–Win Relationship	Customer	C1 Continually delight the targeted consumer C2 Improve dealer/distributor profitability	• Share of segment in key markets • Mystery shopper rating • Dealer/distributor margin on gasoline • Dealer/distributor survey

Safe and Reliable
 	
Competitive Supplier
 	
Good Neighbor
 	
On Spec
On Time
	Internal	I1 Marketing
		  1. Innovative products and services
		  2. Dealer/distributor quality
		
		I2 Manufacturing
		  1. Lower manufacturing costs
		  2. Improve hardware and performance
		
		I3 Supply, Trading, Logistics
		  1. Reducing delivered cost
		  2. Trading organization
		  3. Inventory management
		
		I4 Improve health, safety, and environmental performance
		I5 Quality
			• Non-gasoline revenue and margin per square foot
			• Dealer/distributor acceptance rate of new programs
			• Dealer/distributor quality ratings
			• ROCE on refinery
			• Total expenses (per gallon) vs. competition
			• Profitability index
			• Yield index
			Delivered cost per gallon vs. competitors
			• Trading margin
			• Inventory level compared to plan and to output rate
			• Number of incidents
			• Days away from work
			• Quality index

Motivated and Prepared	Learning and growth	L1 Organization involvement L2 Core competencies and skills L3 Access to strategic information	• Employee survey • Strategic competitive availability • Strategic information availabiilty

monitor strategy implementation. Kaplan and Norton provide this account of the use of the balanced scorecard at FMC:

> Strategists came up with 5- and 10-year plans, controllers with one-year budgets and near-term forecasts. Little interplay occurred between the two groups. But the [balanced] scorecard now bridges the two. The financial perspective builds on the traditional function

performed by controllers. The other three perspectives make the division's long-term objectives measurable.[4]

Another example that helps you understand the integrating power of the balanced scorecard can be seen at Mobil Corporation's North American Marketing and Refining business [NAM&R]. NAM&R's scorecard is shown in Exhibit 11–8. Assisted by Kaplan and Norton, an unprofitable NAM&R adopted the scorecard methodology to better link its strategy with financial objectives and to translate these into operating performance targets tailored to outcomes in each business unit, functional departments, and operating processes within them. They included measures developed with key customers from their perspective. The result was an integrated system where scorecards provided measurable outcomes through which the performance of each department and operating unit, team or activity within NAM&R was monitored, adjusted, and used to determine performance-related pay bonuses.[5]

The balanced scorecard reflects continuous improvement in management thought about how to better manage organizations. Our coverage of the concept is brief, and you are encouraged to seek additional information and resources suggested in various footnotes or through your own current Web search. Strategic control, continuous improvement, specific measurable feedback and inclusion of everyone in some way responsible for customer satisfaction and organizational success are important developments in the art of strategic management and the science of its succesful application.

Summary

Three fundamental perspectives—strategic control, continuous improvement, and the balanced scoreboard—provide the basis for designing strategy control systems. Strategic controls are intended to steer the company toward its long-term strategic goals. Premise controls, implementation controls, strategic surveillance, and special alert controls are types of strategic control. All four types are designed to meet top management's needs to track the strategy as it is being implemented, to detect underlying problems, and to make necessary adjustments. These strategic controls are linked to the environmental assumptions and the key operating requirements necessary for successful strategy implementation. Ever-present forces of change fuel the need for and focus of strategic control.

Operational control systems require systematic evaluation of performance against predetermined standards or targets. A critical concern here is identification and evaluation of performance deviations, with careful attention paid to determining the underlying reasons for and strategic implications of observed deviations before management reacts. Some firms use trigger points and contingency plans in this process.

The "quality imperative" of the last 20 years has redefined global competitiveness to include reshaping the way many businesses approach strategic and operational control. What has emerged is a commitment to continuous improvement in which personnel across all levels in an organization define customer value, identify ways every process within the business influences customer value, and seek continuously to enhance the quality, efficiency, and responsiveness with which the processes, products, and services are created and supplied. This includes attending to internal as well as external customers. The "balanced scorecard" is a control system that integrates strategic goals, operating outcomes, customer satisfaction, and continuous improvement into an ongoing strategic management system.

---

[4] R. Kaplan and D. Norton, "Putting the Balanced Scorecard to Work," *Harvard Business Review* (September–October, 1993), p. 147.

[5] "How Mobil Became a Strategy-Focused Organization," Chapter 2 in R. Kaplan and D. Norton, *The Strategy-Focused Organization* (Boston: Harvard Business School Press, 2001). For an online version of the Mobil NAM&R case study, see www.bscol.com.

Questions for Discussion

Questions for Discussion

1. Distinguish strategic control from operating control. Give an example of each.

2. Select a business whose strategy is familiar to you. Identify what you think are the key premises of the strategy. Then select the key indicators that you would use to monitor each of these premises.

3. Explain the differences between implementation controls, strategic surveillance, and special alert controls. Give an example of each.

4. Why are budgets, schedules, and key success factors essential to operations control and evaluation?

5. What are key considerations in monitoring deviations from performance standards?

6. What are five key elements of quality management? How are quality imperative and continuous improvement related to strategic and operational control?

7. How might customer value be linked to quality, efficiency, and responsiveness?

8. Is it realistic that a commitment to continuous improvement could actually replace operational controls? Strategic controls?

9. How is the balanced scorecard approach similar to continuous improvement? How is it different?

Chapter 11 Discussion Case

BusinessWeek

The Web of Quality: Worldwide Links Mean Better Products

1   Just a decade ago, U.S. businesses were crowing about the promise of new quality-improvement programs. Since then, the U.S. quality movement has altered and improved business practices, and many American companies have matched Japan's vaunted quality benchmarks. Industrial offices buzzed with phrases such as "total quality management (TQM)" and "Six-Sigma accuracy." Such catchphrases are heard less frequently because they've been replaced by Internet jargon. And that raises a question: Where does quality stand in the Internet age?

2   Concerns about quality have by no means disappeared. Rather, at most successful companies, quality has become internalized, says quality consultant Joseph A. DeFeo, CEO of Juran Institute Inc. in Wilton, Conn. The special software and management practices associated with the movement are now in everyday use, he says, so quality has become less self-conscious. But it has reemerged as a critical issue because of the rapid development of Internet links among companies. Quality is no longer the concern of just a single factory but of whole supply chains. As companies outsource more of their work, they need to take increasing care to make sure their partners measure up on quality, says Michael J. Burkett, a senior analyst at Boston's AMR Research Inc., a manufacturing consultant.

3   This report explores the role of quality in today's increasingly networked world. The first section looks at how a unit of General Electric Co. is blazing new quality trails in a field it helped pioneer. The second lifts the lid on efforts by Mexico's manufacturers to meet the quality demands of customers in North America and overseas.

GE: ZERO TO 60, NO SKID MARKS

4   Never before has General Electric Co. cranked out gas-powered turbines in such quantities. Given the growing preference for gas-powered generating plants over their much dirtier coal-burning cousins, demand is booming—with no sign of slowing. In May, GE's Power Systems unit installed five times the number of turbines it did a year earlier. Yet despite the problems of grappling with such a huge increase in production, GE has become progressively better at making good on delivery date promises. Indeed, the company has actually delivered many units ahead of schedule (see chart on p. 344). GE Power's success at managing its huge runup in output is a much-discussed success story among GE insiders—and a major reason they view Power Systems head Robert L. Nardelli as a top contender for GE's CEO job when Jack Welch retires.

5   While GE is hardly complaining about this upturn, executives realized that the runup would pose huge risks. In particular, they worried about maintaining their grip on quality, continuing to fill orders on time, and keeping customers happy. The last thing they wanted was to become another example of a company that lost control when it tried to goose production quickly after getting bombarded by orders. The production snafus at Boeing Co. in 1997 offered an ominous example of how things can go wrong in a big rampup. And when GE execs began taking notice in 1998 of industry numbers showing that electrical-power reserves in the United States were shrinking to alarming levels, Boeing's difficulties were painfully fresh.

6   OUTSIDE RISKS. To prepare for the projected hike in orders, GE Power Systems' managers visited companies that had lived through similar explosions in their businesses. They made a point of flying to Seattle to glean insights from Boeing officials. One thing became evident right away: The biggest risk to GE was outside the company. Suppliers that lacked GE's financial resources might not be able to expand production rapidly enough. At Boeing and other casualties of too-fast growth, most breakdowns occurred when

suppliers overestimated their production capacity. Since more than 50% of a turbine's components are purchased from outside vendors, GE wasted no time shoring up its supply chain. In 1998, GE Power Systems launched an exhaustive study of the suppliers that provide key components for the gas turbines. After first screening 250 of its suppliers, it intensively audited 85 that posed the greatest risk. Teams consisting of specialists in supply sourcing, research and development, finance, and management spent up to two weeks at supplier facilities across the United States and around the world.

7   Since the last major rampup in production at Power Systems in the late 80s, GE had two new tools to help it avoid supply-chain problems, says Victor R. Abate, general manager of fulfillment at Power Systems. One was the Internet. But more important was the company's vaunted Six-Sigma program, adopted in 1996. Six sigma is statistics-speak for 99.9999976%. Applied to manufacturing, it means a quality level of no more than 3.4 defects per million products. At GE, the Six-Sigma program also includes guidelines and tools for boosting productivity and wringing inefficiencies out of its manufacturing and service processes. Mark M. Little, a vice-president at GE Power Systems, says that with Six-Sigma's tools, GE no longer has to rely on bludgeoning suppliers to deliver. Instead, GE's auditors have the wherewithal to determine whether suppliers can hand over parts in time.

8   GE's vendor-checkers scrutinize myriad details right down to the individual machine tools that suppliers use to produce turbine parts. GE also evaluates the supplier's suppliers—their production capacity, shipping and delivery systems, and how rigorous their quality programs are. And the exam doesn't end there. Because a supplier might need to boost hiring, GE checks to see whether the company keeps a stack of résumés on hand. In the end, GE eliminated some suppliers and found backups for suppliers with obvious weaknesses. And they tagged some 350 potential problems that continued to be monitored until fixed by the suppliers.

9   INVALUABLE ASSET. Perhaps most important, the initial evaluation allowed GE to establish a framework for ensuring the quality of its supply chain as production rolled forward. Says analyst Nicholas P. Heymann of Prudential Securities Inc., who formerly worked as a GE auditor: "How many companies today have guys that can go into another company and fully assess where the flaws are—and not only that but also fix them? They've executed Six-Sigma all the way through the supplier chain."

10   That was an invaluable asset as orders flowed in and the stress on production systems mounted, both internally and among suppliers. With its new predictive tools, deep knowledge of its suppliers, and the ability to share information quickly via the Internet, GE could identify problems earlier and avoid potentially costly bottlenecks. "Whenever we see variation, we just attack it," Abate says.

11   Example: GE last year realized that a supplier of a core turbine component was poised to fall behind. Although the company was consistently delivering to GE on time, GE's Six-Sigma audit had found the supplier would be unable to keep up as GE went from producing 25 turbines to 45 per quarter in late 1999. GE sent a team to the company, and a settlement was reached: The supplier would lease additional equipment to keep up with GE's production track. "With these very rigorous tools," says Little, "we now know what the leading indicators are, and we can act fast."

12   The Internet has made a big difference, too. When GE engineers are in the field, checking on deliveries at customers sites anywhere in the world, they can report on a problem on their laptops, and this information is available instantly throughout GE Power Systems. Before the Net, the field engineers would typically resolve each problem at the plant site—but GE managers would remain blissfully unaware of the solution, which would have to be engineered all over again the next time.

13   So what's the customer's view of how well GE is coping with its production surges? Duke Energy North America (DENA, a unit of Charlotte-based Duke Energy Corp.) is clearly satisfied. It placed a huge order with GE in the fall of 1998 to outfit nearly two dozen generating plants with gas turbines, four of which will be on line by month's end. Including service agreements, it was a $4 billion order. So far, everything has gone according to schedule or slightly ahead of it, says

James M. Donnell, CEO of DENA. For Duke, there's a lot at stake. With summer already starting to stroke demand for electricity, each day that a gas-turbine plant isn't producing means a huge revenue loss. A 640-megawatt plant running at maximum capacity for 16 hours on a summer day, for example, translates into $1.75 million in gross revenues.

14   For GE the stakes are high, too. The company boasts that it has grabbed a 75% share of current turbine orders. With the power industry relying so heavily on one supplier, more eyes than ever will be watching to see if Power Systems can keep managing the boom.

Spinning Up Quality at GE

Thanks to its six-sigma program, turbine production soared and far more turbines were delivered ahead of schedule.

Total Deliveries
- Early
- All other

7

8

61

11

Total Commissioned: 15
May 1999

Total Commissioned: 72
May 2000

Source: Petty, John, When Near Enough is Not Good Enough. Australian CPA, May 2000. Pp. 34–35.

Subject Index